IARIA

UBICOMM 2016

The Tenth International Conference on Mobile Ubiquitous Computing, Systems, Services and Technologies

October 9 - 13, 2016

Venice, Italy

UBICOMM 2016 Editors

Sergey Balandin, FRUCT, Finland / ITMO University, Russia

Michele Ruta, Technical University of Bari, Italy

Moeiz Miraoui, Umm al Qura University, KSA

Printed from e-media with permission by:

Curran Associates, Inc.
57 Morehouse Lane
Red Hook, NY 12571

Some format issues inherent in the e-media version may also appear in this print version.

Printed by Curran Associates, Inc. (2016)

International Academy, Research, and Industry Association (IARIA)
412 Derby Way
Wilmington, DE 19810

Phone: (408) 893-6407
Fax: (408) 527-6351

petre@iaria.org

Additional copies of this publication are available from:

Curran Associates, Inc.
57 Morehouse Lane
Red Hook, NY 12571 USA
Phone: 845-758-0400
Fax: 845-758-2633
Email: curran@proceedings.com
Web: www.proceedings.com

TABLE OF CONTENTS

UBICOMM 1: UBIQUITOUS SOFTWARE AND SECURITY

UBICOMM 2: MOBILITY

UBICOMM 3 / CISSS: CONTEXT-AWARENESS IN INTELLIGENT SYSTEMS AND SMART SPACES

UBICOMM 4: UBIQUITOUS MOBILE SERVICES

UBICOMM 5: TRENDS AND CHALLENGES

UBICOMM 6: USERS, APPLICATIONS, AND BUSINESS MODELS

UBICOMM 7: UBIQUITOUS DEVICES AND OPERATIVE SYSTEMS

UBICOMM 8: COLLABORATIVE UBIQUITOUS SYSTEMS

UBICOMM 9 / SSIT: SMART SPACES AND INTERNET OF THINGS

UBICOMM 10 / TETHYS: TOWARD EMERGING TECHNOLOGY FOR HARBOUR SYSTEMS AND SERVICES

UBICOMM 2016

Forward

The Tenth International Conference on Mobile Ubiquitous Computing, Systems, Services and Technologies (UBICOMM 2016), held between October 9 and 13, 2016 in Venice, Italy, continued a series of events addressing fundamentals of ubiquitous systems and the new applications related to them.

The rapid advances in ubiquitous technologies make fruition of more than 35 years of research in distributed computing systems, and more than two decades of mobile computing. The ubiquity vision is becoming a reality. Hardware and software components evolved to deliver functionality under failure-prone environments with limited resources. The advent of web services and the progress on wearable devices, ambient components, user-generated content, mobile communications, and new business models generated new applications and services. The conference created a bridge between issues with software and hardware challenges through mobile communications.

Advances in web services technologies along with their integration into mobility, online and new business models provide a technical infrastructure that enables the progress of mobile services and applications. These include dynamic and on-demand service, context-aware services, and mobile web services. While driving new business models and new online services, particular techniques must be developed for web service composition, web service-driven system design methodology, creation of web services, and on-demand web services.

As mobile and ubiquitous computing becomes a reality, more formal and informal learning will take pace out of the confines of the traditional classroom. Two trends converge to make this possible; increasingly powerful cell phones and PDAs, and improved access to wireless broadband. At the same time, due to the increasing complexity, modern learners will need tools that operate in an intuitive manner and are flexibly integrated in the surrounding learning environment.

Educational services will become more customized and personalized, and more frequently subjected to changes. Learning and teaching are now becoming less tied to physical locations, co-located members of a group, and co-presence in time. Learning and teaching increasingly take place in fluid combinations of virtual and "real" contexts, and fluid combinations of presence in time, space and participation in community. To the learner full access and abundance in communicative opportunities and information retrieval represents new challenges and affordances.

Consequently, the educational challenges are numerous in the intersection of technology development, curriculum development, content development and educational infrastructure.

The event was very competitive in its selection process and very well perceived by the international scientific and industrial communities. As such, it has attracted excellent contributions and active participation from all over the world. We were very pleased to receive a large amount of top quality contributions.

The conference had the following tracks:

- Ubiquitous Software and Security
- Mobility
- Context-awareness in Intelligent Systems and Smart Spaces
- Ubiquitous Mobile Services
- Trends and Challenges
- Users, Applications, and Business models
- Ubiquitous Devices and Operative Systems
- Collaborative Ubiquitous Systems
- Smart Spaces and Internet of Things
- Toward Emerging Technology for Harbor Systems and Services

We take here the opportunity to warmly thank all the members of the UBICOMM 2016 technical program committee, as well as the numerous reviewers. The creation of such a high quality conference program would not have been possible without their involvement. We also kindly thank all the authors that dedicated much of their time and effort to contribute to UBICOMM 2016. We truly believe that, thanks to all these efforts, the final conference program consisted of top quality contributions.

Also, this event could not have been a reality without the support of many individuals, organizations and sponsors. We also gratefully thank the members of the UBICOMM 2016 organizing committee for their help in handling the logistics and for their work that made this professional meeting a success.

We hope UBICOMM 2016 was a successful international forum for the exchange of ideas and results between academia and industry and to promote further progress in the field of ubiquitous systems and the new applications related to them.

We also hope that Venice, Italy, provided a pleasant environment during the conference and everyone saved some time to enjoy the unique charm of the city.

UBICOMM Advisory Committee

UBICOMM Industry/Research Chairs

Korbinian Frank, German Aerospace Center - Institute of Communications and Navigation, Germany
Carlo Mastroianni, CNR, Italy
Michele Ruta, Technical University of Bari, Italy
Jose Manuel Cantera Fonseca, Telefonica Investigacion y Desarrollo, Spain
Yulin Ding, Defence Science & Technology Organization Edinburgh, Australia
Korbinian Frank, German Aerospace Center - Institute of Communications and Navigation, Germany
Cornel Klein, Siemens AG/Corporate Research and Technologies - Münich, Germany
Reinhard Klemm, Avaya Labs Research-Basking Ridge, USA
Serena Pastore, INAF- Astronomical Observatory of Padova, Italy
Jyrki T.J. Penttinen, Finesstel Ltd, Finland
Jorge Pereira, European Comission, Belgium
Miroslav Velev, Aries Design Automation, USA
Christoph Steup, FIN - OvGU, Germany

UBICOMM Publicity Chairs

Raul Igual, University of Zaragoza, Spain
Andre Dietrich, Otto-von-Guericke-University Magdeburg, Germany
Rebekah Hunter, University of Ulster, UK
Francesco Fiamberti, University of Milano-Bicocca, Italy
Sönke Knoch, German Research Center for Artificial Intelligence (DFKI GmbH), Germany

UBICOMM 2016

Committee

UBICOMM Advisory Committee

Jaime Lloret Mauri, Polytechnic University of Valencia, Spain
Sathiamoorthy Manoharan, University of Auckland, New Zealand
Zary Segal, UMBC, USA
Yoshiaki Taniguchi, Kindai University, Japan
Ruay-Shiung Chang, National Dong Hwa University, Taiwan
Ann Gordon-Ross, University of Florida, USA
Dominique Genoud, Business Information Systems Institute/HES-SO Valais, Switzerland
Andreas Merentitis, AGT International, Germany
Timothy Arndt, Cleveland State University, USA
Tewfiq El Maliki, Geneva University of Applied Sciences, Switzerland
Yasihisa Takizawa, Kansai University, Japan
Jens Haupert, German Research Center for Artificial Intelligence (DFKI), Germany

UBICOMM Industry/Research Chairs

Korbinian Frank, German Aerospace Center - Institute of Communications and Navigation, Germany
Carlo Mastroianni, CNR, Italy
Michele Ruta, Technical University of Bari, Italy
Jose Manuel Cantera Fonseca, Telefonica Investigacion y Desarrollo, Spain
Yulin Ding, Defence Science & Technology Organization Edinburgh, Australia
Korbinian Frank, German Aerospace Center - Institute of Communications and Navigation, Germany
Cornel Klein, Siemens AG/Corporate Research and Technologies - Münich, Germany
Reinhard Klemm, Avaya Labs Research-Basking Ridge, USA
Serena Pastore, INAF- Astronomical Observatory of Padova, Italy
Jyrki T.J. Penttinen, Finesstel Ltd, Finland
Jorge Pereira, European Comission, Belgium
Miroslav Velev, Aries Design Automation, USA
Christoph Steup, FIN - OvGU, Germany

UBICOMM Publicity Chairs

Raul Igual, University of Zaragoza, Spain
Andre Dietrich, Otto-von-Guericke-University Magdeburg, Germany
Rebekah Hunter, University of Ulster, UK

Francesco Fiamberti, University of Milano-Bicocca, Italy
Sönke Knoch, German Research Center for Artificial Intelligence (DFKI GmbH), Germany

UBICOMM 2016 Technical Progam Committee

Afrand Agah, West Chester University of Pennsylvania, USA
Aristotelis Agianniotis, Institute of Information Systems, HES-SO Valais, Switzerland
Rui Aguiar, Universidade de Aveiro, Porutgal
Tara Ali-Yahiya, Paris Sud 11 University, France
Mercedes Amor, Universidad de Málaga, Spain
Timothy Arndt, Cleveland State University, USA
Mehran Asadi, Lincoln University, U.S.A.
Zubair Baig, Edith Cowan University, Australia
Sergey Balandin, FRUCT, Finland
Matthias Baldauf, Vienna University of Technology, Austria
Michel Banâtre, IRISA - Rennes, France
Oresti Banos, Kyung Hee University, South Korea
Felipe Becker Nunes, Federal University of Rio Grande do Sul (UFRGS), Brazil
Simon Bergweiler, German Research Center for Artificial Intelligence (DFKI), Germany
Aurelio Bermúdez Marin, Universidad de Castilla-La Mancha, Spain
Bruno Bogaz Zarpelão, State University of Londrina (UEL), Brazil
Jihen Bokri, ENSI (National School of Computer Science), Tunisia
Lars Braubach, University of Hamburg, Germany
Bernd Bruegge, Institut für Informatik - Technische Universität München, Germany
Diletta Romana Cacciagrano, University of Camerino, Italy
Jose Manuel Cantera Fonseca, Telefonica Investigacion y Desarrollo, Spain
Juan-Vicente Capella-Hernández, Universidad Politécnica de Valencia, Spain
Rafael Casado, Universidad de Castilla-La Mancha, Spain
Everton Cavalcante, Federal University of Rio Grande do Norte, Brazil
Davut Cavdar, Middle East Technical University, Turkey
José Cecílio, University of Coimbra, Portugal
Bongsug (Kevin) Chae, Kansas State University, USA
Konstantinos Chatzikokolakis, National and Kapodistrian University of Athens, Greece
Jingyuan Cheng, German Research Center for Artificial Intelligence (DFKI), Germany
Jun-Dong Cho, Sungkyunkwan University, Suwon, South Korea
Sung-Bae Cho, Yonsei University - Seoul, Korea
Mhammed Chraibi, Al Akhawayn University - Ifrane, Morocco
MyoungBeom Chung, Sungkyul University, Korea
Michael Collins, Dublin Institute of Technology, Dublin, Ireland
Andre Constantino da Silva, IFSP, Brazil
Stefano Cresci, IIT-CNR, Italy
Pablo Curiel, DeustoTech - Deusto Institute of Technology, Spain
Klaus David, University of Kassel, Germany
Malcolm Dcosta, University of Houston, USA

Sun-Yuan Hsieh, National Cheng Kung University, Taiwan
Shaohan Hu, UIUC, USA
Xiaodi Huang, Charles Sturt University - Albury, Australia
Javier Alexander Hurtado, University of Cauca, Colombia
Raul Igual, University of Zaragoza, Spain
Marko Jaakola, VTT Technical Research Centre of Finland, Finland
Tauseef Jamal, University Lusofona - Lisbon, Portugal
Jongpil Jeong, Sungkyunkwan University, South Korea
Jun-Cheol Jeon, Kumoh National Institute of Technology, Korea
Ming Jin, UC Berkeley, USAVana Kalogeraki, Athens University of Economics and Business, Greece
Faouzi Kamoun, Zayed University, UAE
Fazal Wahab Karam, Gandhara Institute of Science and Technology, Pakistan
Nobuo Kawaguchi, Nagoya University, Japan
Subayal Khan, VTT, Finland
Brian (Byung-Gyu) Kim, SunMoon University, South Korea
Kyungbaek Kim, Chonnam National University, South Korea
Soo-Kyun Kim, Samsung Electronics, South Korea
Sung-Ki Kim, Sun Moon University, South Korea
Manuele Kirsch Pinheiro, Université Paris 1 Panthéon Sorbonne, France
Cornel Klein, Siemens AG/Corporate Research and Technologies - Münich, Germany
Reinhard Klemm, Avaya Labs Research-Basking Ridge, USA
Sönke Knoch, German Research Center for Artificial Intelligence (DFKI), Germany
Eitaro Kohno, Hiroshima City University, Japan
Shin'ichi Konomi, University of Tokyo, Japan
Dmitry Korzun, Petrozavodsk State University / Aalto University, Russia / Finland
Natalie Kryvinski, University of Vienna, Austria
Jeffrey Tzu Kwan Valino Koh, National University of Singapore, Singapore
Frédéric Le Mouël, INRIA/INSA Lyon, France
Nicolas Le Sommer, Université de Bretagne Sud - Vannes, France
Juong-Sik Lee, Nokia Research Center, USA
Valderi R. Q. Leithardt, Federal University of Rio Grande do Sul, Brazil
Pierre Leone, University of Geneva, Switzerland
Jianguo Li, Conversant Media, USA
Yiming Li, National Chiao Tung University, Taiwan
Jian Liang, Cork Institute of Technology, Ireland
Kai-Wen Lien, Chienkuo Institute University - Changhua, Taiwan
Bo Liu, University of Technology - Sydney, Australia
Damon Shing-Min Liu, National Chung Cheng University, Taiwan
David Lizcano Casas, Open University of Madrid (UDIMA), Spain
Jaime Lloret Mauri, Polytechnic University of Valencia, Spain
Jaziel Souza Lobo, Instituto Federal de Sergipe, Brazil
Juan Carlos López, University of Castilla-La Mancha, Spain
Gustavo López Herrera, Research Center on Information and Communication Technologies

Agis Papantoniou, National Technical University of Athens (NTUA), Greece
Kwangjin Park, Wonkwang University, South Korea
Ignazio Passero, Università degli Studi di Salerno - Fisciano, Italy
Serena Pastore, INAF- Astronomical Observatory of Padova, Italy
K. K. Pattanaik, ABV-Indian Institute of Information Technology and Management, India
Misha Pavel, Northeastern University, USA
Wen-Chih Peng, National Chiao Tung University, Taiwan
Jyrki T.J. Penttinen, Finesstel Ltd, Finland
Jorge Pereira, European Comission, Belgium
Nuno Pereira, CISTER/INESC TEC - ISEP, Portugal
Welma Pereira de Jesus, Institute for Pervasive Computing - Johannes Kepler University Linz, Austria
Thuy Thi Thanh Pham, Hanoi University of Science and Technology, Vietnam
Dinh Phung, Deakin University, Australia
Yulia Ponomarchuk, Kyungpook National University, Republic of Korea
Daniel Porta, German Research Center for Artificial Intelligence (DFKI) - Saarbrücken, Germany
Evangelos Pournaras, ETH Zurich, Switzerland
Ivan Pretel, DeustoTech - Deusto Institute of Technology, Spain
Chuan Qin, University of Shanghai for Science and Technology, China
Muhammad Wasim Raed, King Fahd University of Petroleum & Minerals, Saudi Arabia
Elmano Ramalho Cavalcanti, Federal Institute of Education, Science and Technology of Pernambuco, Brazil
Juwel Rana, Luleå University of Technology, Sweden
Maurizio Rebaudengo, Politecnico di Torino, Italy
Hendrik Richter, LMU - University of Munich, Germany
Jose D. P. Rolim, University of Geneva, Switzerland
Alessandra Russo, Imperial College London, UK
Michele Ruta, Technical University of Bari, Italy
Kouichi Sakurai, Kyushu University, Japan
Johannes Sametinger, Institut für Wirtschaftsinformatik, Austria
Luis Sanchez, Universidad de Cantabria, Spain
Josè Santa, University Centre of Defence at the Spanish Air Force Academy, Spain
Andrea Saracino, University of Pisa, Italy
Yucel Saygin, Sabanci University, Turkey
Michael Ignaz Schumacher, HES-SO Valais-Wallis, Switzerland
Zary Segall , Royal Institute of Technology, Sweden
Sandra Sendra Compte, Universidad Politecnica de Valencia, Spain
Anton Sergeev, St. Petersburg State University of Aerospace Instrumentation, Russia
MªÁngeles Serna Moreno, University College Cork, Ireland
Ali Shahrabi, Glasgow Caledonian University, Scotland, UK
Shih-Lung Shaw, University of Tennessee, U.S.A.
Qi Shi, Liverpool John Moores University, UK
Kazuhiko Shibuya, The Institute of Statistical Mathematics, Japan
Catarina Silva, Polytechnic Institute of Leiria, Portugal

Marjorie Skubic, University of Missouri, USA
Luca Stabellini, The Royal Institute of Technology - Stockholm, Sweden
Radosveta Sokullu, Ege University, Turkey
Animesh Srivastava, Duke University, USA
Xiang Su, University of Oulu, Finland
Álvaro Suárez Sarmiento, University of Las Palmas de Gran Canaria, Spain
Kåre Synnes, Luleå University of Technology, Sweden
Apostolos Syropoulos, Greek Molecular Computing Group, Greece
Ryszard Tadeusiewicz, AGH University of Science and Technology, Poland
Tetsuji Takada, The University of Electro-Communications - Tokyo, Japan
Kazunori Takashio, Keio University, Japan
Yoshiaki Taniguchi, Kindai University, Japan
Adrian Dan Tarniceriu, Ecole Polytechnique Federale de Lausanne, Switzerland
Markus Taumberger, VTT Technical Research Centre of Finland, Finland
Nick Taylor, Heriot-Watt University, Edinburgh, UK
Saïd Tazi, LAAS-CNRS, Université de Toulouse / Université Toulouse1, France
Manos Tentzeris, Georgia Institute of Technology, USA
Tsutomu Terada, Kobe University, Japan
Maurizio Tesconi, IIT-CNR, Italy
Stephanie Teufel, University of Fribourg, Switzerland
Parimala Thulasiraman, University of Manitoba, Canada
Lei Tian, University of Nebraska-Lincoln, USA
Marco Tiloca, University of Pisa, Italy
Piotr Toczyski, Maria Grzegorzewska University, Warsaw, Poland
Jan Top, Wageningen UR - Vrije Universiteit Amsterdam, Netherlands
Chih-Cheng Tseng, National Ilan University, Taiwan
Jean Vareille, Université de Bretagne Occidentale - Brest, France
Dominique Vaufreydaz, INRIA Rhône-Alpes, France
Miroslav Velev, Aries Design Automation, USA
Massimo Villari, Universita' di Messina, Italy
Baobing Wang, Facebook HQ, USA
Wei Wei, Xi'an University of Technology, China
Woontack Woo, Korea Advanced Institute of Science and Technology (KAIST), South Korea
Chao-Tung Yang, Tunghai University, Taiwan
Xiao Yu, Aalto University, Finland
Zhiwen Yu, Northwestern Polytechnical University, China
Mehmet Erkan Yüksel, Istanbul University Turkey
Hao Lan Zhang, Zhejiang University, China
Gang Zhao, National University of Singapore, Singapore
Nataša Živić, University of Siegen, Germany
Claudia Liliana Zuñiga, University of Santiago de Cali, Colombia

Private Data Protection in Ubiquitous Computing

Malika Yaici

Laboratoire LTII
University of Bejaia
Bejaia, 06000, Algeria
yaici_m@hotmail.com

Samia Ameza*, Ryma Houari† and Sabrina Hammachi‡

Computer Department, University of Bejaia
Bejaia, 06000, Algeria
*ameza_samia@yahoo.fr †ri.houari@hotmail.fr
‡hassiba_rima@yahoo.fr

***Abstract*—A system in ubiquitous computing consists of a large amount of heterogeneous users and devices that communicate with each other. Users in this dynamic field communicate with lightweight and autonomous devices, which accentuate security problems and make them more complex. The existing mechanisms and solutions are inadequate to address new challenges mainly for problems of authentication and protection of privacy. In this paper, a new security architecture called Tree Based distributed Privacy Protection System is proposed. It supports protection of users private data and addresses the shortcomings of systems like GAIA, OpenID and User-directed Privacy Protection (UPP). Furthermore, it takes into account the domain dissociation property, in order to achieve decentralized data protection.**

Keywords–Ubiquitous Computing; Security; Private Data Protection; Privacy; Integrity.

I. INTRODUCTION

The growing number of Internet users and the integration of mobile clients has changed distributed computer science, by allowing the creation of smart and communicating environments, thus offering to the user the opportunity to make interactions with its environment and its equipments easily and transparently leading to the concept of ubiquitous computing.

Its origins date back to 1991, when Mark Weiser [1] presented his futuristic vision of the 21st century computing by establishing the foundations of pervasive computing. It aims to integrate computer technology in man's everyday life in various fields (Health, Public services, etc.). To improve interactivity, it offers the user the ability to access various features and services of its environment and from any mobile device (personal digital assistant PDA, tablet computer, smartphone, etc). The emergence of these devices has created new security problems for which solutions and existing mechanisms are inadequate, especially concerning the problems of authentication and users' private data protection. In such a system, the existence of a centralized and homogeneous security policy is in fact not desirable. It is therefore necessary to give more autonomy to security systems, mainly by providing them with mechanisms establishing dynamic and flexible cooperation and collaboration.

Mobile devices and the Internet of Things (IoT) present some problems such as incorrect location information, privacy violation, and difficulty of end-user control. A conceptual model is presented in [2] to satisfy requirements which include a privacy-preserving location supporting protocol using wireless sensor networks for privacy-preserving childcare and safety where the end-user has authorized credentials anonymity.

In [3], the author uses the framework of contextual integrity related to privacy, developed by Nissenbaum in 2010 [4], as a tool to understand citizen's response to the implementation of IoT related technology in a supermarket. The purpose was to identify and understand specific changes in information practices brought about by the IoT that may be perceived as privacy violations. Issues identified included the mining of medical data, invasive targeted advertising, and loss of autonomy through marketing profiles or personal affect monitoring.

Dhasarathan et al. [5] present an intelligent model to protect user's valuable personal data based on multi-agents. A hybrid hash-based authentication technique as an end point lock is proposed. It is a composite model coupled with an anomaly detection interface algorithm for cloud user's privacy preserving (intrusion detection, unexpected activities in normal behavior).

In [6], the authors focus on information privacy protection in a post-release phase. Without entirely depending on the information collector, an information owner is provided with powerful means to control and audit how his/her released information will be used, by whom, and when. A set of innovative owner-controlled privacy protection and violation detection techniques have been proposed: Self-destroying File, Mutation Engine System, Automatic Receipt Collection, and Honey Token-based Privacy Violation Detection. A next generation privacy-enhanced operating system, which supports the proposed mechanisms, is introduced. Such a privacy-enhanced operating system stands for a technical breakthrough, which offers new features to existing operating systems.

Efficiency and scalability become critical criteria for privacy preserving protocols in the age of Big Data. In [7], a new Private Set Intersection (PSI) protocol, based on a novel approach called oblivious Bloom intersection is presented. The PSI problem consists of two parties, a client and a server, which want to jointly compute the intersection of their private input sets in a manner that at the end the client learns the intersection and the server learns nothing. The proposed protocol uses a two-party computation approach, which makes use of a new variant of Bloom filters called by the author Garbled Bloom filters, and the new approach is referred to as Oblivious Bloom Intersection.

Private Information Retrieval (PIR) protocols allow users to learn data items stored on a server which is not fully trusted, without disclosing to the server the particular data element retrieved. In [8], the author investigates the amount of data disclosed by the the most prominent PIR protocols during a single run. From this investigation, mechanisms that limit the PIR disclosure to a single data item are devised.

Releasing sensitive data while preserving privacy is a problem that has attracted considerable attention in recent years. One existing solution for addressing the problem is differential privacy, which requires that the data released reveals little information about whether any particular individual is present or absent from the data. To fulfill such a requirement, a typical approach adopted by the existing solutions is to publish a noisy version of the data instead of the original one. The author of [9] considers a fundamental problem that is frequently encountered in differentially private data publishing: Given a set D of tuples defined over a domain Ω, the aim is to decompose Ω into a set S of sub-domains and publish a noisy count of the tuples contained in each sub-domain, such that S and the noisy counts approximate the tuple distribution in D as accurately as possible. To remedy the deficiency of existing solutions, the author presents PrivTree, a histogram construction algorithm that adopts hierarchical decomposition but completely eliminates the dependency on a predefined limit h on the recursion depth in the splitting of Ω.

Middleware is an essential layer in the architecture of ubiquitous systems, and recently, more emphasis has been put on security middleware as an enabling component for ubiquitous applications. This is due to the high levels of personal and private data sharing in these systems. In [10], some representative security middleware approaches are reviewed and their various properties, characteristics, and challenges are highlighted.

The objective of our work is to develop an architecture that meets the security constraints of the ubiquitous systems that support the protection of user's private data. The idea is to consider the separation of different user data on separate domains, so that an intruder never reaches all of the user's private information and protect them against unauthorized and unwanted access and limit the transmission of such sensitive data.

The paper is organized as follows: after this introduction, some existing research works on the domain are presented in Section 2 (Ubiquitous environment security requirements) and Section 3 (GAIA, OpenID and UPP) with a comparison between them. Then, in Section 4, the proposed system is given with an illustrative example. An improved solution based on a tree structure is presented in Section 5 with some algorithms and a comparison with the pre-cited existing solutions. A conclusion and some perspectives finish this paper.

II. Security in Ubiquitous Systems

Ubiquitous systems are mainly distributed, reactive to context, and deal with user personnel data. It is therefore necessary to give more autonomy to their security systems, mainly by providing them with mechanisms through dynamic and flexible cooperation and collaboration to ensure the smooth flow of data in this system. We must develop robust protocols that ensure high confidence in the services and minimize the vulnerabilities of such systems.

A. *Ubiquitous features*

The main features of ubiquitous environment are the user mobility and the proliferation of light devices, communicating through light and wireless infrastructure. Thus, the convergence of terrestrial infrastructure (Local Area Network LAN, fiber optic, etc.) and mobility (Global system for mobile GSM, 4G and WIFI) enables users to have access to a vast and limitless network of information and services regardless of place and time. All these features create complex security problems. This requires the introduction of advanced authentication methods, the management and distribution of security keys between the various entities on the network, while respecting the constraints of wireless networks, such as the radio interface capacity and mobile devices, resources that represent the bottleneck of such networks.

B. *Security Requirements*

The main issues that must be addressed in terms of security are [10]:

1) Authentication mechanisms and credential management
2) Authorization and access control management
3) Shared data security and integrity
4) Secure one-to-one and group communication
5) Heterogeneous security/environment requirements support
6) Secure mobility management
7) Capability to operate in devices with low resources
8) Automatic configuration and management of these facilities.

To guarantee the security of ubiquitous systems, they must meet the following requirements as defined in [11]:

- Decentralization: Ubiquitous environment is designed to allow the user and all its resources to be accessible anywhere and anytime. The mobile user must have access to his attributes, and prove his identity in this environment without claiming all the time the centralized server of his organization. The security policy implementation should be as decentralized as possible.
- Interoperability: The heterogeneity is a feature of ubiquitous applications. The proposed solution involves the implementation of a decentralized system for collaboration and interaction between heterogeneous organizations.
- Traceability and non-repudiation: The design of a completely secure ubiquitous system is impossible. But, the implementation of mechanisms to quickly identify threats or attacks (such as non-repudiation / tracking) provides an acceptable issue.
- Transparency: Ubiquitous computing aims to simplify the use of its resources. In ubiquitous applications and environments, the problems of authentication are more complex because of the lack of unified authentication mechanism. Several techniques have been designed to make user authentication easy and done in a transparent manner (Single Sign On).

- Flexibility: New authentication techniques have emerged such as biometrics, Radio frequency identification (RFID), etc.. Thus, a security system for ubiquitous environment must be able to integrate these different means of identification and adapt authentication mechanisms to the context of the user, and the capacity and the type of used devices.
- Protection of Privacy: The identity and attributes of a person are confidential information that is imperative to protect. To secure these data we must implement protocols that protect and ensure confidentiality.

III. Privacy in Ubiquitous Systems

The implementation of security solutions in ubiquitous environments has many constraints, like limited capacity of batteries, device mobility and limited time response. Several security systems providing authentication have been proposed and we chose to detail three of them: GAIA, OpenID and UPP.

1) GAIA: GAIA [12] is a system proposed by the University of Illinois which provides an infrastructure to build applications for the ubiquitous environment. GAIA security is integrated as a component of the architecture known as the GAIAOS Security, which includes a central service Cerberus integrating authentication and access control. GAIAOS Security uses the identity as a basis and provides the ability to authenticate the user regardless of the capacity of used devices by using different methods such as conventional mechanisms login / password or smart cards.

2) OpenId: OpenID is an authentication system designed for the World Wide Web. It allows users to authenticate to multiple sites (which support this technology), without having to remember one login for each, but using only once a unique identifier of type URI (Uniform Resource Identifier) which is obtained by one of the OpenID providers [13]. Three main actors are involved in authentication:

- The end user (client)
- The Consumer (Relying Part: RP)
- The identity provider (OpenID Provider: OP / IDP Identity Provider)

The authentication process during a connection is as follows (Figure 1):

1) The client provides URI of his profile OpenID to the consumer site (RP).
2) The RP contacts the OpenID provider's site (OP).
3) Both RP and OP exchange digital information generating a "shared secret"
4) The consumer site (RP) redirects the client in a transparent way to OP.
5) The client authenticates to the provider site (OP).
6) The provider site (OP) redirects the client to the consumer (RP) with the authentication result.

3) User-directed Privacy Protection: The authors in [14] proposed an architecture named User-Directed Privacy Protection (UPP) that allows users to control their information themselves in order to access services. The UPP architecture consists of two parts:

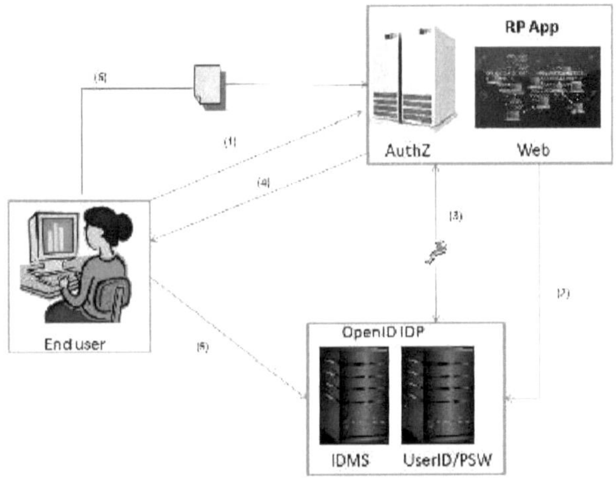

Figure 1: OpenId authentication process [13]

- Authentication Manager: manages the personal information and authentication information.
- Control Center: the part that controls the equipment and contents.

The user uses a personal device (a PDA for example) to authenticate to the security manager of a domain, in order to request a service. The service provider checks if the user manages its list of access information (login, password) himself. If so, before entering the service, he transfers its access policy to the domain manager. The latter "negotiates" the policy with the user and sends this information to a general manager. The authentication process is as follows (Figure 2):

1) Pre-authentication of each security manager of a domain will be established by the manager of global certification.
2) The user authenticates to the security manager of the new domain, it issues a temporary certification to the user by using an encrypted channel.
3) If the user requests a service to the new domain, it requires a new user authentication for access to Global Authentication Manager.
4) The new domain requires a certification to the manager of global certification, and it confirms the request (offer a certificate).
5) The manager of global certification requests personal information to the Global Authentication Manager. The latter provides the necessary information.

A. Synthesis

In this section, we will compare the different approaches based on the requirements of ubiquitous computing security.

- Decentralization: Security systems described here are based on the centralization of user data. Security GAIAOS backups user data in server Cerberus, OpenID has a third party (the identity provider OP) which is the only dedicated server for data storage and users

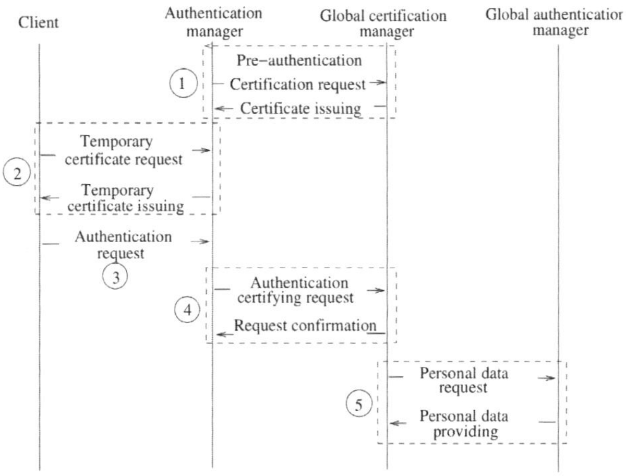

Figure 2: UPP authentication algorithm [14]

authentication, and the manager of the global authentication server is the only server that architecture UPP uses to collect users' certificates.

- Interoperability: Users must have mobile access to the site to which they are affiliated, and to the other remote sites, in order to obtain the desired services. The interoperability of different security policies is essential. OpenID is a great innovation in terms of interoperable solutions for authentication and identity management on the Internet. GAIAOS Security does not support collaboration between organizations, which restricts the security policy to the local domain only.
- Traceability: Traceability is very important; it is based on mechanisms to ensure non-repudiation in order to track any person who committed the fraud. GAIA, OpenID and UPP have the advantage of traceability that allows the account owner to have a history of its subscriptions.
- Transparency: GAIAOS and OpenID provide a way to reduce the interaction of the user during the authentication process. The UPP architecture and the propositions given in [2] and [6] do not provide this feature because users control their information themselves to access services.
- Flexibility: the diversity of devices used in ubiquitous computing ensures that the mobile user has the ability to connect and interact with its environment by using different techniques of identification. GAIAOS, UPP and OpenID provide the ability to authenticate the user regardless of the capacity of the used devices.
- Protection of Privacy: It is necessary to protect the identity and private data of mobile users. OpenID, GAIA and UPP are interesting approaches that allow the protection of private data of mobile users, but has the disadvantage of storing different user privileges on a server that is accessible all the time, this makes these systems vulnerable.

IV. Proposition of a New Management System of Private Data

A. *Problem Positioning*

The development of Web services, the vast heterogeneity of the connection techniques and conditions of communication (including bandwidth), the proliferation of mobile devices, and the heterogeneity of protocols and their deployment in mobile and ubiquitous computing increase significantly the risks related to the protection of user's privacy. Implemented security policies impose protocols that enable the conservation and management of personal data, and limit their transmissions from mobile devices as well as their movement within the network. This is a good approach to avoid some attacks like sniffing.

The security solutions presented previously are typically based on backing up data on a single server. The private data of the user are stored on a single server, the invocation (request) to a secure service by a user, will acquire its data from the server after an authentication procedure. These solutions however suffer from two deficiencies: the first is the inability to access the data without a reliable connection, secure, permanent and fast server, a set of conditions difficult to meet in any environment. The second is the centralization of data on a single server which represents a vulnerability because if the server is compromised the entire system will be.

As part of our project, we will mainly deal with the following two issues:

- How to protect private data of the mobile user in a transparent way, easily and without being intrusive?
- How to decentralize the data and the user's personal information in a fast and secure manner?

B. *The Proposed Architecture*

To satisfy ubiquitous environmental security requirements such as decentralization, flexibility and protection of private data, we opted for a hierarchical architecture. The principle of this solution is the distribution of the user data on a set of servers so that each of them contains only the information needed for user authentication and the servers (nodes) are distributed randomly over a virtual structure. This data is scattered in the system as follows:

- Personal data is not on a single server, but on multiple different servers.
- No server owns the totality of a particular client personal data.

The entities involved in this architecture are as follows:

- The user: a human being (client), who is the consumer of the service.
- Generator of identifier (GenID): a node that is responsible for generating a unique identifier for users during their registration in the system.
- Domains: A domain represents a business, a service provider (music, videos, bank, etc.).

The architecture is based on the following hypothesis:

- The architecture is ephemeral and only the request message and the transmission of personal information uses the links.
- No node knows the entire structure.
- A node knows only its successors and its predecessor.
- A pre-authentication of the domains of the environment is performed using a third party authentication.
- Each user has at least one certificate (issued by his domain of affiliation) and can acquire others in other domains.

Each user has a universal identifier, distributed among all domains at its first registration in the system, which allows gathering its data. Some user data can be replicated on some servers, but each of them stores the personal information necessary to it and the additional information obtained from other nodes are deleted.

C. Illustrative Example

Suppose Alice has an identity certificate containing her name, photograph, date of birth, address, Social Security number, fingerprint, account number, her public key and her profession.

Alice complete identity certificate → {
- Alice
- Professor
- Birth date
- Security ID
- Photo
- Fingerprint
- Public key
- Address
- Bank account ID

If she wants to rent a car, Alice must present a document (certificate) confirming the user name and some personal information such as her photo and address. However, the same document may contain other information that Alice does not wish to divulge, such as age or job.

Car rental→ {
- Alice
- ~~Professor~~
- ~~Birth date~~
- ~~Security ID~~
- Photo
- ~~Fingerprint~~
- ~~Public key~~
- Address
- ~~Bank account ID~~

This case is not unique. During a consultation with a doctor, Alice must be able to present a document showing only the name, date of birth and social security number. This illustrates the need for mechanisms for the decentralization of personal information in order to protect the private data of users.

Doctor→ {
- Alice
- Birth date
- Security ID
- Photo

Bank→ {
- Alice
- Professor
- Fingerprint
- Bank account ID

D. The Broadcast Distributed Privacy Protection System Architecture

To achieve decentralization of private data, we proposed a distributed architecture named Broadcast distributed privacy protection system (BDPPS) based on the decentralization of private data, so a hierarchical architecture is needed. To reflect structural relationships and hierarchies, we used a binary tree. The advantages of binary trees are well known: flexibility, easy construction and management (searching, insertion), etc.

The basics of this architecture are as follows:

- Private user data is distributed on a set of servers so that each one contains only the information necessary for its operation.
- The domains are distributed over the nodes of the tree in a random manner.
- If a domain needs the private data of a user who depends on another domain, a search request will be broadcasted on all system nodes.
- Upon receipt of the response, there is a deadline for the additional data to be deleted.

The major drawback of this architecture is the large number of requests sent through the tree when searching private information. To remedy this problem we decided to improve this proposal, based on how to divide the domains in the system.

V. Improved Solution

To minimize the number of messages circulating in the tree and increase the quality of service, we proposed an improved architecture named Tree Based distributed privacy protection system (TBDPPS). The idea is to increase the probability of finding the sought data by depth-first traversal of the tree, and to arrange these data in a complementary manner with between two close nodes (servers).

The organization of services is done in a manner allowing the users data to be structured in a complementary and easy way. The sent request follows a tree structure in depth in order to increase the probability of finding the researched data. If a server needs more information, instead of asking the user, it retrieves them from the nearest server in the tree. Each node server is supposed to receive a request from a parent node or a

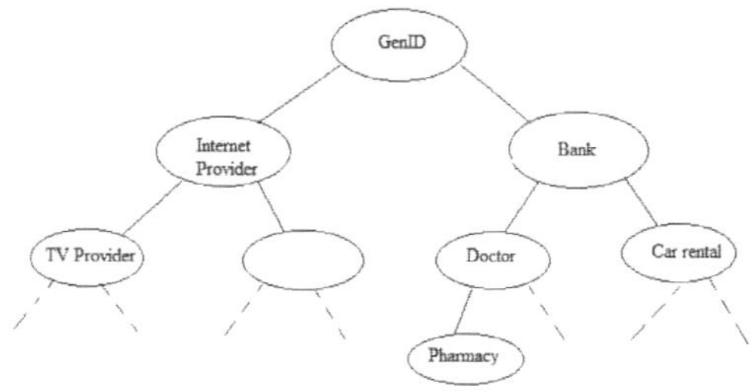

Figure 3: The tree broadcast distributed privacy protection system principle

child node for some specific information that he has but they don't.

For example a service that has an activity like downloading videos, music, etc., it would be better to have the bank node as a closest neighbour, in order to complete the transaction process as quickly as possible (Figure 3).

This distribution of domains offers various advantages:

- Message number Reduction flowing in the tree.
- Increase in the quality of service.
- Simplicity and ease of personal data management.

A. Example

Following the previous example, by using her PDA Alice was authenticated with a car rental service to rent a car. According to the proposed architecture, it is the car rental server that will retrieve data about the payment (account Identifier).

The server prepares a query that contains the necessary parameters such as domain code, the user ID and the needed data (Bank account ID), and then sends them to his child nodes on the tree. The latter seeks the ID of the user and the account number, if they have the desired data they send the response request containing the necessary information, if not they send the request to their child nodes and so on. If no child node exist then the request is sent to its parent node. The car rental service node and the bank node belong to the same subtree, as shown in Figure 3.

B. Algorithms

In the following section, the different algorithms executed by the tree's nodes are described and they use the following defined variables:

`codD`: The domain code which sends the research request.

`reqID` : Request identifier.

`userID` : User identifier.

`privateData` : The set of private data belonging to a domain.

`Ldata` : the set of sought data by the request issuer.

`data` : the set of data conveyed by requests/responses.

`found` : a Boolean variable (initially `FALSE`).

1) User registration: When a user submits a registration request to a domain in the system for the first time, this domain sends a request to the GenID node. This node first verifies the validity of the request (a real new user), if it is valid it generates a unique identifier (a numeric or alphanumeric string), then broadcasts it on the tree. The algorithm implemented on the GenID node is given in Algorithm 1.

Algorithm 1 User registration

Require: Request by a new user
Ensure: User identifier `userID`.

```
if new user then
    if current node code = GenID code then
        generate a userID to user
    end if
    register user to domain
    send(codD, reqID, userID) to child nodes.
end if
```

2) Service request: When a user requests a service to a domain the latter searches its database to retrieve the user's private data. If there is a lack of information necessary for a proper operation of the service, the server propagates a request containing some parameters in its sub-tree to find the missing data simultaneously. If the answer obtained from its sub-tree is negative then the request will be sent to the parent node.

The search stops when the initiator domain has recovered all the necessary data, or has received the request sent by a node (child for the root node or parent for other domain) and the variable found is false. The main steps are as follows:

Step1: The user submits a service request to a domain as given in Algorithm 2.

Algorithm 2 Service request Algorithm

Require: Request by a user affiliated to domain
Ensure: Satisfaction of a service

```
if data ⊂ privateData then
    service satisfied
else
    send(codD, reqID, userID, data, found) to
    child nodes
end if
```

Step2: The receipt of the request by another domain: Upon receipt of this request, the domain checks if the user ID and data exists, if yes it will formulate a response containing the found data and sends to the sender (`codD` of the request), otherwise it sends the request to his child nodes, if they exist, or to its parent node. The result is given in Algorithm 3.

The statement `data←privateData` concerns only the wanted data from the set `privateData`.

Step3: The receipt of the request by the issuer: Upon receipt of the request, the issuer verifies the boolean variable `found` if it is true. Then it compares the data received with the data sought and if all the data are found then the service is executed, otherwise the issuer will make another request by omitting

Algorithm 3 Request reception Algorithm

```
Require: Request(codD, reqID, userID, data, found)
Ensure: Collect missing private data
if (userID ∈ domain) && (data ⊂ privateData then
    found ← TRUE
    data←privateData
    send(codD, reqID, userID, data, found) to codD node
else
    if ∃ child nodes then
        send(codD, reqID, userID, data, found) to child node
    else
        send(codD, reqID, userID, data, found) to parent node
    end if
end if
```

all the found data and sending it to another child if it exists or to the parent to explore another sub-tree. The service is unsatisfied when the issuer receives the request by one of its neighbors (child for the root and parent for other nodes) and the variable `found` is `FALSE`. The term "`card`" stands for the cardinal of a set. Algorithm 4 illustrates this step.

Algorithm 4 Issuer request reception Algorithm

```
Require: Request(codD, reqID, userID, data, found)
Ensure: Satisfaction of a service.
if found=TRUE then
    if card(Ldata) = card(data) then
        Service satisfied
    else
        data ← Ldata-data
        send(codD, reqID, userID, data, found) to child node
    end if
else
    if parent node not visited then
        send(codD, reqID, userID, data, found) to parent node
    else
        Service not satisfied
    end if
end if
```

The statement `data ← Ldata-data` concerns the case when `data` contains more than one item, so the found items are retrieved from the set `data` to continue the search for the rest of items.

If a service is satisfied the `Ldata` is deleted after a fixed delay. If all the links of the tree exist, then all the needed data exist on the tree and it will be found. In this case the searching time will be at maximum the time of parallel browsing of the tree (height size).

A service cannot be satisfied if the needed data is not found, and this is possible only if the concerned server node (which has the data) or the links are down. In this case a request is repeated after a random delay.

VI. SYNTHESIS

We have proposed a solution that solves the problem of data privacy for mobile users. Our proposal is to define a new architecture that takes into account the separation of different domains in the system and corresponds to a tree. The user's personal data are distributed across a set of servers so that none will ever have all the user's private data except those required for its operation.

- Decentralization: In the proposed system, the different domains making up the ubiquitous environment do not share user's private data. Each domain maintains a subset of the user's necessary data.
- Interoperability: the collaboration between the nodes of the system is done to allow a collection of different private data that a domain needs. Each system node can communicate with other remote nodes across his neighbors, by sending the different requests.
- Transparency: the TBDPPS system reduces the interaction of the user during the authentication process and service request. Indeed, a user authenticates first to a service then can acquire other services in an easy and intuitive way, because it is the first server that will retrieve the rest of user private data.
- Traceability: transactions in our system are made via certificates that guarantee non-repudiation of users (certificates owners) in order to identify any performed transactions.
- Flexibility: The system TBDPPS offers the user the possibility to be authenticated regardless of the capacity of the devices used and the different identification methods.
- Privacy protection: Taking into account the separation of the different data on separate domains of the system, so that an intruder cannot have the totality of the user's private information and protect these data against unwanted disclosure, the proposed architecture allows the protection of users private data and overcomes the problems of their storage on a vulnerable single server.
- Data distribution: The propositions given in [7] and [9] deal with distributed private data but the client is an actor, so no transparency. For the latter, it even preconizes a tree architecture but noisy information are included. In our proposition only the private data is distributed, which means less data transmission.
- Autonomy: The proposed system operates without the client intervention. So a hacker cannot get a user's private data. Attacks like sniffing cannot succeed because only some of private data is circulating on the network. Finally, the only dangerous attack is a non-trusted or corrupted server (node), but we supposed that all the domains are authenticated using a third-party protocol.
- Number of messages: Only one type of message will be used. A request is used to collect the missing private data and the same request is used to send the response to the request issuer.

- Algorithmic complexity: the complexity of the proposed method is given depending on the type of trees (from the best to the worst);

Type of binary tree	Complexity
Complete tree	$O(\log n)$
Full tree	$O(\log n)$
One-branch tree	$O(n)$

and on each situation.

Situation	Complexity
Registration	$O(\log n)$
Full private data present	$O(1)$
One missing item	$O(2 * \log n)$
More than one missing	$O(2 * \log n)$

The variable n is the number of domains/nodes in the system/tree.

- Figure 4 shows the results of a small simulation (using Matlab) of the time response of the proposed method depending on the size of tree and the number of missing items in the data. The time response depends on the tree height ($log(n)$ and, even if the number of missing items increases, the parallel parsing of the tree is done once.

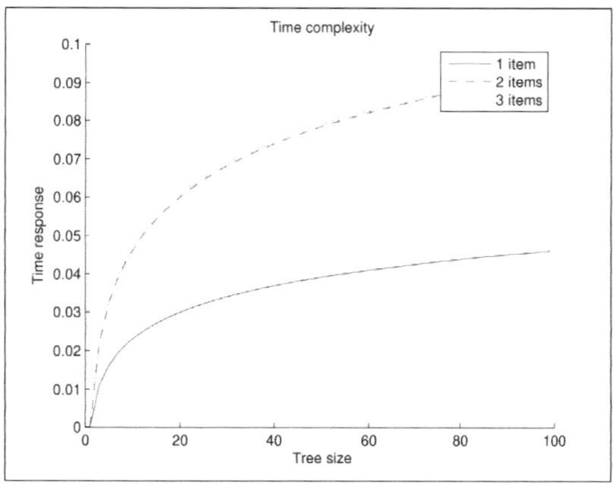

Figure 4: Time response for a single request

VII. Conclusion

Ubiquitous environment allows performing the appropriate actions to the user while adapting to environmental conditions, preferences and user profile. Building such an environment is very difficult given the user's everyday environments composed of heterogeneous devices leading to a dynamic system.

Existing solutions like GAIA, OpenID and UPP systems are very convenient structures for the organization of private data, but the critical point of these projects is the centralization of data on a single server, making data protection of mobile users very vulnerable.

We proposed a solution to protect user's private data which overcomes the aforementioned deficiency and takes into account decentralization and the method of domain dissociation to make communication easy and flexible. The number of domains is limited so the tree size is limited and, since it is a binary tree, its construction will be easier.

As future work, it would be interesting to consider a dynamic construction method of the virtual tree. Only the one-to-one links of the tree are to be built by identifying the parent-child link. This may be done at the first request by the Generator of identifiers node. To achieve this a method for domains dissociation in the system based on private data located in each node would be necessary.

References

[1] M. Weiser, "The computer for the 21st century," Scientific American, vol. 265, 1991, pp. 94–104, ISSN: 0036-8733.

[2] J. Kim, K. Kim, J. Park and T. Shon, "A scalable and privacy-preserving child-care and safety service in a ubiquitous computing environment," Mathematical and Computer Modelling, vol. 55, 2012, pp. 45-57, ISSN: 0895-7177.

[3] J. S. Winter, "Surveillance in ubiquitous network societies: normative conflicts related to the consumer in-store supermarket experience in the context of the Internet of Things," Ethics and Information Technology, vol. 16, March 2014, pp. 27-41, ISSN: 1572-8439.

[4] H. Nissenbaum, Privacy in context: technology, policy, and the integrity of social life. Stanford University Press, Stanford, 2010, ISBN: 0804752370.

[5] C. Dhasarathan, S. Dananjayan, R. Dayalan, V. Thirumal and D. Ponnurangam, "A multi-agent approach: To preserve user information privacy for a pervasive and ubiquitous environment," Egyptian Informatics Journal, vol. 16, 2015, pp. 151-166, ISSN: 1110-8665.

[6] Y. Zuo and T. O'Keefe,"Post-release information privacy protection: A framework and next-generation privacy-enhanced operating system," Information Systems Frontiers, vol. 9, 2007, pp. 451-467, ISSN: 1387-3326.

[7] C. Dong, L. Chen and Z. Wen,"When Private Set Intersection Meets Big Data: An Efficient and Scalable Protocol," in Proceedings of the 20th ACM Conference on Computer and Communications Security (CCS), November 4-8, 2013, Berlin, Germany. ACM Communications, Nov. 2013, pp. 789–800, ISBN: 978-1-4503-2477-9.

[8] N. Shang, G. Ghinita, Y. Zhou and E. Bertino,"Controlling Data Disclosure in Computational PIR Protocols," in Proceedings of the 5th ACM Symposium on Information, Computer and Communications Security (ASIACCS) April 13-16, 2010, Beijing, China. ACM Communications, Apr. 2013, pp. 310–313, ISBN: 978-1-60558-936-7.

[9] J. Zhang, X. Xiao and X. Xie,"PrivTree: A Differentially Private Algorithm for Hierarchical Decompositions," in Proceedings of the International Conference on Management of Data (SIGMOD), June 26–July 01, 2016, San Francisco, CA, USA. ACM Communications, Jul. 2016, pp. 155–170, ISBN: 978-1-4503-3531-7.

[10] J. Al-Jaroodi, I. Jawhar, A. Al-Dhaheri, F. Al-Abdouli and N. Mohamed, "Security middleware approaches and issues for ubiquitous applications," Computers and Mathematics with Applications, vol. 60, 2010, pp. 187–197, ISSN: 0898-1221.

[11] R. Saadi, The chameleon : A security system for nomadic users in collaborative and pervasive environments. PhD Thesis, Institut National des Sciences Appliques de Lyon, France, Jun. 2009.

[12] M. Roman, R. H. Campbell, R. Cerqueiray and C. K. Hess, "Gaia: A development infrastructure for active spaces," Internal document, Department of Computer Science, University of Illinois at Urbana-Champaign, USA, 2001. URL: http://gaia.cs.uiuc.edu/papers/GaiaSubmitted3.pdf [accessed: 2016-05-08].

[13] H. Ludvigsen, L. Valtola, T. W. Kim, H. Shu, A. Johnsen and K. Moen, "Signicat openid," 2008. URL: http://www.idi.ntnu.no/emner/tdt4290/Rapporter/2008/g6.pdf [accessed: 2016-05-08].

[14] J. H. Lee, J. K. Park and S. W. Kim, "User-directed privacy protection in the ubiquitous environment," in Proceedings of IEEE/IFIP International Conference on Embedded and Ubiquitous Computing Dec. 17–20, 2008, Shangai, China. IEEE, Dec. 2008, pp. 37–42, ISBN: 978-0-7695-3492-3.

Browser-to-Browser Authentication and Trust Relationships for WebRTC

Ibrahim Tariq Javed, Khalifa Toumi, Noel Crespi
Institut Mines-Telecom
Telecom SudParis, Evry, France
Email: {Ibrahim_Tariq.Javed, Khalifa.Toumi@telecom-sudparis.eu}, Noel.crespi@mines-telecom.fr

***Abstract*—WebRTC enables browsers to communicate in a Peer to Peer fashion without the use of any plug-ins. This technology is expected to lead a wave of disruptive yet innovative new communication services over the Web. However it also brings significant security and privacy concerns for the users. In WebRTC, authentication is decoupled from the website allowing users to validate each other directly using third party identity providers. User's privacy and security highly depends upon the mechanism used for end-to-end authentication. To achieve security and enhance user privacy it is also essential to define trust between various entities involved in WebRTC security architecture. Therefore, in this paper, we analyze the identity architecture in detail to provide a comparison of suitable authentication protocols. A clear definition of trust is presented by defining various trust relationships that exist in WebRTC identity architecture.**

Keywords*—*WebRTC; P2P; Identity Management; Authentication; Trust.

I. INTRODUCTION

Advancements in HTML standards and the introduction of Web Real Time Communications (WebRTC) has allowed browsers to send real time media in a Peer-to-Peer (P2P) manner [1]. WebRTC is independent of any type of browser, platform or device and enables users to communicate with any HTML compatible device. WebRTC is expected to transform the communication landscape over the Web by introducing real-time communication capabilities to any Web page with just a few lines of code.

However, the open source nature of this technology introduces new security and trust requirements presented in [2] and [3], respectively. Amongst the various security challenges introduced in [4], the most crucial one is to have reliable end-to-end authentication between communicating peers using trusted third party Independent Identity Providers (IdP) [5]. Several significant security issues and architectural challenges faced by the IdP based authentication mechanisms are presented in [6]–[8]. However, all of these existing studies analyze Single Sign On (SSO) solutions over Web, which allow users to sign once and have their identities automatically verified by each application. In contrast, WebRTC requires authentication protocols for end-to-end identity provisioning that enables users to directly receive and verify the identity of their communicating remote peers.

Another security issue that is critical to WebRTC is the clear definition of a trust. The rise of browser to browser communication has generated several questions including how to define trust in WebRTC, what are the different trust relationships and how to evaluate trust for each relationship. To the best of our knowledge, there is no study that provides a generic definition of the trust in WebRTC. Several surveys have been conducted on trust management in various emerging fields [9]–[14]. However, the concept of trust in WebRTC arena is yet to be explored.

The first contribution of this paper is to provide a review of suitable Web based IdP mechanisms for the purpose of identity provisioning. This study will help developers to choose the appropriate protocol for their applications as well as prompt researchers to propose new mechanisms adapted to the security and privacy requirements identified in this paper. A comparative study in terms of user privacy and security is conducted by mapping IdP based authentication mechanisms over WebRTC identity architecture. The second contribution of this paper is to provide a wider vision of trust in browser to browser communications by identifying various trust relationships, their objectives and the context and parameters influencing trust.

The rest of this paper is structured as follows: Section II gives a brief introduction of WebRTC identity architecture and Section III explains the process of authentication. Section IV lists several requirements for identity provision in WebRTC. Section V describes suitable Web authentication protocols that can be applied over the identity architecture of WebRTC whereas various trust relationship of WebRTC communications are presented in Section VII and the paper concludes with Section VIII.

II. WEBRTC IDENTITY ARCHITECTURE

WebRTC is an open-source Web application that resides within the browser to exchange media in a P2P fashion. WebRTC identity architecture [15] aims to provide maximum amount of authentication with the minimum possible level of trust in Web Calling Site/Calling Server (CS). The multi domain call model of WebRTC is presented in Figure 1. Each CS is responsible for providing a JavaScript (JS) application that operates over the browser and initiates the PeerConnection component [16]. By calling appropriate JS APIs PeerConnection (PeerC) establishes direct media connection between browsers. CS is also responsible for implementing signaling where Session Description Protocol (SDP) is used to exchange reachable addresses and session parameters.

In order to authenticate a user from IdP, PeerC downloads JS code "IdP proxy" from a specific location defined in the IdP domain. The Browser is responsible for segregating JS codes into sandboxes therefore restricting each script to interact with resources from the same origin. Thus IdP proxy is only able to communicate with its IdP in order to authentication user. In response, IdP generates user Identity Assertion (IA), which

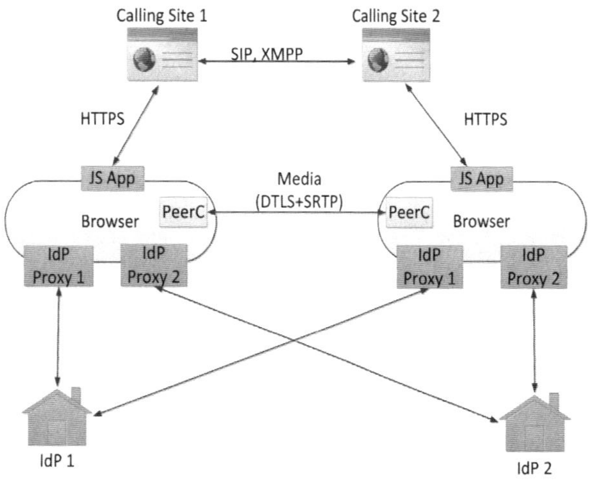

Fig. 1. WebRTC Communication Model

is included in the identity attribute of SDP descriptor message by the browser. The concept of IdP proxy allows the browser to support any type of IdP or authentication protocol as long as it is able to download and run the JS code from IdP.

The browser that establishes user identity by authenticating itself with the IdP is the Authenticating party (AP) whereas the browser which verifies the AP identity from the IdP is called the Relying Party (RP) [15]. In order for communicating parties to authenticate each other, both browsers will act as an AP and as an RP in the process of end-to-end authentication.

III. Authentication in WebRTC

There are two types of authentication that apply to WebRTC communications. First, it is the authentication of the CS/IdP in which the browser validates the ownership of origin by verifying the received digital certificate from the issuing certificate authority. The major drawback is that the browser will trust any certificate that is validated by the trusted issuing authority and has no means of verifying that the certificate truly belongs to the owner. Thus, for WebRTC efficient authentication mechanisms should be introduced to allow browsers to accurately verify that a digital certificate received is the correct certificate used by that website. The second type of authentication is between communicating peers. User identity information in the form of IA are exchanged between peers via the CS and are verified from the same IdP that generated them [17]. There are two major drawbacks of WebRTC identity provision process. Firstly, the IA are sent unencrypted, which allows CS to extract user identity information and track user activities based on identities across communications. Secondly the standard allows CS to force the selection of IdP which does not allow the user to select its own choice of IdP. In order to use the services of CS, user will have to authenticate to CS defined IdP which it may not trust.

The identity provision procedure presented in Figure 2 for end-to-end authentication in WebRTC is explained as follows:

A. *Identity Assertion Generation*

AP PeerC generates request for assertion by attaching fingerprint of DTLS-SRTP certificate. The request also contains the origin of CS which allows IdP to always be aware of the CS the user is using to communicate. IdP proxy is able to access user cookies which allows IdP to check whether the user is already logged in or not. If the user is not authenticated then the IdP proxy returns an error including the URL for entering user credentials. This error is handled by the JS Application or the CS as the IdP proxy is sandboxed and cannot directly demand the user to login. After successful authentication, IdP generates and returns IA. The IA includes user identity information and DTLS fingerprint. The received IA is attached to the SDP message by PeerC and is sent to the remote party via CS.

B. *Identity Assertion Verification*

The RP PeerC extracts the IA from the received SDP message. The domain name of IdP from IA is used to construct the URL in order to downland the IdP proxy. For identity verification, the user is not required to authenticate himself. Upon successful verification the verified IA is returned. PeerC verifies IdP by comparing name-space of received identifier in IA with domain name of IdP. In case of non-authoritative IdP where the name-space of identifier is not the same as domain name, the IdP should be explicitly configured as trusted in browser. Before establishing connection PeerC matches fingerprint in IA with DTLS certificate received over the media channel. This is to ensure that the party establishing peer connection is same as the one which provided the IA.

IV. Requirements for WebRTC Identity Provisioning

We derive a new set of trust requirements based on the weaknesses of identity architecture identified in the previous section. These requirements address the privacy, security and trust concerns raised during end-to-authentication.

(i) ***Identity Unlinkability:*** IdP needs to be able to provide user identity confidentiality against CS.
(ii) ***Identity Encryption:*** IdP needs to be able to provide encryption to user IA.
(iii) ***IdP Selection:*** User needs to select its own choice of IdP without being forced by CS.
(iv) ***CS Unlinkability:*** User needs to be able to hide the information about origin of CS from IdP.
(v) ***Identity Information Control:*** User needs to be able to select the identity information included in IA.
(vi) ***Certificate Verification:*** User needs to be able to verify that the digital certificate provided by CS for authentication is the correct certificate used by it.
(vii) ***User Anonymity by IdP:*** User needs to be able to acquire anonymous identity from IdP.

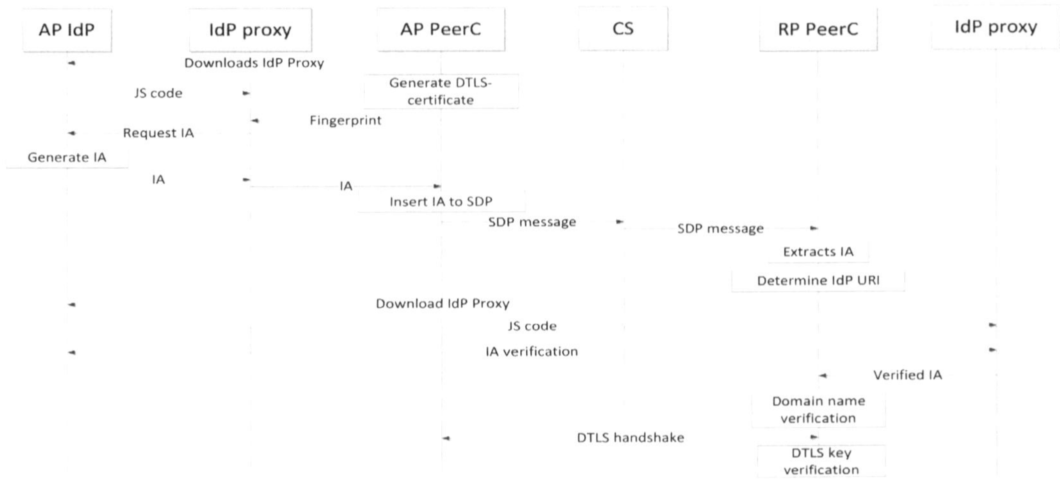

Fig. 2. End-to-End Authentication Flow Diagram

(viii) ***Privacy awareness:*** IdP needs to inform user about how privacy will be handled during P2P authentication.

In order to fulfill these requirements, new solutions/modifications to the architecture and procedures of WebRTC should be proposed.

V. Authentication protocols for Identity Provisioning

WebRTC proposes the use of existing SSO [18] protocols which are designed for client server login. However using these protocols for WebRTC in order to have P2P authentication may require certain modifications. The use of IdP proxy makes WebRTC to be protocol independent. However the selection of a particular authentication protocol will profoundly affect the overall security and privacy of WebRTC communication. We tried to compare the two mechanisms, BrowserID and OAuth2.0 recommended by RTCWeb working group [19] by mapping them over the WebRTC identity architecture [15]. The third protocol applied is OpenID connect (OIDC) which constitutes a set of extensions on top of OAuth for the purpose of authentication.

A. BrowserID

BrowserID allows any website to receive assertion of email address ownership from the user [20]. The website is the RP whereas the browser is considered to be the client. In BrowserID specifications [21], client send Backed Identity Assertion (BIA) to the RP. The BIA is combination of User Certificate (UC) and IA. UC carries user email address and user public key, which is digitally signed by the IdP to certify the ownership of the email address and the public key of the user. Whereas IA contains the request to login into specific RP is signed by the user private key as shown in Figure 3. However when applied to WebRTC instead of the website browsers will authenticate each other. BrowserID can be mapped to WebRTC architecture as follows:

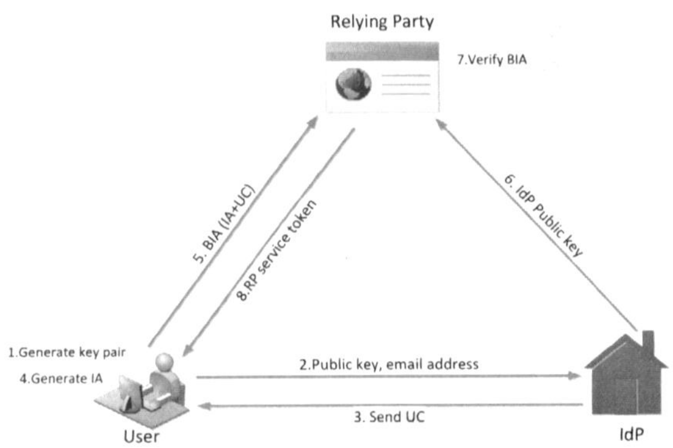

Fig. 3. BrowserID Authentication Overview

Identity Assertion Generation: A public private key pair is generated by the AP browser for asymmetric encryption. PeerC downloads the IdP proxy and requests the IdP to generate UC by including the user public key. After valid authentication of the user, IdP generates UC by signing the user identity (public email address) and public key. The PeerC generates the DTLS-SRTP key for establishing the media connection and sends the fingerprint to IdP proxy. The IA is generated by IdP proxy by signing the fingerprint with user private key. It should be noted that in BrowserID browser is not required to send the fingerprint to IdP as it generates the final assertion. Lastly the PeerC generates the final assertion BIA and includes it into the identity attribute of the SDP.

Identity Assertion Verification: The RP PeerC receives the SDP message and extracts IA and UC. The domain name is used to download IdP proxy to request the public key from the IdP. PeerC performs two checks, firstly it matches the received public key with the signature inside UC, secondly it verifies

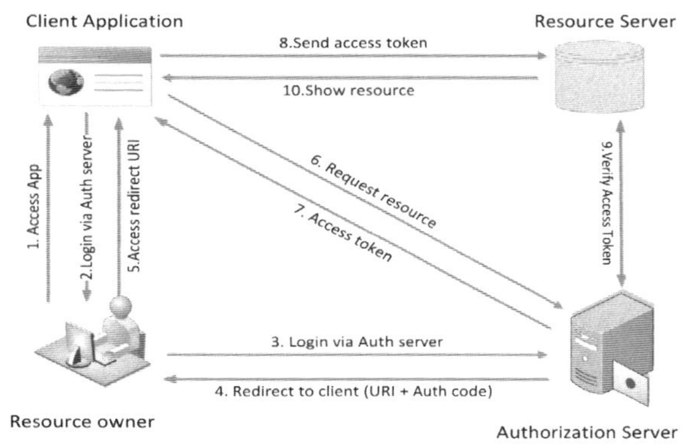

Fig. 4. OAuth Authorization Overview

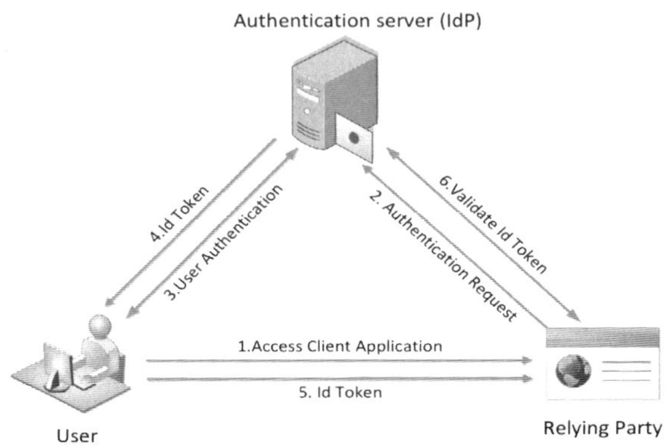

Fig. 5. OIDC Authentication Overview

user public key inside UC with the signature inside IA.

B. OAuth 2.0

OAuth 2.0 [22] being an authorization protocol allows client applications to access resources hosted on a Resource Server (RS) owned by Resource Owner (RO) as shown in Figure 4. The authorization to access resource is provided by the Authorization Server (AS) on behalf of the RO. However before accessing the resource client has to register with AS using the clientid [23]. The process of authorization is described in Figure 4.

To map OAuth protocol onto WebRTC architecture the client application can be considered as RP browser, the RO as the AP browser whereas the IdP acts as AS as well as RS.

Identity Assertion Generation: The AP PeerC using the IdP proxy authenticates the user to the IdP and registers an identity resource with IdP including the fingerprint of DTLS certificate. The IdP in return sends the IA which contains the authorization code. PeerC attaches the authorization code to the SDP and sends it to RP browser via the CS.

Identity Assertion Verification: The RP PeerC receives the SDP message and extracts the authorization code from the identity attribute of SDP. The IdP proxy sends the authorization code and receives the access token from the IdP. Upon receiving the access token the IdP proxy retrieves the identity and fingerprint. The RP PeerC verifies the fingerprint with DTLS certificate received over the media channel.

C. OpenID Connect

OIDC adds an identity layer on top of the OAuth 2.0 protocol. It enables client to verify the identity of user based on the ID Token [24] that contains claims about the user authentication. The ID Token incorporates user (AP) identity information, the IdP identifier and the audience (RP) for which the token is intended for. The ID token is signed by the IdP and can optionally be encrypted. The authentication procedure for OIDC implicit flow is presented in Figure 5.The OIDC protocol can be applied to WebRTC identity architecture as follows:

Identity Assertion Generation: AP PeerC sends authentication request to IdP containing fingerprint and the audience (RP identity) to which the ID Token is intended for. The request may also indicate the type of identity information to be returned in the ID Token. The ID Token is generated and signed by the IdP which contains AP identity information, fingerprint, RP identity and the IdP identifier. PeerC includes the ID Token to the SDP and sends it to the RP.

Identity Assertion Verification: The RP PeerC receives the SDP message and downloads IdP proxy by using identifier domain name. It also extracts the ID Token and fingerprint from the identity attribute. The IdP proxy requests the IdP to validate the ID Token. IdP verifying the signature and returns the verified Identity to the RP. The RP PeerC then verifies the fingerprint with DTLS certificate received over the media channel.

D. Comparison in terms of User Privacy

In WebRTC, user privacy mainly deals with protection of user identity and associated profile information. Table 1 provides a quick comparison of authentication protocols in terms of user privacy properties [25] and features defined as follows:

(i) *Identity Verification*: User ability to verify the identity of remote party.
(ii) *Anonymity*: The inability of remote party and CS to learn user identity.
(iii) *Unlinkability from CS*: The inability of CS to track user activities based on user identities.
(iv) *Unlinkability from IdP*: The inability of IdP to track user activities across different CS.
(v) *Pseudonymity*: The ability of IdP to provide user with psedunonyms as anonymous identities.
(vi) *Identity Encryption*: The ability of IdP to encrypt user identity to achieve confidentiality from CP.
(vii) *Browser Centric*: The ability of browser to generate the identity assertion
(viii) *Information Control*: The ability of user to control the type of information IdP includes in the IA.

TABLE I: Comparison of Authentication Protocols for WebRTC

Authentication Protocols	Identity Verification	Anonymity	Unlinkability from CS	Unlinkability from IdP	Pseudonymity	Identity Encryption	Browser Centric	Information Control	Audience Verification	IdP Centric
BrowserID	✓			✓			✓			
OAuth2.0	✓	✓		✓	✓					✓
OIDC	✓	✓	✓	✓	✓	✓		✓	✓	✓

(ix) *Audience Verification*: The ability of IdP to disclose identity information exclusively to the person which it was intended for.

(x) *IdP Centric*: The ability of user to enforce rules and policies through a trustworthy IdP.

Browser centric approach of BrowserID makes it the simplest protocol that can be applied to WebRTC architecture for identity provisioning. When compared with OAuth and OIDC the considerable drawback of this protocol is the adoption of public email address as user identity. Firstly, it does not allow user to stay anonymous/unidentifiable during the communication. Secondly unlinkability from CS can never be achieved as public email address will always allow it track user activities. When having BrowserID for authentication users will have to trust their CS with their identity information.

However the fact that final IA is generated by the browser without the need of sending DTLS fingerprints to IdP makes BrowserID more reliable in case of distrusted IdP. In contrast to BrowserID protocol, OAuth and OIDC operate in an IdP centric format where IdP is responsible for generating and verifying the IAs. IdP centric nature will allow users to enforce policies and rules through their IdPs. Other than this Anonymity in both these protocols can easily be achieved by the user of pseudonyms.

In OAuth protocol, the redirection between browsers is impossible to achieve as browsers do not have the capability to accept HTTP connection from other browsers. Thus when using OAuth for P2P authentication AP browser is never aware of who is accessing its identity resource whereas IdP is unable to verify that RP has the authority to access AP identity. This brings about serious security concerns for WebRTC communication as any unauthorized party having access to authorization code will be able to obtain user identity information.

OIDC seems to be a better candidate than OAuth in terms of identity confidentially and unlinkability. The feature of encryption and audience in the ID Token does not allow any unauthorized party such as Man-in the middle or CS to obtain user identity information. The audience field in OIDC allows the AP to specify the identity of RP to which the information is intended for. This requires AP to be aware of RP identity before P2P authentication which may be communicated though the CS. Lastly OIDC gives user much more control over their identity information to be shared by indicating it in the authentication request.

VI. Trust Management Objectives

The choice of authentication protocol presented in Section V will further influence the extent to which entities are required to trust each other. For example in the case of BrowserID, user will have to put more trust in their CS as it will be able to track user activities based on its identities. In WebRTC, trust needs to be computed for each entity and displayed to user before connection is established. For now trust in WebRTC is based on valid authentication. However merely authenticating an entity never guarantees that the entity is trusted. Similarly unauthenticated entity does not imply that it may never be trusted for a particular task.

For the wide adaptation of WebRTC technology an efficient trust management framework is essential. To ensure trustworthiness in whole communication system a holistic trust management framework is required with the following objectives:

1) Trust Information Collection: Trust framework that is able to gather and combine information to evaluate trust. Appropriate information collection models are required based on the parameters influencing trust in each relationship.
2) Trust Evaluation: Trust models that are able to compute trust based on the context and parameters influencing trust. These models should be dynamic in nature in order to commute trust variations over time.
3) Privacy Preservation: Privacy enhanced trust models to measure the degree of confidence that a user can have in terms of preserving their privacy. User information should be preserved according to the expectations of each user.
4) Quality of Service: Trust management should ensure that communication and authentication services are offered at exactly the right place and time to the right person.
5) Human-Computer Interaction: Users should be able to interact with the browser in a secure and efficient manner in order to set their communication preferences.
6) Identity Trust: A scalable and efficient identity management system capable of authenticating each entity in a credible and verifiable manner.

VII. Trust Relationships

We define trust as a relation between two entities, a truster and a trustee. The entity that trusts the target entity is known as the truster whereas entity that is being trusted is the

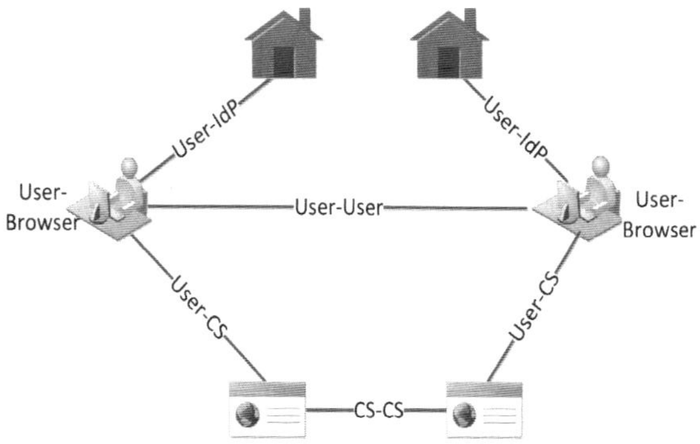

Fig. 6. Trust Relationships in WebRTC

trustee. Thus any trust relationship is described as truster trusting trustee at a given time for a particular context. Trust relationships can be expressed in terms of a trust vector wherein each element of the vector represents a parameter that contributes towards the trust value:

$$(Truster \xrightarrow{c} Trustee)_t = [K^{te}_{tr}, E^{te}_{tr}, R^{te}_{tr}, A^{te}_{tr}] \quad (1)$$

Where context 'c' is the information which characterizes the situation of the entities involved. The context of trust can be expressed as the combination of trust purpose and trustee aspects. Therefore a truster will always trust the ability of a trustee to perform a specific action with regards to certain trustee characteristic. For example, truster A trusts trustee B's security to access a resource that the truster controls. Time 't' is used to characterize the dynamic behavior of a trust relationship whereas the parameters used for evaluating trust are described as follows:

- Knowledge parameter K^{te}_{tr} is based on truster's awareness about the abilities of trustee in a specific context.
- Experience parameter E^{te}_{tr} is the cumulative effect of previous interactions between a trustee and a truster in a particular context and over a specified period of time.
- Reputation parameter R^{te}_{tr} is the sum of recommender's judgment about trustee in relation to the truster in a specific context. Each recommendation is weighted by the truster trust in recommender within that context.
- Authentication parameter A^{te}_{tr} defines the strength in the authentication process. The server identity will be verified form the certificate authority whereas the communication participant identity will be verified from the IdP. Therefore this parameter will be weighted with the amount of trust in IdP or the certificate authority.

We identify four trust relationship that exist in WebRTC: User-CS, User-User, User-IdP, CS-CS and User-Browser represented in Figure 6.

A. User-IdP Trust Relationship

IdP provides user the functionality of storing and managing their identity information while allowing them to authenticate. The purpose of trust in User-IdP relationship is to trust an IdP's ability to provide authentication services while considering its ability to preserve privacy. We provide a set of IdP's attributes that should be considered while evaluating trust in IdP:

- *Privacy Protection*: An IdP's ability to provide identity confidentiality in terms of unlinkability from CS;
- *Anonymity*: An IdP's ability to provide anonymity by means of pseudonyms;
- *Encryption*: An IdP ability to provide encrypted IA;
- *Authentication Mechanism*: The type of authentication protocol being used by IdP; and
- *IdP Type*: If an IdP is authoritative or non-authoritative.

B. User-CS Trust Relationship

CS provides JS application that allows browser to communicate in a P2P fashion. CS is also responsible for implementing signaling for the exchange of session parameters, identities, call answer/offer request and user reachable addresses between communicating parties. The purpose of trust in a User-CS relationship reflects the CS ability to provide communication services whereas CS aspects that needs to be considered are security and reliability. For the evaluation of trust in CS the following should be considered:

- *Malware Detection*: Undesirable software installations by a CS;
- *Software Vulnerabilities*: Weaknesses detected in the JS code provided by CS;
- *Attack Detection*: The CS's ability to detect and prevent attacks;
- *Mixed Content*: The content loaded from an HTTP origin onto the HTTPS page of a CS; and
- *IdP Selection*: The IdP selection enforced by the CS.

C. User-User Trust Relationship

Before an exchange of real time media, each user needs to verify the identity of its communicating participant. The purpose of trust is user identification. Subjective aspects are considered such as user's honesty, accuracy and integrity while receiving the identity information. We present set of attributes that should be considered for the evaluation of trust in the received identity assertion:

- *Identity Proofing*: How strongly the identity information of user has been verified and vetted by the IdP;
- *Credential Verification*: How easily a user's credential can be spoofed or stolen;
- *Assertion Strength*: Proof that the identity was actually asserted by IdP for a given transaction;
- *Encryption*: If received IA is encrypted or not;
- *Audience Protection*: The received IA contains the audience identity for which the assertion is intended; and
- *Anonymity*: The use of an anonymous identity by the communicating participant.

D. CS-CS Trust Relationship

Several efforts are being made to achieve cross domain interoperability [26], [27], [28] where users from different domains are allowed to contact and communicate with each other. Each CS will be responsible for sharing availability status, identity information and the reachable addresses of users from different domains. Trust between CS needs to be computed and displayed to the subscribers of each CS before they decide to interact with the users of another domain. The purpose of trust in this relationship is to achieve interoperability whereas the aspects of a CS that need to be considered for trust assessment are its security and reliability.

E. User-Browser Trust Relationship

The browser is responsible for running JS codes in isolated sandboxes to connect with various entities on behalf of a user. The identity of each entity is verified by the browser before communication takes place. The overall security of WebRTC communication is highly dependent upon the selection of a trustworthy browser. Security in WebRTC can never be achieved if a browser is compromised. Therefore, it is essential for users to select trustworthy browsers that can be relied upon completely. However trust between browser and user is subjective and may not be computed.

ACKNOWLEDGMENT

This work has received funding from the European Union's Horizon 2020 research and innovation program under grant agreement No 645342, project reTHINK.

VIII. CONCLUSION

WebRTC technology is envisioned to lead innovative ways to share information and communicate over Web. The vast adaptation of this highly potential P2P communication technology requires an efficient identity and trust management framework. This paper aims (1) to analyze the end-to-end authentication procedure between browsers and (2) to give a clear definition of trust in WebRTC.

A study of WebRTC identity architecture and authentication mechanisms suitable for the purpose of end-to-end user identification is conducted. To address the security and privacy concerns identified in this paper we prompt the community to develop mechanisms particularly suitable for WebRTC communications. In order to have a wider vision of trust, we define various trust relationship, the context of trust and parameters influencing trust computation for browser to browser communication.

REFERENCES

[1] S. Loreto and S. P. Romano, "Real-time communications in the web: Issues, achievements, and ongoing standardization efforts," *IEEE Internet Computing*, vol. 16, no. 5, pp. 68–73, Sept 2012.

[2] E. Rescorla, "Security Considerations for WebRTC," Internet-Draft, Tech. Rep., February 2015.

[3] V. Beltran, E. Bertin, and S. Cazeaux, "Additional Use-cases and Requirements for WebRTC Identity Architecture," Internet-Draft, Tech. Rep., March 2015.

[4] R. L. Barnes and M. Thomson, "Browser-to-browser security assurances for webrtc," *IEEE Internet Computing*, vol. 18, no. 6, pp. 11–17, Nov 2014.

[5] A. Vapen, N. Carlsson, A. Mahanti, and N. Shahmehri, "A look at the third-party identity management landscape," *IEEE Internet Computing*, vol. 20, no. 2, pp. 18–25, Mar 2016.

[6] J. Torres, M. Nogueira, and G. Pujolle, "A survey on identity management for the future network," *IEEE Communications Surveys Tutorials*, vol. 15, no. 2, pp. 787–802, Second 2013.

[7] E. Maler and D. Reed, "The venn of identity: Options and issues in federated identity management," *IEEE Security and Privacy*, vol. 6, no. 2, pp. 16–23, 2008.

[8] E. Ghazizadeh, M. Zamani, J. I. Ab Manan, and A. Pashang, "A survey on security issues of federated identity in the cloud computing," in *Cloud Computing Technology and Science (CloudCom), 2012 IEEE 4th International Conference on*, Dec 2012, pp. 532–565.

[9] J. H. Cho, A. Swami, and I. R. Chen, "A survey on trust management for mobile ad hoc networks," *IEEE Communications Surveys Tutorials*, vol. 13, no. 4, pp. 562–583, Fourth 2011.

[10] Z. Yan, P. Zhang, and A. V. Vasilakos, "A survey on trust management for internet of things," *Journal of Network and Computer Applications*, vol. 42, pp. 120 – 134, 2014.

[11] W. Sherchan, S. Nepal, and C. Paris, "A survey of trust in social networks," *ACM Comput. Surv.*, vol. 45, no. 4, pp. 47:1–47:33, Aug. 2013.

[12] A. Jsang, R. Ismail, and C. Boyd, "A survey of trust and reputation systems for online service provision," *Decision Support Systems*, vol. 43, no. 2, pp. 618 – 644, 2007, emerging Issues in Collaborative Commerce.

[13] S. Marti and H. Garcia-Molina, "Taxonomy of trust: Categorizing p2p reputation systems," *Comput. Netw.*, vol. 50, no. 4, pp. 472–484, Mar. 2006.

[14] L. Margaret and M. Jeffrey, "Machine to machine trusted behaviors," in *The Eighth International Conference on Mobile Ubiquitous Computing, Systems, Services and Technologies (UBICOMM)*, Aug 2014.

[15] E. Rescorla, "WebRTC Security Architecture," IETF Internet Draft, Standards Track, June 2016.

[16] A. Bergkvist, D. C. Burnett, C. Jennings, A. Narayanan, and B. Aboba, "WebRTC 1.0: Real-time Communication Between Browsers," W3C Working Draft, Tech. Rep., May 2016.

[17] V. Beltran and E. Bertin, "Unified communications as a service and webrtc: An identity-centric perspective," *Computer Communications*, vol. 68, pp. 73 – 82, 2015.

[18] A. Pashalidis and C. J. Mitchell, "A taxonomy of single sign-on systems," in *Information security and privacy*. Springer, 2003, pp. 249–264.

[19] Web working group. [Online]. Available: http://tools.ietf.org/wg/rtcweb/charters

[20] D. Fett, R. Ksters, and G. Schmitz, "An expressive model for the web infrastructure: Definition and application to the browser id sso system," in *2014 IEEE Symposium on Security and Privacy*, May 2014, pp. 673–688.

[21] Browserid. [Online]. Available: https://github.com/mozilla/id-specs/blob/prod/browserid/index.md

[22] D. Hardt, "The OAuth 2.0 Authorization Framework," IETF RFC: 6749, Standards Track, Tech. Rep.

[23] B. Leiba, "Oauth web authorization protocol," *IEEE Internet Computing*, vol. 16, no. 1, pp. 74–77, Jan 2012.

[24] J. Bradley, B. de Medeir, and C. Mortimore, "Openid connect core 1.0," *The OpenID Foundation*.

[25] A. Pfitzmann and H. Tschofenig, "Terminology for Talking about Privacy by Data Minimization: Anonymity, Unlinkability, Undetectability, Unobservability, Pseudonymity, and Identity Management," Internet-Draft, Tech. Rep., July 2010.

[26] S. Becot, E. Bertin, J. M. Crom, V. Frey, and S. Tuffin, "Communication services in the web era: How can telco join the ott hangout?" in *18th conference on Innovations in Clouds, Internet and Networks (ICIN)*, Feb 2015, pp. 208–215.

[27] L. Li, W. Chou, Z. Qiu, and T. Cai, "Who is calling which page on the web?" *IEEE Internet Computing*, vol. 18, no. 6, pp. 26–33, Nov 2014.

[28] I. Javed and et al., "Global identity and reachability framework for interoperable p2p communication services," in *19th conference on Innovations in Clouds, Internet and Networks (ICIN 2016)*, March 2016.

Towards Trusted Operated Services in the Internet of Things

Pascal Urien
LTCI UMR 5141
Telecom ParisTech
23 av d'Italie, 75013, Paris, France

Abstract— **This paper presents an innovative concept for the Internet of Things (IoT), in which objects work over TLS stacks running in secure elements. We notice that most of today IoT architectures are secured by the DTLS or TLS stack. Furthermore, tamper resistance, secure communications and storage are consensual requests for the emerging IoT frameworks. We demonstrate that it is possible to design cheap secured and trusted systems based on Javacards plugged in commercial nano-computers. Finally we detail the structure of an innovative JAVA framework able to provide trusted operated services, in a way similar to mobile network operators (MNO) managing smartphone fleets thanks to Subscriber Identity Modules (SIMs).**

Keywords-. IoT; Secure Elements; TLS; DTLS; Security.

I. INTRODUCTION

The Internet of Things (IoT) is a major topic for the development of the digital economy; in [8] it is defined as "*a network of connected things*". According to [1] about 50 billion of connected objects are forecasted by 2020, about 6.6 per human being. It is expected [2] that "today households, across the OECD (*Organisation for Economic Co-operation and Development*) area, have an estimated 1.8 billion connected devices, in 2017 this could be 5.8 billion and in 2022, 14 billion devices". More than 50 connected objects could be located in four people house, such as computers, smartphones, tv, cars, internet connected power sockets, energy consumption display, thermostat, camera, and connected locks.

According to [6] the digital industry roadmap for next decades will not be centered on Moore's law but will deploy networks with hundred trillions of devices [7]. In that context [7] "*Security is projected to become an even bigger challenge in the future as the number of interconnected devices increases... In fact, the Internet of Things can be viewed as the largest and most poorly defended cyber attack surface conceived by mankind*".

As an illustration [3] introduces an IoT service-oriented architecture (SoA), based on the following four layers (see Figure 1) :

- The Sensing layer that comprises hardware objects and acquisition protocols.
- The Network layer, which is the infrastructure needed for the information transport. New wireless networks such as SigFox [4] or Lora [5] have been recently designed for low throughout interactions with sensors.
- The Service layer that manages services needed by users or applications.
- The Interfaces layer that includes API (*Application Programming Interface*) and applications front ends.

This model suggests that some objects could be remotely managed by dedicated service providers. For example, in a smart grid context, connected plugs are remotely switched on in order to enable the battery recharge of electric cars. As underlined in [7] security is a major prerequisite and "*a short list of requirements includes tamper resistance and secure communications and storage*".

In this paper we propose a new perspective for the IoT security, based on cheap secure elements enforcing secure communications for connected devices. Most of legacy devices are monitored thanks to the HTTPS protocol. The IETF (*Internet Engineering Task Force*) comity is currently pushing a framework based on the CoAP (*Constrained Application Protocol*) protocol [12] whose security natively relies on the DTLS (*Datagram Transport Layer Security*) protocol and soon on TLS (*Transport Layer Security*) protocol [13]. We present an innovative concept in which TLS servers are fully running in secure elements. We describe a Java framework that enables the integration of such tamper resistant components in cheap boards, for example fuelled by nano-computer such as the popular *Raspberry Pi* (*www.raspberrypi.org*).

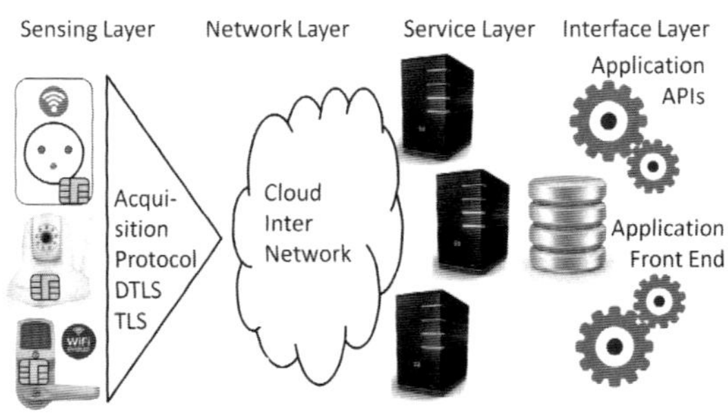

Figure 1. An IoT service-oriented architecture (SoA), based on four layers

The paper is constructed according to the following outline. Section 2 details some acquisition protocols in today IoT systems. Section 3 introduces the concept of TLS server running in secure elements. Section 4 describes an experimental JAVA framework designed for nano-computers, such as the popular Raspberry Pi, whose communication security, is enforced by secure elements. Finally, section 5 concludes this paper.

II. ACQUISITION PROTOCOLS

Today many connected devices are using HTTPS, i.e. communication with web servers secured by the TLS protocol. As an illustration the popular Nest thermostats work [7] with JSON (*JavaScript Object Notation*) formatted data POSTed to their web servers; some connected plugs [8] use *Home Network Administration Protocol* (HNAP) a proprietary network protocol based on SOAP (*Simple Object Access Protocol*), invented by Pure Networks, Inc. and acquired by Cisco Systems, which allows identification, configuration, and management of network devices.

The *Constrained Application Protocol* (CoAP) [12] is designed according to the *Representational State Transfer* (REST) architecture [11], which encompasses the following six features: 1) Client-Server architecture; 2) Stateless interaction; 3) Cache operation on the client side; 4) Uniform interface ; 5) Layered system ; 6) Code On Demand.

CoAP is an efficient RESTfull protocol easy to proxy to/from HTTP, but which is not understood in an IoT context as a general replacement of HTTP. It is natively secured by DTLS (the datagram adaptation of TLS), and works over a DTLS/UDP/IP stack. Nerveless the IETF is currently working [13] on a CoAP version compatible with a TLS/TCP/IP stack.

0 1	2 3	4 5 6 7	0 1 2 3 4 5 6 7	0 1 2 3 4 5 6 7 0 1 2 3 4 5 6 7
V	T	TKL	Code	Message ID
Token (if any)				
Options (if any)				
11111111		Payload (if any)		

Figure 2. The CoAP Header

The CoAP header is illustrated by Figure 2. Version (V) is the protocol version (01). Type (T) indicates if the message is of type Confirmable (CON), Non-confirmable (NON), Acknowledgement (ACK) or Reset. Token Length (TKL) is the length of the Token field (0-8 bytes). The Code field identifies the method and is split in two parts a 3-bit class and a 5-bit detail documented "c.dd" where "c" is a digit from 0 to 7 and "dd" are two digits from 00 to 31. For example methods named GET, POST, PUT and DELETE are respectively noted 0.01, 0.02, 0.03, and 0.04. The attribute Message ID matches messages ACK/Reset to messages CON/NON previously sent; it is usually noted inside two brackets ([0xMessageID]). The Token (0 to 8 bytes) is used to match a response with a request. Options give additional information such as *Content-Format* dealing with proxy operations.

According to the CoAP model objects act as "servers". Clients deliver requests to servers that return responses and may proxy HTTP requests.

Some IoT frameworks (for example the ARM® mbed™ IoT Device Platform, see Figure 3) are supporting the MQTT (*MQ Telemetry Transport*) protocol [14], a Client Server publish/subscribe messaging transport protocol that is secured by TLS.

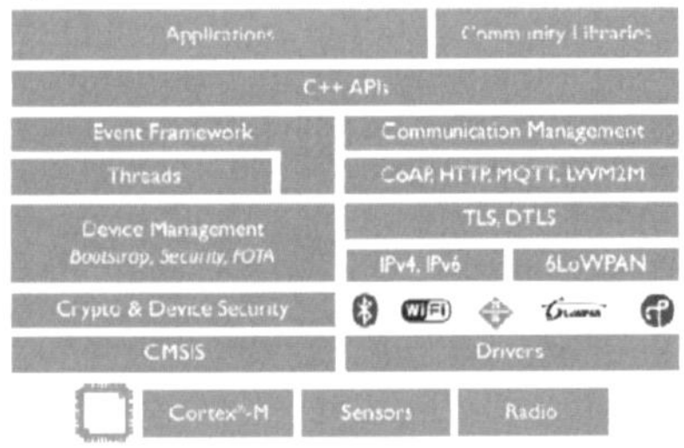

Figure 3. MBED stack from the ARM company

From the above lines it appears that TLS and DTLS are the security cornerstones of many IoT stacks. We believe that the integration of TLS servers in cheap tamper resistant chips enforcés secure communications and storage. It could enable trusted and operated IoT infrastructure. Furthermore TLS/DTLS servers perform strong mutual authentication with clients when both entities are equipped with private keys and certificates, used for object identities.

III. TLS SERVERS FOR SECURE ELEMENTS

A secure element [19] is a secure micro controller, whose area is about 5x5 mm^2. ISO7816 standards specify electrical and logical interfaces; small messages whose size is less than 256 bytes are exchanged over serial or USB interfaces. It is usually glued in PVC rectangular supports referred as smartcards. Nerveless these tamper resistant devices can be shrunk in other electronic dies such as NFC controllers or SD memories. Most of secure elements include a Java Virtual Machine (JVM) and therefore run applications written in the javacard language [18], a subset of JAVA. They include cryptographic libraries providing symmetric procedures (3xDES, AES), asymmetric algorithms (RSA, ECC) and hash functions (MD5, SHA1, SHA2..).

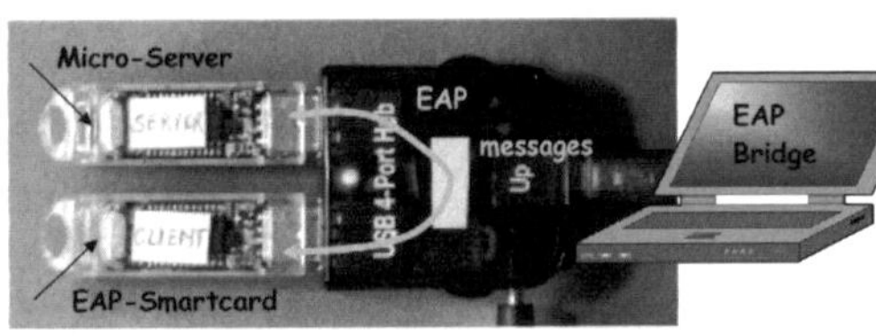

Figure 4. The first TLS micro-authentication server [15], 2005

The first micro-authentication server, illustrated by Figure 4 was introduced ten years ago in [15]. It was running in a javacard , including a TLS stack embedded application. This former TLS stack booted a TLS session in about 30s.

Ten years later, secure elements perform this task in about 1 to 10s for TLS full sessions and about 0,5 to 5s for TLS resume sessions.

According to [16] embedded TLS server interface is based on the EAP-TLS protocol, whose packets are transported over ISO 7816 messages. Figure 5 illustrates the choreography of these exchanges.

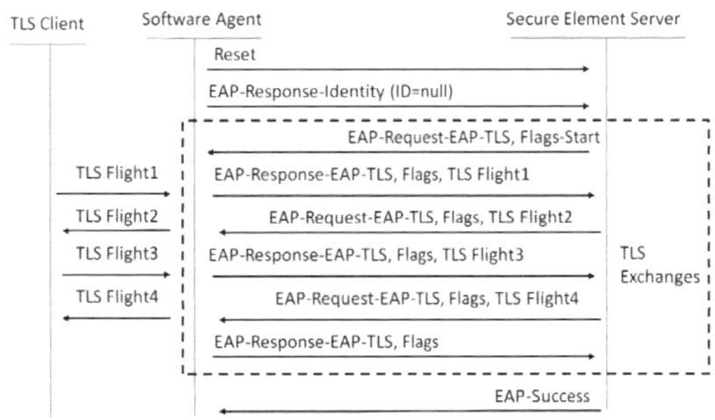

Figure 5. Booting of a TLS session from a secure element with an interface based on EAP-TLS over ISO 7816 [16][17]

A recent IETF draft [17] introduces TLS/DTLS security modules dedicated to secure elements. TLS/DTLS sessions are booted according to [16], but afterwards the TLS secure channel can be used for the decryption of data sent by the client or the encryption of information to be transmitted to the client (see Figure 6). Software agents mentioned in Figure 5 and 6 are logical entities that drive the secure elements. They act as a logical bridge between the network transporting TLS packets over TCP/IP and the secure element dealing with EAP-TLS messages shuttled in ISO7816 requests/responses.

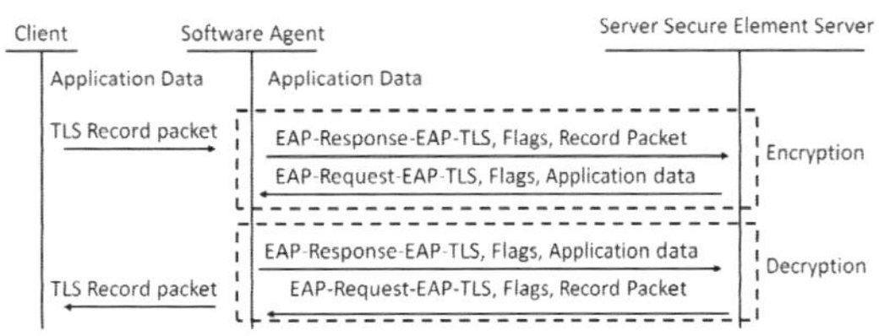

Figure 6. Application data encryption and decryption performed by a TLS server (i.e. a RecordLayer) running in a secure element [17].

It should be noted than in a previous work [20] we suggested to export TLS sessions from secure elements according to a technology named *TLS-Tandem*. Therefore, upon opening a TLS session two choices are possible : 1) processing TLS packet ciphering/deciphering in the secure element OR 2) performing this task in the application that drives the tamper resistant chip.

The TLS server javacard application is designed according to the *OpenEapSmartCard* framework previously detailed in [21] and illustrated by Figure 7.

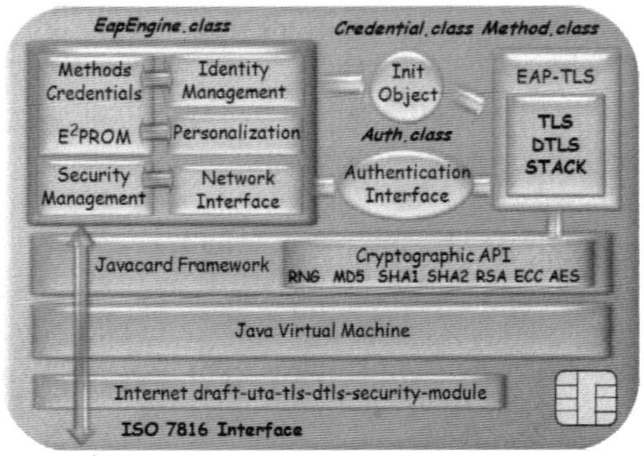

Figure 7. Javacard TLS/DTLS stack framework according to the OpenEapSmartcard [21] framework.

IV. JAVA FRAMEWORK

Today many objects are working in a LINUX software environment. For example the popular Raspberry Pi nano computer is powered by a DEBIAN operating system (see Figure 8). It supports the PCSC-Lite (*Personal Computer/Smart Card*) middleware developed by the M.U.S.C.L.E (*Movement for the Use of Smart Cards in a Linux Environment*) organization. Furthermore the JAVA framework (up to the 1.5 version) is also available. PCSC-Lite can be easily linked with the javax.smartcardio JAVA package, which provides a set of smartcard I/O APIs.

Figure 8. TLS Server satck embeded in secure element, in a Raspberry Pi environnment.

Therefore it is possible to deploy TLS servers running in secure elements for this class of objects and to control these chips, thanks to a dedicated API (SE-TLS API) described below. This approach facilitates the design of secure communications and storage.

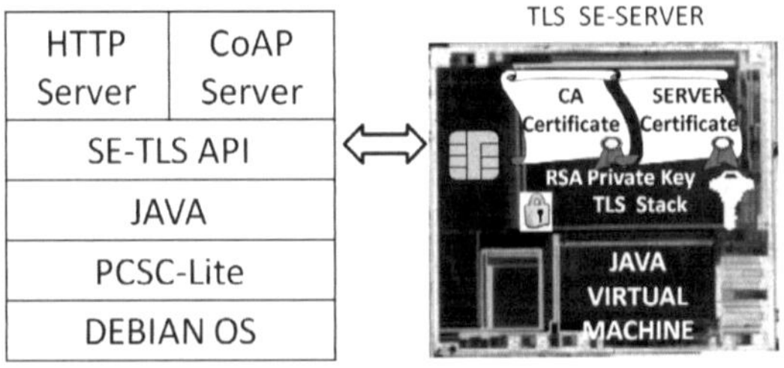

Figure 9. Software stack for SE based TLS server, such as HTTP or CoAP

The software for HTTP and CoAP servers based on secure elements is depicted by Figure 9. The main JAVA package needed by a server daemon is the SE-TLS API, which comprises three logical components: the core implementation, the ServerTLS thread, and the GenericServer class.

The *core implementation* of the server daemon is illustrated by Figure 10. It begins by the instantiation of a tls-tandem object (named *myserver*) that initializes a TLS socket server (on the 443 port) and resets the secure element. The secure element embedded TLS stack, written in javacard, is identified by the parameter AID. It requires a PIN value, and is associated to an identity attribute "server" defining a set of cryptographic attributes such as certificates and private key.

```
public static void ServerDaemon()
{
 tls-tandem myserver= new
 tls-tandem(tls_tandem.SERVER, readername,
           AID, PIN , "server");
 myserver.ServerTLS.rdv   = false;
 myserver.ServerTLS.InUse = false;

 while(true)
 { //myserver.ServerTLS.rdv = true;
   recordlayer RecordLayer =
   myserver.OpenSession();
   myserver.ServerTLS.rdv =    false;
   myserver.ServerTLS.InUse = false;
 if (RecordLayer == null);
 else
 { GenericServer myGS= new
   GenericServer(myserver,RecordLayer);
  // myserver.CloseSession(RecordLayer);
  }
 }
```

Figure 10. Core implementation of a SE based TLS server

During the instantiation of the tls-tandem class, the ServerTLS thread (see Figure 11) is created. It deals with two control (boolean) flags *rdv* and *InUse*.

The Rendez Vous mechanism is a fundamental paradigm for a SE based server. An incoming TCP connection is denied if no logical entity is ready for its processing; this availability is indicated by the *rdv* flag. Afterwards the *InUse* flag is set and the ServerTLS thread will remain idle until its resetting. The *InUse* variable means that the secure element is currently computing a TLS session, implying that no new incoming client can be processed. In that case incoming TCP sessions are stored in the backlog queue, whose size is fixed by the JAVA constructor of the ServerSocket class (see Figure 11). According to the JAVA documentation the default value is set to 50. The backlog queue size tunes the number of TLS sessions that can be delayed before being processed by the secure element.

The OpenSession() method (see Figure 10) provided by the tls-tandem object initializes a Rendez Vous (rdv= true) with a TCP client. The secure element is thereafter in use (InUse =true) and a software agent (as illustrated by Figure 5) boots the TLS session. Upon success a RecordLayer object is created (see Figure 10) and returned by the OpenSession() procedure.

At this step the Rendez Vous is cancelled (rdv =false). The RecordLayer class manages a TCP socket and provides the procedures (see Figure 12) needed for exchanging TLS record packets over TCP/IP. If the TLS session is exported from the secure element then the InUse flag may be reset. Otherwise the secure element remains busy (inUse= true) and incoming TCP connections are delayed.

```
// ServerTLS Thread

ServerSocket soq = new
ServerSocket(443,backlog,
InetAddress.getByName("0.0.0.0"));
InUse=false;
while(true)
{ client = null ;
  try {Socket client= soq.accept();}
  catch(IOException e){client=null;}
  if (!rdv)
  { try {client.close();client=null;}
    catch(IOException f){}
  }

  if (client != null) InUse=true;
  while(InUse)
  {try  { Thread.sleep((long)100);}
   catch (InterruptedException e){};
  }
  if (client != null)
  { try { client.close();}
    catch(IOException e){};
  }
}
// End of ServerTLS
```

Figure 11. The ServerTLS thread

The GenericServer class (see Figure 10) is an implementation of an HTTP or CoAP server; as illustrated by Figure 6 it is a functional subset of the Software Agents. It uses services provided by the RecordLayer object (see

Figure 12) dealing with TLS packets reception and decryption, or TLS packets encryption and transmission. These operations may be performed in the secure element or by pure software means if the TLS session has been previously exported.

```
byte[] buf = RecordLayer.recv();
if (buf !=null);
buf = RecordLayer.decrypt(buf);

byte[] buf=RecordLayer.encrypt(buf;
int err = RecordLayer.send(buf) ;
```

Figure 12. TLS packets processing by the RecordLayer object.

V. Conclusion

In this paper, we have demonstrated a TLS server running over a secure element in an object environment, i.e. a cheap nano-computer with an LINUX operating system, similar to many devices already available on the IoT. Thanks to this innovation we claim trusted and secured communications booted from a strong mutual authentication. In a way similar to SIM modules managed by mobile network operator (MNO) we believe that this paradigm is a step towards IoT infrastructure remotely controlled by IoT operators.

References

[1] D. Evans, "The Internet of Things How the Next Evolution of the Internet Is Changing Everything", Cisco, White Paper, 2011

[2] OECD, "Building Blocks for Smart Networks", OECD Digital Economy Papers, No. 215, OECD Publishing, 2013

[3] L. D. X. Shancang Li and S. Zhao, "The internet of things: a survey", Information Systems Frontiers, vol. 17, pp. 243–259, 2015.

[4] LoRa Alliance, "LoRaWAN™ Specification", Version: V1.0, January 2015

[5] SigFox, "One network A billion dreams", M2M and IoT redefined through cost effective and energy optimized connectivity", white paper, 2015

[6] M. Waldrop, "More Than Moore", Nature, February 2016 Vol 530

[7] SIA/SRC, "Rebooting the IT Revolution: A Call to Action", 2015

[8] K. Pretz, "The Next Evolution of the Internet", March 2013, http://theinstitute.ieee.org/technology-focus/technology-topic/the-next-evolution-of-the-internet

[9] http://stackoverflow.com/questions/15482257/how-nest-thermostat-communicates, seen June 2016.

[10] http://www.devttys0.com/2014/05/hacking-the-d-link-dsp-w215-smart-plug/, seen June 2016

[11] R. Fielding, "Architectural Styles and the Design of Network-based Software Architectures", 2000,

[12] Z. Shelby, K. Hartke, C. Bormann, "The Constrained Application Protocol (CoAP)", RFC 7252, June 2014

[13] C. Bormann ET al, "A TCP and TLS Transport for the Constrained Application Protocol (CoAP)", IETF draft April 2016

[14] A. Banks and R. Gupta, "MQTT Version 3.1.1", OASIS Standard September 2014.

[15] P. Urien, P, M. Dandjinou, M.Badra, "Introducing micro-authentication servers in emerging pervasive environments", IADIS International Conference WWW/Internet 2005, Lisbon, Portugal, October 2005.

[16] P. Urien, "EAP Support in Smartcard", draft-urien-eap-smartcard-29.txt, July 2015

[17] P.Urien, "TLS and DTLS Security Modules", draft-urien-uta-tls-dtls-security-module-00.txt, June 2015

[18] Z. Chen, "Java Card™ Technology for Smart Cards: Architecture and Programmer's (The Java Series)", 2002, Addison-Wesley, ISBN 020170329

[19] T.M. Jurgensen ET. al., "Smart Cards: The Developer's Toolkit", Prentice Hall PTR, 2002,, ISBN 0130937304.

[20] P. Urien, "TLS-Tandem: A Smart Card for WEB Applications", Consumer Communications and Networking Conference, 2009. CCNC 2009. 6th IEEE, January 2009.

[21] P. Urien, P and M. Dandjinou, M, "The OpenEapSmartcard platform", Fourth IFIP International Conference on Network Control and Engineering for QoS, Security and Mobility, Lannion, France, November 2005, Springer 2007.

Memguard: A Memory Bandwidth Management in Mixed Criticality Virtualized Systems
Memguard KVM Scheduling

Nicolas Dagieu, Alexander Spyridakis, Daniel Raho

Virtual Open Systems
Grenoble - France
Email: {n.dagieu,a.spyridakis,s.raho}@virtualopensystems.com

Abstract*—Memory bandwidth in standard computing architectures using DRAM (Dynamic Random Access Memory) is one of the most critical parts of the system, mainly responsible for performance degradation in memory bandwidth demanding computations. Memguard is a kernel module designed to solve this issue, created with the goal to schedule memory bandwidth at the CPU (Central Processing Unit) core level and enabling bandwidth regulation functionalities. In this paper we propose a new implementation of Memguard that can also be utilized in mixed-criticality virtualized computing environments. This involves the regulation of memory bandwidth at the guest level and forwarding memory bandwidth needs to the host, where the requests are enforced. Introduced changes include modifications to the CFS (Completely Faire Scheduler) Linux scheduler to work with the modified Memguard kernel module. The original kernel module and the proposed implementation have been tested on an ARMv8 platform to demonstrate the performance and viability of such extensions on future embedded systems. A specific benchmark suite was used to stay as close as possible to common scenarios, measuring the memory bandwidth and the performance gain when scheduling at this level is introduced.

Keywords–Memguard; memory bandwidth scheduling; CFS; virtualization; KVM/ARM.

I. Introduction

Nowadays, computers and embedded systems are based on a multi-component architecture, which requires at least a microprocessor, some RAM (Random Access Memory) and other optional peripherals and storage devices. Over the last decades the performance of CPUs (Central Processing Unit) has been increasing steadily but memory, on the other hand, has not followed this trend, as such, computer systems are facing the Memory Wall problem [1][2]. Even if new solutions like HBM (High Bandwidth Memory) or stacked memory are attempts to solve this problem [3], most actual platforms are based on standard DRAM (Dynamic Random Access Memory). In this context, it is difficult to provide a guaranteed bandwidth to an application, especially real-time (i.e., soft or hard real-time) applications executed together with other tasks, as such, memory-bandwidth remains the most critical part of the system, especially on multicore systems (where memory is shared).

The performance bottleneck of memory bandwidth has been extensively studied, and several solutions [4] have been implemented. Most of them are hardware solutions [5][6], at the memory controller level. Few solutions have been proposed at the software level [7][8][9], mostly for server distributed large scale systems [10]. In this paper, memory bandwidth management has been considered as a solution to regulate virtualized environments.

A. Contribution of this paper

The existence of memory bottlenecks in actual computing systems is highlighted which results in degraded performance. In a mixed criticality and virtualized system, it also decreases the interactivity (interrupts processing can be slowed down). There is a need to implement a memory bandwidth reservation service to solve this issue.

A solution, called memguard was chosen as the memory bandwidth reservation system. The need to experiment with memory bandwidth regulation features on an embedded system, resulted in porting Memguard from x86 to the ARMv8 architecture and benchmarks demonstrate that even on ARMv8 Memguard can be beneficial as a memory bandwidth reservation system.

In the context of virtualization and embedded mixed-criticality systems, a communication interface between guests and the host was designed which forwards memory bandwidth requests to the Memguard kernel module. This new design also makes use of CFS [11] to sync the memory bandwidth reservation of tasks with the default scheduler of Linux.

An ARMv8 platform [12] was used to run experimental tests, which represents actual high-end embedded computer systems. This platform was selected to demonstrate that actual systems can optimally run mixed-criticality workloads by utilizing a memory bandwidth mechanism with virtualization in mind. Qemu/KVM (Kernel-base Virtual Machine) [13] was used as the virtualization solution to run experiments, as it is the most popular embedded virtualization solution.

B. Organization of the paper

The rest of this paper is organized as follows. Section II describes the state of the art of Memguard. Then, Section III lists the problems with virtualized mixed-criticality systems. Methods and benchmarks are explained and detailed in Section IV while initial results are reported in Section V. Possible implementations and solutions are detailed in Section VI and experimental results in Section VII. Finally, Section VIII summarizes the findings and directions for future work.

II. MEMGUARD KERNEL MODULE

Memguard [14][15] is a memory bandwidth aware scheduler, it distinguishes memory bandwidth in two parts, guaranteed and best-effort. It provides guaranteed bandwidth for temporal isolation and best-effort bandwidth to use as much as possible available bandwidth [16] (after all cores are satisfied). Memguard is designed to be used on actual systems using DRAM as main memory.

The common DRAM architecture consists of banks with different rows/columns [17]. Maximum memory bandwidth can be achieved in the case where data are located in different banks [18], in other cases the memory bandwidth can be limited and in such cases, Memguard can improve performance by scheduling the memory bandwidth to provide the desired Quality of Service.

A. Memguard architecture

Memguard is implemented as a linux kernel module, which is based on the use of the Performance Monitor Unit (PMU). It captures the memory usage of each core by reading the Performance Counter Monitor (reading memory request if used with PCM lower than 2.4 and memory reads and writes if PCM upper than 2.4).

The module architecture is based on two parts, the first being the Reclaim Manager which stores and provides bandwidth allocation to all per-core B/W regulators, while the other part is the per-core B/W regulator that monitors (thanks to the PCM) and regulates the memory bandwidth usage of each core. Memguard is linked to physical cores, the regulation process works only at the core level. Due to this architecture, regulating a process running on several cores at once is not easily feasible.

We can summarize the Memguard architecture components as follows:

The global budget manager aka Reclaim manager, which handles the memory budget on each core of the CPU. Every scheduler tick (1 ms), if the predicted budget of each core is under the assigned (fixed) budget of the overall system, a memory budget tank is set to give more bandwidth during the future time slice for tasks that need to access more B/W than required (and some B/W is available in the reclaim manager).

The per core bandwidth regulator, handles the memory management for each core, updating the actual used budget with the PCM (Performance Counter Unit) value, and configuring the PCM to generate an overflow when all memory budget is used. Additionally it requests more bandwidth from the reclaim manager if needed.

B. Memguard functionalities and use-cases

Beside this architecture, Memguard has different features. Its major functionality is the bandwidth limiting management, allowing users to set a limit (in MB/s, weight or in percent). Another feature is the per-task mode, where it uses task priority as the core's memory weight. The last major feature is the reclaim bandwidth functionality, distributing any leftover bandwidth that was not consumed, enabling the most effective use of memory bandwidth. When not in use, the available bandwidth is equal to the max-bandwidth setting set at start (or updated later).

The simplest use case for Memguard is to balance workloads, reducing the memory bandwidth of a task to preserve memory bandwidth for others. Memguard usage is linked to the physical cores of the CPU, consequently application level use is complicated and must be done manually. Memguard usage requires to set the bandwidth manually, thus users must be aware of application B/W needs and on which core they are being executed.

III. MEMORY MANAGEMENT IN EMBEDDED VIRTUALIZED ENVIRONMENTS

A. Context of use

In the past most actual embedded systems were designed to handle standalone actions within simple scenarios. Nowadays, more and more autonomous and network related tasks are utilized for embedded systems, as well as multimedia applications and database analysis workloads. At the same time embedded systems are designed with several small micro-controllers to communicate with each other (and/or with a master), resulting in increasing costs and decreasing the MTBF (mean time before failure).

As more demanding usage patterns emerge, most actual multi-chip embedded systems are being replaced by a central unit, performing most of the computation and networking related workloads. This paradigm shift raises the problem of mixed-criticality which is at the heart of the system, if a single platform is used to run different criticality software, additional resource and safety constraints are created.

Mixed-criticality is essentially the concurrent execution of hard real-time application together with soft real-time or standard applications [13] on the same processing unit. As such, this kind of system needs to provide spatial and temporal isolation of system resources, and in addition proper scheduling between hard and soft real time processes, as well as Quality of Service.

Virtualization is the last component of a future unified embedded system architecture. Virtual Machines give the possibility to ensure the security and resource isolation between tasks. Each task, for example a video processing task (capture video from a sensor and proceeding the image to find particular patterns) could run at the same time as a video playback workload and/or additional critical tasks. Each task can then be executed in a separate VM with all the software needed and the correct amount of processing/memory bandwidth reserved.

B. Requirements

In this context, the memory bandwidth management becomes the bottleneck of the system not only because all cores use the same memory but also because all different VMs are running simultaneously. Each VM handles its own software environment, with a specific priority and memory bandwidth. The priority of the guest is already solved with a priority scheduling mechanism[14], but for memory bandwidth this is not the case and it must be managed to reduce memory performance degredation.

As Memguard was designed to be used at the core level, its use at the Guest level in a virtualized environment involves to utilize Memguard in a different manner and to modify/extend parts of it. For now Memguard is restricted to be used with cores, and can't be linked to a program executed on different cores (scheduler balancing activated). As a result it's impossible to set a memory bandwidth policy on a guest to restrict its bandwidth and allow other guests make use of the remaining available bandwidth.

The primary target of this paper is to suggest a solution which enables a guest to set its memory bandwidth requirements. This would allow to set manually or automatically memory bandwidth in order to use it as efficiently as possible. The second target is to produce a tool which schedules the bandwidth between guests in order to limit some of them while letting others to maximize their usage. The possibility to schedule in that way, would allow to preserve some tasks (guests), making sure that they always have the correct amount of bandwidth. This would create a temporal memory separation and provide even more security between guests.

IV. Methods and Benchmarks

This paper uses a specific benchmark suite, composed by a virtualized environment and various software benchmarks. The experimental environment is based on the Linux 4.3.0 kernel with an open-embedded file-system, while Qemu/KVM is the selected virtualization solution. The actual benchmark platform is a Juno r0 development board with 2 Cortex-A57 and 4 Cortex-A53 cores. Only A57 cores are used to run the needed number of guests, as the memory bandwidth difference between A57 and A53 cores is too large to include both types of cores (from 2500MB/s to 1500MB/s). The taskset utility is used to set guests on specific cores, which they are based on 4.3.0 Linux and a minimal file-system, including the benchmark software suite.

The first benchmark used is a program used by the original author of memguard, this program is used to get a point of comparison between our platform and the author's one. It consists of a simple buffer copy-process application which utilizes a large amount of memory bandwidth, while providing a number of processed frames per second. The second program is the well-known Mplayer video suite. Mplayer was chosen to represent multimedia use-case in a mixed-criticality environment and is used with the benchmark option to see if a high-bitrate video decoding (two videos are used, 5Mb/s and 1Mb/s) process is runnable in the benchmark environment. The last benchmark is an FFT program, simulating a capture and process workload in soft real-time constraints. The FFT benchmark is called periodically and allocates a memory buffer for FFT computations, the output is a number of buffers processed per second.

V. Experimental Results

A. Memory bandwidth limitation

The first test (Fig. 1) highlights the memory bandwidth limitation mechanism. For this purpose, four different tasks will be launched at the same time. A different memory bandwidth weight will be associated to each core/task. Each task is running on a specific core (one core = one task).

During the first 120 seconds, Memguard is not loaded. After 220 seconds, Memguard is working with different weights to highlight the memory bandwidth limitation on each task. Task 1 has the maximum weight while task 4 has the lowest

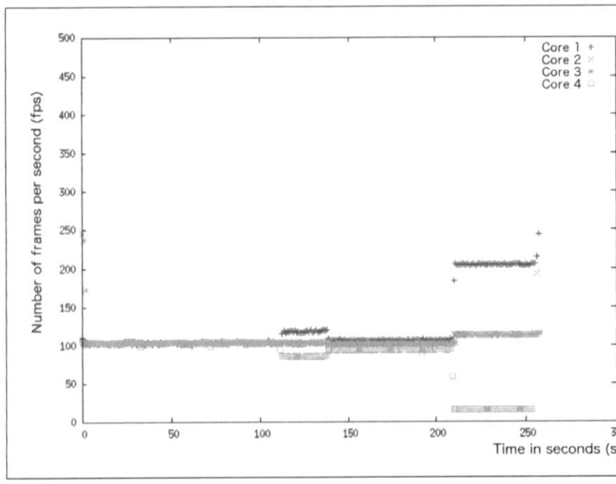

Figure 1. Memory bandwidth reservation on different cores

(tasks 2 and 3 have the same weight). The results are equivalent to the author ones, and show that Memguard is regulating the memory bandwidth of each task.

B. Memory bandwidth reclaim feature

The second experiment (Fig. 2) highlights the reclaim feature, a simple task is used to test if Memguard can release more bandwidth than the applied limit.

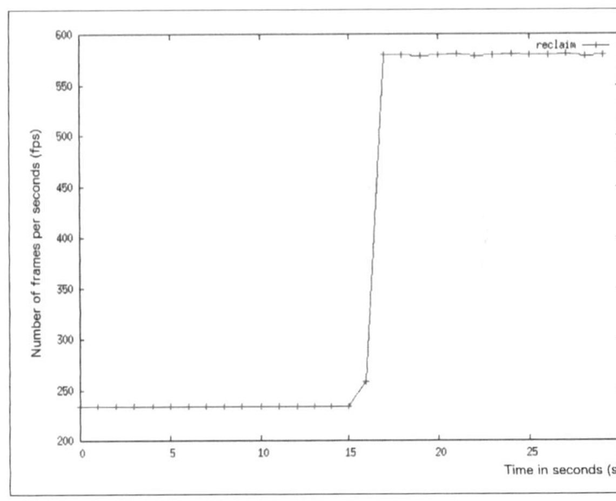

Figure 2. Memory bandwidth reclaim feature

The task is running between 0 to 15 seconds with an under-estimated memory bandwidth limit. The limit was set to 240MB/s, and when the reclaim feature is enabled the memory bandwidth reaches 590MB/s. This experiment shows that the reclaim feature can provide more than twice the original memory bandwidth limitation if more bandwidth is available.

C. Memguard's overhead

The CPU overhead of Memguard was measured to understand how to efficiently use Memguard in order to reduce this overhead as much as possible. The experiment uses Memguard with the reclaim feature activated.

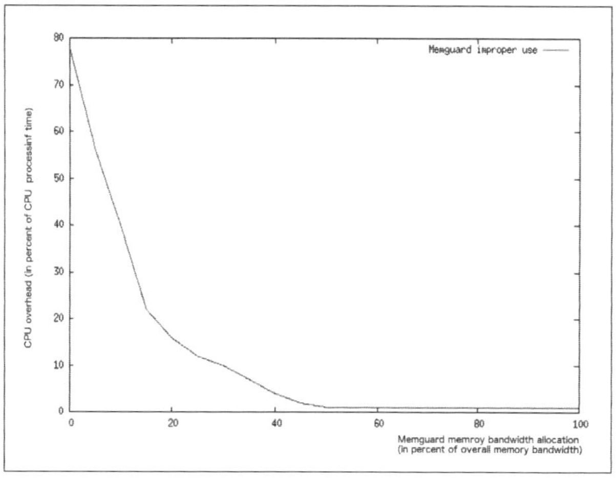

Figure 3. Relation of memory bandwidth allocation and CPU utilization

Depending on the memory reservation policy set by the user, Memguard can introduce a significant overhead to the system, in terms of CPU utilization. Fig. 3 shows the relation between CPU utilization and memory bandwidth allocation of an application. In cases where a large memory bandwidth is allocated, CPU utilization remains low, but when memory bandwidth for an application is underestimated, Memguard produces a large overhead due to the reclaim feature. This feature throttles the core and reallocates a fixed memory bandwidth amount, if the available bandwidth is too high, the produced overhead can reach up to 78 percent of CPU usage.

D. Example of use

In order to understand the way Memguard can be used in real-life computation, an experiment with video playback has been done (Table I).

TABLE I. VIDEO DECODING BENCHMARK

Environment of execution	*Processing time*
Plain linux 2 cores running same video task (mplayer)	Core 1 : 60.318s (decoding time) Core 2 : 60.320s (decoding time)
Memguard with under estimated bandwidth : 20 MB/s on all cores	Core 1 : 313.313s (decoding time) Core 2 : 311.306s (decoding time)
Memguard with correct estimated b/w core 1 (250 20 20 20)	Core 1 : 58.836s (decoding time) Core 2 : 276.001s (decoding time)
Memguard with correct estimated b/w core 1 and best-effort policy activated	Core 1 : 59.881s (decoding time) Core 2 : 95.619s (decoding time)

This experiment highlights the memory-bandwidth reservation capabilities of Memguard. When standalone Linux is executed, 60s (approx.) are needed to decode the video, whereas when Memguard is enabled, decoding lasts 58s. The interest of Memguard resides in the memory-bandwidth temporal reservation. A core can be limited to let other cores to use as much as possible the remaining memory-bandwidth (last case).

E. Memory bottleneck

Memory bottleneck conditions are highlighted in the first experiment (Fig. 1). Executed applications are all performing with similar results at the start of the test, where the bandwidth is divided equally to the guests. When Memguard is enabled, task number 1 reaches more than twice of the original memory bandwidth usage. The memory bottleneck is obvious, and if the user wants to prioritize a task due to its criticality, it's impossible to do so without Memguard. As such, memory bandwidth is the limiting parameter of the whole system, introducing increased latency and overall reduced performance.

F. Embedded virtualization problems

Since with QEMU/KVM a virtual machine is just another task to be scheduled by the host, memory bandwidth can have a significant role in performance. Every guests is using the same memory bandwidth and no hierarchy is implemented (like in a CPU scheduler) between guests. This memory-bandwidth bottleneck can eventually affect the performance of guests in scenarios where memory is aggressively utilized.

When Memguard is used to regulate guests, the user must launch each guest on one specific core (or several but, at least one core must be reserved to each guest), reducing the interest of using Linux with KVM, with the load balancing between cores. From the host's viewpoint, VMs are highly dynamic processes with varying workloads that may need different amounts of memory bandwidth. This results in the need for Memguard to be more flexible and be able to regulate on a process granularity instead of cores.

VI. SOLUTION

The aforementioned problem in virtualized environments can be solved using a memory bandwidth scheduler.

A. Architecture and implementation

The solution is based on a new architecture involving all layers of the virtualized computing chain (from the guest to the host kernel), which can deliver messages and regulate the memory bandwidth dynamically.

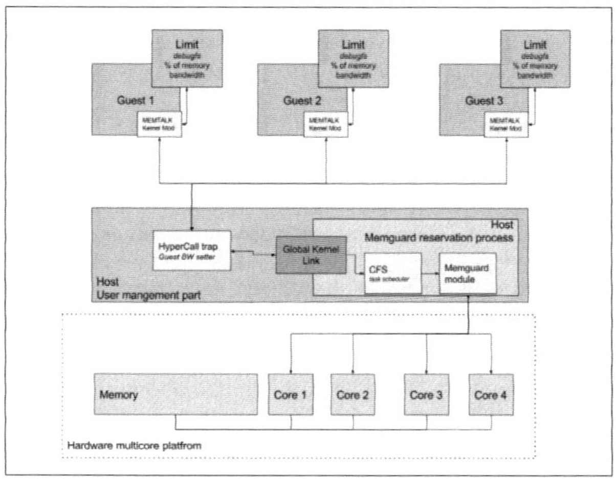

Figure 4. Proposed extensions to Memguard's architecture

The architecture of the solution is split in three main parts, the guest level API, the host message exchange mechanism and parts of Memguard linked to CFS. The selected architecture helps to keep a simple yet flexible mechanism. The first part is composed of a simple debugfs interface, enabling the user

```
memguard_guest_update(cpu_number){
    if next_task = a_guest_in_the_list
        callback_to_memguard()
}
```

Figure 5. Pseudo code to call memguard from CFS

```
update-budget-sched(int cpu-n, long bw-n){
    convert-bandwidth-to-cache-event()
    set-the-core-budget()
    initialize-the-memguard-statistics()
}
```

Figure 6. Pseudo code to update the per-core budget, called from CFS

to write/read from a simple file to set the needed memory bandwidth value, which also allows to set the bandwidth from other applications (e.g., a local resource manager).

Every call is made with the following:
ID of request: Host is aware that this call is a guest request
Request type: Host is notified if a guest wants to update bandwidth or be removed from the guest reservation process
Value: A general purpose 64bit variable to send information (e.g., bandwidth need: 70 percent of total BW)

The second part is the HyperCall module, which is processed by KVM in the host; every HyperCall is trapped, filtered and processed by the hypervisor. The HyperCall process has been described in detail previously[4], it traps the guest memory bandwidth request and stores it in the GlobalKernelLink.

The GlobalKernelLink is the bridge between the frontend (guest's API) and the backend, which is a hidden mechanism regulating the guest's memory bandwidth. A structure composed of several variables, exported across the host kernel called the GlobalkernelLink is responsible for handling all needed information for the solution, composed of
Memguard_sched_guests: number of guests running with memguard reservation enabled
Memguard_sched_PID: Tab to store guests PID
Memguard_sched_BW: Tab to store Bandwidth need of guests
Memguard_update_bandwidth: pointer to memguard callback function

The third part is the mechanism which regulates the bandwidth, applying the requested memory-bandwidth that was previously stored. This part is composed of two components, CFS, the Linux scheduler and Memguard, the kernel module, regulating memory-bandwidth at core level. CFS was selected because it is the main Linux scheduler and is fair between tasks. We implemented a method to call Memguard when guests are running.

When CFS has scheduled the next task, a callback to Memguard is executed which then enforces the memory bandwidth regulation. It is also worth mentioning that Memguard had to be also modified in order for it to handle the callback from CFS. This function in Memguard updates the memory bandwidth of the core corresponding to the linked guest.

CFS is an asynchronous scheduler, no fixed length scheduling clock is used during the scheduling (except the minimum execution time 4ms). Contrariwise Memguard has a fixed length scheduling clock (1ms), this scheduling mechanism difference raises a problem when merging both parts of the proposed solution. In order to address this issue, Memguard was modified to start a new scheduling period when CFS is calling-back Memguard. The resulting solution synchronizes both parts, CFS is unchanged and Memguard's scheduling tick is synchonized with CFS. Changes made in CFS introduce a small slowdown due to the processing time needed to check tasks' membership.

B. Benefits

The actual implementation has several benefits. The first one is the limited overhead due to a change in the memory-bandwidth requested by the guest, as a HyperCall is performed only when needed, reducing the total time spent when adjusting the value. The second benefit relates to the use of the CFS scheduler. This significantly reduces the complexity of integrating the solution, and the overhead is kept to a minimum. The last benefit comes from the Memguard callback, which provides memory bandwidth reservation and limitation functionalities.

C. Mixed criticality enhancement

As discussed previously, the target of the actual paper is to define a virtualized mixed-criticality solution to regulate memory-bandwidth. The solution provides a global answer in order to schedule dynamically memory-bandwidth, as the guest user can either set the needed bandwidth manually or let an automatic system take care of it. This results in the possibility to dynamically adjust the memory bandwidth and to regulate tasks between them, reducing the bandwidth of a task to let others use the remaining.

VII. Experimental Results with New Memguard Architecture

In this section, experiments and benchmarks are presented in order to highlight how Memguard extensions can be used in a mixed-criticality virtualized system.

The first benchmark (Fig. 7) shows the problem of the memory bottleneck. When two guests are running on the same core, the memory bottleneck limits the memory-bandwidth of both tasks. As in the first experiment (Fig. 1), in a virtualized environment, the bottleneck is the same.

This second experiment (Fig. 8) shows the interest of Memguard solution, at first both tasks are memory-bandwidth scheduled, the first curve (top one) at 70 of the guaranteed bandwidth and second curve (bottom one) at 20 of the memory bandwidth. When Memguard is disabled (around 13 seconds to 20 seconds) the first guest can reach the maximum bandwidth; after 20 seconds the second guest increases its memory-bandwidth reservation, resulting in less bandwidth available for the first guest. The interest is that both guests are running

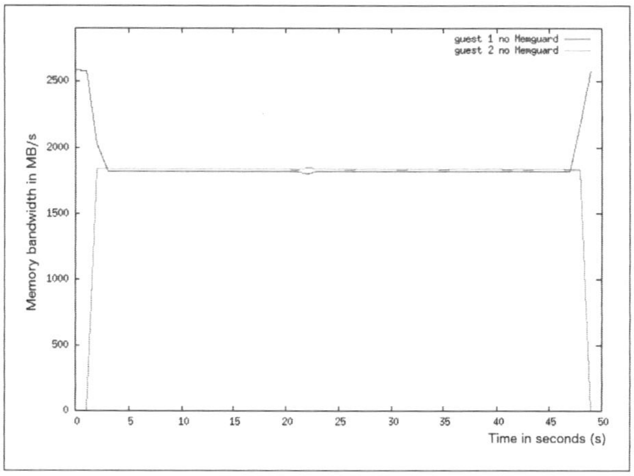

Figure 7. Memory bandwidth degradation between two guests

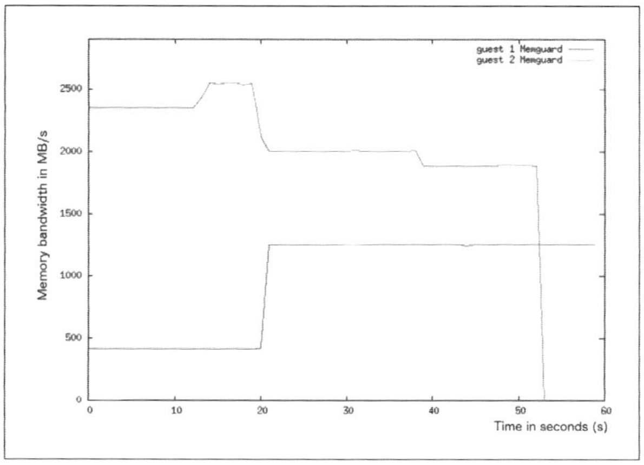

Figure 8. Guest memory bandwidth separation with Memguard

at different memory-bandwidth limits enabling a memory-bandwidth hierarchy between them.

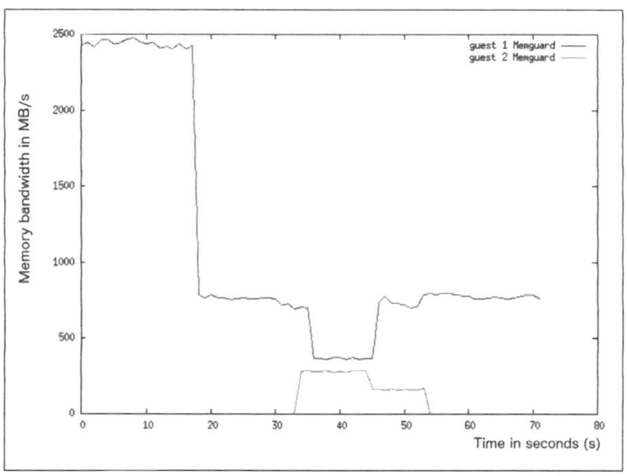

Figure 9. Guest memory bandwidth separation with Memguard (1 core of execution)

The third benchmark (Fig. 9) demonstrates the memory separation between guests. The first guest (top curve) is running unregulated at start, after 17 seconds, a limit is set, and a second guest (bottom curve) is launched after 33 seconds with a limited bandwidth. The reduction of bandwidth is due to the CPU time shared between both guests (running on the same core), when both guests are running, each has a specific memory bandwidth allocation which highlight the memory separation of guests running on the same core.

TABLE II. Video decoding benchmark

Environment of execution	*Processing time*
Plain linux 2 cores running same video task (mplayer)	Guest 1 : 62.112s (decoding time) Guest 2 : 67.968s (decoding time)
Memguard with under estimated bandwidth : 20 MB/s on all cores	Guest 1 : 386.893s (decoding time) Guest 2 : 384.655s (decoding time)
Memguard with correct estimated b/w core 1 (250 20 20 20)	Guest 1 : 57.947s (decoding time) Guest 2 : 312.014s (decoding time)
Memguard with correct estimated b/w core 1 and best-effort policy activated	Guest 1 : 60.911s (decoding time) Guest 2 : 97.665s (decoding time)

The Mplayer benchmark (Table II) was accomplished with an Mplayer decoding process running on two Guests. The results are following the ones done with no Virtualized environment and it demonstrates that the solution is not reducing the performance of the overall system.

TABLE III. FFT "real time" benchmark

Process used	*Processing speed*
FFT	78 033 sec/frame
FFT Database	148207 sec/frame 1450 MB/s
FFT (high priority) Database (BW reduced)	81014 sec/frame 800 MB/s

The last Benchmark (Table III) involves two guests, one is a camera capture-process VM and the second one is a memory intensive program (equivalent to a database explore task). Overall we can see that with Memguard plus the virtualization extensions, the performance of mixed-criticality use cases can improve significantly due to the additional QoS features implemented. When Memguard is not used, the FFT task has a large slowdown due to a lack of available memory-bandwidth, where if Memguard keeps the database task to a certain level of memory-bandwidth usage (800 MB/s), the FFT task can almost reach its full performance.

VIII. Conclusion and Future Works

In this paper, we highlighted the memory bottleneck on multi-core CPUs and the need to use a memory bandwidth reservation mechanism. In answer Memguard has been tested and extended for its use on ARM platforms. Due to the pervasive nature of virtualization even on embedded systems, Memguard has been adapted to fit this need.

A new architecture forwarding guests' memory requirements to Memguard has been implemented, working with CFS, Memguard has been modified to be synced with the scheduler. In result we obtained a memory reservation service which can throttle memory-bond tasks in favor of high criticality tasks. The actual implementation has several benefits and allows to increase the performance of tasks in mixed-criticality use cases. The overhead is kept to a minimum and the communication mechanism is easy to use from user space or other applications.

The proposed extensions to Memguard are still a proof of concept, and some improvements can be achieved when several guests are running on the same core to improve the tasks' memory separation.

ACKNOWLEDGMENT

This project has received from the European Unions FP7 research and innovation programme, Dreams, under grant agreement N 610640. This work reflects only authors view and the EC is not responsible for any use that may be made of the information it contains

REFERENCES

[1] S. Rixner, W. J. Dally, U. J. Kapasi, P. Mattson, and J. D. Owens, Memory access scheduling. ACM, 2000, vol. 28, no. 2.

[2] D. Field, D. Johnson, D. Mize, and R. Stober, "Scheduling to overcome the multi-core memory bandwidth bottleneck," Hewlett Packard and Platform Computing White Paper, 2007.

[3] S. H. Pugsley, J. Jestes, H. Zhang, R. Balasubramonian, V. Srinivasan, A. Buyuktosunoglu, A. Davis, and F. Li, "Ndc: Analyzing the impact of 3d-stacked memory+ logic devices on mapreduce workloads," in Performance Analysis of Systems and Software (ISPASS), 2014 IEEE International Symposium on. IEEE, 2014, pp. 190–200.

[4] Y. Kim, D. Han, O. Mutlu, and M. Harchol-Balter, "Atlas: A scalable and high-performance scheduling algorithm for multiple memory controllers," in High Performance Computer Architecture (HPCA), 2010 IEEE 16th International Symposium on. IEEE, 2010, pp. 1–12.

[5] K. Srinivasan, "Optimizing Memory Bandwidth in Systems-on-Chip," ESC conference, 2011, http://sonicsinc.com/wp-content/uploads/2012/09/Presentation_Multicore_final.pdf.

[6] E. Ipek, O. Mutlu, J. F. Martínez, and R. Caruana, "Self-optimizing memory controllers: A reinforcement learning approach," in Computer Architecture, 2008. ISCA'08. 35th International Symposium on. IEEE, 2008, pp. 39–50.

[7] K. W. Batcher and R. A. Walker, "Dynamic round-robin task scheduling to reduce cache misses for embedded systems," in Proceedings of the conference on Design, automation and test in Europe. ACM, 2008, pp. 260–263.

[8] E. Ebrahimi, R. Miftakhutdinov, C. Fallin, C. J. Lee, J. A. Joao, O. Mutlu, and Y. N. Patt, "Parallel application memory scheduling," in Proceedings of the 44th Annual IEEE/ACM International Symposium on Microarchitecture. ACM, 2011, pp. 362–373.

[9] W. Jing, "Performance isolation for mixed criticality real-time system on multicore with xen hypervisor," 2013.

[10] Y. Kim, M. Papamichael, O. Mutlu, and M. Harchol-Balter, "Thread cluster memory scheduling: Exploiting differences in memory access behavior," in Microarchitecture (MICRO), 2010 43rd Annual IEEE/ACM International Symposium on. IEEE, 2010, pp. 65–76.

[11] J.-P. Lozi, B. Lepers, J. Funston, F. Gaud, V. Quéma, and A. Fedorova, "The linux scheduler: a decade of wasted cores," in Proceedings of the Eleventh European Conference on Computer Systems. ACM, 2016, p. 1.

[12] ARM, "Technology Preview: The ARMv8 Architecture," ARM white paper, https://www.arm.com/files/downloads/ARMv8_white_paper_v5.pdf.

[13] Qumranet, "KVM: Kernel-based Virtualization Driver," White paper, http://www.linuxinsight.com/files/kvm_whitepaper.pdf.

[14] H. Yun, "Memguard: Memory bandwidth reservation system for efficient performance isolation in multi-core platforms," in Real-Time and Embedded Technology and Applications Symposium (RTAS), 2013 IEEE 19th. IEEE, 2013, pp. 55–64.

[15] H. Yun, G. Yao, R. Pellizzoni, M. Caccamo, and L. Sha, "Memory bandwidth management for efficient performance isolation in multi-core platforms," 2013.

[16] H. Yun, "Improving real-time performance on multicore platforms using memguard," 2013.

[17] V. Cuppu, B. Jacob, B. Davis, and T. Mudge, "A performance comparison of contemporary dram architectures," in ACM SIGARCH Computer Architecture News, vol. 27, no. 2. IEEE Computer Society, 1999, pp. 222–233.

[18] IBM, "Understanding DRAM Operation," Application note, https://www.ece.cmu.edu/ ece548/localcpy/dramop.pdf.

Intelligent Wearables

Alexiei Dingli
University Of Malta
alexiei.dingli@um.edu.mt

Luca Bondin
University Of Malta
luca.bondin.13@um.edu.mt

Abstract— **Wearable devices are ever more becoming an asset in our everyday lives. This shift to ubiquitous computing has also led to the development of systems that make these wearable devices behave intelligently according to a user's need, when deployed in various scenarios. The system discussed here, is envisaged to be deployed in a tourism environment as a personalized suggestion generation that relays information back to the user through an Augmented Reality framework. The implementation explored the use of various techniques in literature, and a series of tests were performed in order to evaluate the system's personalization capabilities and its perceived efficiency. The Precision rate obtained was 81%, while Recall and F-Measure, stood at 60% and 65% respectively. Future work on this study opens the door to the implementation of such systems that allow for the development of intelligent wearable devices that can be both useful in increasing accessibility or simply entertainment.**

Keywords- Profiling; Ontology; Augmented Reality; Intelligent recommendations; Implicit data gathering; Explicit data gathering; rule-based approach; Synsets; Precision; Recall; F-measure; tf-idf

I. INTRODUCTION

Artificial Intelligence (AI) "is the science and engineering of making intelligent machines, especially intelligent computer programs" [1]. Therefore, it is fair to conclude that the design and implementation Intelligent Wearable devices, devices that can adapt to the user's needs and behavior, is at the very core the field of Artificial Intelligence. We are now witnessing a shift to ubiquitous computing that has made it possible to have intelligent systems operate as effectively on mobile devices, and deployed in various scenarios without compromising on performance while incorporating new technologies such as Augmented Reality. One scenario where such systems can be deployed effectively is in the tourism domain in the form of Landmark Recommendation engines for tourists.

The tourism industry is an ever growing industry which caters for people of all ages, who come from various areas of life and more importantly, whose travel interests tend to differ. One such major difference would be that, while members of the older generations tend to prefer going on organized tours where a person is giving out information about any landmarks in the surroundings, members of the younger generation would rather roam freely about the city discovering what there is to be discovered by themselves. In addition, people tend to look out for different attractions when they are abroad which vary from tourist to tourist depending on the person's interests.

The development of wearable devices that behave intelligently, and that can be deployed in such scenarios would not only be interesting from the point of view of research, but also a step into what will soon be the norm for most devices we have around us [6][8]. The aim of this research is to make such wearables act intelligently by having the device generate recommendations tailor made for the individual. Acting intelligently also involves the presentation of relevant information to the user at the time when this is actually required. Such tasks involve the implementation of user-profiling mechanisms in order to be able to understand the traits of the user and in turn generate recommendations that are as accurate as possible. Deployed in the aforementioned domain, such devices would ensure that any tourist visiting a foreign city gets the opportunity to explore the city better, without hindering his visit with the cumbersome tasks of having to carry with him devices which are not very user friendly. Therefore, finding the right techniques with which to gather information, present it in structured formats, and, more importantly, infer user traits from the data at hand, is pivotal in the creation of such systems.

Section 2 gives an insight into the Aims and Objectives that this paper aims to achieve. While Section 3 provides an overview of related work, Sections 4 and 5 provide a description of the design and the implementation of the system respectively. Section 6 presents the results from the evaluation carried out and Section 7 provides an insight into future work. Finally, Section 8 provides a conclusion for the work carried out.

II. AIMS AND OBJECTIVES

The aim of this research is to investigate the best practices and techniques of building an accurate user profile from social media, to provide accurate recommendations that will sustain the operations of the intelligent wearable device. In order to achieve this, the following objectives were identified:

1. Building and representing a user profile from any source of data relevant to the cause and ensuring that mechanisms employed keep a representative profile which is up-to-date. Returning the recommendations of landmarks which may be interesting to a user, and extracting information from web sources to be returned to the system user.

2. Through the use of the mobile application notify the user whenever he is close to the landmark and provide on screen tailored information through an augmented reality framework.

The extent to which each of these objectives was satisfied by this study is as follows:

- The first objective was ultimately achieved through the personalization component. Through the tests performed accuracy results for this component were recorded at 0.81 precision average, 0.6 recall average and 0.65 f-measure average.

- The second objective was achieved through the information visualization component.

III. RELATED WORK

Research carried out focused primarily on personalization systems, mainly on how to construct efficient and effective user profiles. The ultimate goal of user-adaptive systems is to provide users with what they need without them asking for it explicitly. The idea of Automatic Personalization is central to such systems [2]. The ability of a personalization system to tailor content and recommend items implies that it must be able to infer what a user requires on previous and current interactions with the user. Tourist recommendation systems are all the more becoming an integral contributor to the concept of e-tourism services. Most recommendation systems tend to focus on helping the user select the travel destination while others tend to focus only on some aspects of the holiday. For example, Entrée [3] uses domain knowledge about restaurants, foods and cuisines to recommend restaurants to users while MastroCARonte provides personalized tourist information (hotels,restaurants, places to see or visit) on-board vehicles. In 2012, F.-M. Hsu et al. [9], came up with an intelligent recommendation system for tourist attractions [8]. Similarly, one can find CAPA, a personalised restaurant recommender that rather than being browser based, works on a mobile device. Systems such as the GUIDE system [4] and WebGuide [5] give the user a personalised experience when visiting cities such as Lancaster, Heidelberg and Vienna, through the way in which information is fed back to him. Other systems such as IMA provide services in a wide geographical area. CRUMPET proposes touristic sights' and uses advertisements to promote all kinds of services that may be helpful to any tourist [9].

IV. DESIGN

For development purposes, the system was drawn up into a number of components and subcomponents that communicate with each other to achieve the final goal of an application that works on a wearable device. Figure 1, shows an abstract representation of the proposed system and its main components. For the scope of this study, Android mobile applications, especially in view of the ease with which to create such applications, are ideal to implement the application component while Apache servers provide an ideal platform on which to host server side scripts that help the application with its tasks. Having the system planned out in this manner return provides many advantages mainly for the fact that by delegating the heaviest tasks to the server, the application on the mobile device can focus its resources on other areas. Also, any future updates to the system would require the alteration of some scripts on the server rather than having to modify the application's structure.

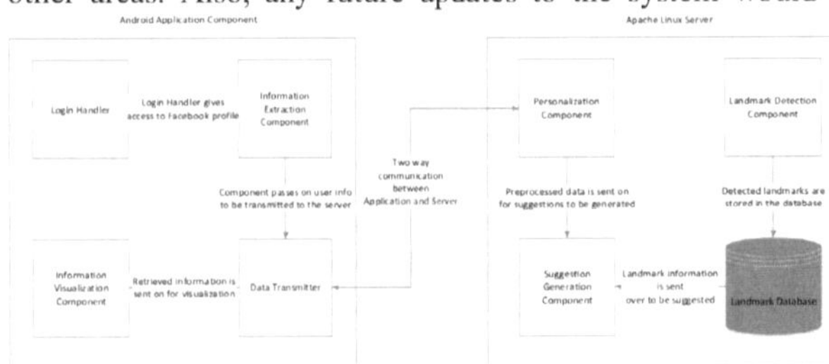

Figure 1. A diagram of the proposed system.

The first major component of the system is the Android Application component, which is first and foremost responsible for handling login operations that will in turn ask for information from a about the user and then triggering and handling the results obtained by the operations of the other sub components. For this function, social media was considered, mainly due to the fact that social media accounts tend to have an enormous amount of wealth of information about the user. The second component is an Apache Linux server component that through communication with the application that will be deployed on a wearable device, reduces much of the computational burden from the application side by handling the more cumbersome components of the system mainly, the personalization component. This component is also responsible for handling the presentation of the final system results.

The application component, as shown in the diagram below has a number of sub-components each responsible for handling specific tasks that give the application, and the whole system, its functionality. These components include a login handler component, an Information Extraction component, a JavaScript Object Notation (JSON) transmitter and an Information Visualization Component. The Login Handler component, as the name suggests is responsible for handling social media login requests by the user and works in tandem with the Information Extraction component to obtain the required information from the social media profile. Given that the application must in some form or another send and also receive data from the second component, the JSON transmitter component is critical for what the system is trying to achieve. This component provides the means of communication between the application and the server through the device's network services. The final module in the application component is the Information Visualization component. This component is responsible for displaying graphically the information that the application component receives from the server. Taking into consideration the various types of wearable devices, the most suitable device for such this proposed system is a head-mounting device. However, this is not its only use, as this component is also responsible for handling location tracking for the device and also for performing arithmetical operations to know when the device is actually required to display the retrieved information.

The server component has a number of sub-components as well, which components are responsible for handling specific tasks in relation to the personalization capabilities of the system. These components include a personalization module that prepares the received data for the generation of recommendations, and a Suggestion Generation module. The latter is tasked with building the user profile from the information retrieved from the application, and generating the suggestions based on the user profile built earlier. These suggestions are then transmitted back to application. In addition to these two modules, the server component also consists of a database that contains the information about landmarks in the city being visited, from which the suggestions are to be drawn.

V. IMPLEMENTATION

A. *Information Gathering*

The first task of the application is to gather information about the user. As previously discussed, this information is to be extracted from social media profiles and for this reason Facebook was chosen as the platform from which to gather the required information. The choice to go for this particular social media platform stems from the fact that as of 2016 it is estimated that Facebook has 1.59 billion users and therefore it is fair to say that it is one of the most popular platforms in the area. More importantly, Facebook profiles tend to be much more indicative about their users given the type of information people share. Facebook's Graph API is therefore used to obtain the desired information which information varies from personal information, such as demographics, to particular likes such as interests, artistic groups, and so on. The information is supplemented with information from the user's social media feed in order to ground it within a temporal context. The idea is to make the harvesting of the information as implicit as possible requiring only a minimal amount of explicit data input from the user. The user's 100 most recent likes and 25 most recent posts to his or her social media profile are taken into consideration and are later on analyzed to achieve the personalization objective. This amount of data is ideal since it finds a balance between having just about the right amount of data to be able to perform user profiling without overloading the application with information to be sent to the server, and eventually read back, making the application process too slow. In addition, this amount of information provides an ideal temporal context that makes sure that the information being used to achieve personalization is in fact based on the user's most recent activity which is indicative of his or her present interests.

B. *User Personalisation*

The first step in user personalization involves preparing the data for analysis. Essentially what this step does is that it receives the data and performs tokenization and stop-word removal. For the purpose of this implementation sentences were tokenized in order to be able to see the data in the form of words which makes it more practical to analyze. Stop-word removal, on the other hand, removes from a list of words very commonly occurring words that more often than not do not have any relevance to the subject of the sentence. Through the application of stop-word removal it is ascertained that the tokens that will be analyzed actually have a certain degree of importance and would actually contribute to the end result to be obtained by the system. Finally, after applying the aforementioned techniques, the system uses an ontology, in this case WordNet, in order to find the synonyms of all the remaining tokens in the gathered data. At the end of this process, the system is left with two data items that are crucial for the continuation of the profiling process. These are the list of remaining words after applying stop-word removal and a list of words with their synonyms. Upon termination of the first phase, the data next needed to be passed on for further processing.

C. *User Profiling*

User profiling can only start taking place when the data is properly prepared after completion of the above mentioned steps. However not until a further few steps are carried out, can the actual task of building the user profile be carried out. The first of these steps involves the introduction of tf-idf in order to be able to classify the words in the gathered data according to their importance. What this means is that if a word occurs more times than others then it will have a higher tf-idf value than the other words, which is precisely what is needed in this case. For the purpose of this implementation, the corpus includes all the information retrieved from the user's profile. Through calculation of tf-idf values the system creates a data structure consisting of data-pairs where each pair contains the word and its perceived importance, and how it is able to identify the most commonly occurring words. These words are considered to be the most important words which in turn will be used to base any assumptions for building the user profile. This reasoning stems from the thought that if a person talks or searches about some specific things, then one can deduct that the person is interested in these things. Consequently, these most commonly occurring words are considered to be indicative of the user's interests. For the purpose of this study the 200 most commonly occurring words are taken into consideration. It was felt that such a dataset size can give a sufficiently vast dataset on which to perform the remaining tasks.

1) Building the user profile

User-profiling adopts a hybrid approach between Weighted Key-word representation and the Semantic representation. It finally employs categorization into specific groups in order to improve uniformity. There are twelve identified categories which are: "photography", "shopping", "history", "military", "food", "religion", "art", "technology", "science", "music", "sport" and "nature". These identified categories also correspond to the categories of landmarks as classified by TripAdvisor. For each interest category identified, the synonyms were also identified once again through WordNet as a reference ontology, and the use of Node.js modules.

The profiling process is split up into three phases in order to ensure utmost veracity when the final results are achieved. The first stage involves comparing a set of words, deemed to be the most frequently used words by the user after analysis of the gathered data to the groups that correspond best to the landmark categories. Thus if the list of most commonly occurring words contains some word that is found in the list of identified interests, then that particular interest category is marked as relevant. Although this is one form of classifying the user, it was deemed too trivial and too risky when considering the result accuracy. As a second measure of profiling the word ontology results are introduced by which the system compares the synonyms of the most frequently used words to the stereotype categories. To further complement this, in the final stage of categorization, the system also looks at the synonyms of the landmark types and performs one final check in order to categorize the user into the most representative categories based on his interests. This ensures that if the list of most commonly occurring words does not contain the exact name of an interest field, then more checks are carried out to increase the chances of obtaining a hit. At the end of this cycle the result would be a user profile consisting of the interest fields that are deemed to be of interest to the user.

2) Generating suggestions

The only remaining task to do at this stage for the system is to generate the recommendations. The identified interest fields have a set of allocated landmarks which will, in turn, be recommended to the user by the wearable device. For example, if the user profile has the 'food' category ticked, then the system will return to the user a list of all the landmarks that fall under the 'food' category in the landmark database.

This database is generated through calls to the Google Places API. These calls in addition to returning the name of the landmark, its geographical location and reviews about the place, also returns a list of categories under which these landmarks can be classified. It is through these returned categories that the landmarks are classified in the landmark database and eventually recommended back to the user. This component makes the system extremely flexible, in the sense that with just a simple update of the landmark database through API calls, the system can be deployed virtually everywhere that is covered by Google Maps. These suggested landmarks are then returned to be visualized on screen.

D. Information Visualization

The final component of the system is the Information Visualization component, which is responsible for visualising the suggestions on the wearable device and which is implemented in its entirety on the application side. In order to achieve a functional Location-based Augmented Reality, which is the approach chosen for this implementation, the undertaking of the following steps was necessary prior to the actual Augmented Reality framework construction:

- Getting the GPS location of the device
- Getting the GPS location of destination point
- Calculation of the theoretical azimuth based on GPS data
- Getting the real azimuth of the device
- Comparing both azimuths based on accuracy to then call an event

1) User Location and Azimuth Angles

Keeping in mind the application's objective, it is imperative for the application to constantly know the user's location in order to be able to augment the user's view with information that is relevant to landmark which is in view. Location details are obtained through the device's GPS whereby, with the use of listeners, the user's coordinates are updated periodically. This was implemented by GoogleApiClient requesting location updates at a predefined interval between each request. When the application senses that there is a change in movement, location is updated.

The system must also calculate the user's azimuth angle since the implementation approach chosen is based on the geodesy theory. Calculation of this angle is necessary for triggering the on-screen visualization of the landmark information, and the process of getting this calculation relies heavily on the use of the device's sensors.

2) Object Identification

Location data is pivotal to achieve whatever needs to be done in this component since the system adopts a Location-based Augmented Reality approach. What this approach entails is that the device does not know what the landmark actually looks like, but rather where it is. Since the system is being deployed in a scenario where it is required to suggest landmarks to its user, this approach fits the requirement perfectly because a landmark is hardly ever going to move, and should it move, for example if a restaurant relocates, the system can work just as fine with a simple update of the landmark database.

As already mentioned the system keeps track of the user's location at regular intervals and this data is, in turn, used to augment the screen with the landmark information. Apart from this it also makes sure that whatever data is presented on screen, it is relevant to the landmark actually in view. In order to be able to function, the Visualization Component relies on the landmark data file transmitted by the server. As soon as this is available the component becomes active. It first reads every suggested landmark from the retrieved list, and then creates a data structure of landmark objects where each object contains the landmark name, its location and any relevant reviews. When the application is fully aware of what landmarks exist then visualization can begin.

The aim of the application is to be able to return information on screen whenever a landmark is in view. It does not require to have multiple pieces of information about various landmarks at any one time on screen. This, however, required the implementation of a method that is able to identify the nearest Point Of Interest (POI) which would allow the application to augment the screen with the relevant information pertaining to the landmark which is closer to where the user is at a point in time. It is in this manner that Object Identification was implemented. The application constantly updates its knowledge about the landmarks. At any one time it knows that when a user is at a particular location, the nearest location is the object whose information is to be visualized.

However, although this already achieves, to some degree, the Object Identification requirement, it is still not enough to display the information correctly on the screen. It is for this reason that the application also calculates the landmark's azimuth angle. The application gets the co-ordinates of the POI and forms a right angled triangle between the user's location, a point directly in front of the user projected on the plane that the POI is on, and the POI location itself. Using conventional trigonometric functions the azimuth angle is calculated and the system would know whether to display information on the screen or not depending on the resultant azimuth angle.

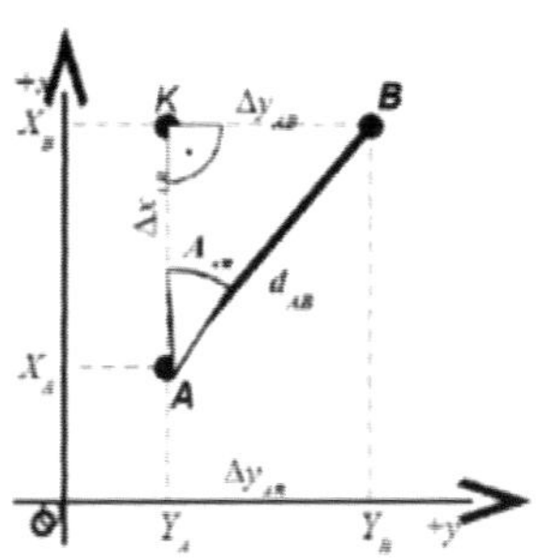

Figure 2. Calculation of Azimuth Angle in principle. If A is where the device is and B is the landmark, then the azimuth angle is the angle between AB and AK.

In this manner, the application is able to perform Object Identification quite effectively. When an augmentation is indeed triggered, a marker appears on screen showing the landmark together with the relevant reviews.

Figure 3. Output of the Visualization Component where the landmark is pointed out by the icon appearing at the center of the view, and the landmark name and any reviews are displayed at the bottom.

VI. Results and Evaluation

In order for the system and methodology of this study to be evaluated properly, a number of different aspects were analyzed. The first tests were carried out in order to analyze the performance of the system's personalization capabilities, more specifically, the system's ability to generate accurate user profiles representing its users. In order to complete this evaluation, a number of individuals were invited to participate in the process. Through this crowdsourcing, data could be gathered which would in turn mock a real world scenario where the system would be deployed, and the system's performance could then be analyzed.

The second tests carried out focused more on the general deployment of such a system to a wearable device and how would the general public, when given a wearable device that performs in this manner, reacts to its use. This evaluation focused on the complete package that includes both the personalization components, and the landmark detection and Augmented Reality components of the system, and again involved the participation of a number of users

A. Crowdsourcing demographic analysis

In order to determine the quality of the relevance of the data obtained through crowdsourcing, and thus evaluate the completion of both objectives, it is essential to analyze the background of the test subjects that provided it. Sixty people were invited to participate in the evaluation through completion of the questionnaire. The information extracted from the demographic part of the questionnaire, consisting of age and the user's perceived level of use of social media, was thus extracted and analyzed.

As can be seen from the charts in Figures 4. and 5., the majority of the participants were between 20 and 30 years old. The people belonging to this age group are considered to be the most avant-garde when it comes to trying out new technologies and are also the most active on social media [10]. Therefore, they provide an ideal basis on which to build the evaluation. However, other age groups were also taken into consideration in order to evaluate the system's performance according to different user behavior.

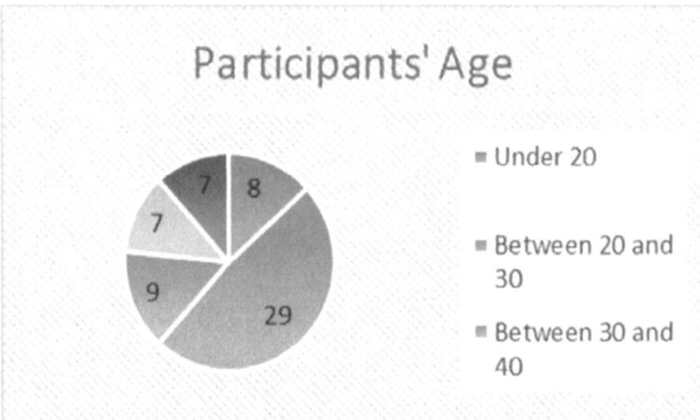

Figure 4. Pie chart showing age distribution between participants in this study. (Source: Luca Bondin, Intelligent Wearables)

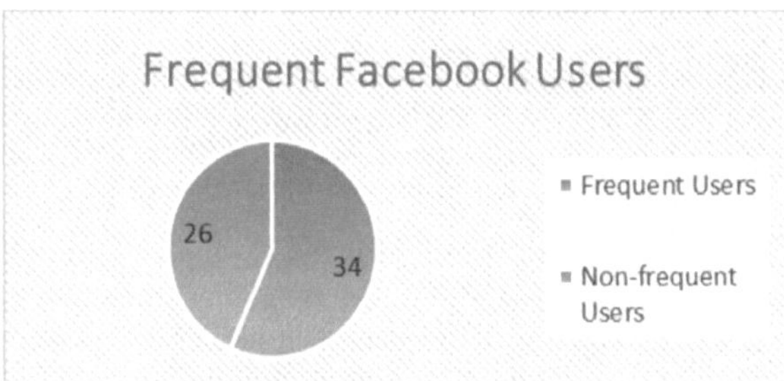

Figure 5. Pie chart showing distribution of participants according to perceived use of Facebook (Source: Luca Bondin, Intelligent Wearables)

As for the test users' level of use of social media, the questionnaire asked users whether they consider themselves as frequent Facebook users. 34 respondents said they were regular Facebook users while the remaining 26 said otherwise. This distribution was ideal as while the system and the methodology could be evaluated on profiles that are regularly updated, it could also be evaluated on other profiles whose owners do not share as much information frequently.

B. Profiling accuracy analysis

In order to complete the evaluation of the profiling components of the system the participants were first asked to explicitly mark which of the interest fields they thought best described their interests. Next, they were asked to make use of the system, through the aforementioned web agent, that makes use of the system's scripts to extract the participants' social media profiles and generate a user profile accordingly. The generated user profile is then compared to the interest fields marked by the user. Given the set-up of the system and what the system is aiming at achieving, it was decided that calculation of Precision and Recall values was the optimal way of evaluating the accuracy and suitability of the system for the purpose it is intended. Finally, F-Measure is used to provide a single measurement for the system.

The average Precision rate obtained by the system was 0.81 meaning that there is an 81% chance that the system will at least classify the user into one correct category and return relevant suggestions. On the other hand the Recall values returned by the system were somewhat smaller. Although the highest Recall value achieved is 1.0, the average Recall value obtained stood at 0.60 meaning that there is a 60% probability that a relevant interest field is found in the user profile. Again these results may have been compromised with previously mentioned issues with users not sharing information which is entirely relevant and indicative of their interests. Surprisingly though, the system still performed reasonably well in cases when the test user listed down that he or she was not a frequent Facebook user. Therefore, one may speculate that rather than being a case of whether a user is making frequent use of his profile or not, it is rather the case of what content the user decides to share through the social media profile. The average f-measure value obtained from the conducted tests stands at 0.65.

TABLE I. THE RESULTS AFTER EVALUATION

	Minimum	Maximum	Average
Precision	0.33	1	0.81
Recall	0.17	1	0.60
F-Measure	0.29	1	0.65

C. System Design Evaluation

The second evaluation included the evaluation of the system as a whole and how people would react at being given the opportunity to use such a system. In order to complete this evaluation, the participants were presented with a scenario where such a system could be deployed on a wearable device, and were presented with the system's abilities when making use of it. The participants were then asked a number of questions to determine whether they would make use of such a system, whether they would feel comfortable using such a system due to issues that may arise with the way the system is designed to work, and finally whether they think that such a device would truly enhance their visit to a city and why.

The results for this evaluation are overwhelmingly positive. All the participants think that such a system does indeed enhance one's visit to a city and would indeed be willing to use such a device should it be given to them. While some mention that such a device would allow them to roam freely without following tours, others mention that such a device would render their lives easier in the sense that it reduces the need for them to do endless research before going on their trips. This trend is evident amongst all age groups. However, some issues do seem to exist as people of all ages are becoming more conscious of what information they share and who they share this information with. These issues arise due to the system's use of a user's personal data. A number of people express their concern at such systems requiring, and eventually extracting, personal information from their social media profiles to achieve their functionalities.

Upon analysis, the results obtained provide further indication that the objectives set out at the start were indeed reached. For the purpose of this implementation the efficiency of implicit data gathering could be deduced from the results obtained through the evaluation of the personalization components. This evaluation shows that taking into consideration the various limitations that exist, especially with the user data, the implementation still yielded satisfactory results, most notably through the fact that the system provided suggestions for all the test profiles. There were occasions where it managed to profile the user perfectly. On the whole, the 81% precision rate was quite good, although the recall rate achieved was slightly disappointing. As mentioned, there are quite a good number of variables that may in fact influence these results and all in all, considering the effort done in trying to overcome any issues that the approach adopted might have, the results obtained were satisfactory. Certainly, with more uniform information fed to the system to perform personalization, the results are bound to improve even further.

VII. Future Work

More work could be done to improve the performance of the system with respect to its personalization capabilities, more specifically, to improve on the Ontology-based approach adopted in this study. The first issue that should be tackled is the cold-start problem that the system might encounter when working on some profiles. This problem could be tackled by looking at alternative sources through which it could acquire data for personalization, which may be other social media platforms or through mild forms of explicit data gathering. Also, the use of a hybrid approach to personalization would perhaps be ideal. At the moment, the system performs profiling by performing comparisons between words and their synsets to the interest fields and their synsets, but what if the system could analyze whole sections of data and know what they actually are? For example, if a person writes about some football team then the system knows that what the user has written about is actually a football team and it determines that the user is interested in sport without actually finding the exact word "sport" or a word pertaining to its synset.

Boosting the personalization capabilities of the system could also be achieved through obtaining more information about the user from other sources. There is a reluctance to move towards explicit data gathering but the need for better input data is clear. This can be achieved from other sources such as a user's browser history and from some form of mild explicit data gathering.

Secondly, work could be done to improve both the Augmented Reality approach of the implementation as well as some minor tweaks that make the implementation work more intelligently such as the ability for the system to know in which city it is at a point in time, and automatically make calls to the Google API and update the landmark database with landmarks that are in the vicinity. Also, the Location-based approach could be strengthened with an implementation of computer vision methods in order to improve performance.

Finally, when the hardware is available the system should be deployed on a wearable device that could satisfy the system requirements and allow it to operate at its full computational abilities.

VIII. Conclusions

The approach chosen for implementation was able to produce a system that can profile a user to a reasonably high degree of precision. The rule-based approach, aided by traits derived from both the weighted key-word profile and the ontology-based approach to personalization systems was pivotal in achieving the set objective, and the 81% Precision rate and 60% Recall rate prove the efficiency of the said approach. A definite strong point of the system is however its flexibility of the system in terms its structure and the way it is intended to work. As shown from the evaluation results, such a system deployed on a wearable device would greatly enhance a person's visit to a new city, increasing both accessibility and comfort, while the fact that it is able to be deployed in any city around the world with the same performance results sets it apart from other systems of its kind.

This study opens the door to a better understanding on how intelligent systems that are designed to work on a wearable device may be implemented, which is a positive step in the development of such devices which are becoming ever more popular and essential. Along with improvements on the approach taken and future work cited, such a system would be both revolutionary, as well as provide an innovative solution on how such systems could be developed to act intelligently with respect to the user's ever changing demands.

References

[1] J. McCarthy, [Online]. Available: http://www-formal.stanford.edu/jmc/whatisai/node1.html [30/9/2016]

[2] B. Mobasher, 2007. Data mining for web personalization. In The adaptive web (pp. 90-135). Springer Berlin Heidelberg.

[3] R. Burke, 2002. Hybrid recommender systems: Survey and experiments.User modeling and user-adapted interaction, 12(4), pp.331-370.

[4] K. Cheverst, N. Davies, K. Mitchell, A. Friday, and C. Efstratiou, 2000, April. Developing a context-aware electronic tourist guide: some issues and experiences. In Proceedings of the SIGCHI conference on Human Factors in Computing Systems (pp. 17-24). ACM.

[5] J. Fink and A. Kobsa, 2002. User modeling for personalized city tours. Artificial intelligence review, 18(1), pp.33-74.

[6] https://www.microsoft.com/microsoft-hololens/en-us [30/9/2016]

[7] A. Pretschner and S. Gauch , 1999. Ontology based personalized search. InTools with Artificial Intelligence, 1999. Proceedings. 11th IEEE International Conference on (pp. 391-398). IEEE.

[8] S. Poslad, H. Laamanen, R. Malaka, A. Nick, P. Buckle, and A. Zipl , 2001. Crumpet: Creation of user-friendly mobile services personalised for tourism.

[9] M. Van Setten, S. Pokraev, and J. Koolwaaij, 2004, January. Context-aware recommendations in the mobile tourist application COMPASS. In Adaptive hypermedia and adaptive web-based systems (pp. 235-244). Springer Berlin Heidelberg.

[10] http://www.statista.com/statistics/187041/us-user-age-distribution-on-facebook/ [30/9/2016]

[11] M. Pazzani and D. Billsus, 1997. Learning and revising user profiles: The identification of interesting web sites. Machine learning, 27(3), pp.313-331.

[12] S. Gammeter, A. Gassmann, L. Bossard, T. Quack, and L. Van Gool, 2010, June. Server-side object recognition and client-side object tracking for mobile augmented reality. In Computer Vision and Pattern Recognition Workshops (CVPRW), 2010 IEEE Computer Society Conference on (pp. 1-8). IEEE.

[13] H. Bay, T. Tuytelaars and L. Van Gool, , 2006. Surf: Speeded up robust features. In Computer vision–ECCV 2006 (pp. 404-417). Springer Berlin Heidelberg.

[14] M. Minio and C.Tasso, 1996. IFT: un'Interfaccia Intelligente per il Filtraggio di Informazioni Basato su Modellizzazione d'Utente. AI* IA Notizie IX (3), pp.21-25.

[15] S.E. Middleton, N.R. Shadbolt and D.C. De Roure, 2003, October. Capturing interest through inference and visualization: Ontological user profiling in recommender systems. In Proceedings of the 2nd international conference on Knowledge capture (pp. 62-69). ACM.

[16] S. Fox, K. Karnawat, M. Mydland, S. Dumais and T.White, 2005. Evaluating implicit measures to improve web search. ACM Transactions on Information Systems (TOIS), 23(2), pp.147-168.

[17] K. Kabassi, "Personalising Recommendations For tourists," Telematics and Informatics, pp. 51-56, 2009.

[18] M. Wasim, I. Shahzadi, Q. Ahmad and W. Mahmood, 2011, December. Extracting and modeling user interests based on social media. In Multitopic Conference (INMIC), 2011 IEEE 14th International (pp. 284-289). IEEE.

[19] S. Schiaffino and A. Amandi, 2009. Intelligent user profiling. In Artificial Intelligence An International Perspective (pp. 193-216). Springer Berlin Heidelberg.

[20] A. Ansari, S. Essegaier and R. Kohli, 2000. Internet recommendation systems. Journal of Marketing research, 37(3), pp.363-375.

[21] M. Montaner, B. López, and J.L. de la Rosa, 2004, April. Evaluation of Recommender Systems Through Simulated Users. In ICEIS (3) (pp. 303-308).

[22] P. Srisuwan and A. Srivihok, 2008. Personalized trip information for e-tourism recommendation system based on Bayes theorem. In Research and Practical Issues of Enterprise Information Systems II (pp. 1271-1275). Springer US

[23] A. Jagielski, 2014. Geodezja II. Wydawnictwo

[24] R. Malaka, 2000. Artificial intelligence goes mobile. In R. Malaka (Ed.) Artificial Intelligence in Mobile Systems–AIMS2000, Workshop in conjunction with ECAI 2000 (pp. 5-7).

[25] R.D. Burke, K.J. Hammond, and B.C. Young, 1996, August. Knowledge-based navigation of complex information spaces. In Proceedings of the national conference on artificial intelligence (Vol. 462, p. 468).

An Application and Hardware for Repetition Images in Special Effects Shooting

Myoungbeom Chung
Division of Computer Engineering
Sungkyul University
Anyang City, South Korea
e-mail: nzin@sungkyul.ac.kr

Abstract—**In this paper, we propose an application that can be used to take repetition images for special effects shooting in movies or television using the Bluetooth technology of smart devices. After the application saves the control data for a specific period (based on the user's selection), the proposed application can move the motors of the hardware mounted on the camera to perform the same motion several times via Bluetooth communication. We do not permit users to control the camera motors for the repeated movements, so we can keep the same start and end positions after saving the moving data. The camera motors are only moved remotely by the application's saved data. We developed the proposed application and hardware, which work with camera motors for performance evaluation. Then, we confirmed that the proposed application repeated exactly the same motion with the camera motors several times, according to the saved data. Therefore, because the proposed application can take same images by remotely controlled camera motors, it will be a useful technology for special effects shooting of movies or television.**

Keywords-special effects shooting; repeated images; smart devices; application; same-movement.

I. INTRODUCTION

With the rapid development of smart devices and wireless communication, many technologies, such as data sharing, near wireless transmission, and hardware control methods are using the communication function of smart devices. The communication technologies included in smart devices are Bluetooth, socket transmission using Wi-Fi, and Wi-Fi Direct; these are developed from control research involving robots, smart devices, Remote Control (RC) cars, etc. [1-4].

From the growth of these control technologies, equipment for broadcast shootings has been applied to remote control technologies. ARRI Co. has sold equipment and software to control the Motion Control Camera (MCC) called Scorpio Mini Head SB92 [5], and CamRanger co. has released an MP-360 tripod head that can be controlled by a smart device or computer [6]. These control technologies are set up and used in dangerous recording positions, such as high places or quickly moving vehicles, and especially in difficult-access areas. Because the MCC has a built-in memory card for special effects shooting, it can record moving shots during a two minute period and it can shoot the same motion consistently. Thus, the MCC can record the same scene with the same camera moving a dozen times. When wired controls are used for the MCC, the scene being shot through the monitor can be seen immediately, and electric power can be directly supplied to the MCC. However, when we use wireless controls for the MCC, a wireless control desk is need, and the MCC can only save four movements according to the number of built-in memory cards. Because most MCC equipment is very expensive, we cannot use it frequently. On the other hand, the MP-360 is cheaper than MCC equipment and it can be controlled wirelessly. Since the MP-360 uses a tripod, we can adjust it to making a movie or video. However, the MP-360 can make panning and tilting motions, but not rolling motions.

In this paper, we propose an application based on smart devices and hardware that can repeat the same movement consistently for special effects shooting. The proposed application and hardware have the advantages of both the MCC and the MP-360. The proposed application sends the movement data to the hardware via Bluetooth, and the hardware mounted on the video camera can repeat the same movement numerous times. The hardware is composed of four motors (one motor for the panning motion, one motor for the tilting motion, and two motors for the rolling motion), a Micro Controller Unit (MCU) board for data transmission and control, and a Bluetooth module.

To evaluate the performance of the proposed application and hardware, we developed an application based on smart devices and hardware, and we conducted a control experiment with the same movements repeated during two, three, and four minute periods. The results showed that the proposed application and hardware moved to the same position without error during the two and three minute periods. Moreover, during the four-minute phase, the error rate was only 0.18% for the rolling motion. Thus, because the proposed application and hardware can work as well as the MCC and because they do not require an extra control desk, the proposed application and hardware can replace the MCC. Since the proposed equipment can be used in dangerous regions or places people difficult for people to access, it will be useful for special effects shooting.

This paper is organized as follows. Section 2 explains some of the equipment used for special effects shooting and how to make a special effect using the MCC. In Section 3, we describe the proposed application based on smart devices and hardware mounted on video cameras. In Section 4, we describe the application and hardware that we developed, and we discuss the results of the control experiment in terms of the performance of the proposed technologies. Finally, in Section 5, we present the conclusions and our further research.

II. RETATED WORK

In this section, we explain some of the equipment required for special effects shooting. Many kinds of broadcast shooting equipment exist for special effects shooting and Computer Graphics (CG), such as the MCC, Body-Cam (body camera), Steadicam, or wireless controllers for lens focusing. The body-cam is a video camera attached to the body of an actor using hardware, and it can capture scenes for the first person narrative, following up the actions of the actor and creating a sense of immediacy [7]. Steadicams capture a steady scene even if the actor of the scene runs or walks [8]. While running or walking with a Steadicam, the camera operator cannot focus the lens. Therefore, when the distance between the actor and the movie camera is changed, a wireless controller is often used to focus the Steadicam lens.

For special effects shooting, the MCC is used to repeat the same camera movement though actors move differently during each take. For example, we can shoot the same motion with the same camera using the MCC, as shown in Fig. 1 [9].

Fig. 1 (a) is a tree plate scene: the base scene for special effects shooting. Fig. 1 (b) is a tracking plate, which includes a guideline for CG special effects. Fig. 1 (c) is a reference plate, where a silver pipe stands in for a stream of water that will be added later by CG effects. Fig. 1 (d) is a main plate that will compose the background of a scene with applied CG effects. After we combine each scene with CG effects, we can make a special effects scene, as shown below in Fig. 2 [9].

In Fig. 2, the stream of water that was based on the reference plate is now visible in the main plate, which did not show any water originally.

Recently, broadcast equipment for special effects shooting has mostly been comprised of the Remote Head series of ARRI co.; of this series, the Classic Head HD and Mini Head HD are capable of tri-axis movements [10]. However, the Remote Head series of ARRI co. requires a hand-wheel to control the head manually and a wireless control desk to control the head wirelessly. Thus, we cannot use Remote Head equipment often, and movie companies or advertisement companies use it most, because renting the hardware is expensive.

(a) (b) (c) (d)

Figure 1. Each plate is an example of how to create CG and special effects for a movie scene: (a) tree plate, (b) tracking plate, (c) reference plate, (d) main plate

Figure 2. Final shot using special effects implementation and CG

III. An Application and Hardware for Same-Movement Shooting

In this section, we describe an application based on smart devices that can control hardware via Bluetooth, and we describe the hardware mounted on the video camera that can do the same movement multiple times. Wireless transmission control between the application and the hardware connects with Bluetooth pairing, and the work flow is shown in Fig. 3.

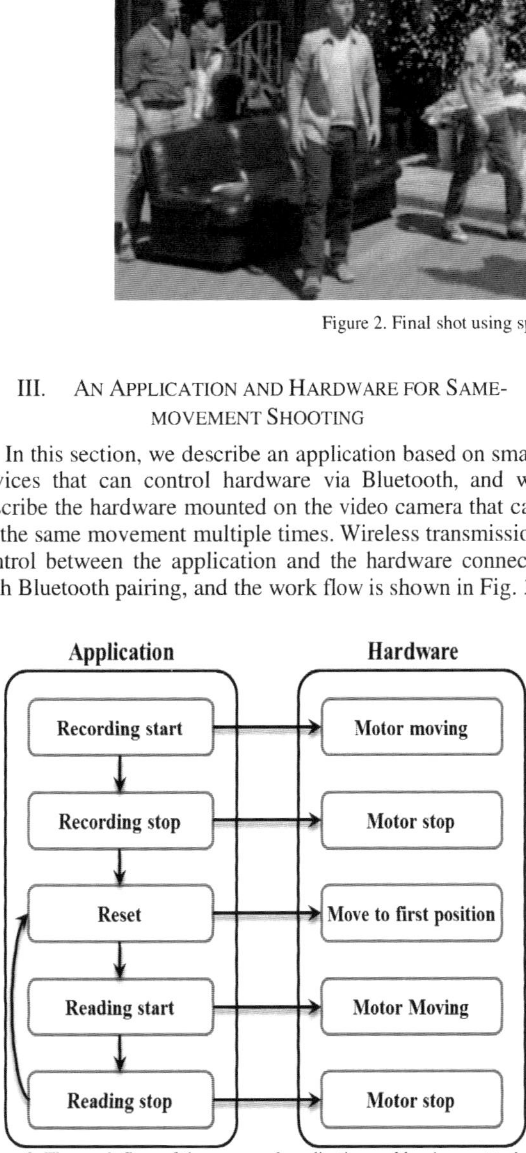

Figure 3. The work flow of the proposed application and hardware attached to the camera

As shown in Fig. 3, the hardware is not moved from shooting start to shooting end without the proposed application. When the proposed application moves the hardware after "Recording start" is selected, the application saves the movement data to built-in memory, according to the user's control. If the user finishes shooting a scene, he or she can stop the application from recording via the "Recording stop" button, and the application finishes by saving control data. At the same time, the hardware stops each camera motor. When the proposed application executes the "Reset" function, the hardware moves to the first position recorded by the application's movement data. Next, if we execute the "Reading start" button, the application sends movement data to the hardware, which then moves according to the movement data provided. If the application's saved movement data ends, the application stops reading movement data and the hardware stops each motor. Then, the "Reset, Reading start, Reading stop" operating process repeats until enough scenes are obtained for CG special effects. A screen shot of the proposed application based on smart devices is portrayed in Fig. 4, and the menu of the application is categorized into three headings: Recording, Reading, and Setting.

Fig. 4 shows the control functions of the "Recording" menu, which allows the user to move the hardware via many directional buttons, such as Panning (Left, Right), Tilting (Up, Down), and Rolling (Left, Right). These buttons can move the hardware even if the "Recording Start" button is not executed. When the user wants to save a hardware movement, the user touches the "Recording Start" button. Then, the "Recording time" increases, and the application saves the camera movement data. Simultaneously, the application moves the hardware via Bluetooth, and the user can take a shot needed for special effects shooting via the Panning (Left, Right), Tilting (Up, Down), and Rolling (Left,

Right) buttons. When the shooting is ended, the user touches the "Recording Stop" button, and the application stops to save the camera movement data. The camera movement data is saved in the built-in memory of the smart device, and we can see the saved data from the application's "Reading menu" (shown below in Fig. 5).

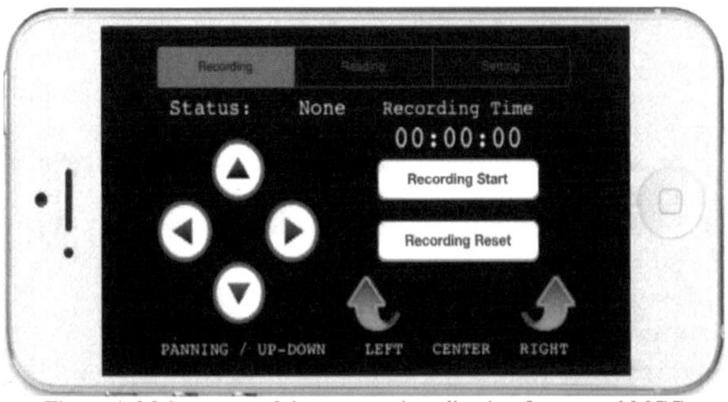

Figure 4. Main screen of the proposed application for control MCC

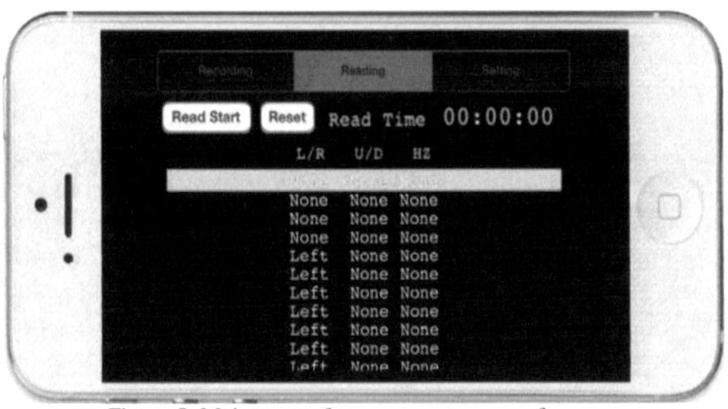

Figure 5. Main screen for repeat movement of camera

In Fig. 5, the hardware's position should be moved to the first position, because the position of hardware is the ending position after shooting is finished. Thus, the hardware goes to the first position as the user touches the "Reset" button in the "Reading" menu. If the user does not touch this button but touches the "Read Start" button, the application shows an alert message and the hardware does not move. When the user touches the "Read Start" button after touching the "Reset" button, the application sends movement data to the hardware in consecutive order, and the video camera attached to the hardware takes another shot of the same scene. The color of the control message line changes to red when a control message exists, and it changes to green when no control message exists. Next, the "Setting" menu has three slide bars to regulate the control speed, as shown in Fig. 6. As shown in Fig. 6, each slide bar ranges from 1 to 10; the chosen value can increase or decrease the motor speed of the hardware. If the value is low, the motor speed is slow and the hardware will move slowly. Conversely, if the value is high, the motor speed is fast and the hardware will move quickly. The "Remaining Time" switch sets how the "Read time" of the Reading menu will be displayed. If the switch is off, the "Read time" shows a time counter. If the switch is on, the "Read time" shows the remaining time.

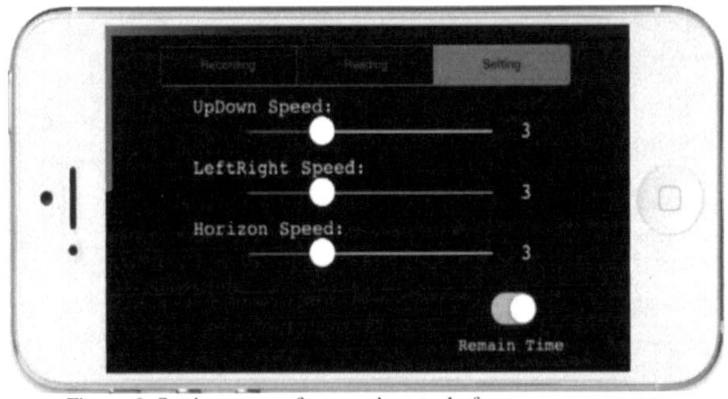

Figure 6. Setting screen for speed control of camera movements

Finally, the composition of the hardware mounted on the video camera is shown in Fig. 7.

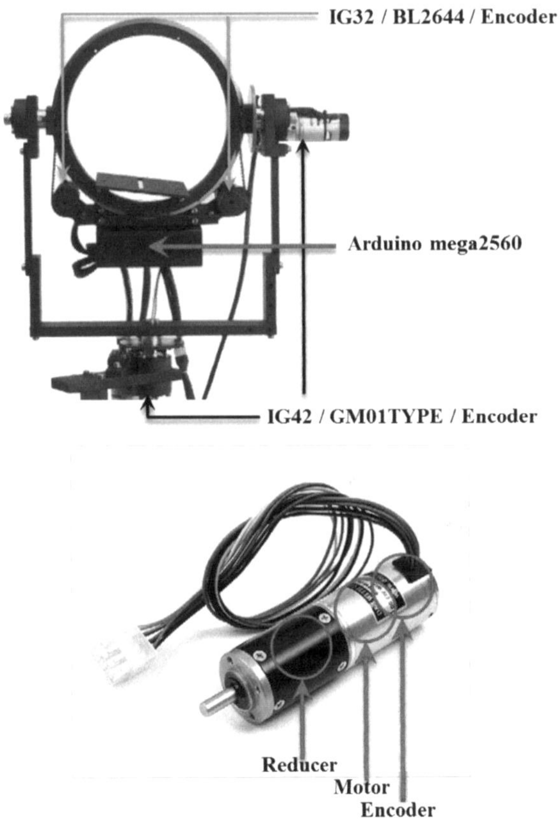

Figure 7. The composition of the proposed hardware to be attached to the camera

In Fig. 7, each motor is composed of a reducer, a motor, and an encoder. For rolling movements, we used two motors that are composed of an IG 32 reducer, a BL2644 motor, and a dual channel 26-pulse encoder. We used a 5GT type pulley and pulley belt to connect these two motors. For panning and tilting movements, we used one motor for each. This motor is composed of an IG42 reducer, a GM01-Type DC motor, and a dual channel 26-pulse encoder. Next, MCU and communication modules for controlling each motor are shown below in Table 1.

TABLE I. THE CONTROLLER COMPOSITION OF THE PROPOSED HARDWARE

Equipment	Model name
MCU	Arduino mega 2560
Communication	BLE Shield SLD09041M
BLDC driver	NT-BL3V
DC driver	NT-VNH20SV1
Power	5V for Board, 24V for BLDC

MCU not only controls all motors from control data via Bluetooth Low Energy (BLE) but also supplies information about current motor status and position to a computer for experiment and analysis. The BLE shield is a module for communication between the smart device and the hardware, while the Brushless DC (BLDC) driver controls the BL2644 motor and retrieves its position information. The DC driver is meant to control the GM01-Type motor and to get its position information, and power equipment is to supply additional electric power to MCU and each motor.

IV. Experiments and Evaluation

This section explains the experiments and evaluation of the proposed application and hardware. The aim of the experiments was to verify how well the wireless application and hardware worked and how exact (i.e., without error) the position of the hardware was throughout its repeated movements. Fig. 8 shows how the user can control the proposed application and hardware according to the user's purpose.

Fig. 8 illustrates the user touching the "Left" button of the proposed application for left-panning. The hardware was turning from right to left in the following order: (a), (b), (c), (d), (e), and (f). We tested not only panning movements but also tilting and rolling movements, and the proposed application and hardware worked as well for all movements as movement of left-panning.

Next, we did an experiment about whether the hardware maintained the same position after being moved several times to shoot the same scene. We could check the position value of each motor from a PC via USB serial communication, because we used Arduino mega 2560 as MCU and motor driver to get the position value of each motor. We saved movement control data in the "Recording" menu, and we checked the start position and end position values of each motor at the "Reading" menu at 5, 10, and 20 repetitions. At these times, the setting speed of the panning, tilting, and rolling movements was three and the control duration of the hardware was two minutes, which was the maximum saving time of MCC of ARRI co., three minutes, and four minutes. The results of this experiment are presented in Table 2.

The value of each cell is the error rate of the hardware's end position value via the proposed application. In Table 2, the error rates for panning and tilting movements were 0% at two, three, and four minutes, though the hardware was moved several times. In contrast, the error rate for the rolling movement was 0.18% at four minutes, even though the error rates were 0% at two and three minutes. A possible explanation is that we used a 5GT type pulley and pulley belt to connect the two motors for the rolling movement.

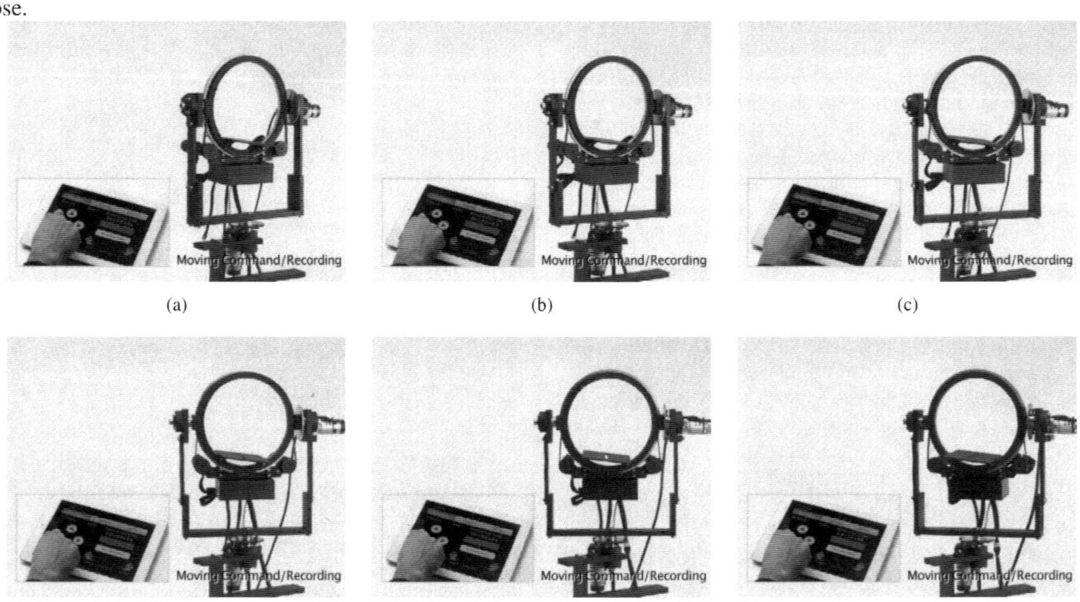

Figure 8. Images of the stages of left-panning via the proposed application, controlled by the hardware

TABLE II. THE ERROR RATES OF END POSITION VALUE OF THE HARDWARE VIA THE PROPOSED APPLICATION

	Motor direction	2 min	3 min	4 min
5 times	Panning	0 %	0 %	0 %
	Tilting	0 %	0 %	0 %
	Rolling	0 %	0 %	0.17 %
10 times	Panning	0 %	0 %	0 %
	Tilting	0 %	0 %	0 %
	Rolling	0 %	0 %	0.18 %
20 times	Panning	0 %	0 %	0 %
	Tilting	0 %	0 %	0 %
	Rolling	0 %	0 %	0.18 %

We expect that the rolling movement error occurred when the motor stopped, because the 5GT type pulley belt has a 3 mm furrow. If we had used a pulley belt that was smaller than the furrow of the 5GT pulley belt, we think we could have decreased the error rate for rolling movements. From the results of the experiment, it is clear that the proposed application and hardware worked exactly according to the user's purpose.

V. CONCLUSION AND FUTURE WORK

In this paper, we have proposed an application based on smart devices that can control hardware movements and save the movement data; we have also proposed hardware that can conduct the same movement repeatedly for special effects shooting for movies or dramas. From the experiment results, we showed that the application and hardware were working well during two, three, and four minute periods without any error for panning and tilting movements. A marginal error of the application and hardware occurred only during the four minute period for the rolling movement. Thus, the proposed application and hardware could not only work like the MCCs of ARRI co., but they also do not require any wireless control desk or extra controller. Therefore, the proposed application and hardware would be a useful technology for special effects shooting at dangerous locations and difficult-access areas.

In future research, we will look into other options to replace the 5GT type pulley and pulley belt, and we will do more experiments using these options. Furthermore, we will test whether the accumulated shots of the same hardware movement overlap exactly when we use the proposed application the hardware.

ACKNOWLEDGMENT

This research project was supported in part by the Ministry of Education under Basic Science Research Program (NRF-2013R1A1A2061478) and (NRF-2016R1C1B2007930), respectively.

REFERENCES

[1] C. J. Ryu, "The design of remote control car using smartphone for intrusion detection," In Computer Science and its Applications, pp. 525-533, 2012.

[2] C. Y. Wang and A. F. Lai, "Development of a mobile rhythm learning system based on digital game-based learning companion," Proceedings of 6th International Conference on E-learning and Games, Edutainment 2011, pp. 92-100, 2011.

[3] Chopper 2, http://majicjungle.com/chopper2_iphone.html, retrieved Sept. 2016.

[4] PadRacer, http://padracer.com/, retrieved Sept. 2016.

[5] Scorpio mini head SB 92, http://www.cinecrane.com/en/ScorpioSB92.html, retrieved Sept. 2016.

[6] CamRanger PT Hub, http://camranger.com/camranger-pan-tilt/, retrieved Sept. 2016.

[7] Facecam, http://tvtropes.org/pmwiki/pmwiki.php/Main/Facecam, retrieved Sept. 2016.

[8] R. Ofria Jr, "Steady camera mount system." U.S. Patent No. 6,027,258. 22 Feb. 2000.

[9] Visual distractions Ltd., "Fuji Finepix 3d – City Trip", http://vd-fx.com/project/fuji3d, retrieved Sept. 2016.

[10] ARRI Remote Heads, http://www.arrirental.de/grip/remote-heads/remote-heads/, retrieved Sept. 2016.

A modification of Wu and Palmer Semantic Similarity Measure

Djamel Guessoum
Dept. of Electrical Engineering
École de Technologie Supérieure,
Montréal, Canada
e-mail: djamel.guessoum.1@ens.etsmtl.ca

Moeiz Miraoui
university of Gafsa,
Gafsa, Tunisia
e-mail: moeizmiraoui@gmail.com

Chakib Tadj
Dept. of Electrical Engineering
École de Technologie Supérieure,
Montréal, Canada
e-mail: Chakib.Tadj@etsmtl.ca

***Abstract*-Context-aware applications are intended to facilitate the adaptation of services in a pervasive computing system. The semantic similarity between contexts and the application of a semantic similarity measure as a mechanism for service adaptation are topics that have yet to be thoroughly explored in the literature. The most developed semantic similarity measures are those applied to the ontological / taxonomic representation of the context. The Wu and Palmer semantic similarity measure is one of these measures that is characterized by its simplicity and high performance, but it can give inaccurate results because two concepts in the same hierarchy of an ontology may show a lower similarity than two concepts belonging to different hierarchies. In this work, we present a modification to improve the accuracy of this measure.**

Keywords-semantic similarity; Wu and Palmer; Taxonomy; context.

I. INTRODUCTION

Semantic similarity measures are used in various fields with different types of applications. In pervasive computing, the application of these measures is linked to the concept of "context" and its impact on the adaptation of services provided to the user. Several studies apply these measures to service recommendation systems [10], in which context is represented by the user's profile-related preferences. K. Ning and D. O'Sullivan [11] developed the similarity measure between ontological concepts of [3] by including context and allocating the weight of relations between concepts.

Mention should be given to applications of similarity measures in other domains that can be used in the field of pervasive computing, such as data mining [8], or the research of Slimani et al. [19], which improved the semantic similarity measure of Z. Wu and M. Palmer [22] by taking into account the context of the measure.

A pervasive computing system is designed to provide services to a user by minimizing his direct involvement, and to this end, the few studies applying semantic similarity measures have each given a particular definition to the context and its specific purpose. Examples include M. Kirsch-Pinheiro et al. [7], who proposed a dynamic adaptation of services to solve the problem of incomplete information in the process of choosing the adequate service in a particular context. Y. Benazzouz [1] used the same type of similarity measures for clustering data in order to determine the particular situations triggering a particular service.

The remainder of this paper is organized as follows. Section 2 introduces some applications of the semantic similarity between contexts in pervasive computing, while Section 3 introduces the semantic similarity measures and context variables. In Section 4, semantic similarity measures applied to ontologies are shown and finally, in Section 5 we introduce our proposed modification of the Wu Palmer measure. The conclusion is presented in Section 6.

II. RELATED WORK

The identification of the current context is defined by the contextual information related to the triggering of a service as well as a situation or "current context" in the set of current contextual information, similar to a known situation or context [1], with each identified situation being linked to one or more of the services to be provided. This identification forms the basis of the rule-based adaptation mechanism, which is a set of conditional rules with the form: if (contextual information I) then (service S).

Identifying a context is based on data mining techniques. Once identified, semantic similarity measures are applied in order to compare it with contexts with known services. P.Y Gicquel [4] modeled the spatio-temporal context of a museum visitor in an ontological form, with the semantic similarity measures being used to recommend artwork similar to the interests of the user by comparing the properties of two concepts in the knowledge base. The similarity measure is a modified version of the similarity proposed by G. Pirró, and J. Euzenat [12], which combines the similarity calculation based on Tversky's model with that of informational content.

Y. Benazzouz [1] and F. Ramparany et al. [14] applied semantic similarity measures to group data and "pure" contexts based on the measures of [13] [23].

A similar approach was proposed by M. Kirsch-Pinheiro et al. [6] for the adaptation of content found in an intelligent device with a Pervasive Computing System (PCS). The authors used semantic similarity measures to assess the degree of matching between the predefined profiles of situations and the current context of the user with the aim of prioritizing them, using a graph-modeled context [25].

Semantic similarities between contexts in a PCS are thus based on the collection of one or several elements of contextual data that are relevant to one or several services. The description and semantic relations of these services are described in an ontological form, thus allowing the application of known semantic similarity measures.

Many variations of the Wu and Palmer measure are present in the literature. We will mention the work of Slimani et al. [19] in which a penalty function is integrated in the measure to penalize concepts belonging to different hierarchies and the measures of C. Leacock, and M. Chodorow [8] and Y. Li et al. [9], where each trying to make adjustments on a particular aspect of the measure of Wu and Palmer. All these measures are difficult to implement and add an extra computational load to the original measure.

III. SEMANTIC SIMILARITY MEASURES AND CONTEXT VARIABLES

The most frequently cited definition of context is that of A. K. Dey [2] who defines context in the following manner: "any information that can be used to characterize the situation of an entity (person, object or physical computing." This definition clearly resembles that of B. Schilit et al. [20] since the context is conceived as a set of information collected from a user environment (person), physical environment (physical object), or system environment, with the purpose of data collection being the characterization of these environments.

The data set that characterizes a context is collected from several sources of information, for example, physical sensors in the environment, intelligent devices, virtual sensors, Internet access, or even telecommunication service providers; this information is thus very heterogeneous. In accordance with several previous studies [5][10], The contextual information can be categorized in 3 classes, as shown below:

1. Quantitative variables are expressed in scalar or vector form (i.e., temperature, latitude, longitude, altitude).
2. Quantifiable variables are expressed in qualitative or ordinal form (i.e., large, small, first, second).
3. Categorical variables are not quantifiable. Variables of this type are described as a set of characteristics (e.g., standing, sitting).

The global approach to measuring the similarity between contexts is primarily based on calculating local similarities between attributes or context variables [16]. The global similarity (1) can then be calculated based on these local similarities by weighting each attribute:

$$Similarity(Context_{new}, Context_{old}) = \frac{\sum_{i=1}^{n} w_i \times Sim(a_i^{Context_{new}}, a_i^{Context_{old}})}{\sum_{i=1}^{n} w_i} \quad (1)$$

where w_i is the weight of the attribute a_i, $a_i^{Context_{new}}$ is the attribute i of the new context, and $a_i^{Context_{old}}$ is the attribute i of the existing context.

IV. NOTION OF SEMANTIC SIMILARITY

In pervasive computing, where the notion of context plays a very important role, the semantic similarity measure is a tool to evaluate the resemblance between instances of a context. It allows services to be chosen and classified according to their relevance to a given query, and a user's profile and preferences

A. *Semantic similarity measures applied to ontologies*

The most developed semantic similarity measures in recent years, based on the ontological representation of knowledge and especially in its taxonomic form, were described by D. Sánchez et al. [17]. The authors categorised the semantic similarity measures on the counting of arcs, characteristics of concepts, and information content.

Semantic similarity measures based on the counting of arcs were introduced by R. Rada et al. [13]. The basic notion for these measures was the fewer the number of arcs separating two concepts, the greater their similarity.
Among the studies using this approach we find:

- *Rada measure*

It is based on the fact that we can calculate the semantic similarity between two concepts in a hierarchical structure (ontology) with links, such as "is-a" by calculating the shortest path between these concepts.

- *Wu and Palmer measure*

Several variants based on the Rada measure have been proposed to improve some aspects, such as Z. Wu, and M. Palmer [22] applied to an ontology O (Fig. 1), who considered the depth of ontology in the measure, because two concepts in lower levels of ontology are more specific and are more similar. This measure is given by:

$$Sim_{WP}(X,Y) = \frac{2 \times N}{N_1 + N_2} \quad (2)$$

where Sim_{WP} is Wu and Palmer similarity, N_1 and N_2 are the number of arcs between the concepts X , Y and the ontology root R and N is the number of arcs between the LCS and the ontology root R.

We chose to modify the semantic similarity measure proposed by Z. Wu, and M. Palmer [22] (2) because it is simple to implement in a pervasive computing system where the context is modeled using an ontology and gives realistic similarity results. Nevertheless, we modified the Wu and Palmer measure to eliminate an inherent disadvantage, in which two concepts in the same hierarchy may show a lower similarity than two concepts belonging to different hierarchies [16] [18] [19].

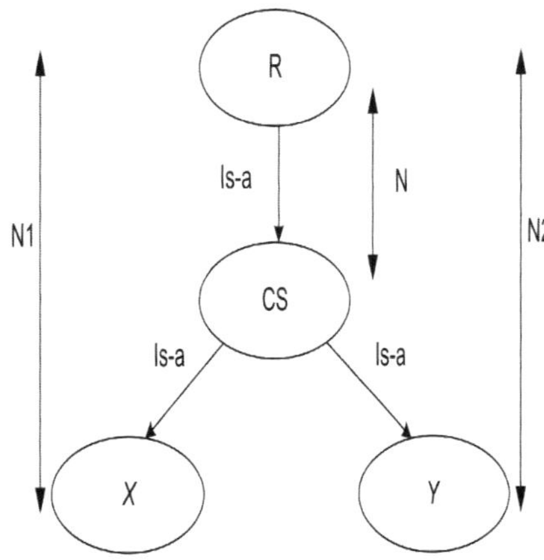

Figure 1. Wu and Palmer Ontology example

Several other measures were subsequently introduced by C. Leacock, and M. Chodorow [8] and Y. Li et al. [9], as the authors attempted to make adjustments for a particular aspect of Wu and Palmer's measure.

Semantic similarity measures based on the characteristics of concepts derive from the similarity model of [21], in which two concepts are more similar if 1) they share more common characteristics and 2) less non-common characteristics. However, the determination of the weighting parameters represents a major challenge for this type of measures.

Finally, semantic similarity measures based on the information content of a common concept involving two concepts to be compared were first introduced by P. Resnik [15]. Their dependency on the design of the ontology and their lack of consideration for the context are some of their limitations.

V. MODIFIED WU AND PALMER SIMILARITY MEASURE

As it was shown from the disadvantages of the Wu and Palmer semantic similarity measure, is that with this measurement one can obtain inaccurate results [16] [18] [19]. See the following example (Fig. 2):

$Sim_{WP}(c1,c2) = \frac{2*1}{(1+4)} = 0.4$ (LCS=Person, N=1, N1=1, N2=4)

$Sim_{WP}(c2,c3) = \frac{2*2}{(4+3)} = 0.57$ (LCS=Employee, N=2, N1=4, N2=3)

It is clear that the semantic similarity measures applied to the UnivBench ontology (Ontology from the educational field, used to describe data on universities and their departments [19] [24], $Sim_{WP}(c1,c2) < Sim_{WP}(c2,c3)$, despite the fact that the concepts c1 and c2 belong to the same hierarchy.

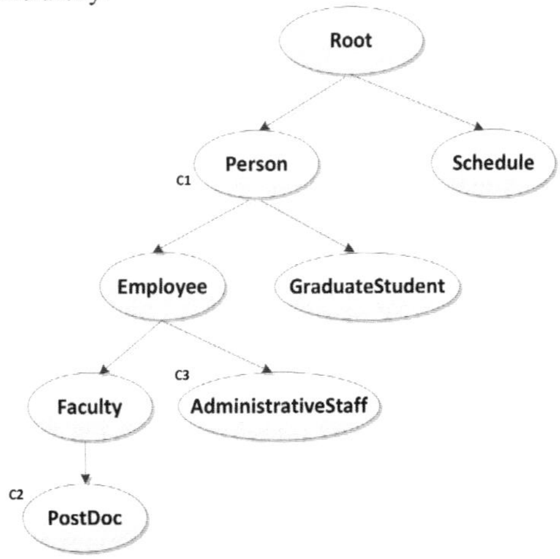

Figure 2. Extract from UniveBench. Ontology

The following modification is proposed to remedy this disadvantage (Fig. 3):

$$sim(c1,c2) = \begin{cases} Sim_{WP}(c1,c2) = \dfrac{2N}{N1+N2} & if\ N1 \neq \mathrm{N}\ and\ N2 \neq \mathrm{N} \\ \dfrac{2N}{N2-N}\ if\ (N1 = N)\ and & \dfrac{2N}{N1-N}\ if\ (N2 = N) \end{cases}$$

1- Two concepts belong to different hierarchies if: $N1 \neq \mathrm{N}\ and\ N2 \neq \mathrm{N}\quad sim(c1,c2) = Sim_{WP}(c1,c2)$

2- Two concepts belong to the same hierarchy if : N1=N or N2 =N,

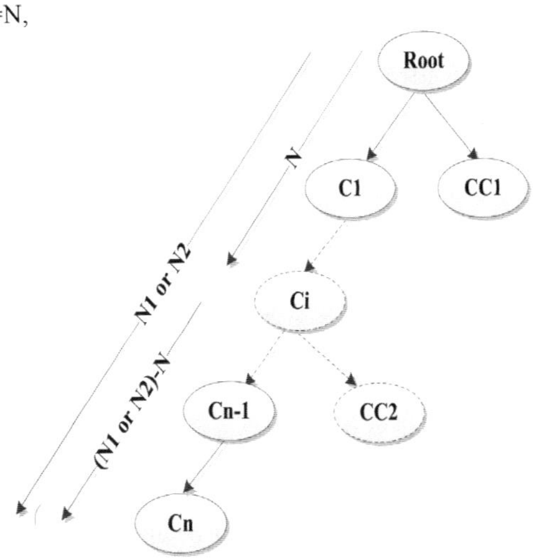

Figure 3. Modified Wu and Palmer Measure

Sim(Ci,Cj)> Sim(Ci,CC) ∀ i,j=1,...n

Where: Ci,Cj are two concepts of the same hierarcy and CC is a different hierarchy concept.

1- If N1=N, $\frac{2N}{N2-N} > \frac{2N}{N1+N2} \leftrightarrow N2 - N < N1 + N2$

2- If N2=N, $\frac{2N}{N1-N} > \frac{2N}{N1+N2} \leftrightarrow N1 - N < N1 + N2$

The proposed modification meets the four criteria of similarity measures: non-negativity, identity, symmetry, and uniqueness, as defined below:

1) non-negativity: Sim(A, B)≥0,
2) identity : Sim (A, A) = Sim (B,B)=1
3) symmetry: Sim (A, B) = Sim (B, A)
4) uniqueness : Sim (A, B)=1 → A=B

It is also clear that the semantic similarity between two concepts that belong to the same hierarchy is inversely proportional to the distance between these two concepts (N2-N or N1-N) and is always greater than the semantic similarity between a concept of that hierarchy and another concept from another hierarchy. It has all the advantages of the Wu and Palmer measure, namely its implementation simplicity and expressiveness.

This modified Wu and Palmer measure applied to the example of Fig. 2 gives the following results:

$Sim\ (c1, c2) = \frac{2*1}{(4-1)} = 0.66$
(LCS=Person, N=1, N1=1, N2=4)
$Sim\ (c2, c3) = \frac{2*2}{(4+3)} = 0.57$
(LCS=Employee, N=2, N1=4, N2=3)

VI. CONCLUSION

The proposed modification of the Wu and Palmer semantic similarity measure retains all the benefits of this measure namely its implementation simplicity and power to give close similarities to the reality unlike several other changes proposed in the literature. It also meets the criteria of semantic similarity measures namely the non-negativity, the identity, the symmetry and uniqueness. Its advantage is the fact that all the concepts in the same hierarchy must be more similar to each other than other concepts of a different hierarchy and the similarity between the concepts in the same hierarchy also depends on the distance between these concepts.

REFERENCES

[1] Y. Benazzouz, "Context discovery for the automatic adaptation of services in ambient intelligence," (Doctoral dissertation, Ecole Nationale Supérieure des Mines de Saint-Etienne), pp. 71-98, 2011.

[2] A. K. Dey, "Understanding and using context," Personal and Ubiquitous Computing, 5, 4-7, pp. 4, 2001..

[3] P. Ganesan, H. Garcia-Molina, and J. Widom, "Exploiting hierarchical domain structure to compute similarity," ACM Transactions on Information Systems (TOIS), 21(1), pp. 64-93, 2003.

[4] P.Y Gicquel, "Semantic and contextual similarities for informal learning in mobility," RJC EIAH'2012, pp. 45-50, 2012.

[5] K. C. Gowda and E. Diday, "Symbolic clustering using a new similarity measure," IEEE Transactions on Systems, Man, and Cybernetics, 22(2), pp. 368-378, 1992.

[6] M. Kirsch-Pinheiro, M. Villanova-Oliver, J. Gensel, and H. Martin, "A personalized and context-aware adaptation process for web-based groupware systems," In 4th International Workshop on Ubiquitous Mobile Information and Collaboration Systems, CAiSE'06 Workshop, pp. 884-898, 2006.

[7] M. Kirsch-Pinheiro, Y., Vanrompay, and Y. Berbers, "Context-aware service selection using graph matching," In 2nd Non Functional Properties and Service Level Agreements in Service Oriented Computing Workshop (NFPSLA-SOC'08), ECOWS. CEUR Workshop proceedings, Vol. 411, pp. 10-12, 2008, November.

[8] C. Leacock, and M. Chodorow, "Combining local context and WordNet similarity for word sense identification," In WordNet: An electronic lexical database, MIT Press, pp. 265-283, 1998.

[9] Y. Li, Z. Bandar, and D. McLean, "An Approach for Measuring Semantic Similarity between Words Using Multiple Information Sources," IEEE Transactions on Knowledge and Data Engineering, 15, pp.871-882, 2003.

[10] L. Liu, F. Lecue,, N. Mehandjiev, and L. Xu, "Using context similarity for service recommendation," In Semantic Computing (ICSC), 2010 IEEE Fourth International Conference on , pp. 277-284, 2010, September.

[11] K. Ning and D. O'Sullivan. "Context modeling and measuring for context aware Knowledge Management," International Journal of Machine Learning and Computing 2, no. 3, 2012.

[12] G. Pirró and J. Euzenat, "A feature and information theoretic framework for semantic similarity and relatedness," In The Semantic Web–ISWC 2010, , Springer Berlin Heidelberg, pp. 615-630, 2010.

[13] R. Rada, H. Bicknell, E. Mili, and M. Blettner, "Development and application of a metric on semantic nets," IEEE Transaction on Systems, Man, and Cybernetics, 1(19), pp. 17-30, 1989.

[14] F. Ramparany, Y. Benazzouz, J. Gadeyne, and P. Beaune, "Automated context learning in ubiquitous computing environments," In SSN, pp. 9-21, 2011.

[15] P Resnik, "Using information content to evaluate semantic similarity," In Proceedings of the 14th International Joint

Conference on Artificial Intelligence, August 20-25; Montréal Québec, Canada, pp. 448-453, 1995.

[16] M. Richter, Weber, Rosina "case based reasoning," Textbook, , Springer Heidelberg New York Dordrecht London , p. 546, 2013,

[17] D. Sánchez, M. Batet, D. Isern, and A. Valls, , "Ontology-based semantic similarity: A new feature-based approach," Expert Systems with Applications, 39(9), pp. 7718-7728, 2012.

[18] K. C. Shet and U. D. Acharya, "A New Similarity Measure for Taxonomy Based on Edge Counting," arXiv preprint arXiv:1211.4709, 2012.

[19] T. Slimani, B. B. Yagahlane and K. Mellouli. "A new similarity measure based on edge counting," Proceedings of the World Academy of Science, engineering and Technology 17, pp. 3, 2006.

[20] B. Schilit, N. Adams and R. Want, "Context-aware computing applications," In IEEE Workshop on Mobile Computing Systems and Applications . Santa Cruz, CA, US, pp. 85-90, 1994.

[21] A. Tversky, "Features of similarity," Psycological Review, 84(4), 1977.

[22] Z. Wu and M. Palmer, "Verbs semantics and lexical selection," InProceedings of the 32nd annual meeting on Association for Computational Linguistics, pp. 133-138. Association for Computational Linguistics, 1994, June.

[23] J. Zhong, H. Zhu, J. Li, and Y. Yu, , "Conceptual graph matching for semantic search," In Proceedings of the 10th International Conference on Conceptual Structures (ICCS), Springer-Verlag, London, pp. 92-196, 2002.

[24] M. Dean, G. Schreiber, S. Bechhofer, F. van Harmelen, J. Hendler, I. Horrocks, and L. A. Stein, "OWL web ontology language reference," W3C Recommendation February, 10, 2004.

[25] D. Guessoum, M. Miraoui, and C. Tadj, "Survey of semantic similarity measures in pervasive computing," International journal on smart sensing and intelligent systems, 8(1), pp. 125-158, 2015.

Energy Saving in a Smart Waiting Room Using Context-aware Services Adaptation

Moeiz Miraoui
Al-leith computer college,Umm Al-Qura University
Makkah, KSA
email: mfmiraoui@uqu.edu.sa

Manel Guizani
Higher institute of information and communication techniques, University of sousse
Hammem sousse, Tunisia
email: guizani.manelprof@gmail.com

***Abstract*—Smart spaces have become an active research field over the last few years. The main objective of such spaces is to provide intelligent services to the user for improved comfort and energy saving. The recent advances in sensors network and embedded systems have helped a lot in the realization of smart spaces. In order to provide adapted services to the users, such spaces should operate in a proactive manner and according to the current context. The degree of intelligence of such spaces could be enormously enhanced with the context-awareness aspect. Defining context and establishing its components are basic steps for context-aware services adaptation in a smart space. In this paper, we propose a context-aware services adaptation for a smart waiting room which could improve both person's comfort and energy saving in such spaces. We describe the context using a clear and concise definition and use the naïve Bayes machine learning technique for the adaptation.**

Keywords-waiting room, context; service; adaptation; naïve Bayes.

I. INTRODUCTION

The main aim of smart spaces or intelligent environment is to assist inhabitants (resp. occupants) to live comfortably by not bothering them from concentrating on setting and configuring home appliances. The most common definition of a smart space is the one proposed by Cook and Das [1]: "Smart space is able to acquire and apply knowledge about its environment and to adapt to its inhabitants in order to improve their experience in that environment". Smart spaces should provide intelligent services in order to improve the quality of life, energy saving and safety of inhabitants. Smart spaces should provide adapted services in a proactive manner (without explicit intervention from user). In order to improve the intelligence of these spaces, services should be provided according to the current context. One example of smart spaces is the waiting rooms where people can wait (generally sitting) for some kind of services. An important issue in such spaces is energy saving. In several cases appliances of the waiting room such as light bulbs, cooling/ heating system and TV or radio/music player operate even when there is no person inside the waiting room which causes a great loss of energy. Context-awareness has become an important aspect of smart spaces. It could enhance both the person's comfort and energy saving of the waiting room and helps it to operate smartly by adapting services according to the current context. Context-aware services adaptation should be preceded by an important and basic step which consist of defining the context element and establishing its components. Several approaches for context-aware services adaptation were proposed for either pervasive systems or smart spaces. Most of them have the following same weakness point: not based on a clear definition of context and do not propose a clear method for context elements establishment which limit their use and affect the quality of services adaptation. In this paper, we propose a context-aware services adaptation for a waiting room which could enhances energy saving and comfort of waiting persons. Our approach is based on a clear definition of context and clear steps to extract context elements. The adaptation task is done using the naive Bayes machine learning technique.

The rest of this paper is organized as follows. Section II provides some background information about related work. Section III describes the overall environment of an exemplary waiting room. In Section IV we discuss details about context identification. Section V presents our context-aware services adaptation approach. The conclusion and future work will be given in Section VI.

II. RELATED WORK

Several approaches for context-aware services adaptation for smart spaces have been proposed over the last few years. Most of them were proposed for a particular type of smart spaces namely smart homes.Li et al.[2] developed a context-aware lightning control system for smart meeting rooms. They used an ontology-based context modeling approach and a rule based system for context reasoning. Madkour et al. [3] used a Weighted Case Based Reasoning (WCBR) for enabling context awareness. They illustrated the elaboration of an adaptive and autonomous control of heating Ventilation and Air Conditioning (HVAC). Ni et al. [4] proposed a case-based reasoning technique for services adaptation in a smart home. Chahuara et al. [5] presented an audio-controlled smart home based on a framework composed of knowledge representation module using a two level ontology, a situation recognition module based on the Semantic Web Rule Language *(SWRL)* logic reasoner and a decision making module based on the markov logic network (using weighted logic rules) to deal with uncertainty and imprecision of context information. Miraoui et al. [6] proposed a context-aware services adaptation approach for a smart living room using two machine learning techniques namely naive Bayes and neural network. Humayun et al. [7] presented a context-aware application which can provide service according to the predefined choice of user. It uses Mahalanobis distance based k nearest neighbor's classifier technique for inference of predefined service. They combined the features of supervised and unsupervised machine learning in the proposed application. This application can also adapt itself when the choice of user is changed by using Q-learning reinforcement learning algorithm. Badlani & Bhanot [8] proposed an adaptive smart home system for optimal utilization of power, through Artificial Neural Network (ANN). Kumar et al. [9] presented a semantic policy adaptation technique and its applications in the context of smart building setups. Humayun et al. [10] presented a machine learning based context-aware system which can provide service according to the trained model. Two effective learning algorithms: Back propagation Neural Network, and Temporal Differential (TD) class of reinforcement learning are used for prediction and adaptation respectively.

III. SMART WAITING ROOM

A. *Description of a typical waiting room*

A waiting room is a special place where people can wait (generally sitting) for a service. One can find waiting rooms in several locations: at doctor's office, at a lawyer office, at several government offices, at banks, etc. The main aim of a waiting room is to keep people waiting for their services in a comfortable state. An exemplary waiting room is composed of a set of appliances and furniture which can be mainly categorized in three classes: a) light system, composed of a set of light bulbs and window blinds, b) cooler/ heater system which is composed of a heater and a cooler or embedded in one air conditioner which can either make cooling or heating, c) entertainment system, which is composed of a TV and/or a radio/music player and d) a set of chairs (Fig. 1).

Figure 1. Main components of an exemplary waiting room

B. *Expected running of a smart waiting room*

In order to improve waiting people's comfort and saving energy, a smart waiting room should provide services according to the current context and proactively (without explicit user intervention) in an unobtrusive manner. In the initial and final state (the waiting room is empty), all the appliances should be off in order to save energy. As soon as at least one person enters the waiting room (state 1), the light system composed of window blinds and a set of light bulbs starts to adjust the inside light. When the system perceives at least one person sitting, it moves to state 2. In addition to running the light system, the smart waiting room should start the heating/cooling system to adjust the temperature inside the waiting room. After a few seconds, the entertainment system composed of the TV or the radio/music player should start and the waiting room goes to state 3. At any state, if the smart waiting room system perceives no one inside the waiting room, it should go to the initial state and put all appliances off or go to temporary state (state 3) during office hours where all appliances should be set at low energy consumption. Fig. 2 shows the state diagram of the overall operation of the smart waiting room.

IV. CONTEXT IDENTIFICATION

Context-awareness is a highly desirable property for smart spaces which allows them to provide proactively (without explicit intervention of users) adapted services according to the context of use. The first step of developing context-aware systems consists of defining context in a clear manner and establishing its components. In spite of the great number of definitions proposed for context, until now there are no agreed definition. Most of these definitions remain vague and general and do not provide clear steps or method to extract context elements. Some of the proposed definitions were based on enumerating contextual information (localization, nearby people, time, date, etc.) like those proposed in [11] [12] [13]. Others were based on providing more formal definitions in order to abstract the term, like the one proposed by Dey [14]. In our previous work [15], 16], we have made a survey of existing definitions of context and proposed a service-oriented definition of context for pervasive and ubiquitous computing environments which could be easily adapted to smart spaces. Our definition states that the context is: "Any information that triggers a service or changes the quality (form or mode) of a service if its value changes." This definition is sufficiently abstract and helps to limit the set of contextual information. We believe that this definition is more expressive, because it is simple, clear, and complete; in addition, it covers all aspects of the context. Establishing context elements is a three-steps process consisting of: 1) specify for each equipment the provided service and the set of information that could trigger the service, 2) specify for each service the set of forms through which the services can be provided. We should also specify for each form of service the set of information whose change will change the form of a service and 3) make the union of the two previous sets to get the final list of contextual information and define the set of possible values for each context element. This information will compose the global context.

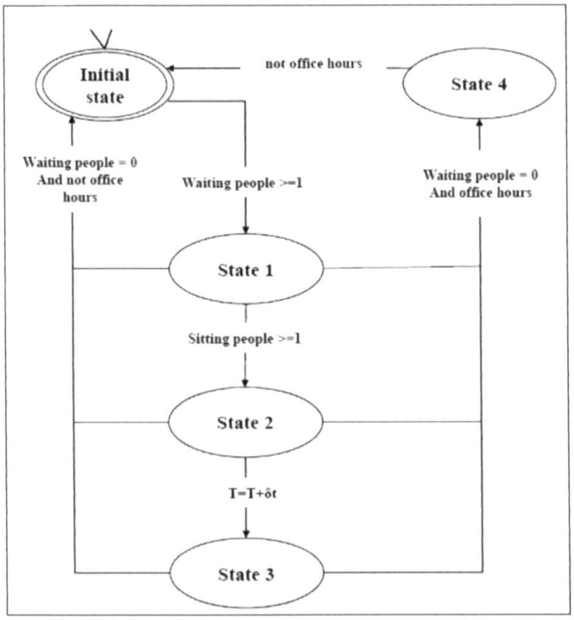

Figure 2. The state diagram of the overall operation of the smart waiting room

By applying our context definition and context components establishment method to the smart waiting room, we have got the result of each step as indicated in Table I, Table II and Table III.

TABLE I. CONTEXT ELEMENT ESTABLISHMENT (STEP 1)

Equipment	Service	Triggering information
heater	heating	Seated person
cooler	cooling	Seated person
window blinds	lighting	Person presence
light bulbs	lighting	Person presence
TV and Radio/music player	entertainment	Seated person

TABLE II. CONTEXT ELEMENT ESTABLISHMENT (STEP 2)

Equipment	Service's Forms	Forms changing information
heater	Off, low, average, high	Indoor temperature, time
cooler	Off, low, average, high	Indoor temperature, time
window blinds	Closed, mostly closed, half-opened, mostly opened, closed	Indoor light, outdoor light, time
light bulbs	Off, low average, high	Indoor light, outdoor light, time
TV and Radio/music player	On, Off	Seated person

TABLE III. CONTEXT ELEMENT ESTABLISHMENT (STEP 3)

Context element	Possible values
Person presence	Yes, no
Seated person	Yes, no
Indoor temperature	Very low, low average, high, very high
Indoor light	Dark, low, average, high
Outdoor light	dark, low, average, high
Time	Office hours, not office hours

It is clear that our method for context elements establishment which is composed of the above three steps is easy to perform and leads to the set of global context required for services adaptation inside the waiting room. The possible values of each context element (values domain) could be adjusted according to the implementation.

V. CONTEXT-AWARE SERVICES ADAPTATION

The aim of context-aware services adaptation is to render appliances of the waiting room operating in a proactive manner with minimum human intervention and to provide services with minimum energy consumption. Based on the previous context definition and its element's establishment, we propose in this Section a context-aware services adaptation for a waiting room. The waiting room should operate according to the current context which is composed of the following elements: person presence, seated person, indoor temperature, indoor light, outdoor light and time.

Whenever a person enters the waiting room, the light system should start adjusting the ambient light by setting the window blinds and light bulbs according to the rules presented in Table IV. There are also two particular context situations related to energy saving (Table V). The first one is when there is no person inside the waiting room and it is outside of office hours so the light system should be set off. The second one is when there is no person inside the waiting room and it's during office hours so the system should set the light on its minimum energy consumption mode which is window blinds opened and light bulbs off. The symbol "?" means whatever value.

The cooler/heater system should operate according to the current context whenever the system perceives at least one person seated inside the waiting room. The possible context-aware configurations of the cooler/heater system are given by Table VI. Alike the light system, there are also some particular context situations related to energy saving. The first one is when there is no person inside the waiting room and it's not office hours so the cooler/heater system should be set off. The other ones are when there is no person inside the waiting room and its office hours so the system should set the cooler/heater on its minimum energy consumption mode, which is shown in Table VII.

TABLE IV. CONTEXT-AWARE LIGHT SYSTEM CONFIGURATION

In light	Out light	Window blinds	Light bulbs	Person presence	Seated person	Time
Dark	Dark	Closed	High	yes	?	Office hours
Dark	Low	Opened	Average	yes	?	Office hours
Dark	Average	Mostly opened	Low	yes	?	Office hours
Dark	high	opened	Off	yes	?	Office hours
Low	Dark	Closed	High	yes	?	Office hours
Low	Low	Opened	Average	yes	?	Office hours
Low	Average	Mostly opened	Low	yes	?	Office hours
Low	high	Half opened	Off	yes	?	Office hours
Averag e	Dark	Closed	High	yes	?	Office hours
Averag e	Low	Opened	Off	yes	?	Office hours
Averag e	Average	Mostly opened	Off	yes	?	Office hours
Averag e	high	Half opened	Off	yes	?	Office hours
High	Dark	Closed	Off	yes	?	Office hours
High	Low	Opened	Average	yes	?	Office hours
High	Average	Half opened	Low	yes	?	Office hours
high	high	Mostly closed	off	yes	?	Office hours

TABLE V. ENERGY SAVING MODE OF THE LIGHT SYSTEM

Indoor light	Outdoor light	Window blinds	Light bulbs	Person presence	Seated person	Time
?	?	opened	off	no	no	office hours
?	?	closed	off	no	no	Not office hours

The entertainment system composed of the TV or music/radio player is triggered whenever the system perceives at least one person seated in the waiting room. Otherwise, it should be set off both during office hours or out of office hours in order to save energy as mentioned in Table VIII.

The above tables of possible appliances configuration will form the training set for a naïve Bayes classifier chosen as a machine learning technique for the context-aware services adaptation of the smart waiting room. The Bayesian Classification represents a supervised learning method as well as a statistical method for classification. For each new sample they provide a probability that the sample belongs to a class. Training is very easy and fast, no need for complicated training process as in neural networks. Naïve Bayes is fast and space efficient. It can provide an optimal decision making system even in presence of violating independence assumption. We have used the free machine learning tool Waikato Environment for Knowledge Analysis(WEKA) [17] to implement the context-aware adaptation system.

TABLE VI. CONTEXT-AWARE COOLER/HEATER SYSTEM CONFIGURATION

temperature	Cooler	heater	time	Person presence	Seated person
Very low	off	high	Office hours	yes	yes
Low	off	average	Office hours	yes	yes
Almost low	off	low	Office hours	yes	yes
Average	off	off	Office hours	yes	yes
Almost high	low	off	Office hours	yes	yes
High	average	off	Office hours	yes	yes
Very high	high	off	Office hours	yes	yes

TABLE VII. ENERGY SAVING MODE OF THE COOLER/HEATER SYSTEM

temperature	Cooler	heater	time	Person presence	Seated person
?	off	off	Not office hours	no	no
Very low	off	low	Office hours	no	no
Low	off	low	Office hours	no	no
Almost low	off	low	Office hours	no	no
Average	off	off	Office hours	no	no
Almost high	low	off	Office hours	no	no
High	low	off	Office hours	no	no
Very high	low	off	Office hours	no	no

TABLE VIII. CONTEXT-AWARE ENTERTAINMENT SYSTEM CONFIGURATION

TV or radio/music player	time	Person presence	Seated person
On	office hours	yes	yes
off	Office hours	no	no
off	Not office hours	no	no

In order to make a principal step toward our system validation, we performed three series of tests. Each one is composed of ten possible context situations. We have got satisfactory results with acceptance rate of 92%. Such rate was very encouraging.

VI. CONCLUSION AND FUTURE WORK

Context-awareness could enormously improve the quality of services for smart spaces. It helps to provide proactive services which enhance both user's comfort and energy saving. The most important task in building context-aware systems consists of defining the context in a clear manner and establish its components. In this paper, we have proposed a context-aware services adaptation for a particular smart space namely smart waiting room using the naive Bayes learning machine technique. Our approach could help a lot the energy saving in such space in addition to improving person comfort. Our future work consists of applying the same approach for other types of smart spaces, such as smart office, smart classroom, etc.

REFERENCES

[1] D. J. Cook & S. Das, "Smart environments: Technology, protocols and applications". John Wiley & Sons, New york pp. 153-174, 2005

[2] C. Li, L. Sun and X. Hu, "A context-aware lighting control system for smart meeting rooms". Systems Engineering Procedia, Volume 4, Information Engineering and Complexity Science-Part II, pp. 314–323, 2012

[3] M. Madkour et al., "Living Campus: Towards a Context-Aware Energy Efficient Campus Using Weighted Case Based Reasoning", AAAI Workshops, Workshops at the Twenty-Ninth AAAI Conference on Artificial Intelligence, pp. 42-48, 2015

[4] H. Ni, X. Zhou, D. Zhang, K. Miao and Y. Fu, "Towards a Task Supporting System with CBR Approach in Smart Home", ICOST '09 Proceedings of the 7th International Conference on Smart Homes and Health Telematics: Ambient Assistive Health and Wellness Management in the Heart of the City, Springer, pp.141-149, 2009

[5] P. Chahuara, F. Portet and M. Vacher, "Making Context Aware Decision from Uncertain Information in a Smart Home: A Markov Logic Network Approach". Fourth International Joint Conference on Ambient Intelligence, Dublin, pp. 78-93, 2013

[6] M. Miraoui, R. Cherif, N. Rtimi and C. Tadj, "Context-aware services adaptation for a smart living room" Computer Applications & Research (WSCAR), 2014 World Symposium on, IEEE press, pp. 1-5, 2014

[7] M. Humayun Kabir, M. Robiul Hoque and S. H. Yang, "Development of a Smart Home Context-aware Application: A Machine Learning based Approach", International Journal of Smart Home Vol. 9, No. 1, pp. 217-226, 2015

[8] A. Badlani and S. Bhanot, "Smart Home System Design based on Artificial Neural Networks", Proceedings of the World Congress on Engineering and Computer Science 2011 Vol I WCECS 2011, October 19-21, 2011, San Francisco, USA, pp. 2011

[9] V. Kumar, A. Fensel and P. Froehlich, "Context Based Adaptation of Semantic Rules in Smart Buildings", IIWAS '13 Proceedings of International Conference on Information Integration and Web-based Applications & Services Pages 719, 2013

[10] M. Humayun Kabir, M. Robiul Hoque, H. Seo and S. H. Yang, "Machine Learning Based Adaptive Context-Aware System for Smart Home Environment", International Journal of Smart Home, Vol. 9, No. 11, pp. 55-62, 2015

[11] S. Schilit and M. Theimer, "Disseminating Active Map Information to Mobile Hosts", IEEE Nenvork, Vol. 8(5) p.22-3, 1994.

[12] P. J. Brown, J. D. Bovey and X. Chen, "Context-aware Applications: From the Aboratory to the Marketplace", IEEE Personal Communications, Vol. 4(5) pp. 58-64, 1997

[13] N. Ryan, J. Pascoe and D. Morse, "Enhanced Reality Fieldwork:the Context -Aware Archeological Assistant", Computer Applications in Archeology, pp. 269-274, 1997

[14] A. K. Dey, "Understanding and Using Contex"," Journal of Personal and ubiquitous computing, pp. 4-7, 2001

[15] M. Miraoui and C. Tadj, "A service Oriented Definition of Context for Pervasive Computing", in Proceedings of the 16th International Conference on Computing, Mexicocity, Mexico, Nov. 2007. pp. 1-6, 2007

[16] M. Miraoui, C. Tadj and C. Ben Amar, "Context Modeling and ContextAware Service Adaptation for Pervasive Computing Systems", International Journal of Computer and Information Science and Engineering, Vol. 2(3): p. 148-157, 2008

[17] WEKA tool web site (retrieved: 09, 2016): http://www.cs.waikato.ac.nz/ml/weka/downloading.html

Machine Learning Technologies in Smart Spaces

Somia Belaidouni
MMS Laboratory, Quebec University,
École de technologie supérieure
Montréal, Canada
email :belaidounisoumia@yahoo.fr

Moeiz Miraoui
High institute of applied sciences and technology
University of Gafsa, Tunisia
email: moeizmiraoui@gmail.com

Abstract— **Context-awareness is a key element for building a smart environment that responds to users needs. The goal of such environment is to provide proactively services according to the demand of users by considering the user's context information. Machine learning techniques can provide several benefits. They can be applied in many context-aware systems to help provide services. They have the possibility to make better prediction and adaptation than other techniques. In this paper, we present the main goals of machine learning and some learning algorithms applied in smart space.**

Keywords-context-awareness; smart environment; machine learning; prediction; adaptation; performance.

I. INTRODUCTION

A smart environment can be defined as an environment that is able to acquire and apply knowledge about the environment and its inhabitants in order to improve their experience in that environment [1]. In effect, such environment can perceive the state of the space using sensors, analyzes the state using learning and reasoning techniques and adapt behaviors according to users in order to provide easy daily life by increasing their comfort. Dynamism and complexity are very important characteristics in smart spaces [2]. Indeed, there are different devices networked via an infrastructure of heterogeneous access technologies. Also, the user behaviour or preferences may change at any time.

In addition, the awareness of context is a key feature to develop an adaptable smart system which has the ability to sense and to react according to context modifications. Also, smart space should be able to control and to adapt services automatically with minimum user intervention. Machine learning techniques have been widely used for this objective. Machine learning as a domain capable of supporting the solution of complex problems is able to provide significant help [3]. These algorithms can be applied in a predictive sense or to investigate internal relationships of a dataset [4]. They can be divided into four main groups: supervised learning, unsupervised learning, semi-supervised learning and reinforcing. Each of these groups has their advantages and drawbacks and utilizes different approaches to target different goals.

This paper is organized as follows. Section 2 describes important goals of machine learning in smart environments. Section 3 shows the principal necessary phases in the learning process. Section 4 discusses the different types of machine learning and some techniques applied in smart spaces. Section 5 concludes the paper.

II. MACHINE LEARNING GOALS

One important feature of smart environments is that they possess a high degree of autonomy, adapt themselves to changing environments, and communicate with humans in an easy way. Application of machine learning in context aware systems can be employed to achieve specific goals. Generally, these goals belong to 4 main classes.

A. Recognition

Several approaches already exist devoted to recognition problem to identify events or activities of users in smart environments. The activity recognition is usually done through two steps: activity pattern clustering and activity type decision [5]. In most cases, recognition problems are processed by supervised learning algorithms which assumes that a training set is consisting of a set of instances that have been properly labeled by hand with the correct output.

B. Prediction

The aim of prediction is to predict what is going to happen in the future. In a smart environment, prediction allows providing information useful for future locations and activities. It helps to predict the most probable event or subsequent activity. This type of problem can be solved by online training approach which can learn from input data over time, to predict the output data [4].

C. Adaptation

Adapting user services according to the current context aims to provide the proper services by considering the user and the environmental information. Machine learning algorithms provide several benefits for context-aware systems. Indeed, it can be applied to support reasoning, inferences and also to deal with complex or fuzzy information [6].

D. Optimization

Optimization is a very important feature in smart environments. It aims to increase their performance and effectiveness. It can be solved by using reinforcement algorithms that can explore idealized learning situations and evaluate the effectiveness of various learning methods [7].

III. LEARNING PROCESS IN SMART ENVIRONMENTS

Machine learning techniques used in smart environments offer major opportunities to provide context-aware services. Context-awareness is about capturing a broad range of contextual attributes (such as the user's current positions, activities, and surrounding environment) to better understand what the user is trying to accomplish, and what services the user might need [8]. In consequence, learning becomes important and indispensable for reasoning and for making the best decision. It is considered necessary for knowledge creation [9]. In addition, artificial intelligence includes several subcategories such as detection, knowledge representation and machine learning, machine perception, among others [10]. In this paper, we focus mainly on four processes namely detection, interpretation, learning and reasoning as illustrated in Fig 1. First, the detection phase is accomplished using different sensors installed in the environment in order to capture current context. After that, interpretation is done in order to interpret raw data to get a useful and significant context. After acquiring the sensed context, learning mechanisms take the useful context and try to classify and to organize the observations according to a specific algorithm. Finally, the reasoning phase allows using the context information knowledge acquired through learning to achieve its objectives.

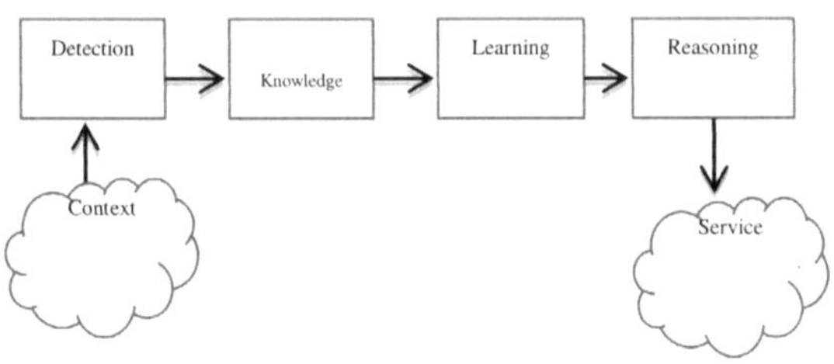

Figure 1. The main steps for learning process in a context-aware system.

IV. MACHINE LEARNING APPLICATION IN SMART ENVIRONMENTS

Diverse machine learning algorithms have been developed to cover a variety of data and problem types in smart environment. Machine learning has branched into several subfields dealing with different types of learning tasks. We give a rough taxonomy of learning paradigm. Mainly, there are four categories: Supervised learning, unsupervised learning, semi-supervised learning and reinforcing algorithms. The next section presents some learning strategies applied for different objectives in smart environment.

A. Supervised learning

Supervised machine learning is the search for algorithms that perform reasoning on externally supplied instances to produce general hypotheses, which then make predictions about future instances [11]. Mainly, supervision is provided in the form of a set of labeled training data, each data point having a class label selected from a fixed set of classes [12]. The use of the supervised activity classification approaches has shown promising results [13].

Supervised learning methods are widely used in smart environments to solve several problems. The ACHE system used neural networks and reinforcement learning to control devices [14]. Bourobou et al. [15] proposed a hybrid approach consisting of the neural network algorithm based on temporal relations and K-pattern clustering to recognize and predict user activities in IoT (internet of things) based smart environments. Neural network was used for inferring the users viewing preferences to develop a personalized contextual TV recommendation system [16]. Fleury et al. [17] used SVM (support vector machine) algorithm to classify the activities of daily living in a Health Smart Home. In [18], authors used Decision tree based on context history to infer the preferences of the user in order to provide personalized services using context-aware computing. A naïve Bayes Classifier was used to learn user activity and availability directly from sensor data according to given user feedback [19].

B. Unsupervised learning

In unsupervised learning no information about the input is given and thus the system cannot know anything about the correctness of the outcome [2]. It tries to directly construct models from unlabeled data either by estimating the properties of their underlying probability density (called density estimation) or by discovering groups of similar examples (called clustering) [20]. The use of an unsupervised approach was applied for different activities recognition in smart spaces when it is difficult to have labels for the data [21]. Authors used a statistical approach based on hidden Markov models in a regression context for the joint segmentation of multivariate time series of human activities. Hidden Markov models (HMM) were also used in [22] for both segmentation and recognition of 3-D Human action to enable real-time assessment and feedback for physical rehabilitation.

C. Reinforcement learning

Reinforcement learning is a learning paradigm concerned with learning to control a system so as to maximize a numerical performance measure that expresses a long-term objective [23]. Q-learning [24] is a model-free reinforcement learning method based on learning the expected utility given a state decision. Li and Jayaweera [25] proposed a Q-learning algorithm to provide a more efficient way for on-line decision making, with more flexibility and adaptiveness with relatively good performance. This algorithm was also implemented in simulation to demonstrate how the performance of the new Markov Decision Process (MDP) representation is comparable to that of a Linear Time-

Invariant (LTI) one on a reference-tracking scenario [26]. Reinforcement algorithms are used in Mavhome project [27] to acquire an optimal decision policy to automate basic functions in order to maximize the inhabitants' comfort and minimize the operating cost of the home.

D. *Semi-supervised learning*

Semi-supervised learning is a learning paradigm concerned with the study of how computers and natural systems such as humans learn in the presence of both labeled and unlabeled data [28]. The goal of semi-supervised learning is to combine a large amount of unlabeled data, together with the labeled data, to build better classifiers [29]. This category requires less human effort as well as building costs.

There are some popular semi-supervised learning models, including self-training, mixture models, co-training and multi-view learning, graph-based methods and semi-supervised support vector machines. Authors in [30] combined between supervised and semi-supervised learning to recognizing ADL (assisted daily life) activities and to provide context-aware services, such as health monitoring and intervention in different smart space.

V. PERFRMANCE COMPARISON OF MACHINE LEARNING ALGORITHMS

Machine learning algorithms that have been used for solving different problems in context-aware smart spaces generally fall into the categories of being supervised, unsupervised, semi-supervised or with reinforcement. Nevertheless, the advantages or disadvantages of each one depend on what learning algorithm wants to solve.

Neural networks are the most widely used supervised learning. Indeed, they offer a number of advantages including requiring less formal statistical training, ability to implicitly detect complex nonlinear relationships between dependent and independent variables, ability to detect all possible interactions between predictor variables and the availability of multiple training algorithms [31]. On the other hand, disadvantages include its "black box" nature, greater computational burden and proneness to over fitting. Decision trees algorithm are non-parametric algorithm and easy to interpret and explain. Their main disadvantage is that they easily over fit. SVMs could work well with an appropriate kernel even when data isn't linearly separable, they have a high accuracy and nice theoretical guarantees regarding over fitting. Whoever, they are hard to interpret.

In unsupervised learning, there is no outcome measure; we observe only the features and the goal is to describe the associations and patterns among a set of input measures [32]. Its major disadvantage is the lack of direction for the learning algorithm and that the absence of any interesting knowledge discovered in the set of features selected for the training. Clustering is a form of unsupervised learning that consists of finding patterns in the data by putting each data element into one of K-clusters, where each cluster contains data elements most similar to each other [33].

Semi-supervised learning is an interesting field. It is a hybrid between clustering and supervised learning, potentially useful on scenarios where labeling effort is not ready available or expensive. These algorithms try to solve a supervised learning approach using labeled data, augmented by unlabeled data. So, by adding cheap and abundant unlabeled data, one is hoping to build a better model than using supervised learning alone.

Reinforcing learning algorithms learn more control policies, especially in the absence of a priori knowledge and a sufficiently large amount of training data. However, they suffer from a major drawback: high calculation cost because an optimal solution requires that all states be visited to choose the optimal one.

VI. CONCLUSION

In this paper, we have discussed the importance of the use of machine learning techniques in context-aware systems. We have presented the major goals of learning methods. We have also shown the main steps to achieve the learning process in context-aware smart spaces. This process must acquire the context of the environment to be able to adapt services to users according to the current context. A discussion of the most important and commonly used learning algorithms was provided to solve different problems in smart environments.

REFERENCES

[1] S. K. Das, D. J. Cook, "Designing and modeling smart environments," Proceedings of the 2006 International Symposium on on World of Wireless, Mobile and Multimedia Networks. IEEE Computer Society, pp. 490-494, 2006.

[2] S. Stenudd, "Using machine learning in the adaptive control of a smart environment," Utigivare, Vuorimiehentie, 2010.

[3] A. Smola and SVN. Vishwanathan, "Introduction to machine learning, " Cambridge University, UK, vol. 32, pp.34, 2008.

[4] A. J. Stimpson, "A machine learning approach to modeling and predicting training effectiveness, ". Thèse de doctorat. Massachusetts Institute of Technology, 2015.

[5] S. T. M. Bourobou and Y. Yoo, "User activity recognition in smart homes using pattern clustering applied to temporal ann algorithm, " Sensors, vol. 15, no 5, pp. 11953-11971, 2015.

[6] V. G. Motti, N. Mezhoudi and J. Vanderdonckt, "Machine Learning in the Support of Context-Aware Adaptation, ". In : CASFE. 2012.

[7] R. S. Sutton, A. G. Barto and G. Andrew, "Reinforcement learning: An introductio, " Cambridge : MIT press, 1998.

[8] WP. Lee, "Deploying personalized mobile services in an agent-based environment, " Expert Systems with Applications, vol. 32, no 4, pp. 1194-1207, 2007.

[9] G. D. Bhatt and J. Zaveri, "The enabling role of decision support systems in organizational learning, ". Decision Support Systems, vol. 32, no 3, pp. 297-309, 2002.

[10] M. Bkassiny, M. Li and S. Jayaweera, "A survey on machine-learning techniques in cognitive radios," IEEE Communications Surveys & Tutorials, vol. 15, no 3, pp. 1136-1159, 2013.

[11] S. B. Kotsiantis, I. Zaharakisand P. Pintelas, "Supervised machine learning: A review of classification techniques," 2007.

[12] T. Mitchell, "The role of unlabeled data in supervised learning, " In :Proceedings of the sixth international colloquium on cognitive science. pp. 2-11, 1999.

[13] K. Altun, B. Barshan and O. Tuncel, "Comparative study on classifying human activities with miniature inertial and magnetic sensors," Pattern Recognition, vol. 43, no 10, pp. 3605-3620, 2010.

[14] M. C. Mozer, "The neural network house: An environment hat adapts to its inhabitants," In : Proc. AAAI Spring Symp. Intelligent Environments, 1998.

[15] S. T. M. Bourobou and Y. Yoo, "User activity recognition in smart homes using pattern clustering applied to temporal ann algorithm, " Sensors, vol. 15, no 5, pp. 11953-11971, 2015.

[16] S. H. Hsu, M. H. Wen and M. H. Lee, "A personalized TV recommendation system, " In : European Conference on Interactive Television. Springer Berlin Heidelberg, pp. 166-174, 2007.

[17] A. Fleury, M. Vacher and N. Noury, "SVM-based multimodal classification of activities of daily living in health smart homes: sensors, algorithms, and first experimental results, " IEEE transactions on information technology in biomedicine, vol. 14, no 2, pp. 274-283, 2008.

[18] J. S. E. Hong and J. Kim, "Context-aware system for proactive personalized service based on context history, " *Expert Systems with Applications*, vol. 36, no 4, p. 7448-7457, 2009.

[19] M. Muhlenbrock, O. Brdiczka and D. Snowdon, "Learning to Detect User Activity and Availability from a Variety of Sensor Data, " In : PerCom. pp. 13-22, 2004.

[20] G. T. Chen, S. haxun, X. Tao, "An unsupervised approach to activity recognition and segmentation based on object-use fingerprints, " Data & Knowledge Engineering, vol. 69, no 6, pp. 533-544, 2010.

[21] D. Trabelsi, S. Mohammed, F. Chamroukhi, "An unsupervised approach for automatic activity recognition based on hidden Markov model regression, " IEEE Transactions on Automation Science and Engineering, , vol. 10, no 3, pp. 829-835, 2013.

[22] F. LV and R. Nevatia, "Recognition and segmentation of 3-d human action using hmm and multi-class adaboost, ". In : European conference on computer vision. Springer Berlin Heidelberg, pp. 359-372, 2006.

[23] C. Szepesvari, "Algorithms for Reinforcement Learning (Synthesis Lectures on Artificial Intelligence and Machine Learning, " Morgan and Claypool, 2010.

[24] C. Watkins and P. Dayan, "Q-learning. Machine learning, " vol. 8, no 3-4, pp. 279-292, 1992.

[25] D. Li and S. K. Jayaweera, "Reinforcement learning aided smart-home decision-making in an interactive smart grid, " In : Green Energy and Systems Conference (IGESC), pp. 1-6, 2014.

[26] E. C. Kara and M. Berges and B. Krogh, "Using smart devices for system-level management and control in the smart grid: A reinforcement learning framework, " In : Smart Grid Communications (SmartGridComm), IEEE Third International Conference on. pp. 85-90, 2012.

[27] D. J. Cook, G. M. Youngblood and E. O. Heierman, "MavHome: An Agent-Based Smart Home, " In : PerCom. pp 521-524, 2003.

[28] X. Zhu, A. Goldberg, "Introduction to semi-supervised learning. Synthesis lectures on artificial intelligence and machine learning, vol. 3, no 1, pp. 1-130, 2009.

[29] X. Zhu, "Semi-supervised learning literature survey, ". 2005.

[30] D. j. Cook, "Learning setting-generalized activity models for smart spaces, " IEEE intelligent systems, vol. 2010, no 99, pp. 1, 2010.

[31] J. V. Tu, "Advantages and disadvantages of using artificial neural networks versus logistic regression for predicting medical outcomes, " Journal of clinical epidemiology, vol. 49, no 11, pp. 1225-1231, 1996.

[32] M. Ramon, F. M. Pastor and O. L. G. A. Felipe, "Taking advantage of the use of supervised learning methods for characterization of sperm population structure related with freezability in the Iberian red deer, ". Theriogenology, vol. 77, no 8, pp. 1661-1672, 2012.

[33] B. Wooley, "Scaling Clustering for the Data Mining Step in Knowledge Discovery, ". 1999.

Toward SoC/SoPC Architecture in Low Power Consumption for Wireless Sensor Networks

Manel Elleuchi, M.Wassim Jmal, Mohamed ABID
CES research unit, National School of Engineers of Sfax
Digital Research Center (CRNS)
Sfax, Tunisia
e-mail : manelelleuchi@gmail.com, wassim.jmal@gmail.com, mohamed.abid@enis.rnu.tn

Abdulfattah M. Obeid, Mohammed S. Ben Saleh
National Center for Electronics, Communications and Photonics
King Abdulaziz City for Science and Technology
Riyadh, Kingdom of Saudi Arabie
e-mail : obeid@kacst.edu.sa, mbensaleh@kacst.edu.sa

***Abstract*—Maximizing sensor nodes' lifetime is an essential issue for wireless sensors networks applications. Therefore, it is necessary to control the energy consumption of the sensor node from the first stages of the design flow. Modeling nodes using system on chip is among the typical solution used to minimize energy consumption. Thus, many studies are currently focusing on proposing new designs and architectures based on system on chip technology. In this paper, we present a new solution, based on system on chip technology, aimed at improving performance. A detailed study of different parts of proposed solution is presented.**

Keywords-component; Wireless sensor networks(WSNs); Power consumption; System on Chip(SoC)

I. INTRODUCTION

Innovation in sensor devices is required due to the wide variety of wireless sensor network applications that have been emerging. With the huge number of domains, low power, low cost and highly integrated System on Chip (SoC) WSN nodes are needed. Nowadays, most of the sensor nodes are developed based on the SoC platforms in order to be very useful for WSNs applications and minimize energy consumption. In this paper, we focus on the study of different proposed hardware implementations of routing protocols in order to minimize power consumption. These implementations are executed in many architectures and platforms such as field-programmable gate array (FPGA) [15] and complex programmable logic device CPLD [10][11][12]. We present, also, the study of different proposed SoC architectures of wireless sensor network nodes. The main objective of our work is to introduce the field of wireless sensor networks, browse the existing solutions and then propose an architecture that minimizes energy consumption based on SoC/System on programmable chip(SoPC). The rest of the paper is structured as follows: The hardware implementation is presented in Section II. Section III present a study of low-power SoC architectures in WSN. Our proposed architecture (SoC/SoPC) is detailed in Section IV. We finish with a conclusion in Section V.

II. RELATED WORK

In literature, several works use reconfigurable hardware as a solution to limit energy consumption in sensors nodes when implementing routing protocols [10]-[13].

In [10] and [12], the authors introduced a platform that uses a reconfigurable device (CPLD) to enhance the processing power of the sensor nodes and reduce overall energy consumption in the common tasks, such as routing and security and header processing. In [10], the used routing protocol is XMesh for its performance when applied in real sensor networks. To implement the proposed platform, they connected a CPLD to a sensor. They used the Digilent X-Board, which connects a Xilinx CoolRunner -II CPLD with the necessary circuit to connect the reconfigurable device. The used sensor node is Crossbow's IRIS with the MDA100 sensor and data acquisition board, which includes a number of sensors and a general prototype space. Multiplication function was chosen to be implemented on reconfigurable device to improve the performance of the routing protocol and to reduce the energy consumption. According to the authors, the measured energy consumption is reduced by 71.49 %, compared to the software approach. From the results that have been found, the authors explain the interest of using CPLD as a hardware accelerator. In [12], a "Pioneering Platform" is introduced, using all the advantages of CPLDs in order to improve the processing power of the sensor nodes and, more importantly reduce the overall energy consumption in heavy demanding tasks such as the routing and processing of the header. This platform accelerates the cost estimation algorithm routing protocol XMesh by 606 times. There is also a reduction of the energy consumption measured by 97%. In addition, the proposed system in [12] can accelerate the control calculation scheme by three orders of magnitude and it consumes up to 96% less energy than the corresponding standard software implementations.

Brokalakis et al propose in [11] the use of a Turbo Code system to increase the robustness and efficiency of communication between end nodes and base stations in the single- hop topologies. In fact, the reconfigurable hardware device was used to perform the coding scheme. The approach in [11] reduces the overall energy consumption of a node by more than 40 % compared with a Turbo code system implemented in software, as well as more than 70% compared with transmission systems of traditional WSNs that do not support any type of Forward Error Correction. A platform that combines WSNs with a reconfigurable device (CPLD) to reduce energy consumption Turbo coding task was proposed. The reconfigurable device is used for data processing to improve the overall energy efficiency of the WSNs infrastructure. A Turbo encoder was used and the entire coding process has been performed by CPLD. To measure the energy consumption of the platform an oscilloscope was used. The authors in [13] suggest unloading the task of data compression to a CPLD to be connected to the main node of WSN for reducing the overall energy consumption. According to [13] and from experiments, the authors show that it can reduce the energy consumption by a minimum of 46%.

The majority of the related work use CPLD in hardware implementations, but there is another architecture, which can be better than CPLD such as FPGA. In fact, FPGAs offer more logic flexibility and more sophisticated system features than CPLDs: clock management, on-chip Random Access Memory (RAM), Digital Signal Processor (DSP) functions, (multipliers), and even on-chip microprocessors and Multi-Gigabit Transceivers. These benefits and opportunities of dynamic reconfiguration, even in the end-user system, are an important advantage [14]. FPGAs are used for larger and more complex designs and have special routing resources to implement binary counters, arithmetic functions like adders, comparators and RAM. Moreover, FPGA can contain very large digital designs, while CPLD can contain only small designs. The high static (idle) power consumption prohibits use of CPLD in battery-operated equipment. Nevertheless, FPGA idle power consumption is reasonably low. IGLOO FPGAs can be considered to offer revolutionary possibilities in power, size, lead-times, operating temperature, and cost [16]. Among the FPGA implementation that we find in literature is the implementation of the GPSR routing protocol in [15]. In fact, a hardware implementation based on FPGA was used. In the experimental steps, the authors use two different development boards: a Digilent XUPV5 hosting a high-end Xilinx Virtex-5 FPGA device (XC5VLX110T) and a Digilent XUPV2P board with a low-cost Virtex-II ProFPGA (XC2VP30). In both platforms, the FPGA is connected with an Intel Board, which hosts an integrated Intel Dual-Core Atom 330 processor [15]. Via real-world experiments, the authors demonstrated that their system is 31 times faster than an existing CPU-based system, and the overall energy consumption was reduced by more than 90%. The authors explained, also, that the platform could adapt to a different routing protocol in such cases. According to the advantages of FPGA, it can be chosen as a base architecture in our proposed SoC/SoPC architecture, which will be presented in the next sections. A study on the use of SoC for routing protocol in WSNs will be detailed.

III. LOW-POWER SOC ARCHITECTURES IN WSNS

With the goal to make the wireless sensor network nodes small in size, light in weight, cheap in cost, as well as low in power consumption, projects have been carried out to develop sensor node based on SoC technology.

In [1] Wisenet was proposed. It is a platform of low power consumption developed by the Swiss Centre for Electronics and Micro technology for the implementation of wireless sensor networks based on SoC design. It is a distributed wireless sensors network, that combines detection, local signal processing and wireless communication capabilities of short-range in a compact system with low-power consumption. The WiseNET platform uses a design approach that combines a radio with WiseMAC, a control protocol in low power and a complex SoC node. The authors in [1] explained that the WiseNET solution consumes about 100 times less energy with simulation validation than other comparable solutions .

In [2], the authors proposed an approach named EasiSOC, which is a general "sensors node on chip" approach with two typical SoC architectures for different application areas. The basic functionalities, which execute simple tasks, are supported by the first architecture of the sensor node. The second architecture of sensor node supports complex functionalities [2]. The authors presented the design, implementation and simulation of hardware security coprocessor and a program protection mechanism based on (SoC) technology for WSNs. The design is mapped in FPGAs and ASICs. The authors explained that the hardware design overhead is 9.6% lower than previous designs and the design time is only 0.2% of general-purpose processors. These results were obtained with real experiments.

A SoC architecture of a sensor node for the ZigBee protocol was presented in [3]. The proposed architecture in [3] can be used as a stand-alone chip or be incorporated as a component of a larger system at a time. The complete architecture has been designed with each block coded and verified. Blocks like the CRC Unit, AES Unit and the MAC units have been synthesized and preliminary power figures have been obtained. Power and gate count of implemented units(AES UNIT, CRC UNIT, MAC UNIT) are computed. The power Figures are obtained using magama tools on 0.13 micron Technology. The proposed SoC is based on microcontroller.

The authors in [4] present the modeling and simulation of nodes composed by a system-on-chip for applications in WSNs using systemC/TLM. The SoC contains a microprocessor without interlocked pipeline stages (MIPS) processor, a memory, a bus, a timer, a transceiver and a battery. As a case study, the authors conducted a simulation of WSN in star topology and they showed the energy consumption of each node, with a discussion about the computational load. The authors proposed that their approach is flexible and can be adapted to simulate more complex systems and topologies.

In [5], the authors proposed a novel solution, which uses the reconfigurable technology RSoC. They minimized the energy consumption with the use of FPGA nodes that are equipped with "tiny rechargeable units" to recharge the batteries. This solution is designed for specific applications "border control and forest fire monitoring". Energy consumption is not indicated. Table I presents a summary of the majority of the words presented here.

TABLE I. SYNTHESIS

Ref	Energy consumption	Real Experiences	Simulation
[1]	100 times less energy	-	+
[2]	Low power consumption	+	-
[3]	Low power consumption	+	-
[4]	Low power consumption	-	-
[5]	not indicated	-	-

From this study, we conclude the efficiency of using SoC architecture in WSNs. In fact, the majority of related works confirm the minimization of energy consumption using SoC solution. In this context, we propose a new efficient solution based on SoC/SoPC architecture that reduces power consumption and helps to maximize sensor lifetime, which ameliorates the WSNs operation. This solution will be detailed in the next sections.

IV. PROPOSED SOC/SOPC ARCHITECTURE

In this section, we provide the details of a study in order to propose a novel architecture. To find the most appropriate approach with WSNs characteristics and SoC, an in-depth study is essential for different parts such as the design approach, the SoC design environment, the refinement environment, the validation environment, the processor cores and the operating systems. Fig. 1 below presents the Flow of system design of SoC.

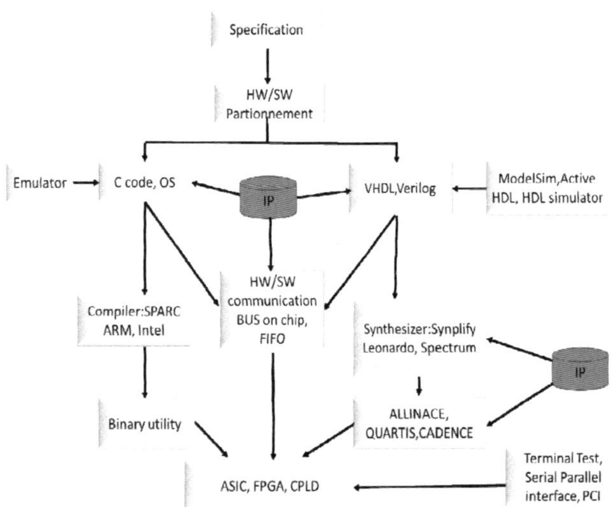

Figure.1. Flow of system design of SoC

Fig.1 presents the flow of system design of SoC, which presents the SoC design environment. Design tools for software and hardware parts form this environment. A detailed description will be done in the next sub-sections for all different parts.

A. Study of design approaches for routing in WSNs

The easiest solution is to use a CPU. However, this solution cannot be the only response to the constraints of complexity of operations needed in WSNs. Another solution is to use a special processor for the complex treatments of algorithms, which has many advantages compared to the classical processor (time, energy, acceleration). For the design, there exists many choices to have the appropriate processor. For the processor, one choice is the Harvard processor Digital Signal Processor (DSP), which allows parallelism due to the very long instruction word (VLIW) architecture. The second solution is the possibility to use a specific approach and choose a specific processor dedicated to common parts. This approach is the most effective in terms of treatment, but, due to its specificity, it cannot be used for other applications. This solution implies many restrictions in terms of possible applications. The reconfigurable approach consists in integrating a reconfigurable processor core (as an example FPGA). The main advantage of this approach lies in its flexibility with the possibility to synthesize other algorithms if necessary.

B. SoC design environment

This environment is composed of software and hardware design tools. Currently, there are specific language systems that can describe both hardware and software components in a unified manner. These languages require the presence of refinement tools to move to the prototyping level from a high level of specification. Moreover, it is possible to specify the software and hardware parts with two separate specification language.

In our case, we find interesting to adopt the second type based on a separate design, due to the availability of refinement and simulation tools. To construct a system based on SoC, we need to specify all parts of the system.

C. Software refinement environment in SoC

SoC need a specific compiler for the architecture of the processor (Intel, Sparc, PowerPC, etc.) for generating executable code. On the other hand, executable programs generated by compilers will be downloaded in electronic target modules (RAM, ROM, Flash memory, etc.), so there is a need to have binary tools that allow specific binary codes for a target electronic module.

In addition to the binary and compilation tools, the software environment supports an operating system that can make the link between the software and the hardware.

D. Hardware refinement Environment in SoC

The hardware environment refinement is based on flow circuit design. Indeed, this environment contains synthesis tools, placement tools and simulation tools. Due to that, the goal of SoC design in our solution is the implementation of complex applications in routing in terms of architecture and functions. It is necessary to have a robust design environment that can support this complexity. For this reason, the researchers are moving towards the use of commercial hardware description language (HDL) simulation tools (ModelSim, Cadence NC-Verilog) and synthesis tools (Altera's Integrated VHSIC Hardware Description Language (VHDL) / Verilog HDL Tool Leonardo Spectrum, Synplify Pro, Synopsys FPGA Express tool, etc.). However, the major problem with these tools is their refinement runtime, which is very long and can take many days for complex applications. On the other hand, the installation of these commercial tools demands efficient execution platforms in terms of operating systems and memory size. In addition to that, these refinement tools target a specific range of FPGA families, for example, there is a specific simulation tool for Altera FPGA family (ModelSim-Altera) or Xilinx (ModelSim Xilinx Edition). Therefore, a study to find hardware refinement tools with an acceptable runtime, non-specific and a consistent execution platform is necessary to have an efficient system in WSNs.

E. Validation environment in SoC

The design of our solution based on SoC requires validating the functionality of the system through all levels of abstraction in order to reduce the time of design and to avoid the propagation of error in the design flow. The validation technique is based first, on the use of emulators to validate the functionality of the system at an abstract level such as the SIS (SPARC Instruction Simulator). Each processor architecture needs a specific emulator. Second, the validation technique is based on HDL simulator. It is possible to test the functionality of HDL module due to the existing library (library for reading binary files) for RTL or logic level. The HDL simulator allows the test after synthesis phase with some libraries (Vital and UNSIM). Nevertheless, the major disadvantage of this simulator is the enormous computing time, especially for complex systems. Thirdly, the validation technique is based on communication terminals, which are communication interfaces between the prototyping cards and the workstation. As examples of communication terminals, we find XSTOOLs, JTAG Programmer and iMPACT of Xilinx. The problem with these communication terminals is the requirement to use a form of strict and well-defined file and a limited range of prototyping board that reduces the flexibility of these terminals.

F. Comparative study of processor cores

For the proposed solution, we will integrate a SoC based on one or more core processors. It is in this context that our architecture will be proposed. It is necessary to make a study about processors in order to find the most suitable for the implementation of the routing protocols. To do this, a comparative study between different synthesizable processors should be done. The architecture of the adopted processor should be studied in order to determine the adequacy of its architecture and the appropriate routing algorithm (Algorithm Architecture Adequacy(AAA)). Routing algorithms have many steps that require a huge amount of calculation and many characteristics that make very interesting the realization on dedicated architectures. The use of embedded software by processor cores implemented on programmable devices and integrated on a single chip is an inevitable trend. These processor cores can be of three types: general purpose processors, processors specific to a domain and the processors that incorporate functional units and a set of specific instructions for a specific application. The choice of the target architecture can be based on three criteria: real-time constraints, the flexibility of the system and the time to market.

In our case, we can find that the most suitable is the general purpose processor due to its flexibility and facility of integration. In fact, this type of processor can quickly and easily make treatments in WSNs and guarantee the possibility of integration of new services, as well as follow the scalability of applications in WSNs. Among processor cores, we find LEON [6], ARM [7], MicroBlaze (Xilinx), OpenRISC1200, Openfire [8] and NIOS [9] (Altera).

A comparative study of the different characteristics and parameters of processors is required to find the most suitable type for the implementation of the routing algorithms on SoC.

G. Comparative study of Operating Systems

For our proposed solution, we need to have an embedded operating system characterized by the limited availability of resources, low price, low power consumption and should be a real time operating system. These operating systems will be used for management of memory, network access time, etc. Among the embedded operating systems, there is Symbian OS, Linux, µCOS, RTEMS, etc. A comparative study of the different characteristics and parameters of operating systems will be done as future work to find the most suitable one.

The proposed SoC architecture is presented in Fig. 2 below.

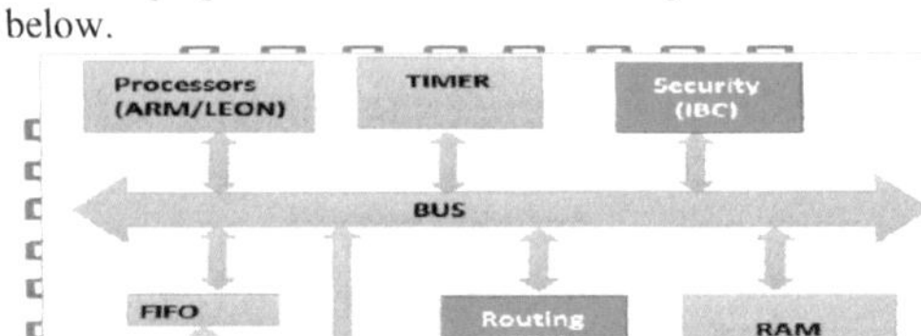

Figure 2. Proposed SoC architecture

The proposed solution includes processor, which can be LEON or ARM, a TIMER, a routing accelerator, a memory (ROM and RAM) and a reconfigurable part. The system components connect to the processor over a bus structure. The implementation and the validation of this proposed architecture will be done as future works.

V. CONCLUSION

The recent developments of WSNs have caused sensor nodes to encounter energy optimization problems. In fact, a sensor node must have the capability of sensing, treating and routing. Routing is the most energy consuming activity in WSNs. In this context, several works proposed many solutions to reduce power consumption and enhance the lifetime of the sensor nodes. Developing a sensor node based on SoC technology has emerged as an effective solution to minimize energy consumption, especially in the routing phase. In this paper, we presented related works according to SoC architecture of wireless sensor network node. We detailed, also, a study about the design of SoC/SoPC architecture in WSN. Following to this study, we propose a novel solution. For the proposed architecture, FPGA can be used for prototyping and testing designed system, which will be studied in future work with the implementation and the validation of the architecture.

REFERENCES

[1] C. C. Enz, A. El-Hoiydi, J.-D. Decotignie, A.-S. Porret, T. Melly, and V. Peiris "WiseNET: an ultralow-power wireless sensor network solution," Analog Circuit Design, pp. 91-122, 2004, 8 doi: 10.1007/978-1-4020-2805-2_5.

[2] Xi Huang, Ze Zhao, and Li Cui," EasiSOC: Towards Cheaper and Smaller ", Proc. First International Conference, MSN 2005, Wuhan,

[3] Ninad B. Kothari, T.S.B. Sudarshan, S. Gurunarayanan1, and Chandrasekhar3, "SOC design of a Low Power Wireless Sensor network node for Zigbee Systems", Proc. International Conference on Advanced Computing and Communications, ADCOM, pp. 462-466 2006.

[4] Heider M.G de Medeiros, J.E.G., da Costa, J.C., Beserra, and G.S., "system level power consumption modeling of a soc for wsn applications" Proc. IEEE 2nd International Conference on Networked Embedded Systems for Enterprise Applications (NESEA), pp. 1-6, 2011.

[5] Ali Elkateeb, " SOC-Based Sensor Mote Design", International Journal of Mobile Network Communications & Telematics (IJMNCT),Vol. 3, No.4, p1, August 2013.

[6] Gaisler, J. www.gaisler.com, the LEON Processor User's Manual.15-17 Nov. 2010,pp. 148 – 153.Version2.4.0 Novembre 2011.

[7] www.arm.com. February 2016.

[8] http://www.altera.com/devices/processor/nios2/ni2-index.html, January 2016.

[9] S. Craven, C. Patterson, and P. Athanas, "Configurable soft processor arrays using the openfire processor," Proc. MAPLD International Conference, pp. 250–256, 2005.

[10] G-G. Mplemenos, K. Papadopoulos, and I.Papaefstathiou, "Using Reconfigurable Hardware Devices in WSNs for Reducing the Energy Consumption of Routing and Security Tasks", Proc. IEEE Global Telecommunications Conference (GLOBECOM 2010), 6-10 Dec. 2010, 10.1109/GLOCOM.2010.5683605.

[11] A. Brokalakis and I.. Papaefstathiou, "Using hardware-based forward error correction to reduce the overall energy consumption of WSNs," Proc.IEEE Wireless Communications and Networking Conference (WCNC), pp. 2191-2196, 2012.

[12] G. G. Mplemenos, P. Christou, and I. Papaefstathiou, "Using reconfigurable hardware devices in WSNs for accelerating and reducing the power consumption of header processing tasks", Proc. IEEE International Symposium on Advanced Networks and Telecommunication Systems (ANTS), pp. 12235-12264, 2009.

[13] G. Chrysos and I. Papaefstathiou, "HeavilyReducing WSNs'Energy Consumption by employing Hardware Based Compression ", Ad-Hoc, Mobile and Wireless Networks, Vol. 5793, pp. 312-326, 2009.

[14] http://asic-soc.blogspot.com/2007/11/what-is-difference-between-fpga-and.html. March 2016.

[15] G-G. Mplemenos and I. Papaefstathiou, "Fast and Power-Efficient Hardware Implementation of a Routing scheme for WSNs" Proc. IEEE Wireless Communications and Networking Conference (WCNC), pp.1710 – 1714, 2012.

[16] http://www.microsemi.com/products/fpga-oc/fpga/igloo-nano. December 2015.

Design of Multiple Clouds based Virtual Desktop Infrastructure Architecture for Service Mobility

Dongjae Kang, Sunwook Kim, Youngwoo Jung
High Performance Computing Research Department
Electronics and Telecommunications Research Institute
Daejeon, Korea
e-mail: {djkang, swkim99, ywjung}@etri.re.kr

***Abstract*—Cloud service mobility has been more and more important for the next-generation Cloud service to support limitless movement and stable Quality of Service (QoS). But, existing virtual desktop infrastructure (VDI) solution has been provided from the fixed and dedicated single Cloud. In the situation, it makes several issues to long distance service users in aspect of response time, performance and QoS and so on. To improve the upper needs and problems, we propose multiple Clouds based virtual desktop infrastructure architecture and its functional blocks. Finally, we described use case of the VDI service in the proposed environment. The proposed VDI architecture can significantly improve the response time and stability of VDI service in case user moves to cross-border location.**

Keywords-Virtual desktop infrastructure; Cloud service brokerage; Multiple clouds; Service mobility; Interoperability.

I. INTRODUCTION

Recently, many companies and organizations start to use smart work environment through virtual desktop infrastructure (VDI) service to reduce the cost of management and infrastructure itself. And it is helpful for enhancing security level and realizing green computing. Moreover, the client devices of VDI service are transferring to diverse mobile devices from static PC and server according to mobile work trend. The VDI service may include company-specific business applications with high level security, office SW to handle various documents or favorite personal applications and so on.

In case that the employees in Korea leave on a business trip to another country, e.g., Germany, they still want to use their own VDI service to continuously perform the business work, to access to specific data or to enjoy favorite personal application. But, QoS of VDI service in Germany will be very serious because of degraded response time and performance by long distance transferring. Although this kind of inconvenient situation is occurred, they have to connect to the VDI service provided from Korea. This is very time consuming and troublesome job.

To ease the upper problems, we proposed the architecture and functional blocks of virtual desktop infrastructure in the multiple Clouds environment for enhancing the degraded QoS of VDI service when the user moves to another place, e.g., border-across movement. In the proposed architecture, the VDI service can be freely transferred among multiple Clouds according to user location (User Neighboring Service) and it makes the user to get more stable and high-quality VDI service in anywhere regardless of location.

II. RELATED WORKS

A. *Cloud Service Brokerage*

According to Gartner [2], Cloud service brokerage system is a role of intermediary, in which a company or other entity adds value to one or more cloud services on behalf of one or more consumers of those services. The Cloud service brokerage system offering will also often include some combination of capabilities that fall under three primary roles, aggregation brokerage, integration brokerage, customization brokerage. Gartner's Intermediation encompasses these three primary roles.

In [4], open source based Cloud service brokerage solutions are compared, according concerns like, system category and type, core capabilities, core features and advanced features, architecture and interoperability, service languages, programming model and service engineering, and quality. In this research, the authors place emphasis on the emergence of cloud service brokerage solutions on top of cloud management, the need for further separation of marketplaces and cloud service brokerage solutions and service description mechanisms to commoditize the cloud. Several organizations active in the cloud technology area have identified cloud service brokerage as an important architectural challenge. Architecture and programming model concern is key enabler of any service brokerage solution that mediates between different providers by integrating, aggregating and customizing services from different providers [5].

Cloud service brokerage system generally consists of three main parts that include user portal, brokerage core engine and Cloud connection management [3]. User portal is the front-end of the Cloud service brokerage system for Cloud service consumers and providers and it includes various business support functionalities. Brokerage core engine supports key functionalities for service brokerage, such as request verification, service provisioning, arbitrage, monitoring, service lifecycle management and so on. Finally, Cloud connection management is in charge of the interaction between Cloud service brokerage system and Cloud infrastructures by IaaS providers.

B. Virtual Desktop Infrastructure Service

Virtual Desktop Infrastructure (VDI) is used to run desktop operating systems and applications inside virtual machine that reside on servers. The desktop operating systems inside the virtual machines are referred as the virtual desktops. Through network, users access to the virtual desktops using VDI client that can be thin client, zero client or PC client. The client receives screen data of VM and displays it to the client display. Keyboard and mouse input of the client are captured and transmitted to the VM. Nowadays, there are several VDI solutions provided by VMware, Citrix, Microsoft, and KVM. The VDI systems are combination of the hypervisor and the VDI protocol. The representative VDI protocols are PCoIP, ICA/HDX, and RDP/RemoteFX. In the VDI system, Network Interface Card (NIC) for the virtual desktop is emulated by the hypervisor in software, and the emulated NIC is called as vNIC (Virtual NIC) [6].

The service flow of virtual desktop in single cloud is shown in Figure 1.

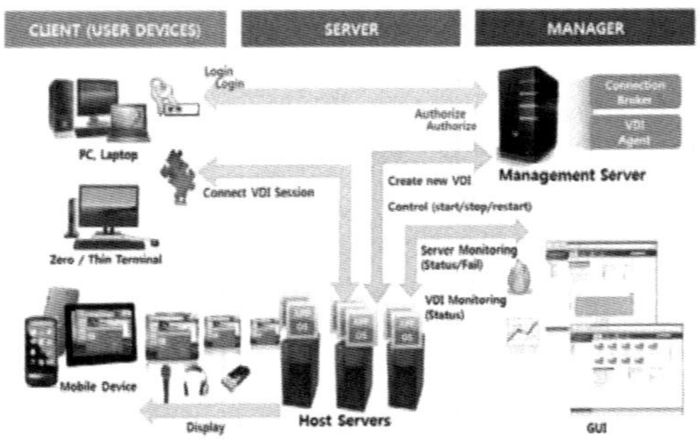

Figure 1. General VDI service architecture in single Cloud

VDI hosts a virtual desktop environment in a virtual machine that runs on a centralized or remote server. And user may access to the assigned VDI service through a variety of terminals. In general, VDI has three components as follows: one is a VDI client, which is user devices to connect to the VDI service, a VDI server in which user's virtual desktop exists, and a VDI manager that administrates and controls virtual desktop system. Virtual desktops in VDI server are transmitted to users' terminal using display protocol on network. These components are interconnected to support VDI service on network.

C. Nested Virtualization

In classical machine virtualization, a hypervisor runs multiple operating systems simultaneously, each on its own virtual machine. These solutions lack interoperability with each other, meaning that a VM running on one hypervisor cannot be easily migrated to another hypervisor, because it differs in several aspects, e.g., virtualization technique, virtual hardware devices, image formats and so on [7]. In nested virtualization, a hypervisor can run multiple other hypervisors with their associated virtual machines. It enables complete abstraction of underlying cloud infrastructure from the application virtual machines and allows deployment of existing VMs into the cloud without any modifications, mobility between the clouds and easy duplication of the entire deployment [8]. In this work, using multi-dimensional paging and multi-level device assignment, it can run common workloads with overhead as low as 6-8% of single level virtualization.

III. THE ARCHITECTURE OF MULTIPLE CLOUDS BASED VIRTUAL DESKTOP INFRASTRUCTURE

In this section, we proposed the architecture of multiple Clouds based VDI and its functional blocks.

A. Architecture of multiple Clouds based VDI

In this section, we describe the concept and whole architecture design of multiple Clouds based VDI service. The system enables the unified management of heterogeneous cloud service providers and make VDI service to be moved across the diverse Clouds.

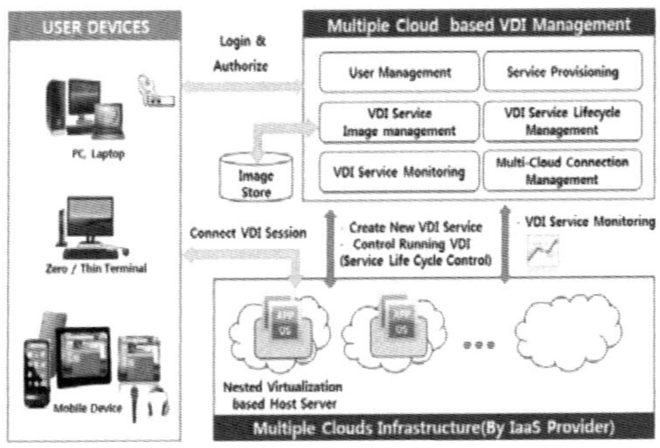

Figure 2. Architecture for multiple Clouds based VDI service

As showed in Figure 2, multiple Clouds based VDI service is consist of three separated parts, user devices, multiple Cloud based VDI management and Multiple Clouds Infrastructure. User devices are a kind of service terminal for VDI service users and it can be personal computer, thin client, laptop, mobile devices and others. Multiple Clouds based VDI management supports provisioning and management of the VDI host server and VDI service on multiple cloud environment. It interacts with diverse Cloud infrastructures and connects to the agent in each VDI host server for controlling VDI service lifecycle. Nested virtualization based host server is a shape of virtual machine including VDI host server. It enables complete abstraction of underlying cloud infrastructure from VDI host server in virtual machines and allows deployment of existing VDI host server into the cloud without any modifications between different hypervisors, e.g., KVM, Xen, VMware. Multiple Clouds Infrastructure consists of the diverse Cloud infrastructures provided by private and public Cloud service provider, that is, Amazon, KT, Rackspace, OpenStack and so on. And each part requires below features.

1) User devices
- Browser-based client system using HTML5
- Adaptive client service based on client resources
- On/Offline virtual desktop service

2) Multiple Cloud based VDI management
- Hierarchical management structure for large scale system
- Modular architecture for easy and quick virtual desktop provisioning
- Fast user image management system
- Web-based management interface

3) Nested Virtualization based Host Server
- Nested hypervisor, virtual hardware, network and storage configuration support
- Ability to run multiple VDI service on single host virtual machine
- Common abstraction and decoupling virtualized VDI server from resources provided by IaaS providers

4) Multiple Clouds infrastructure
- Diverse resource specification support
- Geographically dispersed Cloud resources
- Price, resource, security and other features can be selectable

B. Functional blocks of the multiple Clouds based VDI management

Multiple Clouds based VDI management is the essential part in the proposed VDI architecture and it intermediates most functions between user device and Multiple Clouds Infrastructures. In this section, we explained role of the detailed functional blocks in the Multiple Clouds based VDI Management. Figure 3 and figure 4 show its details and relationships between blocks.

VDI user portal receives various requests from users in the defined form and returns processed result via GUI interfaces. Users can control and manage their provisioned VDI services on multiple Clouds through it. User authentication and management has two kinds of roles, one is user authentication for VDI service and the other is account mapping between VDI service and each user or user group. Service provisioning is initial process to provide VDI service to user. It includes finding best-fit Cloud infrastructure for VDI services and makes required configuration and deploys VDI service on the selected Cloud infrastructure. VDI service lifecycle management reacts from monitoring alert, especially, SLA status monitoring and applies pre-defined policies to maintain recommended QoS. Possible reaction can be restart, stop, resume, suspend and move to another Cloud. User system image management is a kind of image repository which stores and retrieves VDI host server and VDI service image from/to IaaS provider's infrastructure. And it manages the version of specific user or tenant's VDI service image to keep the final updated information on the image. VDI service monitoring is responsible for measuring the Key Performance Indicators (KPIs) of the VDI services. In the proposed systems, it provides the data primarily for service accounting / billing and SLA management. Monitoring helps to diagnose hardware and software problems, to enhance the resource utilization and to ensure the service's performance and security.

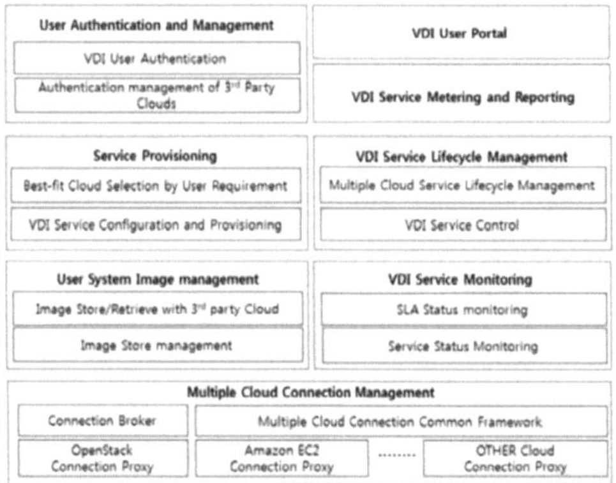

Figure 3. Functional blocks of multiple Clouds based VDI management

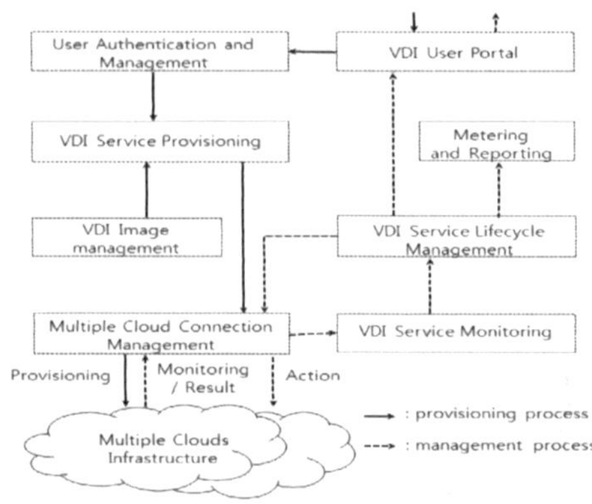

Figure 4. Relationship among main functional blocks

Multiple Cloud connection management deals with the interoperability interface between the VDI management system and the collection of heterogeneous Cloud providers. This component translates the requests from the provisioning and configuration component into understandable provider API calls. And connection proxy abstracts the existing API's heterogeneity through a common framework in the proposed system. It is also in charge of connection and management of VDI host server through connection broker with host server agent.

IV. USE CASE

In this section, we described the use case of the multiple Cloud based VDI service. In this use case, we assumed VDI service user moves to EU from Korea and wants to use his preferred existing VDI service in EU without service delay. Figure 5 shows overall operational sequence for the use case.

VDI Management server can interacts with diverse Cloud infrastructures through Multiple Cloud Connection Management block and communicate with deployed virtualized VDI host servers on it by host server agent. Virtualized host server is created by using nested virtualization technique. It enables complete abstraction of underlying cloud infrastructure from virtual VDI host servers and allows deployment of existing host server into the cloud without any modifications between the Clouds. The use case sequence is as below.

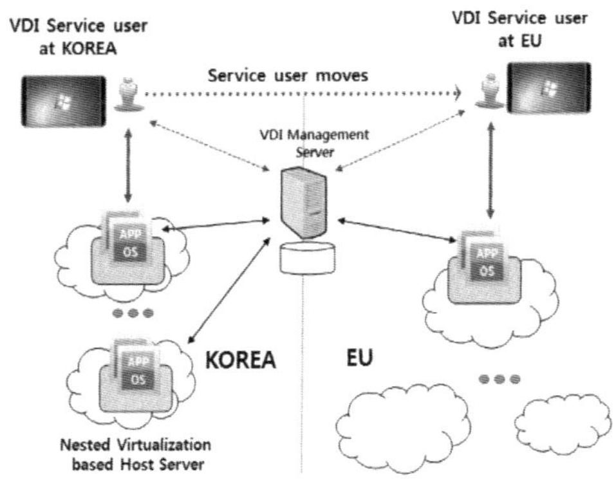

Figure 5. Use case for multiple Clouds based VDI service

1) User login VDI Management server to uses VDI Service in Korea.

2) VDI Management server deploys a VDI service in Korea Cloud and returns connection information to the user.

3) User connects to the allocated VDI service and uses it.

4) Service user has business trip to EU from Korea. Before moves to EU, user connects to VDI Management Server and finds best-fit Cloud infrastructure where user's VDI service will be migrated. To search best-fit Cloud, users can inputs diverse conditions, e.g., location, price, security level, usage period and so on.

5) VDI Management server recommends several EU Cloud infrastructures satisfying user's requirements and user selects and confirms the best one.

6) VDI Management server deploys VDI host server using existing virtualized server image.

7) VDI Management server connects to the agent in deployed virtualized host server and creates new VDI service. And it reflects differential data from existing VDI service to new created VDI service to maintain up-to-date status.

8) VDI Management server stop the existing VDI service in Korea and launches new VDI service in EU.

9) User in EU login VDI Management server and it returns new connection information to user.

10) User enjoys same VDI service from another Cloud infrastructure in EU without additional delay.

V. Conclusion

Most people have used the diverse and huge number of personal devices and they move frequently from one area to another. So, Cloud service mobility is very important for the next-generation Cloud service to support limitless movement and stable QoS. To satisfy the upper described needs, we proposed the architecture of multiple Clouds based VDI service and use case on its environment and designed the functional blocks of multiple Clouds based VDI management and defined the relationships among them. The proposed system architecture can improve the mobility and stability of VDI service in case the user move to cross-border location. Multiple Cloud based VDI service supports flexible service mobility using geographically dispersed Cloud providers and can be dynamically brokered to the best-fit Cloud infrastructure according to emerging demands.

In future plan, to verify usability of this work, we will compare service performance and stability between traditional VDI and the proposed VDI service. And we also consider container based architecture for better performance.

Acknowledgment

This work was supported by the European Union's Horizon 2020 research and innovation programme under grant agreement no. 723131 and from ICT R&D program of Korean Ministry of Science, ICT and Future Planning no. R0115-16-0001

References

[1] N. Grozev, and R. Buyya, "Inter-Cloud architectures and application brokering : taxonomy and survey," Software Practice and Experience, March 2014, Vol. 44, Issue 3, pp. 369–390, doi: 10.1002/spe.2168.

[2] "The Role of CSB in the Cloud Services Value Chain," Gartner, G00218960, Oct. 2011.

[3] S. H. Son, D. J. Kang, S. P. Huh, W. Y. Kim, and W. Choi, "Adaptive trade-off strategy for bargaining-based multi-objective SLA establishment under varying cloud workload," Journal of Supercomputing, April 2016, Vol. 72, Issue 4, pp. 1597–1622, doi:10.1007/s11227-016-1686-y.

[4] F. Fowley, C. Pahl, and L. Zhang, "A Comparison Framework and Review of Service Brokerage Solutions for Cloud Architectures," Service-Oriented Computing, 2014, LNCS Vol 8377, pp. 137-149, doi:10.1007/978-3-319-06859-6_13.

[5] J. Tordsson, R. S. Montero, R. Moreno-Vozmediano, and I. M. Llorente, "Cloud brokering mechanisms for optimized placement of virtual machines across multiple providers," Future Generation Computing Systems, 2012, Vol. 28, Issue 2, pp. 358-367, doi:10.1016/j.future.2011.07.003.

[6] D.-A. Dasilva, L. Liu, N. Bessis, and Y. Zhan, "Enabling Green IT through Building a Virtual Desktop Infrastructure," 2012 Eighth International Conference on Knowledge and Grids (SKG), Oct. 2012, pp. 32-38, doi:10.1109/SKG.2012.29.

[7] A. Fishman, M. Rapoport, E. Budilovsky and I. Eidus, "HVX: Virtualizing the Cloud," 5th USENIX Workshop on Hot Topics in Cloud Computing, June 2013.

[8] M. Ben-Yehuda, M. D. Day, Z. Dubitzky, M. Factor, N. Har'El, A. Gordon, A. Liguori, O. Wasserman and B.-A. Yassour, "The Turtles project: Design and implementation of nested virtualization," 9th USENIX conference on Operating systems design and implementation, Oct 2010, pp. 1-6.

Verifying Scenarios of Proximity-based Federations among Smart Objects through Model Checking

Reona Minoda
Graduate School of Information Science
and Technology, Hokkaido University
Sapporo, Hokkaido 060–8628, Japan
Email: minoda@meme.hokudai.ac.jp

Yuzuru Tanaka
Meme Media Laboratory
Hokkaido University
Sapporo, Hokkaido 060–8628, Japan
Email: tanaka@meme.hokudai.ac.jp

Shin-ichi Minato
Graduate School of Information Science
and Technology, Hokkaido University
Sapporo, Hokkaido 060–8628, Japan
Email: minato@ist.hokudai.ac.jp

***Abstract*—In this paper, we show a formal approach of verifying ubiquitous computing scenarios. Previously, we proposed "a proximity-based federation model among smart objects", which is intended for liberating ubiquitous computing from stereotyped application scenarios. However, we faced challenges when establishing a verification method for this model. This paper proposes a verification method of this model through model checking. Model checking is one of the most familiar formal verification approaches and it is often used in various fields of industry. Model checking is conducted using a Kripke structure which is a formal state transition model. We introduce a context catalytic reaction network (CCRN) to handle this federation model as a formal state transition model. We also give an algorithm to transform a CCRN into a Kripke structure and we conduct a case study of ubiquitous computing scenario verification, using this algorithm and the model checking.**

Keywords*—*ubiquitous computing; catalytic reaction network; formal verification; model checking; smart object.

I. Introduction

Today, we are surrounded by a lot of devices with computation and communication capabilities. These devices are called *Smart Objects* (SOs). SOs include PCs, smart phones, embedded computers, sensor devices and radio frequency identifier (RFID) tags. Here, we use the term *federation* to denote the definition and execution of interoperation among resources that are accessible either through the Internet or through peer-to-peer ad hoc communication. SOs' communication capabilities make it possible to form federations of SOs. Our real world environment is now steadily laying the foundation for the concept of ubiquitous computing which Mark Weiser had foreseen [1].

It has been almost quarter of century since Weiser proposed the notion of ubiquitous computing. In the meantime, a lot of different frameworks have been proposed to realize ubiquitous computing. However, regardless of specific research areas in ubiquitous computing, these researches typically only consider two types of application scenarios. One is "*location transparent service continuance*" (i.e., a user can use a service wherever the user goes). The other one is "*context-aware service provision*" (i.e., a user can use different kinds of services depending on where the user is). Robin Milner thought that the lack of models for describing ubiquitous computing application scenarios limited application scenarios to these two types [2]. Besides, according to Milner [2], it is not possible to describe all concepts of ubiquitous computing by using a single model. Milner argued that the hierarchy structure of models (Milner called it "*a tower of models*") was necessary. In a tower of models, each higher model should be implemented by a lower model.

Following the notion of a tower of models, Yuzuru Tanaka once proposed the basic idea for describing ubiquitous computing application scenarios using a catalytic reaction network model [3]. This idea includes the following three models:

- At the first (lowest) level, the port matching model describes the federation mechanism between two SOs in close proximity to each other.
- At the second (middle) level, the graph rewriting model describes the dynamic change of federation structures among SOs.
- At the third (highest) level, the catalytic reaction network model describes application scenarios involving mutually related multiple federations.

In our previous work, Julia and Tanaka brushed up these three models and established a concrete tower of models by proving that a higher model surely implements a lower model [4]. Moreover, Julia's model implementation has error handling mechanisms assuming unexpected situations such as the connection failures between two SOs. Therefore, we can focus on the catalytic reaction network model for describing application scenarios of ubiquitous computing.

However, there are still challenges of establishing the verification method of the catalytic reaction network model. So far, when we made a scenario using the catalytic reaction network model, we could not prove easily whether a particular federation would occur because federations of multiple devices are formed by proximity sensitive connections between SOs. So when we discuss a scenario using the catalytic reaction network, we also need to consider the proximity relations of SOs.

In this paper, we propose a verification method of device-federation model based on catalytic reaction network. Basically we transform a scenario into a well-known state-transition model such as Kripke structure. This enables us to apply existing model checking verifiers. With this method, we can discuss the following things:

- Determining whether a property described in a linear

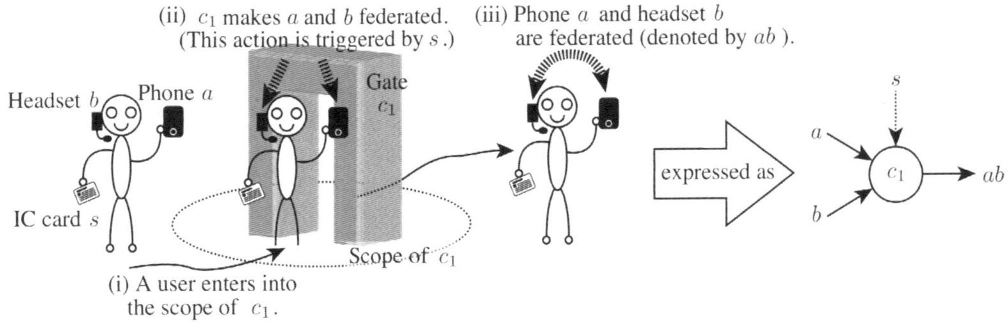

Figure 1. Example of a Catalytic Reaction

temporal logic (LTL) specification (e.g., a particular federation *finally* occured) is satisfied or not in the given scenario described by the catalytic reaction network model.
- Showing a counterexample if there is any case violating the property described above.

In a scenario using original catalytic reaction network model, there are so many proximity relations among SOs (n SOs would have 2^n proximity relations). This sometimes causes the state explosion problem in the model checking. We need to constrain the proximity relations in the original catalytic reaction network model. For this reason, we will first define the constrained model called "*Context Catalytic Reaction Network* (CCRN)." Then, we will propose the method to transform CCRN into a well-known state transition model such as a Kripke structure that can apply existing model checking verifiers.

The rest of this paper is organized as follows. The rest of this section introduces related work of our research. Section II provides preliminaries of this paper, such as basic definitions and notations. Using them, we define a CCRN in Section III. Then, we propose the verification method of a CCRN in Section IV. Section V introduces the case study of the verification. Finally, we summarize the results of this paper in Section VI.

A. Related Work

1) Formal Verification of Cyber Physical Systems: Similarly to ubiquitous computing, a lot of devices such as sensors measure physical phenomena such as temperature, humidity, acceleration and so on, while actuators manipulate the physical world, like in automated robots. The combination of an electronic system with a physical process is called cyber physical system (CPS). In the field of CPS, Drechsler and Kühne use *timed automata* [5] as a state transition model to conduct formal verifications of given systems' properties [6].

2) Context Inconsistency Detection: In the field of ambient computing, Xu and Cheung propose a method of context inconsistency detection [7]. This method detects inconsistencies from a series of gathered events such as "a user entered a room" and "the temperature of room is 30°C" by logical deduction. Unlike a formal verification, this method can be applied only after the system begins to work. Instead, a formal verification can find the failed cases from a given system *in advance*.

II. Preliminaries

In this section, we give definitions and notations which is necessary for this paper.

A. Basic Definitions and Notations

Let X and Y be any two sets, we use $X \cup Y$, $X \cap Y$ and $X \setminus Y$ to denote the union, intersection and difference of X and Y respectively. For a set X, we denote its power set (i.e., all subsets) by 2^X and its cardinality by $|X|$. For a family M of sets (i.e., a set of sets), we denote the union and the intersection of all sets in M by $\bigcup M$ and $\bigcap M$ respectively.

B. Catalytic Reaction Network

A catalytic reaction network was originally proposed by Stuart Kauffman in the field of biology to analyze protein metabolism [8]. Based on this model, Tanaka applied it to the field of ubiquitous computing as the way to describe an application scenario involving mutually related multiple federations among SOs [3]. In this paper, we mean the latter by the term "catalytic reaction network".

A catalytic reaction network is a set of catalytic reactions. Each catalytic reaction takes input materials and transforms them into output materials. And each catalytic reaction has a catalyst which is called *context*. It may be also possible to include a catalyst in input materials. We call this kind of catalyst *stimulus*. A catalytic reaction occurs when all required SOs are in the proximity of each other. We use the term "*scope*" to denote the inside of the proximity area (we assume a range of Wi-Fi radiowave, and so on). The scope of a SO o is represented as a set of SOs which are accessible from the SO o. Tanaka assumed that all scopes of the context and SOs involved in a catalytic reaction are considered [3]. However, as we mentioned in previous section, this causes the state explosion problem during the model checking. For this reason, in this paper, we assume that only the scopes of contexts are considered instead. In other words, we consider

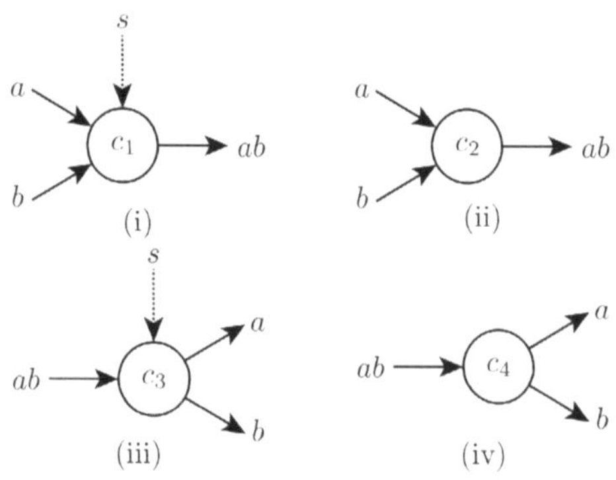

Figure 2. Four Types of a Catalytic Reactions

that the catalytic reaction occurs if all required SOs just enter into the scope of the corresponding context.

Fig. 1 shows an example of single catalytic reaction. In this example, there is a gate c_1 regarded as a context and a user has three SOs i.e., a phone a, a headset b and an IC card s. If the user enters into the scope of c_1, c_1 makes a and b federated. This action is triggered by s. After that, phone a and headset b are federated. We denote federated SOs such as a and b by a concatenation of a and b, i.e., ab. During this process, c_1 and s work as catalysts. In particular, s is a stimulus in this reaction. We express this reaction as the right hand side diagram of Fig. 1.

In catalytic reaction networks, there are four types of catalytic reactions as we show in Fig. 2. We categorize these four types of reactions into two groups. One group is the *composition* reaction group (Fig. 2 (i) and (ii)), the other group is the *decomposition* reaction group (i.e., Fig. 2 (iii) and (iv)). A catalytic reaction of Fig. 1 is a type (i) catalytic reaction. We also consider the catalytic reaction without a stimulus such as Fig. 2 (ii). In type (ii), if a user who has SO a and SO b enters into the scope of context c_2, c_2 makes a and b federated *without a stimulus*. In a similar way, we consider the decomposition reactions such as Fig. 2 (iii) and (iv). In type (iii), if a user who has two SOs that are federated into ab enters into the scope of context c_3, c_3 decomposes these SOs ab into a and b triggered by SO s. Type (iv) is a decomposition reaction without a stimulus.

The output SO of a reaction may promote other reactions as a stimulus or become an input SO of other reactions. In this way, catalytic reactions form a network of reactions.

Now we define a catalytic reaction network formally. First, let O be a set of SOs, we give a definition of a federated SO o_f by $o_f \in 2^O \setminus \emptyset$ where $|o_f| > 1$. If $|o_f| = 1$, we treat o_f as a single SO. Next, we define a catalytic reaction as follows:

Definition 1 (Catalytic Reaction): Let O and C be a set of SOs and a set of contexts respectively, a catalytic reaction is defined as a tuple (c, M, N) where

- $c \in C$, $M \subseteq 2^O \setminus \emptyset$, $N \subseteq 2^O \setminus \emptyset$
- $\forall o_f \forall o'_f \in M.(o_f \neq o'_f \rightarrow o_f \cap o'_f = \emptyset)$
- $\forall o_f \forall o'_f \in N.(o_f \neq o'_f \rightarrow o_f \cap o'_f = \emptyset)$
- $\bigcup M = \bigcup N$, and
- $(|M \cap N| + 1 = |N|, |M| > |N|) \vee$
  $(|M \cap N| + 1 = |M|, |M| < |N|) \quad (*)$

The former of the last condition (signed by $(*)$) and the latter of the last condition correspond to a necessary condition for composition reaction and decomposition reaction respectively.

We give some examples of catalytic reactions. Given $C = \{c_1, c_3\}, O = \{a, b, s\}$, a catalytic reaction of Fig. 2 (i) and (iii) can be defined by $(c_1, \{\{a\}, \{b\}, \{s\}\}, \{\{a, b\}, \{s\}\})$ and $(c_3, \{\{a, b\}, \{s\}\}, \{\{a\}, \{b\}, \{s\}\})$ respectively.

Finally, a catalytic reaction network is defined as follows:

Definition 2 (Catalytic Reaction Network): A catalytic reaction network is a set of catalytic reactions.

C. Model Checking

A model checking is a method to verify a property of a state transition system. It has been often used in various fields, which range from electronic-circuit-design verification [9] to secure-network-protocol (e.g., Secure Sockets Layer (SSL) protocol) design verification [10]. In the model checking, it is typically assumed to use a Kripke structure as a state transition system. The property of a Kripke structure is described by a modal logic. There are two kinds of commonly used modal logics such as *linear temporal logic (LTL)* and *computational tree logic (CTL)*. In this paper, we use LTL to describe the property of the Kripke structure.

1) Kripke Structure: Before we consider the details of a model checking, we give the definition of a Kripke structure [11] which is necessary for a modal logic and a model checking.

Definition 3 (Kripke Structure): Let *AP* be a set of atomic propositions, *a Kripke structrue* M is a tuple (S, I, R, L), where

- S is a finite set of states,
- $I \subseteq S$ is a set of initial states,
- $R \subseteq S \times S$ is a set of transition relation such that R is left-total, i.e., $\forall s \in S$, $\exists s' \in S$ such that $(s, s') \in R$, and
- $L : S \rightarrow 2^{AP}$ is a labeling function.

2) Linear Temporal Logic: LTL is a well-known modal logic. LTL was first proposed for the formal verification of computer programs by Amir Pnueil in 1977 [12]. First, we give a definition of LTL syntax.

Definition 4 (Linear Temporal Logic Syntax): Let *AP* be a set of atomic propositions, a linear temporal logic formula ϕ is defined by the following syntax recursively.

$$\phi ::= \top \mid \bot \mid p \mid \neg\phi \mid \phi \vee \phi \mid \mathbf{X}\,\phi \mid \mathbf{G}\,\phi \mid \mathbf{F}\,\phi \mid \phi\,\mathbf{U}\,\phi$$

where $p \in AP$.

These right-hand terms denote true, false, p, negation, disjunction, next time, always, eventually and until respectively.

Next, we define a transition path π of a Kripke structure M.

Definition 5 (Transition Path): Let M be a Kripke structure, $\pi = (\pi_0, \pi_1, \pi_2, \dots)$ is a transition path in M if it respects M's transition relation, i.e., $\forall i.(\pi_i, \pi_{i+1}) \in R$. π^i denotes π's ith suffix, i.e., $\pi^i = (\pi_i, \pi_{i+1}, \pi_{i+2}, \dots)$.

Also it can be shown that

$$\begin{aligned}(\pi^i)^j &= (\pi_i, \pi_{i+1}, \pi_{i+2}, \dots)^j \\ &= (\pi_{i+j}, \pi_{i+j+1}, \pi_{i+j+2}, \dots) \\ &= \pi^{i+j}.\end{aligned}$$

Now we focus on the semantics of linear temporal logic. First, we define the binary satisfaction relation, denoted by $\models$, for LTL formulae. This satisfaction is with respect to a pair – $\langle M, \pi \rangle$, a Kripke structure and a transition path. Then we enumerate LTL semantics as follows:

- $M, \pi \models \top$ (true is always satisfied)
- $M, \pi \not\models \bot$ (false is never satisfied)
- $(M, \pi \models p)$ iff $(p \in L(\pi_0))$ (atomic propositions are satisfied when they are members of the path's first element's labels)

And there are two LTL semantics of boolean combinations as follows:

- $(M, \pi \models \neg\phi)$ iff $(M, \pi \not\models \phi)$
- $(M, \pi \models \phi \vee \psi)$ iff $[(M, \pi \models \phi) \vee (M, \pi \models \psi)]$

And there are four LTL semantics of temporal operators as follows:

- $(M, \pi \models \mathbf{X}\ \phi)$ iff $(M, \pi^1 \models \phi)$
- $(M, \pi \models \mathbf{F}\ \phi)$ iff $[\exists i.(M, \pi^i \models \phi)]$
- $(M, \pi \models \mathbf{G}\ \phi)$ iff $[\forall i.(M, \pi^i \models \phi)]$
- $(M, \pi \models \phi\ \mathbf{U}\ \psi)$ iff $[(\forall j < i.(M, \pi^j \models \phi)) \wedge (M, \pi^i \models \psi)]$

3) Model Checking Problem: Intuitively saying, a model checking problem is to judge whether a given Kripke structure M satisfies a given property described in a modal logic formula ϕ. A model checking problem is formally stated as follows.

Definition 6 (Model Checking Problem): Given a desired property described by a modal logic formula ϕ (in this paper, we use LTL) and a Kripke structure M, a model checking problem is a decision problem whether the following formula

$$\forall \pi.(M, \pi \models \phi)$$

is satisfied or not. Note that a set $\{\pi \mid (M, \pi \not\models \phi)\}$ is particularly called *counterexamples*.
It is known that a model checking problem can be reduced to a graph search if M has finite states.

There are several implementations of the model checking verifier such as **S**imple **P**romela **IN**terpreter (SPIN) [13], **L**abel **T**ransition **S**ystem **A**nalyzer (LTSA) [14], **N**ew **S**ymbolic **M**odel **V**erifier version **2** (NuSMV2) [15] and so on. In this paper, we use a model checking verifier NuSMV2.

III. Context Catalytic Reaction Network

In this section, we introduce a segment graph and a CCRN.

A. Segment Graph

As we discussed in the previous section, a catalytic reaction occurs when the required SOs enter into the scope of the corresponding context. To analyze the property of a given catalytic reaction network as a state transition system, it is necessary to formalize the movement of SOs. For example, in Fig. 3 (i), there are contexts c_1 and c_2 and these scopes have an *overlap*. A user can walk around the path $\alpha\beta$ shown in Fig. 3 (i). This situation can be represented as a segment graph shown in Fig. 3 (ii). We consider that the user walks around this segment graph and the user is always located at one of the nodes of this segment graph. Each node of a segment graph has a corresponding set of scopes of contexts. In this way, the given situation like Fig. 3 (i) including overlaps of scopes of contexts can be represented as a discrete structure.

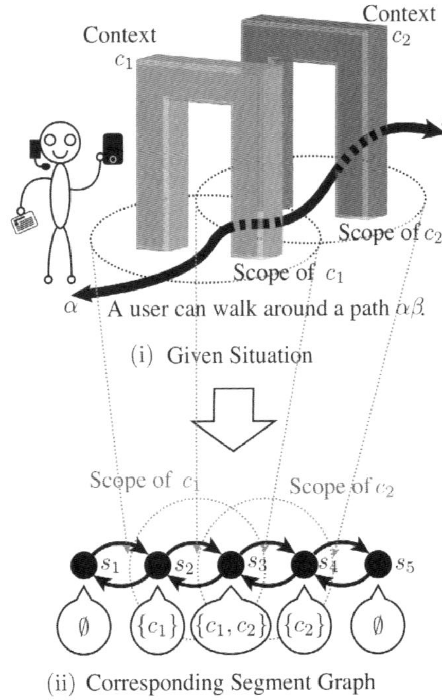

Figure 3. Example of Segment Graph

Now we define a segment graph as follows.

Definition 7 (Segment Graph): Let C be a set of contexts, a segment graph G is a tuple (S, E, F), where

- S is a finite set of segments,
- $E \subseteq S \times S$ is a set of directed edges between two segments, and
- $F : S \to 2^C$ is a function returning scopes of contexts at corresponding segments.

B. Context Catalytic Reaction Network

A context catalytic reaction network (CCRN) is a discrete structure of a situation involving SOs in a catalytic reaction network. A CCRN is defined as a conbination of a segment graph and a catalytic reaction network.

Definition 8 (Context Catalytic Reaction Network): A *CCRN* is a tuple $(O, C, R, G, L_{\mathrm{FIX}}, l_0)$, where

- O is a set of smart objects,
- C is a set of contexts,

- R is a set of catalytic reactions,
- G is a segment graph (S, E, F),
- $L_{\mathrm{FIX}} \subseteq O \times S$ is the locations of fixed SOs, and
- $l_0 \in S$ is the initial segment locating mobile SOs (mobile SOs can be represented as $O \setminus \{o \in O \mid \exists s \in S.((o, s) \in L_{\mathrm{FIX}})\}$).

IV. VERIFICATION METHOD OF A CCRN

In this section, we propose a verification method of a CCRN. Before discussing the details of the method, we assume that all mobile SOs are carried together (by a single user). A state of a CCRN can be represented as a combination of the location of mobile SOs (e.g., mobile SOs are located at segment s) and the presence of federated SOs (e.g., federated SOs o_f and o'_f are existing) and we regard these two kind of facts as atomic propositions. We use the following atomic propositions (AP):

- $loc_{O_{MOB}}(s)$: mobile SOs are located at segment s
- $fed(o_f)$: federated SOs o_f is existing

While mobile SOs move around a segment graph, more than one federated SOs may appear. For example, federated SOs $\{a, b\}$ and $\{c, d\}$ may appear at the same time. For that reason, we define a single state of the presence of federated SOs as the subset of 2^O (e.g., $\{\{a, b\}, \{c, d\}\}$ is a subset of $2^{\{a,b,c,d\}}$). But each SO can not be a part of more than one federated SOs. For example, we do not permit federated SOs like $\{a, b\}$ and $\{b, c\}$ are presented at the same time because SO b is a part of both of these two federated SOs. Considering this constraint, a set of states of presence of federated SOs can be represented as $O_F = \{\emptyset\} \cup \{o_F \mid o_F \subseteq 2^O, \forall o_f, o'_f \in o_F.(o_f \neq o'_f \rightarrow o_f \cap o'_f = \emptyset, \forall o_f \in o_F.(|o_f| > 1)\}$. Finally, we represent a state of a CCRN as $state(s, o_F)$ where s is the segment at which mobile SOs are located and o_F is the set of federated SOs. For example, $state(s_0, \{\{a, b\}, \{c, d\}\})$ means mobile SOs are located at segment s_0 and federated SOs $\{a, b\}$ and $\{c, d\}$ are existing.

Using the above representation of a state of a CCRN and atomic propositions, we conduct verification of a CCRN by constructing a Kripke structure from a given CCRN. Here we give an algorithm in Fig. 4 to construct a Kripke structure from a given CCRN. After constructing a Kripke structure from a CCRN, now we describe properties of a CCRN by LTL formulae. We enumerate examples of LTL formulae:

- $\mathbf{G}(\neg fed(o_f) \rightarrow \mathbf{F}(fed(o_f)))$
  Informally and intuitively saying, federated SOs o_f finally exists if o_f does not exist at the beginning and this always happens.
- $\mathbf{G}((\neg fed(o_f) \rightarrow \mathbf{F}(fed(o_f))) \vee (\neg fed(o'_f) \rightarrow \mathbf{F}(fed(o'_f))))$
  This means federated SOs o_f finally exists if o_f does not exist at the beginning. Similarly, federated SOs o'_f finally exists if o'_f does not exist at the beginning. At least one of these phenomena always happens.

Finally, we conduct the model checking, giving a Kripke structure and LTL formulae. This can be done by various implementations of model checking verifiers which we introduced in previous section.

Input: CCRN $(O, C, R, (S, E, F), L_{\mathrm{FIX}}, l_0)$
Output: Kripke Structure $(\mathcal{S}, \mathcal{I}, \mathcal{R}, \mathcal{L})$

Initialization :

$O_{MOB} = O \setminus \{o \in O \mid \exists s \in S.((o, s) \in L_{FIX})\}$
$O_F = \{\emptyset\} \cup \{o_F \mid o_F \subseteq 2^O, \forall o_f, o'_f \in o_F.(o_f \neq o'_f \rightarrow o_f \cap o'_f = \emptyset), \forall o_f \in o_F.(|o_f| > 1)\}$
$AP = \{loc_{O_{MOB}}(s) \mid s \in S\} \cup \{fed(o_f) \mid o_f \in o_F, o_F \in O_F\}$
$\mathcal{S} = \{state(s, o_F) \mid s \in S, o_F \in O_F\}$
$\mathcal{I} = state(l_0, \emptyset)$
$\mathcal{R} = \emptyset$

Loop Process :

for each $o_F \in O_F$ **do**
  for each $s \in S$ **do**
    $\mathcal{L}(state(s, o_F)) = \{loc_{O_{MOB}}(s)\} \cup \{fed(o_f) \mid o_f \in o_F\}$
    $S' = \{s' \mid (s, s') \in E\}$
    for each $s' \in S'$ **do**
      $R' = \{(c, M, N) \in R \mid c \in F(s'), \{o_f \in M \setminus N \mid |o_f| > 1\} \subseteq o_F, O(c) \supseteq \bigcup M\}$ where $O(c \in C) = O_{MOB} \cup \{o \in O \mid \exists s'' \in S.(c \in F(s''), (o, s'') \in L_{FIX})\}$
      if $R' \neq \emptyset$ **then**
        for each $(c, M, N) \in R'$ **do**
          choose $o'_F \in O_F$ s.t. $o_F \setminus o'_F = \{o_f \in M \setminus N \mid |o_f| > 1\}$, $o'_F \setminus o_F = \{o_f \in N \setminus M \mid |o_f| > 1\}$
          $\mathcal{R} = \mathcal{R} \cup \{(state(s, o_F), state(s', o'_F))\}$
        end for
      else
        $\mathcal{R} = \mathcal{R} \cup \{(state(s, o_F), state(s', o_F))\}$
      end if
    end for
  end for
end for
return $(\mathcal{S}, \mathcal{I}, \mathcal{R}, \mathcal{L})$

Figure 4. Algorithm for transforming CCRN into Kripke structure

V. CASE STUDY OF THE VERIFICATION

We have conducted a case study of a verification of a given CCRN, using a model checking. We assume that a CCRN is given by the designer who intend to design applications of ubiquitous computing. Here, we use an example of museum as shown in Fig. 5. A CCRN of this example is represented as a tuple $(O, C, R, (S, E, F), L_{FIX}, l_0)$ where

- $O = \{a, b, d, e, s\}$,
- $C = \{c_1, c_2, c_3, c_4, c_5, c_6\}$,
- $R = \{(c_1, \{\{a\}, \{b\}, \{s\}\}, \{\{a, b\}, \{s\}\}),$
  $(c_2, \{\{a, b\}, \{d\}\}, \{\{a, b, d\}\}),$
  $(c_3, \{\{a, b, d\}\}, \{\{a, b\}, \{d\}\}),$
  $(c_4, \{\{a, b\}, \{e\}\}, \{\{a, b, e\}\}),$
  $(c_5, \{\{a, b, e\}\}, \{\{a, b\}, \{e\}\}),$
  $(c_6, \{\{a, b\}, \{s\}\}, \{\{a\}, \{b\}, \{s\}\})\ \}$,
- $S = \{s_1, s_2, s_3, s_4, s_5, s_6, s_7, s_8, s_9\}$,

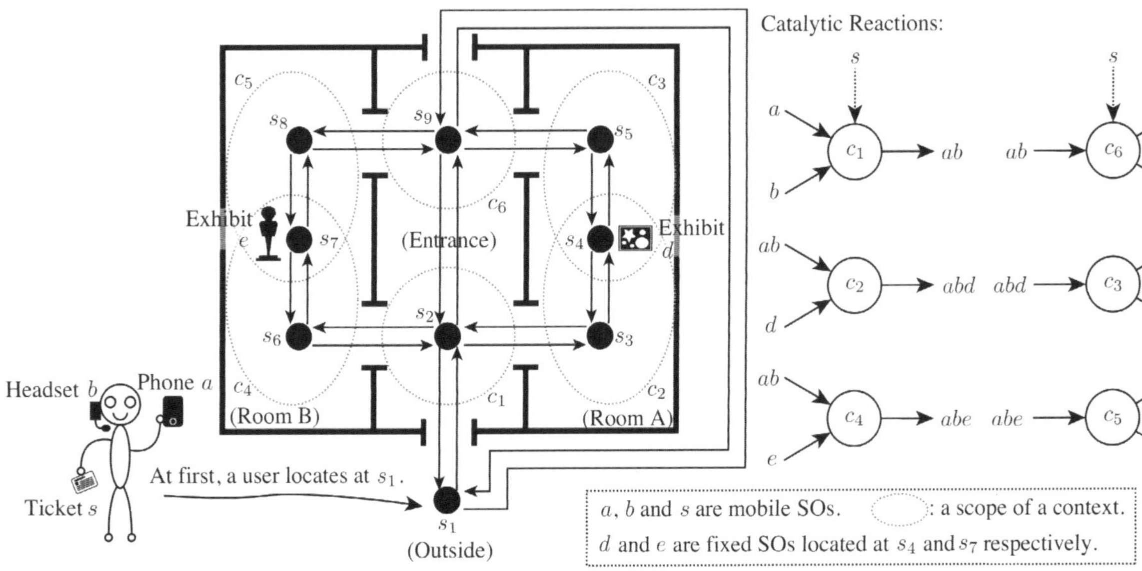

Figure 5. Example of Museum

- $E = \{(s_1, s_2), (s_2, s_1), (s_2, s_3), (s_3, s_2), (s_3, s_4), (s_4, s_3), (s_4, s_5), (s_5, s_4), (s_5, s_9), (s_9, s_5), (s_2, s_6), (s_6, s_2), (s_6, s_7), (s_7, s_6), (s_7, s_8), (s_8, s_7), (s_8, s_9), (s_9, s_8), (s_9, s_1), (s_1, s_9)\}$,
- $F = \{(s_1, \emptyset), (s_2, \{c_1\}), (s_3, \{c_2\}), (s_4, \{c_2, c_3\}), (s_5, \{c_3\}), (s_6, \{c_4\}), (s_7, \{c_4, c_5\}), (s_8, \{c_5\}), (s_9, \{c_6\})\}$,
- $L_{FIX} = \{(d, s_4), (e, s_7)\}$, and
- $l_0 = s_1$.

In this example, a user enters the entrance of a museum, carrying a phone a, a headset b and a ticket s. Once the user entered the entrance, the phone a and the headset b are federated by a reaction associated with the scope of c_1, which is triggered by the ticket s. Then, the federated SOs ab are worked as a voice guide of the museum. Next, if the user enters into room A, the federated SO ab and an exhibit d are federated by a reaction associated with the scope of c_2. By the federated SO abd, an explanation of the exhibit d can be provided to the user. After this, the user leaves the room A and the federated SO abd is decomposed and becomes ab again by a reaction associated with the scope of c_3. A similar reaction occurs in the room B, which is for an explanation of an exhibit e. If the user leaves one of the exhibition rooms and returns to the entrance, the federated SO ab is decomposed before leaving the museum.

Now we verify a CCRN of this example. Using an algorithm shown in Fig. 4, we can obtain a Kripke structure M. Then, the designer may give desired properties of the given CCRN by LTL formulae such as:

- $\phi_1 = \mathbf{G}(\neg(\mathit{fed}(\{a, b, d\}) \wedge \mathit{fed}(\{a, b, e\})))$, and
- $\phi_2 = \mathbf{G}(\ (\neg \mathit{fed}(\{a, b, d\}) \rightarrow \mathbf{F}(\mathit{fed}(\{a, b, d\}))) \vee (\neg \mathit{fed}(\{a, b, e\}) \rightarrow \mathbf{F}(\mathit{fed}(\{a, b, e\})))\ )$.

Intuitively saying, ϕ_1 means that no more than one federation for the explanation of exhibits exists at the same time and ϕ_2 means that if a user enters into one of the exhibition rooms, an explanation of each exhibit is always provided to a user.

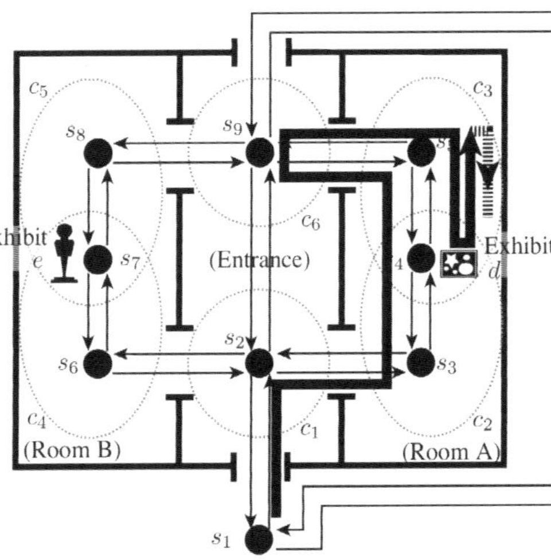

Figure 6. A Counterexample of Museum Example

Now we verify a CCRN using a generated Kripke structure M, ϕ_1 and ϕ_2. To conduct model checking, we used NuSMV2 as a model checking verifier. We have confirmed that $\forall \pi.(M, \pi \models \phi_1)$ is satisfied. However, $\forall \pi.(M, \pi \models \phi_2)$ is *not* satisfied. A model checking verifier also give a counterexample π_c such as

$$\pi_c = (\mathit{state}(s_1, \emptyset), \mathit{state}(s_2, \{\{a, b\}\}), \mathit{state}(s_3, \{\{a, b, d\}\}), \mathit{state}(s_4, \{\{a, b\}\}), \mathit{state}(s_5, \{\{a, b\}\}), \mathit{state}(s_9, \emptyset), \mathit{state}(s_5, \emptyset), \mathit{state}(s_4, \emptyset), \mathit{state}(s_5, \emptyset), \mathit{state}(s_4, \emptyset) \dots).$$

A bold line in Fig. 6 is the visualization of π_c. First, the

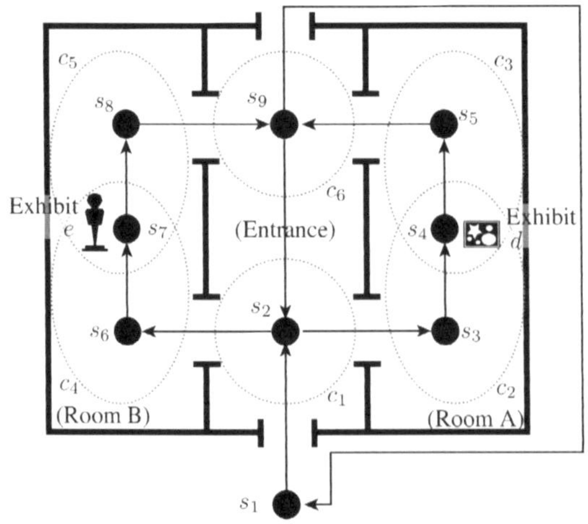

Figure 7. Revised Museum Example

user enters the entrance of the museum, then, the user goes to room A and goes away from room A. But the user enters the room A again from where the user goes away. Finally, the user stays there. In this situation, we never obtain the federated SO abd again since the user stays in the room A. To resolve this problem, we need appropriate constraints on the segment graph not to cause any counterexamples of ϕ_2 during model checking.

Now we *debug* the system to satisfy all properties of a given CCRN given by LTL formulae. To do so, we need to revise the segment graph of a given CCRN of this example. We have rewritten E of the given CCRN as follows (Fig. 7 is the visualization of this revision):

$$E = \{(s_1, s_2), (s_2, s_3), (s_3, s_4), (s_4, s_5), (s_5, s_9), (s_2, s_6), (s_6, s_7), (s_7, s_8), (s_8, s_9), (s_9, s_1)\}.$$

This revision indicates that the user should follow the *regular route* of the museum.

Then, we have conducted the model checking again using the revised Kripke structure M, ϕ_1 and ϕ_2. Finally, we have confirmed that both $\forall\pi.(M, \pi \models \phi_1)$ and $\forall\pi.(M, \pi \models \phi_2)$ are satisfied. If all of these two LTL formulae are satisfied, this museum meets all of requirements defined by the designer of this museum. Of course, the designer can try other properties within range of LTL, using a combination of two kinds of atomic propositions.

In this case study, we show that our method actually helps designers of applications to find exceptions of the design of applications and to debug these exceptions using counterexamples provided by model checking verifiers through trial and error. Using our method, we can discuss the property such as the validity and the safety of applications consisting of mutually related multiple federations among SOs. Formal approaches, such as this kind of verification, are important because they can avoid specifications errors of ubiquitous computing applications in advance of actual implementations of these applications, which may incur additional costs.

VI. Conclusion and Future Work

In this paper, we proposed a verification method of applications which is described by a CCRN using model checking. Using our framework, various properties of scenarios of ubiquitous computing can be discussed by logic such as LTL. At this time, we have considered only the case of a single user but in future work, we will also consider the case of multiple users. Namely, more than one user moves around, carrying SOs simultaneously. This will enable us to consider more complex applications of ubiquitous computing.

Acknowledgment

Our work is partly supported by JSPS KAKENHI(S) 15H05711.

References

[1] M. Weiser, "The Computer for the 21st Century," *Scientific American*, vol. 265, no. 3, pp. 94–104, sep 1991.

[2] R. Milner, "Theories for the global ubiquitous computer," in *Foundations of Software Science and Computation Structures*. Springer, 2004, pp. 5–11. [Online]. Available: http://www.springerlink.com/index/h0261v5xde0qegef.pdf

[3] Y. Tanaka, "Proximity-based federation of smart objects: liberating ubiquitous computing from stereotyped application scenarios," in *Knowledge-Based and Intelligent Information and Engineering Systems*. Springer, 2010, pp. 14–30. [Online]. Available: http://www.springerlink.com/index/103TL30123728248.pdf

[4] J. Julia and Y. Tanaka, "Proximity-based federation of smart objects," *Journal of Intelligent Information Systems*, vol. 46, no. 1, pp. 147–178, feb 2016. [Online]. Available: http://link.springer.com/10.1007/s10844-015-0357-4

[5] R. Alur and D. L. Dill, "A theory of timed automata," *Theoretical Computer Science*, vol. 126, no. 2, pp. 183–235, apr 1994. [Online]. Available: http://linkinghub.elsevier.com/retrieve/pii/0304397594900108

[6] R. Drechsler and U. Kühne, Eds., *Formal Modeling and Verification of Cyber-Physical Systems*. Wiesbaden: Springer Fachmedien Wiesbaden, 2015. [Online]. Available: http://link.springer.com/10.1007/978-3-658-09994-7

[7] C. Xu and S. C. Cheung, "Inconsistency Detection and Resolution for Context-aware Middleware Support," *Proceedings of the 10th European Software Engineering Conference Held Jointly with 13th ACM SIGSOFT International Symposium on Foundations of Software Engineering*, pp. 336–345, 2005. [Online]. Available: http://doi.acm.org/10.1145/1081706.1081759

[8] S. Kauffman, *Investigations*. Oxford New York: Oxford University Press, 2002.

[9] J. Burch, E. Clarke, K. McMillan, and D. Dill, "Sequential circuit verification using symbolic model checking," in *27th ACM/IEEE Design Automation Conference*, vol. 13, no. 4. IEEE, 1994, pp. 46–51. [Online]. Available: http://ieeexplore.ieee.org/lpdocs/epic03/wrapper.htm?arnumber=114827

[10] J. C. Mitchell, V. Shmatikov, and U. Stern, "Finite-state Analysis of SSL 3.0," in *Proceedings of the 7th Conference on USENIX Security Symposium - Volume 7*, ser. SSYM'98. Berkeley, CA, USA: USENIX Association, 1998, p. 16. [Online]. Available: http://dl.acm.org/citation.cfm?id=1267549.1267565

[11] S. A. Kripke, "Semantical Analysis of Modal Logic I Normal Modal Propositional Calculi," *Zeitschrift für Mathematische Logik und Grundlagen der Mathematik*, vol. 9, no. 5-6, pp. 67–96, 1963.

[12] A. Pnueli, "The temporal logic of programs," *18th Annual Symposium on Foundations of Computer Science (sfcs 1977)*, pp. 46–57, 1977.

[13] G. Holzmann, "The model checker SPIN," *IEEE Transactions on Software Engineering*, vol. 23, no. 5, pp. 279–295, may 1997.

[14] J. Magee and J. Kramer, *Concurrency State Models and Java Programs*. New York, New York, USA: John Wiley and Sons, 1999.

[15] A. Cimatti, E. Clarke, and E. Giunchiglia, "Nusmv 2: An opensource tool for symbolic model checking," *Computer Aided Verification*, vol. 2404, pp. 359–364, 2002. [Online]. Available: http://link.springer.com/chapter/10.1007/3-540-45657-0_29

Network Layer Dependability Benchmarking: Route Identification

Maroua Belkneni
University of Tunis El Manar
Tunis, Tunisia
Email: belknenimaroua@gmail.com

M.Taha Bennani
and Samir Ben Ahmed
University of Tunis El Manar,University of Carthage
Tunis, Tunisia
Email: Taha.Bennani@enit.rnu.tn
Email: Samir.benahmed@fst.rnu.tn

Ali Kalakech
Lebanese University
Beirut, Lebanon
Email: akalakech@ul.edu.lb

Abstract—**The use of wireless sensor networks (WSN) is widespread; it covers, particularly, environmental and critical systems monitoring. Since the structure of the WSN has various layers including the application, the routing, the transfer, the Media Access Control(MAC) and the Radio Frequency(RF) Media, its dependability evaluation can be challenging. This paper defines the essential components of the network layers' benchmark, which are: the target, the execution profile, and the robustness measure. The dependability assessment is addressed in our benchmark by focusing on three standard protocols: Ad-Hoc on Demand Distance Vector Protocol (AODV), Optimized Link State Routing Protocol (OLSR) and Destination Sequence Distance Vector Routing Protocol (DSDV). The NS-3 simulator was used for the test bed. After the evaluation campaigns, we noticed that the DSDV and AODV protocols have an equivalent robustness. OLSR is the least robust but it is a fail-safe protocol.**

Keywords–Dependability; WSN; route discovery; assessment.

I. INTRODUCTION

A sensor node is made up of a processing unit, memory, RF transceiver, power source, and boards various sensors and actuators [2]. A large number of sensor nodes gathered in a wireless sensor network communicate in an ad hoc fashion and transmit measurements to the end user to monitor, track or detect the region in which they are deployed. Threats such as natural catastrophes, criminal or terrorist attacks have targeted Critical infrastructures (CI). Therefore, the use of WSN [8] based solutions could be a real shield to protect CIs. The deployment of such a solution helps avoid failures and possible loss of human life.

The goal of dependability benchmarking is to provide generic ways to characterize the behavior of components and computer systems in the presence of faults, which allows the quantification of reliability measures [5]. To perform such analysis, a widely accepted technique in the literature is the fault injection. It represents the observation of the system behavior in response to deliberately introduced faults. Thus, meeting the challenging task of developing dependable sensor networks requires not only the fault-tolerant sensing and actuating capabilities but also the evaluation and validation of their dependability attributes. We use a fault injection-based evaluator that deliberately accelerates the occurrence of faults to evaluate the quality of error handling mechanisms and, more generally, to analyze the dependability of the sensor network [1]. The remainder of this paper is organized as follows: Section 2 surveys some of the most relevant research works on dependability benchmarking for WSN. In Section 3, we describe the benchmark target. Next, in Section 4, the execution profile is held. Section 5 defines the faultload specification. Section 6 describes measurements and simulation results. Finally, Section 7 concludes the paper and presents directions for future studies.

II. RELATED WORKS

Some works propose a survey on adopted techniques of reporting the aspects and characteristics of some research studies. Here, we analyze the current state of the art of the WSN dependability assessment approaches in order to identify the most performant and to discuss the ongoing challenges.
A recent bibliography has categorized the approaches evaluating the WSN dependability attributes into three classes: experimental, simulative, and analytical [9]. For example, authors in [14] introduce an algorithm identifying faulty sensors which misbehave through calibration error, random noise error, and complete malfunctioning. In [15], authors present an analytical approach using an adapted probabilistic graph to model the network behavior. They associate an operational probability to each node, achieved using a data analysis field on the real sensors. The authors claim that components wear out, power failures and in some cases, natural catastrophes may lead to failures. They proved that evaluating the reliability of an arbitrary WSN is a non-deterministic polynomial-time hard problem for random networks. In [6], Heinzelman et al. provide an analytical model used to forecast the power consumption and thus the lifetime of the network. In [7], Mini et al. present a network state model to forecast the network residual energy. This work can have two different objectives, namely the evaluation of performance or dependability. In the first case, a set of measures is usually used to compare different solutions. Corson et al. [16] describe a number of quantitative parameters that can be used to evaluate the performance of MANET routing protocols, such as, packet delivery ratio, routing overhead, normalized routing overhead, Average End-to-End Delay (second), Packet Loss and Throughput (packet / second). In [17], Rahman et al. present the following measures: Remaining Battery Power, Power Consumed and MAC Load Dropped Packets. In contrast the dependability measures, rather we use the following measures: Network reliability, Sensing reliability, time-to-failure, timeto-recovery [12]. We can also use Node Uptime and Mean Time To Failure (MTTF), which were defined as reward variables in the Mobius tool [18]. In [13], Koushanfar et al. define a taxonomy for the faults of WSNs. Inconsistent measurement provided by a sensor, offset bias, death of a sensor, and idle reading are four different kinds of faults. Network reliability, sensing reliability, time-to-failure, and time-to-recovery are the key components of the

dependability measurements used by Chipara et al. [12].
To perform such analysis, a widely accepted technique in the literature is the fault injection. It consists in the observation of the system behavior as a response to deliberately introduced defects. Thus, meeting the challenging task of developing reliable sensor networks requires not only the fault-tolerant sensing and actuating capabilities but also the definition of the evaluation process to validate the dependability attributes. Our goal is to set the foundations of a fault injection-based evaluator that handles errors and analyzes the reliability of the sensor network [1].

III. Benchmark target

The network layer provides two services, namely, route identification and route maintenance. This paper addresses the dependability assessment of the first service. The MANET routing protocols maintain the routes of the MANET and do not require any infrastructure to connect with other nodes in the network. Ad hoc routing protocols can broadly be classified into proactive, reactive and hybrid protocols. Proactive protocols, also known as table-driven protocols (i.e., DSDV, OLSR, Fisheye State Routing (FSR)), maintain routes between nodes in the network at all times, including the situation when the routes are not currently being used. Reactive protocols, also known as on-demand protocols (i.e., AODV, DSR, Temporally Ordered Routing Algorithm (TORA)), involve discovering routes to other nodes only when they are needed. A route discovery process is invoked when a node wishes to communicate with another for which it has no route table entry. There exists another class of protocols, such as zone routing protocols (ZRP), which employs a combination of proactive and reactive methods [19]. Even though similar studies have been carried out previously [10][11], this paper provides a comparative succinct view of DSDV, OLSR and AODV protocols. Hence, the OLSR builds up a route by maintaining a routing table at every node of the network. The topology information, which is exchanged using Topology Control (TC) packets builds the routing table. OLSR uses the HELLO messages to find its one-hop neighbors and its two-hop neighbors through their responses. The sender can, as a result, select its MultiPoint Relays (MPR) based on the one-hop node that identifies the best routes to the two-hop nodes. In DSDV, each node maintains an entry to the table containing the address' identifier of the destination, the shortest known distance metric to that destination measured in terms of hops, and the address identifier of the node that is the first hop on the shortest path to the target [4]. In reactive routing, AODV broadcasts a Route Request (RREQ) to all its neighbors. Then it propagates the RREQ through the network, unless, it reaches either the destination or the node holding the newest route to the destination. The destination node sends back an RREP response to the source to prove the validity of the route [3].
The "`send()`" operation responsible for sending the packet, a protocol data unit (PDU) messages and delivers it to the lower layers, whereas the "`Receive()`" operation provides the requests response. These two activities define services offered by the Transport Layer. All studied network protocols, AODV, OLSR, and DSDV, have the same provided service. Nevertheless, several differences exist and belong not only to the handled message's structure but also to the mechanisms used to establish, deliver and retrieve the exchanged communications.

IV. Execution profile

The execution profile activates the target system with either a realistic or a synthetic workload. Unlike performance benchmarking, which includes only the workload, the dependability assessment also needs the definition of the faultload. In this section, we describe the structure and the behavior of the workload.

A. *Workload structure*

To apply our approach to a real structure, we chose to monitor the stability of a bridge. Figure 1 introduces the topology of the nodes which is a 3D one. In our experiments, we vary the number of nodes within the range of 10 to 50 (see Table I). The more nodes we define, the more dependable the structure. With ten nodes, the structure has one redundant path between the source node and the sink. Then, even though one node had failed, the emitter node would have transmitted a packet to the sink. When the structure has more nodes, it will tolerate more than one node failure.

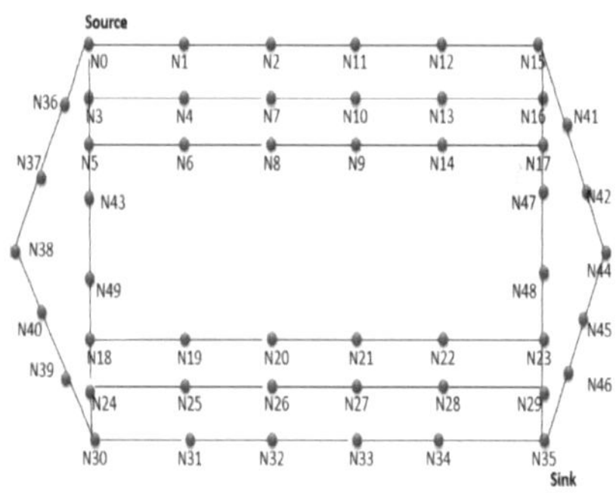

Figure 1: Scheme of the considered bridge and resulting topology

B. *Workload behavior*

As the assessed service is the route establishment by the network protocols, our workload consists of the sending of a packet from a source to the sink node. Table I below summarizes the simulation parameters.
Our study is carried within the NS-3 simulator, and Table I depicts the simulations' parameters implementing our experiments. We use the wireless channel and Mac802.11 to send the information throughout the nodes of the wireless sensors network. Before sending 512 bytes of useful data information, network protocol builds up the route between the sender node and the sink. We target, in our experiments, three different and

TABLE I: SIMULATION PARAMETERS

Network Simulator	NS3
Channel type	Channel/Wireless channel
MAC type	Mac/802.11
Routing Protocol	AODV, OLSR, DSDV
Simulation Time	100 s
Number of Nodes	10, 20, 30, 40, 50
Data payload	512 bytes
Initial energy	10J

representative network protocols: AODV, OLSR, and DSDV. Different scenarios may raise various observations within a variable time duration; then each simulation lasts 100 seconds. To avoid running out of energy, we initialize our network with 10 joules.

V. FAULTLOAD SPECIFICATION

It would be troublesome to identify the origin of the failure using multiple modifications. Therefore, to avoid the correlation drawback, our benchmark assesses the WSN behavior using a single fault injection. As the source node triggers the communication and the route construction, we will inject faults within the packets it creates. Nevertheless, we have designed three different origins of flaws: the source, the gateway, and the destination. Even though the failures' root is not the emitters' node, we will inject various faults, described in Table II below, within the parameters of the primitive "send" belonging to the interface of the network layer.
The Table II introduces three set of elements: Fixed variables,

TABLE II: THE VARIABLE DECLARATION

Fixed variables (fault injection)	
F_Model	Fault model (injection into the source, the intermediate or the destination node)
F_Type:	Fault node or non existing node.
saddr:	The source IPV4 address.
Crpd_saddr:	The corrupted source address.
daddr:	The destination IPV4 Address.
Crpd_daddr:	The corrupted destination address.
sport:	The source port number.
Crpd_sport:	The corrupted source port number.
dport:	The destination port number.
Crpd_dport:	The corrupted destination port number.
RS:	The source IPV4 route address.
Crpd_RS:	The corrupted source route address.
RD:	The destination IPV4 route address.
Crpd_RD:	The corrupted destination route address.
RG:	The gateway IPV4 route address.
Crpd_RG:	The corrupted gateway route address.
State variables	
NP	The number of control packets.
Rate	The rate of injection.
NCP_Total	The total number of control packet.
Control functions	
SetDestination(Ipv4Address dest)	Set destination address.
SetGateway(Ipv4Address gw)	Set gateway address.
SetSource(Ipv4Address src)	Set source address.

state variables, and control functions which are mandatory to specify the faultload. Fixed variables are the elementary parameters of the fault, they identify the packet's fields, which are the saddr, daddr, etc. and their relative corrupted values, that are the Crpd_saddr, Crpd_daddr, etc. Also, the fault model specifies the faulty node which could be the source, intermediate or destination node and the fault type initializes the node's address using a random value belonging to the network or an imaginary one. All these values have to stay constant during one simulation. The state variables identify the behavior of the simulation evolution using three different variables: Total number of control packets (NCP_Total), the number of packets (NP) and the injection ratio (Rate). The three functions, belonging to the "Control functions", change the source, gateway or destination addresses.

The Computation Tree Logic (CTL) formulae written below specify the faultload used to assess the dependability of the routing layer.
The expressions (1), (6) and (10) specify the fault model respectively, a fault injection within the source, gateway and destination node. The fault type can take a false value of another node within our architecture or a value of a non existing one. When we inject in the source node, the fault may cover three fields: Saddr(3), sport(3) or route (source)(4). The expression (8) indicates that the fault targets the route (gateway). In the destination injection, the fault may alter these following fields: Daddr(12), dport(12) or route (destination)(13). Fault injection is realized by an injection rate which is the ratio of modified packets over the total number of control packets sent as shown in the expressions (5), (9) and (14).

Source injection:

$$(F\_Model = source \wedge \quad (1)$$
$$(F\_Type = fault \vee non\_existing) \wedge \quad (2)$$
$$(saddr = Crpd\_saddr \vee sport = Crpd\_sport \vee \quad (3)$$
$$RS = SetSource(Crpd\_RS))) \quad (4)$$
$$\models \Box \quad (NP \leqslant rate * NCP\_Total) \quad (5)$$

Gateway injection:

$$(F\_Model = gateway \wedge \quad (6)$$
$$(F\_Type = fault \vee non\_existing) \wedge \quad (7)$$
$$(RG = SetGateway(Crpd\_RG))) \quad (8)$$
$$\models \Box \quad (NP \leqslant rate * NCP\_Total) \quad (9)$$

Destination injection:

$$(F\_Model = destination \wedge \quad (10)$$
$$(F\_Type = fault \vee non\_existing) \wedge \quad (11)$$
$$(daddr = Crpd\_daddr \vee dport = Crpd\_dport \vee \quad (12)$$
$$RD = SetDestination(Crpd\_RD))) \quad (13)$$
$$\models \Box \quad (NP \leqslant rate * NCP\_Total) \quad (14)$$

VI. MEASUREMENTS AND SIMULATION RESULTS

In addition to the performance measures as the remaining energy and the route identification time, we define the robustness :

- Remaining energy: Is the average of remaining energy of all nodes.
- Time of route identification: It is the time taken by a protocol to find a route to the destination.
- Robustness: the limit injection rate beyond which the protocol does not discover the route.

We will present the results and analyze them. The obtained simulation results are viewed in the form of line graphs. The study of AODV, OLSR and DSDV is based on the varying of the workload and the faultload.

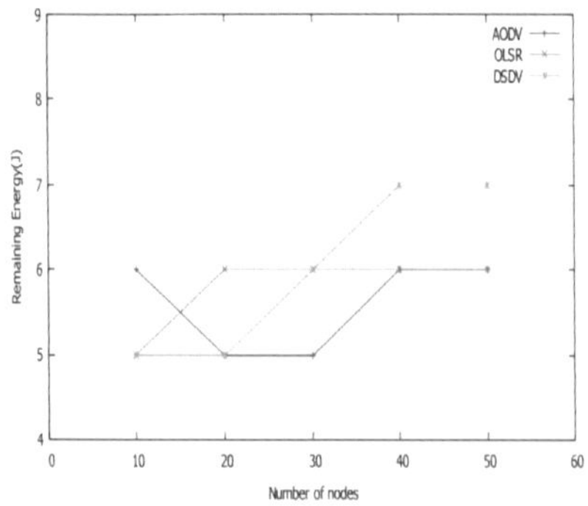

Figure 2: Fault free simulation: Remaining Energy

Figure 2 shows that DSDV consumed less energy than AODV and OLSR, especially when the number of nodes increases because the area size increases and consequently the nodes send more control packets to determine the route which preserves energy. The flow of AODV and OLSR are very close to each other, but AODV used the highest amounts of energy with 20 and 30 nodes.

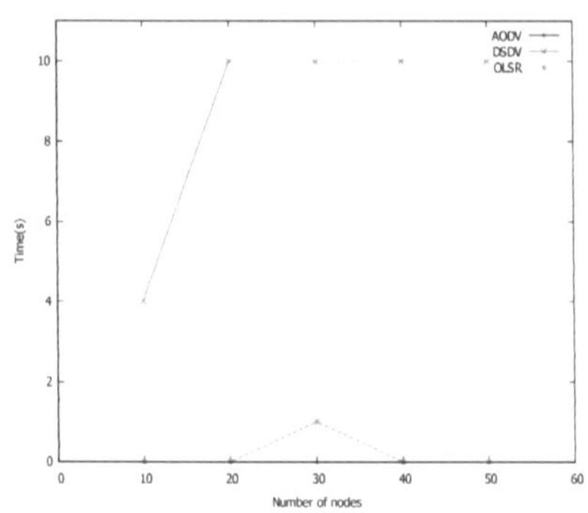

Figure 3: Fault free simulation: Identification time

In Figure 3, we note that AODV is the fastest protocol to find the route and OLSR the slowest one. DSDV has to continuously update the whole routing table periodically and when needed, which leads to a slight delay in delivery compared to AODV.

The three protocols are robust to the saddr and daddr fields injection, i.e., they identify the route. Moreover, the perfermances remain unchanged.

OLSR is not robust to the sport and route(source) fields injection. That is to say, it does not identify the route and it does not consume energy. However, AODV and DSDV are robust to the injection and, in addition, they keep the same performance as the fault free scenario.

DSDV is robust by contribution to the injection into the dport fields without changing perfermance. However AODV cannot find the route, but it preserves the energy consumption. OLSR shows a robustness rate equal to 97%. As shown in Figs. 4 and 5, the remaining energy and the time of route identification with OLSR, increases proportionally with the injection rate. However, the energy consumption decreases because the control packet does't require an increased energy consumption.

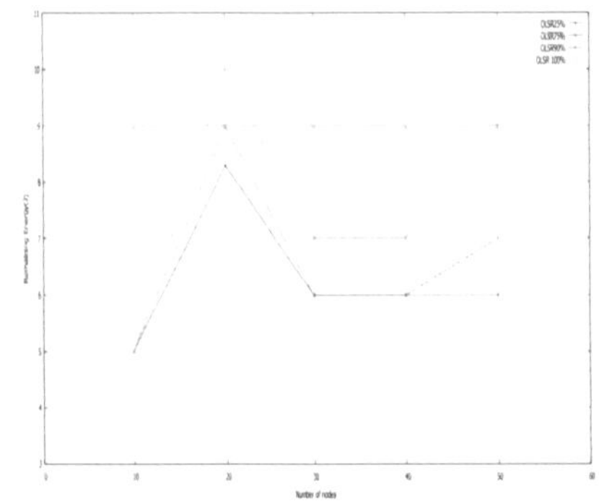

Figure 4: OLSR measures: Remaining Energy

As shown in Figure 4, the 25% injection curve is the lowest and the 90% curve is the highest one because the protocol sends more control packets. On the other hand the 100% injection curve is constant because OLSR does not identify the route and it does not consume energy.

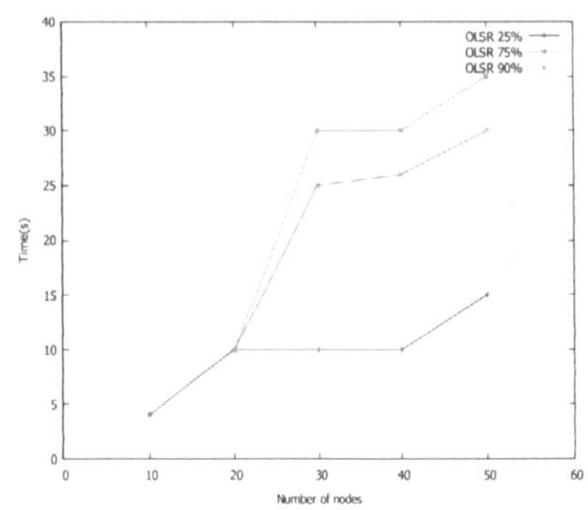

Figure 5: OLSR measures: Identification time

Figure 5 shows that OLSR takes more time to identify the route when the injection rate increases.

AODV is robust to the injection in route(destination) field. OLSR does not realize the service and does not consume energy. The DSDV behavior is based on the fault injection rates and the node number. However, with 10 nodes it crashes with 75% injection. 80% with 20 nodes, 90% with 30, and 95% with 40 and 50 nodes, as shown in Figure 6.

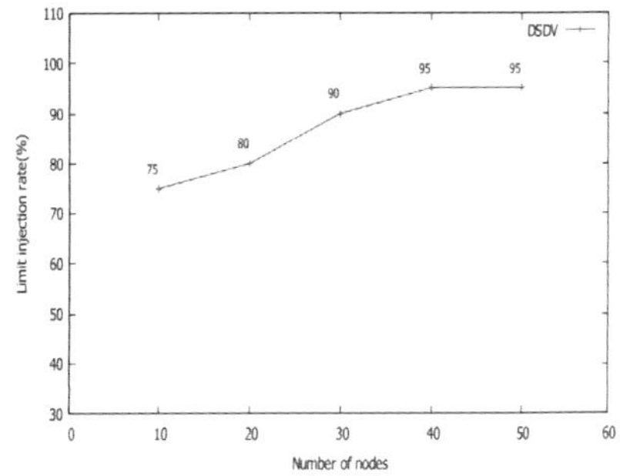

Figure 6: DSDV robustess

The three protocols are not robust to the route(Gateway) injection. Nevertheless, the fault injection leads to a total decrease in energy consumption with AODV and DSDV. It explains that all packets are either a control or a routing (RTR) packet. In fact, we notice the OLSR does not consume energy because it stops quickly. The limit injection rate of DSDV is 95% and of OLSR is lower than 10%.

Figure 7 shows a summary description of protocols robustness.

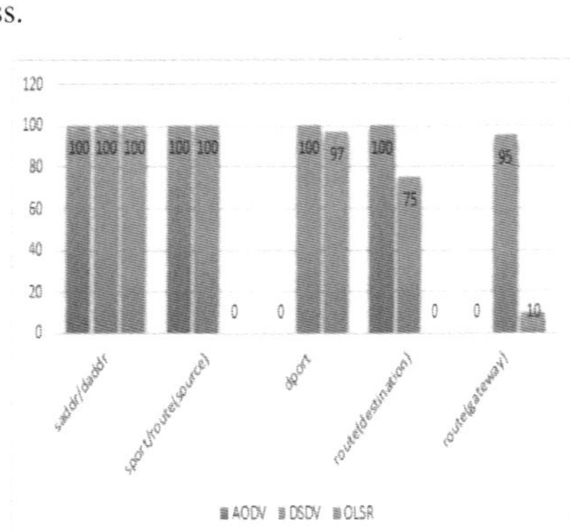

Figure 7: Protocols robustness

VII. Conclusion

The absence of an appropriate system for WSN dependability forces developers to conduct exhausting testing campaigns. Independent verification of each network layer reliability is not sufficient to guarantee the dependability of WSN, but rather makes a comparison between two or three layers. To tackle this problem, we have presented a network layer dependability benchmarking. We started by introducing the dimensions of the benchmark such as the target system, workload, faultload and measurements. We defined the robustness measure that represents the injection rate beyond what the service is no longer provided. After the evaluation campaigns, we noticed that the DSDV and AODV protocols have an equivalent robustness. The first one fails with the route(gateway) and route(destination) fields injection. The second is sensitive to the route(gateway) and dport injections field. OLSR is the least robust but it is a fail-safe protocol. However at the injection, the route is not discovered, but the energy is preserved. Our future work will include a new fault profile and a consideration of sensor nodes mobility with a real world case and the second service dependability (route maintenance).

References

[1] F. Sailhan, T. Delot, A. Pathak, A. Puech, and M. Roy, *Dependable Sensor Networks*, Atelier sur la GEstion des Donnes dans les Systmes d'Information Pervasifs (GEDSIP) au sein de la confrence INFormatique des ORganisations et Systmes dInformation et de Dcision (INFORSID), May 2010, pp. 1-15.

[2] I. F. Akyildiz, W. Su, Y. Sankarasubramaniam and E. Cayirci, *Wireless Sensor Network: A Survey*, IEEE Communications Magazine, Vol. 40, No. 8, 2002, pp. 102-114.

[3] S. Kumari, S. Maakar , S. Kumar and R. K. Rathy, *Traffic pattern based performance comparison of aodv, dsdv and olsr manet routing protocols using freeway mobility model*, International Journal of Computer Science and Information Technologies, 2011, pp. 1606-1611.

[4] E. Spaho, M. Ikeda, L. Barolli, F. Xhafa, M. Younas and M. Takizawa, *Performance of olsr and dsdv protocols in a vanet scenario: Evaluation using cavenet and ns3*, 2012 Seventh International Conference, 2012, pp. 108-113.

[5] K. Kanoun and Y. Crouzet, *Dependabiliy Benchmark for Operating Systems*, International Journal of Performability Engineering, July 2006, pp. 275-287.

[6] W. Heinzelman, A. Chandrakasan and H. Balakrishnan, *Energy efficient routing protocol for wireless microsensor networks*. "In Proc. of Hawaii International Conference on System Sciences", HICSS00, 2000, pp. 1-2.

[7] A. Mini, B. Nath, and A. Loureiro, *A probabilistic approach to predict the energy consumption in wireless sensor networks*. "4thWorkshop de Comunicao sem Fio e Computao Mvel", So Paulo, Brazil, 2002.

[8] L. Buttyan, D. Gessner, A. Hessler, and Peter. Langendoerfer, *Application of wireless sensor networks in critical infrastructure protection: challenges and design options [Security and Privacy in Emerging Wireless Networks]*, "IEEE Wireless Communications is designed for individuals working in the communications and networking communities", Vol. 17, No. 5, 2010, pp.44-49.

[9] M. Cinque, D. Cotroneo, C. Di Martinio, and S. Russo, *Modeling and Assessing the Dependability of Wireless Sensor Networks*, Reliable Distributed Systems, SRDS 2007. "26th IEEE International Symposium on", 2007, pp. 33-44.

[10] G. Z. Santoso and M. Kang, *Performance analysis of AODV, DSDV and OLSR in a VANETs safety application scenario*, Advanced Communication Technology (ICACT), 2012 14th International Conference on 2012, pp. 57-60.

[11] R. Kaur and C. Sharma, *Review paper on performance analysis of AODV, DSDV, OLSR on the basis of packet delivery*, IOSR Journal of Computer Engineering (IOSR-JCE), Issue 1 (May. - Jun. 2013), pp. 51-55.

[12] O. Chipara, C. Lu, T.C. Bailey, and G.-C. Roman, *Reliable Clinical Monitoring Using Wireless Sensor Networks: Experiences in a Step-down Hospital Unit*, "Proceedings of the 8th ACM Conference on Embedded Networked Sensor Systems", Vol.14, 2010, pp. 155-168.

[13] F. Koushanfar, M. Potkonjak, and A. Sangiovanni-Vincentelli. *Online fault detection of sensor measurements*. "Proceedings second IEEE international conference on sensors (Sensors 03)", Vol.2, 2003, pp. 974979.

[14] J. Chen, S. Kher and A. Somani. *Distributed fault detection of wireless sensor networks*. "DIWANS 06: Proc. of the 2006 workshop on Dependability issues in wireless ad hoc networks and sensor networks", 2006, pp. 6572.

[15] HMF AboElFotoh, SS. Iyengar, and K. Chakrabarty. *Computing reliability and message delay for Cooperative wireless distributed sensor networks subject to random failures*. "Reliability, IEEE Transactions on", 2005, pp. 145155.

[16] S. Corson and J. Macker, *Routing Protocol Performance Issues and Evaluation considerations*, RFC2501, IETF Network Working Group, January 1999.

[17] A. Rahman, S. Islam, and A. Talevski, *Performance Measurement of various Routing Protocol in Ad-Hoc Network* , "IMECS", Vol. 1, March 2009, pp. 321-323.

[18] W. H. Sanders and L. M. Malhis. Dependability evaluation using composed SAN-based reward models. "Journal of Parallel and Distributed Computing 15",1992, pp. 238254.

[19] A. Kumar, M. Q. Rafiq, and K. Bansal, *Performance Evaluation of Energy Consumption in MANET*, "International Journal of Computer Applications (0975 8887)", Vol. 42, No.2, March 2012.

Towards Security Solutions in IoT Sensor Network and Middleware

A Systematic mapping

Cícero Woshington Saraiva Leite
FJN-Faculdade de Juazeiro do Norte
Juazeiro do Norte, Brasil
email:cicerow.ordb@gmail.com

Leonardo Lourenço Lacerda
CESAR-Centro de Estudos e Sistemas Avançados do Recife
Maceió, Brasil
email:leonardolacerda.as@gmail.com

Fábio Lucas Faleiro Naves
CESAR-Centro de Estudos e Sistemas Avançados do Recife
Iporá, Brasil
email:fabionaves@gmail.com

Cícero Samuel Clemente Rodrigues
FJN-Faculdade de Juazeiro do Norte
Juazeiro do Norte, Brasil
email:samuelclerod@gmail.com

Geiziany Mendes da Silva
FJN-Faculdade de Juazeiro do Norte
Juazeiro do Norte, Brasil
email:geiziany.mendes@gmail.com

Abstract — Internet of Things (IoT) is present in several environments, from houses to large health care institutions. Data flows from small sensors and actuators to large data centers and cloud computer services. Small sensors and actuators need to guarantee data confidentiality, availability and integrity, even with limited resources. This paper presents a systematic mapping outlining problems and solutions studied in the last three years about middleware and sensors network security. The process used to select, filter and analyze articles is described and the results indicate efforts to certify integrity, availability and, especially, confidentiality.

IoT; Middleware; Sensor Network.

I. INTRODUCTION

The term Internet of Things (IoT) was first proposed in 1999, in an article of the RFID Journal, when a supply chain was interconnected with an enterprise using Radio Frequency Identification (RFID) [1]. According to Khan, an IoT environment has to promote connectivity with everything and everyone [2], through a group of interconnected sensors, providing a set of relevant information for a computer decision support system.

According to Business Insider, almost $6 trillion must be invested in solutions using IoT in the next five years [24]. IoT is one emergent technology in Gartner's IT Hype Cycle [3], as seen in Fig. 1.

In the last years, concepts about IoT have been implemented in many sectors, such as health care, public services, transport and so forth. This paradigm of interconnected things increases the challenge to develop and maintain an infrastructure to assist this demand without security problems.

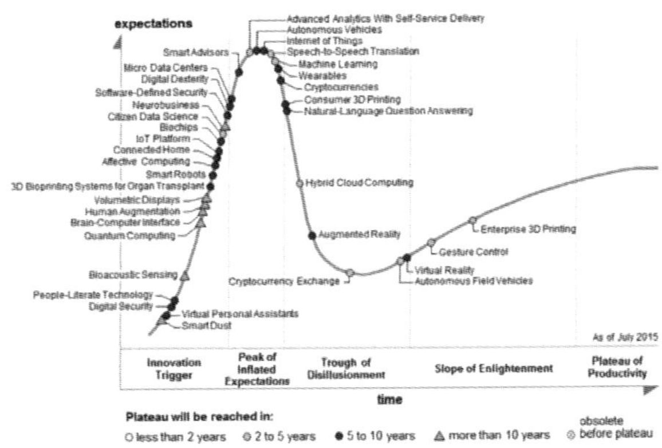

Figure 1. Gartner's IT Hype Cycle [3]

An architecture proposed by Tan and Wang (2010) and Wu et al. split the components used in IoT environments in 5 layers: perception (device), transport, processing (middleware), application and business [4]. This work will focus on the perception, transport and processing layers of this model.

Every computing system may have security problems and the same can be said about IoT. A secure computing system has to guarantee the following pre-requisites:

- Availability: related to the computing system's level of availability.
- Integrity: related to the guarantee that information was not modified in its source or on its path.
- Confidentiality: related to the assurance that only an authorized person can access the data.

In IoT, the perception layer is mainly composed of sensors, which are small, autonomous, with low processing and low power consumption [5]. These features, combined with its wide dispersion, make it even more complex to guarantee privacy and security to the information collected without the considerable increase in power consumption and processing in these wireless sensor networks [6].

This work intends to do a systematic mapping of problems and solutions in security communication within sensor networks and middleware used in IoT environments between devices in the perception and processing layers. According to Petersen (2008), systematic mapping involves a search in literature to verify the nature, extension and quantity of published articles [7]. IoT was the object of multiple studies over the last years and this work has the purpose of identifying and categorizing problems and solutions related to sensor networks and middleware security in IoT, resulting in a reference to related studies.

This work is organized in five sections: Section 2 presents the theoretical principles of IoT, its concepts and components. After that, Section 3 explains the process used in systematic mapping detailing the process of search. It also specifies the academic databases included in the research and the criteria for their inclusion and exclusion. Moreover, Section 4 analyzes and classifies the data collected and, finally, Section 5 presents the conclusion of this work.

II. THEORETICAL PRINCIPLES

A. Internet of Things (IoT)

IoT is a model that uses several objects (or things) to establish a pervasive presence around us [9]. These objects are present in houses, offices, industries, etc., providing information about the context where they work [10]. Applications use the Internet to consume such information and to serve reasoning and semantic data, intelligent and responsive services, big data analysis, and so on. Thus, a network of objects, services and people is ordered. Atzori et al. show the interaction of these elements, as shown in Fig. 2 [9].

The top circle in Fig. 2 lists some of the objects used in an IoT environment. Almost all of these objects are small electronic sensors and actuators capable of interacting with the real environment. Nonetheless, there are many technologies to develop and to implant these objects. The technologies shown in Fig. 2 are only a short enumeration.

Usually, sensors and actuators have a small amount of resources to process or store data (even none). Some of these sensors are integrated with smartphones and other small computing platforms (like Arduino and Raspberry PI). Finally, all these objects need a way to connect to the Internet moving from the top circle to the left circle. Sometimes, middlewares are necessary to assure the compatibility of elements. Sensors, actuators and communication devices cover mold, what is called "things" oriented vision [9]. The initial efforts to implant IoT platforms over the years were concentrated in the top circle elements and there are plenty of technologies in the market about this.

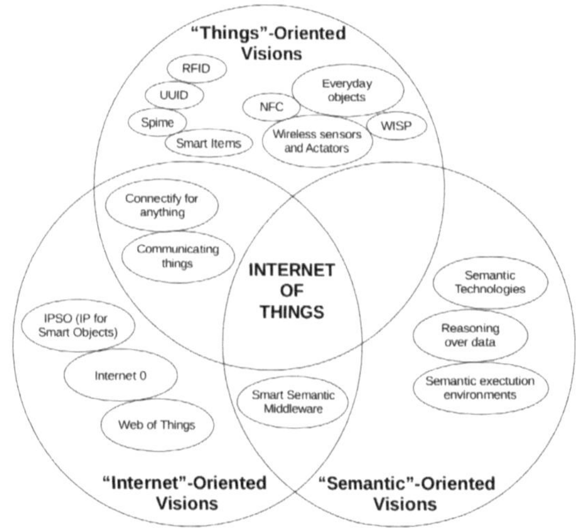

Figure 2. "Internet of Things" paradigm as result of the convergence of different visions [9].

Nowadays, another concept is being studied. Quantum Lifecycle Management (QLM) messaging is a standard based on IoT that defines changes in a life cycle of information between different IoT products [11].

The left circle in Fig. 2 presents some technologies used to provide applications that interact with objects, such as those presented in the top circle. The "Internet"-oriented vision is the connection between humans and objects in the IoT concept. Humans, using a computer or a smart device, can receive a data summary from sensors and send commands to the actuators.

There is another modern approach to understand this part of the concept. For example, Guo et al. present the opportunistic IoT to provide networks compatible with the movement and opportunistic contact of the human nature. Then, a person who interacts with an environment of objects (sensors and actuators) will find other people to provide the network to share and feed the applications used in the left circle [11]. Thus, smart mobile devices connected in ad-hoc networks are the center of this concept to reflect the human-human interaction against the human-computer interaction reflected in network layout. Therewith, the IoT environment will reproduce the human behavior more than objects behavior, changing and improving the context of information.

Moving to the right circle, the applications designed to interact with humans have to interact with other applications to extend their capability. The elements called Web of Things (WoT) must implement new interfaces to computers over the network or Internet. Again, new middleware is necessary to exchange data between these elements. Some technologies, such as Simple Object Access Protocol (SOAP) or Representational State Transfer (REST), are examples in this case. REST is a lightweight integration technology introduced in 2000 by Roy Fielding. Rettig et al. present a research work in which REST is applied in this context [13].

Finally, in the right circle, the analysis of the data collected and processed in the left circle will provide some new real time information. At this stage, the analysis will focus on providing knowledge more than information. The objective is not to understand the responses of sensors, but to interpret this information comparing it with another environment with the same context or even to compare it with other contexts to create new knowledge about this. According to Atzori et al., to represent, store, interconnect, search and organize the magnitude of information generated by so many devices will be a great challenge [9].

B. Middlewares

Rocha et al. affirm that distributed systems generate new problems because they are not centralized. Among the questions regarding distributed systems is: how to make it easy the development of distributed systems and the integration with legacy systems? One of the responses to this question is middlewares [14].

Maciel et al. (2004) define middleware as a software layer that permits communication between distributed applications. In other words, middlewares are responsible for interoperating between systems, providing a layer to allow transparent communication, minimizing complexity and providing a homogeneous environment for the few or several systems that might be involved [15].

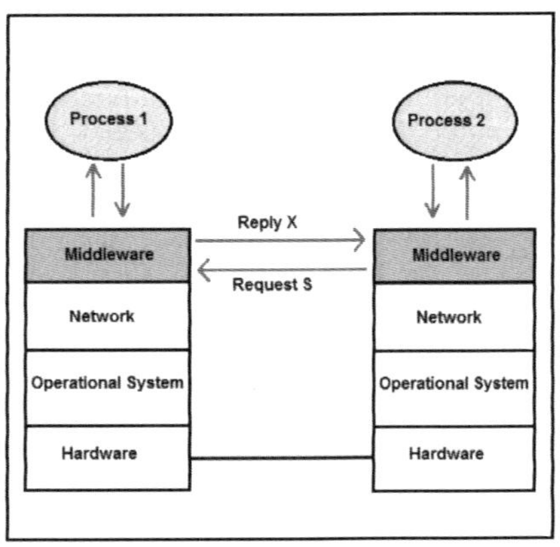

Figure 3. Communication between middleware [15].

Fig. 3 shows a usage example of a middleware. The middleware layer is inside the structure and it is responsible for providing communication between existent systems. The process is transparent to the applications (processes 1 and 2) and the middleware handles the communication in a heterogeneous environment.

According to Cavalcanti et al., the main middleware features are [16]:

- Hiding the information distributed.
- Hiding the hardware components heterogeneity from several operating systems and communication protocols.
- Providing high-level uniform interfaces to applications and developers.
- Supplying a set of common services to execute some general functions, avoiding effort duplication and facilitating collaboration between applications.

Middleware is gaining market over the past years in order to integrate legacy systems with new systems and also to simplify the integration by developing new services to both systems.

Nowadays, middleware is used in several scenarios, including IoT, from e-health to smart houses where middleware is responsible for providing communication between some sensors and interoperating them with other systems.

C. Sensors Networks

When the Internet was proposed, the objective was to create a long distance decentralized communication network. The client/server paradigm suggests an application with one human interacting directly, with a client side and one computer at the server side.

Despite this, sensor networks designed for an IoT environment involve communication between a sensor and a transport device without a human being in the circuit. These components are installed at a short distance in the same environment for almost all cases. Finally, sensors, actuators and transport devices have reduced capacity to store and process data and it is difficult to connect the sensor network to the Internet because the data from the sensors cannot be transmitted in long distance with the limitation of these transmission protocols. With low power of processing data, even none, sensors are not able to execute complex algorithms to cypher information [17].

In this scenario, to ensure security features, especially confidentiality, can be a great challenge. Many different studies try to solve this problem with diverse approaches: "small sized keys, reduce communication exchanges, operate under the assumption of insecure communication channels, etc." [18], but the discussion along this work shows the challenge is only in its beginning. To face various different scenarios, with singular needs and features, using distinct technologies and implementing particular sets of protocols is necessary to stablish more solutions with different cost/benefit relations. This justifies the relevance of the systematic mapping conducted to understand the most recent studies about this topic.

III. SYSTEMATIC MAPPING

The systematic mapping adopted in this work is based on the process proposed by Petersen et al. (2008) that describes five steps [7]:

1. Research questions definitions;
2. Primarily relevant studies research;
3. Classification (first filter);
4. Summary keyword (second filter);
5. Data extraction and mapping.

Usually, questions in a systematic mapping must be general, of an exploratory nature, while systematic revisions may use more specific questions [8]. This way, this work focuses on the following questions:

- (Q1). Which are the main problems related to communication security in sensors network and middleware used in IoT?
- (Q2). Which are the solutions to communication security in sensors network and middleware used in IoT?

The academic databases chosen to be part of this research were ACM Digital Library, Elsevier (Science Direct) and IEEE Xplore. The elected research keywords were: IoT, security and sensors networks. To classify the articles, the following criteria for inclusion were established:

- Articles from 2014 or newer;
- For articles about the same research subject, only the most recent were selected;

Exclusion criteria were:

- Any article about other subjects, not analyzed in this paper;
- Secondary studies such as summary, presentations and so forth;

The first search returned a total of 649 papers. The first filter (reading the titles and abstracts in order to apply inclusion and exclusion criteria) reduced the number of articles to 94. The second filter (reading the introductions) reduced the number to 60 after we applied applied again the inclusion and exclusion criteria. The result is presented in Table I.

TABLE I. ARTICLES NUMBERS

BASE	First Filter	Second Filter	Final Selection
ACM Digital Library	199	42	24
Elsevier (Science Direct)	222	22	12
IEEE Xplore	225	30	24
Total	646	94	60

To answer the first question (Q1) the articles were arranged in groups: Confidentiality, Availability, Integrity and ALL, presented in Section 1 of this paper. To resolve the second question (Q2), the articles were classified according to the presented solution:

- Cryptography – key generator: key generation solutions;
- Cryptography – key management: key management and distribution solutions;
- Anonymity: guarantees privacy solutions;
- Internal prevention of attacks: prevents attacks from devices inside sensor network;
- Architecture: proposed architecture to implant security;
- Physical attack: physical attacks to devices, for instance to steal or to break;
- Authentication: guarantees both, identity and source of information;

IV. ANALYSIS

This section presents details about the study and the collected information during the classifying process. Fig. 4 shows the relation between academic databases and the articles classified. The analysis draws 24 (39,7%) articles from ACM, 24 (39,7%) from IEEE Xplore and 12 (20,7%) from Elsevier.

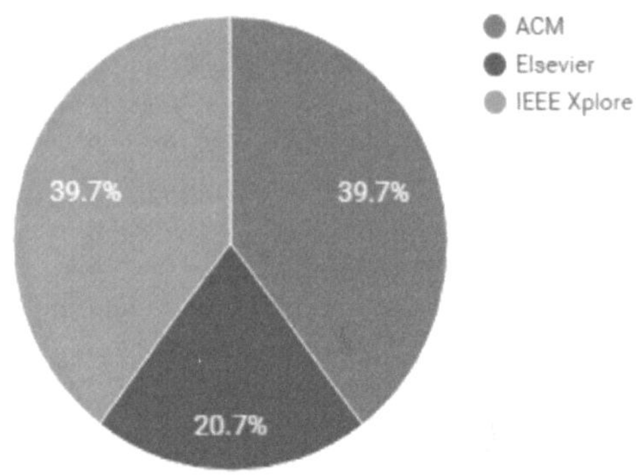

Figure 4. Counts of Base

In all the articles included, 60% enumerate confidentiality as the main problem to be solved by security middlewares in sensor networks in an IoT environment. As proposed by Baker (2009 apud Ntul et al. 2016) [19], capturing data or doing a physical attack in a sensor network means that "the attacker can clone the device, install new firmware or learn sensitive information". The hacked device might be used in other complex and destructive attacks. Belsis and Pantziou [20], Gope and Hwang [21], and others show the risk of intercepting and infering data about patients and location in a medical monitoring environment in a likely IoT approach. Something between sensors and gateways must assure the privacy of people and accuracy of the health information. It can be applied to other environments. Caron et al. [22] discuss the privacy to the Australian citizen and the legal guarantees to protect personal information. The center of the discussion features how secrecy, anonymity and solitude can be applied to almost every country in the modern world. Nonetheless, low cost devices have limited processing power and have to use simple cryptographic and sign functions [23]. Fig. 5 shows the percentage of distribution of security problems of this study.

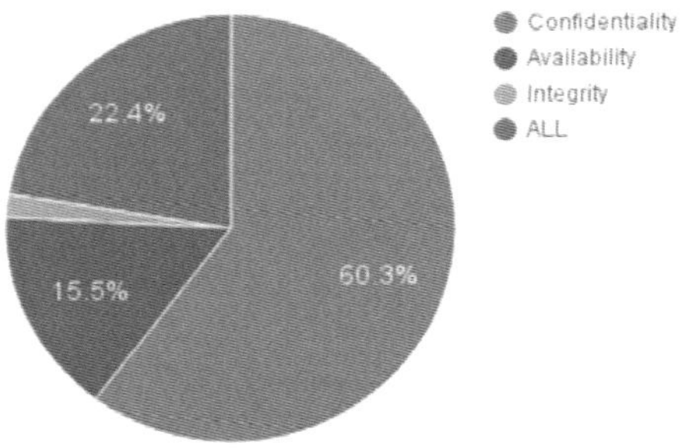

Figure 5. Percentage of security problems

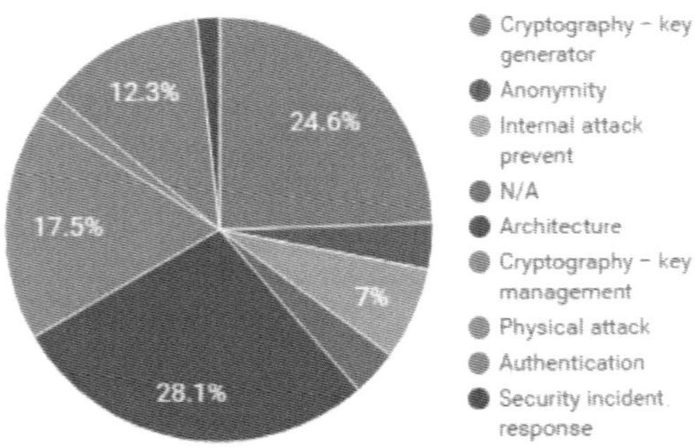

Figure 6. Percentage of security solutions

Among the identified problems, a few proposed solutions were identified. Those were arranged in categories. Fig. 6 represents the distribution of categories for solutions and percentage from the selected articles.

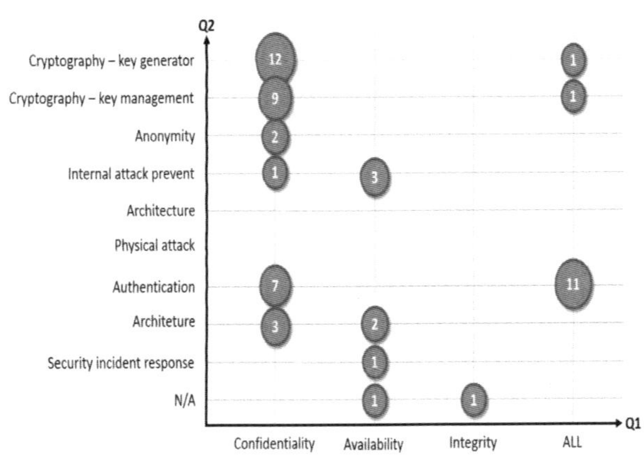

Figure 7. Mapping

The main concerns found about the solutions were: Cryptography - Key Management (17.5%), Cryptography - Key Generator (24.6%) and Architecture (28.1%). These represent 70,2% of all solutions found. Solutions based in Architecture represent 28.1%, but solutions based in Cryptography are more recurring representing 45,6%, almost half of all solutions. About the Architecture category, many solutions were proposed, such as network architecture to middleware model, including specific security issues with focus in data confidentiality and integrity. The N/A category groups articles without proposed solutions. Fig. 7 shows the articles distribution comparing the two questions: problems (Q1) and proposed solutions (Q2).

V. CONCLUSION

The set of technologies that defines an IoT environment is rapidly evolving. The concerns with security are reflected in the articles discussed in this paper and others that did not meet the outlined criteria. The same way, different approaches suggest solutions to different scenarios.

The aim of this work was to map security problems and respective solutions to sensors networks in IoT environments. Four categories of problems and nine solution categories were defined, presenting uneasiness with the lack of confidentiality and suggestion, especially in cryptography.

The superficial analysis in this paper suggests a deeper study to compare effectiveness and application of presented solutions is necessary. It is important to work and understand what makes confidentiality the most exposed problem and explore best applicable approaches. A survey is a great suggestion to continue the research in future papers.

REFERENCES

[1] K. Ashton. "That 'internet of things' thing.", RFiD Journal, vol. 22, no.7, 2009, pp. 97-114.

[2] R. Khan, S. U. Khan, R. Zaheer and S. Khan. "Future internet: the internet of things architecture, possible applications and key challenges." Frontiers of Information Technology (FIT), 2012 10th International Conference on. IEEE, 2012, pp. 257-260.

[3] B. Burton and M. Walker. "Hype Cycle for Emerging Technologies, 2015.", 2015.

[4] L. Tan and N. Wang. "Future internet: The internet of things." 2010 3rd International Conference on Advanced Computer Theory and Engineering (ICACTE), vol. 5. IEEE, 2010, pp. 376-380.

[5] M. Chaqfeh and N. Mohamed, "Challenges in middleware solutions for the internet of things", In Collaboration Technologies and Systems (CTS), 2012 International Conference on. IEEE, 2012, pp. 21-26.

[6] P. Kumari, M. Kumar, and R. Rishi, "Study of Security in Wireless Sensor Networks" In

Proceedings of International Journal of Computer Science and Technology, vol. 1, no. 5, 2010, pp. 347-354.
[7] K. Petersen, R. Feldt, S. Mujtaba and M. Mattsson, "Systematic mapping studies in software engineering" In Proceedings of the international conference on Evaluation and Assessment in Software Engineering, 2008, pp. 68-77.
[8] B. A. Kitchenham and S. Charters, "Guidelines for performing systematic literature reviews in software engineering", Technical Report EBSE 2007-001, Keele University and Durham University Joint Report, July 2007. 2.4, 2.4, 3.1, 3.2.1, 3.2.2, 4.1, 5.1, C.2, C.3
[9] L. Atzori, A. Iera, and G. Morabito. "The Internet of Things: a Survey", Computer Network, vol 54, no. 15, pp. 2787-2805, 2010.
[10] A. Rodrigues. A. Ordóñez, H. Ordóñez, and R. Segovia, "Adapting NSGA-II for Hierarchical Sensor Networks in the IoT" Procedia Computer Science, vol. 61, pp. 355-560, 2010.
[11] K. Främling and M. Maharjan, "Standardized Communication Between Intelligent Products for the IoT" IFAC Proceedings, vol. 46, no. 7, pp. 157-162, 2013.
[12] B. Guo, D. Zhang, Z. Wang, Z. Yu, and X. Zhou, "Opportunistic IoT: Exploring the harmonious interaction between human and the Internet of things", Journal of Network and Computer Applications, vol 36, no 6, pp. 1531-1539, 2012.
[13] A. Rettig, S. Khanna, and R. Beck "Open source REST services for environmental sensor networking" Applied Geography, vol 60, pp. 294-300, 2014.
[14] V. Rocha, F. Ferraz, H. Souza, and C. Ferraz. "ME-DiTV:A Middleware Extension for Digital TV", unpublished.
[15] R. Maciel and S. Assis. "Middleware: Uma solução para o desenvolvimento de aplicações distribuídas". ClenteFico, Year IV, vol. 1, 2014.
[16] A. Cavalcanti, C. Albuquerque, and A. Furtado. "A Study on middleware for IoT", unpublished.
[17] Q. Zhu, R. Wang, Q. Chen, Y. Liu, and W. Qin "IOT Gateway: Bridging Wireless Sensor Networks into Internet of Things" International Conference on Embedded and Ubiquitous Computing on IEEE, 2010, pp. 347-352.
[18] I. Chatzigiannakisa, A. Vitalettia, and A. Pyrgelis "A Privacy-Preserving Smart Parking System based on an IoT Elliptic Curve Based Security Platform" Computer Communications vol. 89-90, pp.165-177, 2010.
[19] N. Ntul and A. Abu-Mahfouz "A Simple Security Architecture for Smart Water Management System" Procedia Computer Science, vol. 83, pp. 1164-1169, 2016
[20] P. Belsis and G. Pantziou "A k-anonymity privacy-preserving approach in wireless medical monitoring environments" Pers Ubiquit Computing, vol. 18.1, pp. 61-74, 2014
[21] P. Gope and T. Hwang "BSN-Care: A Secure IoT-based Modern Healthcare System Using Body Sensor Network" IEEE Sensors Journal, vol. 16, no. 5, pp. 1368-1376, 2016
[22] X. Caron, R. Bosua, S. Maynard, and A. Ahmad "The Internet of Things (IoT) and its impact on individual privacy: An Australian perspective" Computer Law & Security Review, vol. 32, no. 1, pp. 4-15, 2016.
[23] K. Mandal, X. Fan, and G. Gong "Design and Implementation of Warbler Family of Lightweight Pseudorandom Number Generators for Smart Devices" Department of Electrical Engineering, University of Washington, vol. 15, no. 1, 2016
[24] Greenough. "How the 'Internet of Things' will impact consumers, businesses, and governments in 2016 and beyond" Business Insider, 2016.

Primary Access Procedures in M2M Networks

Abdullah Balcı, Radosveta Sokullu
EEE Dept., Faculty of Engineering, Ege University
Izmir, Turkey
email : abdullah.balci@ege.edu.tr, radosveta.sokullu@ege.edu.tr

Abstract — **The immensely increased number of networked devices in the last several years is believed to be only the beginning of a new era of machine-to-machine (M2M) communications, where billions of devices will connect over the network and react to events in the environment without human intervention. This emerging technology poses new challenges to the existing connectivity mechanisms. Current network access methods rely on random access (RA) back-off based mechanisms with inherent control of the congestion and the delay. In M2M communications, devices will be sending only very small amounts of data (several bytes so several kilobytes) but their excessive numbers and the possibility that many of them will try to connect simultaneously will cause high collision rate and unacceptable delays. A lot of active research is directed to these subjects and the goal of this paper is to summarize and classify the suggested methods in order to provide a clear picture of the open research issues.**

Keywords-M2M communications; random access procedure; congestion; delay

I. INTRODUCTION

A lot of research in recent years is concentrated on new technologies, enabling the communication between "things", "machines" and "devices" like "the Internet of Things" (IoT), "Machine-to-Machine" (M2M) and Device-to-Device (D2D) communications. The basic idea behind these concepts is that "things" or "objects" will be able to communicate with each other and perform actions without human intervention [1]. In 2015, 604 million machines were connected to the internet and the number is predicted to rise over 3,075 million by 2020. This amazing growth in terms of number of devices and data volume is faster than the growth of human population and consequently has resulted in a new paradigm defined as M2M communications [2][3].

The aim of M2M networks is to connect devices together and enable them to make smart decisions based on the generated and transferred data. The characteristic of these M2M networks are quite different from those of current wired and wireless networks. Human-to-human (H2H) communications focus on high data rates and high QoS, while M2M communications aim generally at low data rates with very strict time constraints. Furthermore, because of the large number of devices, the number of simultaneous attempts to connect to the network will be much greater than those in H2H centered networks. This renders existing access algorithms ineffective resulting in high collision rate and extreme delays and has forced major standardization organizations such as ETSI and 3GPP to concentrate their efforts on these issues [4]. Specifically 3GPP is working on network architectures that allow the integration of M2M communications with cellular networks such as LTE and LTE-A. In LTE, the devices have to perform the RA procedure to connect to the network using the Physical Random Access Channel (PRACH) in the uplink direction. With H2H communications this procedure gives satisfactory results but is not suitable for M2M scenarios. Furthermore, since both H2H and M2M devices will perform this procedure on the same uplink resources, it will also cause significant degradation in the QoS for H2H users and this is quite an active research area [4].

In this paper, we focus on the challenges arising in the RA procedure due to the introduction of an extremely large number of M2M devices. The paper is organized as follows: first a brief overview of the RA procedure in LTE is presented, then in Section III, the RA challenges are defined and the existing solutions are summarized introducing a clear taxonomy of the suggested methods. Section IV concludes the paper by defining the major open research issues.

II. RANDOM ACCESS PROCEDURE IN LTE

The two most important situations when the Random Access (RA) procedure is initiated by a device are: when it is turned on and it has no allocated uplink resources, and when handing over from one eNB to another. The devices can send their access request only on the allocated PRACH, which consists of 6 Resource Blocks (RB). There are 16 different RA resource configurations for different system bandwidth and different number of cells per eNB. LTE allows two types of RA procedure: contention based where the devices compete for the channel access, and contention-free. The first one is used by UEs for initial establishing a connection and synchronization, while the second one is reserved only for new downlink requests or handover, which are very time-sensitive operations [6]. The contention-based RA procedure has four steps:

Step 1: Preamble Transmission: The RA procedure begins with the selection (from a predefined set) of a preamble, which is used as a signature. Each device randomly selects one of the 64-N_{cf} orthogonal pseudo-random preambles, reserved for contention-free requests, without knowing which is already selected or used. When the cell size is large, a longer preamble will improve the reliability of reception at the cell edge. If a preamble is selected by more than one device, a collision can occur in step 3. Otherwise, the different preambles are easily detected by eNB because of orthogonality. After the transmission is completed, the device waits for the response from eNB.

Step 2: Random Access Response: For each successfully decoded preamble, the eNB sends a random access response (RAR) on the PDSCH, and a Random Access Radio Network Temporary Identifier (RA-RNTI), which identifies the time-frequency slot where the preamble was detected. The RAR message includes the identity of the detected preamble, a timing alignment instruction to synchronize the uplink transmission, an initial uplink resource grant for transmission of the "step 3" message, an assignment of a temporary Cell Radio Network Temporary Identifier (C-RNTI), and a back-off indicator, which determines the waiting time before a new RA attempt. Each device expects to receive the RAR within a time window, specified and broadcasted by eNB. The earliest subframe can occur 2 ms after the end of the preamble sub-frame but typical delay is 4 ms. If the device does not receive a RAR within this time window, it selects and transmits another preamble. If multiple devices select the same preamble in the same time-frequency resource, they would both receive the same RAR.

Step 3: Connection Request: The "step 3" message is the first scheduled uplink transmission on the Physical Uplink Shared Channel (PUSCH) sent using HARQ. It conveys the C-RNTI and the actual RA message, such as Radio Resource Control (RRC) connection request or scheduling request. If multiple devices select the same preamble in step 1, these devices will be allocated the same time-frequency resource by eNB, and a collision will occur at the eNB. If no acknowledgement is received by the eNB, the devices will retransmit the same message after the timeout expires.

Step 4: Contention Resolution Message: The contention resolution message is addressed to the C-RNTI as an answer to the connection request message, which is sent in step 3. Upon reception of the contention resolution message there are three possibilities: 1) the UE correctly decodes the message, detects its own identity and sends back a positive ACK; 2) the UE correctly decodes the message, discovers that it contains another device's identity, then it sends nothing back; 3) the UE fails to decode the message or misses the resource allocation.

III. RACH CHALLENGES AND POSSIBLE SOLUTIONS

A. RACH Challanges

As mentioned above, one of the major characteristic of M2M communication is the unprecedented high number of devices which leads to much higher access request rate as compared to H2H communication. Many devices may simultaneously try to connect to the network to send only small amounts of data. So the bottleneck is not high network traffic in general but the burst traffic created during accessing the channel. The high collision probability (CP) and low success rate in network access will cause unexpected access delays, waste of resources, and extra energy consumption. Our simulation results (Table 1) confirm that while for uniform distribution of the access requests (typical for H2H – light grey) the burst arrival traffic (typical for M2M – dark grey) creates much larger CP and AD for large number of devices.

TABLE I. RACH RESULTS FOR UNIFORM AND BURST ARRIVALS

Performance Metrics	**Number of Devices**			
	5000	***15000***	***25000***	***30000***
Collision Probability (CP)	0.005%	0.05%	0.16%	0.23%
	0.39%	5.23%	42.63%	46.49%
Access Success Probability	100%	100%	100%	100%
	100%	99.9%	38.34%	29.11%
Number of Preamble Transmissions	1.42	1.46	1.49	1.5
	1.55	2.12	3.36	3.28
Access Delay (AD) (ms)	26.61	27.67	28.63	28.87
	30.23	47.45	75.7	80

The RA procedure allows some devices to establish connections but does not solve the overload of repeated attempts. The results in Fig.2 show the increased number of unsuccessful attempts for burst arrival traffic.

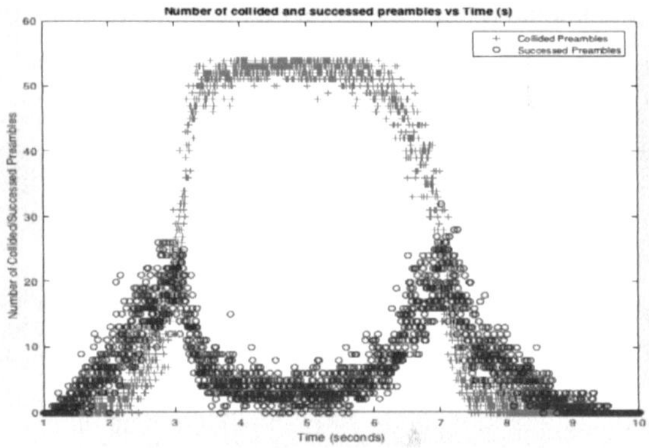

Figure 1. Number of successful and collided preambles for burst traffic

B. Suggested Solutions

Efficient overload mechanisms are required for M2M communication over LTE. In [7], the authors suggest application level schemes to control the congestion by scheduling the M2M devices in less loaded periods (midnights), but these solutions bring inconvenience to the end user and greatly limit the application areas of M2M communication, making them undesirable for providers and costumers. 3GPP [8] defines the following major criteria for access methods to be used with M2M communications:

- M2M integration shouldn't affect the H2H performance,
- Access delay should be considered predicting the behavior of M2M device in the radio access network
- Access methods should be easy to integrate and minimize the effect M2M have on the existing network.

Complying with these major criteria there are a number of various solutions proposed for the primary access to the RACH. The main goal of our paper is to present a taxonomy that allows comparing these solutions and pointing out the areas where more research is needed. The general structure of the suggested taxonomy is provided in Fig.2.

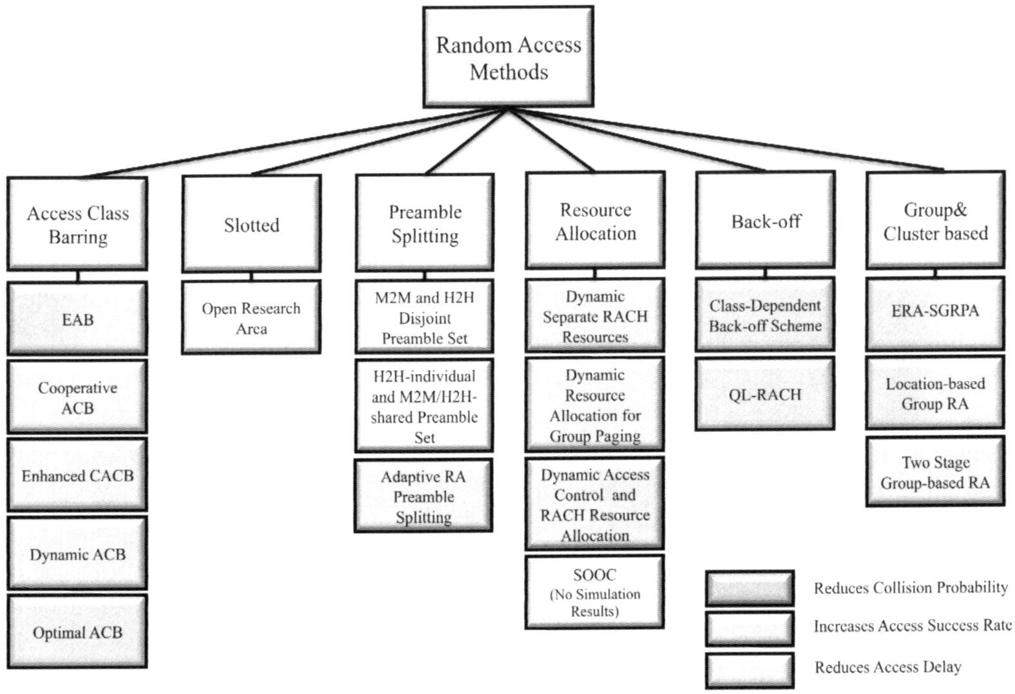

Figure 2. Random Access Methods

C. *Access Class Barring Schemes*

A large group of solutions is based on Access Class Barring (ACB) access algorithm, where the eNB groups incoming requests into several classes according to their service requirements and broadcasts a barring factor (ACB parameter) and a barring time. When a device initiates the RA process, it draws a random number and compares it with the barring factor. If the number is less than the barring factor, it continues with its RA process, otherwise, it waits for a period equal to the barring time before reinitiating the RA process. Since the probability of collision is reduced, the throughput of RACH is improved but barring increases the access delay because devices may be barred for an undesirably long time. A version of ACB, the Extended Access Class Barring (EACB) is proposed in which delay-tolerant applications are not permitted to perform the RA process if there is congestion. [5] Thus the number of channel access attempts as a whole is reduced at the price of increased access delay for delay-tolerant applications.

Lien et al [10] proposed a Cooperative Access Class Barring (CACB) scheme in a heterogeneous multi-tier network with picocells and macrocells. In this scheme, neighboring eNBs select the barring factor jointly based on the network congestion level. CACB achieves around 30% improvement both in the average access delay and the worst case delay performance. A major drawback is that it requires devices to be located in more than one eNBs coverage area. Hsu et al [11] proposed the Enhanced Cooperative ACB (ECACB), where they add the number of M2M devices attached to an eNB to determine the M2M device access probability and obtain the barring factor. The ECACB continues to monitor the M2M resource allocation after the devices have been successfully attached to network. It presents a new RRM method that reserves a fixed amount of Physical RBs (PRBs) for M2M devices. The number of reserved PRBs is based on the access rate of M2M device. Results show that ECACB has a lower access delay than CACB even in the worst case scenario. Duan et al [12] proposed a Dynamic ACB (DACB) scheme to reduce the congestion in RACH. Their goal is to manage the access attempts of the M2M devices instead of dismissing the access requests. They propose a novel algorithm that reduces both congestion and access delay by changing the barring factor adaptively. As expected reducing of access delay is reduced but at the price of increased complexity since continuous monitoring is required. The authors of [13] use ACB mechanism together with timing advance information to reduce the RA overload. A novel algorithm is proposed to estimate the number of devices requiring access to the eNB in a given RA slot. They try to find the optimal ACB using the fact that for stationary devices propagation delay is nearly constant. Each device stores the timing advance value for a successful RA run, and compares it with the timing advance value in the next RA run. If the two are the same, the device continues to send the connection request message in step 3. Results show that using ACB together with time advance information allows around 50% of the RA slots be saved for M2M devices when compared to other schemes, which use only timing advance information, only ACB, or only cooperative ACBs.

The main advantage of ACB based solutions is the decreased probability of collision; however, the access delay may be increased a lot and is difficult to predict. This is unacceptable for delay-intolerant emergency applications and event-driven applications where the congestion can rise considerably in very short periods of time. An interesting point is covered in the [14]. Using simulation, the study investigates the RACH performance based on a combination of different barring factors (0.9, 0.7, 0.5) and different RA attempt periods (10 s, 60 s). While almost all devices access the network successfully when the attempt period is set to 60 s, for the same barring factor the access probability falls to 60-70% when the attempt period is reduced to 10 s, i.e., for short attempt periods the barring factor considerably affects the collision rate and the access probability. The results provide valuable insight into the operation of ACB schemes under light and congested conditions.

D. *Slotted Schemes*

In telecommunication systems, media access is either contention-based (Aloha, CSMA in IEEE 802.11), or is channelized, where the frequency or time is shared between users based on pre-defined slots (FDMA, TDMA). The main advantages of TDMA-type access methods are that there is no collision and slots can be assigned on demand. However, slotted-type methods require very precise synchronization. 3GPP proposed [5] a slotted access method for RA in which the slots are dedicated to M2M devices and each M2M device only accesses in its dedicated slot. However, such contention-free mechanisms are exclusive to two use cases: when the device is in connected state but needs uplink synchronization information to be able to transmit positive or negative ACK or when the device is performing handover from one cell to another.

Slotted mechanisms, well known from many MAC layer protocols, solve collision issues but for their operation the number of participating devices has to be known ahead. Previous research in some related areas (i.e., wireless sensor networks) has shown that very good results in terms of resource efficiency can be achieved if slotted schemes are combined as two stage solutions with contention based methods. How approaches like these can be utilized in the context of M2M communications is a research area to be exploited in the future.

E. *Preamble Splitting Schemes*

One of the main criteria for integrating M2M communication over LTE is minimizing the effects of M2M communication on H2H communication performance. 3GPP described 64 different preambles for random access procedure that are used by both M2M and H2H devices. So the probability of selecting the same preamble will increase, degrading H2H devices. For this reason, some researchers investigate the possibilities for separation of RA preambles for M2M and H2H devices as an indirect way of reducing congestion and ensuring QoS. Lee et al [15] compare the throughput of two methods for separating RA preambles. The first method is to completely split the set of available RA preambles into two disjoint subsets one for M2M and one H2H communication. The other method is split the set into two subsets – one individually for H2H devices, the other common for both H2H and M2M devices. They demonstrate that method 2 is slightly better than method 1, but their proposal does not examine the effects on decreasing the congestion. Another study on splitting preambles is [16], where Kim et al propose the Adaptive RA Preamble Splitting (PS) to evaluate three history-based PS schemes in terms of access success rate by using the ratio of non-contention based RA preambles to the total number of RA preambles. These and some other studies using PS show that access success probability can be increased but they do not discuss the effects these methods have on delay performance.

F. *Resource Allocation*

Another approach to combat congestion on the RACH channel is to separate the RACH resources for H2H and M2M devices [17]. If RACH resources are shared between M2M and H2H devices, the large amount of M2M devices will negatively affect the performance of H2H devices. The RACH resources may be wasted by collisions created by the enormous amount of M2M devices trying to access the network. 3GPP proposed a general algorithm, Dynamic Separate RACH resources (DSRR) in which M2M devices are categorized by types and only devices of the same type contend for the PUSCH resources. Each M2M device listens to the environment before accessing the channel. If there is any activity from devices of the same type, it starts a contention process with them on the dedicated resources; otherwise it is permitted to contend with H2H devices in the PRACH by following the normal RA procedure. Separating M2M from H2H devices in the uplink and classifying the M2M devices increases the access probability for both M2M and H2H devices as well as ensures the performance and access delay for H2H communication. In [18], the authors focus on RA opportunities (RAOs) for group paging. Group paging is a RAN overload control scheme that uses a single paging message to inform a group of M2M devices for system information changes and emergency notifications. In group paging, the eNB assigns a unique group identity to a group of M2M devices. When the group of devices receives the paging message, the devices simultaneously transmit randomly chosen RAOs in the first RA slot. The RA preamble is determined in terms of RAOs and the number of RAO is equal to the number of frequency bands in RA slot times the number of preambles. When a collision occurs, the collided M2M device will perform the back-off algorithm and perform RA procedure with a new chosen RAO in a new RA slot. Because with group paging the number of devices decreases, it is suggested to dynamically allocate RAOs in each RA slot. The proposed method improves the utilization of resources by at least 65% compared to static RAO allocations. Oh et al [19] propose a Dynamic Access Control and RACH Resource Allocation algorithm, which has two phases; "estimating the number of M2M devices" and "access control and RAOs allocation". The last two studies are similar in the sense that they adjust the RAOs, however the first one applies it to group paging, while the other one integrates it with an ACB mechanism. Both show that improving the utilization of RAOs maximizes the RA efficiency while guaranteeing the average delay. Lo et al [20] propose a novel overload control scheme called Self-Optimizing Overload Control Scheme (SOOC). SOOC integrates several multiple control schemes (RACH resource separation scheme, the ACB, the SAS and the p-persistent scheme) in order to provide a more efficient, step-by-step congestion control. A M2M device can easily detect an overload on the PRACH channel when it fails to receive a response in the step 4. It assumes there is a state ofnetwork overload and performs an ACB algorithm as described before. Since the collided devices would collide again in the next RA slot, the p-persistent algorithm is used to minimize the chance of a second collision. In the p-persistent algorithm, a device senses the medium and if found idle, transmits with probability p, or else keeps sensing the medium continuously until it becomes idle and then transmits with probability p. A small p leads to long access delay. In SOOC, each device keeps track of the overload indicator and increases it when an access attempt fails. This situation also means that the congestion level of the PRACH channel is rising. That is why each device includes the overload indicator in the step 3 message and according to that the eNB dynamically increases or decreases the number of RA-Slots for PRACH. Unfortunately, the algorithm proposed in this paper is not supported by any simulation or theoretical results.

Separating RACH resources can reduce the impact on H2H devices by only slightly reducing the M2M communication performance as compared to the non-separate RACH case [14]. However, the improvement is limited at high congestion levels. The study also shows that while the dynamic allocation of RACH resources increases the general performance, under heavy traffic the PUSCH resources are extensively allocated for RA procedure.

G. *Back-off Scheme*

The methods in this group explore different possibilities of adjusting back-off time after collision to regulate the RA procedure. In [21], it is proposed to prioritize H2H devices by using a separate back-off scheme. If the random back-off time for M2M devices is based on a separate back-off parameter, larger than the one assigned to H2H devices, M2M devices will perform RA after a longer time. This increases the success probability for H2H devices. Jian et al [22] suggest M2M class-dependent back-off prioritization to reduce the RACH overload in RAN. They also propose to combine back-off scheme with ACB to control the number of devices that are allowed to start the RA procedure. The suggested algorithm consists of two stages; the ACB stage and the class-dependent back-off stage. The results show that the probability of collision is reduced and the throughput improved by 2-5%. But the disadvantage of this algorithm is increasing the access delay. Bello et al [23] propose a Q-learning based RA scheme (QL-RACH) where a virtual RA slot frame (M2M-frame) is designed specifically for M2M devices. Each RA slot keeps a value according to the success probability in the virtual frame and this value is used in the future to find the best slot for placing an access request. Here the back-off scheme is implemented on top of QL-RACH. Both H2H and M2M devices can use the same frame for initial access. However, after a collision, H2H and M2M devices use different back-off frames, which are restricted for each group, M2M devices cannot transmit in H2H frames and vice versa. The results show an enormous throughput increase by around 70%, but the incurred access delay is not discussed.

Back-off based schemes have only limited potential to improve overall performance and cannot handle overload if the intensity of arrivals is very high. However, they give good results when combined with other schemes; a research question, which can be pursued further [13].

H. *Group&Cluster-Based Scheme*

In many cases it is required that applications are grouped into clusters based on a specific criteria like; geographic location, application type, QoS requirements, etc. and it is convenient that M2M devices access the RA slot as a group. In the M2M architecture proposed by 3GPP, the resource restricted M2M devices connect to an M2M gateway, which communicates with the eNB on their behalf. Cluster-based access methods have been exploited in WSN quite a lot to provide promising results (e.g. the LEACH protocol, which introduced a revolutionary distributed cluster formation technique enabling self-organization of large number of nodes [24]). Such ideas are quite relevant to M2M communications where clusters can be help increase the efficiency in using the RACH. Kim et al [25] propose to use spatial clustering of devices for preamble reuse during the RA procedure (ERA SGRPA). Preamble reuse for two different devices is suggested when the difference of preamble detection time is larger than the delay spread. All group parameters such as number of groups, a set of group distance, and a set of preambles allocated for each group are broadcasted by eNB. Each device knows its distance from the eNB through the RSS value and determines the affiliated group in a distance based manner. Then, each device selects a preamble set, allocated for its group to start the RA procedure. The proposed method reduces the probability of collision to 1.65% when the number of devices in a cell is 50.000, which is about 9 times less than conventional RA schemes. Another scheme proposed by Lee et al [26] uses location information to form groups. Changes in the RA procedure adapt it to group-based communication. An M2M device periodically transmits the group preamble on behalf of all members. When the eNB receives the group preamble, it sends multiple RARs, which carry information for uplink grant in a RAR-window. Then, each device selects a RAR in the frame and gets the uplink grant. The results show considerable enhancement in the access delay where 95% of the devices successfully complete the RA procedure within 200 ms, which is 40% higher than the devices in legacy RA procedure. A main drawback is that the number of devices in each group must be known before dedicating the resources. Kao et al [27] propose a two-stage group based RA scheme to reduce the collision of M2M devices. The RA procedure is controlled by the M2M gateway for each group. The first M2M device to send a RA request becomes a group leader (M2M gateway) and the eNB broadcasts its identity to all group members. Data transmission is done at two stages: Local Network Stage (LNS) – between M2M device and

M2M gateway - and Global Network Stage (GNS) - between M2M gateway and eNB. Devices contend to send requests to the M2M gateway and the M2M gateway assigns them a RA slot. Each M2M device waits for the arrival of the allocated RA slot and an ACK from the M2M gateway. Finally, the device can perform the ordinary RA procedure on the allocated RA slot. There is no priority between M2M devices and they perform the local contention within the group before GNS. The results show that the access probability is increased nearly 7 times compared to traditional schemes; however the authors do not discuss the delay problem.

IV. CONCLUSION

In this study, we have discussed existing methods for controlling the RA procedures in M2M networks. We have pointed out three major problems arising from the abundance of devices trying to connect to the network simultaneously: increased collisions creating congestion and extreme delays, reduced throughput and reduced QoS for H2H users. We have suggested a taxonomy of the existing solutions and provided their comparative evaluation. ACB based methods alleviate collisions, preamble splitting methods help preserve the H2H QoS but both lead to uncontrollable delays. Resource allocation methods score well on both counts but reduce the general throughput, similar to back-off based ones. Finally, most promising are cluster based and adaptive, two-stage solutions, which require further research.

REFERENCES

[1] L. Atzori, A. Iera, and G. Morabito, "The Internet of Things: a survey," Computer Networks, vol. 54, no. 15, pp. 2787–2805, Oct. 2010.

[2] Cisco Systems, Visual Networking Index. Available: http://www.cisco.com/c/dam/assets/sol/sp/vni/forecast_highlights_mobile/index.html, July 2016.

[3] G. Andrews, H. Claussen, M. Dohler, S. Rangan, and M. C. Reed, "Femtocells: Past, present, and future," IEEE J. Sel. Areas Comm., vol. 30, no. 3, pp. 497–508, Apr. 2012.

[4] 3GPP TR 22.868 V8.5.0, "TSG Service and System Aspects," Study on Facilitating M2M Comm. in 3GPP Systems, Mar. 2007.

[5] 3GPP TR 37.868, "RAN Improvements for Machine-type Communication", 3GPP Technical Specification Group Services and System Aspects (Release 11), 2011.

[6] S. Sesia, I. Toufik, and M. Baker, Eds., LTE, the UMTS long term evolution: From theory to practice. UK, Wiley-Blackwell, pp. 371-406, 2011.

[7] 33GPP:TSG-RAN-WG2-69, "RACH congestion for MTC," 3GPP TSG RAN WG2 69bis,Beijing, China, 2010.

[8] 3GPP:R2-105623, "Comparison on RAN loading control schemes for MTC," Alcatel-Lucent, Alcatel-Lucent Shanghai Bell, 2010.

[9] 3GPP:R2-100182, "Access control of MTC devices," 3GPP TSG RAN WG2 Meeting 68bis, Valencia, Spain, 2010.

[10] S.Y. Lien, T.H. Liau, C.Y. Kao, and K.C. Chen, "Cooperative access class barring for M2M communi-cations," IEEE Trans. Wireless Comm., vol. 11, no. 1, pp. 27–32, Jan. 2012.

[11] Y.H. Hsu, K. Wang, and Y.C. Tseng, "Enhanced cooperative access class barring and traffic adaptive radio resource management for M2M communications over LTE-A," APSIPA, pp. 1–6, Oct. 2013.

[12] S. Duan and V.W.S. Wong, "Dynamic access class barring for M2M communications in LTE networks," Proc. of IEEE GLOBECOM, Altlanta, GA, Dec. 2013.

[13] Z. Wang and V.W.S. Wong, "Optimal Access Class Barring for Stationary Machine Type Communication Devices with Timing Advance Information," IEEE Trans. On Wireless Comm., vol. 14, no. 10, pp 5374-5387, Oct. 2015.

[14] 3GPP:TSG-RAN-WG2-71, "MTC simulation results with specific solutions," 3GPP TSG RAN WG2 #71, Madrid, Spain, 2010.

[15] K.-D. Lee, S. Kim, and B. Yi, "Throughput comparison of random access methods for M2M service over LTE networks," Proc. IEEE GLOBECOM Workshops, pp. 373-377, Dec. 2011.

[16] D. Kim, W. Kim, and S. An, "Adaptive RA preamble split in LTE," 9th IWCMC, pp. 814–819, July. 2013.

[17] 3GPP:R2-113328, "Dynamic separate RACH resources for MTC," 3GPP TSG RAN WG2 74, Institute for Information Industry (III), Coiler Corporation, 2011.

[18] R.Cheng, F.A.Taee, J.Chen, and C.Wei, "Dynamic resource allocation scheme for group paging in LTE-A networks," IEEE IoT Journal, vol. 2, no. 5, pp. 427–434, Oct. 2015.

[19] C. Oh, D. Hwang, and T. Lee, "Joint Access Control and Resource Allocation for Concurrent and Massive Access of M2M Devices," IEEE Trans. Wireless Commun., vol. PP, no. 99, pp. 4182–4292, Aug. 2015.

[20] A. Lo, Y. Law, M. Jacobsson, and M. Kucharzak, "Enhanced LTE-Advanced Random-Access Mechanism for Massive Machine-to- Machine (M2M) Communications," Proc. 27th Meeting of Wireless World Research Form, Oct. 2011.

[21] 3GPP:TSG-RAN2-70, "Separate backoff scheme for MTC," 3GPP TSG RAN2 70bis,Stockholm, Sweden, 2010.

[22] X. Jian, Y. Jia, X. Zeng, and J. Yang, "A novel class-dependent back-off scheme for machine type communication in lte systems," Wireless and Optical Communication Conference (WOCC), pp. 135–140, 2013.

[23] L.M. Bello, P. Mitchell, D.Grace, and T. Mickus, "Q-Learning Based RA with Collision free RACH Interactions for Celullar M2M," Next Gen. Mobile App. Services and Tech., pp. 78-83, 2015.

[24] W. B. Heinzelman, A. P. Chandrakasan, and H. Balakrishnan, "An application-specific protocol architecture for wireless microsensor networks," IEEE Trans. Wireless Comm., vol. 1, no. 4, pp. 660 – 670, Oct. 2002.

[25] T. Kim, H. S. Jang, and D. K. Sung, "An Enhanced Random Access Scheme with Spatial Group Based Reusable Preamble Allocation in Cellular M2M Networks," IEEE Commun. Lett., vol. 19, no. 10, pp. 1714-1717, 2015.

[26] K. Lee et al., "A group-based communication scheme based on the location information of MTC devices in cellular networks," Proc. IEEE ICC, pp. 4899-4903, Jun. 2012.

[27] H.W. Kao, Y.H. Ju, and M.H. Tsai, "Two-stage radio access for group-based machine type communication in LTE-A," on IEEE International Conference on Communications, pp. 3825-3830, June 2015.

Problems in Adopting Middleware for IoT : A Survey

Marcos Gregório, Roberto Santos, Cléber Barros and Geiziany Silva
CESAR – Recife Center for Advanced Studies and Systems
Recife, Brazil
e-mail:{demarcosluiz, robertosf90, cleberbarros.ti, geiziany.mendes}@gmail.com

Abstract – **In this paper, we present initial concepts of Internet of Things (IoT), whose technology combines Internet and day-to-day objects. We present, as well, the concept of middleware, which is a piece of software that connects software and hardware. After studying several scientific publications, we cover and analyze problems and challenges identified in the implementation of middleware for IoT. Applying knowledge acquired from these documents, we list the principal, recurring problems in adopting middleware for IoT, presenting and describing these problems in detail. Finally, we conclude on how these problems can affect and harm the adoption of middleware for IoT.**

Keywords: Internet of Things; Middleware; Heterogeneous network.

I. INTRODUCTION

The term "Internet of Things" was possibly introduced in 1999, during a lecture delivered by the British innovator Kevin Ashton at Procter & Gamble (P&G) [1]. According to Ashton, computers are very dependent on humans. His idea is that "things" could generate information without needing a human being. He claims that this would bring many benefits to the industry and to humanity, such as, increased information extraction, increased productivity, reduced losses in the energy economy, improvements in security and education, and much more.

In the IoT environment, we have heterogeneous devices and networks. These differences, as well as the complexity, may potentially increase with new technologies. The middleware for IoT facilitates the use of these devices and takes into account their heterogeneity to protect the software from the changes that would be needed to adapt to each device the software is connected to [2]. The IoT changes the way that we understand the world, using sensors to continuously monitor the environment around us, providing more information about traffic, weather, health, fleet management, vehicle control, allowing the Information Systems to provide value-added information for every single person.

The adoption of middleware helps to avoid some common problems in IoT development, such as:

- Hides the heterogeneity of hardware components, operation systems and communication protocols
- Interconnects parts running in distributed locations
- Provides uniformly high level of standard interfaces for developers and application integrators, making these applications easy to build, reuse and inter-operate
- Provides a set of common services to perform various general purpose functions, avoiding repeated efforts of the developing team [3]

However, in spite of the benefits, the adoption of middleware for IoT also brings problems. This paper presents a vision of the most common problems in adopting middleware for IoT based on the work done by different authors.

The rest of the paper is structured as follows. In Section II, we present an overview of the main concepts of IoT. In Section III, we present a review of the concepts related to middleware. In Section IV, we present the most common problems when middleware is adopted in IoT development. Finally, Section V presents the conclusion and final considerations.

II. INTERNET OF THINGS

Internet of Things is a new technology that is growing and gaining prominence. Every year several new devices are developed and software is applied to this new concept. However what is IoT and when did this term appear?

IoT is a technological revolution that has been growing increasingly since 2009. The tendency is to last for much greater time [4]. Even so, according to IDC, by the end of 2020, there will be somewhere around 30 billion devices connected to the IoT world and the IoT market will see an elevation of approximately seven billion dollars [5].

As previously mentioned, IoT is a new way to use applied technology in devices and applications, which allows for communication between day-to-day objects (e.g. washing machines, refrigerators, air conditioning units) to the Internet, for the purpose of supplying access to real-world information. [6].

IoT can also be defined as a dynamic global network infrastructure with auto-configuration capabilities based on standard communication protocols, which are inter-operable and virtual, in which things have physical attributes and virtual personalities use intelligent interfaces being seamlessly integrated into the information network [7].

IoT has the ability to contribute to society by better integrating devices and people, because the amount of information made available by IoT is enormous, and based on this information decisions that will bring benefits to the entire world population can be taken.

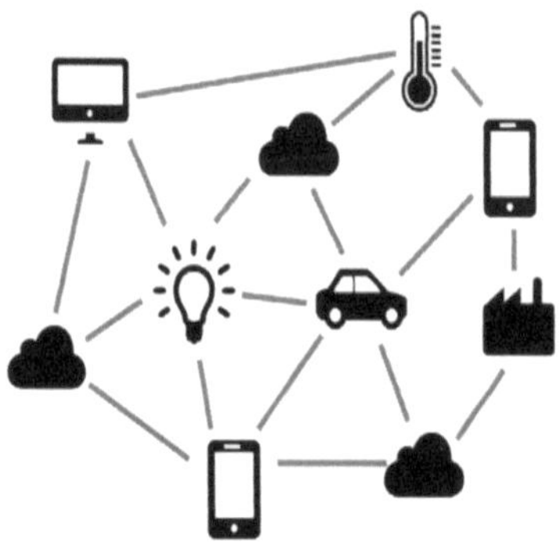

Figure 1. Connection between "things" using the Internet [7]

Figure 1 illustrates all connections between "things" with the Internet. Another feature of IoT is that it allows things and people to be connected anywhere, anytime, with anything or anyone.

As mentioned above, IDC says that in the coming years, there will be over 20 billion devices. Because of that immense amount and variety of devices, they will vary according to their physical characteristics, features and manufacturers. This enormous diversity causes the IoT to be seen from different viewpoints [8].

The differences in these viewpoints refer mainly to the differences between developers of devices, specifically everyday objects. From the point of view of the developer, this is owing to the fact that each developer has his or her favorite programming language, and, as is well known, each language has special features. In order to abstract the language and the complexity that the developer used to access the service provided, one of the best solutions is to use the middleware.

III. MIDDLEWARE

Middleware is a layer or set of software sub-layers interposed between levels of operational and communicative application [9]. The middleware has several features, the primary being to hide details from different technologies, protocols, network environments, data replication, and parallelism. Another feature of middleware is to exempt the programmer from issues that are not directly linked to final application, because middleware masks the heterogeneity of computer architectures, operating systems, programming languages, and network technologies [10]. In other words, middleware acts as the glue. The goal is to connect different systems, abstracting the diverse heterogeneous hardware components, operating systems and communication protocols, as well as to provide an immense amount of interfaces for developers to integrate the final application.

In recent years, middleware obtained greater importance in its use. Deuged says that this is due to the fact that the middleware simplifies the development of new services, old integrations, and new technologies [11].

Companies and business corporations are increasingly using middleware as a solution for connecting their old systems. Because their applications are old and often inherited, the integration of new systems becomes totally impractical financially, and integration is often prohibited due to several factors, for example, to ensure data security. Proper functioning of the features is one of the most important motives that prohibit the integration. However, with the use of middleware, the integration with the different departments and systems becomes easier and its cheaper maintenance [10].

The future of the IoT will consist of a variety of sensors connected to a network that will store all information for all users [10]. The article says, as well, that the IoT must be supported by middleware that enables consumers and IoT developers to interact in a friendly manner.

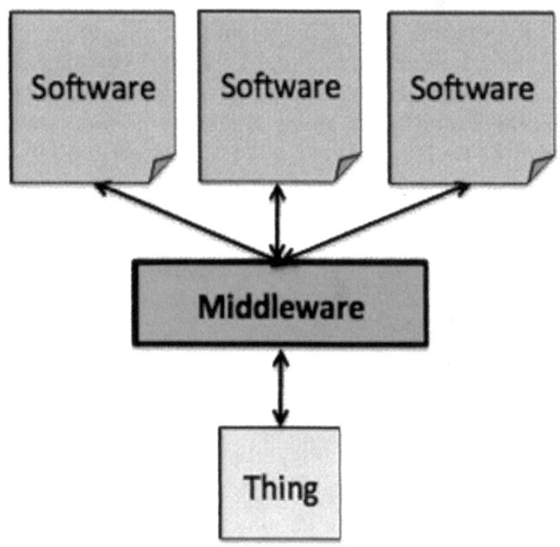

Figure 2. Interaction between software and things using middleware [12]

Figure 2 illustrates how the IoT works with middleware. The idea is that middleware will support a lot of different software and allow for connection with "things."

However, even with all these features and benefits, using middleware with the IoT may present some challenges, such as inter-operability, scalability, abstraction, spontaneous interaction between "things," distributed infrastructure, security, privacy, and variety of middleware types [10].

Regarding the problems cited above, the proposed article focuses on citing the main problems in the use of the IoT with middleware. The problems and difficulties listed in this article result from studies conducted by researchers.

IV. PROBLEMS/DIFICULITIES WITH MIDDLEWARE FOR IOT

A. Security problems in IoT plataforms

Everything indicates that the IoT will have a great impact on humanity because of the fact that it uses objects from our everyday lives. Despite all the benefits that can be gained with this technology, one topic that demands a lot of attention is security in the IoT. This security problem has even been the subject the BlackHat and DEFCON conference on issues related to hacking [13].

In a report published by [14], 70% of the IoT devices are vulnerable to attack. The study was based on the top ten devices most currently used. It found 250 flaws [15]. On average, 25 vulnerabilities were found per each device tested. The top vulnerabilities highlighted were:

- Privacy concerns
- Insufficient authorization
- Lack of transport encryption
- Insecure web interface
- Inadequate software protection

The following scenario illustrates how complicated the problem is: suppose a person is driving his or her car and suddenly, without receiving the driver's command, the steering wheel turns alone and the driver loses control of the car, causing a serious accident. This situation may eventually become reality, as hackers recently broke into a state-car system and took full control of direction [16]. In addition, other functions may be affected in the event of an invasion in the car system, such as turning off the seatbelts or triggering the airbag. Research also suggests that the traditional platforms of Web and data networks may suffer from Denial of Service (DoS) attacks.

A major concern in the development of middleware for the IoT has been to try to avoid security problems and data theft, seeing that the IoT does not refer only to computers, but also to multiple devices, "things," which eventually will be exposed to attacks.

A survey of low-level protocols to ensure security and privacy in centralized and distributed scenarios of IoT is presented in [17], and the research community aims to improve the protocols constantly in order to address these security challenges.

In [18] an analysis and review of available platforms for IoT and a vision regarding security and privacy are presented.

As seen above, the negative impacts caused by this problem lead to one of the primary reasons that security problem in IoT should be looked into with caution and care.

Middleware developers need to be attentive to this major concern as regards the creation of new platforms for IoT. The lack of well-defined protocol security could jeopardize the advances in IoT and adoption by companies and users [31]. A security barrier can be imposed based on the limitations of the infrastructure of IoT itself, which still needs to evolve in this direction so that it can have a more solid basis for the possibility of more robust implementations.

Figure 3 shows that security has different levels of complexity and scale in the case of security and privacy [19]. This article does not aim to explain in detail the greater security as a whole, but it is important to show that IoT security needs to be studied and analyzed with great care and attention, because, as previously explained, any error or security problem would cause the device in question to be discontinued, or, in worse cases, the company that developed the device could suffer loss or lawsuit.

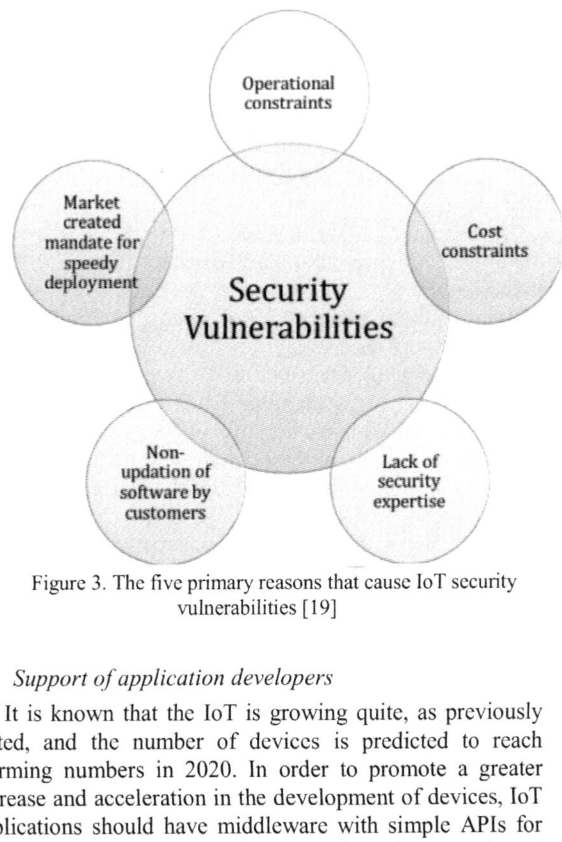

Figure 3. The five primary reasons that cause IoT security vulnerabilities [19]

B. Support of application developers

It is known that the IoT is growing quite, as previously stated, and the number of devices is predicted to reach alarming numbers in 2020. In order to promote a greater increase and acceleration in the development of devices, IoT applications should have middleware with simple APIs for the desired features, preferably with high levels of abstraction. Moreover, these APIs should be developed and made available in a standard way, as far as possible, so that the development of new applications and devices will be more efficient and effective [18].

Mineraud says that most IoT platforms currently offer a public API to use services. According to the same, the APIs are generally based on RESTful principles allowing the use of common operations, such as: PUT, GET, PUSH, or

DELETE. These four operations provide support and interaction of devices connected to the platform. But not all platforms include the REST API to help and facilitate the development of web services [18].

To mitigate the above problem, many platforms provide open source libraries to carry out the connections of different programming languages to the APIs available in the middleware. Mineraud is still more emphatic in stating that these links do not make a significant improvement on developer support, seeing that these libraries offer only basic functions such as access keys [18].

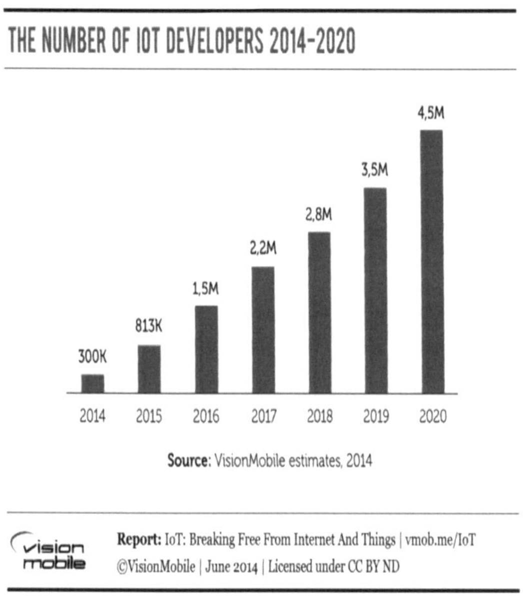

Figure 4. Number of IoT developers [30]

Figure 4 shows that the number of IoT developers is constantly growing, which means that application developer support is more complicated, because the problem affects not only the larger growth of IoT devices, but also the larger growth of IoT developers.

Finally, Mineraud concludes by starting, "We believe that this approach should be more generalized within IoT solutions to maximize usability of the services provided by the IoT platforms."[18]

C. Processing and data sharing

The volume of data used in IoT platform tends to be large, and the applications typically present requirements which need to be met in real time. This volume of data presents a stream of unlimited data, which often varies according to time. Because of this variability, data can be unreliable and incomplete, and there is not a desirable quality and information regarding communication loss account [20]. It is also worth mentioning that this data is represented in various shapes and models. The example is a great challenge to use directly the low-level data that the sensors of the devices generate without having a data model and knowledge.

The information and knowledge behind the data collected are the core and basis of the wealth produced by IoT. Therefore, the processing devices and data sharing must be developed to ensure that the data captured by the IoT can be used in various applications. Today, IoT solutions do not support processing and data sharing in a dynamic format. However, it remains possible to combine multiple simple applications in a dynamic format, provided that the URI to the source of the desired information is known. However, it represents a very challenging technique for application developers and platforms IoT [21].

The Ericsson IoT framework provides mechanisms for virtual integration that can be combined with dynamic sites to analyze statistical data. Furthermore, different techniques of processing and data sharing are adapted for IoT. According to Tsai et al. [22], mining technology research data for the IoT try to improve the processing and sharing of large data stream generated by IoT devices.

D. Privacy concerns

Many IoT devices collect personal information such as name, address, date of birth, health information, and even credit card numbers. Those concerns are multiplied when one adds in cloud services and mobile applications that work with the device [23]. Too much personal information is collected, and it is very common that this information is not properly protected. In the end, users are not given the choice to allow what type of data will be collected.

According to The Open Web Application Security Project (OWASP) [24], in order to verify if the IoT device has privacy concerns, it is necessary to determine the following:

- Whether all data types that are being collected by the device are identified,
- Whether the device and its various components collect only what is necessary to perform its function,
- Whether identifiable information can be exposed when not properly encrypted while at rest on storage mediums and during transit over networks,
- Who has access to personal information that is collected,
- Whether data collected can be de-identified or anonymized,
- Whether data collected is beyond what is needed for proper operation of the device and whether the end-user has a choice for this data collection,
- Whether a data retention policy is in place.

An IoT device can ensure the privacy concerns by minimizing the data collection, anonymizing the collected data or giving the end user the ability to decide what data is collected [25]

E. Integration detection technologies and activation

The essence of the IoT platform is to establish a connection detecting and triggering heterogeneous systems with different capabilities and limitations. In the absence of a common standard of communication and detection, different suppliers become accustomed to the vice of writing and implementing their own interaction patterns and implement different sets of communication protocols. Thus, the IoT platform ends up having multiple and different protocols available. Unfortunately, as a result, IoT platform value has increased. This increase grows proportionally with the amount and versatility of the devices supported by the platform. An ideal platform for IoT must provide a group or set of protocols for communication that are standardized and thus every device 'manufacturer can choose the set of protocols that best adjustment in the device.[27]

For a quiet and harmonious integration with detection and actuation of IoT devices, it is essential to define standardized protocols for all devices, for example, in the manner done today with constrained devices by IEFT [27] and communications ETSI M2M and 3GPP [28]

However, the current solutions found for IoT bring a different approach to the issue of different devices. Usually the question of interoperability with others devices in IoT is guaranteed through the implementation of a gateway, which usually features an expanded capacity with the help of plug-ins that make it possible to support new devices in a IoT platform, thus not featuring a standardization of protocols. In order to accelerate integration of new pattern models devices, such as those recommended in the Smart Objects Guidelines [29], they should be integrated in a broad and systemic way [30].

V. Conclusion and Final Considerations

The IoT presents numerous benefits to consumers and has the potential to change the ways that people interact with technology.

After a brief explanation of IoT and middleware this survey proposes to clarify the difficulties in adopting middleware for IoT development.

From all exposed difficulties and problems in this research, we realize that the security problem in IoT platforms, presented in section 4, is the difficulty that requires the greatest attention from the IoT developers. Software for IoT involves distribution and data sharing, thus increasing the risks of data theft.

From a security and privacy perspective, the introduction of sensors and devices into currently intimate spaces such as the home, the car, wearable objects, or everyday things to detect and share observations about us increasingly deserves special attention and concern.

There is no denying the utility of middleware assists IoT development, but we have to be aware of some concerns about the difficulties and problems that this survey covers in its study.

For future researches, there is good opportunity to apply solutions to all problems listed above or, perhaps, to choose security as the problem most relevant to the use of middleware for IoT.

References

[1] K. Ashton, That 'Internet of Things' Thing [Online]. Available from: http://www.rfidjournal.com/articles/view?4986 2016.08.11

[2] Z. Shirin, Middleware for Internet of Things, University of Twente, November 2013

[3] K. Sacha, "Introduction to Middleware", 2003. Available at http://middleware.objectweb.org/index.html. 2016.08.11

[4] IDC, Worldwide Internet of Things (IoT) 2013-2020 Forecast: Billions of Things, Trillions of Dollars, October2013.

[5] IDC, Worldwide Internet of Things Spending by Vertical Markets 2014-2017Forecast, February 2014.

[6] P. Guillemin and P. Friess, "Internet of things strategic research roadmap," The Cluster of European Research Projects,Tech., September 2009, Available at http://www.researchgate.net/publication/267566519_Internet_of_Things_Strategic_Research_Roadmap 2016.08.10

[7] X. Feng, T. Y. Laurence, W. Lizhe and V. Alex., Internet of Things

[8] L. Atzori and A. Iera, G. Morabito, The Internet of Things: A Survey, Computer Networks., , p.2787-2805, October, 2010

[9] C. Aércio, A. Carlos and F. Ana Paula, "A Study on Middleware for IoT," International Conference on Internet Computing. Athens., pp.32-37, 2016.

[10] C.D Igill and W.D. Smart, Middleware for robots? In: AAAI Spring Symposium on Intelligent Distributed and Embedded Systems. Stanford Proceedings. Stanford:2002

[11] S. De Deugd, R. Carroll, K. Kelly, B. Millett and J. Ricker, SODA: service oriented devide architecture, IEEE Pervasive Computing., pp. 94-96, 2006

[12] M. Koster (2014, May 28). Design Patterns for an Internet of Things [Online]. Available from: https://community.arm.com/groups/internet-of-things/blog/2014/05/27/design-patterns-for-an-internet-of-things 2016.08.11

[13] P. McMillan (2014, Aug 7). DEFCON [Online]. Available: https://defcon.org/images/defcon-22/dc-22-presentations/Mcmillan/DEFCON-22-Paul-Mcmillan-Attacking-the-IOT-Using-timing-attacks.pdf 2016.08.11

[14] D. Miessler. (2014, Jul 7) [Online]. Available: http://h30499.www3.hp.com/t5/Fortify-Application-Security/HP-Study-Reveals-70-Percent-of-Internet-of-Things-Devices/ba-p/6556284 2016.08.11

[15] N. Dhanjani (2014). Abusing the Internet of Things [Online]. Available: https://www.blackhat.com/docs/asia-14/materials/Dhanjani/Asia-14-Dhanjani-Abusing-The-Internet-Of-Things-Blackouts-Freakouts-And-Stakeouts.pdf 2016.08.11

[16] NIC Videos (2014, jan 7) What is IPV6. [Online] Available: https://www.youtube.com/watch?v=_JbLr_C-

HLk&list=PLQq8-9yVHyObGmdqA-aD_QaLrZaC_tkOI 2016.08.10

[17] R. Roman, J. Zhou and J. Lopez, On the features and challenges of security and privacy in distributed internet of things, Computer Networks 57 (10) (2013) 2266–2279, towards a Science of Cy- ber Security and Identity Architecture for the FutureInternet. doi:http://dx.doi.org/10.1016/j.comnet.2012.12.018. URL http://www.sciencedirect.com/science/article/pii/S1389128613000054 2016.08.10

[18] Mineraud, Julien, et al. "A gap analysis of Internet-of-Things platforms." arXiv preprint arXiv:1502.01181 (2015).

[19] S. Schuermans and M. Vakulenko (2014, Jun 26). IoT: Breaking Free From Internet and Things [Online] Availabre from: http://www.visionmobile.com/blog/2014/06/who-will-be-the-ios-and-android-of-iot 2016.08.11

[20] J. Gubbi, R. Buyya, S. Marusic and M. Palaniswami, Internet of Things (IoT): A vision, architectural elements, and future di- rections, Future Generation Computer Systems 29 (7) (2013) 1645–1660. doi:10.1016/j.future.2013.01.010. URL http://dx.doi.org/10.1016/j.future.2013.01.010

[21] A. Maarala, X. Su and J. Riekki, Semantic data provisioning and reasoning for the internet of things, in: Internet of Things (IOT), 2014 International Conference on the, 2014, pp. 67–72. doi:10.1109/IOT.2014.7030117.

[22] C.-W. Tsai, C.-F. Lai, M.-C. Chiang and L. Yang, Data mining for internet of things: A survey, Communications Surveys Tu- torials, IEEE 16 (1) (2014) 77–97. doi:10.1109/SURV.2013. 103013.00206.

[23] Internet of things HPE Security Research Study, Craig Smith and Daniel Miessler, HPE Fortify, June 2014

[24] OWASP. (2016, Feb 5) Top 10 2014-I5 Privacy Concerns [Online]. Available: https://www.owasp.org/index.php/Top_10_2014-I5_Privacy_Concerns 2016.08.10

[25] H. Kate et al. OWASP IoT Top Ten Infographic avaliable at https://www.owasp.org/images/8/8e/Infographic-v1.jpg 2016.08.10

[26] C. Bormann, A. Castellani and Z. Shelby, CoAP: An application protocol for billions of tiny internet nodes, IEEE Internet Com- puting 16 (2) (2012) 62–67. doi:10.1109/MIC.2012.29.

[27] I. Ishaq, D. Carels, G. K. Teklemariam, J. Hoebeke, F. V. d. Abeele, E. D. Poorter, I. Moerman and P. Demeester, IETF stan- dardization in the field of the Internet of Things (IoT): A survey, Journal of Sensor and Actuator Networks 2 (2) (2013) 235–287. doi:10.3390/jsan2020235.

[28] T. Klinpratum, C. Saivichit, A. Elmangoush and T. Magedanz, To- ward interconnecting M2M/IoT standards: interworking proxy for IEEE1888 standard at ETSI M2M platform, in: The 29th International Technical Conference on Circuit/Systems Com- puters and Communications, 2014

[29] IPSO Alliance, Ipso smartobject guideline, Tech. rep., Internet Protocol for Smart Objects (IPSO) Alliance (2014). URL http://www.ipso- alliance.org/ technical-information/ipso- guidelines 2016.08.10

[30] S. Satyadevan, B. Kalarickal and M. Jinesh, Security, trust and implementation limitations of prominent iot platforms, in: S. C. Satapathy, B. N. Biswal, S. K. Udgata and J. K. Mandal (Eds.), Proceedings of the 3rd International Conference on Frontiers of Intelligent Computing: Theory and Applications (FICTA) 2014, Vol. 328 of Advances in Intelligent Systems and Computing, Springer International Publishing, 2015, pp. 85–95. doi:10. 1007/978- 3- 319- 12012- 6_10.

[31] R. Roman, J. Zhou and J. Lopez, On the features and challenges of security and privacy in distributed internet of things, Computer Networks 57 (10) (2013) 2266–2279, towards a Science of Cy- ber Security and Identity Architecture for the Future Internet. doi:http://dx.doi.org/10.1016/j.comnet.2012.12.018. URL http://www.sciencedirect.com/science/article/pii/S1389128613000054 2016.08.12

A Review of User Interface Description Languages for Mobile Applications

Nikola Mitrović*, Carlos Bobed*†, Eduardo Mena*†
*Dept. of Computer Science & Systems Engineering
University of Zaragoza, Spain
†Aragon Institute of Engineering Research (I3A), Spain
Email: mitrovic@prometeo.cps.unizar.es, {cbobed,emena}@unizar.es

Abstract—**Adapting a graphical user interface (GUI) for various user devices is still one of the most interesting topics in today's mobile computation. The benefits of separating the specification of the GUI from its implementation are broadly accepted. However, it is not clear which are the benefits and disadvantages of current GUI specification languages in order to define and develop multiplatform mobile applications which can adapt dynamically to different devices with different features. In this paper, we review User Interface Description Languages (UIDLs) that can be used currently to specify GUIs in mainstream mobile platforms. We analyze their features and usefulness for dynamic adaptation of GUIs to heterogeneous mobile devices. All reviewed UIDLs are suitable for developing mobile applications; however, there are no UIDLs that will truly be able to operate across multiple platforms.**

***Index Terms*—Adaptive GUI; Mobile Computing.**

I. Introduction

The use of mobile devices and applications is increasing. Adapting GUIs to different mobile devices is still one of the most interesting problems in mobile computing as modern devices vary considerably in their properties (e.g., screen size, resolution, user input controls). The benefits of working with User Interface Definition Languages (UIDLs) [1] to specify GUI is that such a specification can be re-used and adapted to different devices automatically. This approach has been accepted by the GUI researchers a long time ago [2], and it has been applied to multiple devices in the Personal Digital Assistant (PDA) era [3]. However, there does not exist yet a standard UIDL that is widely used by software developers, let alone by mobile apps developers.

In this paper, we review main User Interface Description Languages (UIDLs) that can be used currently to specify GUIs in mainstream mobile platforms. While there is a large number of research-based UIDLs (such as UIML [2], UsiXML [4], or Maria XML [5], to name a few), these UIDLs have limited support and implementation code outside their respective research institutions, and, thus, we will focus on the *mainstream* UIDLs that have strong adoption in at least one of the significant technology ecosystems.

Previous UIDL reviews [6][7][8] focused on theoretical UIDLs, devices and platforms of the time, and their usefulness for Human-Computer Interaction adaptation in general, as opposed for mobile application suitability. These prior reviews did not analyze modern, industry accepted, UIDLs such as Android XML [9] or XAML [10], and did not consider today's mainstream mobile devices and their market uptake. We analyze the features of mainstream UIDL languages, and evaluate them from the point of view of being used by mobile applications to allow a dynamic adaptation of such specifications to heterogeneous modern mobile devices. We focus on their ease of use, and the availability of visual tools, among other parameters. We consider the following two categories of UIDLs, based on their relationship with the mobile platforms and Web browsers:

1) *UIDLs specific for mobile devices.* These UIDLs are specifically developed for a particular mobile platform, e.g., Android or iOS devices.
2) *UIDLs associated with Web browsers.* These UIDLs are linked to one or more Web browsers, and can be used for mobile application development.

Finally, for the purpose of this review, we use as an example a simple currency converter, which converts numeric amounts between three currencies. This example application was developed for each UIDL that is reviewed in this paper in order to evaluate the usefulness of the provided tools, and its applicability to multi-device and multi-platform use. Full specifications of the example application in different UIDLs can be found in [11].

The remainder of this paper is structured as follows. Section II presents the UIDLs used in popular mobile platforms. In Section III, we review UIDLs that are associated with Web browsers. In Section IV, we analyze and compare the above approaches. Finally, Section V gives some conclusions and future work.

II. UIDLs Specific for Mobile Devices

In this section, we review the UIDLs used in the market leading mobile platforms, namely, Android XML (Android) and Storyboards (iOS); both platforms together reach a 92% of market share [12]. We also include other relevant UIDLs for mobile devices such as XAML (Windows 10), and QML (Ubuntu OS).

A. Android XML

Android is the most widely used operating systems when it comes to mobile devices (i.e., smartphones and tablets): Android market share is estimated at 60.99%. It is a Linux-based operating system whose middleware, libraries, and APIs are written in C. Android supports Java code as it uses a Java-like virtual machine called *Dalvik* (substituted by ART from Android 5.x onward). In Fig. 1, we show an excerpt of the Android XML code of our example application and a screenshot rendered in an Android N emulator.

```
<LinearLayout
  ...
    <TextView android:layout_width="wrap_content"
        android:layout_height="wrap_content"
      android:text="Currency Converter"
            android:id="@+id/textView" />
  <LinearLayout android:orientation="horizontal" ... >
    <TextView ... android:id="@+id/textView2"
            android:text="Quantity:" />
    <EditText ... android:id="@+id/Qty" .../>
  </LinearLayout>
  <LinearLayout android:orientation="horizontal" ... >
    <TextView ... android:id="@+id/textView3"
            android:text="From:" />
    <RadioGroup ...   android:id="@+id/From">
      <RadioButton ... android:id="@+id/eurFrom"
              android:text="Euros" ... />
      <RadioButton ... android:id="@+id/usdFrom"
              android:text="US Dollars" ... />
      <RadioButton ... android:id="@+id/gbpFrom"
              android:text="British Pounds" ... />
    </RadioGroup>
    <TextView ...
            android:id="@+id/textView4"
              android:text="To:" />
        ...
  </LinearLayout>
  <LinearLayout android:orientation="horizontal" ...
    <TextView ... android:id="@+id/textView5"
            android:text="Result:" />
    <TextView ... android:id="@+id/output" />
  </LinearLayout>
  <Button ... android:id="@+id/convert"
    android:text="Convert" />
</LinearLayout>
```

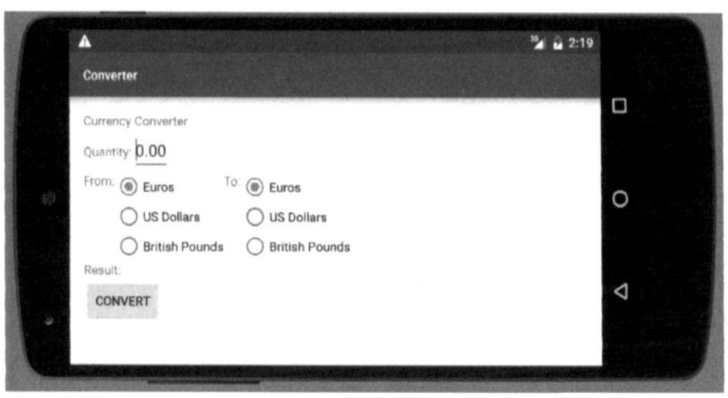

Fig. 1. Excerpt of the Android XML specification and rendering for the sample app.

Android applications are built using *Activities*, which can be regarded as windows in a usual desktop environment, and *Services*, which are background processes without GUI. Graphical User Interfaces are defined using a XML-based notation named Android XML [13][9].

Given the heterogeneity of Android devices, support for GUI adaptation to different devices is provided using layout elements and visual behavior policies. Android also provides further mechanisms to deal with different device display capabilities and adapt the interface, but it is the developer who is in charge of developing the application in a responsive and plastic way [14].

The developer can specify behavioral aspects in Android XML in different ways, such as event handling. Moreover, within the Android XML document, the application developer can state implicit navigation via the definition of *Intents*, objects which represent the intention of the application, and allows development of applications in a service oriented way. This service oriented model allows applications to use activities from other applications using a built-in broker mechanism.

GUI and UIDL development can be performed using the Android Studio SDK's visual editor. Android XML is sufficiently developer-friendly and can be edited manually when required, e.g., to refine GUI behavior.

B. Storyboards (iOS)

Similarly to Android, Apple's iOS also adopts a XML-driven interface via *Storyboards* [15]. Apple's approach goes further than Android: Storyboards use *views* (similar to Android's *activities*), but they can also explicitly include navigation aspects of user interaction in the GUI specification. Thus, a storyboard provides a comprehensive view of the whole application and the workflow of interactions.

The set of elements provided by iOS to define UIs does not contain some common visual elements such as radio and check button widgets (although the platform allows custom widgets to be developed if required). In Fig. 2, we present a screenshot of our example application rendered in iOS emulator; note that choices are made using switches, not radio or check buttons. We have not included the iOS storyboard code due to space limitation (the full code is available in [11]).

Fig. 2. Sample app as rendered in iOS emulator from its storyboard specification.

The model adopted by iOS devices is more closed than the one adopted by Android. When developing applications for iOS, the developer has lower heterogeneity of devices than Android, but the interface guidelines are more strictly dictated by the environment. The definition of the application appearance is done via a visual editor integrated in Apple's Xcode environment. While in Android (and other used UIDLs) the interface definition can be easily defined (or at least edited) by the developer without visual help, storyboard XML language is clearly designed to be machine-generated and not edited manually. The application logic in iOS can be developed using Objective-C or Swift programming languages.

C. XAML: eXtensible Application Markup Language

XAML [10] is the UIDL developed by Microsoft and has been used in several of their technologies (e.g., .NET 4.0, Silverlight). XAML is also used to specify GUIs for the Windows 10 platform. This makes XAML available not only on fixed Windows computers but also on mobile devices. See Fig. 3 for an excerpt of the XAML code of our example application developed as an UWP application, and its rendering on a Windows 10 Desktop.

```
<Page x:Class="Converter.Converter" ... ">
   <StackPanel >
      <StackPanel >
         <TextBlock> Currency Converter</TextBlock>
         <StackPanel Orientation="Horizontal">
            <TextBlock Text="Quantity:"/>
            <TextBox Text="0.00" x:Name="Qty"/>
         </StackPanel>
         <StackPanel Orientation="Horizontal">
            <TextBlock Text="From:"/>
            <StackPanel>
               <RadioButton x:Name="EurFrom"
                  GroupName="From">Euros</RadioButton>
               <RadioButton x:Name="UsdFrom"
                  GroupName="From">US Dollars</RadioButton>
               <RadioButton x:Name="GbpFrom"
                  GroupName="From">British Pounds
               </RadioButton>
            </StackPanel>
            ...
         </StackPanel>
      </StackPanel>
      <StackPanel Orientation="Horizontal">
         <TextBlock Text="Result:"/>
         <TextBlock x:Name="Output" Text=""/>
      </StackPanel>
      <Button x:Name="Convert">Convert</Button>
   </StackPanel>
</Page>
```

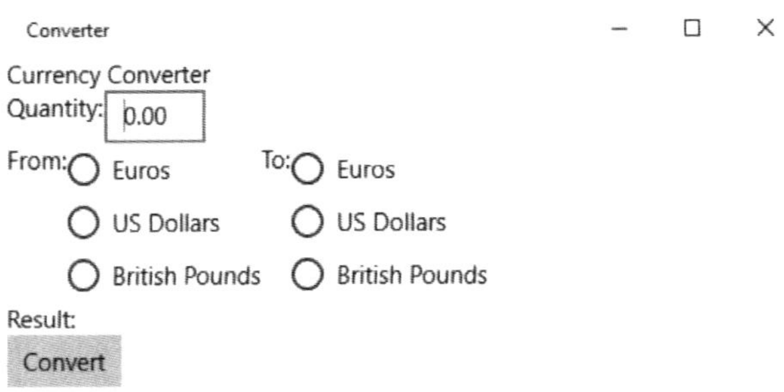

Fig. 3. Example of the XAML specification and rendering for the sample app.

Microsoft made an important effort to unify development of applications for different Microsoft platforms under the Universal Windows Platform (UWP) programme [10]. UWP applications share a basic API and GUI elements which are then extended and specialized for specific device families. As long as the developer restricts its application to the use of the basic API and XAML elements the application will run on all devices that are compatible with UWP.

Although XAML is used only in Windows-based devices, there is still a need to adapt GUIs to different devices. This adaptation is quite similar to Android: developers need to provide layout elements and policies in order to adapt (to a certain extent) automatically the GUI to the specific device.

D. QML

QML is an UIDL associated to Qtgraphical libraries [16] and it has been adopted as UIDL for Ubuntu OS applications. QML is a JSON-like language, where graphical elements are grouped in libraries which can be imported as needed (thus providing an extension mechanism). Fig. 4 shows an QML code excerpt for our example application and a screenshot of the GUI as rendered by Qt Designer (Ubuntu Mate Desktop).

```
import QtQuick 2.1 ...
ApplicationWindow {
   id: applicationWindow1
   title: qsTr("Converter")
   ColumnLayout {
      id: columnLayout1
      anchors.rightMargin: 0
      anchors.bottomMargin: 0
       ...
       Label {
        id: label1
        ...
        text: qsTr("Currency Converter")
   }
      RowLayout {  /* From Radio button */
         id: rowLayout2
         ...
        Label {
           id: label3
           ...
           text: qsTr("From:") }
        ColumnLayout {     /* inside RowLayout */
           id: columnLayout3
           ...
           ExclusiveGroup {id:from}
           RadioButton {
              id: eurFrom
              ...
              text: qsTr("Euros")
              checked: true
              exclusiveGroup: from }
           RadioButton {
              id: usdFrom
              ...
              text: qsTr("US Dollars")
              exclusiveGroup: from }
           RadioButton {
              id: gbpFrom
              ...
              text: qsTr("British Pounds")
              exclusiveGroup: from}
             }...}...}...}
```

Fig. 4. Example of the QML specification and rendering for the sample app.

Being a general purpose UIDL language, QML (since Qt 5.1) also provides layout mechanisms in order to support device adaptation. Previously, Qt Quick support for windows resizing (not device adaptation) was limited to the use of *positioners* for items, and *anchors* to layout children GUI elements. Qt provides bindings to multiple programming languages and platforms, which makes the adoption of QML a feasible solution for multiplatform development. Moreover, as with Android XML and XAML, the specification is developer-friendly and can be edited using visual tools or manually.

III. UIDLs Associated with Web Browsers

Apart from developing ad hoc apps for each of the mobile platforms, the development of applications using Web technologies has increased as Web browsers are broadly available for fixed and mobile devices. These applications use the Web browser (or its engine) as a kind of runtime middleware, where an application can be deployed independently of the underlying mobile platform (with some limitations). This section reviews two UIDLs that are used by Web browsers: HTML5, the most widely used UIDL as it is supported by both mobile and desktop computers, and eXtensible User Interface Definition Language (XUL), used by the Mozilla Foundation.

A. HTML5

HTML5 [17] is a the new version of HyperText Markup Language, the language for structuring and presenting content on the Web. While HTML5 can be considered to be mainly content-oriented, it offers several form tags to interact with the user, which makes it also suitable to define user interfaces. For our review, we are considering plain HTML5, without any JavaScript library extensions.

Fig. 5 shows an excerpt of the HTML5 specification for the sample app and a screenshot of its rendering in Firefox. Note that plain-HTML tag `<table role="presentation">` was used to specify the layout of the GUI. The use of this tag has been discouraged by the W3C HTML5 Recommendation Document and use of CSS [17] is advised instead. This requires GUI developers have to manage both HTML5 and CSS descriptions to specify the required GUI layout.

HTML5 introduces new tags to include different types of content that are now directly supported by browsers (e.g., `<video>`, `<audio>`, `<canvas>`, `...`). Several new control forms [17] are introduced too (e.g., date, color, search, etc.). Moreover, some tags have been included to define a basic web document layout (e.g., `<header>`, `<nav>`, `<footer>`, `...`). However, responsiveness and layout adaption is delegated to CSS (usually combined with JavaScript).

The technology stack HTML5+CSS+JavaScript has gained momentum in mobile applications thanks to: 1) ubiquity of Web browsers, 2) the usefulness of client-server model to allow frequent content updates (rather than providing application updates), and 3) the introduction of cross-platform HTML5 code engines, such as Apache Cordova [18] or Crosswalk [19]. Firefox OS [20] and Ubuntu OS applications can also be implemented using this technology stack. While multiplatform applications can be developed using HTML5 and Cordova or Crosswalk, such applications need to be installed on each computer in the same way as regular applications (to run, some of them have to be bundled along with a particular runtime).

```
<html> ... <body>
 <table role="presentation">
  <tr> <td> Currency Converter </td> </tr>
  <tr> <td>
   <table>
    <tr> <td>
     <table role="presentation">
      <tr> <td> Quantity </td>
       <td>
        <input type="text"
          id="Qty" value="0.00"/> </td> </tr>
     </table> </td> </tr>
    <tr> <td>
     <table role="presentation">
      <tr> <td> From: </td>
       <td>
        <input type="radio" name="From"
          value="eurFrom"> Euros <br>
        <input type="radio" name="From"
          value="usdFrom"> US Dollars <br>
        <input type="radio" name="From"
          value="gbpFrom"> British Pounds </td>
       ...
     </table> </td> </tr>
    <tr> <td>
     <table role="presentation">
      <tr> <td> Result: </td>
       <td id="output"> </td>  </tr>
     </table> </td> </tr>
    <tr> <td>
     <table role="presentation">
      <tr> <td>
        <input type="button" name="Convert"
          value="Convert">
       </td> </tr>
     </table> ...
 ...
</body> </html>
```

Fig. 5. Example of the HTML5 specification and rendering for the sample app.

B. XUL: eXtensible User interface definition Language

XUL [21] is the UIDL developed and supported by Mozilla in its Gecko engine. XUL allows development of multiplatform interfaces by providing a GUI specification that is very abstract and not related to any specific devices or platforms. In Fig. 6, we present an excerpt of the XUL specification of our sample app and its rendering in Firefox.

In order to provide adaption to the different capabilities of the devices, XUL relies both on predefined layouts, and customization via CSS and JavaScript. While it is mainly oriented to window-based GUIs, the widgets and basic layouts provide developers with a higher level abstraction than other similar languages (e.g., HTML5).

```
...
<window title="Converter" xmlns=" ... /there.is.only.xul">
<vbox>
   <label control="lblAll" value="Currency Converter"/>
   <hbox>
      <label control="lblQty" value="Quantity:"/>
      <textbox value="0.00" id="Qty"/>
   </hbox>
   <hbox>
      <label control="lblFrom" value="From: "/>
      <radiogroup orient="vertical" id="From" ...>
         <radio id="EurFrom" label="Euros"/>
         <radio id="UsdFrom" label="US Dollars"/>
         <radio id="GbpFrom" label="British Pounds"/>
      </radiogroup>
      ...
   </hbox>
   <hbox>
      <label control="lblOutput" value="Result: "/>
      <label id="Output" control="Output" value=""/>
   </hbox>
   <hbox>
      <button id="Cnv" label="Convert" oncommand="convert()"/>
   </hbox>
</vbox>
</window>
```

Fig. 6. Example of the XUL specification and rendering for the sample app.

XUL has been adopted as the UIDL for developing extensions for Firefox Web browser, but this use might be discontinued in favor of adopting WebExtensions (mainly due to security reasons). In fact, Firefox OS apps are developed using the full Web technology stack (HTML5, CSS, and JavaScript). The application logic for XUL applications using Gecko engine is mainly developed using JavaScript.

IV. Comparison

After defining our sample Currency Converter application in all the reviewed UIDLs to grasp the philosophy of each language, we analyze the pros and cons of each of them from the point of view of using them to develop the GUI of applications that must run on very different fixed or mobile computers. Thus, in Table I, we can see different appealing characteristics related to multiplatform development, namely:

- Multi-device: It refers to whether the UIDL takes into consideration devices with different characteristics (e.g., screen size).
- Multi-OS: Considers if the UIDL can be used outside the boundaries of a particular OS (or mobile platform).
- Multi-language: It refers to whether the UIDL can be used with different programming languages to develop the application logic.
- Visual Editor: Considers existence of tools that allow developers to design UIDL-based GUIs in a visual manner, abstracting developers from UIDL's syntax.
- Friendly Markup: Considers, regardless the existence of a visual editor, whether the UIDL specification can be edited manually by the developer easily or, alternatively, is the UIDL too difficult to edit manually due to e.g., complexity and number of UIDL elements.
- Layout Support: It refers to whether the UIDL allows developers to select predefined GUI layouts.

Regarding multi-device support, all the analyzed languages can be used in a multi-device target environment. However, it has to be noted that both HTML5 and XUL require a Web browser (or an engine) to be available for each device. Regarding operating systems support for UIDLs, Android XML and Storyboard are tightly bounded with Android and iOS, respectively. Moreover, note that XAML, while is suitable to develop GUIs for several platforms, is restricted to work within Windows devices.

Concerning supported programming languages, the logic of the applications developed with Android XML is, at first, restricted to Java. In iOS (Storyboards), the developer can use Objective-C or Swift. XAML can be used by different programming languages that are available under the .Net platform (e.g., Java, C#, etc.). For QML, JavaScript is recommended for developing apps in Ubuntu OS, but many other languages can be used when used alongside Qt libraries (if appropriate language bindings are available). The application logic of applications in HTML5 needs to be developed in JavaScript. Last but not least, there are some efforts to use XUL with different languages (such as Java) but they seem discontinued.

The existence of a friendly visual editor is not a problem for any analyzed language but for XUL. However, XUL has a really friendly markup which can be easily used to define the UIs. On the other side, in practice, iOS Storyboards require a visual editor due to the verbosity of its GUI specifications.

Finally, all languages but HTML5 support layout elements (and mechanisms) that help the developer to describe the interfaces in an adaptive way, which is a very important feature for multidevice application development. The case of HTML5 is special as layout is delegated almost completely to the use of complementary CSS (there are tags that are used to serve as entry points for this, i.e., `<div>`).

V. Conclusions and Future Work

In this paper, we have reviewed several popular User Interface Definition Languages (UIDLs) from the point of view of their use in the context of mobile applications. The objective of our evaluation was to understand usefulness, benefits, and drawbacks of UIDLs when adapting to multiple mobile devices or different user contexts. We defined an example application in each UIDL to help the evaluation.

TABLE I
COMPARISON OF THE REVIEWED UIDLS.

Feature	Android XML	Storyboard	XAML	QML	HTML5	XUL
Multi-device	✓	✓	✓	✓	✓[2]	✓[2]
Multi-OS	×	×	✓[1]	✓	✓[2]	✓[2]
Multi-language	×	✓	✓	✓[3]	×	✓
Visual Editor	✓	✓	✓	✓	✓	×
Friendly Markup	✓	×	✓	✓	✓	✓
Layout Support	✓	✓	✓	✓	×	✓

[1] Provided that all devices are Windows-based.
[2] Provided a suitable engine (e.g., Web browser or app engine) is available.
[3] Provided there is a binding of Qt libraries to such a language.

As summary, all reviewed UIDLs can be used in mobile applications and adapted to multiple devices. However, we found that the most popular languages have strong dependency on their underlying platform and vendor (Android XML, XAML, Storyboards). These UIDLs are used only on Android, Apple, or Microsoft devices and do not have any support on other platforms. QML, whilst being less vendor-specific, requires language and platform bindings which may not be available or are difficult to use. On the other side, HTML5 is widely accepted as UIDL but requires several technologies to be combined in order to deliver GUIs (i.e., CSS, JavaScript, Web Browser). This makes the development of applications more complex and potentially less portable between different device-platform combinations. Mozilla's XUL, on the other hand, appears to be combining the features of other UIDLs and allows applications to be developed outside the Mozilla platform (i.e., without having a Web Browser).

We have shown that currently there does not exist a good multi-OS oriented UIDL which can be broadly adopted for developing applications whose GUI is correctly presented on very different mobile devices. Whenever an application needs to be delivered on multiple platform-device combinations, the user interface is not likely to be reused unless in vendor-specific situations (e.g., XAML for Microsoft environments, or Android XML for Android). HTML5, as stated before, requires several technologies to deliver a functional GUI description. Finally, XUL may offer the best chance of redeploying the user interface given that there are some implementations outside Mozilla's Web browser engine, albeit some of these appear to be discontinued.

As future work we plan to test different UIDLs by implementing more complex applications in multiple devices and user contexts. Furthermore, we will analyse performance implications of choosing a specific UIDLs, and their usefulness for advanced GUIs.

ACKNOWLEDGMENT

This work was supported by the CICYT project TIN2013-46238-C4-4-R and DGA-FSE.

REFERENCES

[1] N. Mitrović, E. Mena, and J. A. Royo, *Chapter XIX - Adaptive Interfaces in Mobile Environments: An Approach Based on Mobile Agents.* Information Science Reference, 2007, pp. 302–317.

[2] M. Abrams, C. Phanouriou, A. L. Batongbacal, S. M. Williams, and J. E. Shuster, "UIML: an appliance-independent XML user interface language," *Computer Networks*, vol. 31, no. 1116, pp. 1695–1708, 1999.

[3] N. Mitrović and E. Mena, "Adaptive user interface for mobile devices," in *Proceedings of the 9th International Workshop on Interactive Systems. Design, Specification, and Verification (DSV-IS'02)*, vol. 2545. Springer LNCS, June 2002, pp. 47–61.

[4] J. Gonzalez-Calleros, J.-P. Osterloh, R. Feil, and A. Ldtke, "Automated UI evaluation based on a cognitive architecture and UsiXML," *Science of Computer Programming*, vol. 86, pp. 43–57, 2014.

[5] F. Paterno, C. Santoro, and D. S. Lucio, "MARIA: a universal, declarative, multiple abstraction-level language for service-oriented applications in ubiquitous environments," *ACM Transactions on Computer-Human Interaction*, vol. 16, no. 4, pp. 219–224, 2009.

[6] J. Guerrero-Garcia, J. M. Gonzalez-Calleros, J. Vanderdonckt, and J. Muoz-Arteaga, "A theoretical survey of user interface description languages: Preliminary results," *Latin American Web Congress*, pp. 36–43, 2009.

[7] N. Souchon and J. Vanderdonckt, "A review of xml-compliant user interface description languages," in *Proceedings of the 10th International Workshop on Interactive Systems. Design, Specification, and Verification (DSV-IS'03)*, vol. 2844. Springer LNCS, 2003, pp. 377–391.

[8] J. Engel, C. Herdin, and M. Christian, "Review of user interface definition languages," in *Proceedings of the 6th Forum Medientechnik.* VWH, 2014, pp. 183–198.

[9] J. Morris, *Android User Interface Development.* Packt Publishing, 2011.

[10] A. Nathan, *Building Windows 10 Applications with XAML and C# Unleashed (2nd Edition).* Sams, 2016.

[11] N. Mitrovic, C. Bobed, and E. Mena, ADUS: Full UIDL code and samples at http://sid.cps.unizar.es/projects/ADUS/UIDLs, last accessed 30th Aug 2016.

[12] MarketShare, http://www.netmarketshare.com/, last accessed 30th Aug 2016.

[13] R. Rogers, J. Lombardo, and M. Blake, *Android Application Development.* O'Reilly, 2009.

[14] A. Demeure, G. Calvary, J. Coutaz, and J. Vanderdonckt, "The comets inspector: Towards run time plasticity control based on semantic network," in *Proceedings of 5th International Workshop on Task Models and Diagrams for UI Design (TAMODIA'06)*, vol. 4385. Springer LNCS, October 2006, pp. 324–338.

[15] M. Neuburg, *Progamming iOS 9.* O'Reilly, 2015.

[16] R. Rischpater, *Application Development with Qt Creator (2nd Edition).* Packt Publishing, 2014.

[17] W3C, HTML5 W3C Recommendation, http://www.w3.org/TR/html/, last accessed 30th Aug 2016.

[18] J. M. Wargo, *Apache Cordova 4 Programming.* Addison Wesley, 2015.

[19] Crosswalk-Project, http://www.crosswalk-project.org, last accessed 30th Aug 2016.

[20] T. Pant, *Learning Firefox OS Application Development.* Packt Publishing, 2015.

[21] V. Bullard, K. T. Smith, and M. C. Daconta, *Essential XUL Programming.* Wiley, 2001.

A Motivational Study Regarding IoT and Middleware for Health Systems

A Comparison of Relevant Articles

André Pedroza dos Santos, Dalfrede Welkener Soares Lima, Fhelipe Silva Freitas, Geiziany Mendes da Silva
CESAR – Recife Center for Advanced Studies and Systems
Recife, Brazil
e-mail:{anron@hotmail.com, welkener@gmail.com , freitaslouvor@gmail.com , geiziany.mendes@gmail.com}

***Abstract*—In this paper, we present the main concepts of the Internet of Things (IoT), which consists of a mix of smart devices, sensors and the Internet itself. In this research, we also address the concept of middleware, which is a platform that links both sensors and devices on IoT. In addition, we analyze selected research on IoT in order to gather information to construct a synopsis of the main facts in these articles. We identified paramount facts studied in each of these articles, so that we could perform a comparative analysis to highlight similarities with broader relevance.**

Keywords - IoT; middleware; e-health; health systems.

I. INTRODUCTION

In the last few years, we have witnessed a great excitement about the Internet of Things, also known as IoT. It is possible to notice the engagement of both companies and universities searching for solutions to make the concept of the "Internet of Things" become real. Each day new researches, studies and tools emerge and innovative ideas are born, creating a vast exploration of the field.

Nowadays, we live surrounded by electronic devices, at home, at work or in in the simplest environments. Even inside people's bodies, they have many different roles which makes us believe that the era of interconnected things has already began.

In health, we find an opened and motivated field in the search of technological solutions in order to achieve better efficiency in business and also to be accessible by a larger percent of the population. This way, patients who are informed daily about their health can take a proactive role in health care [1]. The contribution acquired by the evolution of interactive technologies is deeply linked to a significant improvement of productivity and quality of life.

In this context, e-health is introduced. It is defined as the use of electronic devices and other technologies in order to help with the practice of health care. That includes electronic medical prescriptions and remote monitoring of patients [2]. The possibility of using wireless sensors on one's clothes or body increases comfort, convenience and the effectiveness of the patients' health treatment. Considering that these can be monitored at distance without affecting the patients' routine [3].

The IoT is growing impressively in the scope of health and general medical care. Such great expansion generates increasingly interactive manners to deal with the patients' clinical situation through apparatuses such as wireless sensors and nanotechnology. It is remarkable the fact that the medical monitoring can be done in real-time through various devices, allowing patients to check their situation and getting new orientations via smartphones or tablets. Although, the immense potential brought by the insertion of the IoT in e-Health brings forward some facts that demand to be evaluated. The observable fact here is the interoperability among gadgets, considering that it demands transparency about the data shared on the devices. As Bui and Zorzi have put it [4] this constitutes a myriad of heterogeneous devices from many different manufacturers, each having their own interfaces and this way creating operational barriers. Besides that, another great concern points to a massive amount of data transmitted in a single network, which raises questions involving privacy and security.

The corcern in the questions above will mainly consist in the insertion of middleware platforms. These have been created to provide interoperability and to manage a variety of objects associated with the users and interconnected applications [5]. To e-health, the middleware platform can be described as a moderator for the data shared, integrating different devices of a heterogeneous environment and providing users the possibility of consulting their information through the Internet.

Baring the mentioned factors in mind, this study has as its main objective to focus on investigating and presenting articles that discuss the reasons of the motivation for creating a middleware to helpful gadgets concerning human health care, as well as the examples of mildware that already exists.

II. INTERNET OF THINGS

Giving the definition for the Internet of Things is not an easy job, since it is such an abstract idea, and yet there is much more to be done until its concept is built. In her article published in 2012, Talyta Singer [6] addresses various concepts of IoT from different authors. As she describes there, the IoT concept is an allusion to a global network in which devices can interact among themselves without human interference. This definition permeates one of the many views about the concept of IoT, leading to us believe that a lot has already been done. However, there is still a long road until it becomes real.

This article holds no intention on formalizing or defining the meaning of IoT, but only to point its use in health care. When it comees to IoT, Atzori [7] points out three great pillars: middleware, sensors and a basic knowledge to be stimulated. So, it is confirmed the need to show some of the reasons and implicationswhen using this technology concerning well being, monitoring, prevention and treatment of any disease [8].

IoT connects countless smart devices to a specific network. This way, technology may improve services in hospitals, health care centers and the practice of home care. To Paiva [9] the IoT is something that has to be present in our daily routine and is a source of great motivation in the health care research field for being a very promising area. The perspective for such an event grows through the popularization of the "Wearables", which can collect data without the need of human intervention. The data that comes from these devices, such as pulse rate, temperature and else, can go into a database, allowing medical monitoring from distance. The benefits of IoT are quite notorious when it comes to efficient diagnosis.

Figure 1. IoT –Health System Scenario. Source: [33]

It is clear that the IoT has very high potential for solving communication problems between health care centers and patients, this way, revolutionizing the treatment of diseases.

III. MIDDLEWARE

The IoT's environment is characterized by the heterogeneity among many devices and softwares involved; Those can execute various functions through distinct protocols, which makes it a challenge to implement such technology. To unify many resources of IoT, it is necessary to provide models of high-level interfacing, abstracting physical devices and services and guaranteeing a good interoperability.

The interoperability can be described as the possibility of interconnection in heterogeneous environments with transparency, as Marcondes and Sayão have said [10]. This unique interface doesn't demand the users to know about where and how their data is stored. In addition, to achieve a cohesive interoperability it is necessary to establish a pattern of communication among the gadgets. The model that offers such integration with transparency is what we call a middleware.

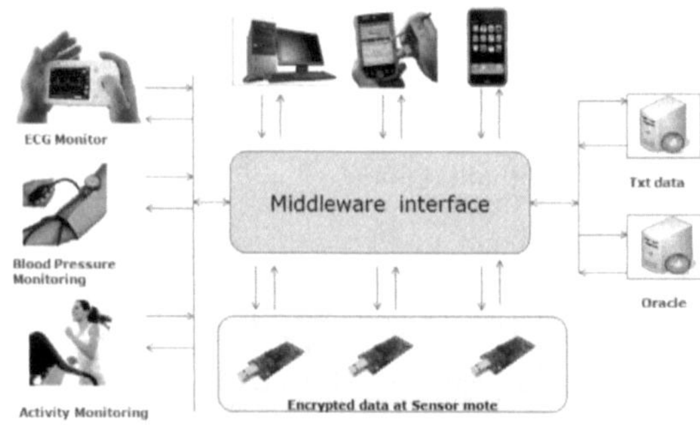

Figure 2. Middleware Interface in Personal Healthcare Information System [28]

For IoT, the middleware is the platform that integrates the applications and involved gadgets, as well as processing their communication. The middleware yet foments the reuse of generic services in order to streamline the development of applications, once it helps developers to deal directly with the specifications of both devices and network. We can also infer that the middleware mediates systems that are in different layers. The use of an intermediate middleware layer is needed to make interactions with the database from specific XML [11],[12],[13].

The differentiated middleware platform for IoT is being studied, but, for Teixeira [14] these proposals have not yet reached a stage of maturity. Also according to the author, several researches reveal points that require concentration on analysis and even more research, such as: robust infrastructures tolerant to failures able to manage and process the data collected through integrated intelligent devices; a better management of uncertainties and resolution of conflicts; and an adequate support to adapt environment and dynamic applications in order to minimize the overload of relevant security functions on the platform of the middleware.

When searching a better foundation, it is necessary to present the main requirements and elements of a middleware platform that includes the IoT environment, according to Maia [15]:

- A scalable interoperability support for the myriad of heterogeneous devices to enable intelligent objects (things) to communicate with users, Internet service and with each other;
- Mechanisms for detection and management of efficient devices that allow dynamic integration of new devices in the IoT's environment, as well as to manage the condition and location of these devices;
- Awareness of capacity for data processing management;
- An efficient dynamic support, since IoT's environment is inherently dynamic and applications

can be reconfigured at runtime according to the changes in such environments;
- The management of large amounts of data collected from smart devices that must be made available to applications and/or final users;
- Issues related to security and privacy, authenticity and integrity, which are important highlights, especially in critical applications; and;
- Providing a high-level interface to access heterogeneous devices transparently. Hiding the specifications of the integrated device applications and/or final users;

This way, the middleware platform comes as a promising solution for promoting interoperability between the IoT's devices and applications, as well as the final users.

IV. E-HEALTH SCENERY

Standards for interoperability have been proposed in the past twenty years to allow information exchange within a health care environment and the establishment of an accessible Electronic Health Record (EHR) to any health institution and/or patient. Standards for interoperability in health care need rules for sharing typical information of an EHR, as the description of health status, treatments given and results [16] Most standards currently broadcast use messages in text mode or Extensible Markup Language (XML) documents to provide health information that can be exchanged between systems. Nevertheless, there is still not a finished and worldwide used standard, which indicates that the interoperability of health systems can still be considered one of the greatest challenges to be faced in the field of health [17]

The use of a standard for interoperability allows any local system to interpretate data using universal concepts and terminology [18] Based on this definition, the idea of using a standard for interoperability in health to integrate distinct systems and use these same concepts and standardized terminologies to access data internally, or to access the database emerged itself. Representing requests by sending messages according to syntax and semantics established by a health standard model makes it possible to maintain compatibility and consistency between systems and database.

V. ANALYSIS OF RELEVANTS ARTICLES

In this section, we present a summary of the most relevant articles for this research; the analysis criteria was made based on the number of references and respective year of publication.

In the article "A Web Platform For Interconnecting Body Sensors And Improving Health Care", [19] the authors present the Health Care Devices' Ecosystem EcoHealth (EcoHealth), a web middleware platform that allows you to connect and approach doctors and patients through the use of body sensors, and thus provide better monitoring of health and diagnosis for patients. EcoHealth is supposed to integrate the information gathered from multiple heterogeneous devices in order to provide subsidy to monitor, process, display, store and send notifications about the patients' health as well as vital signs in real-time by using Internet standards. The article also presents the EcoHealth's proposed models, its logical architecture, implementation and propitious scenario for the use of middleware. Thus, the article shows relevance to this research by the extent of middleware information, IoT and e-health, and presents the implementation of EcoHealth middleware, which we will analyze in a further study.

During the analysis of these researches, we also selected the study "On Middleware for Emerging Health Services" [20] due to the fact that it shows the initial implementation process of a middleware for emergency health services. It also addresses the middleware requirements and challenges arising from the development of technologies applied in health care. Finally, this study describes the specific requirements of the middleware "SBUS" since its early stages.

The article "Uma Plataforma de Middleware para Integração de Dispositivos e Desenvolvimento de Aplicações em E-Health" [21] is another research that contributes immensely to this research. This detailed study presents the EcoHealth middleware platform to promote the integration of heterogeneous body sensors to allow remote monitoring of patients. It also brings an evaluation of the Eco Health platform performance, considering an eHealth application developed as proof of concept. It yet shows the main objectives of the applicability of middleware, consisting of monitoring through body sensors. Variables related to environmental health enable diagnosis via control, visualization, processing and real-time data storage, enabling the performance of hardware platforms in order to provide emergency aid to patients at risk. The evaluation showed that this platform can support a lot of physical devices working with appropriate frequencies for monitoring vital signs. Validating the middleware EcoHealth.

The article "E-Performance Modeling Of Proposed GUISET Middleware For Mobile Healthcare Services In E Marketplaces GUISET" [22] proposes middleware for using in South Africa. The referred platform provides useful services for small and medium-sized companies in the context of mobile services. The results of this study show that the average unconditional waiting time remains the same with the reduction of this as a priority in relation to the preferred model. It is expected to be beneficial in mobile health services where events are prioritized and attention has to be given to urgencies.

In "Service Oriented Middleware Architecture for Mobile Personal Health Monitoring" [23] the authors present a middleware service oriented approach. This platform aims to facilitate the development of health and welfare applications, enabling semantic interoperability of heterogeneous objects, services and applications. They also demonstrate the functionality of collecting values of medical devices, fusion of many sensors data, service orchestration, and export of medical data in a service-oriented approach.

A connectivity kit of medical devices to access the middleware available for developers to create applications based on open standards is also displayed.

Another selected article was the "AMBIENT HEALTHCARE SYSTEMS, Using The Hydra Embedded Middleware For Implementing An Ambient Disease Management System" [24], which presents the Hydra middleware. This platform consists of a modular approach that solves interoperability problems among devices used in health care environments. Hydra provides an interfacing between interactive devices, such as the biosensors and data from the software to be involved. The approach of this middleware is in three layers, which guarantees structured design applications and extensions. The Hydra is still established as an effective platform for health ecosystems that integrate foundations, as well as the services offered by others.

We also selected the study "SIXTH: A Middleware For Supporting Ubiquitous Sensing In Personal Health Monitoring" [25]. This article brings a middleware called SIXTH, which was motivated by the importance of identifying the context in an AAL configuration and how this can be best achieved through the convergence of various sources of heterogeneous data. This study's middleware is open, extensible and offers integration of typical AAL settings and wearable smart devices.

The "CORBAMed And DHE: Middleware Service Approach In Healthcare Information Systems" [26] analyses both situation and challenges health care system faced nowadays, besides introducing two structures of middleware systems of information, the CORBAMed and the DHE. According to the authors, these two architectures can meet the requirements of a system of health information due to the maturity, scope and availability of middleware offered.

The article "Middleware For Heterogeneous Healthcare Data Exchange: A Survey." [27] Brings a survey about the HL7 middleware directed to the area of health. The presented middleware is an international standard, based on the model Open System Intercommunication (OSI), which sets a pattern of exchange and transport information among health organizations. This study is a survey of various middleware cataloged through an exploratory research in the archives of the Association for Computing Machinery (ACM) and the Institute of Electrical and Electronics Engineers (IEEE). After the analysis of the selected researches presented in this paper is an overview of the resource selected middleware.

Another selected article is the study entitled "A Novel Middleware Architecture for Personal Healthcare Information System" [28] has a progressive middleware architecture directed to the medical sector and personal health. The approached architecture is not just a middleware, but provide a tool for analysis of data coming from the sensors deployed in the patient's body. In this article we implemented a Ubiquitous healthcare prototype that has a data analysis report for physicians, patients and health centers. The main data were obtained by a series of sensors used in the experiment such as the ECG, temperature that are considered important aspects for basic health.

VI. COMPARATIVE ANALYSIS OF THE ARTICLES

In this section, we decided to address the issues that we considered of vital importance to the thematic context and its applicability in the real context.

The IoT already permeates the lives of many people in the world, so the possibility of using it for better quality of life is what instigates the surveys conducted. As there are countless devices involved with different manufacturers, protocols and through different communication, it becomes a challenge to face insertion of such technology. Currently, the key focus areas of the IoT have developed massively with the creation of middleware platforms.

Another important challenge for this issue is to ensure interoperability in order to provide back the need of the users. Thus, the articles were selected, [19],[20],[21],[22],[23],[24],[25],[26],[27],[28],[29],[30],[31] to support the motivational research in middleware development for IoT in e-health.

In general, the articles that were the basis for this research are characterized by an attempt to solve these problems in the e-health environment. Most of the studies propose the development of a middleware architecture to mediate devices, trying to solve the interoperability problems applied to e-health. The results show that there are several middleware platforms being developed, what shows a tendency of use of the IoT to improve the monitoring process in general health.

VII. CONCLUSION

This article made a simple introduction about Internet of Things, middleware, and e-health, and the relationship between these elements. This study also showed a range of researches related to the insertion of middleware for e-health, leading us to believe that there is a significant motivation for this feature. In many parts of the researches, the authors encourage new ways of carrying out mediation between interconnected devices on the Internet of things, so that, creating new middleware ideas.

Although this paper was not meant to go deeper into the development of a middleware, it was intended to foment subsidy for a better comparison among the existing ones.

For further research, we plan to explore a middleware architecture model best suited to the unique system of Brazilian health. After a more appropriate analysis of the advantages and disadvantages, to make a comparison study of each middleware platform presented in this work.

REFERENCES

[1] PEREIRA NETO, André; BARBOSA, Letícia; SILVA, Adriano da; DANTAS, Monica Lúcia Gomes (2015). O paciente informado e os saberes médicos: um estudo de etnografia virtual em comunidades de doentes no Facebook. In: HCS-Manguinhos vol.22 supl. Rio de Janeiro Dec. 2015.

[2] Boric-Lubecke, O et al. (2014) "E-healthcare: Remote monitoring, privacy, and securi- ty", Proceedings of the 2014 IEEE MTT-S International Microwave Symposium, USA, pp. 1–3.

[3] Yuce, M. R. (2013) "Recent wireless body sensors: Design and implementation", Pro- ceedings of the 2013 IEEE MTT-S

International Microwave Workshop Series on RF and Wireless Technologies for Biomedical and Healthcare Applications, IEEE, USA, pp. 1–3.

[4] Bui, N., Zorzi, M. (2011) "Health care applications: A solution based on the Internet of Things", Proceedings of the 4th International Symposium on Applied Sciences in Biomedical and Communication Technologies, ACM, USA.

[5] Bandyopadhyay, S., Sengupta, M., Maiti, S., Dutta, S.. Role of middleware for Internet of Things: A study. International Journal of Computer Science & Engineering Survey 2011;2(3):94–105.

[6] SINGER, Talyta. Tudo conectado: conceitos e representações da internet das coisas. In: Simpósio em tecnologias digitais e sociabilidade. 10 e 11 out. 2012, Salvador. Available in: Andlt;http://www.simsocial2012.ufba.br/modulos/submissao/Upload/44965.pdf Andgt; Accessed in: 06 Jun. 2016.

[7] Atzori, L. et al. (2010) "The Internet of Things: A survey", Computer Networks, vol. 54, no. 15, pp. 2787–2805.

[8] LORENZETTI, Jorge; TRINDADE, Letícia de Lima; PIRES, Denise Elvira Pires de and RAMOS, Flávia Regina Souza. Tecnologia, inovação tecnológica e saúde: uma reflexão necessária. Texto contexto - enferm. [online]. 2012, vol.21, n.2, pp.432-439. ISSN 0104-0707.

[9] PAIVA.Fernando. Internet das Coisas vai produzir "tsunami" de sinalização nas redes móveis. Available in: <http://www.teletime.com.br/16/04/2015/internet-das-coisas-vai-produzir-tsunami- de-sinalizacao-nas-redes-moveis/tt/409242/news.aspx> Accessed in: 06 Jun. 2016.

[10] MARCONDES, C. H. e SAYÃO, L. F. Integração e interoperabilidade no acesso a recursos informacionais em C&T: a proposta da Biblioteca Digital Brasileira. Ciência da Informação, Brasília, v. 30, n. 3, p. 24-33, set./dez. 2001.

[11] KO, L. F.; LIN, J. C.; CHEN, C. H.; CHANG, J. S.; LAI, F.; HSU, K. P.; YANG, T. H.; CHENG, P. H.; WEN, C. C.; CHEN, J. L.; HSIEH, S. L. HL7 middleware framework for healthcare information system. In: INTERNATIONAL CONFERENCE E-HEALTH NETWORKING, APPLICATIONS AND SERVICES, 8, 2006, New Delhi. Proceedings... India: Institute of Electrical and Electronics Engineers (IEEE), 2006. p. 152-156.

[12] AL-WASIL, F. M.; GRAY, W. A.; FIDDIAN, N. J. Establishing an XML metadata knowledge base to assist integration of structured and semi-structured databases. In: AUSTRALASIAN DATABASE CONFERENCE, 17.; ACM INTERNATIONAL CONFERENCE, 2006, Hobart. Proceedings... Darlinghurst: Australian Computer Society, Inc., 2006. p. 69-78.

[13] COLLINS, S. R.; NAVATHE, S.; MARK, L. XML schema mappings for heterogeneous database access. Information and Software Technology, v. 44, n. 4, p. 251-257, 2002.

[14] Teixeira, T., Hachem, S., Issarny, V., Georgantas, N.. Service-oriented middleware for the Internet of Things: A perspective. In: Abramow-icz, W.,Llorente, I.M.,Surridge, M.,Zisman,A.,Vayssie`re, J.,editors.Proceeding soft 4th European Conference Towards Service-Based Internet; vol. 6994 of Lecture Notes in Computer Science. Germany: Springer-Verlag Berlin Heidelberg; 2011, p. 220–229.

[15] Maia, P. et al. (2014) "A Web platform for interconnecting body sensors and improving health care", Procedia Computer Science, vol. 40, pp. 135–142.

[16] CEUSTERS, W.; SMITH, B. Strategies for referent tracking in electronic health records. Journal of Biomedical Informatics, v. 39, n. 3, p. 362-378, 2006.

[17] BICER, V.; LALECI, G.; DOGAC, A.; KABAK, Y. Artemis message exchange framework: semantic interoperability of exchanged messages in the healthcare domain. ACM Sigmod Record, v. 34, n. 3, p. 71-76, 2005.

[18] ONABAJO, A.; BILYKH, I.; JAHNKE, J. Wrapping legacy medical systems for integrated health network. migration and evolvability of long-life software systems. In: WORKSHOP AT THE CONFERENCE NETOBJECTDAYS, 2003, Erfurt. Proceedings... Germany: Springer, 2003.

[19] MAIA, Pedro ; BATISTA, T. V. ; CAVALCANTE, Everton R. de Sousa ; BAFFA, Augusto ; DELICATO, Flavia C. ; PIRES, Paulo F. ; ZOMAYA, Albert . A Web Platform for Interconnecting Body Sensors and Improving Health Care. Procedia Computer Science , v. 40, p. 135-142, 2014.

[20] Singh, Jatinder, and Jean M. Bacon. "On middleware for emerging health services." Journal of Internet Services and Applications 5.1 (2014): 1-19.

[21] MAIA, Pedro P. C. ; BAFFA, AUGUSTO ; CAVALCANTE, E. R. ; DELICATO, Flavia C. ; BATISTA, T ; PIRES, P. F. . Uma Plataforma de Middleware para Integração de Dispositivos e Desenvolvimento de Aplicações em e-health. In: XXXIII Simpósio Brasileiro de Redes de Computadores e Sistemas Distribuídos - SBRC 2015, 2015, Vitória - ES. Anais do Simpósio Brasileiro de Redes de Computadores e Sistemas Distribuídos, 2015.

[22] Akingbesote, Alaba Olu, et al. "Performance Modeling of Proposed GUISET Middleware for Mobile Healthcare Services in E-Marketplaces." Journal of Applied Mathematics 2014 (2014).

[23] Ahlsén, Matts, et al. "Service-oriented middleware architecture for mobile personal health monitoring." Wireless Mobile Communication and Healthcare. Springer Berlin Heidelberg, 2011. 305-312.

[24] Eikerling, Heinz-Josef, et al. "Ambient Healthcare Systems Using the Hydra Embedded Middleware for Implementing an Ambient Disease Management System." (2009).

[25] Carr, Dominic, et al. "SIXTH: a middleware for supporting ubiquitous sensing in personal health monitoring." Wireless Mobile Communication and Healthcare. Springer Berlin Heidelberg, 2012. 421-428.

[26] Zhang, Dongsong, and Ralph Martinez. "CORBAMed and DHE: Middleware Service Approach in Healthcare Information Systems." Effective healthcare information systems (2002): 249.

[27] Petry, Karine, et al. "Utilização do Padrão HL7 para Interoperabilidade em Sistemas Legados na Área de Saúde." XI CONGRESSO BRASILEIRO DE INFORMÁTICA EM SAÚDE. Vol. 11. 2008.

[28] Taleb, Tarik, Dario Bottazzi, and Nidal Nasser. "A novel middleware solution to improve ubiquitous healthcare systems aided by affective information." IEEE transactions on information technology in biomedicine 14.2 (2010): 335-349.

[29] Ko, Li-Fan, et al. "HL7 middleware framework for healthcare information system." IEEE Healthcare 1 (2006): 50-165.

[30] Kamal, Rossi, Nguyen H. Tran, and Choong Seon Hong. "Event-based middleware for healthcare applications." Communications and Networks, Journal of 14.3 (2012): 296-309.

[31] Zhang, J. K., W. Xu, and D. Ewins. "System interoperability study for healthcare information system with web services." Journal of Computer Science 3.7 (2007): 515-522.

[32] Power, Gemma, et al. "An adaptive middleware applied to the ad-hoc nature of cardiac health care." Proceedings of the 5th Annual International Conference on Mobile and Ubiquitous Systems: Computing, Networking, and Services. ICST (Institute for Computer Sciences, Social-Informatics and Telecommunications Engineering), 2008.

[33] Gffhealthcare <http://gtt.com.br/gtthealthcare/blog/wp-content/uploads/2015/08/IoT.png

Vehicular Ad Hoc Networks: A Focused Survey

Advances and Current Issues

Priscila Copeland Palmeira, Marcos Pereira dos Santos
Computer Science Department, Tiradentes University
Sergipe, Brazil
Emails: {priscilacopeland, marcospereira.ufs}@gmail.com

Abstract **– Vehicular networks are a kind of technology that requires continuous researcher. In this article, we give an overview of the ITS (Intelligent Transportation System), showing current known problems in the VANETs (Vehicular Ad Hoc Networks) and proposed solutions in existing literature, with emphasis on the following topics: geo-localization, QoS (Quality of Service), and traffic safety.**

Keywords – VANET; issues; geo-localization; QoS; traffic safety.

I. Introduction

Due to population growth and industrial development around the world, vehicle traffic load is getting heavier every day, increasing the likelihood of accidents. This prompts automobile industries to manufacture their vehicles with ITS, in order to ensure a more secure and comfortable vehicle traffic.

To support ITS, the IEEE 802.11 group has produced the IEEE 802.11p protocol [1], which developed applications that include the exchange of data among vehicles using the road infrastructure, thus bringing the Internet to the car framework. Using dedicated wireless DSRC (Device Short-Range Communication), cars are able to communicate with each other through VANETs, i.e., vehicles have intelligent sensors able to detect the road conditions.

VANETs correspond to a field of vehicular networks which is widely recognized as an essential element for ITS. VANETs have the potential to support a wide range of applications and services [2]. So far, the focus has been mainly on security applications, such as road awareness, accident warning, traffic surveillance, which have a huge impact on avoiding traffic accidents and increase the safety of road transport [3][4].

One of the known definitions of VANETs is a type of wireless network where each node is a moving vehicle on the road; the vehicles communicate with each other in order to make the traffic safer and generally better. This type of node acts as a router transmitting a message to another node. This network has two types of communication, V2V (vehicle-to-vehicle), and V2I (vehicle-to-infrastructure). Its main function is to provide secure applications in real-time to users, thus delivering the data at the right time, reducing accidents and delays [18].

However, there are security-related issues, and problems with the management of the media. Wireless network, like VANETs, have a number of communication requirements to work well. The communication requirements have a large number of adverse effects on the characteristics of VANETs, e.g., multi-path disappearance and shading the wireless channel, fluctuating density nodes in different scenarios, and quick changes on the network topology.

Another problem is the creation of flexible services, able to adapt easily to their environment, so that one can connect to any device, while ensuring the safety and performance of the communication.

VANETs support from the simple exchange of information to the integration of highly complex infrastructure. The general application framework takes into account the dissemination of warning messages from those vehicles that could find accidents or dangerous situations, in order to provide useful information for drivers, wherever they might be, in restaurants, hotels and service stations, as well as entertainment: Internet, download multimedia, or chat among vehicles [5].

The rest of the paper is organized as follows. Section II presents the related work; Section III describes the current problems and the proposed solutions; and Section IV shows the conclusion and future works.

II. RELATED WORK

Many researchers have been interested in solving issues related to VANETs and improving their advances. Some of these researches focus on an overview related to the general information pertaining to VANETs and others tackles a more specific topic. In this article, our approach is to tackle both of these scenarios, taking a better look at specifics problems and advances related to VANETs.

Gupta et al. [19] present general idea about VANETs, showing an overview that include basic information. The authors provide focus on the various aspects of VANETs, such as architecture, characteristics, challenges, glimpse of routing protocols, and simulation models used for VANETs. They clarify the advantages and disadvantages associated with sending information protocol among the nodes of VANETs; showing the difference to sending information on the highway and in the cities. Delay and interference are associated with each case. Their results show that the speed and distance influence the efficiency of information exchange, as there is a maximum time for sending such information. In an attempt to improve algorithms for sending and receiving data, they suggest that the network nodes should work as routers using routing tables.

Eze et al. [20] provide an overview of the current research state, challenges, potentials of VANETs as well as the ways forward to achieving the long awaited ITS. The authors present: a comparison of high-speed wireless communication technologies for vehicular networks, spectrum allocation issues in VANETs, message broadcasting, routing protocols, congestion control techniques in inter-vehicle communication, security, privacy, anonymity and liability, reliability and cross-layer approach between the transport layer and the network layer. With their analysis, they have determined the minimal prerequisites to QoS applications in VANETs. Then, the high reliability and the low latency are not guaranteed by any of the revised algorithms in their paper. The paper suggests that the challenge to develop a security solution capable of supporting the exchange of authentication, accountability and privacy, according to each vehicle's information should be disclosed to appropriate government agencies (transport authority) over the network. It is one of the biggest problems of security and privacy in VANETs.

Sanguesa et al. [21] show a clear guideline of the benefits and drawbacks associated with different schemes. The authors did an analysis of the most relevant broadcast dissemination available in a fair comparative scheme analysis by evaluating them according to the same environmental conditions, focusing on the same metrics, and using the same simulation platform, specially designed for VANETs, highlighting their features, and studying their performance under the same simulation conditions. The paper describes one of the biggest problems that the researchers have found when comparing their results with the existing state-of-art. Most researches have taken different approaches and they try to prove which approach has the best performance. They have proven those approaches in different environments with unrealistic parameters leaving inaccurate and unrepresentative conclusions. For this reason, their work has reproduced simulations using the same metrics for different tools, comparing the methods to the same simulation conditions in order to determine which method is the best for each situation.

Other researches, in these cases with specifics subjects, such as [5], designed a collaborative virtual environment that unifies the knowledge and is integrated with vehicles to endow the final user with the necessary information. The authors developed a model-driven approach that generates a groupware application to improve the collaborative work and access to services. The implemented tool facilitates the development and implementation of collaborative frameworks in VANETs. In this kind of collaborative system, it is not essential for all data to be received in a single node, which reduce duplication of information and increases the data flow exchange. However, this system does not consider the vehicle speed, or the environmental changes or handoff that could happen, showing that this solution requires other features in order to function in any VANETs structure.

Tabassum et al [7] developed an interference-aware high-throughput channel allocation mechanism, called HT-CAM that addresses the unique challenges of CRVANETs. They created conflict graphs of link-band pairs to extract non-interfering OBU (On Board Unit) pairs that can communicate simultaneously on a given channel, increasing the spatial reuse of the available channels. In addition, their work formulates a high-throughput channel allocation problem as a MILP (Mixed-integer Linear Programming) problem, showing that the proposed HT-CAM provides a better network performances compared to state-of-the-art protocols. The comparative graphs show that the HT-CAM technique can improve decision-allocation in the most efficient channel for communication in VANETs. To test the new technique efficiency they compared the TE-CAM [33] and CC-VANET [34] methods. As its results, Tabassum et al. [7] proved that their technique outperforms the other two methods in terms of network throughput, channel use, and the late delivery of end-to-end packages.

Gonzalez et al. [12] present an analysis of several protocols proposed in literature for message dissemination in VANETs. The authors proposed a protocol that sets and wait a time to relay candidates. They have demonstrated that it is possible to reduce the delay needed to cover a given area. For that, when they stop the beacon transmissions a warning message is detected and it does not provide a significant performance improvement. Nonetheless, by allowing a continuous channel access, it proves that the performance of any protocol might be greatly increased.

The state-of-art in VANETs is constantly developing, though much more research is required, as many fundamental issues remains. This paper differs from others because of the approach, bringing information and solutions by different authors in the same paper.

III. CURRENT ISSUES AND PROPOSED SOLUTIONS

Many important topics in VANETs are currently under intensive research and discussion. These issues and their background are presented in this section.

A. General Issues

The ordinary issues to VANETs are limitation in bandwidth utilization, frequent link disconnection, small effective diameter, security and privacy, among others [19].

Issue 1: Limitation in bandwidth utilization - There is no central coordinator that controls communication. The main idea is to allow usage of all users in this network to share the same bandwidth without causing harmful interference. VANETs face bandwidth allocations challenges due to the random number of users in the application. The time delay related to this issue is reduced by fair bandwidth utilization. If a vehicle wants to send a message and there is no medium for transmission, then it has to wait, which leads to high latency. Bandwidth is important to the congestion control. Bandwidth utilization is very important for sending large amounts of information, otherwise the system will be overload.

Issue 2: Frequent link disconnection - VANETs changes all the time and this happens dynamically and fast. This brings changes in the network topology. Because of the network high mobility and frequent fragmentation, the link disconnects often due to the short connection time between nodes in VANETS.

Issue 3: Small effective diameter - Maintaining complete global topology is impossible due to weak connectivity between nodes and results in issues when applying the existing algorithm.

Issue 4: Security and privacy – In VANETs, vehicles connect with other random vehicles without knowing their intention. It brings vulnerability to the users to succumb to different malicious attacks. The detection and prevention of attacks in VANETs should be properly designed to ensure the safety of users are not violated, in a real-time framework.

Issue 5: Routing protocols - Due to the above challenges, designing an effective protocol, which transfers maximum packets in minimum time, is not easy to implement. So the design of an efficient routing protocol demands advancements in MANET's architecture, to accommodate the fast mobility of the VANETs nodes in an efficient manner.

For the above issues, the proposed solutions are showing in Table I.

TABLE I. ISSUES IN VANETS AND PROPOSED SOLUTIONS IN THE LITERATURE.

Issue	Proposed Solution
Limitation in bandwidth	Use an algorithm that control congestion
Link disconnection	OLSR (Optimized Link State Routing Protocol)
Small diameter	Position-based Protocol
Security and Privacy	SMT (Secure Message Transmission)

To solve issue 1, the solution proposed by Dongre et al. [22], implements an algorithm that can control and detect the traffic congestion and can send only one message broadcasted by the vehicle, which reduces the overhead on the network, improving bandwidth utilization.

To solve issue 2, it is possible to use the OLSR (Optimized Link State Routing) or its variations. OLSR is an optimization over a pure link state protocol as it compacts the size of data sent in the messages, and reduces the number of retransmissions to flood these messages in the entire network [23]. Today the OLSR has its variations. Gautami et al. [24] have proposed a Meta-heuristic algorithm as optimization of the OLSR protocol to enhance the performance of individual search methods in VANETs.

To solve issue 3, the proposed solutions include position-based protocols, e.g., MFR (Most Forward within Radius) [27], LAR (Location-Aided Routing Protocol) [28], EGR (Energy-Aware Geographic Routing) [29]; they assume that the vehicle is equipped with GPS (Global Positioning System) device in order to find its own geographic position.

To solve issue 4, a combined group of protocols was presented, but the final choice was SMT (Secure Message Transmission) protocol [13]. The data is only transmitted in the communication among registered vehicles. This protocol ensures that the vehicle IDs are not exposed for anyone. SMT utilizes MAC (Message Authentication Code) to check the integrity and authentication of its origin.

B. *Geo-localization*

Currently, navigation technologies are GPS-dependent, which has several problems. The most important problem is price, especially if one is looking for an accurate GPS system. Cheap GPS devices are not precise and can become unusable for autonomous navigation [16].

Therefore, current researches intend to develop technology to obtain information about the position in real-time applications such as real time navigation, traffic behavior studies, and applications related to the location, such as forward collision warning application of the vehicle based central server [1].

In Fig. 1, we show the issues that the papers bellow tries to focus on.

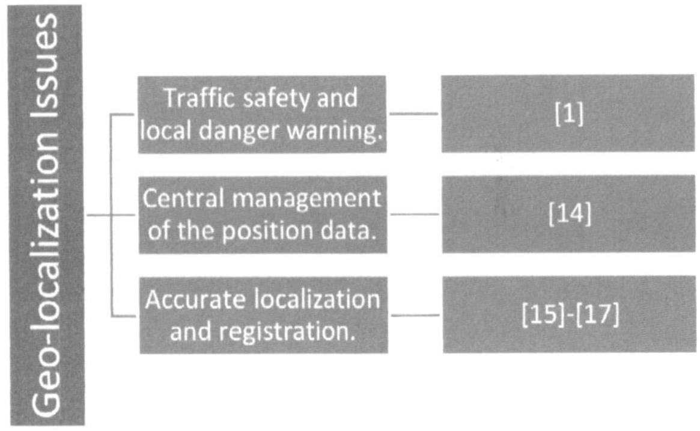

Figure 1. Relation between surveys and issues in VANETS.

Thenmozhi et al. [1] propose vehicle-to-vehicle model that allows moving vehicles to send geographical and speed data over VANETs to prevent accidents. Their method uses Dedicated Short Range Communication (DSRC) Wireless Devices and a repeater in vehicles that solves issues in four-way interior road junctions by sending the data signal for longer distances during local danger circumstances.

Mo et al. [14] consider the vehicle movement patterns (position, speed, and direction) can be stored in the form of a dynamic vector, which has implemented position updating in central MOD (Moving Object Database). It has a vehicle position data updating strategy with packet repetition based on Kalman filter prediction. An algorithm with packet repetition was designed; it can not only generate a position updating data according to a preset threshold, but also decides the packet repetition mode related to the distance of two adjacent vehicles in order to reduce data loss. The simulated results show that vehicle position data updating frequency was obviously reduced and the reliability of the communication is greatly improved through packet repetition mechanism by using this position updating strategy. Their experiment uses the colored noise Gauss to simulate the noise of the Kalman filter to predicted background. They choose the colored noise instead of white noise for the Kalman filter, which does not cover all the noise that might be generated. They also consider that the delay transmission is extremely small, which is not consistent with reality. As justification, they assume that the presence of transmission delay always makes position updating data outdated, so they decided not to allow position data to be stored in the database. For this situation they intend, as work, to research about how to ensure the positional deviation error under the control in the condition of high time delay.

Costea and Leordeanu et al. [15] have proposed a complete system to geo-localization from aerial images in the absence of GPS information. Their proposed pipeline includes contributions with efficient methods to road and intersection detection, intersection recognition with geometric alignment to accurate localization, followed by road detection enhancement. It proves that using learned high-level features is feasible and it is possible to achieve a high level of accuracy. It can be used as a GPS alternative, or in conjunction with GPS, bringing valuable contributions to the literature and to many applications that require offline or online, real-time processing. The limitation of this approach is that the high level of accuracy only happens if the geolocation is from images alone.

Gupta et al. [16] propose new approach to geo-localization position of a mobile platform. Their intent is to solve the problem of accurate mobile platform geo-localization as a combination of approximate geo-localization and accurate relative localization. The article presents the algorithmic and implementation details of their method and demonstrates it for several different types of maps from different regions of the world. The relevance of their results is a system that can provide a fully automatic global localization at a low infrastructure cost.

Ounia et al.'s [17] have as objective to minimize and simplify the computing process in the MS (Mobile Station) during its geo-location phase needed especially to handover. This work additionally considers designing EToA (Extended Time of Arrival) as extended version of ToA (Time of Arrival), following the same principle, using another aspect of the computational process. As a result, the proposed technique is convergent within a reduced number of iterations. Moreover, the implementation simplicity and low computational overhead constitute their major advantages.

C. QoS

Until now, no project has achieved a reliable, flexible and adaptable way that meet the requirements of safety and autonomous driving applications.

In order to guarantee the exchange of information and the reliability in ad hoc networks, the researches should take into account the implementation of QoS, where the routing protocols are the main idea. These protocols aim to choose the best route from source to destination, meeting the QoS requirements, and calculating the QoS parameters. The selection and improvement of these protocols have fundamental importance to improve QoS in VANETs [9].

The current proposed solutions give us an idea of the performance gains that were achieved so far, however, they are specific to a particular application and context and applied in all environments [8].

Nowadays, in the literature, the majority of routing protocols that implement QoS require additional exchange of messages control to determine the QoS parameters and do not consider the problem of congestion during transmission of the data. These protocols actually increase the overhead of routing, causing wear in time and energy during a device discovery path, increasing packet loss [9].

In Fig. 2, we present the issues most searched on QoS in VANETs that are presented in [4][8][9].

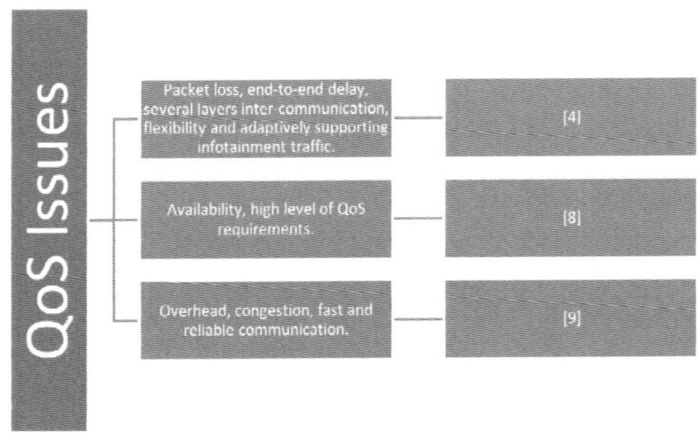

Figure 2. Relation between research and QoS issues in VANETS.

The main idea of the work by Rizzo et al. [4] is to design an architecture for the provision of various levels of QoS in VANETs. The basis of their approach is in CONTACT (Contact and Content Aware Communications for QoS support in VANETs). It was developed through the investigation of several communication strategies capable of adapting, at the same time, to the highly volatile and unstable vehicular environment, to content attributes and properties, and to a diversified set of application performance requirements.

Sumra et al. [8] present the SBC (Secure Business Communication) model and explain the components of the proposed model. It uses TPM (Trusted Platform Mobile) as its core component and TPM ensures a secure communication between user and business parties in VANETs.

With the purpose of reducing the overhead introduced to collect information from neighbor nodes and to obtain an accurate estimate of QoS parameters, Al-Ani et al. [9] describe a new approach for calculating QoS parameters locally and avoiding congestion during data transmission. It uses the SNMP (Simple Network Management Protocol) to estimate these values locally. With the help of the SNMP agent, the QoS parameters are calculated locally without exchanging any additional control message and without synchronization. Their approach evades any network overhead for QoS computation as compared to other QoS-aware routing protocols. This approach uses parallel and global search abilities of ACO (Ant Colony Optimization) algorithm to find multiple paths to the destination satisfying the specified QoS requirements. Their results show that the approach of QoS QoRA (Routing based on Ant Colony Optimization) protocol is scalable and performs well in high mobility, being a model to the congestion avoidance mechanism that evades any network overhead for QoS computation as compared to the other QoS-aware routing protocols.

D. *Traffic Safety*

In general, vehicle network applications are classified as secure applications and non-secure applications. Safety applications are used to notify drivers of urgent events on the road to avoid accidents. Non-secure applications are applications used by drivers or passengers to access the wireless network for entertainment as browsing websites, access email, and play games [10].

Emergency messages are considered an effective solution to improve road safety conditions. The notification allows drivers to have more time to react to avoid accidents, and to improve the safety of drivers and passengers. For this, the vehicles are equipped with intelligent sensors that help to detect road conditions, trying to minimize the problems of local risk and improves traffic management [1].

For the efficiency of these notifications to be immediate, the latency of transmission should be kept within the tolerable range, falling on the subject of QoS.

Among the articles referred in this work, three have related issues with traffic safety, as seen in Fig. 3.

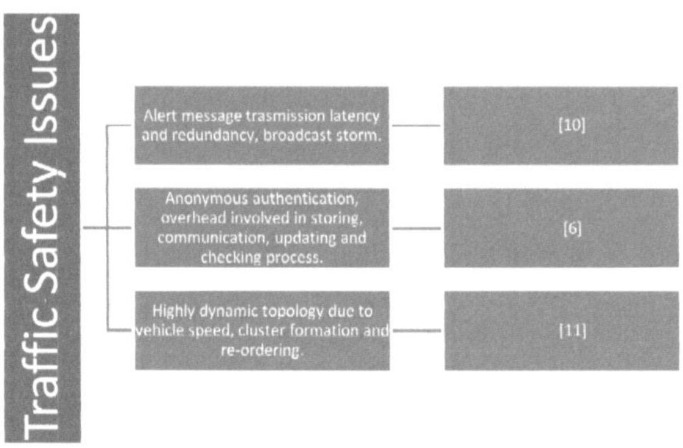

Figure 3. Relation between referred work and Traffic Safety issues in VANETS.

Chang et al. [10] have focused on the alert message dissemination in VANETs. Their idea proposes a fault-tolerant broadcasting protocol for disseminating the alert messages on highway. The proposed protocol designates two vehicles, which are the farthest and sub-farthest vehicles in the transmission range of the source vehicle as the relay candidates. In addition to this, they created an exponential back-off method that can effectively reduce the number of alert messages. This method improves not only the transmission delay of the alert messages but also the number of the alert messages in vehicular wireless networks, increasing the reliability of the system. Their simulation results showed that the fault-tolerant broadcast protocol outperforms the flooding method and the ACK (Acknowledgement) based broadcast protocol, in terms of the number of the alert messages, the number of the ACK messages and the total number of messages. However, it does not outperform the transmission delay of alert messages and penetration rate.

Wang et al. [6] introduce ECPB (Efficient Conditional Privacy-Preserving) authentication scheme based on group signature for VANETs. Though group signature is widely used in VANETs for security requirements, the existing schemes based on group signatures suffer from longer computational delays in the CRL (Certificate Revocation List) checking and in the signature verification process, leading to lower verification efficiency. In their scheme, membership validity (a validity period) is required when a vehicle applies for a group membership and this validity is used to check whether the vehicle is still a group member or not, which can be used as a substitute for the CRL checks. Neglecting the CRL checks will sharply decrease the costs incurred in the signatures verification. In addition, the proposed scheme also supports batch verification. Their experimental analysis proves that the proposed scheme exhibits improved efficiency over the existing schemes, in terms of verification delay and average delay. The security analysis and experimental results show that ECPB delivers higher efficiency verification requirements of VANETs, and satisfies the Privacy-preserving Communication for VANETs.

Ambareish et al. [11] proposed a beacon-based clustering algorithm achieving a significantly higher cluster stability than previous methods, like the CBLR (Cluster Based Location Routing) algorithm [11]. The basis of their approach is to use local mobility measure to decide which cluster heads should remain in their roles and which should change their state. In addition to the already existing states, the authors introduced an EN (Emergency State) for ambulances, police, and other emergency vehicles. In Table II, we present two characteristics of VANETs that result in the consequences that their paper tries to solve.

TABLE II. VANETS CHARACTERISTICS WITH RELATED ISSUES AND ITS CONSEQUENCES.

VANETs Characteristics	Related Issue	Consequences
Frequent connection drop of the network Highly changing topology	Frequent cluster formation and re-ordering	Decreases cluster stability

IV. CONCLUSION AND FUTURE WORK

This paper provided a summary of the most important subdivisions of vehicular networks, presenting the most accurate work in each subject of VANETs in order to enrich and encourage research and future work for the development of vehicle networks. It is worth noticing that the topics covered in the articles studied highlighted the need for performance improvements, control and management of VANET networks, as the main ideas of this work.

For future work, we intend to find a method to reduce the delay on transmission messages in VANETs, comparing our results with the existing methods in the state-of-art.

ACKNOWLEDGMENT

The Information Technology Department of Tiradentes University supports this work.

REFERENCES

[1] R. Thenmozhi and S. Govindarajan, "Safety related services using smart vehicle connections", International Journal of Applied Engineering Research, vol. 11, no. 4, pp. 2384-2387, 2016.

[2] T. L. Willke, P. Tientrakool, and N. F. Maxemchuk, "A survey of intervehicle communication protocols and their applications", Communications Surveys & Tutorials, IEEE, vol. 11, no. 2, pp. 3–20, 2009.

[3] W. G. Najm, J. Koopmann, J. D. Smith, and J. Brewer, "Frequency of target crashes for intellidrive safety systems", Tech. Rep., 2010.

[4] G. Rizzo, M. R. Palattellay, T. Braunz, and T. Engely, "Content and context aware strategies for qos support in VANETs", IEEE 30th International Conference on Advanced Information Networking and Applications (AINA), pp. 717 – 721, March 2016.

[5] R. Lacuesta, J. Gallardo, J. Lloret, and G. Palacios, "Integration of data from vehicular ad hoc networks using model-driven collaborative tools", Mobile Information Systems, vol. 2016, Article ID 4291040, 15 pages, 2016.

[6] Y. Wang, H. Zhong, Y. Xu, and J. Cui, "ECPB: Efficient Conditional Privacy-Preserving Authentication Scheme Supporting Batch Verification for VANETs", International Journal of Network Security, vol. 18, no. 2, pp. 374-382, March 2016.

[7] M. Tabassum, M. A. Razzaque1, M. M. Hassan, A. Almogren and A. Alamri, "Interference-aware high-throughput channel allocation mechanism for CR-VANETs", EURASIP J. Wireless Comm. and Networking 2016, in press.

[8] I. A. Sumra and H. B. Hasbullah, "Using trusted platform module (tpm) to secure business communciation (sbc) in vehicular ad hoc network (VANET)", International Conference on Recent Advances in Computer Systems (RACS-2015), January 2015.

[9] A. Al-Ani and J. Seitz, "Qos-aware routing in multi-rate ad hoc networks based on ant colony optimization", Network Protocols and Algoritms, vol. 7, no. 4, pp. 1 – 25, 2015.

[10] Y. Chang, T. Chung, and T. Wang, "A fault-tolerant broadcast protocol for reliable alert message delivery in vehicular wireless networks", 7th International ICST Conference on Communications and Networking in China (CHINACOM), pp. 475 – 480, August 2012.

[11] B. Ambareesh , M. Aneesh , S. Anshad, D. Deepak, S. Vishnu, K. Praveen, and D. K. Daniel, "A New Cluster Based Protocol for Vanets", Imperial Journal of Interdisciplinary Research (IJIR), vol. 2, no. 5, pp. 22 – 25, 2016.

[12] S. Gonzalez and V. Ramos, "Preset delay broadcast: a protocol for fast information dissemination in vehicular ad hoc networks (VANETs)", Journal on Wireless Communications and Networking, in press.

[13] K. Kaushik and S. Tayal, "VANET's Security Requirements and Attacks – A Review", International Journal of Advances in Engineering Sciences, vol. 6, no. 1, pp. 15-25, 2016.

[14] Y. Mo, D. Yu, J. Song, K. Zheng, and Y. Guo, "Vehicle position updating strategy based on kalman filter prediction in vanet environment", Discrete Dynamics in Nature and Society, vol. 2016, Article ID 1404396, 2016.

[15] D. Costea and M. Leordeanu, "Aerial image geolocalization from recognition and matching of roads and intersections", Cornel University Library (ARXIV), in press.

[16] A. Gupta, H. Chang, and A. Yilmaz, "Gps-denied geo-localisation using visual odometry", ISPRS Annals of the Photogrammetry, Remote Sensing and Spatial Information Sciences, vol. III-3, 2016 XXIII ISPRS Congress, 12–19 July 2016, Prague, Czech Republic, in press.

[17] R. Ounia, M. Zaidib, "EToA: New 2D geolocation-based handover decision technique", Special Issue on Positioning Techniques and Applications (ICT Express), vol. 2, no. 1, pp. 28–32, March 2016.

[18] P. C. Palmeira and M. P. Santos, "Survey in vehicular networks using Mixim on OMNeT++", Scientific Interfaces: Exact and Technology, Journal Portal, Tiradentes Group, vol. 1, no. 2, pp. 47 – 56, 2015.

[19] R. Gupta and P. Patel, "A Survey on Vehicular Ad hoc Networks", International Journal of Scientific Research in Science, Engineering and Technology(IJSRSET), Print ISSN : 2395-1990, Online ISSN : 2394-4099, vol. 2, no. 2, pp. 1251-1259, 2016.

[20] E. C. Eze, S. Zhang, E. Liu, and J. C. Eze, "Advances in Vehicular Ad-hoc Networks (VANETs): Challenges and Road-map for Future Development", International Journal of Automation and Computing, vol. 13, no. 1, pp. 1-18, 2016.

[21] J. A. Sanguesa, M. Fogue, P. Garrido, F. J. Martinez, J. Cano, and C. T. Calafate, "A Survey and Comparative Study of Broadcast Warning Message Dissemination Schemes for VANETs", Mobile Information Systems, vol. 2016, Article ID 8714142, 18 pages, 2016.

[22] M. M. Dongre and N. G. Bawane, "Effective Road Model for Congestion Control in VANETS", Intenational Journal of Wireless & Mobile Networks (IJWMN), vol. 8, no. 2, April 2016.

[23] P. Jacquet, P. Muhlethaler, T. Clausen, A. Laouiti, A. Qayyum, and L. Viennot, "Optimized Link State Routing Protocol for Ad Hoc Networks", Johns Hopkins Whiting School of Engineering, 2016.

[24] R. Gautami, R. R. Sedamkar, and H. Patil, "Application of Hybrid Meta-Heuristic Algorithm for OLSR Protocol Optimization in VANET", International Journal of Current Engineering an Technology, vol. 6, no. 3, June 2016.

[25] Y. Han, E. Ekici, H. Kremo, and O. Altintas, "Throughput-efficient channel allocation in multi-channel cognitive vehicular networks", in INFOCOM, 2014 Proceedings IEEE, pp. 2724–2732, 2014.

[26] Z. Lei, L. Tao, L. Wei, Z. Siting, and L. Jianfeng, "Cooperative spectrum allocation with QoS support in cognitive cooperative vehicular ad hoc networks", Communications, China, IEEE, pp. 49–59, 2014.

[27] H. Takagi, and L. Kleinrock, "Optimal transmission ranges for randomly distributed packet radio terminals", IEEE Transactions on Communications, vol. 32, issue 3, pp.246-257, 1984.

[28] Y. B. Ko, and N. H. Vaidya, "Location-aided routing (LAR) in mobile ad-hoc networks", Wireless Networks (ACM), vol. 6, issue 4, pp.307- 321, 2000.

[29] G.Wang, and G. Wang, "An energy-aware geographic routing algorithm for mobile ad-hoc network", 5th International Conference on Wireless Communications, Networking and Mobile Computing, 24th-26th Sept 2009.

R2TCA: New Tool for Developing Reconfigurable Real-Time Context-Aware Framework

-Application to Baggage Handling Systems-

Soumoud Fkaier*†§, Mohamed Romdhani*, Mohamed Khalgui*‡,and Georg Frey§
*LISI Laboratory, INSAT, University of Carthage, Tunis, Tunisia
†Polytechnic School of Tunisia, University of Carthage, Tunis, Tunisia
‡Systems Control Lab, Xidian University, China
§Chair of Automation and Energy Systems, Saarland University, Saarbrucken,Germany
Email:{soumoud.fkaier, georg.frey}@aut.uni-saarland.de , { khalgui.mohamed, mromdhani7}@gmail.com

Abstract—**Context-awareness was introduced in various domains of ubiquitous computing ranging from mobile computing to automated manufacturing. It gained this importance based on the fact that it provides the possibility to handle adaptive systems according to the environment changes. Therefore, a wide variety of frameworks was developed. However, some requirements are still not satisfied, especially those related to resolving functional constraints, such as inclusion, precedence, and shared resources constraints. Dealing with real-time issues also has not been satisfied. In this work, we propose a new tool for developing a context-aware framework able to overcome the mentioned problems. As proof of concept, we simulated a case study and performed results analysis.**

Keywords–Context-aware framework; Reconfigurable system; Real-time system; Functional constraint; Flexible software service.

I. INTRODUCTION

Context-aware systems are characterized by their ability to interact with the surrounding environment [1]. They sense changes in their environment and adapt their behavior accordingly [2]. These changes act as contexts that will induce system reconfiguration. Since the 1990s, this issue has gained the attention of both the academic and manufacturing fields. Thus, many methodologies, middleware and frameworks have been proposed [3][4][5]. One important field of application of this paradigm is developing applications of adaptive control systems. In fact, these systems are self-adapting systems known by the flexibility to adapt their behavior to the environmental dynamic changes [6]. So, this feature can be satisfied based on context-awareness.

Developing a context-aware framework for adaptive control systems is a challenging task. In fact, these systems require a set of particular exigencies. First of all, they have to adapt their behavior properly without losing system effectiveness. Reconfigurations must always be done safely without conflicts or break downs. To clarify, logical relations between the tasks of reconfiguration processes such as rejection rules must be absolutely respected. Similarly, precedence constraint as well as using some shared resources ought to be guaranteed. Just as respecting these relationships, managing the allocation and de-allocation of the used resources has to be insured as well. No doubt, providing the services before their deadlines is of great importance otherwise the services lose their meaning.

It is true that the available literature on context-aware frameworks has evolved over time. Particularly, providing solutions for real-time as well as functional constraints have gained a great attention from researchers. However, these two points of interest are still not developed in clear and efficient way [10] [13] [14]. For this reason, we propose in this paper a new tool for developing context-aware frameworks to solve the aforementioned constraints. It is called Reconfigurable Real-Time Context-Aware (R2TCA) framework. This new tool is dedicated to developing reconfigurable systems running under real-time and functional constraints. It enables to develop applications following a layered architecture composed of four layers [21]. Every layer has a specific role in the adaptation process. We took an example of baggage handling systems as adaptive system in order to prove the suitability of R2TCA. Moreover, system response time as well as the memory utilization rate is calculated so that we prove R2TCA robustness.

This paper is structured in five main sections. In Section 2, we present the state of the art. Section 3 describes the new tool. Section 4 shows the application of the new tool to a case study. Finally, Section 5 concludes the paper.

II. BACKGROUND

Many works have proposed different context-aware frameworks. In this section, we give an overview of these achievements.

Forkan et al. [7] have proposed the Cloud-oriented context-aware middleware in ambient assisted living (CoCaMAAL). They focused on developing a scalable and context-aware framework in order to facilitate both data collection and processing. Forkan et al. [8] have performed a Big Data for Context-aware Monitoring (BDCaM) that is an extension of CoCaMAAL. They proposed a discovery-based approach enabling systems to adapt their behavior at run-time. It enables finding context information using big data. Mcheick et al. [9] have proposed a context-aware architecture for health care systems in which they focused on abstracting the context. They consider that scalability and inter-operability are the key features towards the abstraction. They added an extension for the addition of sensors so that they simplify dealing with sensed data. Edwin and Alvin [10] have defined CAMPUS, which is a middleware for making automated decisions of adaptation at run-time. Their aim was to reduce the effort made by developers by getting rid of the need to predict and maintain adaptation rules. Lei et al. [11] have proposed a tool called PerDe. They focused on designing a domain-specific language. Also, they provided a set of graphical toolkits covering development steps for ubiquitous computing applications. Balland and Consel [12] have introduced DiaSuite which is a tool dedicated to drive the development processes on specific domains of Sense/Compute/Control (SCC). It has a compiler responsible for generating customized basis for every development step. Liu and Cheng [13] have proposed a middleware framework called MARCHES. It aims to support time-critical adaptive vehicle systems. Also, they tried to improve reconfiguration efficiency for these systems in changing environments. Papadopoulou et al. [14] have proposed an approach of development of pervasive systems based on the notion of Personal Smart Space (PSS). In this work, they addressed the issue of sharing resources.

These existing concepts and tools have been developed in order to satisfy adaptive systems requirements. Although, most of them do not propose a clear strategy to handle real-time services. In addition, there are no solutions that have treated functional constraints like managing dependencies relations. In addition, resource sharing was not considered in the majority of the existing works. Moreover, coherence rules, such as inclusion and exclusion rules, were not considered either. That is why we propose in this paper a new context-aware framework in order to overcome these constraints. We implemented a four layers architecture where every layer has its specific role. This new tool is able to satisfy what the existing works do not.

III. R2TCA: New Tool for Reconfigurable Real-Time Context-Aware Systems

The four layers architecture is given as follows: (i) Reconfiguration layer, (ii) Context control layer, (iii) Services layer, and (iv) Communication layer. The technical description and details of the internal models and behavior of each layer is available in a research report at [21]. The goal of this paper is to present the implemented tool and to show its execution.

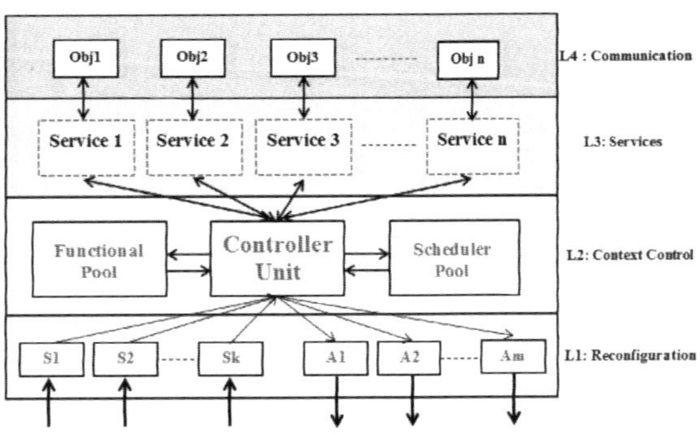

Figure 1. The modules of R2TCA layers.

Fig. 1 presents the superposition of the framework's four layers. The description of layers and their modules is depicted in the next paragraphs.

A. Reconfiguration Layer

This is the first layer in the architecture (see Fig. 2). It is responsible for collecting triggered events in the environment. This collection is ensured thanks to sensors and the layer considers these events as reconfiguration requests. Then, it forwards the reconfiguration requests to the upper layer. The second role of this layer is to transfer commands coming from the upper layer after having checked the constraints to the actuators of the connected devices.

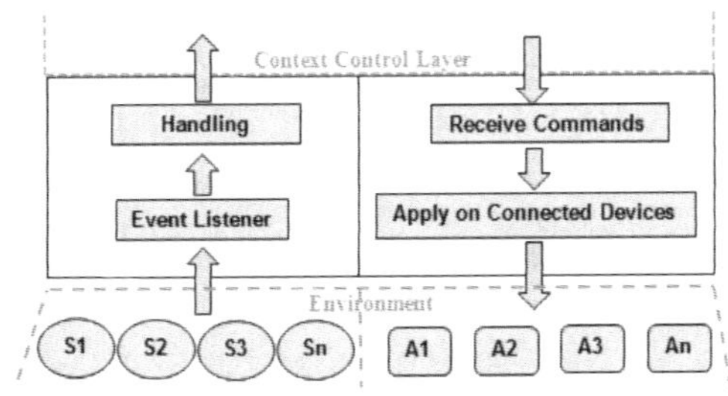

Figure 2. Reconfiguration layer modules.

Fig. 2 shows the composition of this layer. It is composed of four main modules. *Event Listener* is listening for the events. *Handling* is responsible for treating the sensed events and forwarding them to the upper layer. *Receive Commands* is responsible for switching the changes to the environment. *Apply on Command Devices* is responsible for delivering the needed actions to the actuators.

B. Context Control Layer

This is the second layer in the architecture. It is the key layer in the entire proposed framework since it is responsible for controlling the execution of the adaptation process. It is composed of three components, as follows: controller unit, functional pool and scheduler pool.

1) Controller Unit: It is the component responsible for the collaboration between the layers of the architecture and between the components of the context control layer (see Fig. 3). Its role is to receive reconfiguration requests sent by the reconfiguration layer and: (i) decides the modification level that should be processed (whether loading a new service or updating some objects of a service or updating some data of a service), (ii) sends functional constraints to the functional pool to be checked, (iii) sends tasks to be executed to the scheduler pool.

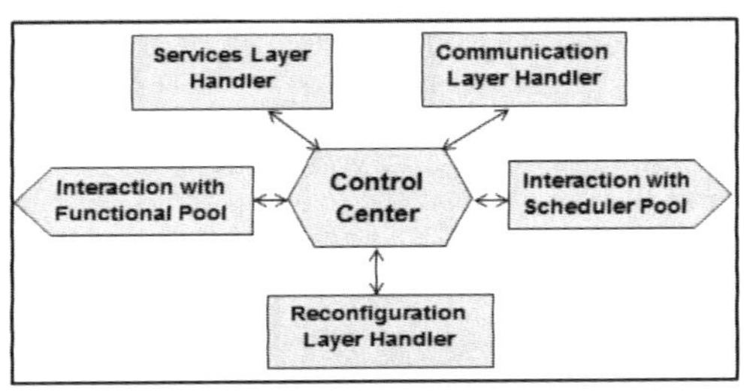

Figure 3. Controller unit modules.

2) Functional Pool: This pool is responsible for checking functional constraints that can be present in adaptive systems. It guarantees the control of dependencies such as using shared resources. Also, it offers the possibility to order the services according to their importance and precedence relation through a priorities table. In addition, it keeps coherent execution of the services by checking inclusion and exclusion rules. Moreover, it provides the ability to allocate and de-allocate resources to be used. Fig. 4 depicts the test levels that guarantee a correct functional behavior.

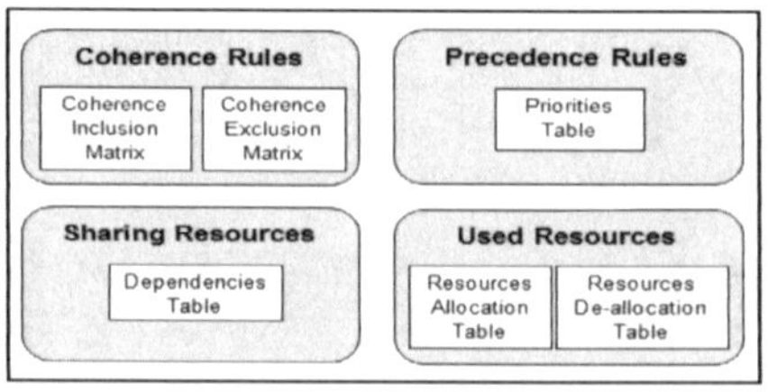

Figure 4. Functional pool modules.

3) Scheduler Pool: This pool is responsible for scheduling real-time tasks. It offers the possibility to employ different categories of scheduling protocols (see Fig. 5). It takes in protocols for scheduling periodic tasks with fixed priorities (Rate Monotonic [15] and Deadline Monotonic [16]) and dynamic priorities (Earliest Deadline First [17] and Least Laxity First [18]). Also, it takes in scheduling of aperiodic tasks thanks to Polling, Deferrable and Sporadic servers [19]. Not only that, but it enables scheduling with regard to sharing resources through Priority Ceiling Protocol [20].

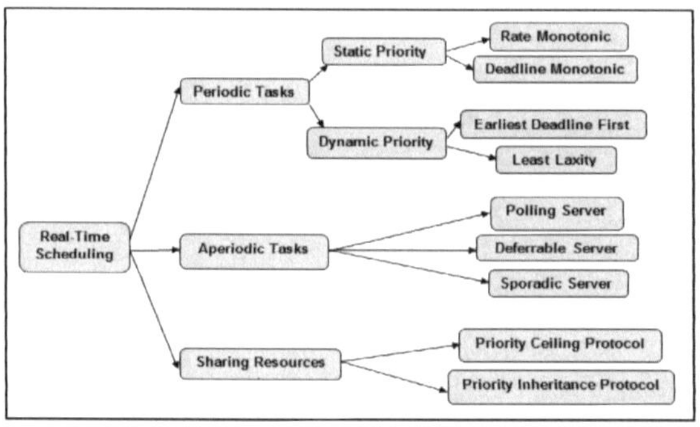

Figure 5. Scheduler pool modules.

C. Services Layer

This is the third layer in the architecture. It contains services containers. In fact, a service is the set of tasks to be accomplished by the system. These tasks are translated in the form of code organized in objects (these objects are classes from the object oriented programming).

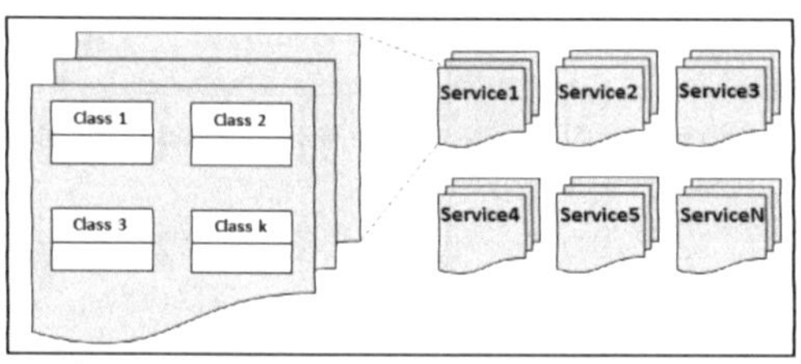

Figure 6. Services layer modules.

Fig. 6 depicts the services containers. Every container is composed of a set of classes including the tasks of the system.

D. Communication Layer

This is the fourth and the last layer in the proposed framework. It represents the interface of the framework to the developers (Fig. 7). It contains a set of interfaces (from object oriented programming) that encapsulates the tasks offered by the services. Each interface represents one service.

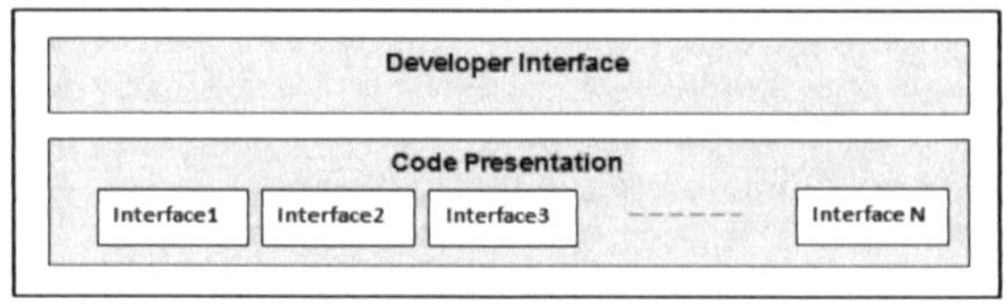

Figure 7. Communication layer modules.

R2TCA is distinguished by the high level of control during leading reconfigurations. It provides a whole component to handle the correctness of the processes execution. Neither deadlocks nor blocking will be faced at run-time thanks to the functional pool. R2TCA solves the problem of system feasibility by including a scheduler pool. This pool guarantees that all services will be executed before exceeding their deadlines.

IV. Application

Based on the R2TCA description presented in the previous section, we have implemented our framework using C# programming language. We have developed the four layers. We proved the suitability of our work by developing a control application of an airport baggage handling system.

A. Baggage Handling System Model and Design

A baggage handling system (BHS) is composed of different devices like conveyor sections, Radio Frequency IDentification (RFID) readers, X-ray sections, pushers, etc. The main target behind using such system is to transport passenger baggage to the right destination at the right time. Fig. 8 depicts an example of BHS. There are various services accomplished by this system: up-stream, down-stream, merging, diverting, tracking, and stop services.

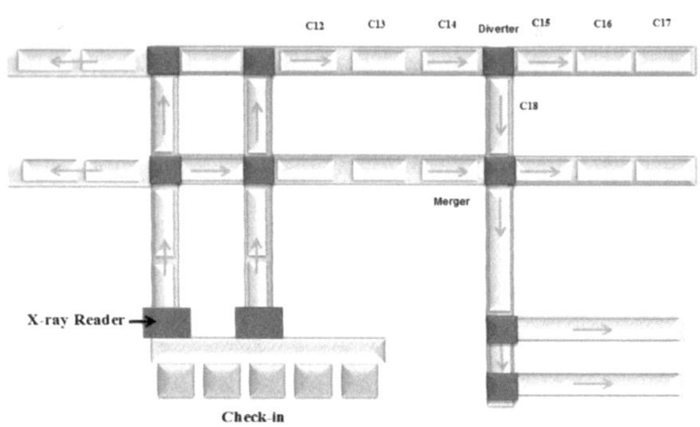

Figure 8. The baggage handling system structure.

To be executed as expected, the BHS has to overcome some problems. First, this system can face reconfigurations at run-time. These reconfigurations can be caused by different reasons like maintenance, failures, human intervention, actions in the environment. So, the system should adapt its behavior accordingly. This adaptation is not a trivial task since putting the system offline or causing some blockage are not acceptable. Thus, controlling functional aspects of reconfiguration processes is really a crucial need. Moreover, conveying the baggage from check-in to the right destination must not take a long time, otherwise the system loses its effectiveness. In this context, we implemented R2TCA a new tool providing the possibility to overcome these problems.

B. Contribution: the new tool R2TCA

In this subsection, we present our developed tool R2TCA. We provide a description of the implementation of the main functionality.

Figure 9. The developers interface of R2TCA.

We have implemented R2TCA which includes the framework services. Fig. 9 depicts its interface. This interface enables developers to access the code of the framework and to use it in order to implement control applications. The folder *Framework* shown in Fig. 10 contains all the packages and classes of our framework. Developers have to use these classes by means of inheritance. They have the possibility to edit the folder *Developer* and create their own project.

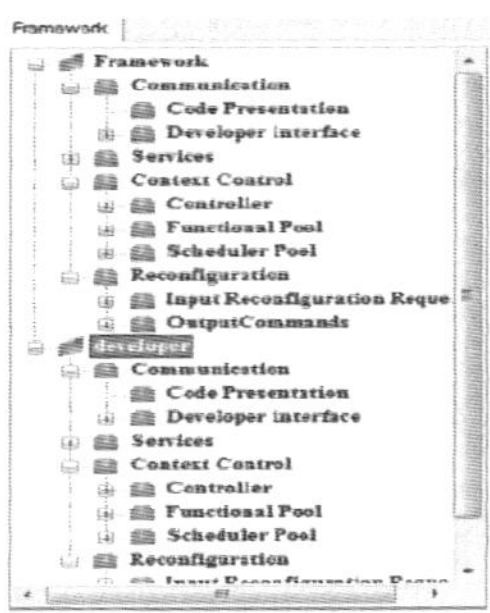

Figure 10. The packages of R2TCA.

In their new projects, developers are free to use the scheduling protocol that fits their needs, they are also free to modify, add, and delete some services (see Fig. 11):

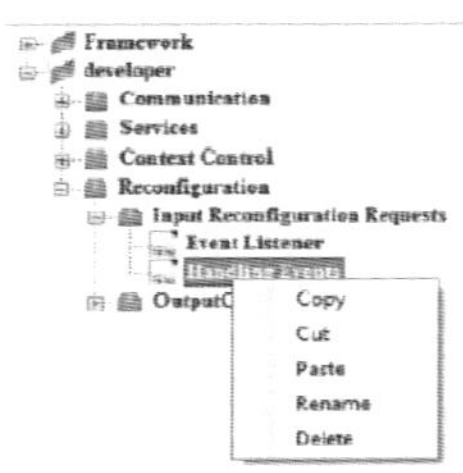

Figure 11. The developer project files.

We have implemented all the scheduling protocols aforesaid in the section of scheduler pool. Feasibility tests and simulations were performed. Let us see how this tool can be used with a baggage handling system.

C. Simulation of the baggage handling system

Before we go to the simulation and test, let us present the developed services and the relations between them.

TABLE I. SERVICES FEATURES.

Name	ID	Priority	included services	excluded services	Resources	Type
Stop	0	1	4	1,2,3,5	R	Real-time
Upstream	1	4	4	0,2	R,Q	Real-time
Downstream	2	4	4	0,1	R,Z	Real-time
Merge	3	3	4	0,5	-	Real-time
Track	4	2	-	-	R	Real-time
Divert	5	3	4	0,3	R,Q	Real-time

As mentioned in Table 1: Service stop has the highest priority, service track has a lower priority, both merge and divert services have equal priorities which is less than track priority, up-stream and down-stream also have the same priority, which is the lowest priority.

The relation between these services can be defined as follows: (i) Services up-stream and down-stream are in exclusion (because they are opposite). (ii) Services merge and divert are also in exclusion. (iii) Service track is in inclusion with all the rest of services. (iv) Service stop is in exclusion with the rest of services. We mentioned also the shared resource R and Q and the type of services (whether they are real-time or not).

We consider the BHS shown in Fig. 8. Baggage has to be transported from the check-in point to the departure gates. Initially, service down-stream and track are running. A reconfiguration scenario arises when the conveyor 16 is broken down. Baggage has to be routed another way, so the control application will load the stop service to stop the down-stream and then to run up-stream until reaching a diverting section (see Fig. 12).

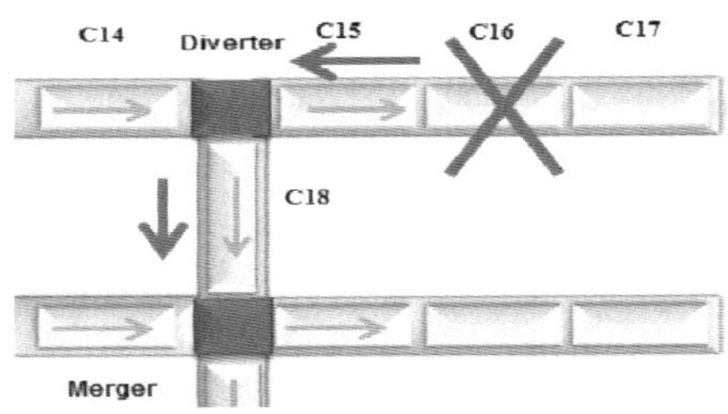

Figure 12. The reconfiguration scenario.

The controller unit begins by selecting down-stream and track service from the services layer (see Fig. 13).

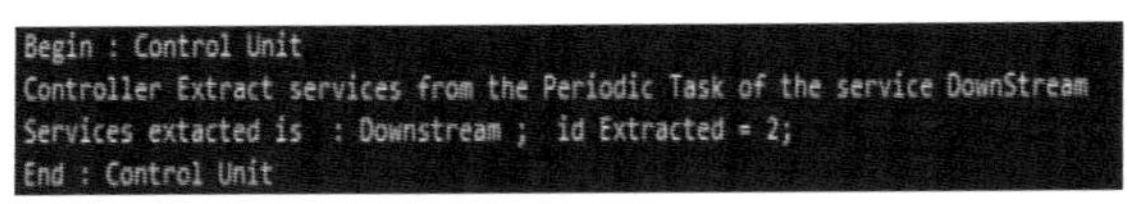

Figure 13. The controller selection of downs-stream service

After that, the controller sends a functional request to the functional pool in order to verify the needed restrictions. Once called, the functional pool creates the necessary tables. It begins with creating the exclusion matrix (this matrix helps to determine which services can work together and which services cannot work together, as we mentioned in Table 1). Similarly, it creates the inclusion matrix that helps to determine which services can be executed simultaneously. Then, it creates priorities, dependencies and resources tables.

After creating all the necessary control matrices and tables, the functional pool starts the verification of the functional requirements of the down-stream service. First of all, it will check the priority of the selected service from the priorities table. The priority of down-stream is 4. The functional pool will verify inclusion and exclusion rules thanks to the created matrices. Then, it checks the dependencies rules using the dependencies table. It verifies if there are shared resources between the services. As shown in Fig. 14, service down-stream uses the resources R and Q, and service track uses the resource R. So, it returns that there are shared resources and Priority Ceiling Protocol has to be used to control these resources. Finally, resources allocation table will be checked to allocate the other needed resources (see Fig. 15).

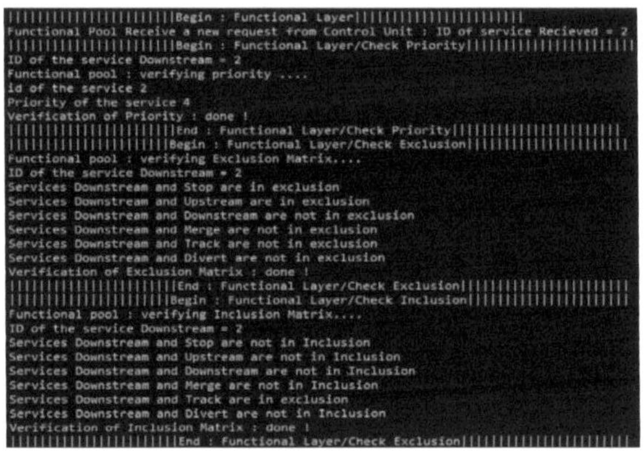

Figure 14. Checking functional constraints (first part).

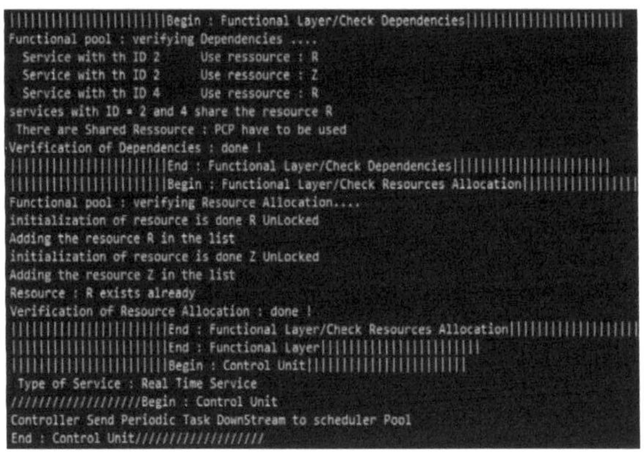

Figure 15. Checking functional constraints (second part).

Once all these constraints are verified, the functional pool sends a positive feedback to the controller. At this level, the controller verifies if the services type is real-time or not. Down-stream is defined as real-time service in our system, so it will be sent to the scheduler pool to be scheduled based on the chosen protocol (in our case, Rate Monotonic is selected to handle periodic tasks and the polling server to handle aperiodic tasks).

The same steps of checking will be repeated with the service track. As seen in Table 1, the downstream and track services are real-time services, so they will be switched to the scheduler pool. The scheduler pool starts the execution of services. At the period of Polling Server (Fig. 16), it checks the list of aperiodic events (reconfiguration events).

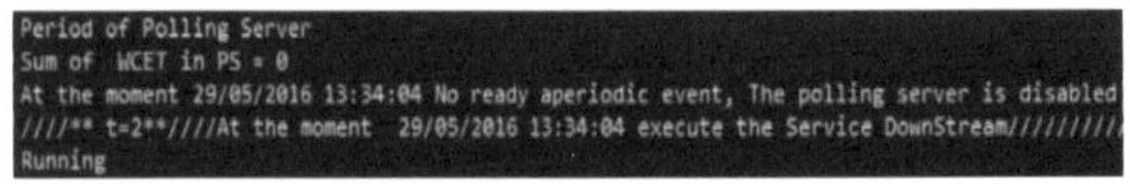

Figure 16. Checking queue of aperiodic tasks.

While our system is running and conveyors are advancing, a problem arises with the motor responsible for conveyor 16, making it unable to execute any command. So, our system should find another valid path to transport baggage to the target destination. This change is picked-up by R2TCA when sensors send an event to stop down-streaming and run up-streaming until reaching a diverting section. Here, stop and up-streaming will be inserted in the queue of aperiodic tasks. This change is considered a reconfiguration scenario.

Before any verification, the controller checks the feasibility of the system and decides if this event will be accepted or not. After verifying this condition, the controller verifies that once accepted, this new event will not cause the lower priority events accepted and not yet executed by the system to miss their deadlines.

After accepting the new event, the controller extracts the ID of the service stop (ID=0), then sends a request to the functional pool. As Table 1 shows, service stop has the priority 0 (the highest priority) and is in exclusion with all the other services except the service track. On the other hand, service stop includes track service. So, the track will not be deleted from the list of competitive services. The functional pool verifies dependencies and resources rules then returns the feedback to the controller. The controller sends the aperiodic event stop to the scheduler pool by putting it in the queue of aperiodic tasks (see Fig. 17).

Figure 17. Controller sends aperiodic tasks to scheduler pool.

The stop service is used in order to stop the down-stream of conveyors. After stopping down-stream, the reconfiguration layer sends a second request to load the service up-stream. Conveyors should move back until reaching a divert point. The controller checks the feasibility, accepts up-stream event, creates a functional request and sends it to the functional pool.

When sensors detect that conveyors reach the diverting position, the controller loads the service divert. Then, it creates a functional request and communicates with the functional pool to verify the functional rules. After that, the controller sends diverting event to the scheduler pool which will add it to the queue of aperiodic events and execute it at the first activation of the polling server. When the target point is achieved, the system should resume its ordinary work.

D. R2TCA Performance

The contribution of R2TCA is that it improves the reconfiguration process and ameliorates the adaptation of system behavior. R2TCA helps systems to shorten the execution time and so to hasten the response thanks to the functional pool. In fact, this pool helps to avoid the time lost in starting the execution of a wrong process. By checking the coherence rules and tasks priorities, developers are confident in the correctness of tasks execution. In addition, the dependencies table plays an important role in minimizing the conflicts, avoiding deadlocks and getting rid of the problem of priorities inversion. We have performed a comparison between two simulation scenarios: with and without the functional pool. The results are shown in Fig. 18.

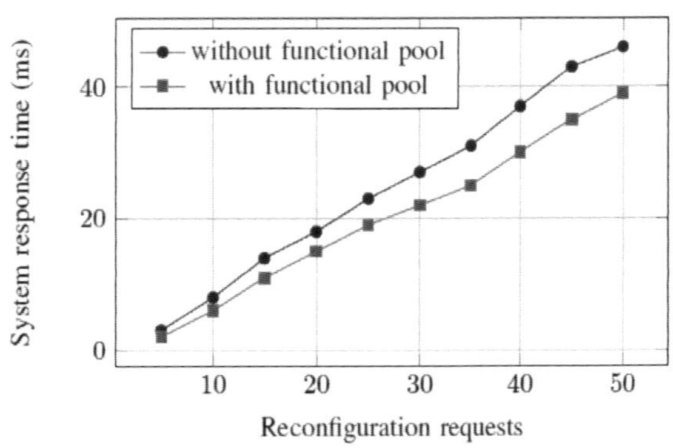

Figure 18. The system response time.

Fig. 18 shows that the red curve (with functional pool) has smaller values than the blue curve (without functional pool). This means that the system response time is faster when using the functional pool. Also, it shows that, by the increasing number of reconfiguration requests, more time is saved compared to using only a few number of requests. Therefore, using the functional pool is an efficient way to save time.

Comparing R2TCA with other related work is beneficial in terms of underlying the differences and highlighting the offered advantages. To this end, we compared R2TCA with CAMPUS [10] development tool. CAMPUS was proposed with the aim of automating context-aware adaptation decisions at run-time. We choose to compare our tool with CAMPUS since its logic of the control process is similar to the logic of R2TCA.

In order to execute an adaptation process when using CAMPUS, if a service is composed of nine tasks and if these tasks are composed of two tasklets, the developers have to prepare 2*9= 18 adaptation rules. The number of these rules will increase with increasing number of services in the system and also with increasing number of taskelts composing each service. In addition, the performed rules have the risk to be tied to a specific application and so it will be less flexible. Instead, by using R2TCA the same number of adaptation rules will be applied in all cases. The functional pool of R2TCA offers the possibility to check six main rules by means of the six tables (Priority, Precedence, Resources Allocation, Resources De-allocation, Inclusion Matrix, and Exclusion Matrix). Table 2 shows a clear view of the gain in terms of adaptation rules provided by R2TCA.

TABLE II. NUMBER OF ADAPTATION RULES OF R2TCA Vs CAMPUS.

	Tasks number	Tasklets number	CAMPUS adaptation rules	R2TCA adaptation rules
Service1	1	6	1*6=6	6
Service2	2	3	2*3=6	6
Service3	8	2	2*8=16	6
Service4	6	3	6*3=18	6
Service5	4	7	4*7=28	6
Service6	3	9	3*9=27	6
Service7	5	3	5*3=15	6
Service8	7	2	7*2=14	6

According to Table 2, CAMPUS and R2TCA have the same number of adaptation rules only in the simple cases where the service has only one task composed of six tasklets or in the case where the service has two tasks composed of three tasklets. Otherwise, R2TCA provides a lower number of functional rules which makes it easier for developers to develop the adaptation process. No doubt, every adaptation rule will use system resources (such as the processor time, the memory, the energy). The number of these resources depends on the complexity of the rule and the controlled entities.

Fig. 19 contains an approximate calculation of the system response time when using R2TCA and CAMPUS.

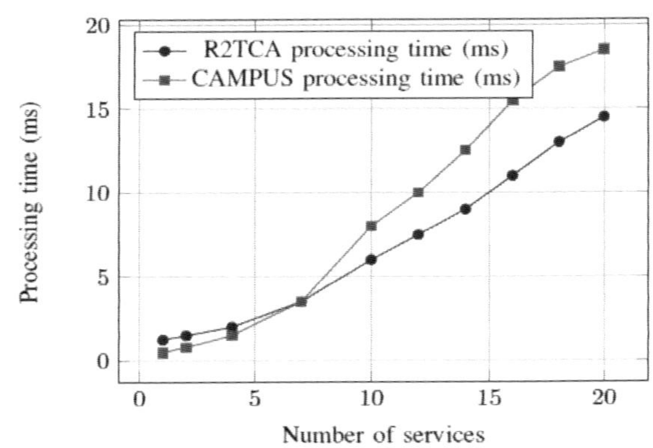

Figure 19. The processing time.

Fig. 19 shows that the processing time of the services is almost the same when using R2TCA and CAMPUS for eight services or less. But when the number of services is higher, R2TCA has a lower processing time compared with CAMPUS.

After that, we wanted to make sure that by adding the extra control pools (functional and scheduler) the system will not be lead to a point of congestion or bottleneck. Processor utilization as well as energy resources have to be absolutely sufficient. No doubt, the memory consumption at run-time is of great importance and it represents a key factor to get a correct reconfiguration process. That is why we have calculated the memory utilization rate when there is an increasing number of reconfiguration requests.

Fig. 20 shows that by increasing the number of reconfiguration requests (receiving 60 requests simultaneously), the system uses 74% of the available memory. This value is considered acceptable since it does not cause the system to be very loaded.

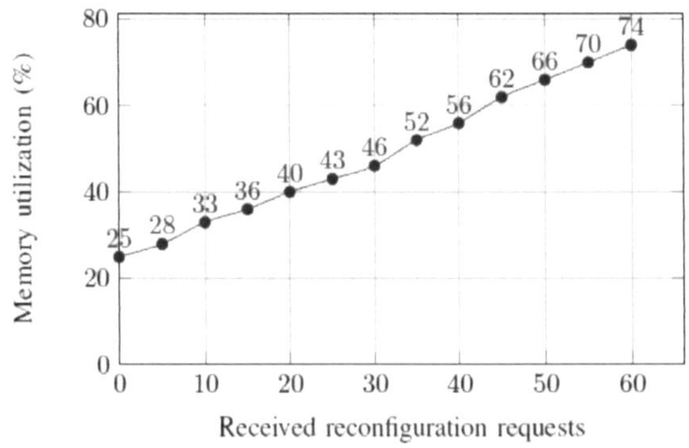

Figure 20. The memory utilization.

V. Conclusion

In this paper, we have presented the new tool R2TCA, a context-aware framework devoted to the development of control applications of adaptive systems. This new tool provides developers with the opportunity to respect both functional and real-time constraints. On one hand, the functional pool helps developers to check the inclusion and exclusion rules as well as to handle the resources to be allocated, de-allocated and shared. On the other hand, the scheduler pool guarantees the feasibility execution of services by offering various types of scheduling protocols. The robustness of R2TCA was proved by implementing our case study (the baggage handling system). R2TCA helps improve the response time of the system. Not only that, but also it is an interesting tool maximizing the resources utilization. In further works, R2TCA can be extended in order to include other control components. We plan to empower our framework by adding artificial intelligence so that we enable the prediction of context. Also, we consider to add a component responsible for quality of service issues.

References

[1] G. D.Abowd, et al. "Towards a better understanding of context and context-awareness." International Symposium on Handheld and Ubiquitous Computing. Springer Berlin Heidelberg, pp. 304-307, 1999.

[2] D. Salber, A. K. Dey, and G. D. Abowd, "Ubiquitous computing: Defining an hci research agenda for an emerging interaction paradigm.", GVU Technical Report;GIT-GVU-98-01, 1998.

[3] X. Li, M. Eckert, J.-F. Martinez, and G. Rubio, Context aware middleware architectures: Survey and challenges, Sensors, vol. 15, no. 8, pp. 20 57020 607, 2015.

[4] U. Alegre, J. C. Augusto, and T. Clark, Engineering context-aware systems and applications: a survey, Journal of Systems and Software, vol. 117, pp. 5583, 2016.

[5] S. Sukode, S. Gite, and H. Agrawal, Context aware framework in iot: A survey, International Journal of Advanced Trends in Computer Science and Engineering, vol. 4, no. 1, pp. 01-09, 2015.

[6] W. Lepuschitz, A. Zoitl, M. Vallee, and M. Merdan, Toward selfreconfiguration of manufacturing systems using automation agents, Systems, Man, and Cybernetics, Part C: Applications and Reviews, IEEE Transactions on, vol. 41, no. 1, pp. 5269, 2011.

[7] A. Forkan, I. Khalil, and Z. Tari, Cocamaal: A cloud-oriented contextaware middleware in ambient assisted living, Future Generation Computer Systems, vol. 35, pp. 114127, 2014.

[8] A. Forkan, I. Khalil, A. Ibaida, and Z. Tari, Bdcam: Big data for context-aware monitoring-a personalized knowledge discovery framework for assisted healthcare, 2015.

[9] H. Mcheick, H. Sbeity, H. Hazimeh, J. Naim, and M. Alameh, Context aware mobile application architecture (camaa) for health care systems, in Humanitarian Technology Conference-(IHTC), 2014 IEEE Canada International, pp. 15, 2014.

[10] E. J. Wei and A. T. Chan, Campus: A middleware for automated context-aware adaptation decision making at run time, Pervasive and Mobile Computing, vol. 9, no. 1, pp. 3556, 2013.

[11] L. Tang, Z. Yu, H. Wang, X. Zhou, and Z. Duan, Methodology and tools for pervasive application development, International Journal of Distributed Sensor Networks, vol. 10 no. 4 516432, 2014.

[12] B. Bertran, et. al Diasuite: A tool suite to develop sense/compute/control applications, Science of Computer Programming, vol. 79, pp. 3951, 2014.

[13] S. Liu and L. Cheng, A context-aware reflective middleware framework for distributed real-time and embedded systems, Journal of Systems And Software, vol. 84, no. 2, pp. 205218, 2011.

[14] E. Papadopoulou, S. Gallacher, N. K. Taylor, and M. H. Williams, A personal smart space approach to realising ambient ecologies, Pervasive and Mobile Computing, vol. 8, no. 4, pp. 485499, 2012.

[15] J. Lehoczky, L. Sha, and Y. Ding, The rate monotonic scheduling algorithm: Exact characterization and average case behavior, in Real Time Systems Symposium, 1989., Proceedings. IEEE, pp. 166 171, 198.

[16] N. C. Audsley, A. Burns, and A. J. Wellings, Deadline monotonic scheduling theory and application, in Control Engineering Practice, vol. 1, no. 1, pp. 7178, 1993.

[17] M. Spuri and G. C. Buttazzo, Efficient aperiodic service under earliest deadline scheduling, in Real-Time Systems Symposium, 1994., Proceedings. IEEE, pp. 211, 1994.

[18] J. Hildebrandt, F. Golatowski, and D. Timmermann, Scheduling co-processor for enhanced least-laxity-first scheduling in hard real-time systems, in Real-Time Systems, 1999. Proceedings of the 11th Euromicro Conference on. IEEE, pp. 208215, 1999.

[19] B. Sprunt, L. Sha, and J. Lehoczky, Aperiodic task scheduling for hard-real-time systems, Real-Time Systems, vol. 1, no. 1, pp. 2760, 1989.

[20] L. Sha, R. Rajkumar, and J. P. Lehoczky, Priority inheritance protocols: An approach to real-time synchronization, Computers, IEEE Transactions on, vol. 39, no. 9, pp. 11751185, 1990.

[21] http://www.aut.uni-saarland.de/mitarbeiter/frey/publications/

Wireframe Mockups to ConcurTaskTrees

A WYSIWYG User Interface Modeling Approach

Miroslav Sili & Christopher Mayer
Health & Environment Department
AIT Austrian Institute of Technology GmbH
Vienna, Austria
e-mail: miroslav.sili@ait.ac.at, christopher.mayer@ait.ac.at

Daniel Pahr
Student at the TU Wien
Vienna, Austria
e-mail: e0906438@student.tuwien.ac.at

***Abstract*— Nowadays, we use a variety of devices to interact with local and cloud-based systems and services and are used to aesthetic and tailored user interfaces. This fact induces challenges for user interface designers regarding additional efforts for the development of multiple user interfaces for (all) available devices. Model-based user interface design tackles this challenge by creating abstract models for a transformation to various devices, but with the disadvantage of additional efforts for using and learning these techniques. Thus, we propose a transformation process deriving an abstract model on the basis of an integrated mockup and wireframe design tool. This allows combining the advantages of model-based user interface design with the world of the classical user interface design process. The engine transfers sketches to an abstract task model in ConcurTaskTrees notation. The model is the input for a separate model interpretation layer generating concrete user interfaces for various device types. The prototype delivers promising results and future research has to focus on extending its applicability by addressing structural constraints and limitations.**

Keywords*— *Wireframe; Mockup; Sketches; User Interface Design; WYSIWYG; ConcurTaskTrees; CTT; UI Model; Adaptivity; Transformation; XSLT

I. INTRODUCTION

The last two decades have seen a growing trend towards mobile and ubiquitous computing. This trend changed the way of Human Computer Interaction (HCI). Nowadays, we use a variety of devices to interact with local and cloud-based systems and services. We also become accustomed to use aesthetic and tailored user interfaces (UI) on different device types. This variety provides some advantages for end-users, but also some significant disadvantages for UI designers. Additional efforts are needed to design and develop multiple UIs for different device types. Considering the number of potential UIs, the classical design approach is not appropriate anymore. At this point, the model-based UI design approach can help to save design resources in terms of time and money. Besides its advantages, it has also some disadvantages. To name a few: the design process is not intuitive enough, additional resources during the learning and training phase are needed and the continuous testing routines require additional efforts. The proposed mixed approach aims to minimize these negative aspects. The idea is to integrate mockup and wireframe design tools, which are common in the classical UI design process, into the model-based UI design process. This What You See Is What You Get (WYSIWYG) - like design helps designers to manifest their vision of concrete UIs without the need to spend too much efforts on specific model-based techniques and language notations.

The remainder of this paper is structured as follows: In Section 2, one finds a short overview of related work. Section 3 provides an introduction to the model-based UI design process, the concept of task models in ConcurTaskTrees (CTT) notation, the evaluation of Wireframe and Sketch-based tools as well as an overview of the chosen tool. Section 4 describes in detail the transformation engine, which is able to transform wireframe mockup output data into abstract UI CTT models. In Section 5, the results are summarized and discussed.

II. RELATED WORK

In the past, similar approaches for the generation of abstract user interface models have been proposed. Those approaches share the employment of WYSIWYG-like editors with our proposed solution and use different abstract models for the representation of the interface.

In [18], the concept of model-driven development is examined with the goal to propose a solution for the automatic generation of user-interfaces. To achieve this, CTT models are introduced into the model driven approach to capture interaction requirements of user interfaces. The proposed tool allows developers to create user interfaces by using sketch-based drawings. However, designers need to provide additional context to UI elements in order to identify them distinctly. This process enables the creation of verifiable, explicit CTT models for a user interface. Using those components a model compiler could automatically create the code for a platform specific user interface.

Gummy [6] uses a WYSIWYG user interface editor to produce an abstract representation in User Interface Markup Language (UIML) format [19]. It offers a live representation of multiple different user interfaces for different platforms while editing. UIML specifications of user interface are very similar to concrete user interface specifications as opposed to the highly abstract nature of CTT used in our proposed solution.

SketchiXML [20] offers an editor more focused on drawing and gesture based interaction than graphical user interfaces. A user can draw its prototype on a canvas and assign a context to the different parts of the sketch to create a user interface model, which in turn, can be viewed on multiple fidelity levels. SketchyXML supports UIML as the main export format but an export to UsiXML [21] is also possible.

III. MODEL-BASED USER INTERFACE DESIGN PROCESS

In contrast to the classical UI design process, model-based design divides the UI generation process into at least two steps. The first step is related to the modeling of an abstract UI, followed by two or more steps related to the generation of concrete UIs. The abstract and declarative model of the first step is composed of components like a user-task model, a user model, a dialog model, a presentation model and a domain model. These models provide a formal representation of the UI design [1]. In the second step, this formal representation can be automatically transformed into concrete UIs by using a separate model interpretation layer, e.g., AALuis [2]-[5]. This (at least) two-step approach offers the opportunity to specify the UI only once, which facilitates the process of changing and editing [6].

Model-based user interface design had its origin in the mid-late 1990s [7]-[9]. Researchers and developers have investigated different model-based techniques in order to structure and automate the user interface design process since then. Some approaches rely, e.g., on State chart XML (SCXML) models [10][11], some on the Business Process Model and Notation (BPMN) models [12][13] and some on CTT models [14][15].

In general, the model-based UI design cannot be declared as an easy and intuitive process. Designers need time to get familiar with the indirect design concept and to learn these model-based techniques and language notations. Furthermore, they also require additional time to test their UI models continuously and to compare the intended output with the automatically generated output. Our proposed transformation engine aims to minimize some of these challenges. Instead of using abstract design elements to model abstract UIs, designers may use existing sketch-based tools to design concrete UI representations. The transformation engine transforms these representations, into abstract UI models. These UI models, in turn, are used in the second phase as input for an automatic transformation into concrete UIs. On the occasion of our current running research and development project YouDo [16][17], which uses abstract UI models in CTT notation, the developed transformation engine also focuses on CTT notation. Nevertheless, the underlying architecture generally allows also transformations into other notations like SCXML notation or BPMN.

A. *Interaction Models in CTT notation*

This paragraph helps to comprehend the main transformation steps by providing a briefly overview about different CTT tasks and temporal operators used in the CTT notation. The CTT notation distinguishes between four task categories, namely interaction, system, user and abstract tasks [14]. Interaction tasks are related to concrete user interactions. These tasks are represented in the final UI, e.g., as control elements or text input elements. System tasks are responsible to receive data from the system and to provide information to the user. User tasks represent internal cognitive or physical activities and abstract tasks are used for complex actions, which need sub-tasks of different categories [23]. Next to these categories, tasks are also classified into different types. Just to mention some, interaction tasks may be of type control, edit or selection. Regarding the proposed transformation engine especially these task types are particularly relevant. As an example, an edit interaction tasks specifies an object which can be manually edited by the user. Depending on the concrete transformation such an edit interaction task may be represented, e.g., by a graphical text field. Next to different task categories and task types the CTT notation specifies also eight temporal operators. Temporal operators are able to describe the relationship between single tasks. [24] provides a detail explanation of the eight temporal operators.

B. *Evaluation of Wireframe and Sketch-based Tools*

Based on a detailed evaluation of existing wireframe and sketch-based tools for user interfaces design, we decide to use the Balsamiq mockup tool [22]. Our evaluation included in total 11 tools and the following set of evaluation criteria: a) the price, b) supported output formats, c) required learning efforts and the tool usability, d) supported platforms, d) available feature set and finally d) the project/tool activity in terms of development and maintenance status. Table I summarizes the list of evaluated tools and some of the mentioned evaluation criteria.

TABLE I. LISTING OF EVALUATED WIREFRAME AND SKETCH-BASED TOOLS AND SOME OF THE EVALUATION CRITERIA

Tool	Price[a]	Supported output formats	Supported platforms	Feature set[b]	Activity[b]
Gummy [26]	/	UIML	Windows	-	-
Glade Interface Designer [27]	/	Libglade, GtkBuilder	Linux, Windows, Mac	+	+
softandGUI [28]	£99	PNG, Word, HTML, XML	Windows	+	+
WireframeSketcher [29]	$99	PNG, PDF, HTML	Linux, Windows, Mac, Eclipse plugin	+	+
iPLOTZ [30]	$99/yr.	JPG, PNG, PDF, iPotz File, XML	Windows & Mac, Web	+	+
Evolus Pencil [31]	/	PNG, HTML, PDF, SVG, ODT	Linux, Windows, Mac, Web	+	+
Mockup-designer [32]	n/a	JSON, PNG	Web	-	n/a
Balsamiq Mockups [22]	$89	BMML (XML-Bas)	Windows, Mac, Web	+	+
Maqetta [33]	/	HTML	Linux, Windows, Mac,	+	-
draw.io [34]	/	XML	Web	+	+
Moqups [35]	19€/mo.	PDF, PNG	Web	+	+

a. Price for the single- user license. The slash symbol </> represents GPL, GPL2 or open source licenses. b. The plus symbol <+> represents positive evaluated criteria whereas the minus symbol <-> represents the opposite.

Balsamiq's easy to use export format Balsamiq Mockups Markup Language (BMML), the cross platform application, or the comprehensive feature list are just some of the positive criteria which influenced our decision. Balsamiq features a very simple, yet powerful, drag and drop-based mockup editor.

A navigation bar presents the user with multiple common user interface elements which can simply be dragged to the canvas. One can then arrange those elements to create a full sketch of a user interface and by using very few basic functions, even create linked user interface prototypes. Such prototypes normally serve to present the look and feel of a finished software product to test it on a specific group of users, or simply to try out the design for developers.

Balsamiq's BMMF file features an XML format. As such, a whole mockup can be viewed like a tree structure with a root node, which has child nodes representing the components of the mockups. Multiple attributes and property nodes can be assigned to the components to mirror the design of the mockup. Furthermore, a grouping function is available, which actually serves to create groups of interface elements and enables the user to move them as a whole. However, in the scope of transformation this function will be more of use to assign identifying objects to UI elements that are inherently without a concrete description, such as text boxes or check boxes. The linking of mockups is also resembled in a simple property node that can be attached to UI elements like buttons.

IV. WIREFRAME TO CTT TRANSFORMATION ENGINE

With Balsamiq mockup files, serving as the input for the transformation engine, the next step was to design mapping rules and to create a concrete transformations from Balsamiq' export file format BMML into the CTT format. Due to the fact that both file formats use an XML structure the Extensible Stylesheet Language Transformation (XSLT) [25] was used to carry out the transformation. XSLT requires a stylesheet template to establish transformation rules which are able to convert a document from one specific XML structure into another XML structure. The transformation itself is carried out by an XSLT processor. For this purpose, we implemented a small Java application.

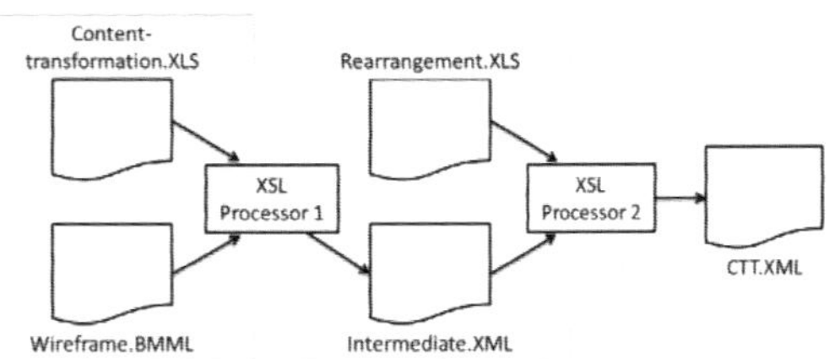

Fig. 1. Illustration of the two-step transformation from Balsamiqs' specific BMML file format into the UI model in CTT notation.

The two underlying XML structures involved in this transformation are fundamentally different. BMML represents the concrete graphic user interface, whereas CTT describes a task model representing a succession of interactions that need to be performed in order to achieve a certain goal. In order to extract sufficient semantic information from a user interface mockup and to limit the number of possible CTT interpretations, the following structural limitations have been introduced:

- Each mockup contains exactly one window, which represents a single static user interface.
- The transformation supports just user interfaces, which can be represented as a set of linked windows.
- The interface must have a designated start point, symbolized by the first window that is presented to the user.
- Each window expresses a so called Presentation Task Set (PTS). A PTS is a set of user interactions, respectively tasks, needed to perform one distinct action. Example: to perform a login action the user needs to fill in the username, the password and to operate the login button within a single window.
- The user input order within a single window is irrelevant.
- One window has at least one control button, which ends users' interaction on that window and forces the system to start the processing of the entered data.
- The system outcome, in turn, is represented by a single window.

Furthermore, due to its complexity the transformation itself takes place in two separate steps: (Step 1) UI content transformation into CTT tasks and their grouping and (Step 2) rearrangement of tasks and the generation of the intended interaction flow using CTTs temporal operators. Fig. 1 illustrates the two-step transformation approach.

1) Step 1 - UI Content Transformation: The UI content transformation consists of two substeps: (substep 1.1) the mapping of Balsamiq UI elements into CTT tasks and (substep 1.2) the grouping of CTT tasks into subtrees, which represent single PTS.

a) Substep 1.1: In this substep, UI elements are translated into semantically corresponding CTT tasks. Table II illustrates the basic set of implemented mapping rules. This approach is also applicable for more complex UI elements like tables, menu groups or street maps. The CTT notation offers the possibility to define interaction tasks of custom type. Thus, one can define an interaction tak e.g., of type table within the XLS transformation. Once implemented, every Balsamiq's table UI element will result in a corresponding table interaction task. Like for any other interaction tasks the CTT interpretation layer is responsible to render these custom interaction tasks accordingly. Additionally due to the possibility to link multiple mockups, a hierarchical structure can be extracted. In this step, single window elements are transformed into CTT subtrees and each UI element nested within the UI window is transformed into a single CTT task.

b) Substep 1.2: In this substep, CTT tasks are grouped into subtrees representing separate PTS. Additionally, each subtree is supplemented by an initial system task (required by the model interpretation layer). The following design patterns are used during the grouping process:

- Each subtree is supplemented by an initial system task. The initial system task is required by the model interpretation layer. The system task causes the layer to pull concrete data values from the backend system. These data values, if present, are used by the layer to perform an auto fill in on the rendered UI elements.
- Each subtree contains one or more interaction tasks of a type unlike control. These interaction tasks are gained from the substep 1.1 using the window UI element and its child UI elements.

- Each subtree contains one or more abstract tasks gained from substep 1.1 using the button UI element. As described in Table II, a button UI element is transformed into a composition of the following three CTT tasks:
  - A single interaction task of type control. This interaction task causes the model interpretation layer to render the concrete final UI element, e.g., a graphical button.
  - A single system task. Like the initial system task, this task is required by the model interpretation layer. In contrast to the initial system task, which pulls data values, this task pushes user input values towards the backend system.
  - If present, an abstract task containing the next PTS in form of a separate subtree. This step applies the design patterns recursively.

2) Step 2 - Rearrangement of PTS tasks and generation of the interaction flow: As already mentioned, after the first step of the transformation, a semi-complete CTT model is produced. The second step consists as well of two substeps in order to complete the CTT model: (substep 2.1) the rearrangement of PTS tasks and (substep 2.2) the generation of the intended interaction flow using CTTs temporal operators.

TABLE II. MAPPING BETWEEN BASIC INTERACTION ELEMENTS IN BALSAMIQ AND CTT TASKS

Balsamiq	CTT	Note
Text field	Interaction task of type edit	
Combo box or Radio button	Interaction task of type single choice	Radio buttons belonging to the same choice need to be grouped together
Check box	Interaction task of type Multiple Choice	Check boxes belonging to the same choice need to be grouped together
Label	Interaction task without explicit task type	
Button	Subgroup of one interaction task of type control, one system task and if present, one abstract task containing the next PTS	Buttons represent the navigations through different PTS
Window	Abstract task containing the current PTS	The title attribute is used to name the abstract task

a) Substep 2.1: Using the complete set of grouped CTT tasks produced in substep 1.2, this substep is responsible to rearrange all tasks within every subtree. The following three ordering rules are used during this process (see for an example Fig. 3):

- Firstly, the initial system task is the first task in the subtree.
- Secondly, all interaction tasks with a type different than "control" follow the initial system task.
- Thirdly, all interaction task of type "control" are arranged lastly in the subtree.

b) Substep 2.2: This is the last processing step performed by the transformation engine. This substep generates the intended interaction flow using CTTs temporal operators. The following rules are applied (see for an example Fig. 3):

- The initial system task is connected to the first interaction tasks with the sequential enabling information processing operator.
- Due to the fact that user inputs do not rely on a specific input order (compare to limitations introduced above), all following interaction tasks with a type different than "control" are connected to the order independence operator.
- The last interaction task with a type different than "control" is connected to the first abstract task (resulting from the UI button element) to the disabling operator.
- Possible following abstract tasks (resulting from the UI button element) are connected to the choice operator.

V. RESULTS

Fig. 2 illustrates an example for a sequence of two simple mockups. The link between the two windows is symbolized by the arrow, leading from the Login-button to the Welcome window.

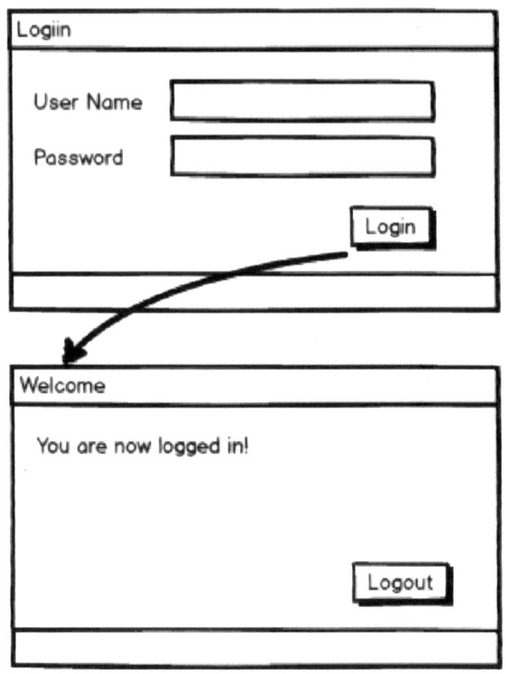

Fig. 2. Illustration of sequence of two simple mockups designed by means of the Balsamiq Mockup Tool

In Fig. 3, one can see the output of the transformation engine when processing the mockups from Fig. 2. Moreover, Fig. 3 provides a comparison of the intermediate semi-complete tree, obtained from the first transformation step and the final task tree, obtained from the second transformation step. The intermediate tree features no temporal operators and the order of the components is not correct. The mockup UI windows "Login" and "Welcome" have been transformed into the corresponding abstract tasks named "Login" and "Welcome". The UI input elements "User Name" and "Password" have been translated to corresponding interaction tasks of type edit. The UI button "Login" has been transformed into an abstract task named "Control Group Login". This, in turn, is composed by an interaction task of type control named "Button_Login", a system task named "Finalization_Login" and finally the already transformed abstract task named "Welcome", which represents the second mockup window. In the final tree, the CTT is complete and all temporal operators have been placed between tasks.

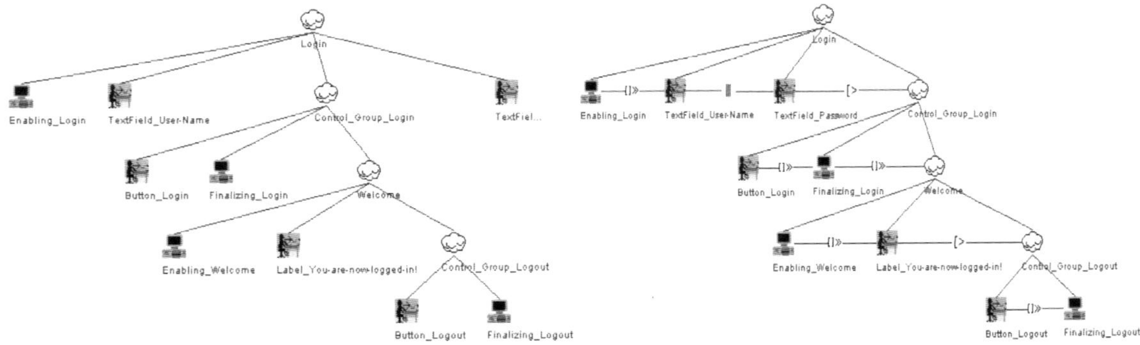

Fig. 3. Illustration of the intermediate semi-complete CTT tree (left) and the complete CTT (right).

The prototype for the proposed transformation tool delivers promising results for the use in combination with an appropriate CTT model interpretation layer, e.g., the AALuis layer. The transformation can be applied to any sequence of mockups following the specified conventions specified. In the moment however, the application of the tool is limited to sequential links that do not contain loops. Such a loop is created when a mockup links to another that has previously appeared on the same path. In future work, the transformations have to be modified to support such interfaces. An idea for further research is the development of a direct presentation of the final user interface, when developing the mockups, thus not only displaying the CTT model as the abstract user interface representation, but as well the transformed user interface.

VI. LIMITATIONS

As mentioned initially, in the model-based UI design process developers are requested to investigate some efforts and practice in order to benefit from model-based generated UIs. The aim of this work is to illustrate one potential solution to minimize these efforts and thus to increase the acceptance of model-based UI development. In our literature review we have been focused on similar practicable and easy to use state-of-the-art solutions and approaches. However, the scope of this work is not on an exhausting listing and detailed comparison of these solutions and approaches, but rather on the description of the proposed solution from a technical and methodological point of view. Moreover, this work tackles the generation of interaction models in CTT notation but not the concrete interpretation of these models. Interpretations concepts have been published previously [2]-[5]. The proposed solution is still under development and requires a detailed validation and evaluation in the scope of performance, acceptance and usability.

ACKNOWLEDGMENT

The project YouDo is co-funded by the AAL Joint Programme (REF. AAL-2012-5-155) and the following National Authorities and R&D programs in Austria, Germany and Switzerland: BMVIT, program benefit, FFG (AT), BMBF (DE) and SERI (CH).

REFERENCES

[1] A. R. Puerta, "A model-based interface development environment," IEEE Software 14.4, pp. 40-47, 1997, doi: 10.1109/52.595902

[2] C. Mayer, M. Morandell, M. Gira, M. Sili, M. Petzold, S. Fagel, S. Schmehl, "User interfaces for older adults," Universal Access in Human-Computer Interaction User and Context Diversity, vol. 8010, Springer Berlin Heidelberg, Jul. 2013, pp. 142-150, doi: 10.1007/978-3-642-39191-0_16

[3] M. Sili, C. Mayer, M. Morandell, M. Gira, M. Petzold, "A Practical Solution for the Automatic Generation of User Interfaces–What Are the Benefits of a Practical Solution for the Automatic Generation of User Interfaces?" Human-Computer Interaction. Theories, Methods, and Tools, vol. 8510, pp. 445-456, Jun. 2014, doi: 10.1007/978-3-319-07233-3_41

[4] C. Mayer, G. Zimmermann, A. Grguric, J. Alexandersson, M. Sili, C. Strobbe, "A comparative study of systems for the design of flexible user interfaces," Journal of Ambient Intelligence and Smart Environments, vol. 8, pp. 125-148, Mar. 2016, doi: 10.3233/AIS-160370

[5] C. Mayer, M. Morandell, M. Gira, K. Hackbarth, M. Petzold, S. Fagel, "AALuis, a User Inter-face Layer That Brings Device Independence to Users of AAL Systems," Computers Helping People with Special Needs, vol. 7382, pp. 650-657, Jul. 2012, doi: 10.1007/978-3-642-31522-0_98

[6] J. Meskens, J. Vermeulen, K. Luyten, K. Coninx,"Gummy for multi-platform user interface designs: shape me, multiply me, fix me, use me," Proceedings of the working conference on Advanced visual interfaces, pp. 233-240, 2008, doi: 10.1145/1385569.1385607

[7] C. Janssen, A. Weisbecker, J. Ziegler, "Generating user interfaces from data models and dialogue net specifications," Proceedings of the INTERACT'93 and CHI'93 conference on human factors in computing systems, pp. 418-423, 1993, doi: 10.1145/169059.169335

[8] A. R. Puerta, H. Eriksson, J. H. Gennari, M. A. Musen, "Model-based automated generation of user interfaces, " AAAI, pp. 471-477, Okt. 1994,

[9] A. R. Puerta, J. Eisenstein, "Towards a general computational framework for model-based interface development systems," Knowledge-Based Systems, vol. 12, pp. 433-442, 1999

[10] J. Barnett, et al. "State chart XML (SCXML): State machine notation for control abstraction." W3C Recommendation, [Online] Available from: https://www.w3.org/TR/scxml retrieved: Jul. 2016

[11] A. Nuno, S. Samuel, T. Antonio, "Multimodal Multi-Device Application Supported by an SCXML State Chart Machine," Proceedings of EICS Workshop on Engineering Interactive Systems with SCXML, 2014

[12] M., Zur Muehlen, J. Recker, "How much language is enough? Theoretical and practical use of the business process modeling notation," InInternational Conference on Advanced Information Systems Engineering, pp. 465-479, Jun. 2008, doi: 10.1007/978-3-540-69534-9_35

[13] H. Trætteberg, "UI design without a task modeling language–using BPMN and Diamodl for task modeling and dialog design," Engineering Interactive Systems, pp. 110-117, 2008, doi: 10.1007/978-3-540-85992-5_9

[14] F. Paternò, C. Mancini, S. Meniconi, "ConcurTaskTrees: A diagrammatic notation for specifying task models," Human-Computer Interaction INTERACT'97, pp. 362-369, 1997, doi: 10.1007/978-0-387-35175-9_58

[15] F. Paternò, C. Mancini, "Developing task models from informal scenarios," CHI'99 Extended Abstracts on Human Factors in Computing Systems, pp. 228-229, 1999, doi: 10.1145/632716.632858

[16] M. Sili, D. Bolliger, J. Morak, M. Gira, K. Wessig, D. Brunmeir, H. Tellioğlu, "YouDo-we help! - An Open Information and Training Platform for Informal Caregivers," Studies in health technology and informatics, vol. 217, pp. 873-877, 2014, doi: 10.3233/978-1-61499-566-1-873

[17] YouDo – we help! [Online] Available from: http://youdoproject.eu Retrieved: Jul. 2016

[18] O. Pastor, S. España, J. I. Panach, N. Aquino, "Model-driven development," Informatik-Spektrum, vol. 31(5), pp. 394-407, 2008, doi: 10.1007/s00287-008-0275-8

[19] M. Abrams, C. Phanouriou, A. L. Batongbacal, S. M. Williams, J. E. Shuster, "UIML: an appliance-independent XML user interface language," Computer Networks, vol. 31(11), pp. 1695-1708, 1999, doi: 10.1016/S1389-1286(99)00044-4

[20] A. Coyette, S. Kieffer, J. Vanderdonckt, "Multi-fidelity prototyping of user interfaces," IFIP Conference on Human-Computer Interaction, pp. 150-164, 2007, doi: 10.1007/978-3-540-74796-3_16

[21] Q. Limbourg, J. Vanderdonckt, B. Michotte, L. Bouillon, V. López-Jaquero, "USIXML: a language supporting multi-path development of user interfaces," International Workshop on Design, Specification, and Verification of Interactive Systems, pp. 200-220, Jul. 2007, doi: 10.1007/11431879_12

[22] Balsmaiq. Rapid, effective and fun wireframing software. | Balsamiq [Online] Available from: https://balsamiq.com Retrieved: Jul. 2016

[23] M. Sili, C. Mayer, M. Morandell, M. Petzold, "A framework for the automatic adaptation of user interfaces," Assistive Technology Research Series, vol. 33, pp. 1298-1303, 2013, doi: 10.3233/978-1-61499-304-9-1298

[24] Concur Task Trees (CTT), W3C Working Group Submission 2 February [Online] Available from http://www.w3.org/2012/02/ctt Retrieved: Jul. 2016

[25] XSL Transformations (XSLT) Version 1.0, W3C Recommendation 16 November 1999, [Online] Available from: http://www.w3.org/TR/xslt Retrieved: Jul. 2016

[26] Gummy-live [Online] Available from: http://research.edm.uhasselt.be/~gummy Retrieved: Aug. 2016

[27] Glade – A User interface Designer [Online] Available from: https://glade.gnome.org Retrieved: Aug. 2016

[28] Wireframing Tools, Application Prototyping, softandGUI - UXToolbox [Online] Available from: http://www.softandgui.co.uk Retrieved: Aug. 2016

[29] Wireframing Tool for Professionals – WireframeSketcher [Online] Available from: http://wireframesketcher.com Retrieved: Aug. 2016

[30] iPotz: wireframing, mockups and prototyping for websites and applications [Online] Available from: http://pencil.evolus.vn Retrieved: Aug. 2016

[31] Home – Pencil Project [Online] Available from: http://pencil.evolus.vn Retrieved: Aug. 2016

[32] Mockup Designer [Online] Available from: http://fatiherikli.github.io/mockup-designer Retrieved: Aug. 2016

[33] Maquetta [Online] Available from: http://maqetta.org Retrieved: Aug. 2016

[34] Flowchart Maker & Online Diagram Software [Online] Available from: https://www.draw.io Retrieved: Aug. 2016

[35] Onine Mockup, Wireframe & UI Prototyping Tool – Moqups [Online] Available from: https://app.moqups.com Retrieved: Aug. 2016

Stochastic Models of Traffic Flow Balancing and Management of Urban Transport Networks

Dmitrii Zhukov
Institute of Information Technologies
Moscow state technical university, MIREA
Moscow, Russia
e-mail: ZhukovDm@yandex.ru

Sergey Lesko
Institute of Information Technologies
Moscow state technical university, MIREA
Moscow, Russia
e-mail: Sergey@testor.ru

Anton Alyoshkin
Institute of Information Technologies
Moscow state technical university, MIREA
Moscow, Russia
e-mail: Antony@testor.ru

Abstract— **In this paper, we developed models and algorithms for managing stochastic flows with indeterminate characteristics of distributing static parameters in urban transport networks. The proposed models describe the dependence of the single nodes blocking probability on the urban traffic parameters changing over time. In addition, we have modeled a city transport network and traffic flow with the traffic lights switching time regulated according to the proposed model and with rigidly set switching regimes (a 'conventional traffic' mode). The conducted research of the line-up lengths appearing at the traffic lights exhibits a double reduction of the traffic jams when using the elaborated model of the 'regulated' traffic lights in comparison with a conventional model of traffic management.**

Keywords-transport network; stochastic dynamics of transport network nodes blocking; traffic flow balancing; traffic flows management algorithms.

I. INTRODUCTION

In order to develop efficient algorithms of information-and-transport systems performance, one should have adequate mathematical models.

The mathematical models used to analyse the traffic networks are diverse according to the tasks they solve, mathematical tools employed and the degree of detailing the traffic flow and the data used.

Therefore, it is impossible to provide an exhaustive classification of the transport models, yet we can tentatively specify three major classes of models based on the tasks solved, i.e.:

- Forecast models. They solve the tasks of defining a number of averaged parameters of the traffic flow, e.g., the flow rate, the quantity of automobiles and passengers on various parts of a road, the transfer volume etc.
- Simulation models. They allow to describe the traffic flow dynamics, reproducing the movement of any single vehicle separately. The application of simulation models lets us estimate the traffic flow dynamics, speed, behaviour and length of line-ups and traffic jams and some other parameters.
- Optimisation models. They aim at optimising trucking or passenger travel routes, improving the calculations of traffic lights regimes, defining optimal configuration of the network model and so on.

The now existing models of traffic flow dynamics can also be classified by their properties and types [1]:

- Macroscopic models. They describe the movement of objects in averaged terms, e.g., density, vehicle cruising speed etc.
- Kinetic model. When describing a traffic flow, one equals it to the flow of some liquid, thus such models are also called hydrodynamic.
- Microscopic models describing the movement of each vehicle more precisely in comparison to the macroscopic models.

A kinetic approach to building transport models is the following. The traffic flow is described via density in the phase space, i.e., in the field of coordinates and speeds of the vehicles [1]. A kinetic equation defines the dynamics of the phase density. A kinetic approach is closer to a micro-level, whereas an averaged description allows transition to a macro-level. The main benefit of the kinetic model is that one can use it to develop macroscopic models. Knowing how phase density changes over time, we can calculate macroscopic features of the traffic flow, e.g., the average speed and the density of the traffic. Kinetic models consider the changes of automobile speeds accounted by processes of interaction. Interaction means the following: if a speedier car catches up with a slower one moving ahead, the former must either slow down or pass it. In a freely moving traffic flow, there is natural distribution of cars by 'desirable' speeds.

Desirable is the speed at which the car could move without any obstacles or interactions. One of the most serious drawbacks of this model is the hypothesis of an automobile chaos. According to it, during mutual interactions of cars there is no connection between their speeds.

Kerner theory [2] of the three-phase traffic flow can be attributed to macroscopic models, as it can predict and explain empirical properties of dense traffic breakdown and resulting space and time structures in the traffic flow.

One of the most efficient micro-models is the cellular automation model (Cellular automata models, CA [3]). Cellular automata are idealised representations of physical systems in which the time and space are represented as discreet, and all elements of the system have some discreet range of possible states.

A road is divided into conditional cells of the same length Δx, at that at each moment the cell is either empty or occupied by a single vehicle. At each time step $t \rightarrow t + 1$, the condition of all cells simultaneously (in a parallel way) updates according to some set of rules. The choice of some set of rules defines the diversity of CA options [4]. Traffic models based on CA can correlate the traffic flow dynamics at a micro-level with the traffic flow behaviour at a macro-level.

We should note that the afore-mentioned models are not universal and have some flaws necessitating the search for new models, e.g., the ones founded on stochastic dynamics.

The rest of the paper is structured as follows. In Section II, we will describe stochastic model of traffic flow. In Section III, we will describe the results of mathematical simulation of the traffic flows in urban transport networks and improvements of road situations when we use the model of 'managed' traffic lights. We conclude in Section IV.

II. A STOCHASTIC MODEL OF TRAFFIC FLOW DISTRIBUTION WITH INDETERMINATE CHARACTERISTICS IN URBAN TRANSPORT NETWORKS

To develop a dynamic model of traffic network performance, we propose decomposing the task set and dividing it into solutions of two levels:

- The level of describing a single node performance dynamics.
- The level taking into consideration the network topology and a single node performance dynamics.

The essence of the model we developed for performance of single nodes is the following. If we consider the change of traffic flow as a random process and we set for each direction, each node of the transport network (a junction) a critically admissible number of cars in line $L_{i,j}$, then we can define the probability $P(L_{i,j}, t)$ of the situation that by moment t the number of cars in a line will not exceed $L_{i,j}$ (there is no traffic jam).

Suppose that over some time interval τ there arrive ε cars and leave ξ cars in the i direction of the line at j junction. The whole data processing will be adding single steps h having duration τ, with $\frac{\varepsilon}{\tau} = \lambda$ being the intensity of the traffic inflow, and $\frac{\xi}{\tau} = \mu$ being the intensity of traffic outflow.

Let us denote by $P_{x-\varepsilon,h}$ the probability of the number of cars $(x-\varepsilon)$ in line after h steps of processing, by $P_{x,h}$ the probability of x cars, and by $P_{x+\xi,h}$ the probability of $(x+\xi)$ cars. Then probability $P_{x,h+1}$ (see Figure 1) of x cars at step $h+1$ will equal:

$$P_{x,h+1} = P_{x-\varepsilon,h} + P_{x+\xi,h} - P_{x,h}$$

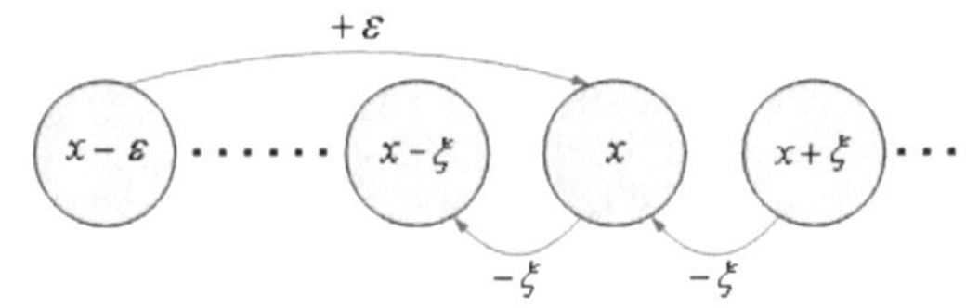

Figure 1. The scheme of probable transitions between the states characterising the number of cars at j junction in i direction at h+1 step of traffic lights performance.

Let us introduce $t=h\tau$, where t is the total time of processing, we thus get:

$$P(x,t+\tau)=P(x-\varepsilon,t)+P(x+\xi,t)-P(x,t)$$

Expanding this equation in a Taylor series, we obtain:

$$P(x,t)+\tau\frac{dP(x,t)}{dt}+\frac{\tau^2}{2}\frac{d^2P(x,t)}{dt^2}+\ldots=$$

$$=P(x,t)-\varepsilon\frac{dP(x,t)}{dx}+\frac{\varepsilon^2}{2}\frac{d^2P(x,t)}{dx^2}-\ldots+$$

$$+P(x,t)+\xi\frac{dP(x,t)}{dx}+\frac{\xi^2}{2}\frac{d^2P(x,t)}{dx^2}+\ldots-P(x,t).$$

The second derivative of t can be excluded as it naturally describes the process at which cars themselves could bear additional cars. Taking into account the members in the left part containing no more than the first derivative of t, and the members of the right part having no more than the second derivative of x, we receive:

$$\tau\frac{dP(x,t)}{dt}=\frac{\varepsilon^2+\xi^2}{2}\frac{d^2P(x,t)}{dx^2}-(\varepsilon-\xi)\frac{dP(x,t)}{dx},$$

$$\frac{dP(x,t)}{dt}=\frac{\lambda^2+\mu^2}{2\mu}\frac{d^2P(x,t)}{dx^2}-(\lambda-\mu)\frac{dP(x,t)}{dx}.$$

Assuming that μ and λ do not depend on x and introducing the insymbol $a=\frac{\lambda^2+\mu^2}{2\mu}$ and $b=\lambda-\mu$, we get:

$$\frac{dP(x,t)}{dt}=a\frac{d^2P(x,t)}{dx^2}-b\frac{dP(x,t)}{dx}.$$

As the function $P(x,t)$ is continuous, we can transgress from probability $P(x,t)$ to the probability density $\rho(x,t)$, which enables us to formulate and solve a boundary problem for describing a stochastic model of processing applications at a single node with indeterminate parameters of the statistical law of their incoming times distribution.

With the number of cars $x=L$ lining up for j junction in i direction, where L is some critical limit number, we assume that the node of processing (j junction in i direction) becomes overloaded and a traffic jam is formed. The probability of detecting such a state will be different from zero, and the probability density defining the traffic flow in state $x=L$ should be put down as 0 (we are trying to avoid this condition), i.e.:

$$\rho(x,t)_{x=L}=0 \qquad \text{(a)}$$

We choose the second limit condition based on the fact that condition $x=0$ defines a standstill in the processing. The probability to detect such a state will be nonzero, however, the probability density defining the traffic flow under condition $x=0$ must be laid down as equal to 0 as well. We must also strive to avoid this condition as it correlates to the case when the traffic lights do not close this direction, and it contradicts the logic of its work, i.e.:

$$\rho(x,t)_{x=0}=0 \qquad \text{(b)}$$

As at time $t=0$ (the start of the calculation) there may be x_0 cars under the processing. Let us set the initial condition in the following form:

$$\rho(x,t=0)=\delta(x-x_0)=\begin{cases}1, x=x_0\\ 0, x\neq x_0\end{cases}$$

Since the initial condition is set as a δ-function, it leads to the fact that the solution of the obtained differential equation remains indiscreet (continuous) at point $x=x_0$ and the equation will suffer derivative discontinuity at this point.

Employing operational calculus methods for probability $P(L_{i,j}, x_0|t)$ of the traffic jam not being formed by some t moment (the number of cars in a line will not exceed $L_{i,j}$), we can obtain the following expression:

$$P(L_{i,j},x_0\,|\,t)=2e^{-\frac{2b_{i,j}x_0+b_{i,j}^2t}{4a_{i,j}}}\cdot$$

$$\cdot\sum_{n=1}^{M}\frac{e^{\frac{b_{i,j}L_{i,j}}{2a_{i,j}}}\sin(\pi n\frac{x_0}{L_{i,j}})+\sin(\pi n\frac{L_{i,j}-x_0}{L_{i,j}})}{(-1)^{n+1}\left\{\pi n+\dfrac{b_{i,j}^2L_{i,j}^2}{4\pi n a_{i,j}^2}\right\}}\cdot e^{-\frac{\pi^2n^2a_{i,j}t}{L_{i,j}^2}} \qquad (1)$$

where $a_{i,j}=\dfrac{\mu_{i,j}^2+\lambda_{i,j}^2}{2\lambda_{i,j}}$ and $b_{i,j}=\lambda_{i,j}-\mu_{i,j}$, $\mu_{i,j}$ are the number of cars leaving j-node of traffic network (junction/traffic lights) in i-direction per unit of time (an outflow), $\lambda_{i,j}$ is the number of cars entering the node per unit of time (an inflow), t is time, x_0 is the number of cars in a line at the start time of traffic lights operation step.

Solving (1) relative to time t allows determining optimal time intervals of traffic lights switch on. Yet it is input-intensive computational task. Taking into consideration that the computations should be simultaneously carried out for multiple directions and junctions, and one should also synchronise (see (2)) the traffic inflows and outflows as neighbouring junctions, it is reasonable to use parallel computations to simulate the traffic flow.

$$x_{0i,j}^{k}=$$

$$x_{0i,j}^{k-1}+\frac{1}{r}\sum_{i-1}^{r}(\mu_{i,j}^{k-1}\tau_{i,j}^{k-1}+\Delta\lambda_{i,j}^{k-1}T_{i,j}^{k-1})-\mu_{i,j}^{k}t_{i,j}^{k} \qquad (2)$$

$$\lambda_{i,j}^{k}=\frac{x_{0i,j}^{k}V_{D1}}{l_{i,j}},$$

where $x_{0i,j}^{k-1}$ is the number of cars which did not manage to get through in direction i of j junction after performing $(k-1)$ step, r is the number of directions at the junction, $\mu_{i,j}^{k-1}$ are the outflows at step $(k-1)$ per each r direction at the chosen junction. Any car from those traffic inflows at step $(k-1)$ can equally likely choose at next k step one of r directions, that is why we introduce a numerical coefficient $(1/r)$ before the summation symbol. $T_{i,j}^{k-1}$ is the time during which the chosen direction was closed by the traffic lights (it is not the 'open' time, but the time of 'idle cycle') between two chained openings. Let us note that opening of all directions at the chosen junction may happen not in the rigidly set periodical sequence. The order of directions openings may vary depending on the traffic behavior. The time interval between two chained openings of the same chosen direction will simply be the 'idle cycle', which value $T_{i,j}^{k-1}$ can change dynamically. $\Delta\lambda_{i,j}^{k}$ is the change of traffic inflow in the chosen direction at the chosen node of traffic flow over time $T_{i,j}^{k-1}$. The total number of cars in the transport network at any time of the day corresponds to the function of the number of cars on the time of the day. $\tau_{i,j}^{k-1}$ is the time during which at $(k-1)$ step the directions of traffic inflows are open while the chosen outflowing direction is closed during time $T_{i,j}^{k-1}$. $\mu_{i,j}^{k-1}$ is the traffic outflow in the chosen direction at step k, $t_{i,j}^{k}$ is the time interval of traffic lights switch on at step k of the chosen direction. It is important to determine the time interval value in order to solve the equation defining probability $P(L_{i,j}, x_0|t)$ of the fact that by time t the number of cars in line will not exceed $L_{i,j}$ (the gridlock do not form). V_{D1} is the recommended speed.

III. Simulating and Balancing the Traffic Flows in Urban Transport Networks on the Basis of the Stochastic Model

To simulate transport network and determine whether it is possible, as a matter of principle, to dynamically change the time intervals of traffic lights switching in a city to prevent traffic gridlock, besides (1) and (2), we should have a model of how the number of cars varies with the time of the day. For modelling, the total number of cars in a transport network may be set, for example, by the function depicted in Figure 2 (The traffic load is measured with 10 generating units (points) and correlated to the situation when all vehicles registered in Moscow or Moscow Region are on the road at the same time. According to statistics, autumn is the busiest time of the year).

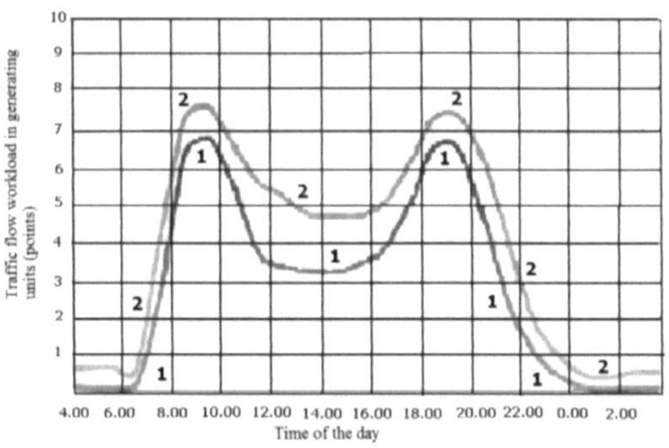

Figure 2. Traffic load in Moscow during a workday (curve 1 represents autumn of 2013; curve 2 is for autumn 2014).

Basing on (1) and (2) as well as on the function in Figure 2, we developed an algorithm of managing the transport network and tested the proposed approach.

For the simulation purposes, we elaborated a number of algorithms and software allowing us to model a city transport network and traffic situations with 'controlled' traffic lights, which are regulated according to the proposed model, and 'uncontrolled' traffic lights which have rigidly set modes of switching (classical traffic).

To serve as a technological concept, we realised the function of maps downloading as Open Street Map (OSM) and wrote a parser of this format, the output of which is a graph of transport network with featured properties of arcs (a road) and peaks (a junction). This is important for simulation and emulation of traffic flow, and the set of WPF (Windows Presentation Foundation) objects is vital for their onto mapping.

At the second stage, we constructed a structural model of a city, which featured all classes of roads, junctions, traffic directions, traffic lights and their modes, as well as cars and line-ups. Besides, we realised the tools for entering the cars according to their per diem spread (see Figure 2) and the tools to set the cars behaviour.

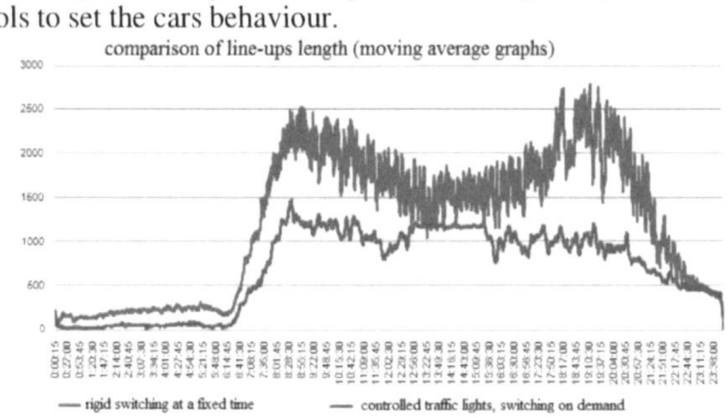

Figure 3. Comparison between performing efficiencies of the proposed model and the traffic lights switching at a fixed time

We chose the index of total length of all line-ups at all junctions of the loaded map to be the simplest efficiency criterion. A traffic jam is a line-up of cars at the traffic lights waiting for the permissive signal.

For the experiment, we downloaded a small real map of Vasilievskiy Island in Saint Petersburg and simulated daily traffic flow. Careful examination of line-ups length (see Figure 3) demonstrates that the number of gridlocks halved when we use the model of 'managed' traffic lights in comparison with the rigid classic traffic mode.

The traffic lights with fixed phases of operation help to solve the problem of regulating the traffic, yet they are less efficient and cannot react to traffic situation changes as they lack feedback. For instance, if cyclical (daily) variations could be accounted for when we develop the traffic lights operational phases, plenty of various accidental (random) factors, such as weather conditions, road works, accidents, cannot be fully factored in.

It is evident that real traffic situation can greatly diverge with the experimental mathematical simulation, but the obtained results allow us to state the adequacy of the proposed model and its potential application in designing control services in automated systems of traffic flow.

IV. Conclusions

We developed models and algorithms of controlling stochastic flows with indeterminate characteristics of statistical parameters spread in urban transport networks; they allow to describe the dependence of single node blocking probability on the traffic flow parameters over time.

In the elaborated mathematical models, we provided a description of how to service junctions (the times of traffic lights switching), accounted for the traffic burden balance of cars in the system and connection of traffic flows between neighbouring junctions. The proposed model enables the creation of a dynamic model using a real transport network map and thus emulating its work and testing the way gridlocks are formed.

Simulation of urban transport network and traffic situation according to the proposed model of 'controlled' switching times of traffic lights in comparison with fixed modes of switching ('classical traffic') shows a double reduction of gridlocks when we use the former model of 'controlled' switching instead of the latter one.

In our future works we plan to develop traffic lights control algorithms based of stochastic models of balancing and flow control that focus not on the "priority of the shortest possible route", but on the load state of each node (or group of nodes). Given the fact that some nodes can be soon overloaded and such nodes should be balanced. Depending on how close node is to critical state in a transport network, the metric for this node can be proportionally increased linearly or nonlinearly (the closer to critical state, the greater value of the metric).

We also note that the above approach can also be applied in case when the transport network is divided into several areas and inner traffic lights within areas have information about the topology of the other parts of the network.

ACKNOWLEDGMENT

This work is supported by Russian Foundation for Basic Research (grant 16-37-00373 mol_a).

REFERENCES

[1] S. Göttlich and A. Klar, "Model hierarchies and optimization for dynamic flows on networks," Modeling and optimization of flows on networks, Cetaro (CS), June 15–19, 2009, C.I.M.E, Courses, 2009. http://php.math.unifi.it/users/cime/Courses/2009/01/200914-Notes.pdf [retrieved: 09, 2016]

[2] B. S. Kerner, "Introduction to Modern Traffic Flow Theory and Control," Berlin: Springer, 2009.

[3] S. Maerivoet and B. De Moor, "Cellular automata models of road traffic," Physics Reports 2005, V. 419, № 1, P. 1–64., 2005.

[4] H. J. Ruskin and R. Wang, "Modeling Traffic Flow at an Urban Unsignalized Intersection," Lecture Notes in Computer Science. 2002. T. 2329. P. 0381.

New Reconfigurable Middleware for Adaptive RTOS in Ubiquitous Devices

Aymen Gammoudi
LISI Laboratory, INSAT
Tunisia Polytechnic School
University of Carthage, Tunisia
IRISA Laboratory, ENSSAT
University of Rennes1, France
aymen.gammoudi@irisa.fr

Adel Benzina
LISI Laboratory, INSAT
Tunisia Polytechnic School
University of Carthage, Tunisia
adel.benzina@isd.rnu.tn

Mohamed Khalgui
LISI Laboratory, INSAT
University of Carthage, Tunisia
SystemsControl Laboratory
University of Xidian, China
khalgui.mohamed@gmail.com

Daniel Chillet
IRISA Laboratory, ENSSAT
University of Rennes1, France
daniel.chillet@irisa.fr

***Abstract*—Energy management is a central problem in battery powered real-time systems design, in particular for periodically reconfigurable embedded wireless devices. This kind of systems can be more or less intensive in computing, but must remain alive until the next recharge. They are not always critical, or at least some treatments are not critical. In this case, modification on tasks parameters of non-critical parts of the system can be done to increase the autonomy of the battery. The objective of this work is to develop a software plugin, called *Reconf-Middleware*, which corresponds to a software layer to be placed above the Operating System (OS). The main role of this software layer is to manage tasks execution for reconfigurable architecture when the battery recharges are done periodically. We integrate also a new scheduling strategy to ensure that the system will run correctly, after any reconfiguration scenario, under memory, real-time and energy constraints until the next recharge. This software component is designed to execute and evaluate the performance, reliability and correctness of some real-time scheduling approaches, which are theoretically validated. The middleware can be integrated into many operating systems and provides good quality both in terms of execution time and energy consumption. We discuss the paper's contribution by analyzing the experimental results that we did on a running example. We propose in this paper a new middleware to be placed above the operating system.**

Keywords–RTOS; Ubiquitous device; Reconfiguration; Real-Time and Low-Power Scheduling; Energy-aware.

I. INTRODUCTION

Reconfigurable real-time embedded systems are used in many application domains, manufacturing process control, telecommunications, robotics, sensor networks, ubiquitous devices and consumer electronics. In all of these areas, there is rapid technological progress, yet, energy concerns are still the bottleneck. In this context, we focus on reconfigurable real-time embedded systems when the battery recharges are done periodically. The minimization of energy consumption is an important criterion for development of rechargeable real-time embedded systems due to limitations in the capacity of their batteries. In addition, battery life can be extended by reducing power consumption [1]. When undergoing a reconfiguration, to reduce the energy consumption, these systems have to be changed and adapted to their environment without any disturbance. Any reconfiguration scenario may increase energy consumption and/or cause some software tasks to violate their deadlines. Concerning the reconfiguration, two policies are defined in the literature: i) Static reconfigurations [2] to be generally applied off-line; ii) Dynamic reconfigurations [3] that can be applied at run-time. Dynamic reconfiguration is important in embedded systems, where one does not necessarily have the luxury to stop a running system. For these reasons, we consider here dynamic reconfiguration and we assume that the system executes n real-time tasks initially feasible towards real-time scheduling. We also assume that the system battery is recharged periodically with a recharge period *RP*. However, development and design of high quality of scheduling middleware for real-time environment is difficult and complex, as it demands several requests such as system implementation, validation and optimization. The recent advance of middleware technologies, that enables communication and coordination in a computing system provides the perfect way to implement real-time middleware solutions. The general goal of this paper is to design a new middleware, called *Reconf-Middleware*, able to reconfigure the execution of the application tasks and to ensure that any reconfiguration scenario changing the implementation of the embedded platform does not violate real-time constraints and does not result in fatal energy over consumption or in memory saturation. A middleware is a software layer located above the operating system. It communicates with it and exploits its functionality to support the development of many reliable solutions. However, the architectures of most of the middleware solutions, do not offer the predictability required to support the real-time behavior in new complex systems, or the reconfigurability required for these middleware solutions to be integrated into various Real-Time Operating System (RTOS). To manage tasks on a reconfiguration architecture, RTOS plays an important role in the system.

As a major contribution of this paper, to respect the memory, real-time and energy constraints, a new middleware is defined where after each reconfiguration scenario, suitable and acceptable modifications are performed on parameters of tasks. *Reconf-Middleware* presents a middleware implemented in RTLinux and describes the transition from the theory to the actual implementation. We implement in *Reconf-Middleware* a new original methodological strategy that proposes quantitative techniques to modify periods, reduce execution times of tasks or remove some of them to ensure real-time feasibility, avoiding memory overflow and ensuring a rational use of remaining energy until the next recharge.

The paper is organized as follows. Section II presents the background of RTOSs for embedded architectures. Section III explains the strategy formalization. The fourth section presents the reconfiguration of tasks with the proposed run-time strategy and the operating mode of *Reconf-Middleware*. We present the Unified Modeling Language (UML) design models for *Reconf-Middleware* in Section V. In Section VI, we present the performance evaluation of the compared techniques presented by Wang et al. [3] and Wang et al. [1]. Finally, we conclude and present our future work in Section VII.

II. Background

Rechargeable reconfigurable embedded systems are composed of a variety of different processing elements, memories, Input/Output devices, sensors, battery, and so forth. The choice of processing elements includes instruction-set processors, application specific fixed-function hardware, and reconfigurable hardware devices. Several distinguished studies deal with rechargeable reconfiguration systems [4][5][6][7]. This type of systems can execute different reconfiguration scenarios at a particular time t. A reconfiguration scenario means the addition, removal or update of tasks in order to manage the whole system at the occurrence of hardware/software faults, or also to improve its performance at run-time. When such a scenario is applied, the system risks a fatal increase in energy consumption, a violation of real time constraints or a memory saturation. In this context, the real-time operating system is required to provide services for memory management, energy management, task scheduling and reconfiguration. To ensure that the system will run correctly until the next recharge, several interesting studies have been proposed in recent years for this kind of real-time operating systems. In this section, we decompose the state of the art into groups, the first corresponding to the work on scheduling of embedded systems with rechargeable periods, the second group concerns scheduling algorithm of embedded system without battery recharges.

A. Real-Time Scheduling

1) Real-Time Scheduling for Embedded Systems with Rechargeable Battery: Real-time scheduling has been extensively studied in the last three decades [8]. These studies propose several feasibility conditions of the dimensioning of real-time systems. These conditions are defined to enable a designer to guarantee that time constraints associated with an application are always met for all possible configurations. Two main classical scheduling are generally used in real-time embedded systems: Rate Monotonic (RM) and Earliest Deadline First (EDF). Several studies have been performed in this context, such as the research works reported in [9][10][11]. Chetto et al. [5][11] are interested in a real-time embedded system that is powered through a renewable energy storage device. They present a scheduling framework called $EDeg$ (Earliest Deadline with energy guarantee) and an exact feasibility test that decides for periodic task sets. EDeg is a variation of EDF able to cope with energy constraints. These studies are interesting, but the authors didnt consider neither the reconfiguration problems, nor the aperiodic tasks. In addition, the authors of the papers [5] and [11] have not studied the rechargeable systems with a well-defined period of recharge.

2) Real-Time Scheduling for Reconfigurable Architectures: Nowadays, a fair amount of research has been done to develop reconfigurable embedded systems. Wigley and Kearney [12] present one of the first attempts to develop an OS dedicated to the management of reconfigurable resources. Steiger et al. [13] discuss the design issues for reconfigurable hardware operating systems and the problem of on-line scheduling of hard real-time tasks for partially reconfigurable devices. They also developed two on-line scheduling heuristics in order to ensure that the system will respect the real-time feasibility. Merino et al. [14][15] split the reconfigurable area into an array of predefined subareas, so-called slots. The operating system schedules tasks to these slots based on a task allocation table that keeps track of currently loaded tasks. As each task fits into one slot, there is again no placement problem involved. Wang et al. [3] propose a study for feasible low-power dynamic reconfiguration of real-time systems where additions and removals of real-time tasks are applied at run-time. They aim to minimize the energy consumption after any reconfiguration scenario. This effort is continued by Khemaissia et al. [16] who propose an intermediate layer to play the role of middleware that will be in interaction with the kernel Linux. This layer will manage the addition/removal/update of the periodic and also aperiodic tasks sharing resources and with precedence constraints. These tasks should respect their deadlines after any reconfiguration scenario. The proposed middleware will divide the tasks into several virtual processors as time slots. The decomposition is done based on the task's category. The first virtual processor executes dependent periodic tasks, the second one executes dependent aperiodic tasks with hard deadlines and the third virtual processor executes dependent aperiodic tasks with soft deadlines. After applying a reconfiguration scenario, some tasks may miss their deadlines and the power consumption may increase. In order to re-obtain the feasibility of the system after such scenario, an agent-based-architecture is defined to modify the parameters of the tasks. The studies of [3][16] present a simple run-time strategy that reduces the energy consumption. They propose to modify the tasks period T_i, assigning a single value to all tasks, which is not reasonable in practice [1]. Another solution proposed is to reduce the Worst Case Execution Time (WCETs) C_i assigning a single value to all tasks, which is not reasonable in practice [1]. The formulas proposed by Wang et al. [1] and Wang et al. [3] are simple with soft calculation, but the main disadvantage is that it is not acceptable for a real-time system to change the period of tasks more than a certain limit according to user requirement. Moreover, if tasks have very diverse periods T_i, tasks that have small periods will be too much affected if they will be aligned with tasks that have large periods. Although these rich and useful contributions provide interesting results, no one is reported to address the problem of dynamic reconfigurations of real-time systems under battery with a periodic recharges and memory constraints. To address this problem, we propose a new middleware *Reconf-Middleware* that implements the methodological strategy proposed by Gammoudi et al. [17]. The principle of this strategy is to evaluate system and battery states and to modify periods, reduce execution times of tasks or remove some of them to ensure real-time feasibility, avoiding memory overflow and ensuring a rational use of remaining energy until the next recharge.

B. RTLinux

The contribution of this paper can be applied for a large number of RTOS. We choose to implement it on RT-Linux since it is an open source. It is a hard real-time RTOS microkernel that runs the entire Linux operating system as a fully preemptive process. Fig. 1 depicts the design of the RT-Linux system. Important aspects are displayed in Figure 1:

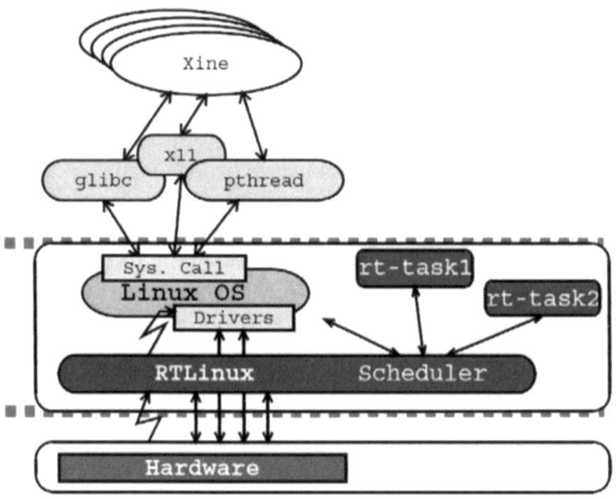

Figure 1. RTLinux system [18].

1) RT-Linux sits between the real hardware and the kernel,
2) It acts as the hardware for the kernel,
3) It treats the kernel as a single big process. RT-Linux receives the interruptions of the hardware layer and sends them to the kernel linux after converting them into software interruptions [18]. Also, the RT-LINUX manages the scheduling of the real-time tasks. According to [19], the kernel is not designed to be reconfigurable.

In this research, we suggest to create a middleware layer *Reconf-Middleware* between the RT-Linux and the hardware. *Reconf-Middleware* will be in interaction with the kernel Linux.

The basic functionality of RTLinux is initialized in a system by inserting five modules into the kernel: rtl.o, rtl_time.o, rtl_posixio.o, rtl_fifo.o and rtl_sched.o.

III. FORMALIZATION

We recall in this section the task and energy models with their characteristics and scheduling constraints [17]. We continue with a description of the memory model. Finally, we define the reconfiguration problem and state our goals.

A. Task Model

A hard real-time system comprises a set of n independent real-time tasks τ_1, τ_2, ..., τ_n. Each task consists of an infinite or finite stream of jobs or requests, which must be completed before their deadlines. A uniprocessor system can only execute one process at a time and must switch between processor. For this reason, the context switching will add more time to the overall execution time when preemption is used. According to [20], we present the following well-known concepts in the theory of real-time scheduling: A periodic task τ_i (C_i, T_i, D_i, MF_i) is an infinite collection of jobs that have their request times constrained by a regular interarrival time T_i, a worst case execution time (WCET) C_i, a relative deadline D_i and a memory footprint MF_i. A real-time scheduling problem is said feasible if there is at least one scheduling policy able to meet the deadlines of all the tasks. A task is valid with a given scheduling policy if and only if no job of this task misses its deadline.

EDF is the earliest deadline first policy for scheduling real-time tasks. EDF schedules tasks according to their deadlines: The task with the shortest deadline has the highest priority. Let $U = \sum_{i=1}^{n} \frac{C_i}{T_i}$ be the processor utilization factor. In the case of synchronous, independent and periodic tasks such that their deadlines are equal to their periods, $U \leq 1$ is a necessary and sufficient condition for this set of tasks to be feasible according to the EDF-based scheduling.

RM is the rate monotonic policy for scheduling real-time tasks. RM schedules tasks according to their periods: The task with the shortest period has the highest priority. A sufficient condition for a set of n tasks to be feasible according to the RM scheduling algorithm $U = \sum_{i=1}^{n} \frac{C_i}{T_i} \leq n(2^{\frac{1}{n}} - 1)$ [20]. We use as a notation for this real-time feasibility analysis : $U = \sum_{i=1}^{n} \frac{C_i}{T_i} \leq \alpha_{policy}$, where α_{policy}=1 for EDF scheduling and α_{policy}=$n(2^{\frac{1}{n}} - 1)$ for RM scheduling.

B. Energy Model

We consider the following energy model as described by Wang et al. [3] and Gammoudi et al. [17]. Each rechargeable embedded system is characterized by i) A quantity of energy available at full recharge E_{max}, ii) An energy available at time t : $\Delta E(t)$, iii) A recharge period RP, and iv) A time remaining until the next recharge Δt. The power consumption P is proportional to the processor utilization U [21]. Then, the power consumption is calculated by:

$$P = k.U^2 = k.(\sum_{i=1}^{n} \frac{C_i}{T_i})^2 \quad (1)$$

We assume in this paper that $k = 1$. To ensure that the system will run correctly until the next recharge, it is necessary that at time t:

$$P(t).\Delta t \leq \Delta E(t) \quad (2)$$

where $P(t)$ is the power consumption at t, that means $P(t) \leq \frac{\Delta E(t)}{\Delta t}$. We define $P_{limit}(t) = \frac{\Delta E(t)}{\Delta t}$. After each reconfiguration scenario, we have to ensure that $P(t) \leq P_{limit}(t)$: This is the energy constraint.

C. Memory Model

We suppose that the memory model in a real-time embedded system is characterized by a memory size MS. Each task occupies at run-time MF_i amount of memory. After each reconfiguration scenario, we must ensure that: $\sum_{i=1}^{n} MF_i < MS$. This is the memory constraint.

D. Problem Formalization

We suppose that the system Sys is initially composed of n tasks and assume that $Sys(t0)$ is feasible. A system is feasible if and only if it satisfies the three constraints (real-time, energy and memory constraints). We assume in the following that the system Sys is dynamically reconfigured at run-time at $t1$ such that its new implementation of tasks is $Sys(t1) = \{\tau_1, \tau_1, ..., \tau_n\, \tau_{n+1}, ..., \tau_m\}$. The subset $\{\tau_{n+1}, ..., \tau_m\}$ is added to the initial implementation $\{\tau_1, \tau_2, ..., \tau_n\}$. To ensure that the system will run correctly after this reconfiguration scenario, at a particular time, it is necessary to check whether the new configuration satisfies the following constraints:

1) Real-time scheduling feasibility constraint, Sys must verify:
$$U = \sum_{i=1}^{m} \frac{C_i}{T_i} \leq \alpha_{policy}$$
2) Energy constraint, Sys must verify:
$$P(t) \leq P_{limit}(t)$$
3) Memory constraint, Sys must verify:
$$\sum_{i=1}^{m} MF_i < MS$$

After each reconfiguration scenario, one or more of these constraints can be violated. We have to find the suitable solution to bring back the system to the feasibility conditions.

IV. Pack Oriented Solution

A. Pack Model

In this section, we present a brief summary about different approaches proposed by Wang et al. [3] and Wang et al. [1] to solve this problem. We also discuss the strategy presented by the authors in [17]. This study is necessary to show the interest of the approach in [17] compared to [3]. Wang et al. [1][3], present a simple run-time strategy to ensure that the system runs correctly after any reconfiguration scenario. They propose to modify the tasks period T_i, assigning a single value to all tasks, which is not reasonable in practice. Another solution proposed is to reduce WCETs C_i of all tasks. These solutions are interesting, but the main disadvantage is that it is not acceptable for a real-time system to change the period of tasks more than a certain limit according to user requirements. To improve these solutions and implement more suitable values, we proposed in a previous paper [17] a new strategy based on the definition of packs of tasks and the management of their parameters. We propose to group the tasks that have "similar" periods in several packs, denoted Pk, by assigning a unique new period T^{New} to all tasks of the first pack Pk_1. Moreover, all new periods affected to pack Pk_j are multiples of T^{New}, the period affected to tasks belonging to pack Pk_1. We have only to compute in this case the suitable T^{New}. This solution controls the complexity of the problem. Let us note that each time a new period T^{New} is affected to a task that has originally a period T_i, the cost is a delay penalty for this task of T^{New} - T_i. This is applicable for tasks of pack Pk_1. For other packs, Pk_j the period is $j * T^{New}$. So the cost for each task of Pk_j is: (T^{New}-(T_i mod T^{New})) mod T^{New}. The total cost for the approach is the sum of all these costs. We compare this strategy in [1][3][17] and show that the cost of delaying tasks is significantly improved. To ensure that the system is feasible after each reconfiguration scenario, we present the following five solutions (Sol A, Sol B, Sol C, Sol D and Sol E) detailed and justified in [17]. The first two solutions can be applied in order to ensure that the system satisfies the real-time constraint. Sol C and Sol D are used if the energy constraint is not satisfied. For each solution, we adjust the new period T^{New} or the new WCET C^{New} to fulfill the real-time or the energy constraints. For each solution, the value of T^{New} or C^{New} is calculated by minimizing the total cost of the solution in terms of delaying tasks. Sol E is used to remove less important tasks according to the importance factor I_i in order to minimize the energy consumption.

B. Operating Mode

Thanks to *Reconf-Middleware*, the system is able to be adapted after any reconfiguration scenario. To satisfy the memory, real-time and energy constraints after any reconfiguration scenario, *Reconf-Middleware* should start by checking the memory availability. If this constraint is respected, then the energy and also the real-time constraints have to be checked. If one or more constraints are violated, then this algorithm ensures a deterministic choice between the solutions A, B, C, D and E. Fig. 2 explains this strategy step-by-step.

V. Contribution: Reconfigurable Middleware

The objective of this section is to integrate the pack-based solution in an RTLinux in order to ensure that the system runs correctly after any reconfiguration scenario.

A. Architecture

We present in Fig. 3 the different services of a classical OS and the additional reconfiguration services. Let us explain some services: i) Memory service: Keeps track of the status of each memory location, either allocated or free. It determines how memory is allocated by processes, decides which one gets memory. When memory is allocated, it determines which memory locations will be assigned. It tracks when the memory is freed or unallocated and updates the status. ii) Garbage collector or just collector: It attempts to reclaim garbage, or memory occupied by objects that are no longer in use by the program. iii) Scheduler and Dispatcher: A scheduler is a component that schedules the system's tasks on a processor. Another component that is involved in the CPU-scheduling function is the dispatcher, which is the module that gives control of the CPU to the process selected by the short-term scheduler. It receives control in kernel mode as the result of an interrupt or system call. iv) Battery service: It is a service that communicates with the battery component and retrieves the level of the system's battery. v) We add another service *Reconfiguration Service* that communicates with the other OS services to apply the proposed strategy that will satisfy the three constraints.

B. Middleware Design

Several research studies [22][23][24] have focused on the UML model of reconfiguration operating system. We present

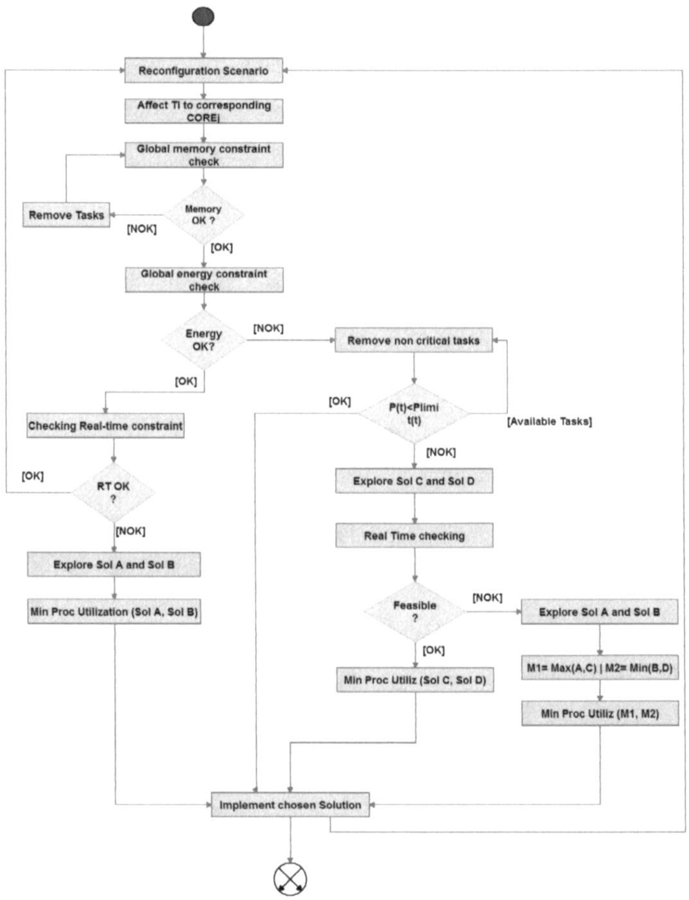

Figure 2. Activity diagram of strategy.

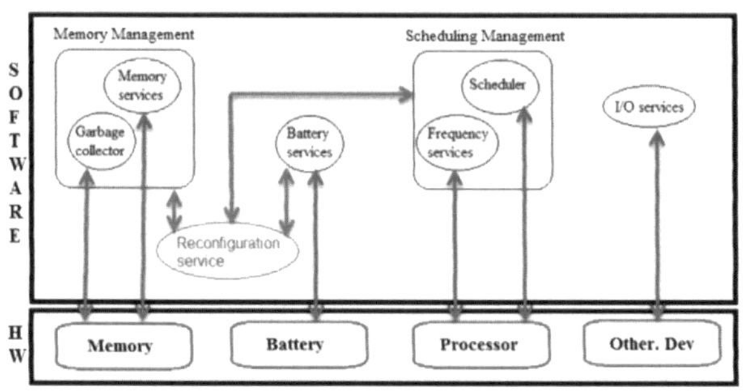

Figure 3. OS services.

in this section the UML [25] class diagram for our middleware: The hardware and software elements and the interactions between them. The diagram (Fig. 4) is divided into three layers: the software layer, the hardware layer and the reconfiguration layer.

Software Layer: It presents the different tasks (periodic and aperiodic tasks). The task scheduling is ensured by this layer. In this paper, we focus on RM and EDF policies. Task class is specified through the typical parameters used in the real-time context: Identification, worst case execution time, importance factor, memory footprint and whether the task is periodic or not. In order to store any interaction between tasks, we define DataAccess class that ensures data storage. The amount of memory needed by each task is indicated in parameter *Data* and its size in *Size*.

Hardware Layer: It contains classes representing the hardware components that are physically implemented in the platform. It includes the processor, battery and memory.

Reconfiguration Layer: It ensures that the system will run correctly after any reconfiguration scenario. Reconfiguration class receives different reconfiguration scenarios taht can violate one or more of the three constraints: real-time feasibility, memory and energy constraints. The Manger class proposes quantitative techniques to modify periods, reduce execution times of tasks or remove some of them to ensure the real-time feasibility, avoiding memory overflow and ensuring a rational use of remaining energy until the next recharge. The PackConst class ensures the grouping of tasks that have "similar" periods or WCETs in several Packs. This idea is formalized in [17].

C. Middleware Overview

The proposed middleware will have the role to reconfigure the OS. Many routines are added to RTLinux in order to apply

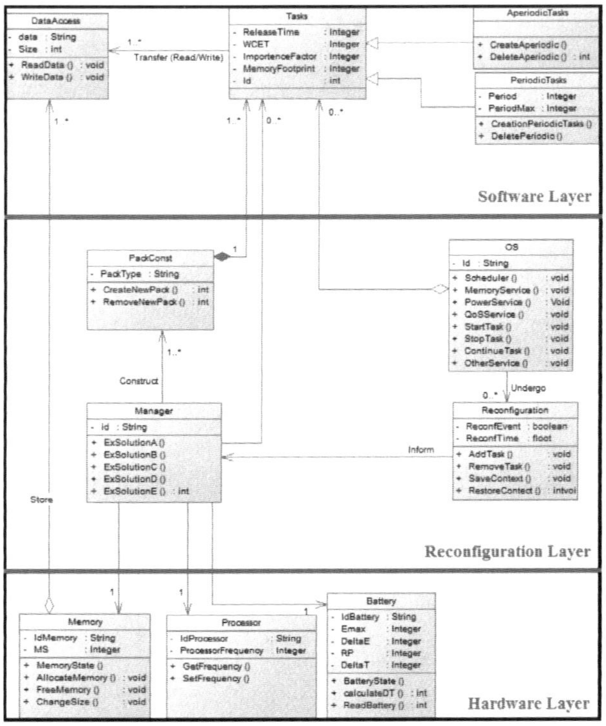

Figure 4. Class Diagram.

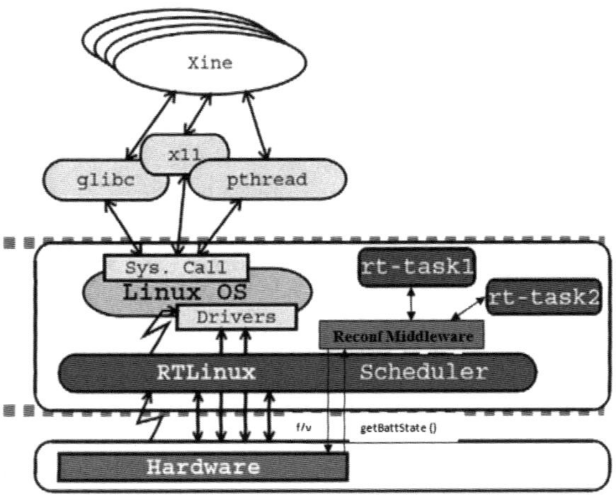

Figure 5. The middleware location.

the different proposed solutions. A routine is a service offered by RTLinux. Fig. 5 represents the Plugin integration. The Plugin will interact with the kernel and the hardware platform.

D. Implementation

The developed middleware *Reconf-Middleware* presents the different possible solutions given by the proposed run-time strategy. After any reconfiguration scenario, our plugin ensures the verification of three constraints (Real-Time, Energy, Memory) using the following functions:

- To obtain the battery level: getBattState()
- To create a task by modifying the period T: int pthread-make-periodic-np(pthread-t thread, hrtime-t start-time, hrtime-t period), Where: pthread-make-periodic-np marks the thread as ready for execution. The thread will start its execution at start-time and will run at intervals specified by a period given in nanoseconds.

The scheduler of RTLinux uses the rtl_sched.h library to ensure that all tasks are schedulable. The data structure of task τ_i is:

```
struct rt_task_struct {
int *stack;
int uses_fp;
int magic;
int state;
int *stack_bottom;
int priority;
RTIME period;
RTIME resume_time;
struct rt_task_struct *next;
RTL_FPU_CONTEXT fpu_regs;
}
```

The data structure that is responsible to store the battery data is:

```
struct battstate { short unsigned int powerstate,
time_hour, time_min; float chargelevel; };
```

To obtain the current battery state, we use the getBattState() function, which is the pointer on the structure of struct battstate.

VI. Evaluation of Performance

In order to evaluate the performance of *Reconf-Middleware*, we implement the same case study presented by Wang et al. [3]. The initial system is feasible with low-power constraint. Then, we add some periodic tasks in order to violate the real-time constraint. To re-obtain the system feasibility, *Reconf-Middleware* must execute Sol A or Sol B. The cost of a solution is the total delay introduced to periods T_i or to WCETs C_i as explained in IV-A.

If we apply the solution A: After the modification of the periods T_i, the processor utilization is reduced and can satisfy the real-time scheduling: **U= 0,99**. Fig. 6 illustrates the considered system of 70 tasks after changing periods by our solution A [17] and by the proposed solution in [3]. Both solutions provide a change on the period of tasks. To evaluate the performance of our solution compared to the approaches in [3], we present the following curves (Fig. 6): The histogram in red is the cost of our solution and the blue one is when applying the solution presented in [3].

As presented in Section IV-A, the cost is a delay penalty for a task i of T^{New} - T_i. Therefore, the total cost for each approach is the sum of all these costs. After the execution of our strategy [17], we note that the total cost is equal to 6940*ms*, but the total cost by using the second strategy [3] is equal to 23036*ms*. Then, our solution is better than that presented in [3]. The introduced delay is only 30% ($\frac{6940}{23036} * 100 \simeq 30\%$) of the introduced delay in [3].

If we apply the solution B: After the modification of the WCETs C_i, the processor utilization is reduced and can satisfy the real-time scheduling: **U= 0,636**. According to (Fig. 7), we

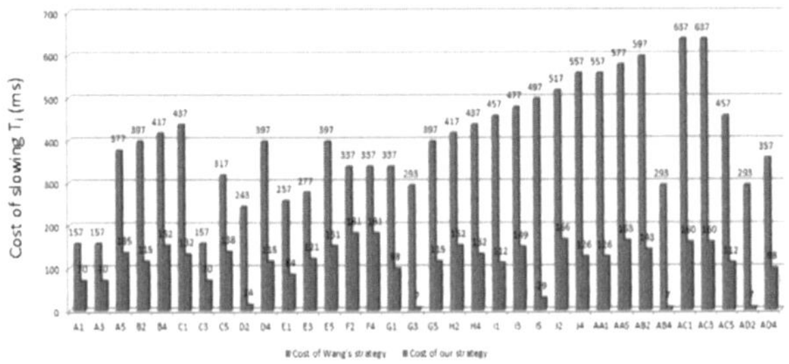

Figure 6. Cost of modification of periods T_i compared with [3].

can notice that our solution is less costly also in case B than the Wang strategy in [3].

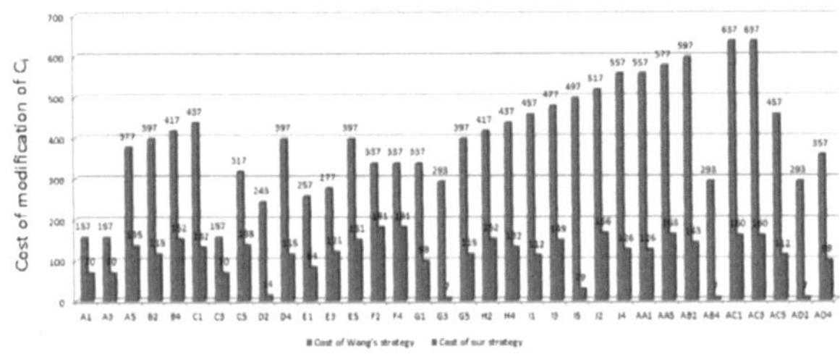

Figure 7. Cost of modification of WCETs C_i (solution B).

The total cost of our strategy is equal to 154ms but the total cost by using the second strategy defined in [3] is equal to 326ms. Then, our solution is better than the solution presented in [3]: The introduced delay is reduced to 45%.

VII. Conclusion and Future Work

Many solutions and scheduling algorithms have been proposed, however, few of them are implemented in real-time systems. To be used and evaluated, theoretical solutions must be deployed into a real-time system. Unfortunately, just few real-time scheduling middleware have been developed to date and most of them require the use of a specific simulation language. In this paper, we are interested in reconfigurable real-time embedded systems when the battery recharges are done periodically. We propose in this paper a new middleware to be placed above the operating system. Thanks to the strategy implemented in this middleware, the system can run correctly after any reconfiguration scenario. We are interested in improving the strategy and generalizing it to multi-core real-time embedded systems.

References

[1] X. Wang, M. Khalgui, and Z.Li, "Dynamic low power reconfigurations of embedded real-time systems," In: Proceedings of the 1st International Conference on Pervasive and Embedded Computing and Communication Systems, Portugal, vol. 6, 2010.

[2] C. Angelov, K. Sierszecki, and N. Marian, "Design models for reusable and reconfigurable state machines," in L.T. Yang et al. (Eds.): Proc. of EUC 2005, LNCS 3824, vol. 12, 2005, pp. 152–163.

[3] X. Wang, I. Khemaissia, M. Khalgui, Z.Li, O. Mosbahi, and M. Zhou, "Dynamic low-power reconfiguration of real-time systems with periodic and probabilistic tasks," IEEE Transactions on Automation Science and Engineering, vol. 14, 2014, pp. 258 - 271.

[4] A. Allavena and D. Mossé, "Scheduling of frame-based embedded systems with rechargeable batteries."

[5] H. Ghor, M. Chetto, and R. Chehade, "A real-time scheduling framework for embedded systems with environmental energy harvesting," Int. Journal of Computers and Electrical Engineering, vol. 26, 2010.

[6] E. Camponogara, A. Oliveira, and G. Lima, "Optimization-based dynamic reconfiguration of real-time schedulers with support for stochastic processor consumption," Industrial Informatics, IEEE Trans. Ind. Informat, vol. 16, 2010, pp. 594–609.

[7] L. George and P. Courbin, "Reconfiguration of uniprocessor sporadic real-time systems: The sensitivity approach," in Book Chapter in IGI Global Knowledge on Reconfigurable Embedded Control systems: Applications for Flexibiliy and Agility, vol. 17, no. 167–189, 2011.

[8] S. Baruah and J. Goossens, "Scheduling real-time tasks: algorithms and complexity," Handbook of Scheduling: Algorithms Models and Performance Analysis, vol. 38, 2003.

[9] W. Yuan and K. Nahrstedt, "Energy-efficient soft real-time cpu scheduling for mobile multimedia systems," ACM SIGOPS Operating Systems Review, vol. 37, no. 5, 2003, pp. 149–163.

[10] F. Gruian, "Hard real-time scheduling for low-energy using stochastic data and dvs processors," Proceedings of the 2001 international symposium on Low power electronics and design, 2001, pp. 46–51.

[11] M. Chetto and H. El Ghor, "Real-time scheduling of periodic tasks in a monoprocessor system with a rechargeable battery," 2009, p. 45.

[12] G. Wigley and D. Kearney, "The first real operating system for reconfigurable computers," Computer Systems Architecture Conference, vol. 9, no. 1-8, 2001, pp. 130–137.

[13] C. Steiger, H. Walder, and M. Platzner, "Operating systems for reconfigurable embedded platforms: Online scheduling of real-time tasks," IEEE Transactions on Computers, vol. 15, 2004, pp. 1393–1407.

[14] P. Merino, J. Lopez, and M. Jacome, "A hardware operating system for dynamic reconfiguration of fpgas," Proc. Int. Workshop Field-Programmable Logic and Applications From FPGAs to Computing Paradigm, vol. 5, 1998, pp. 431–435.

[15] P. Merino, M. Jacome, and J. Lopez, "A methodology for task based partitioning and scheduling of dynamically reconfigurable systems," Proc. IEEE Symp. FPGAs for Custom Computing Machines, vol. 2, 1998, pp. 324–325.

[16] I. Khemaissia, O. Mosbahi, M. Khalgui, and W. Bouzayen, "New reconfigurable middleware for feasible adaptive rt-linux," Parallel and Distributed Processing Symposium, 2006. IPDPS 2006. 20th International, vol. 10, no. 1–10, 2014.

[17] A. Gammoudi, A. Benzina, M. Khalgui, and D. Chillet, "New pack oriented solutions for energy-aware feasible adaptive real-time systems," The 14th International Conference on Intelligent Software Methodologies, Tools and Techniques, vol. 14, no. 1–14, 2015.

[18] F. Lab, "Getting-started-with-rtlinux," vol. 42, 2001.

[19] D. Faggioli, F. Checconi, M. Trimarchi, and C. Scordino, "An edf scheduling class for the linux kernel," 2009.

[20] C. L. Liu and J. W. Layland, "Scheduling algorithms for multiprogramming in a hard-real-time environment," Journal of the ACM (JACM), USA, vol. 15, 1973, pp. 46 - 61.

[21] Y. Shin and K. Choi, "Power conscious fixed priority scheduling for hard real-time systems," Design Automation Conference, 1999. Proceedings. 36th, 1999, pp. 134–139.

[22] F. Verdier, J. Prvotet, a. Benkhelifa, D. Chillet, and S. Pillement, "Exploring rtos issues with a high-level model of a reconfigurable soc platform," vol. 8, 2010.

[23] P. Hastono, S. Klaus, and S. Huss, "An integrated systemc framework for real-time scheduling assessments on system level," In 25th IEEE Int. Real-Time Systems Symposium (RTSS 2004), vol. 4, 2004.

[24] I. Benkermi, "Model and scheduling algorithm for dynamic reconfigurble architectures," Thesis in Computer Science, IRISA, Rennes1 University, France, vol. 140, 2007.

[25] A. B. H. Ali, M. Khalgui, and S. B. Ahmed, "Uml-based design and validation of intelligent agents-based reconfigurable embedded control systems," International Journal of System Dynamics Applications (IJSDA), vol. 1, no. 1, 2012, pp. 17–38.

Comparing IoT Platforms under Middleware Requirements in an IoT Perspective

An fulfillment analysis of IoT middleware requirements in IoT Platforms that uses REST to communicate with external applications

Artur Oliveira, Daniel Melo, Geiziany Silva, Thiago Gregório
CESAR – Centro de Estudos e Sistemas Avançados do Recife
Recife, Brazil
e-mail: artur@arturluiz.com, danielfarias.ti@gmail.com, geiziany.mendes@gmail.com, thiago.gregorio@gmail.com

Abstract—**The increasing number of heterogeneous objects in IoT and the different kinds of software that consume data generated by those objects, have created an opportunity for middleware software to arise acting like an adapter, simplifying communication among them. As Representational State Transfer (REST) is broadly used as communication protocol by Web applications, this paper aims to analyze the fulfillment of Internet of Things (IoT) middleware requirements in IoT Platforms that use REST to communicate with external applications.**

Keywords-IoT; REST; Middleware Requirements; IoT Platforms.

I. INTRODUCTION

Internet of Things (IoT) means everything connected to the Internet, such as sensors, smart objects, clothes, toys, anything at all. The condition is that those things can produce something meaningful. The good news is that, with all people's creative imagination, almost any data may have a meaning under certain circumstances and can become useful information. To show how the IoT is going to be a world changer, it is predicted that the quantity of things in IoT would reach an astonishing number of 212 billion things generating constant data about practically everything in real world [3].

But not all those things (the 'T' from IoT) talk the same language, as they are made by different companies or groups. It is normal that they do not have a common interface to transmit their data directly to services and would be unfeasible that the services have an internal component to understand a wide variety of different components. Having this in mind, middleware software receives this responsibility. In addition to providing a large understanding how to talk to things, it also translates the data to a known language (protocol) by external applications.

Representational State Transfer (REST) is an architectural style based on Hypertext Transfer Protocol (HTTP) and an approach to communications, which has been widely used in integrations between different applications.

This paper's main purpose is to analyze the fulfillment of IoT middleware requirements in IoT Platforms that use REST to communicate with external applications. We start in Section II by presenting concepts related to the Internet of things. Section III continues by presenting an overview of the REST architectural style. Then, Section IV described the concepts of middleware and its different types that have emerged over time. In Section V, the functional and non functional requirements of middleware for IoT are listed. In Section VI, we analyze the fulfillment of IoT middleware requirements in IoT Platforms that use REST. Finally, Section VII concludes the paper.

II. INTERNET OF THINGS

The future of communication and Information technology (IT) is represented by the technological revolution of the Internet of Things [2]. The IoT was leveraged by technological advances in wireless communications, Radio-frequency identification (RFID), and the strong growth of the World Wide Web (www). The main objective of the IoT is to allow anything existing in the world can be identified, addressed, controlled and monitored by the Internet anytime and anywhere, interconnecting the physical and the virtual world through communication between two new dimensions: human-to-thing (H2T) and thing-to-thing (T2T), both promoted by IoT [1].

Through the interconnection of virtual and physical worlds, sensors play a vital role in achieving the connecting bridge between these worlds. The sensors are designed to collect data from their environment, with the intention to generate information about the context, allowing monitoring and controlling anything that can be connected to the environment [2].

Smart objects of IoT are expected to reach 212 billion entities deployed worldwide by the end of 2020. The expectation is that the Machine to Machine (M2M) traffic flow constitutes 45% of all Internet traffic [3]. So, the implantation of the IoT paradigm directly impacts the daily lives of people that will be motivated by the use of new technologies based on the interaction of physical devices [1].

III. REPRESENTATIONAL STATE TRANFER (REST)

The architectural style REST emerged in the mid-2000s, proposed by Roy Thomas Fielding through the doctoral dissertation: "Architectural Styles and the Design of Network-based Software Architectures" [4][5]. This style made people feel encouraged to use protocols and Web features to map requests in various representations, providing the resource management and processing by means of a uniform interface operation [6]. The REST style is based on HTTP protocol, Uniform Resource Identifier (URI), Extensible Markup Language (XML) and HyperText Markup Language (HTML) [7]. The main features around the REST architecture are described below.

A. The Uniform Resource Identifier (URI)

The creation of an identifier for Web resources is necessary in order for anything can be considered as a Web feature, an audio, a video, or an encapsulated process, for instance. The URI is used to identify and address each Web resource, directly navigating to the specific resource. The relationship between resources and URI is that a resource may correspond to multiple URIs, but a URI corresponds only to a single resource that characterizes a relationship of one-to-many [6].

B. Resource Representation Transformation

The representation of a resource defines its current status, including the data itself and metadata. A resource can be represented through the transformation to some known formats: Extensible Hypertext Markup Language (XHTML), Atom, XML, JavaScript Object Notation (JSON), Plain Text, Comma-Separated Values (CSV MPEG-4 Part 14 (MP4) or JPEG [6].

C. Operation Methods GET, POST, PUT or DELETE

In the Web context operations, such as GET, PUT, POST, and DELETE are known as methods standard-based operations on the HTTP protocol. REST emphasizes the semantic use of such methods to perform the desired transactions [6].

D. Stateless Communication

The stateless communication on REST defines that each client request is treated as an independent transaction, and contains sufficient information to be totally understood. Using REST, any request is unrelated to any previous request. So, the communication consists of independent pairs of request and response [6].

E. Why use REST for IOT

The REST structure is designed to accommodate large data transfers efficiently equivalent to hypermedia data [7]. So, through the IOT model that allows anything that exists in the world to be connected and that its control and monitoring is possible [1]. It is easy to see the sensors as a resource on the Web and using RESTful Web service that is nothing more than a simple Web service that uses the HTTP protocol and REST principles, it is a way to combine HTTP and Web Service easily and clearly [8].

IV. MIDDLEWARE

Several definitions have emerged in the literature about distributed systems. One of them can summarize enough: A distributed system is a collection of independent computers that appears to its users as a single coherent system [9]. This means that, transparent to the user, multiple components (computers on the definition) require integration and collaboration between them. In principle, distributed systems must also have high scalability and availability. Users and applications should not notice that parts are being replaced or adjusted, or even that new parts are being added [9].

With the emergence of the need for more robust systems that could operate in a distributed way, the software engineering faced challenges during the development of distributed systems. New problems have arisen which did not exist in the development of centralized systems, such as network saturation or connection problems between the components involved [9]. An infrastructure that supports the development and execution of distributed applications was necessary.

The term middleware first appeared in the late 1980s [10]. There are several definitions for middleware in the literature. The common point between them is that middleware can be defined as a software layer located above the operating system and network software and below applications as shown in Fig. 1. The middleware allows interaction and communication between different applications via Application Programming Interface (APIs) and protocols supported between distributed components [11][12][13][14] proposed the following requirements for middleware: network communication, coordination, reliability, scalability and heterogeneity.

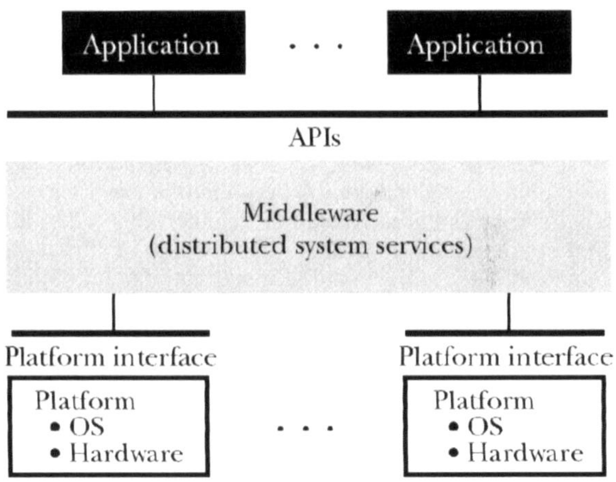

Figure 1. The set of middleware in distributed system, taken from [3..7], p. 89

Middleware gained more importance in recent years for its role in simplifying the development of new services and integration between old and new technologies [12]. In the literature, there are different types of middleware that have emerged over time and according to technological evolution. The most known are: transactional middleware, procedural middleware, object-oriented middleware and message-oriented middleware messages.

A. Transactional Middleware

It is a kind of middleware that is already considered old, which supports transactions between components that are distributed on different servers. Transactional middleware was designed to support synchronous and distributed transactions. Its main function is to coordinate requests between clients and servers that can process these requests [9]. A transaction must support the Atomic, Consistent, Isolated and Durable (ACID) property. Atomic means that transaction either completes or it does not. The "all or nothing" strategy. Consistency should hold the system in a consistent state, independent of the status of the transaction. Isolation is the ability of one transaction to work independently from other transactions. Durability means the ability of the transaction to survive system failures (expected or unexpected) [15].

B. *Procedural Middleware*

Remote Procedure Calls (RPC) was developed by Sun Microsystems, the same responsible for the Java language, in early 80s. Their use enables an application to call functions from other applications running on remote machines. By being a synchronous communication mechanism, the client application waits while processing of the remote function is completed. Another problem caused by the PRC is the high traffic on network, requiring at that time, an evolution for the use of networks with better performance [16]. Examples: Tuxedo from BEA and Customer Information Control System (CISC) from IBM.

C. *Object-oriented Middleware (OOM)*

It is an evolution of procedural middleware. Communication is still synchronous between distributed objects. The interfaces of the services are described by specific languages and the marshalling and unmarshalling (data representation transformation in a format compatible for storage and transmission) are made automatically, unlike the procedural middleware that required this transformation was implemented [17]. Examples: Common Object Request Broker Architecture (CORBA) from Object Management Group (OMG), Distributed Component Object Model (DCOM) from Microsoft and Remote Method Invocation (RMI) from Java.

D. *Message-oriented Middleware (MOM)*

The information (messages) that travels between distributed components can be processed in two ways: message queuing and message passing. In the message queuing way, the communication is indirect, asynchronous and the messages are sent to queues. In the message passing way, the communication is direct, synchronous and operates according to the publish-subscribe model [17].

V. MIDDLEWARE REQUIREMENTS FOR IoT

Due to the nature of IoT middleware, where it is necessary to connect a large number of heterogeneous components (sensors and devices), it is recommended to archive a few minimal requirements to execute this task effectively. In [18], IoT middleware requirements are grouped into functional, those focus are functionalities themselves, and non-functional, those focus is on Quality of Service (QoS) and performance.

Fig. 2 illustrates the set of requirements explored in this paper grouped into functional and non-functional requirements. The following requirements were selected for their relevance level presented in [18]. We list their descriptions below.

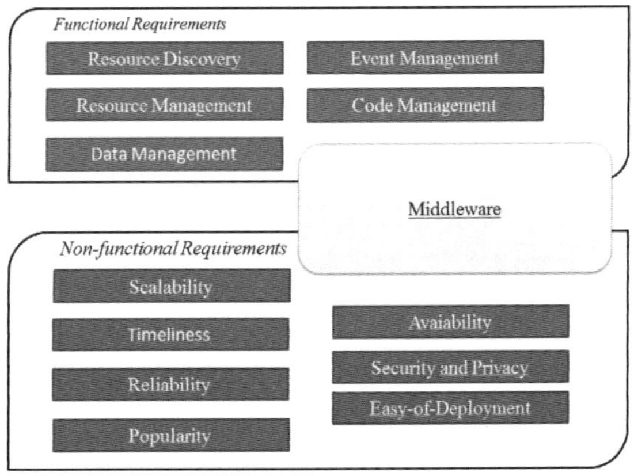

Figure 2 – The set of middleware requirements in an IoT perspective explored in this paper.

Resource Discovery allows middleware service to detect the exact moment when components connect and disconnect, making possible a reliable list of all connected components and to free up unused resources. It is also necessary that such functionalities are automated, due to infeasibility of human intervention in every situation.

Resource Management covers the efficient use of available resources, monitoring of such resources and the release procedure when they are no longer needed. This requirement is necessary due to limited resource components commonly encountered in an IoT environment.

Data Management provides access to data generated by devices and sensors, and data that may have a useful meaning to applications that consume these data from middleware like data related to network health.

Event Management allows external services connected to the middleware to be notified when an event happens in the device network that that middleware controls. Those events may be related to components availability, the interaction between them, network health etc.

Code Management allows users or external applications use a group of devices to solve a defined task, injecting necessary code in those devices. It also includes functionalities that migrate the injected code among other devices.

Scalability is the capacity to support a growing number of connected "things" generating data constantly, and external applications consuming such data with little or no loss of QoS.

Timeliness is the capacity that ensures that data which are dependent on the time they were generated are provided with a time delay which tends to zero. In the IoT context there are many components that fit into this category. This requirement turns out to be essential for a middleware that intends to act in the areas of health, transport, security etc.

Reliability ensures that the middleware is always operating during the execution of a task, even when there are failures. This requirement is totally dependent on devices and sensors that are connected to the middleware, since it is they who generate the data. A failure at the device level can cause the transfer, through the middleware, to consumer systems.

Availability is the capability that the middleware is or appear to be available when necessary. This requires that the frequency of errors and the recovery time is small enough as to become imperceptible to external services connected to the middleware.

Security and Privacy ensures data in the middleware is protected from being read or modified by anyone other than those who have rightful permission and prohibit malicious applications to have access to connected things and connected services.

Ease of Deployment is not an essential requirement. It concerns the low complexity in the installation and upgrade process middleware, causing an advanced technical knowledge not being required for the deployment and maintenance. The ideal scenario is an automated update process that does not interfere with Availability and Reliability requirements.

Popularity is a differential in the IoT middleware platform choosing process. Popularity is directly related to the size of the community that uses the middleware and the amount of contributions that community provides.

VI. IoT PLATFORMS ANALYSIS

IoT has undergone rapid transformation since the variety and the number of devices connected to the Internet have increased exponentially in recent years [19]. IoT has become a mainstream technology with a significant potential for advancing the lifestyle of modern societies. For this reason, there are several companies that heavily invest in the creation of solutions that covers IoT and necessary infrastructure, providing a complete platform for easy development and deployment of applications that consume IoT data.

The list of IoT platforms present in this paper was purely based on the criteria of companies that provide software solutions that enable information processing devices and sensors using REST as integration option.

The selected platforms are: Appcelerator, Amazon Web Service (AWS) IoT Platform, Bosch IoT Suite, Ericsson Device Connection Platform (DCP), EVRYTHNG, IBM Watson IoT Platform, Cisco ParStream and Xively.

Appcelerator is a platform for mobile development, including REST integration and real-time analytics through Titanium [20].

Bosch IoT Suite is composed by different services, they are Analytics, Hub, Integrations, Permissions, Remote Manager, Rollouts and Things, these services are described in [21] [22].

AWS IoT Platform provides integrations from devices to AWS Services and other devices, it also has a security layer for data and interaction [23] [24] [25] [26].

Xively's main focus is to make their clients profit from IoT. For that, they offer from IoT services (management of devices and data) to professional services (specialized consulting for clients) [27].

Ericsson DCP is a M2M platform that handles connectivity and subscription management, supporting a high number of devices and applications [28].

According to [29] "EVRYTHNG collects, manages and applies real-time data from smart products and smart packaging to drive IoT applications".

IBM Watson IoT Platform is a cloud-hosted service that simplifies access to connected devices data providing real-time connectivity throught MQ Telemetry Transport (MQTT) protocol [30] [31].

Cisco ParStream is mainly focused in analysis and time to market. [32] presents a list of its capabilities.

Table 1 shows the analysis of the functional and non functional requirements for IoT middleware depending upon the selected IoT platforms.

Through this analysis we realized that almost all IoT platforms have a requirement "not mentioned" in the documentation available and researched by the authors. This may show that the documentation is not complete enough or that the requirement "not mentioned" cannot really be found on this platform.

Another aspect realized by the analysis is that IBM Watson IoT Platform achieves all requirements presented in this paper, maybe proving to be the best choice among the listed platforms. The non-functional requirements Scalability and Reliability were found in all the chosen IoT platforms, proving to be a main requirement for any IoT platform. A possible cause for timeliness not being mentioned in a few platforms may be that they were not designed for a specific area, but for general use instead.

VII. CONCLUSION

This paper proposed to analyze the fulfillment of IoT middleware requirements in IoT Platforms that use the architectural style REST. After a brief explanation of all the concepts that surround IoT platforms, this paper has analyzed the functional and non functional requirements of middleware for IoT of the current state-of-the-art IoT software platforms.

It also can be seen that all IoT platforms, except the "Appcelerator", satisfy the majority of functional and non functional requirements of middleware for IoT. The analysis focused on requirements, such as resource discovery, resource management, data management, event management, code management, scalability, timeliness, reliability, availability, security and privacy and easy-of deployment.

As future work, we intend to analyze the cost benefit in relation to the total resources needed in the implementation of IoT platforms. Sorting the IoT platforms is more feasible for the cost reserved for this deployment.

TABLE 1 – ANALYSIS RESULTS OF THE FULFILLMENT OF IOT MIDDLEWARE REQUIREMENTS IN IOT PLATFORMS.

	Appcelerator	AWS IoT platform	Bosch IoT Suite	Ericsson DCP	EVRYTHNG	IBM Watson IoT	Cisco ParStream	Xively
Resource Discovery	X	√	√	√	√	√	X	√
Resource Management	X	Not mentioned	√	√	√	√	√	√
Data Management	X	√	√	√	√	√	√	√
Event Management	X	√	Not mentioned	√	√	√	Not mentioned	√
Code Management	X	√	√	√	Not mentioned	√	Not mentioned	√
Scalability	√	√	√	√	√	√	√	√
Timeliness	X	√	Not mentioned	√	√	√	√	Not mentioned
Reliability	√	√	√	√	√	√	√	√
Avaiability	√	√	√	Not mentioned	√	√	√	√
Security and Privacy	√	√	√	√	√	√	Not mentioned	√
Easy-of Deployment	X	√	√	√	√	√	X	√

REFERENCES

[1] P. F. Pires et al. (2014), "A Platform for Integrating Physical Devices in the Internet of Things". Proceedings - 2014 International Conference on Embedded and Ubiquitous Computing, EUC 2014, x'234. http://doi.org/10.1109/EUC.2014.42

[2] L. Tan, "Future internet: The Internet of Things. 2010 3rd International Conference on Advanced Computer Theory and Engineering" (ICACTE), V5–376–V5–377. http://doi.org/10.1109/ICACTE.2010.5579543

[3] A. Al-Fuqaha, M. Guizani, M. Mohammadi, M. Aledhari, and M. Ayyash, "Internet of Things: A Survey on Enabling Technologies, Protocols, and Applications". IEEE Communications Surveys and Tutorials, 2015, 17(4), 2348 http://doi.org/10.1109/COMST.2015.2444095

[4] B. Costa, P. F. Pires, F. C. Delicato, and P. Merson, "Evaluating a Representational State Transfer (REST) architecture: What is the impact of REST in my architecture?". Proceedings - Working IEEE/IFIP Conference on Software Architecture 2014, WICSA 2014, 105. http://doi.org/10.1109/WICSA.2014.29

[5] T. R. Fielding, "Architectural Styles and the Design of Network-based Software Architectures", 2000, Building, 54, 162. http://doi.org/10.1.1.91.2433

[6] Z. Han, Y. Kong, and X. Wang, "Geographic stereo video web service based on the REST architecture". Proceedings - 2011 19th International Conference on Geoinformatics, Geoinformatics 2011, pp2 (40771166). http://doi.org/10.1109/GeoInformatics.2011.5980900

[7] L. Xiao-Hong, "Research and development of web of things system based on rest architecture". Proceedings - 2014 5th International Conference on Intelligent Systems Design and Engineering Applications, ISDEA 2014, 745. http://doi.org/10.1109/ISDEA.2014.169

[8] X. Zhang, Z. Wen, Y. Wu, and J. Zou, "The implementation and application of the internet of things platform based on the REST architecture". BMEI 2011 - Proceedings 2011 International Conference on Business Management and Electronic Information, 2, 43. http://doi.org/10.1109/ICBMEI.2011.5917838

[9] A. Tanenbaum, M. Van Steen, "Distributed Systems: Principles and Pradigms", 2nd ed. Pearson, pp 2-4, 2007.

[10] Middleware white paper [Online]. http://web.cefriel.it/~alfonso/WebBook/Documents/isgmidware.pdf [retrieved: July, 2016].

[11] P.A. Bernstein. "Middleware: a model for distributed system services". Communications of the ACM, pages 86-98, 1996.

[12] R. P. Bob Hulsebosch, Wouter Teeuw. "Middleware tintel state-of-the-art deliverable", 1999.

[13] J. M. Myerson, "The Complete Book of Middleware. Auerbach Publications", 2002.

[14] W. Emmerich, "Software engineering and middleware: A roadmap". Communications of the ACM, pages 117-129, 2000.

[15] D. S. Linthicum, "Application servers an eai", eAI Journal, July/August 2000.

[16] D. S. Linthicum, "Enterprise Application Integration", 1st edition, Addison-Weslley Professional, 1999.

[17] H. Pinus, "Middleware: Past and present a comparison", pp. 1–5, 2004.

[18] M. Razzaque, M. Milojevic-Jevric, A. Palade, and S. Clarke, "Middleware for Internet of Things: a Survey", 4-5. 2016.

[19] M. Dayarathna, "Comparing 11 IoT Development Platforms" [Online]. Available from: https://dzone.com/articles/iot-software-platform-comparison [retrieved: August, 2016].

[20] Appcelerator Open Source. [Online]. Available from: https://www.appcelerator.com/mobile-app-development-products [retrieved: July, 2016].

[21] Bosch IoT Suite Benefits. [Online]. Available from: https://www.bosch-si.com/products/bosch-iot-suite/iot-platform/benefits.html [retrieved: August, 2016].

[22] Bosch IoT Suite white paper brochure. [Online]. Available from: https://www.bosch-si.com/products/bosch-iot-suite/downloads/white-paper-brochure.html [retrieved: August, 2016].

[23] AWS Amazon, How it works. [Online]. Available from: https://aws.amazon.com/pt/iot/how-it-works/ [retrieved: August, 2016].

[24] AWS Amazon, IoT Rules. [Online]. Available from: http://docs.aws.amazon.com/iot/latest/developerguide/iot-rules.html [retrieved: August, 2016].

[25] AWS Amazon, IoT Security Identity. [Online]. Available from: http://docs.aws.amazon.com/iot/latest/developerguide/iot-security-identity.html [retrieved: August, 2016].

[26] AWS Amazon, IoT thing shadows. [Online]. Available from: http://docs.aws.amazon.com/iot/latest/developerguide/iot-thing-shadows.html [retrieved: August, 2016].

[27] N. Sinha, K. E. Pujitha, J. S. R. Alex, "Xively Based Sensing and Monitoring System for IoT",1-4.

[28] Ericsson DCP [Online] . Available from: https://www.ericsson.com/ourportfolio/products/device-connection-platform [retrieved: August, 2016].

[29] Evrythng IoT Platform [Online]. Available from: https://evrythng.com/platform/ [retrieved: August, 2016].

[30] M. Kim et al., "Building scalable, secure, multi-tenant could services on IBM Bluemix", 1-3. 2016.

[31] IBM Watson IoT documentation [Online]. Available from: https://docs.internetofthings.ibmcloud.com/ [retrieved: August, 2016].

[32] Cisco ParStram Analytics Automation [Online]. Available from: http://www.cisco.com/c/en/us/products/analytics-automation-software/parstream/index.html [retrieved: August, 2016].

ZiZo: A Complete Tool Chain for the Modeling and Verification of Reconfigurable Function Blocks

Safa Guellouz, Adel Benzina
LISI Laboratory, INSAT and
Tunisia Polytechnic School,
University of Carthage, Tunis, Tunisia
Email: guellouz.safa@gmail.com,
adel.benzina@isd.rnu.tn

Mohamed Khalgui
School of Electro-Mechanical Engineering,
Xidian University,
Xi'an 710071, China
Email: khalgui.mohamed@gmail.com

Georg Frey
Chair of Automation and Energy Systems,
Saarland University,
Saarbrücken, Germany
Email: georg.frey@aut.uni-saarland.de

Abstract—**Ubiquitous systems support reconfigurable hardware and software self-adapted components to external changes for a better performance. IEC 61499 is the most suitable manufacturing standard that designs distributed ubiquitous systems. All the available IEC 61499 development tools ensure the design, simulation and code generation of function block systems. There is no complete tool chain which supports design, modeling with Petri nets and automatic verification with model checking. This paper presents ZiZo v3 tool that supports the whole process for a new extension of IEC 61499 named Reconfigurable Function Block (RFB). ZiZo automates the transformation from RFB design diagrams to the Generalized Reconfigurable Timed Net Condition/ Event Systems GR-TNCES model that preserves its behavioural semantics and also exports it to the probabilistic symbolic model checker PRISM. A case study is presented to demonstrate the whole process from the design with RFB to verification.**

Keywords–IEC 61499; Reconfiguration; Reconfigurable distributed system; Automatic transformation; GR-TNCES.

I. INTRODUCTION

The flexibility and reconfigurability of manufacturing is one of the major drivers of IEC 61499 [1]. Several works address various aspects of hardware and software reconfiguration using this standard. These include works on down-timeless evolution [2] and real-time implementations [3]. Other works focus on agent-based reconfiguration [4], ontology-based reconfiguration agent [6] and even reconfiguration protocol [7]. We notice that these approaches of reconfiguration following IEC 61499 increase engineering efficiency and also the design complexity. In fact, the number of function blocks and the interconnections between them in the design system become very complex as well as their verification. In order to make the design easier, we propose an extension to the function block, named Reconfigurable Function Block (RFB) that encapsulates many scenarios of reconfiguration related to the changes in the controlled process. We aim to modify first of all the implementation of a function block by modifying the execution control chart model and the interface by adding a new event type to support reconfiguration, as well as the probabilistic aspect. Probabilistic events and scenarios are suggested to add a degree of uncertainty to events, thus it will be possible to evaluate after words the probability of occurrence of some unwanted states or scenarios like deadlocks.

On another hand, the verification and validation of automation software for reconfigurable distributed systems is an especially hard task. Many research works model manually the system with Petri nets [18] to verify it with a model checker. To handle the design and the modeling of systems with RFBs and automate their transformation to GR-TNCES [8], a class of Petri nets that preserves the behavioral semantics of RFB, we developed a complete tool ZiZo v3 as an extension to an existing tool ZiZo v2 [9] that models and simulates adaptive probabilistic discrete event control systems with GR-TNCES. Thanks to ZiZo, the verification of functional and temporal properties becomes easy: The designer can export the GR-TNCES model to PRISM model checker [10]. He/She can verify the functional correctness and safety of individual function blocks and entire control applications.

The remainder of this paper is structured as follows: We begin with the state of the art. In Section III, we present the reconfigurable function block as a new extension to IEC 61499. Then, we discuss the transformation of RFBs models to GR-TNCES model through a well-defined set of transformation rules in Section IV. We continue presenting the way that ZiZo v3 supports and automates the transformation process in Section V. This is followed by a presentation of the BROS system, which we have considered as a case study for our approach. Finally, we summarize this work.

II. STATE OF THE ART

A. IEC 61499 Modeling

Today, in industry, ubiquitous computing software must operate in conditions of radical change [5]. That is why several component-based technologies have been proposed to develop ubiquitous embedded control systems. Among all these technologies, the Industrial International Standard IEC 61499 is a component-based technology that defines Function Blocks (FBs) to model and implement distributed Industrial Process Measurement and Control Systems (IPMCSs).

A function block is an event triggered unit encapsulating some functionalities in algorithms. It contains data/event inputs and outputs to interact with the external environment. The activation of the block is ensured by events while data contain valued information. The algorithms encapsulated in the function block use data associated with incoming events to update internal and output data. The functionality of function block is defined by a state machine called execution control chart. It controls the algorithms execution and produces output events. Each state is assigned to actions (ECAction) that include algorithms to be executed before sending output events. The states are connected to each other with ECtransitions that fire if the corresponding event occurs and the guard conditions are met. The conditions are based on internal variables or data inputs but not events.

Several tools have been developed in the past years to design IPMCSs following the standard: FBDK [11], IsaGRAF [12], nxtSTUDIO [13] and other IEC 61499 IDEs. Nevertheless, they do not offer verification support. The most important tool for that is VEDA [14] that mainly focuses on the modeling and verification of the function block execution control. In fact, the modeling and verification of reconfigurable manufacturing systems attract many researchers. Pang et al. [15] present a prototype model generator, which aims to automatically translate IEC 61499 function blocks into Net Condition/Event Systems following sequential execution semantics. Gerber et al. [16] present a formal model for integer-valued data types. This allows automatic model generation from arbitrary function block programs. Suender et al. [17] present a new formal validation of "on-the-fly" modification of control software in IEC 61499 automation systems. The main objective of modeling with Petri nets is to validate the system before its deployment. The above works use Petri nets to verify the correctness of the IEC61499 designs. But none of them has proposed a way for considering and modeling probabilistic reconfiguration scenarios within the function block paradigm and none has provided a complete tool that supports the design of function blocks, modeling with Petri nets and verification using model checking. In this work, a reconfigurable function block is formalised to support probabilistic reconfigurations in the current standard IEC 61499. Furthermore, a complete tool chain supports the whole process from the design of RFB to verification with model checking.

B. GR-TNCES

Petri nets [18] are widely used for the modeling of distributed control systems and support formal analysis such as model checking. GR-TNCES is a class of Petri nets considering reconfiguration and probability of occurrence of events. A GR-TNCES, as defined in [8], is an extension of the formalism Reconfigurable Timed Net Condition/Event Systems (R-TNCES) [19], which models unpredictable systems under memory and energy constraints and has a real-time probabilistic reconfigurable supervised control architecture. It is defined as a structure $G = \{\sum R - TNCES\}$. $R - TNCES = (B, R)$, where R is the control module consisting of a set of reconfiguration functions. B is the behavior module that is a union of multi TNCES, represented as follows:
$B = (P, T, F, W, CN, EN, DC, V, Z0)$ where: (i) P (respectively, T) is a set of places (respectively, transitions), (ii) F is a set of flow arcs $F \subseteq (P \times T) \cup (T \times P)$, (iii) W: $(P \times T) \cup (T \times P) \rightarrow \{0, 1\}$ maps a weight to a flow arc, $W(x, y) > 0$ if $(x, y) \in F$, and $W(x, y) = 0$ otherwise, where $x, y \in P \cup T$, (iv) CN (respectively, EN) is a set of condition (respectively, event) signals with $CN \subseteq (P \times T)$ (respectively, $EN \subseteq (T \times T)$), (v) DC: $F(P \times T) \rightarrow \{[l, h]\}$ is a super-set of time constraints on output arcs, (vi) V: $T \rightarrow \{\vee, \wedge\}$ maps an event-processing mode (AND or OR) to each transition, (vii) Z0= $(T0, D0)$ where $T0$: $P \rightarrow \{0, 1\}$ is the initial marking and $D0$: $P \rightarrow 0$ is the initial clock position.

A reconfiguration function $r \in R$ is a structure $r = (Cond, P, E, M, S, X)$ where: (a) $Cond \rightarrow \{true, false\}$: The precondition of r, (b) P: $F \rightarrow [0..1]$ is the TNCES probability, (c) E: $P \rightarrow [0..max]$: controls the energy requirements, (d) M: $P \rightarrow [0..max]$ controls the memory requirements, (e) S: $TN(\bullet r) \rightarrow TN(r\bullet)$ is the structure modification instruction for reconfiguration scenario, (f) X: $laststate(\bullet r) \rightarrow initialstate(r\bullet)$ is the state processing function.

We note, finally, that ZiZo v2 is the only tool that models GR-TNCES models. It is an extension to ZiZo v1 [20], developed in LISI Laboratory of INSAT Institute in collaboration with Saarland University in Germany. It edits, simulates and checks adaptive systems modeled with R-TNCES formalism. Furthermore, Zizo v2 allows designers to edit, simulate and export GR-TNCES models to the probabilistic model checker PRISM [10]. PRISM is a useful tool to verify functional and temporal properties of GR-TNCES. We apply it in our work to verify adaptive probabilistic discrete event control systems.

C. Originality

The design of reconfigurable systems following the IEC 61499 standard using the available tools is complex and difficult. To optimize the network of FBs and make it more adjustable to external changes, we propose a new function block named RFB that provides a simple model of reconfigurable systems. An RFB allows several ways of functioning thanks to reconfiguration. Hence, it reduces the number of FBs used in the design as well as its complexity. Consequently, we extend the Petri nets editor ZiZo v2 to support: (i) design with RFB, (ii) automatic transformation from RFB to GR-TNCES model, and (iii) verification with model checking. ZiZo v3 is the only tool that supports the whole process from the design with RFB to verification.

III. RECONFIGURABLE FUNCTION BLOCKS

An RFB is a new extension of IEC 61499 that includes reconfiguration and probability aspects. It encapsulates several reconfiguration scenarios within a single FB and incorporates the probability of triggering each scenario. It is able to self-adapt the behavior of the system when changes occur in the environment. An RFB, as illustrated in Fig. 1, has new events and data of reconfiguration. It has also a specific architecture of the known execution control chart ECC: an $ECC_{controller}$ for the supervision of the elementary ECCs named ECC_{slaves} such that each one executes a scenario of reconfiguration. When an input event of reconfiguration occurs, $ECC_{controller}$ becomes active and reads the associated data of reconfiguration to select which scenario of reconfiguration will be active, and therefore, which ECC_{slave} will be executed. If the guard condition of the transition in $ECC_{controller}$ is met, then the corresponding ECC_{slave} waits for the occurrence of an input event to run the suitable algorithm, updates data and sends output events. At the end of all algorithms execution, $ECC_{controller}$ receives an event from the active ECC_{slave}. It updates the data of reconfiguration and generates output events of reconfiguration to communicate with the next RFBs.

The formalization of an RFB is defined as a tuple:
RFB=($Interface$, $ECC_{controller}$, ECC_{slave}), where:

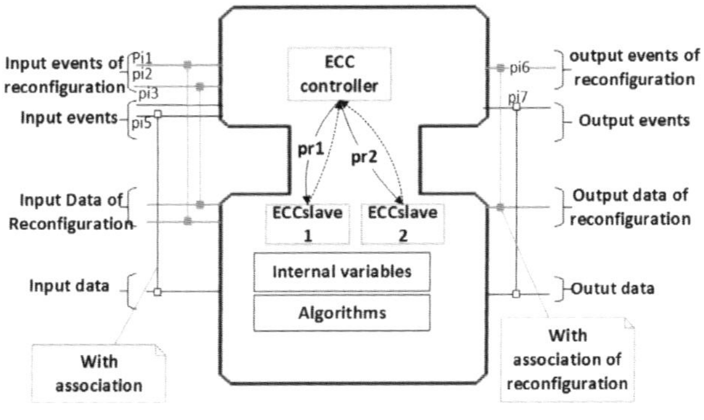

Figure 1. RFB interface.

1) Interface: The interface of an RFB is determined by the tuple $Interface$=(IE, OE, ID, OD, IW, OW, IER, OER, IDR, ODR, IWR, OWR), where (i) IE (respectively OE) is a set of input (respectively output) events; (ii) ID (respectively OD) is a set of data inputs (respectively outputs); (iii) IW (respectively OW) is a set of WITH-associations for inputs (respectively outputs); (iv) IER (respectively OER) is a set of input (respectively output) events of reconfiguration, each $ier \in IER$ has a probability $p \in [0,1]$; (v) IDR (respectively ODR) is a set of input (respectively output) data which corresponds to all distinct ECC_{slaves} in this RFB (respectively in the next RFBs); (vii) $IWR \subseteq IER \times IDR$ is a set of WITH-associations for inputs of reconfiguration. Each input event of reconfiguration is associated with the corresponding $ECC_{slave} \in IDR$ that will be activated; (viii) $OWR \subseteq OER \times ODR$ is a set of WITH-associations for output events of reconfiguration. Each output event of reconfiguration is associated with the corresponding $ECC_{slave} \in nextRFB$ that will be activated. (ix) Each event in the interface has a probability of occurrence $pi_j \in [0,1]$ / $j \in \mathbb{N}$ and each ECC_{slave} has a probability of activation $pr \in [0,1]$.

2) $ECC_{controller}$: Is the main component in an RFB. It controls the activation of ECC_{slaves}, as illustrated in Fig. 2a. It is defined as a tuple: $ECC_{controller}$ = ($State_{controller}$, $Transition_{controller}$, $Condition_{controller}$, $Action_{controller}$), where: (i) $State_{controller}$ is a set of states where $s0 \in State_{controller}$ is the initial state; each state can have zero or more $Action_{Controller}$; (ii) $Transition_{Controller} \subseteq State_{controller} \times State_{controller}$ is a set of arcs representing transitions, a transition may have a probability $pr \in [0,1]$, which corresponds to the probability of activation of an ECC_{slave}. The sum of probabilities of transitions issued from the same state must be equal to one $\sum pr_i = 1$. The probabilities in the interface are the same as those on the $ECC_{controller}$ transitions; (iii) $Condition_{Controller}$ is a guard condition defined on an input event and data of reconfiguration; (iv) $Action_{controller} : State_{controller} \setminus \{s0\} \longrightarrow ECA$ where $ECA = ECC_{slave} \times OER$ is a set of actions. Each action should select one ECC_{slave} and one output event of reconfiguration.

3) ECC_{slave}: Let us consider n $ECC_{slave_i} \in RFB$ where $i \leq n$. Each ECC_{slave_i} is controlled by $ECC_{controller}$, it encapsulates all algorithms to execute. According to the received data of reconfiguration, $ECC_{controller}$ selects the corresponding ECC_{slave}. As illustrated in Fig. 2b, an ECC_{slave_i} =(S, Tr, C, A), where: (i) S is a set of states; (ii) $Tr \subseteq S \times S$ is a set of arcs representing transitions from one state to another; (iii) C is a set of guard conditions defined over input, internal and output variables of RFB; and (iv) A is a set of actions sequences. Each action is related to an algorithm that can change only internal variables and output data of the RFB.

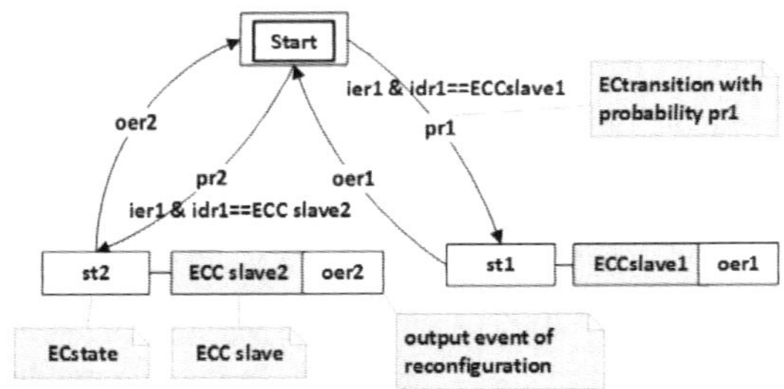

(a) $ECC_{controller}$.

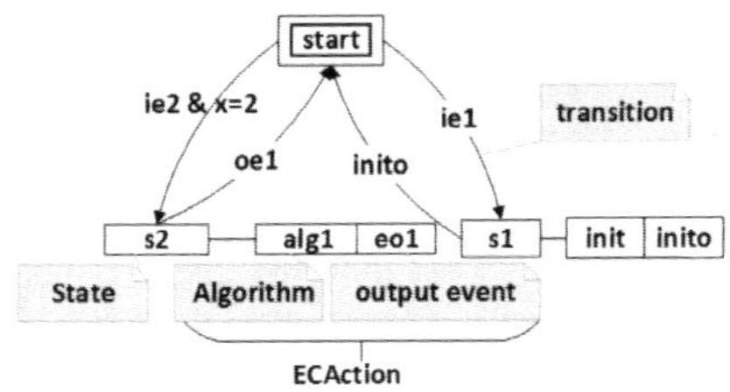

(b) $ECC_{Slave}1$.

Figure 2. RFB components.

As a result, a reconfigurable distributed system is modeled as a network of interconnected RFBs linked by data and event flows. At the end of each scenario of reconfiguration encapsulated in an ECC_{slave}, each output data of reconfiguration contains the next ECC_{slave}, which will be active in the next RFB. When its value is updated, the associated output event of reconfiguration occurs to trigger the suitable RFBs.

IV. TRANSFORMATION RULES

The main objective of this transformation is to validate the system before its deployment. Each functional component of the RFB is modeled by a GR-TNCES [8] module. $RFB = \{G_{Interface}, G_{ECCController}, G_{ECCSlave}\}$ where $G_{Interface}$ =\{ G_{IE}, G_{OE}, G_{ID}, G_{OD}, G_{IER}, G_{OER}, G_{IDR}, G_{ODR}, G_{IW}, G_{OW}, G_{IWR}, G_{OWR}\} where G_X models the X components of the RFB. $G_X = \sum G_{X_i}$. We have G_{X_i}=(B,R) where B=(P, T, F, W, CN, EN, DC, V, Z_0) and $R = \sum r_i$; r_i=($cond$, $P0$, $E0$, $M0$, S, X) a reconfiguration function.

All the input and output events have the same structure. The graphical models presented in Fig. 3 and Fig. 4 explain the transformation rules for all the components. As an example, let us detail the transformation rule for an input event:

Rule1: $ie \in IE \longrightarrow G_{IE_i}$

The objective of this rule is to transform each input event of RFB to a G_{IE_i} module. The graphical model is presented in Fig. 3a. The behavior of G_{IE_i} is composed of: P=\{$p1$,$p2$\};T=\{$t1$,$t2$\}; F=\{(p_1,t_1),(t_1,p_2),(p_2,t_2),(t_2,p_1)\}; W=\{\} ;CN=\{\}; EN=\{$ie1$, $ie2$, $oe1$\}; DC=\{\}; $V(t1)=\wedge$;

$V(t2)$=∧; Z_0={$T0$,$D0$} where $T0(p_1)$=1, $T0(p_2)$=0 and $D0(p_1)$=0;

Rule2: $IW \in Interface$ (respectively OW) is translated to G_{IW}:$G_{IE} \rightarrow G_{ID}$ (respectively G_{IW}:$G_{OE} \rightarrow G_{OD}$) where an output event $oe \in G_{IE}$ (respectively $eo \in G_{OE}$) is linked to an input event $ie \in G_{ID}$ (respectively $ie \in G_{OD}$.
$IWR \in Interface$ (respectively OWR) translated to G_{IWR}:$G_{IER} \rightarrow G_{IDR}$ (respectively G_{IWR}:$G_{OER} \rightarrow G_{ODR}$) where an output event $oe \in G_{IER}$ (respectively $oe \in G_{OER}$) is linked to an input event $ie \in G_{IDR}$ (respectively $ie \in G_{ODR}$).

The $ECC_{Controller}$ transformation rule is different from Rule1, it is modeled in Fig. 5 as follows:

Rule3: $ECC_{Controller} \longrightarrow G_{ECCcontroller}$

An $ECC_{Controller}$ is transformed to a $G_{ECCcontroller}$ module. $G_{ECCcontroller}$ is composed of: An initial marked place and a transition from which emerge n branches such that each one has a certain probability (probability of each reconfiguration scenario) where n is the number of ECC_{slave} in the current RFB. Each branch is composed of: two places and two transitions. The first place is linked to an input condition "ECC_{slave_i} true" ($i \in [1..n]$), which indicates that the ECC_{slave_i} must be activated. This place is linked to a transition T2 from which emerge n output events for activating the ECC_{slave_i} and deactivating the rest of the ECC_{slave}. This ensures that a single scenario of reconfiguration is active at a given time. The second place is linked to an input condition "ECC_{slave_i} finished", which marks the end of execution of the current active ECC_{slave_i}. Each branch finishes with a transition that sends 2 output events: the first one is for setting the output events of reconfiguration $oer \in OER$ and the second one for unsetting the input event of reconfiguration $ier \in IER$. Let us consider that there are n $ECC_{slave}s$ and m output events of reconfiguration in an RFB, the model of the $G_{ECCcontroller}$ has then n reconfiguration function r_i. B will be composed of: $P = \{p_1..p_{2n+1}\}$; $T = \{t_1..t_{n+2}\}$; F= {(p_1,t_1),(t_1,p_2),(t_1,p_3)..(t_1,p_{n+1}), (p_2,t_2),(p_3,t_3)..(p_n,t_n), (t_2,p_{n+2}),(t_3,p_{n+3})..(t_n,p_{2n})..(p_{2n+1},t_{n+2}),(t_{n+2},p_1)}; EN={$oe_1..oe_{2n+1+m}$}; CN= {$ci_1..ci_{2n}$} (for each slave an input condition ECC_{slave} true and an input condition ECC_{slave}finshed); W={}; DC={}; $V(t_i)$=∧; Z_0={$T0$,$D0$} where $T0(p_1)$=1, $T0(p_i)$=0 and $D0(p_1)$=0;

Rule4: $ECC_{slave_i} \in ECC_{Slave} \longrightarrow G_{ECC_{slave_i}}$

An ECC_{slave_i} is transformed to a $G_{ECC_{slave_i}}$ module. ECC_{Slave}, as we aforementioned, is a standard execution control chart so it contains states, transitions and actions.

The initial state is transformed to an initial marked place linked to a transition that is fired with the arrival of an input event for activating ECC_{slave_i}. As shown in Fig. 6, each state is transformed to two places "state run alg" and "state finish alg" as well as a transition between them. Each action is modeled with: an initial place "wait", an initial transition T14 that is fired when the input condition "start algorithm" is *true* and M places linked to M transitions for running $Algo_j$ (where M is the number of algorithms within the action) and $j \in [1..M]$). When all the algorithms in the different actions finish their execution, the ECC_{slave} generates an output condition indicating the end of the slave. Let us consider k states and k actions in ECCslave$_i$, j guard conditions on transition, each action contains an algorithm and an output event of reconfiguration then $B(G_{ECCslave_i})$ is composed of: P={ $p_1...p_{5k+2}$}; T={$t_1...t_{4k+4}$}; $F \subseteq (P \times T)U(T \times P)$; EN={ie_1, ie_2,oe_1,...,oe_k}; CN={ci_1, ci_2, ci_{j+k}} W={};DC={}; $V(t_i)$=∧; Z_0={$T0$,$D0$} where $T0(p_1)$=1, $T0(p_i)$=0 and $D0(p_1)$=0;

V. ZIZO V3

The third version of ZiZo allows to model any reconfigurable distributed system with RFB formalism by modeling the different reconfiguration scenarios and save it as ".nrfb" file. It supports new probabilistic events named "input and output event of reconfiguration" and new data types named "input and output data of reconfiguration" that present the ECC_{slaves}. As shown in Fig. 7, ZiZo v3 is more than a basic RFB editor, but it allows the system designer to transform automatically the RFB system into GR-TNCES that supports random reconfigurations with real-time constraints. Each component of RFB corresponds to a GR-TNCES module. This transformation is from ".nrfb" file to ".zz" file and it helps to verify functional and real-time properties after exporting it to PRISM model checker. During the exportation, a ".pm" file is generated to contain the places and the probability between them. This process is not sufficient to prove the correctness of the RFB system as it lacks the formal properties that is described in computation tree logic (CTL) [19] and Probabilistic Computation Tree Logic (PCTL) [21] language.

VI. CASE STUDY

The presented case study consists of a surgical robotized platform *BROS* [22] that is able to change its behavior in an unpredictable way during run-time processes. BROS [23] is a new automated intelligent platform developed for an optimal orthopaedic surgery to treat supracondylar elbow fractures in children. It is a complex system that contains the following interactive components: An intelligent robotic arm P-BROS to place the pins, two intelligent manipulator arms (B-BROS1 and B-BROS2) for the blocking and the reduction of the fracture respectively, a system browser (BW), a control unit (CU), which orchestrates the various components and finally a middleware between the CU and the BW. The surgeon triggers the system and selects the operating mode. Based on the fracture coordinates determined by BW, the CU calculates the new coordinates to reduce the fracture by B-BROS2 (move the patient arm to the calculated position). CU asks MW to check the correctness of the reduction. If the reduction is successful, then the CU orders B-BROS1 to block the patient's arm. Else, the system repeats the reduction. Under the request of CU and according to the identified fracture type, P-BROS performs the single or double pinning in the elbow. Once the pinning is successful, CU asks B-BROS1 to unblock the limb.

Using "ZiZo v3", we begin with modeling the three robotic arms in BROS with RFB formalism. The whole architecture, as shown in Fig. 8, is composed of four interconnected RFBs (A: RFBmode, B: BBROS1, C: BBROS2 and D: PBROS). RFBMode has five ECC_{slaves} each corresponds to an operating mode. BBROS1 has four ECC_{slaves}: (i) ECC_B offering the automatic blocking; (ii) $ECC_{ManualB}$ deactivating the blocking if $datarec$ is equal to manual; (iii) ECC_U activating the automatic unblocking; (iv) $ECC_{ManualU}$ deactivating the robotized unblocking.

B-BROS2 has two ECC_{slaves}: ECC_R to activate reduction and ECC_{notR} to deactivate the robotized reduction;

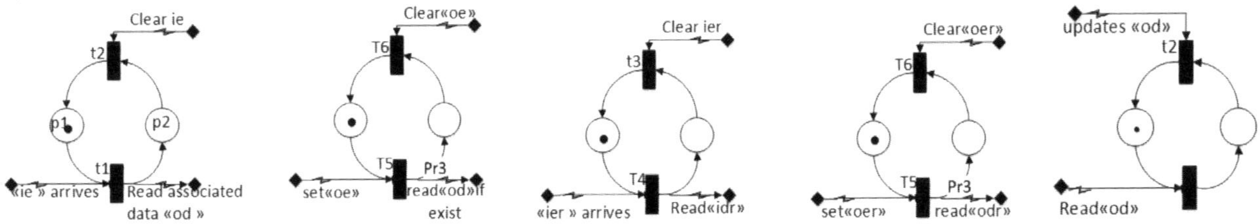

(a) GR-TNCES model of an input event "ie".

(b) GR-TNCES model of an output event "oe".

(c) GR-TNCES model of an input event of reconfiguration "ier".

(d) GR-TNCES model of an output event of reconfiguration "oer".

(e) GR-TNCES model of an output data "od".

Figure 3. GR-TNCES model of events.

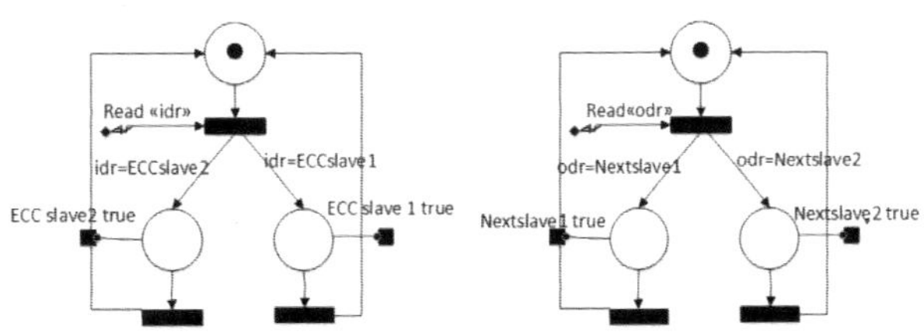

(a) GR-TNCES model of an input data of reconfiguration "idr".

(b) GR-TNCES model of an output data of reconfiguration "odr".

Figure 4. GR-TNCES model of reconfiguration data.

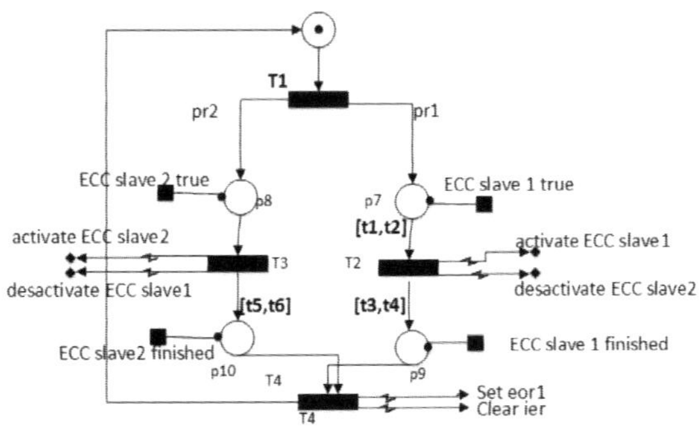

Figure 5. GR-TNCES model of an $ECC_{controller}$.

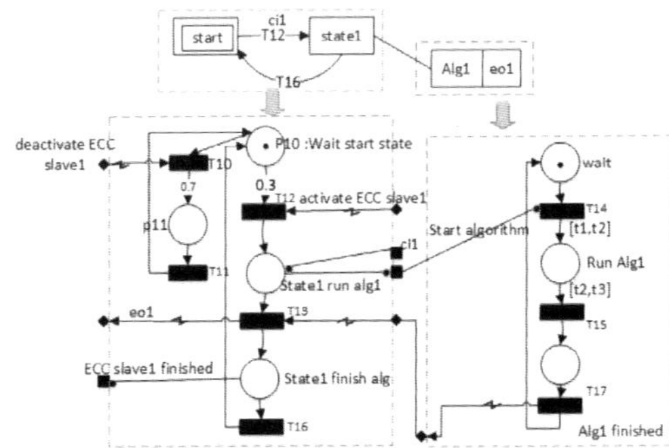

Figure 6. GR-TNCES model of ECC_{slave1}.

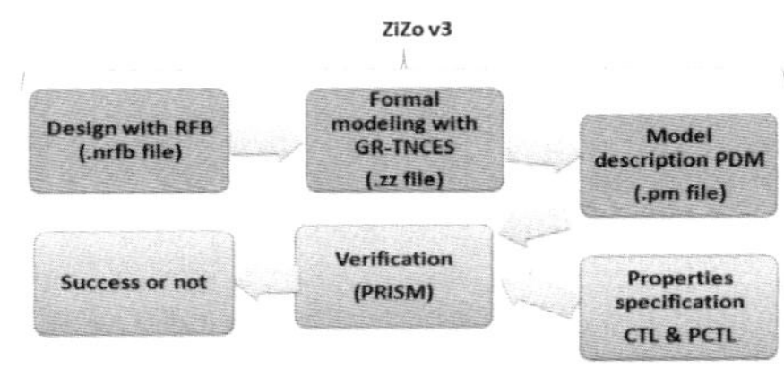

Figure 7. Flow diagram of the verification process using ZiZo and PRISM.

finally, PBROS not only depends on the operation mode but also on the fracture type that determines the pins number. It has $ECC_{ManualP}$, ECC_{1Pin} (respectively ECC_{2Pin}) encapsulating the single (respectively double) pinning algorithms that require the current P-BROS position, P-BROS orientation and the patient arm position. In the case of automatic reduction, blocking or unblocking the CU checks each functionality and returns *reductionOK*, *blockingOK* and *PinningOK* when it is successful. In the other case (manual reduction, manual blocking or manual unblocking), the system waits for these events from the surgeon to continue the operation. When exporting RFB model to GR-TNCES model, a file ".zz" is generated. The transformed model of BROS, according to the transformation rules in Section IV, is composed of four parts, as shown in Fig. 9, where: (i) A= $\sum GR-TNCES$ modules of *RFBmode*; (ii) B=$\sum GR-TNCES$ modules of *B-BROS1*; (iii) C=$\sum GR-TNCES$ modules of *B-BROS2*; (iv) and D= $\sum GR-TNCES$ modules of *P-BROS*.

Let us detail *RFBmode* presented in Fig. 10 that permits to activate one operating mode between five (AM, SAM, DMP, DMB, BM). The $ECC_{controller1}$ of "RFBmode" (Fig. 11a), reads input data of reconfiguration $idr1$. If the guard condition $ier1\&idr1 = AM$ is met (an event of reconfiguration $ier1$ arrives and $idr1$ equal to "AM") then it activates the ECC_{slave} "AM" detailed in Fig. 11b.

Fig. 12 presents the transformed GR-TNCES model of *RFBMode*, which is composed of GR-TNCES modules colored in yellow. Each module is composed of places, transitions, events and conditions that preserve the behavioral semantic of an RFB component. *ier1* module models the input event of reconfiguration $ier1 \in RFBMode$, which is associated to *idr1* that can be equal to one of the ECC_{slaves} (AM, SAM, DMP, DMB or BM). $idr6$ contains the fracture type, which

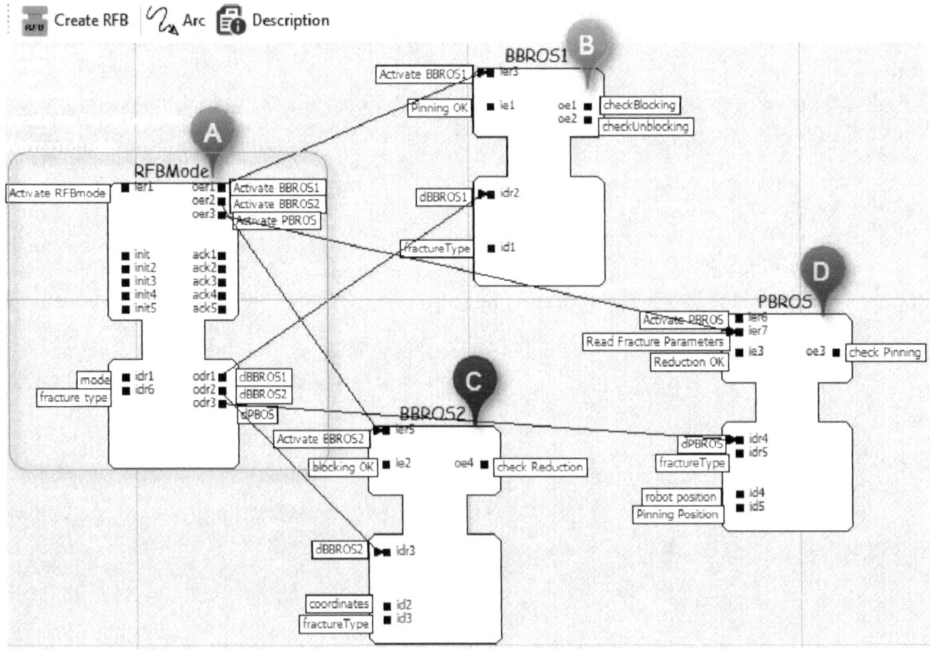

Figure 8. BROS model with RFB.

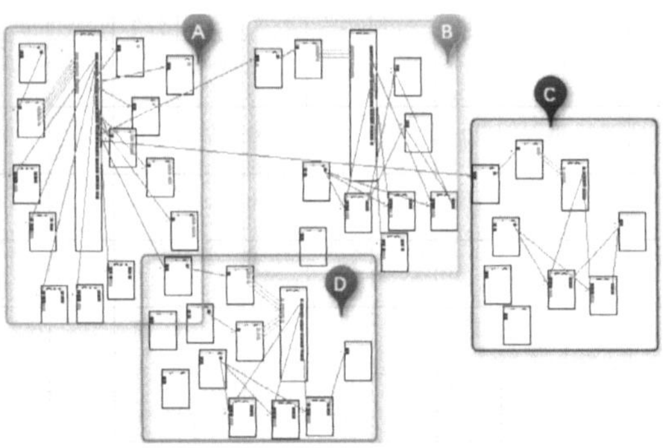

Figure 9. GR-TNCES model of the whole system.

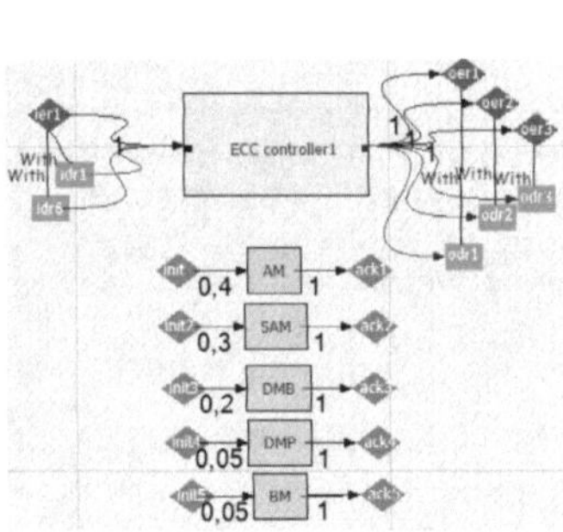

Figure 10. "RFBMode" internal components.

can be equal to IIB or IIC that involves single pin, IIA or III that involves double pins. If the pinning is robotized (the operation mode must be AM, SAM or DMP as detailed in [22]) then BROS must activate ECC_{1Pin} or ECC_{2Pin} according

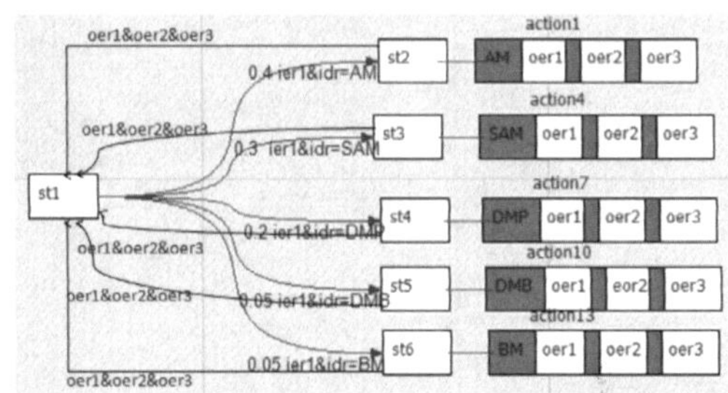

(a) $ECC_{controller}$ of "RFBMode"

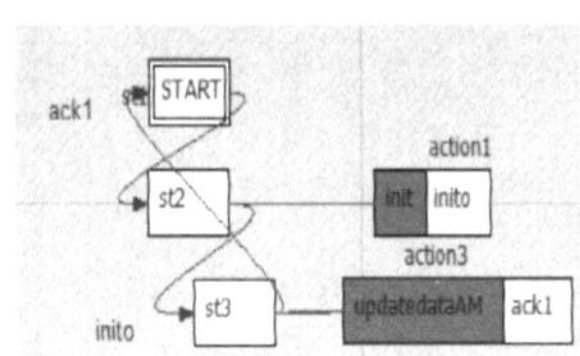

(b) ECC_{slave}AM

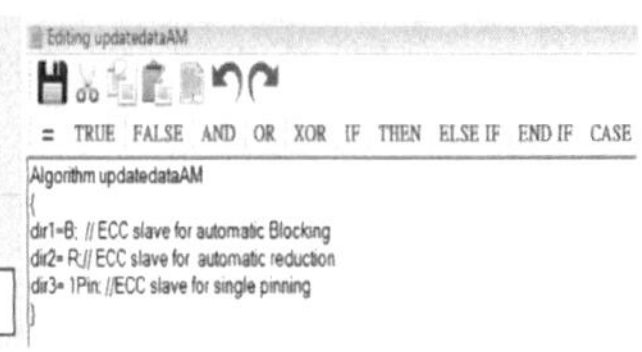

(c) Update data AM algorithm

Figure 11. RFBMode details.

to the fracture type, else $ECC_{ManualP}$ will be executed. The module $idr1$ has five output conditions, only one is true, which corresponds to the selected ECC_{slave}. $ECC_{controller}$, shown in Fig. 13a, activates the scenario to execute and deactivates the others. At the end of the algorithm execution (init0 and UpdatedataAM, UpdatedataSAM, UpdatedataDMP, UpdatedataDMB or UpdatedataBM), the slave depicted in Fig. 13b returns an output condition to the $ECC_{controller}$ and an output event ack_i where $i \in \{1..5\}$. $ECC_{controller1}$ generates three output events of reconfiguration $oer1$, $oer2$

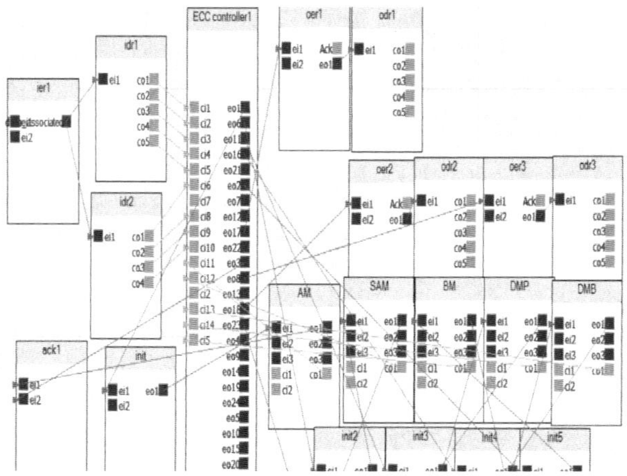

Figure 12. GR-TNCES model of RFBMode.

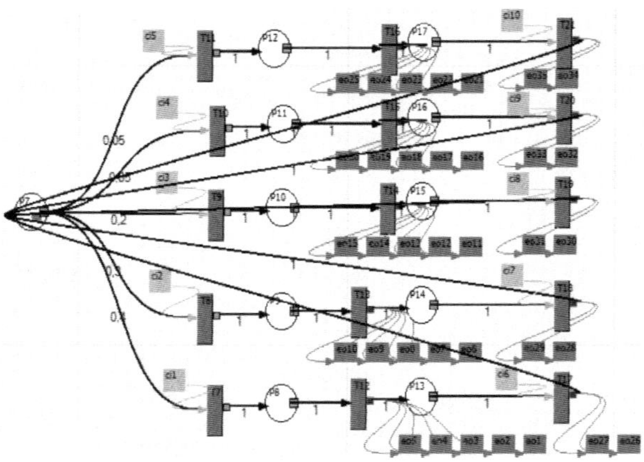

(a) $ECC_{controller}$.

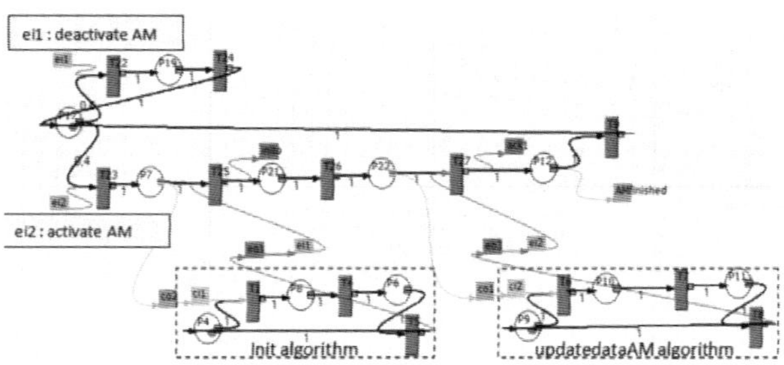

(b) ECC_{slave} AM.

Figure 13. Some GR-TNCES modules of RFBMode.

and $oer3$ that activate respectively the controller of BBROS1, BBROS2 and PBROS. Each output event of reconfiguration is associated with an output data of reconfiguration: $odr1$, $odr2$ and $odr3$ that contain ECC_{slave} in the next RFB. Therefore, $odr1$ module activates ECC_B, ECC_U, $ECC_{ManualB}$ or $ECC_{ManualU}$ module of $BBROS1$ and vice versa.

After transforming the RFB model automatically to GR-TNCES, we have verified the functional correctness and safety of individual RFBs as well as the entire system using PRISM. It is used as a model checker that offers a probabilistic model checking for run-time verification of adaptive systems and analyses systems that exhibit random or probabilistic behaviors.

ZiZo facilitates the verification process by converting the GR-TNCES model to MDP model readable by PRISM. A ".pm" file is generated that contains model descriptions written in the PRISM language. CTL and PCTL are used to check the following safety properties: (i) The deadlock problem in each RFB and in the RFBs system, using the formula: "E[F"deadlock"]", which was proven to be false; (ii) BROS never executes pinning and unblocking simultaneously thanks to the following formula "P=?[F p=1& p=2]", where "p=1" is the unblocking and "p=2" is the pinning, which returns zero. (iii) Let us attach a probability 0 to the event "reductionOK" in *BBROS1*. What is the probability to change the mode of pinning in *PBROS* from automatic to manual? Using the formula "$P = ?[Fp = 11\&(p = 12|p = 13|p = 14|p = 15)]$", where p=11 (AM), p=12 (SAM), p=13 (DMP), p=14 (DMB) and p=15 (BM), we proved that the probability of switching from automatic pinning to manual is 0.9.

VII. CONCLUSION AND FUTURE WORK

In order to enhance and simplify the system design and the verification process of reconfigurable systems, we have defined a new extension to IEC 61499 standard named RFB. We introduce in our RFB the probability associated to each reconfiguration scenario. We defined then a set of transformation rules for the RFB design to GR-TNCES model, implemented by ZiZo v3 that automates the transformation and the verification with PRISM. We have found our approach very helpful in the development process of reconfigurable distributed automation systems. In our future work, we will focus on the code generation of RFB to deploy it in manufacturing. We are also working on translating R-UML requirements to RFB design to promote reusability.

References

[1] V. Vyatkin, "IEC 61499 as enabler of distributed and intelligent automation: State-of-the-art review," Industrial Informatics, IEEE Transactions on, vol. 7, no. 4, pp. 768–781, 2011.

[2] M. N. Rooker et al., "Zero downtime reconfiguration of distributed automation systems: The epsiloncedac approach." in HoloMAS. Springer, pp. 326–337, 2007.

[3] A. Zoitl, G. Grabmair, F. Auinger, and C. Sunder, "Executing real-time constrained control applications modelled in IEC 61499 with respect to dynamic reconfiguration," in Industrial Informatics, 2005. INDIN'05. 2005 3rd IEEE International Conference on. IEEE, pp. 62–67, 2005.

[4] R. W. Brennan, M. Fletcher, and D. H. Norrie, "A holonic approach to reconfiguring real-time distributed control systems," in Multi-Agent systems and applications II. Springer, pp. 323–335, 2001.

[5] T. Kindberg, and A. Fox, System software for ubiquitous computing. IEEE pervasive computing, vol. 1, no. 1, pp.70-81, 2002.

[6] Y. Al-Safi and V. Vyatkin, "An ontology-based reconfiguration agent for intelligent mechatronic systems," in Holonic and Multi-Agent Systems for Manufacturing. Springer, pp. 114–126, 2007.

[7] M. Khalgui, O. Mosbahi, Z. Li, and H.-M. Hanisch, "Reconfiguration of distributed embedded-control systems," Mechatronics, IEEE/ASME Transactions on, vol. 16, no. 4, pp. 684–694, 2011.

[8] O. Khlifi, O. Mosbahi, M. Khalgui, and G. Frey, "GR-TNCES: new extensions of R-TNCES for modelling and verification of flexible systems under energy and memory constraints," in ICSOFT-EA 2015 - Proceedings of the 10th International Conference on Software Engineering and Applications, Colmar, Alsace, France, 20-22 July, 2015., pp. 373–380, 2015.

[9] O. Khlifi, "ZiZo 2015," http://www.aut.unisaarland.de/forschung/forschung-zizo-tool-khlifi/, [accessed: Jun,2016].

[10] M. Kwiatkowska, G. Norman, and D. Parker, "Prism: Probabilistic symbolic model checker," in Computer performance evaluation: modelling techniques and tools. Springer, pp. 200–204, 2002.

[11] Holobloc Inc., FBDK 2.5 - The Function Block Development Kit, http://www.holobloc.com/fbdk2/, [accessed: September,2016].

[12] ICS Triplex ISaGRAF., ISaGRAF Workbench, http://www.isagraf.com, [accessed: September,2016].

[13] NxtControl., nxtSTUDIO - Engineering software for all tasks, http://www.nxtcontrol.com/en/engineering/, [accessed: September,2016].

[14] V. Vyatkin and H.-M. Hanisch, "Verification of distributed control systems in intelligent manufacturing," Journal of Intelligent Manufacturing, vol. 14, no. 1, pp. 123–136, 2003.

[15] C. Pang and V. Vyatkin, "Automatic model generation of IEC 61499 function block using net condition/event systems," Industrial Informatics, 2008. INDIN 2008. 6th IEEE International Conference on, pp. 1133–1138, 2008.

[16] C. Gerber, I. Ivanova-Vasileva, and H.-M. Hanisch, "Formal modelling of IEC 61499 function blocks with integer-valued data types," Control and cybernetics, vol. 39, no. 1, pp. 197–231, 2010.

[17] C. Suender, V. Vyatkin, and A. Zoitl, "Formal validation of downtimeless system evolution in embedded automation controllers," ACM Transactions on Embedded Control Systems, vol. 12, no. 17, pp. 17:1–17:17, 2013.

[18] J. Ezpeleta, J. M. Colom, and J. Martinez, "A petri net based deadlock prevention policy for flexible manufacturing systems," IEEE transactions on robotics and automation, vol. 11, no. 2, pp. 173–184, 1995.

[19] J. Zhang, M. Khalgui, Z. Li, O. Mosbahi, and A. M. Al-Ahmari, "R-tnces: a novel formalism for reconfigurable discrete event control systems," Systems, Man, and Cybernetics: Systems, IEEE Transactions on, vol. 43, no. 4, pp. 757–772, 2013.

[20] M. O. B. Salem, "ZiZo: a tool to model, simulate and verify reconfigurable real time control systems," http://www.aut.unisaarland.de/forschung/forschung-zizo-tool-bensalem/, [accessed: Jun, 2016].

[21] V. Forejt, M. Kwiatkowska, D. Parker, H. Qu, and M. Ujma, "Incremental runtime verification of probabilistic systems," in Runtime verification. Springer, pp. 314–319, 2012.

[22] M. O. B. Salem, O. Mosbahi, M. Khalgui, and G. Frey, "Zizo: Modeling, simulation and verification of reconfigurable real-time control tasks sharing adaptive resources - application to the medical project BROS," in HEALTHINF 2015 - Proceedings of the International Conference on Health Informatics, Lisbon, Portugal, 12-15 January, 2015, pp. 20–31, 2015.

[23] M. O. B. Salem, "BROS: a robotic platform for the treatment of the supracondylar humerus fracture," http://www.aut.unisaarland.de/forschung/forschung-bros-platform/, [accessed: Jun, 2016].

Service and Workflow Engineering based on Semantic Web Technologies

Volkan Gezer and Simon Bergweiler

German Research Center for Artificial Intelligence (DFKI)
Innovative Factory Systems
Kaiserslautern, Germany
Email: firstname.lastname@dfki.de

***Abstract*—This paper presents the concept and implementation of a cloud-based infrastructure platform and tailored tools for graphical user interaction. The goal is the creation of a platform that allows users to generate workflows for their experiments in the field of product design and quality assurance without any knowledge of service engineering and the underlying Semantic Web technologies. An experiment is described as workflow and consists of orchestrated services from several vendors that encapsulate specific tasks. One advantage of this approach is the combination of a cloud-based platform with high-performance computing. Services that encapsulates complex calculation procedures can be outsourced to specific servers. This results in tremendous time savings and allows experts to carry out more experiments with products, which was omitted due to the complexity and the required computing power until now. The possibility to conduct these experiments improves the productive know-how of the companies and enhances the products they are selling.**

***Keywords*–Cloud infrastructure; Semantic Workflows; Semantic Web services; graphical workflow interface.**

I. INTRODUCTION

Nowadays, cloud-based solutions are part of the daily life, and their usage is increasing day by day. These solutions increase the mobility of data by allowing access from multiple locations with minimum effort [1]. In this paper, we present the concept and implementation of a flexible cloud-based platform for the vendor-independent integration of Semantic Web services in the engineering domain. This platform is provided as Infrastructure as a Service (IaaS), and is able to combine and orchestrate Web services. Involving semantic technologies inside a cloud-based solution significantly improves usability by structuring the data in a standardized way that these can be understood by machines and humans. The structured data can be utilized to create interoperable and vendor-independent applications, and thereby avoid vendor lock-in problems [2]. The platform enables experts from various application domains to independently plan and execute their experiments with strong calculation procedures, e.g., to check the quality of products and their compliance with construction rules by comparison of 3D-models, or to identify weaknesses and subsequently improve the positive effects of their products. Each experiment is described as workflow that orchestrates services from different vendors. Each service encapsulates specific tasks, calculation procedures or complex sub-systems and require highly scalable computing clusters for their execution within an acceptable time-frame. Therefore, to provide an added value, the developed platform is combined with a cluster of high-performance computers spread across different virtualization solutions, which take over the calculation of complex tasks. This results in enormous time savings and allows experts to carry out more experiments with products, which was neglected due to the complexity of the task and the required computing resources until now. The developed tailored tools of this cloud-based platform, described below as core components, allow engineering companies or software providers to integrate their Software as a Service (SaaS) and orchestrate them in a specific workflow, seamlessly supported by graphical user interfaces and without requiring specific skills or knowledge of the underlying Semantic Web technologies. The developed solution uses standardized Web-based technologies and all workflows can be executed using a Web browser, requiring no additional software. Due to this distributed architecture, the platform offers optimal conditions for both short and long-running experiments.

Section II introduces used technologies and describes the topics under consideration. For a better understanding, Section III describes the requirements in the engineering domain and leads over to Section IV, methodology and concept of the developed approach. The next section describes the architecture and developed core components. The paper ends with a conclusion and an outlook on future work and extensions.

II. BACKGROUND

Web services are designed to support machine-to-machine interaction over a network and allow interoperable communication [3]. With the help of description languages, which will be discussed in the upcoming sections, Web services create communication between peer-platforms, prevent vendor dependency and increase reusability.

A. Web Services Description Language

The Web Service Description Language (WSDL) is a language- and platform independent XML-based interface definition language, designed with the aim to create a standardized mechanism for the description of Web services. It describes SOAP-based Web services in detail, their technical input and output parameters, ports, data types, and how services must be invoked. With this machine-readable description language, the automatic detection and execution of Web services is possible. A ready-revised language draft was submitted to the World Wide Web Consortium (W3C) [4], but only version 2.0 was standardized and proclaimed as W3C recommendation [5]. Unfortunately, WSDL is a lower level interface description language that addresses the technical mechanisms and aspects of Web services, and it does not reflect the functionality of a service. Furthermore, it is difficult to create and understand for humans. In this approach, WSDL is used for the technical description of Web services, their input and output parameters, and the SOAP messaging mechanism.

B. Technologies of the Semantic Web

The development of the current Web to the "Semantic Web" is pervasive. Efforts are aiming to add annotations to things and objects of daily life. Through the help of annotations, the vision of the Semantic Web allows better cooperation between people and computers; well-defined meanings are attached to information [6]. The Resource Description Framework (RDF) is one of the most important data formats that has been developed to implement this vision. The Semantic Web combines technologies that deal with the description of information and knowledge sources, such as ontologies, RDF triple stores, and Semantic Web services [7] [8]. Ontologies allow the definition of a vocabulary of a dedicated application domain and define for this purpose concepts and properties. These concepts can in turn be connected by relations, which promise a significant value, when conclusions are drawn about these structures. In that field, the W3C defines his recommendations as an open standard like RDF(S) [7][9] and the Web Ontology Language (OWL) [10].

In contrast to a complex and comprehensive infrastructure that tries to solve all problems of the interaction and communication of distributed applications, the Semantic Web Technology Stack, depicted in Fig. 1, is a family of modular standards mostly standardized by the W3C. Each of these standards aims at another part of problem or another sub-problem.

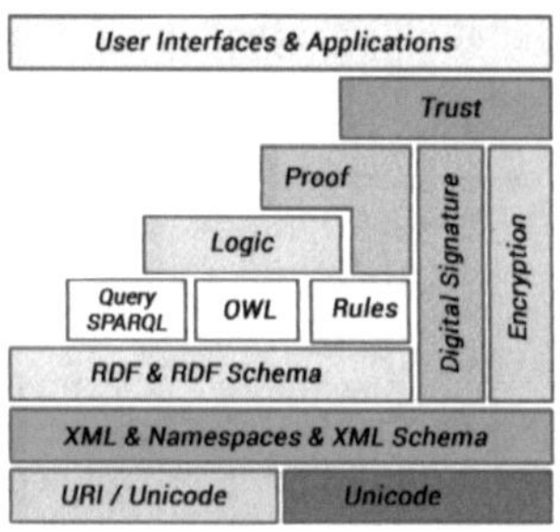

Figure 1. Semantic Web technology stack.

This stack of Semantic Web technologies describes the vision of the W3C to create a Web of linked data. The idea of open data stores on the Web, the ability to build vocabularies, and write rules for handling data based on these empowered technologies, such as RDF, OWL, and the SPARQL Protocol And RDF Query Language (SPARQL) [11].

C. Semantic Web Services

In the recent years, the tendency towards Semantic Web technologies increased the research in the domain, results in an elevated number of available ontologies as well as standards recommended by the W3C. To widen the scope of applicability, one of the submitted ontologies to W3C was the Web Ontology Language for Web Services (OWL-S), which allowed services on the Web to be found, executed, and monitored. The OWL-S ontology is designed on top of OWL with extensions to make service discovery, invocation, composition, and monitoring possible. The provided structure also allowed these operations to be performed autonomously, when desired [12]. Based on the previously described technologies, domain models must be created to form an important conceptual basis. Therefore, parts of the dedicated knowledge domain are categorized and structured in a machine readable form. OWL-S [12] extends this base to a set of constructs that relate to properties, specialties and dependencies of the Web service level and is also machine readable and processable.

A concrete service description in OWL-S is separated in several parts. Fig. 2 shows the main concepts and relations of a service model in OWL-S: service profile, service model, service grounding, and for our approach important, the processes. The *Service Profile* is used for service discovery and describes the functionality of the service and contains information about the service provider. Furthermore, this profile reflects the overall functionality of a service with its precondition, input and output types, features, and benefits.

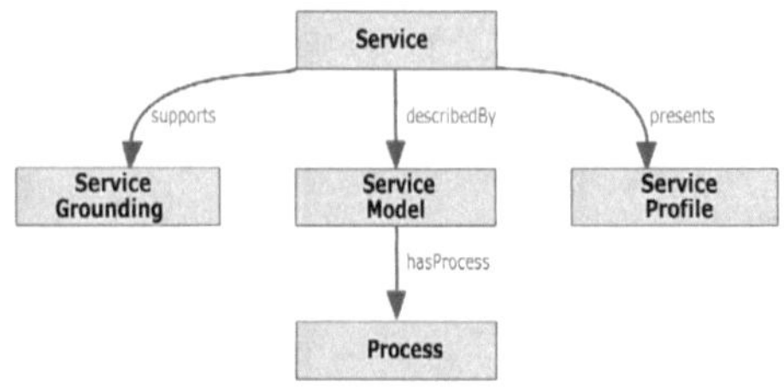

Figure 2. Main Web service concepts in OWL-S.

Any Web services provided with a WSDL description and SOAP interface can be integrated into the infrastructure and converted into semantic descriptions as long as they satisfy the requirements. However, for a Web service that is converted into a Semantic Web service with the help of an upper ontology, the following types of the OWL-S Submission [12] are required:

- The *Service Profile* provides information to describe a service to a requester. The profile provides three types of information: the service creator, the service functionality, and the service characteristics [12].
- The *Service Model* is a mandatory type for the description how a Web service works. The model describes the inputs, outputs, preconditions and effects. It also specifies the *Process* concepts and their execution order. The process description consists of simple atomic processes or complex composite processes that are sometimes abstract and not executable. Each function provided by the service is considered as an *Atomic Process*, whereas combined multiple services are named as *Composite Service*.
- The *Service Grounding* stores the detailed technical communication information on protocols and formats. This concept provides the physical location to the technical description realized in WSDL. This WSDL-file is called when the service is executed, as well as during conversion process to retrieve the technical inputs and outputs of the service.

The listed types provide basis for OWL-S to create relations, which are utilized for improved interoperability. However, the relations generated using only OWL-S ontology form the minimal relationship for services, enough to be operated. If the usage scenario requires involvement of additional relations, these must be defined creating a *meta-ontology* and including it inside a semantic repository [13].

D. Workflows

Services provide functionality for special tasks, but complex tasks in the engineering domain usually consist of multiple steps. Therefore, one service is not sufficient and an orchestration of services is needed. The complete service chain is described in a *workflow*. Depending on the domain, a *workflow* can have multiple definitions, but in the context of this paper, a workflow will be considered as a set and ordered list of chained up Web services provided with a WSDL file and a SOAP interface to perform a specific task with or without user interaction.

Determined by the complexity, multiple workflows can be necessary to finalize the task. In this case, with the help of semantic descriptions, workflows can be grouped and chained up to create "sub-workflows." Workflows as well as sub-workflows are stored in semantic repositories. Similar to Semantic Web services, they are reusable and their descriptions are updated without causing any fragmentation.

E. Triple Stores

Computational tasks often require collection and storage of the results for further usage. Storage of information without a structured form increases the complexity and the time to access the data, and reducing the flexibility for further modifications and enhancements [14] causing to fragmentation problems. To address this issue, databases play the role as containers, which collect and organize the data for swift future access [15].

Semantic repositories are similar to the database management systems (DBMS) in terms of providing functionality for organization, storage, and querying the data, but differ from them in terms of the type of organization and data representation. Unlike DBMS, semantic repositories use schemata to structure the data thus allow defining the data stored to set relations between. Regarding to data representation, semantic repositories work with flexible and generic physical data models, which allow merging other ontologies "on the fly" and relate the data among merged schemata [16]. As OWL-S is based on OWL, which is built on top of RDF, see Section II-B, the data operations are performed using the same RDF structure. This structure provides descriptions to query the data, and allows optimal extension of relations allowing multiple use. The Sesame framework [17] is one RDF store solution, which can be used in this context. It creates, processes, edits, stores, and queries RDF data, therefore it is chosen to serve as a storage for the framework.

F. Related Work

The Business Process Execution Language (BPEL) is a language for describing and executing business processes in general. It provides an XML-based syntax and allows data manipulation for data processing and data flow. It also allows orchestration of services, after specifying the service set and the service execution order [18].

For the languages OWL-S and BPEL, there exist tools for the automated execution of Web services described in WSDL. They also permit implementations in any programming languages as long as they provide valid WSDL descriptions. Different from BPEL, OWL-S facilitates Semantic Web technologies, which make the structure meaningful for human and machines and allow automated design and orchestration of services, whereas BPEL does not [19].

The execution order of services is usually defined using a design tool (textual or graphical) which is then executed and monitored using an engine. For BPEL, Apache BPEL Designer and JBoss Tools BPEL Editor can be given as examples to design tools, whereas Oracle BPEL Process Manager, Apache ODE, IBM WebSphere Process Server, and Microsoft BizTalk Server can be listed as examples for execution and monitoring.

Using OWL-S increases the interoperability and enables automatic orchestration between the services, but it requires a deep knowledge in the domain. Hence, there are few editors available for OWL-S. However, all of them must be locally installed to be used. To create complex workflows, Protégé OWL-S Editor [20], which is a plug-in for Protégé, can be utilized. Nevertheless, the usage of this plug-in also requires advanced knowledge in the domain. To convert Web services into Semantic Web services, a design tool and an execution engine are necessary.

In another approach, created in the context of the THESEUS funding program, a framework for the discovery, integration, processing, and fusion of Semantic Web services is described [21]. According to a user request, the framework identifies and assembles matching services for problem solving and creates a plan for the composition and execution order. The focus is on the matching of heterogeneous services and the fusion of all gathered information in real time. The harmonizing and mapping of knowledge is carried out based on ontologies.

The advantage of our approach is the continuous integration of services, from the UI to an automatic executable experiment, described as a specific workflow. Within the developed infrastructure, specific services can be deployed and assigned to workflows graphically, without detailed knowledge of the underlying Semantic Web technologies.

III. SCENARIO

In the engineering domain, a conventional practice for quality assurance of the manufactured final product are comparison checks against the virtual designed product model. This accuracy check is performed by comparing two 3D models. First a scanning process creates and transfers accurate points, and in this way a virtual 3D model is created. The entire model consists of millions of 3D points, which must be matched and compared with the designed product model to find out the discrepancies by calculating the distances of points in both, the designed model and the virtual clone of the final product [22] [23].

The manufacturer of these big turbine blades uses different tools to perform this comparison task and these supplementary tools generate additional license and training costs. The handling of different software solutions requires many hours of work. By using the workflow and service infrastructure and the distributed High Performance Computing (HPC) solution described here, the comparison time is significantly reduced. These advantages allow the company to focus on quality measurement and also increase the capacity of the company for initiating new projects. Fig. 3 shows a complete Kaplan turbine (a), one blade that is to be evaluated (b) and the scanned and virtualized 3D model with color-coded comparison results (c) [23]. The virtual model is created by an open-source tool for rendering and visualization [24].

To perform such a comparison task, the complete workflow has to be formally described. The workflow description defines that two CAD files must be loaded and compared by the help of additional comparison services. These services make compatibility checks, they check whether components of the production environment created by different tools in different formats for Computer-Aided Design (CAD) and Computer-Aided Engineering (CAE) fit together, by comparing compatible

Figure 3. A complete manufactured Kaplan turbine (a), its single turbine blade (b) and the color-coded comparison of its scan and design (c).

heights and dimensions.

IV. CONCEPT

The cloud-based infrastructure allows to orchestrate services individually, formalized by a workflow. To design the workflow, a special tooling is needed, where each step in the workflow or each state change is assigned to a service. To solve this problem, all available technical Web service interfaces needs to be described using standards, such as WSDL. Based on this technical description with its functions, input, and output types, a semantic Web service model, described in OWL-S, is generated and integrated into the semantic repository. This transformation and conversion is automatically performed by the provided converter libraries, shown in Fig. 4. As depicted, the creator retrieves the service type and the URL of the WSDL file and converts the service into a specific instantiated Semantic Web service description that is stored in the semantic repository. Using the cloud-based approach, it is easily possible to execute the service execution task in an HPC cluster, which extremely saves computation time.

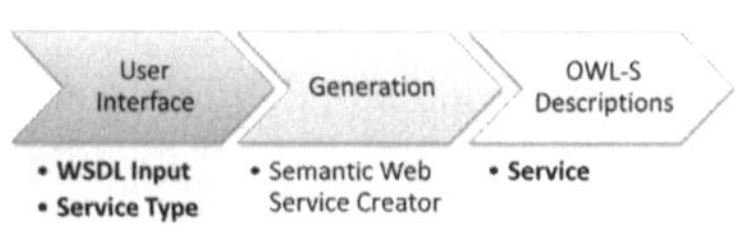

Figure 4. Generation of services in OWL-S.

However, in this approach three service categories must be differentiated:

- Synchronous Service
- Asynchronous Service
- Asynchronous Web Application

These service categories are disjoint, each Web service can only be assigned to one category of the service repository. Standard Web services belong to the *Synchronous Service* category. Whenever a request is made, they must respond within 60 seconds, which is defined as default timeout limit in SOAP. Every service, which does not require an interaction with the user is part of this category. An *Asynchronous Service* is a special category, which returns information whenever the calling component checks the status. Unlike the previous category, asynchronous services can display feedback messages and these services can last days or even weeks to complete. A response to the calling component reports the status by telling either the service is completed or still ongoing. Lastly, the *Asynchronous Web Application* category contains Web services, which are similar to asynchronous services, but without a status check. This type of service is used by interactive Web pages in the Web portal.

With this kind of service categorization, it is possible to support users and their specific needs to complete their tasks with synchronous or asynchronous processes executed in the background. A detailed description of the system design that uses annotations for workflow modeling is given in Section V. A service orchestration is performed by using a component for workflow editing to create a semantic workflow description. Fig. 5 summarizes the generation of workflows. First the workflows define the order in which the services have to be executed. In the process chain, the output of a service is passed to the input of the next service. A tool supporting graphical user input has the advantage that the user must not have a detailed knowledge of OWL-S to describe a workflow. The graphically sketched sequence of services is formalized in a workflow and stored in an XML-based meta-format that serves as input for the conversion into OWL-S.

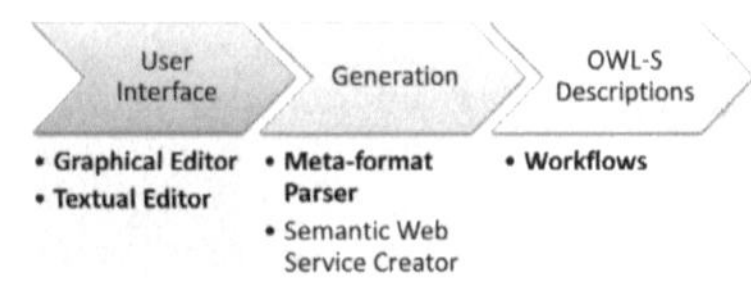

Figure 5. Generation of workflows in OWL-S.

The service domain is structured by an upper model for the generic description and vocabulary of services and workflows in OWL-S. It defines how services must be described and specified, using annotations and technical descriptions. The detailed knowledge of different application domains is represented by several domain ontologies that describe detailed application functionality.

V. INTERACTION OF CORE COMPONENTS

The creation of an interoperable and flexible platform provided as IaaS requires an embodiment of core components, which are compatible with each other. These core components are presented as Web services with a technical interface description in WSDL and form the infrastructure and host all the functionality:

- *Semantic Repository for services and workflows*: This component hosts the OWL-S descriptions of services and workflows.
- *Workflow Editor*: The graphical workflow editor assists in the creation of workflows and associates service functionality. The defined workflows are transferred into an XML-based meta-format, based on a predefined schema.
- *Semantic Web Service Creator*: This component creates the Semantic Web services out of WSDL. In another context, it creates semantic workflow descriptions in OWL-S based on the XML-meta-format, introduced by the Workflow Editor.

- *Workflow Manager process control system*: This component manages, orchestrates, monitors workflows, and checks permissions of the users for the execution.

Vendor specific Web services provide and wrap functionality for specific software components of different complexity levels. Generic services are provided to load data structures with different formats, e.g., Computer-Aided Engineering (CAE) and Computer-Aided Design (CAD) data. Higher services encapsulate complex calculations and comparison operators or even provide the interface to third-party systems to perform complex calculations. The service providers are able to deploy the WSDL description of their Web services via the Workflow Editor (WFE) in the Web portal. The Semantic Web Service Creator uses the absolute URL to the WSDL description of the service to generate the semantic Web service descriptions in OWL-S, and it stores and registers them in the Semantic Repository including the inputs and outputs of the services. The basic requirement for all saved workflows and services are unique names. Each Semantic Repository is based on a central domain model, formalized as an OWL ontology, that describes the input and output types for the matchmaking process of the services.

Fig. 6 gives an overview of the interaction of the core components of the developed platform. The main user interface of the developed platform is a Web portal, and it translates user actions into core component specific requests, e.g., workflow design, workflow and service execution, service monitoring, and result management. With the graphical interface of the Workflow Editor, the user gets access to the services stored in the Service Repository and services dedicated to experiments can be chained up to create dedicated workflows, such as for the comparison of 3D models. Each created workflow is stored in the Semantic Repository and can be found by querying with simple properties. To store the workflows, the graphical contents of the workflows are transferred into a XML-based meta-format. This format serves as input for the Semantic Web Service Creator that generates the workflow descriptions in OWL-S.

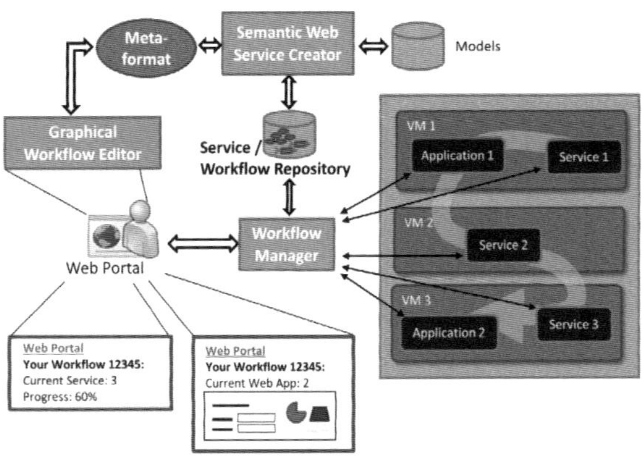

Figure 6. Overview of the interactions of the core components.

The Workflow Manager (WFM) component is used for the management and execution of individual predetermined workflows. Each workflow is a formalized orchestration of Semantic Web services and consists of at least one integrated service or many complex services, defined in sub-workflows. In the execution task, the component processes the individual workflows and accordingly queries the listed services in the defined order. If the service execution is completed and the answer of a service is received, the next step in the sequence is activated. The results of respective services are unified and added to a single representation structure, which is passed at the end of all processing steps to the UI of the Web portal.

For each workflow, the manager initiates processing procedures and tracks the progress individually. Before starting a workflow, it checks whether the user has permission to run it to prevent unauthorized execution. It also provides a monitoring functionality, which allows users to leave the workflow anytime and return at later stage to continue where they left off. This maximizes the benefits of such a cloud-based platform, supporting access anytime and from any desktop or mobile device with internet access. If the workflow does not need user input, the WFM is even able to complete it automatically and display its results to the user at a later time. As explained in the previous sections, services of different vendors can be used that are implemented by different programming techniques and run within the cloud on different application servers. But during the lifetime of a workflow, the user does not need to know, where the services are stored and how the data is forwarded to the next service. The manager component retrieves the service descriptions and performs the tasks without user notification and the complexity of all associated services within a workflow remains hidden from the user.

An example of a graphical workflow is shown in Fig. 7. The execution order is represented by dashed arrows inside WFE and the blue blocks are the individual workflow steps. The green marked block is an HPC sub-workflow, which executes the service in an HPC server environment. This sub-workflow consists of three tasks: (1) *pre-processing task* to generate the command to be executed by HPC process, (2) *HPC command task*, which receives the command by user interface and gives feedback to the user, and (3) *post-processor task*, which converts the output from the HPC process into application specific output.

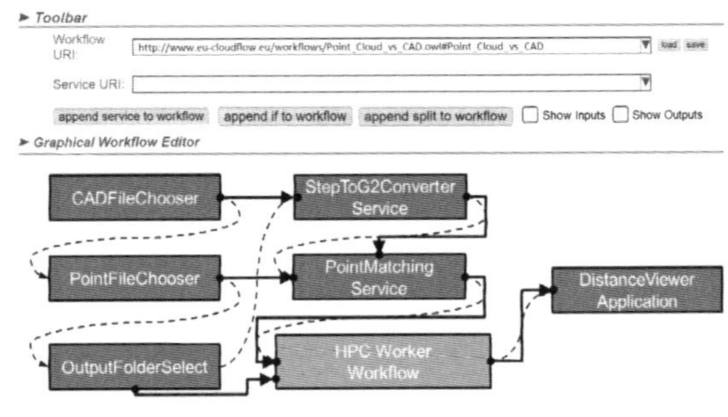

Figure 7. The graphical workflow editor UI shows the scenario workflow.

Based on their defined service types, synchronous or asynchronous, services are differentiated and executed by the execution engine of the WFM. The services for the pre- and post-processing tasks are implemented as *Synchronous Services*. Whereas, the HPC operating procedure is implemented as *Asynchronous Service*. If the duration of a Web service execution cannot be predicted, the service must be implemented as an *Asynchronous Service*, which provides its status via a method. This method is periodically requested by the WFM.

As a result, this method is able to return HTML feedback, which is displayed on the Web portal. The usage of pre- and post-processing tasks varies from application to application.

If a Web service provides an UI to interact, the service must be implemented as an *Asynchronous Web Application*. Services that belong to this category are implemented similar to *Asynchronous Services*, but contrarily do not need to deliver their status. This service type explicitly tells the WFM that the task is completed. After receiving this notification, the WFM performs the next step and gives feedback on the Web portal.

VI. Conclusion and Future Work

This paper explained the concept and realization of a flexible cloud-based infrastructure platform, which involves Semantic Web technologies and tailored tools for the creation, execution, and management of workflows and conducted services by graphical user interface. The realized platform satisfies the requirements for the development and execution of experiments defined as workflows, without requiring knowledge on High Performance Computing or other underlying technologies of the Semantic Web. The platform offers an UI for the integration of Web services, described in WSDL. These services are automatically converted into Semantic Web services, without requiring specific knowledge of used complex Semantic Web technologies, such as OWL and OWL-S. With another graphical user interface, the Workflow Editor, the services can be orchestrated within the meaning of the experiment can be orchestrated and stored as workflow descriptions. For the execution of the experiment, the Workflow Manager uses these descriptions as a basis. One advantage of this approach is the combination of the created platform with high-performance servers. Complex tasks are outsourced to these servers and this results in enormous time savings and allows the experts to carry out more experiments with products, which was omitted due to the complexity and the required computing power until now. Of course, the possibility to conduct these experiments leads to an enormous increase in expert knowledge.

In future, the Workflow Editor will be able to give recommendations to the user, for an easier dynamic workflow design. A dynamic workflow formalizes an orchestration of services, supported by an automated matchmaking process that provides adequate services ordered by their confidence values, which is only possible using Semantic Web technologies. Furthermore, the Workflow Editor automatically inserts converter services into the workflow, just for adjustment of input and output types, e.g., convert units of measurement and file formats.

Acknowledgments

This research was funded in part by the 7th Framework Program of the European Union, project number 609100 (project CloudFlow). The responsibility for this publication lies with the authors.

References

[1] T. Barton, "Cloud Computing," in E-Business mit Cloud Computing. Springer Fachmedien Wiesbaden, 2014, pp. 41–52.

[2] A. Ranabahu and A. Sheth, "Semantics Centric Solutions for Application and Data Portability in Cloud Computing," in Cloud Computing Technology and Science (CloudCom), 2010 IEEE Second International Conference on, 2010, pp. 234–241.

[3] R. Cyganiak, D. Wood, and M. Lanthaler, "Web Services Architecture," W3C Working Group Note, 2004, [retrieved: July 2016]. [Online]. Available: https://www.w3.org/TR/2004/NOTE-ws-arch-20040211/

[4] E. Christensen, F. Curbera, G. Meredith, and S. Weerawarana, "Web Services Description Language (WSDL) 1.1," W3C, W3C Note, March 2001, [retrieved: July 2016]. [Online]. Available: http://www.w3.org/TR/wsdl

[5] R. Chinnici, J.-J. Moreau, A. Ryman, and S. Weerawarana, "Web Services Description Language (WSDL) Version 2.0 Part 1: Core Language," W3C Recommendation, 2007, [retrieved: July 2016]. [Online]. Available: https://www.w3.org/TR/wsdl20/

[6] T. Berners-Lee, J. Hendler, and O. Lassila, "The Semantic Web," Scientific American, 2001, [retrieved: July 2016]. [Online]. Available: http://www.jeckle.de/files/tblSW.pdf

[7] G. Klyne and J. J. Carroll, "Resource Description Framework (RDF): Concepts and Abstract Syntax," W3C Recommendation, 2004. [Online]. Available: http://www.w3.org/TR/2004/REC-rdf-concepts-20040210/

[8] P. Hitzler, M. Krötzsch, and S. Rudolph, Foundations of Semantic Web Technologies. Chapman & Hall/CRC, 2009.

[9] R. Cyganiak, D. Wood, and M. Lanthaler, "RDF 1.1 Concepts and Abstract Syntax," W3C Recommendation, 2004, [retrieved: July 2016]. [Online]. Available: http://www.w3.org/TR/2014/REC-rdf11-concepts-20140225/

[10] P. F. Patel-Schneider, P. Hayes, and I. Horrocks, "OWL Web Ontology Language Semantics and Abstract Syntax," Feb. 2004, [retrieved: July 2016]. [Online]. Available: http://www.w3.org/TR/2004/REC-owl-semantics-20040210/

[11] I. Horrocks, B. Parsia, P. Patel-Schneider, and J. Hendler, "Semantic Web Architecture: Stack or Two Towers?" in Principles and Practice of Semantic Web Reasoning, Third International Workshop, PPSWR 2005, Dagstuhl Castle, Germany, F. Fages and S. Soliman, Eds. Berlin, Heidelberg: Springer Berlin Heidelberg, 2005, pp. 37–41.

[12] D. Martin et al., "OWL-S: Semantic Markup for Web Services," 2004, [retrieved: July 2016]. [Online]. Available: http://www.w3.org/Submission/2004/SUBM-OWL-S-20041122/

[13] S. Bergweiler, "A Flexible Framework for Adaptive Knowledge Retrieval and Fusion for Kiosk Systems and Mobile Clients," in Eighth International Conference on Mobile Ubiquitous Computing, Systems, Services and Technologies (UBICOMM 2014), International Academy, Research, and Industry Association (IARIA). IARIA, 8 2014, pp. 164–171.

[14] C. Casanave, "Designing a Semantic Repository - Integrating architectures for reuse and integration," 2007, [retrieved: July 2016]. [Online]. Available: https://www.w3.org/2007/06/eGov-dc/papers/SemanticRepository.pdf

[15] "Webster Database Definition," [retrieved: July 2016]. [Online]. Available: http://www.merriam-webster.com/dictionary/database

[16] Ontotext, "GraphDB - Semantic Repository," [retrieved: July 2016]. [Online]. Available: http://ontotext.com/products/graphdb/semantic-repository/

[17] Sesame Framework Contributors, "Sesame Java Framework," [retrieved: July 2016]. [Online]. Available: http://rdf4j.org/about.docbook?view

[18] "Web Services Business Process Execution Language Version 2.0," OASIS Web Services Business Process Execution Language (WSBPEL) Technical Commitee, 2007, [retrieved: July 2016]. [Online]. Available: http://docs.oasis-open.org/wsbpel/2.0/OS/wsbpel-v2.0-OS.html

[19] S. Bansal, A. Bansal, G. Gupta, and M. B. Blake, "Generalized semantic Web service composition," Service Oriented Computing and Applications, vol. 10, no. 2, 2016, pp. 111–133.

[20] D. Elenius et al., "The OWL-S editor - a development tool for semantic web services," in ESWC, 2005, pp. 78–92.

[21] S. Bergweiler, "Interactive service composition and query," in Towards the Internet of Services: The Theseus Program. Springer Berlin Heidelberg, 2014, pp. 169–184.

[22] C. Stahl, E. Bellos, C. Altenhofen, and J. Hjelmervik, "Flexible Integration of Cloud-based Engineering Services using Semantic Technologies," in Industrial Technology (ICIT), 2015 IEEE International Conference on, 2015, pp. 1520–1525.

[23] Stellba, "Comparing CAD Models with 3D Scanned Manufactured Parts on the Cloud," [retrieved: July 2016]. [Online]. Available: http://eu-cloudflow.eu/experiments/first-wave/experiment_6.html

[24] C. Dyken et al., "A framework for OpenGL client-server rendering," in Cloud Computing Technology and Science (CloudCom), 2012 IEEE 4th International Conference, 2012, pp. 729–734.

CloudFlow - An Infrastructure for Engineering Workflows in the Cloud

Håvard Heitlo Holm*, Jon M. Hjelmervik* and Volkan Gezer†
*Heterogeneous Computing Group
SINTEF ICT
Oslo, Norway
Emails: havard.heitlo.holm@sintef.no
and jon.m.hjelmervik@sintef.no
†Innovative Factory Systems (IFS)
German Research Center for Artificial Intelligence (DFKI)
Kaiserslautern, Germany
Email: volkan.gezer@dfki.de

Abstract—**In this paper, we present a framework for easy integration of existing software solutions in a cloud environment. We aim to allow software providers to offer their products in the Cloud through a common web portal. Central in the framework is workflows, where independent software solutions can be chained together to solve the users tasks in a unified way. One of the main challenges addressed here, is facilitating workflows spanning multiple software vendors and cloud solutions. The framework is validated by a range of experiments, consisting of both software vendors and end users, from the context of manufacturing industries, and offer unique and ubiquitous access to integrated workflows.**

Keywords–Workflows; Cloud computing; HPC; Semantic descriptions; One-stop-shop.

I. INTRODUCTION

Cloud computing is now a natural part of the daily life, both professionally and for consumers. Users are expecting to have access to all their software and data independent of which computer they are using, which have revolutionized how data is consumed and shared.

Cloud providers are continuously extending and improving their tools to make it easier to deploy software in their solutions. These developments have made cloud computing attractive for software vendors, and many companies offer cloud integration throughout their product range. However, it can also be very tempting to make the cloud integration very tight, which in turn locks the software vendor into the cloud provider's ecosystem. New solutions, including UberCloud [1] and Cloud Modelling Language (CloudML) [2], target this challenge by offering platforms that are neutral to cloud providers, while aiming at making it as easy as possible to offer cloud based solutions for their costumers' software.

Not all tasks can be completed using a single application, but are best solved using a workflow where data is transferred from one application to another. The ideal workflow may consist of software from different vendors, which should seamlessly work together. To achieve this, it is not sufficient to give access to software in a cloud solution, the interoperability between the different applications and software suits must also be targeted. This paper proposes to add semantic descriptions to the available software, as well as their input and outputs. The semantic descriptions are used to chain compatible services into complete workflows. Furthermore, data formats should be based on open standards, or come with conversion tools to and from standard formats. In this paper, we present the CloudFlow Infrastructure, aiming at providing the technology platform for a one-stop-shop for cloud based workflows. This work builds upon the initial results by Stahl et al. [3].

The infrastructure described here can be applied to any business area, however, data formats and descriptions must be adapted to the application domain. However, currently the focus is on manufacturing industries, with a special focus on the needs of small businesses. The examples used in this paper therefore come from this domain, though the technology is neutral to application domain. In manufacturing industries, different software suits are used across the lifetime of their products, from design through numerical analysis through quality assurance and maintenance. Small companies in this market often find it too expensive to install the different solutions locally, due to hardware costs, installation overhead and license costs. This may cause loss in quality of their products due to insufficient analysis, and overly expensive design phases due to inefficient work procedures. For such companies, having access to a cloud solution that spans over different clouds and software providers, all integrated in tailored workflows, will not only save time and cost, but also improve their final product.

Larger companies may already have a server infrastructure and prefer to store their data within their control. These companies may still benefit from the integrated workflows and access from everywhere inside the secure network. It is therefore important that private cloud solutions also are supported to host the CloudFlow Infrastructure.

End users that are familiar with a software solution may be reluctant to shift providers when moving from a desktop application to a cloud based approach. The platform must therefore not only be attractive for end users, but also for software providers. This means that it must be flexible enough to support the wide range of software solutions desired and have a good user experience, while keeping the costs low.

The goal is to provide ubiquitous availability of compute resources, software and data. In contrast to other approaches, the aim here is to integrate existing software solutions into one common platform, combining them to work together and make them accessible through a web portal. Furthermore, the proposed solution supports installation in private clouds as well as access to multiple cloud and High Performance Computing (HPC) providers through one common portal installation. To facilitate a broad selection of existing software solutions, we target cloud solutions offering Infrastructure as a Service, where software providers can install their own operating system and fully control the virtual machines.

In the rest of this paper, we give a short overview of the related work in Section II. The CloudFlow Infrastructure is then presented in Section III, where the focus is on the aspects and infrastructure components related to workflow orchestration and execution, resource monitoring, data storage, authentication, and utilization of HPC clusters. In order to validate the infrastructure and demonstrate the usefulness of CloudFlow, the experimental setup applied through the CloudFlow project is described in Section IV, along with an example workflow. Finally, we conclude and describe some plans for future work in Section V.

II. Related Work

Cloud computing and cloud-based engineering is delivered by multiple providers. One dedicated software vendor delivering such a solution is SimScale [4], offering simulators for computational fluid dynamics, finite element analysis and thermodynamics in the cloud. Based on these simulation tools and web-based visual pre- and post-processing, Simscale targets end users only. Combining their cloud solution with software developed by other vendors is therefore not straight forward.

The cloudSME project [5] combines a business model targeting both end users and software vendors. Software vendors are offered a Platform as a Service solution, where they offer Software as a Service for their existing and new end users. This approach also makes it possible for end users to combine software from different software vendors to perform more complex engineering tasks. CloudSME does however not use any semantic information to orchestrate how to combine the different software, and lacks the use of HPC.

There are several initiatives to simplify cloud deployment and avoid vendor lock-in. Bergmayr et al. [2] propose a modelling approach, where the cloud deployment is described by a vendor independent language CloudML. The deployment model is implemented in this language, which sets up virtual machines, network communication and deploys services accordingly.

Stahl et al. [3] proposed the initial work and the main concepts of the CloudFlow Infrastructure. Among the newly introduced concepts are a unified way to access HPC resources, functionality to use external cloud providers, resource monitoring and a graphical tool to define workflows.

Semantic Markup for Web Services (OWL-S) and *Business Process Execution Language* (BPEL) are two technologies that allow web service execution as processes. BPEL is a language to execute business processes with web services as stated by Mendling [6]. According to its specifications, BPEL executes web services defined using Web Service Description Language (WSDL). It supports orchestration of actions within services, by structuring them as sequences and supporting branches and loops. The structure is described using a syntax based on Extensible Markup Language (XML). OWL-S is a markup that is built on top of Web Ontology Language (OWL) and describes web services semantically introducing an XML-based syntax. It also supports orchestration and due to semantic technologies, structuring the sequences using OWL-S is both machine and human understandable. OWL-S and WSDL are usually used to describe services based on the Simple Object Access Protocol (SOAP) specification. It allows web services to send requests in a predefined structure encoded in a XML format.

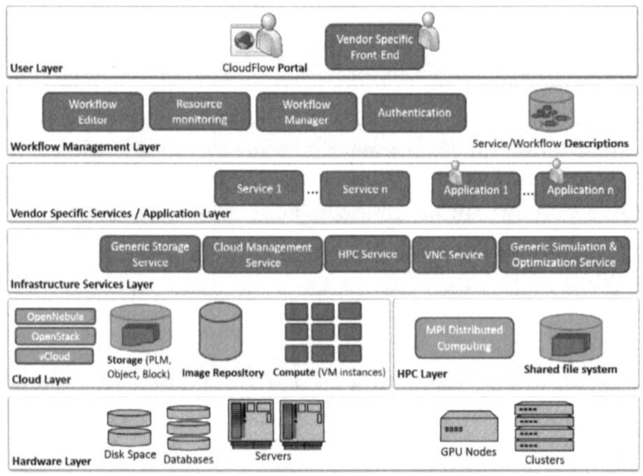

Figure 1. Simplified diagram of the system layers with their main components.

BPEL is similar to OWL-S in terms of orchestration and XML-based syntax, but it lacks utilizing semantic technologies. Therefore, making web services machine-understandable and automating them without user interaction is a non-trivial task using BPEL [7].

The process execution is usually performed by designing an execution order and monitoring it with an execution engine. There are several execution engines designed for this purpose. Execution engines, or managers, introduce an editor or a syntax to specify the order and then track the progress. Depending on the implementations, they can also provide user interface.

One of the available execution engines for BPEL is Process Manager by Oracle. It provides a graphical interface to manage cross-application business processes in a service oriented architecture (SOA) [8]. It also allows designing workflow steps and connecting external systems into the workflow. However, lack of semantic technologies inside BPEL prevents automation of these design steps. Involving semantic technologies would therefore increase the productivity by reducing the time needed to design the task steps, and is hence quite important.

To achieve the goal of CloudFlow, a manager which can facilitate semantic technologies, integrate web services from different providers and locations, and provide automation during the design and execution phase was necessary.

III. Architecture Overview

The components in the CloudFlow Infrastructure can be described as a multilayer architecture to separate functionalities. It consists of six main layers as depicted in Fig. 1. The natural entry point for both end users and software vendors is through the CloudFlow Portal, or just *the Portal*, found in the user layer of the infrastructure. This section presents key components and concepts of the CloudFlow Infrastructure.

A. *Workflow Management*

A workflow is an orchestrated and repeatable pattern of several activities enabled by the systematic organization of resources into processes that transform materials, provide services, or process information. Workflows may be as trivial as browsing a file structure or visualizing a Computer-Aided Design (CAD) model, or they can be more complex, including describing the full set of operations used to design, analyse and prepare for manufacturing of a product. Utilizing semantic technologies such as OWL-S makes it possible to reuse existing workflows as building blocks in more complex ones.

As described in Section I, the main goal of CloudFlow is to host software from different software providers and chain appropriate parts of them to perform end user tasks in workflows within one common platform. In the following, we will describe how web services are integrated into the CloudFlow Infrastructure, and how workflows are designed and executed.

1) Services: A set of complementary reusable functionalities that are provided by a software for different purposes is called "service." More particularly, a web service is a software system designed to support interoperable machine-to-machine interaction over a network [9]. A web service invocation consists of a single request/response pair and is expected to execute in a short time.

The CloudFlow Infrastructure defines some Application Programming Interface (API) requirements to services to be integrated into workflows. The simplest web service that follows those requirements is called a *synchronous service*. These services are useful when the operation ends relatively quickly, and the user does not need progress update during its execution. In contrast, *asynchronous services* do not have any restrictions when it comes to runtime, and they are also allowed to present the user with progress information. Common for the service types are that they represent an operation that takes predefined input parameters and generates output parameters without a user interaction. All communication with the services are performed through SOAP requests which are sent to their endpoints defined through their WSDL files. In addition to services, also *applications* which allow user interaction are supported. The most common application types are web forms for selecting parameters for the following service and visualization applications for inspecting the output. Throughout this paper, the term *CloudFlow service* denotes services and applications compatible with the CloudFlow API.

2) Workflow Definition: In order to define a web service as a CloudFlow service, and then to create workflows from a chain of CloudFlow services, the web services need to be integrated into the infrastructure. This is performed using a graphical tool named *Workflow Editor*.

Workflow Editor (WFE) was mentioned as future work in [3] as an implementation of a workflow modelling tool and it is currently available for use. The developed WFE is based on XML, SOAP, and WSDL standards, and inserts web services into a semantic database by adding semantic descriptions based on their WSDL. The server side functionality of WFE is implemented as web services hence it also provides a SOAP API that can be used directly from 3rd party tools.

In order to make a web service available as a CloudFlow service, the service provider supplies the endpoint for the service's WSDL to WFE, where semantic descriptions of the service itself and its input and output parameters are defined. Based on these semantic descriptions, semi-automatic orchestration of workflows can be made by letting the system suggest services which are compatible with respect to their inputs and outputs. After these parameters are converted into semantic descriptions for the given service, the service is integrated into the infrastructure and can be used as a step in a workflow.

The WFE is also used to chain services into workflows. The creation is offered through both a textual and a graphical editor, combined as a single web page. Using the graphical editor, the CloudFlow services are selected using a dropdown menu and appended to a workflow. The data flow between the services is defined by dragging and dropping outputs of services and connecting them with inputs of others. The execution order is represented using dotted arrows and the data flow is shown using solid lines as shown in Fig. 2. Each action performed using the graphical editor is synchronized with an XML-based meta-formatted textual editor. The XML format contains all information stored in the semantic database, and can be used also for later updates of the workflow.

Even though each CloudFlow service typically represents an individual operation with dedicated input and output parameters, some services naturally belong together. Instead of having to connect the same sequence of services repeatedly for multiple different workflows, such services are modelled as a smaller workflow of their own called *sub-workflows*. Sub-workflows are yet again available to be added into any other workflow as a single component, similar to a regular CloudFlow service. The changes made within a sub-workflow are applied to all workflows using it, reducing time and effort for the workflow designer through avoiding a repetitive task.

3) Workflow Manager: The semantic descriptions created by WFE only contain meta-data and describe how the data is bound. The component *Workflow Manager* (WFM) acts as an execution engine acting on the semantic descriptions. It executes and monitors all services in a workflow providing the input parameters as defined in WFE, either as constant values or outputs from previous steps. The status of each asynchronous service is checked at regular intervals in order to determine if it is finished as well as to present the service's status to the user.

Before executing a workflow, the billing component is asked to verify that the user has the valid licenses for all involved services. Therefore, requests to initiate services that do not originate from the WFM should be rejected, preferably on a network level, e.g., by strict firewall settings. The WFM also tracks execution times by utilizing resource monitoring components which are explained in Section III-B. Usually, the user interacts with the Portal to initiate and monitor workflows. However, this is just one possible way and the Portal is not needed during the execution of workflows. Both synchronous and asynchronous services can be executed even after the user has left the client that initiated the workflow. This is also true for applications, though they will wait for user interaction before the workflow can be continued. Independently on how a workflow is initiated, the Portal can be used to inspect the status of workflows and interact with them during their execution.

B. Resource Monitoring and Billing

To facilitate that CloudFlow becomes a one-stop-shop where software vendors integrate and offer their software for new customers, functionality to monitor the resource usage by each workflow and service is needed. Based on different requirements, the software vendors are able to use different business models, such as offering their software as pay-per-use, or for a fixed monthly or annual fee. For computationally intensive software, that require exclusive access to a hardware resource, there will also be a cost related to the CPU hours

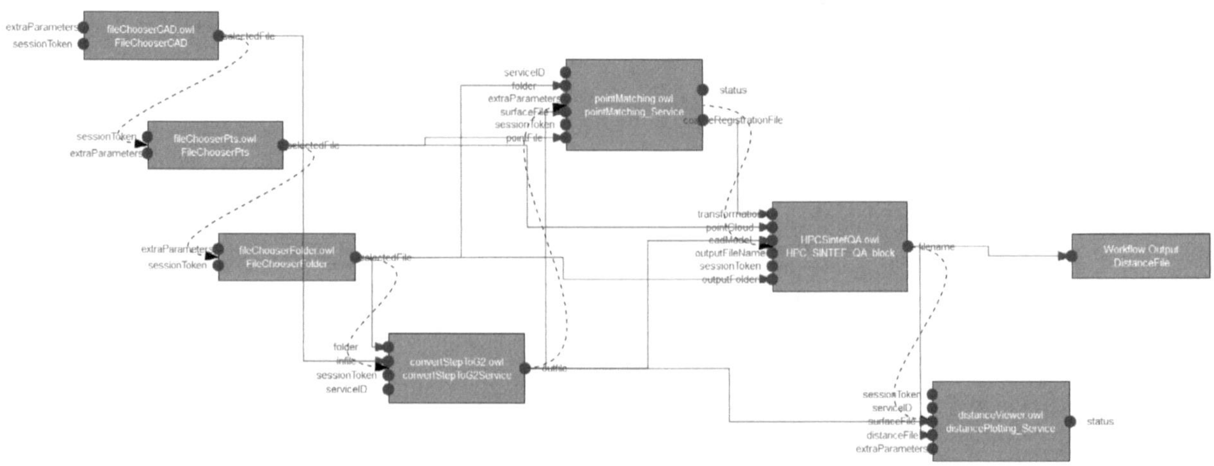

Figure 2. The graphical user interface of WFE, where dotted lines represent flow of services, while solid lines connect parameters from outputs to inputs.

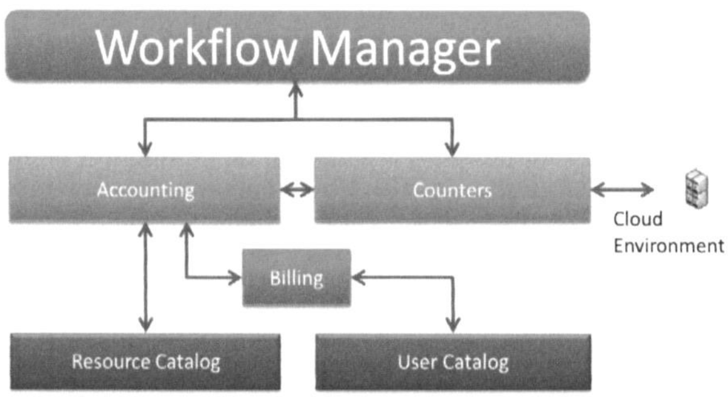

Figure 3. Communication between billing-related components inside infrastructure.

spent. Each service is tagged with which *software package* it belongs to. All license costs related to the software package is described in the *Resource Catalog* component, either as a time based license requirement, runtime cost, or a combination of both. The Resource Catalog also holds information about hardware costs and which vendors the costs belong to. Fig. 3 illustrates how the different components are connected.

As a workflow is executed, the resources consumed through this workflow is gathered, and the related cost for running the workflow is calculated. Collection of this information and cost calculation is performed within the resource monitoring and billing components of the CloudFlow Infrastructure. When an end-user starts a workflow, the WFM lists all software packages within the workflow and checks with *Accounting* service whether the user has the required licences to run them. Later, if the user is allowed to execute the workflow, the *Counter* service is used to track the execution times delivered by the WFM. This service passes these data back to the Accounting service to calculate the bill for CPU usage, as well as the software costs within the workflow.

The Resource Catalog holds a list of software and hardware/data centers, whereas the *User Catalog* keeps a list of organizations or users. The calculations and usage information at the end of each workflow are gathered by the *Billing* component. This component issues bills to the end users and is the only component which users interact with in order to get their usage and cost reports.

C. *Cloud Storage*

In order to follow the loosely-coupled layered architecture design of the CloudFlow Infrastructure (see Fig. 1), the interaction with the cloud storage is designed to be vendor independent. As different cloud storage solutions have different APIs for accessing files, a set of services with a unified API is required. Further, in order to avoid unnecessary network cost and to avoid potential security issues, the files need to be transferred directly between the cloud storage and the client, and not via an intermediate server. To support these requirements, the *Generic Storage Services* (GSS) have been developed within CloudFlow.

The GSS exposes an API consisting of both SOAP and REpresentational State Transfer (REST) web services, and offers functionality for interacting with the cloud storage solutions available in CloudFlow. In contrast to SOAP, RESTful web services come with a smaller overhead and are better suited for transferring large amounts of data. Each available storage solution is added as a back-end to GSS, where information is provided through SOAP services on how to use the native REST interface. The client transfers files directly to and from the cloud storage, with no added overhead. In this way, GSS acts like a look up service telling how to make requests toward the different back-ends, where each back-end is treated as an object storage. Beside transferring files, other functionality such as listing folder content, checking existence of files, creating folders etc., are made directly through the SOAP API.

Files are uniquely defined by file IDs, which includes a prefix indicating which storage back-end the file belongs to. The file ID combined with a valid authentication token is sufficient for downloading any file. As long as all CloudFlow services are implemented using this API, interoperability and vendor independent file access is obtained within CloudFlow workflows. Further, any cloud storage solution with a RESTful API can be made available in CloudFlow by adding an additional back-end in GSS. Existing services can then immediately use the new cloud storage solution without making any changes to their implementation. A cloud storage can also use external authentication solutions, as it is not a requirement that the authentication token used towards the cloud storage is a valid CloudFlow token.

A web-based file browser application is available for all workflows. It is configurable through WFE to tailor its behaviour for each workflow, and has a user friendly interface with a context dependent right-click menu. Here, end users can upload and download files between their computers and the cloud.

Since the CloudFlow services have SOAP interfaces, their parameters should consist of short messages rather than entire files. Because of this, the file browser gives the file ID of the chosen files as output instead of the content of it. This rule illustrate best practice and applies to all CloudFlow services.

Currently, four cloud storage solutions are made available in the CloudFlow Infrastructure through GSS. There are two OpenStack Swift installations (one internal and one external), a product lifecycle management (PLM) system, and a native storage at one of CloudFlow's HPC providers.

D. Authentication and Multi-Cloud

Several of the CloudFlow Infrastructure components need to be available from outside the infrastructure itself. This includes design and execution of workflows, interaction with the cloud storage, and viewing how much resources a user has spent. Since only registered users should be allowed to issue such requests, and since a user should only have access to their own files and resource usage, all web services within the CloudFlow Infrastructure need an authentication parameter representing the user. For this, a token based authentication system is used. Users obtain a token at login which represents them throughout the session, and which contains their appropriate permissions.

As a security measure, tokens have limited life spans, meaning that requests containing old tokens will be unsuccessful. However, workflows (and perhaps especially within manufacturing industries) can consist of services lasting longer than any lifespan given to tokens. Since an expired token can not be used for, e.g., uploading results to the cloud storage, CloudFlow needs an authentication scheme that both invalidates tokens after a certain time while allowing workflows of arbitrary lengths to have access to infrastructure components.

In order to support these requirements, the *Authentication services* are introduced to CloudFlow. These services build on top of OpenStack's Keystone component [10], and extend its with functionality to handle the challenge related to long lasting workflows. In addition, vendor lock-in towards OpenStack is avoided through these services. Changing the communication with Keystone, or exchanging Keystone itself, will require changes in the implementation of the Authentication services only, while the API, and all components relying on the authentication, are kept unchanged.

The problem consisting of tokens expiring during workflow executions are solved by issuing and storing special workflow tokens from the Authentication services. Each time a workflow is started, such a token is created from combining the regular token with the ID of the workflow execution. This workflow token is stored in a database, and is passed to all services within the workflow. During validation, the regular token is checked normally first, but if it has expired and the combination with the execution ID is recognized, the token is still marked as valid. A new regular and valid token can then be generated with the same permissions as the existing token based on the now invalid one. When the workflow later is finished or aborted, the special workflow token is deleted from the database, and is then invalidated.

1) Multi-Cloud: As CloudFlow is not tied to any one cloud, it is possible to use multiple clouds for hosting CloudFlow services. One reason for doing this might be that customers are physically too far away from the main CloudFlow cloud, making a local cloud more attractive in terms of network costs and delays. Other reasons might be that alternative clouds might be cheaper, or equipped with hardware not available in the CloudFlow cloud, for example by offering more powerful processing resources.

The main challenge related to such solutions is authentication across the different clouds. While the external clouds have their authentication methods, they are not necessarily compatible with those used in CloudFlow. Services that are written for multi-cloud settings should therefore be implemented with an additional external token parameter. The semantic information can then describe what cloud the external token should be authenticated against, and external authentication services can be added to such workflows. Such a service will provide a web form where the user can login to the external cloud, and where the external token is passed to the next steps in the workflow. The external token can also be stored in a cookie in the browser, so that if a valid token is already present, this token will be used and the users are spared from typing their username and password more than necessary.

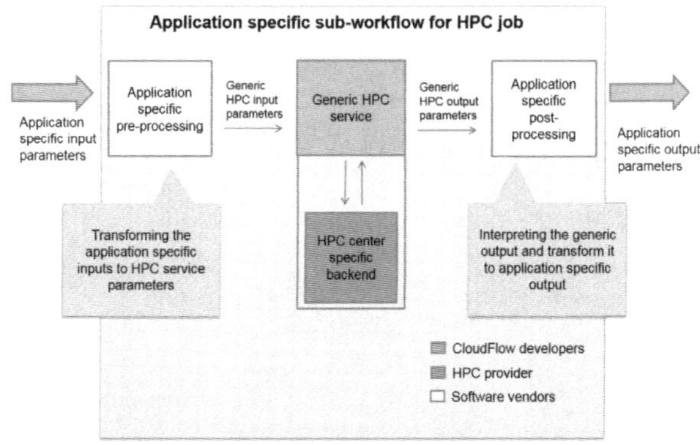

Figure 4. An application specific sub-workflow encapsulating an HPC job.

E. HPC Access

Computationally intensive tasks that benefit from running on HPC clusters are common in many engineering workflows. Because of this, the CloudFlow Infrastructure is required to facilitate seamless and secure integration of such tasks, making it easy for software vendors to run their applications on an HPC cluster as part of a CloudFlow workflow. The solution for this is the design and concept of *HPC application sub-workflows*, with the generic *HPC service* as the central component.

An HPC application sub-workflow is built from three CloudFlow services as shown in Fig. 4; an application specific pre-processing service, the generic HPC service, and an application specific post-processing service. The HPC service is designed to be generic with respect to both the application and the type of job scheduling system used by the HPC provider. This way, the HPC providers can make changes to their queuing systems, or CloudFlow can expand to more HPC centers without requiring the software vendors to make changes to their services or workflows. Even though the HPC service is generic, the application that is executed through it will be part of a software package (as mentioned in Section III-B). The name of the software package it is part of will therefore be hardcoded as input to the HPC service within the application sub-workflow. This information is then used by the service to check with the Resource monitoring component that the user has a license to run the application, and to ensure that the software vendor receives the correct license fees. Other resource management tasks, such as reporting CPU hours spent on the computation, are also reported from within the generic HPC service.

In order to separate the service from the HPC center specific details, the HPC service communicates internally with an HPC back-end. Since user credentials defined in CloudFlow are not necessarily compatible with the user definitions in the HPC cluster, the back-end may perform a mapping between the two sets of user definitions through a method seen fit by the HPC provider. For security reasons, different CloudFlow users should not be assigned the same user on the cluster. The two HPC providers within CloudFlow currently use different approaches to solve this challenge. One provider has set up a pool of HPC users reserved for CloudFlow, where each execution of the HPC service is assigned an arbitrary user from the pool, which is then reserved until that execution has completed. To ensure security, the home directory of each such HPC user is deleted between executions of jobs. The other provider assigns a one-to-one mapping between the two types of users, so that a CloudFlow user is assigned a dedicated HPC user. This second approach is particularly suitable to private cloud installations of CloudFlow, where the same system administrators control both the cloud and compute cluster environments.

The input and output parameters for the HPC service is highly generic, and should support the vast majority of applications that will be run on the compute cluster. As input, the service takes a string containing the set of command lines that will execute the application with its correct input parameters. Additional inputs to the service are the number of cores and nodes to use, as well as a maximum execution time used to limit cost and stop non-converging simulations.

The output from the HPC service is a string which is read from a *result file*, written by the application. As this output parameter will be sent in a SOAP message, output files should not be written in the result file, but rather uploaded to the cloud storage. The file ID of the uploaded file should instead be written as the result.

During the execution of the application, the end user will often appreciate some feedback in the form of a progress report. What kind of progress report that makes sense to provide highly depends on the application, as some applications are only able to provide a progress bar, while others might create a status report including images and text. A reserved *status file* is being monitored by the HPC service, and any content of this file is interpreted as HTML and displayed in the browser for the user. The software vendor can therefore fill this file with any meaningful information seen fit, either directly from the application, or through a background process parsing the log file of the application into the status file.

In order to create the string with the set of command lines, an application specific pre-processing service is required in front of the HPC service. This service is implemented by the software vendor providing the application itself, and takes the same input parameters as the application. Similarly, in order to interpret the output from the HPC service and add semantic descriptions to it, an application specific post-processing service is called. It parses the output from the HPC service, which is the information written in the result file, into application specific output parameters. Since both these operations in most cases are basic string manipulations which finish immediately, both the pre- and post-processing services are usually implemented as synchronous services. In some cases however, it is natural to let the end-user choose how many nodes the application should use. It is then natural to either implement the pre-processing service as a web application instead, or have a web application where this choice is made before the pre-processing.

When the number of nodes is hardcoded within the application specific sub-workflow, all details concerning the HPC is hidden from whoever uses the sub-workflow in a larger workflow. The sub-workflow will have nothing but application specific inputs and outputs, and will therefore have the same interface in WFE as a single CloudFlow service running the same application in the cloud environment. The usage of the compute resources is therefore transparent for the user, and does not require that the end user (or workflow creator) knows the difference between cloud and HPC environments.

IV. Results

The development of the CloudFlow Infrastructure is organized to meet the requirements from end users in manufacturing industries and their software providers. This has given opportunity to validate our choices and arrange validations, where the end users test the platform and the deployed software.

A. *Validation results*

To facilitate the development and validation, three *waves of experiments* have been set up. In the first wave of experiments, all workflows were tailored towards the needs of hydropower engineers. Software from 6 different independent software vendors (ISVs) were integrated with the infrastructure and accessible through the cloud solution, and validated with one common end user. For the second and third wave, European software vendors and end users were invited to test the infrastructure and develop new workflows based on the needs of the end user. In total 14 new experiments were selected, each with one new end user.

The motivation to use the CloudFlow Infrastructure varies among the experiments, including attracting new customers, reducing license cost, reducing time spent to create a new product and improving the design of new products. The overall common goal is to enhance availability of easy to use software and computational resources through

- User friendly interfaces
- Easy access to cloud computing resources

For each experiment, the user requirement group of the project helped the end user to define usability criteria requirements. In parallel, the software vendors developed business plans for

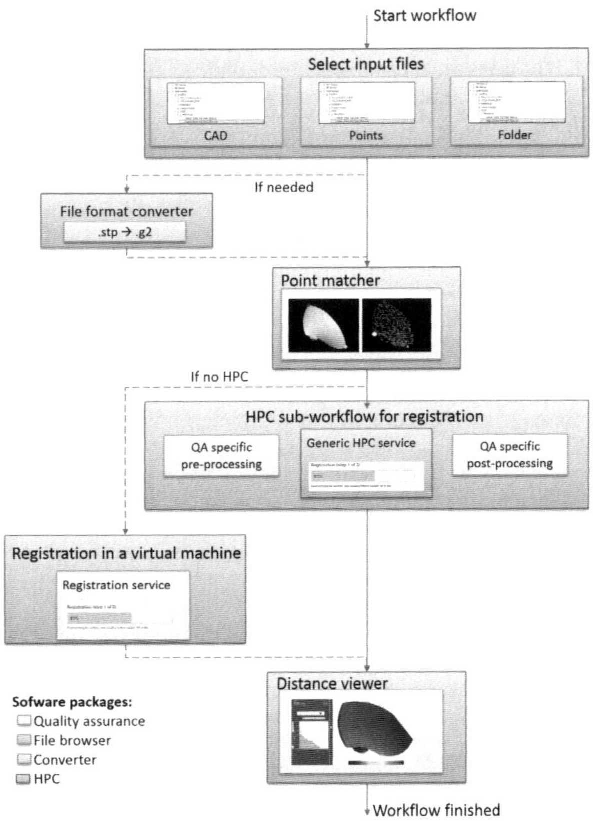

Figure 5. A workflow for quality assurance where a 3D scan of a produced product is compared with the initial CAD model.

how to realize the economical potential benefiting both the end user and software vendors. This way, not only the theoretical potential of the software platform is verified, but also that the final solution can sustain as an attractive option.

At several stages the end users were invited to perform daily tasks using the CloudFlow Infrastructure, validating the success, not only of the experiment but also the infrastructure as a whole.

The end users have demonstrated how to use the software solutions in a daily task. The demonstrations are monitored by the user requirements group to assess the user experience and recommend future improvements. The conclusion from the 13 already finished experiments have been processed and shows that the main goals of all experiments have been reached. Furthermore, the experiments reported that the end users would benefit economically from using more compute resources than today, and that the CloudFlow Infrastructure can make it economically feasible. The validation revealed that the concept is functional and makes it more attractive to use Cloud computing both for software vendors, consultancy companies and end users.

B. *Quality Assurance in the Cloud*

As an example of a workflow using the components and concepts mentioned in Section III, a quality assurance application will be considered. This workflow will compare a CAD model to a 3D scan of the produced product, for this application: a turbine blade. The goal is to confirm that the turbine blade is manufactured according to its design within given tolerances, and later to control wear on the blade after it has been in production for some time.

The quality assurance process consists mainly of three steps, where each step contains one or several CloudFlow services. The main challenge is to properly align the 3D scan data to the CAD model, which usually is a tedious manual process. A fully automated alignment is not necessarily feasible, especially if the CAD model has symmetries or the 3D scan is partial. The first step is therefore a coarse manual alignment, which is performed before an automated alignment process, where an optimization process iterates to make the point cloud fit as close as possible to the surfaces of the CAD model. Thereafter, the result of the registration needs to be reported to the user in an informative and user friendly manner. The entire workflow and the four software packages within it, is shown in Fig. 5.

1) Quality assurance pre-processing: The workflow starts of by letting the user choose the CAD model, 3D point cloud and where to store the results from the registration. This functionality is covered by the File Browser, mentioned in Section III-C.

Since CAD models can be stored in different file formats, and since the services later in the workflow are designed expecting a pre-defined file format, a file conversion might be needed at this point. If so, a conversion service accesses a dedicate virtual machine in the Cloud which runs the conversion. The conversion service is not guaranteed to finish within a HTTP time out, and is therefore implemented as an asynchronous service. The service launches the conversion as a background process, and WFM polls on the service to check if the process is finished or not. Before the conversion finishes, it provides a progress bar along with a text describing the current status. Note that this conversion requires no interaction from the user, allowing the WFM to automatically proceed to the next step of the workflow after the conversion is completed.

The manual alignment step, where the initial guess to the registration is made, is a web application. Here, the CAD model and the point cloud are shown in separate canvases and the user is expected to match corresponding points from the two models. Since the models can be quite large, a hybrid rendering is done through the Tinia framework [11]. The models are rendered server side, generating 3D images that are sent to the web client. The user can freely interact with the local model for an interactive experience, without transferring the CAD model. Similarly to the file browser, WFM awaits a message from the client to proceed in the workflow, and this signal is sent when the user accepts the initial guess.

2) Registration: The registration application is implemented to take advantage of parallel execution, and in order to integrate the application in the CloudFlow Infrastructure, the HPC service along with its design pattern described in Section III-E is used. A registration pre-processing service is implemented to generate the set of command lines required to run the registration based on the file IDs obtained in the file chooser applications, converter and initial guess application. A post-processing service for the registration is also implemented in order to enable semantic descriptions to the result from the HPC service. In this case, it will be the file ID holding the registration results. These three services are then stored as an

HPC registration sub-workflow, before it is modelled into the rest of the quality assurance workflow.

The registration has also been implemented as a single asynchronous service where the registration is run in the cloud environment instead of on the HPC cluster. Since the registration HPC sub-workflow has application specific inputs and outputs, the sub-workflow can be exchanged with the single cloud service directly. This can be useful as a cheaper alternative for users who do not prioritize performance. The service or the HPC block could potentially also be chosen dynamically. If the appropriate HPC queue is filled the execution in the virtual environment can be faster as it does not have to wait in the queue, even though execution itself is slower.

3) Quality assurance post-processing: The results of the registration is visualized by a WebGL application showing both the CAD model and the aligned point cloud in the same view. The distance between the models are illustrated both trough statistical information and color coding of the point cloud. The user will typically view and inspect these results for an unspecified time. The viewer is therefore implemented as a web application, where the user presses a "finish" button to tell WFM that the workflow should move to the next step. As there are no more next steps, the workflow is completed with a list of workflow output parameters. This list can be accessed later through the user's list of finished workflows.

V. Conclusion and Future Work

In this paper, the concept and the realization of a cloud-based platform is explained. The platform allows seamless integration and combination of engineering services, controlled execution, and monitoring of the used resources. The infrastructure components which build the platform utilize standards such as WSDL and SOAP in order to make the integration process simple. Additionally, employment of semantic descriptions allows discovery of compatible services and assists to chain services to form workflows. This type of assistance, semi-automatic orchestration, makes the services aware of each other improving interoperability.

The proposed solution has been validated by a wide range of end users solving different tasks from the manufacturing industries. Software providers will be able to offer their services in a common web portal. Software providers as well as consultancy companies can then combine available software solutions into potential workflows tailored to solve tasks provided by end users. The access to such efficient software solutions together with remote computational resources can dramatically reduce labor intensive tasks while improving the final product.

In the future, these semantic descriptions can be enhanced by expanding the semantic vocabulary so that WFE can orchestrate the creation of workflows fully automated, meaning without a user interaction provided that intermediary services exist. By intelligently orchestration any user can create their own tailored workflows consisting of their favorite software tools. So far, the solution is validated within the manufacturing industries. The technological choices are to little extent based on this choice, but validation in other segments will be needed to fully validate the solution.

Acknowledgement

This research was conducted in the context of the CloudFlow project, which is co-funded by the 7th Framework Program of the European Union, project number 609100. More information and news about CloudFlow can be found on the project website at `http://eu-cloudflow.eu/`.

References

[1] "UberCloud," https://www.theubercloud.com/, retrieved: August 2016.

[2] A. Bergmayr et al., "The evolution of CloudML and its manifestations," in Proceedings of the 3rd International Workshop on Model-Driven Engineering on and for the Cloud (CloudMDE), pp. 1–6, 2015.

[3] C. Stahl, E. Bellos, C. Altenhofen, and J. Hjelmervik, "Flexible integration of cloud-based engineering services using semantic technologies," in Industrial Technology (ICIT), 2015 IEEE International Conference on, pp. 1520–1525, 2015.

[4] "SimScale," https://www.simscale.com/, retrieved: August 2016.

[5] "cloudSME, simulation for manufacturing & engineering," http://cloudsme.eu/, Seventh Framework Programme (FP7) under grant agreement number 608886, retrieved: August 2016.

[6] J. Mendling, "Business Process Execution Language for Web Service (BPEL)," [Online]. Available: https://www.uni-ulm.de/fileadmin/website_uni_ulm/iui.emisa/Downloads/emisaforum06.pdf, retrieved: August 2016.

[7] M. Aslam, S. Auer, and J. Shen, "From BPEL4WS process model to full OWL-S ontology." [Online]. Available: http://bis.informatik.uni-leipzig.de/files/bpel_2_owls_short_paper.pdf, retrieved: August 2016.

[8] Oracle, "Oracle BPEL process manager datasheet,". [Online]. Available: http://www.oracle.com/technetwork/middleware/bpel/overview/ds-bpel-11gr1-1-134826.pdf, retrieved: August 2016

[9] D. Booth, H. Haas, F. McCabe, E. Newcomer, M. Champion, C. Ferris, and D. Orchard, "Web Services Architecture," W3C Working Group Note, 2004. [Online]. Available: https://www.w3.org/TR/2004/NOTE-ws-arch-20040211/, retrieved: August 2016.

[10] "Openstack Keystone," http://docs.openstack.org/developer/keystone/, retrieved: August 2016.

[11] C. Dyken et al., "A framework for OpenGL client-server rendering," in 4th IEEE International Conference on Cloud Computing Technology and Science Proceedings, CloudCom 2012, Taipei, Taiwan, pp. 729–734, 2012.

Intelligent Agent-Based Approach for Real-Time Reconfiguration of Cloud Application

Walid Bouzayen*†, Hamza Gharsellaoui*‡, Mohamed Khalgui*§
*LISI, INSAT Institute, Carthage University, Tunisia
†FST, Tunis El Manar University, Tunisia
‡ENI-Carthage, Carthage University, Tunisia
§SystemsControl Lab, Xidian University, China
Email: {walid.bouzayen, gharsellaoui.hamza, mohamed.khalgui}@gmail.com

Abstract—**This paper deals with the problem of reconfiguration of Internet of Things (IoT) and Cloud Computing (CC) applications which have been widely studied recently. They are composed of a set of interconnected software components running on real-time on remote virtual machines. Virtualization is one of the building blocks for cloud computing and provides the mechanisms to implement the dynamic allocation of resources. Once cloud applications are deployed, they need to be reconfigured in order to react to any disturbance created by the removal or modification of virtual machines or components that make up these machines. In this paper, the original approach proposed for handling these reconfiguration scenarios must preserve the application consistency, feasibility, computing time, low power consumption and respect important architectural invariant related to real-time properties and to software dependencies. Finally, the challenges, advantages of the proposed cloud architecture and future works for the application and implementation are discussed.**

Keywords–Cloud Computing; Reconfiguration Technology; Internet of Things.

I. INTRODUCTION

This work touches areas of Internet of Things (IoT) and Cloud Computing (CC). A system is made of interconnected Virtual Machines (VMs) where each one runs a set of processes. It is usually necessary to reconfigure a process, component or any object of the cloud, which also requires the reconfiguration of the whole system at run-time. CC aims to build a virtual infrastructure providing users with remote computing and storage capacity. CC is rapidly gaining traction in industrial and business ethics. It offers businesses online services on demand and allows them to reduce costs on software, hardware and information technology support [2]. On one hand, dealing with this new technology, CC analyzes the informational duties of hosting companies that own and operate CC datacentres (e.g., Amazon). On the other hand, it considers the cloud services providers leasing "space in the cloud" from hosting companies (e.g., Salesforce, Dropbox) and it examines the private "clouders" and the business using these services.

IoT is a concept of communication between people and smart objects and the CC technology is based on the virtualization. In literature, Srivastava [15] states that IoT represents the greatest level of technological convergence that we can currently imagine. Moving from an Internet of user-generated content to thing-generated content will produce a new level of sensory awareness, with the ultimate goal of increasing our control over time and space. The vision that characterizes the IoT is one where things are connected that we would not previously have considered relevant to computation or feasible to integrate with a network. This change will allow various forms of data to be collected from all kinds of objects around us, from the use of appliances and lighting to door locks, clothes or toothbrushes [16]. Therefore, in the domain of CC, we must deal with two key issues: computing and storage. This latter is increasingly considered as a major research field in the area of CC. Indeed, more and more data intensive applications are attracted by the cloud since cloud storage can provide high scalability, fault tolerance, security, availability and cost-effective data services [1]. The huge number of users of the cloud and the devices makes the control of the performance of different storage nodes very difficult or impossible to the network manager. The cloud network has a huge amount of data written to it by different users on storage devices; a great percentage of this data might be similar or identical. Almost 90% of the data stored in cloud is duplicated [3].

In order to optimize the storage over cloud, many methods and techniques have been used: compression, snapshots and deduplication. Data compression [24] is a technique to reduce storage cost by eliminating redundancies in different files. There exist two types of compression, lossy and lossless. The technology of Snapshot [21] is defined as a virtual copy of a set of files. This technique solves several data backup problems, including backing up large amounts of data and recovering corrupted data. Data deduplication [22] is a technique for reducing the amount of storage space by eliminating redundant data. This is called intelligent compression. Many works related to the cloud reconfiguration have been proposed. Duran and Salaun [20] proposed a reconfiguration scenario on a simple Web application that includes three VMs with the following components: Apache, Tomcat, MySQL. The first drawback is that the reconfiguration scenario poses no major problem and the order of the shutdown and the restart of components/VM is obvious. The other drawback, which seems obvious in the solution proposed in [20] is the systematic shutdown of all components and machines that support them. This solution seems a bit exaggerated and unrealistic. It would be wiser to stop only the components that should be stopped and let those which cannot be stopped run.

Our contribution in this paper is to model and propose an intelligent agent-based architecture, able to manage applications/services with integrated Cloud IoT while meeting performance criteria based on performance running time and power consumption. This work proposes an online reconfiguration algorithm that optimizes both the cost of storing and memory performance. For this reason, we opted for the modeling of a dependency graph whose vertices are the components/objects and edges are connections between these different components/objects, that can be executed on the same VM or different VMs. We also formalized a method of scheduling components/objects such that the start/stop components or objects is done in a consistent manner. As a result, we propose to use a weighted graph. On each arc, we add information that specifies if the shutdown of destination component imposes or not the shutdown of the source component. In this case, when a component needs to be stopped, stopping the component that precedes it will no longer be required, which allows a performance gain. To the authors knowledge, the first work that deals with the real-time reconfiguration of IoT and CC applications is what we propose in this paper which allows a performance gain in storage and power and for this reason we consider it as original work.

The remainder of the paper is organized as follows. Section 2 presents a brief overview of the application and reconfiguration of IoT and CC applications in manufacturing and embedded systems. In Section 3, we present our proposed solutions and implementation. Section 4 describes our case study and Section 5 discusses our experimental studies. Finally, Section 5 concludes this paper and gives avenues for future work.

II. State of the Art

Even though, the proposed approaches that offer cost models for storage devices are known to be particularly difficult, they have attracted the interest of many researchers. In [4], Kim et al. propose a model which optimizes the storage system based on the consumption of energy. Despite having applied this approach to several types of storage devices from the Hard Disk Drive (HDD) to the Solid-State Drive (SSD) [5][6] it seems to be difficult to apply the presented approach on VMs. Indeed, the VMs depend on several factors such as the type of the virtualization, the hypervisor and the VM reconfiguration (adding, deleting and modifying components/ objects) [4]. The model proposed by Kim et al. runs under devices which causes a limited memory, so our main challenge is to propose an intelligent agent-based approach for real-time reconfiguration of cloud applications that will guarantee the storage capacity as a performance factor.

Many other domains such as the transformation of the graph [7], meta-modelling [8], reconfiguration patterns [9], software architectures [10][11] have been addressed by many works in literature. In this sense, the works of Darwin [10] and Wright [11] help users to formally develop dynamic applications. The main characteristics of these formal models are the dynamic reconfiguration (adding or removing links) of component-based systems [17]. The protocol proposed by Salaun et al. [13] has the advantage of knowing the number of VMs, components and their relationships. However, the fact that this protocol is deployed in a cloud environment in a decentralized way does not guarantee the majority of applications that will require reconfiguration due to new requirements, scaling on demand or application techniques for recovery failures. Boyer et al. [14] propose a robust reconfiguration protocol to disconnect ports and to change the state of components. Despite the correctness of the protocol which is proven by the authors in their work, this approach has the inconvenient that all components are hosted on a same VM. In the same sense, a single centralized manager is used to ensure the steps of the reconfiguration protocol.

Other architectures are proposed in the literature and are based on a life cycle model that consists of basic states with a direct implication on the VMs and the Infrastructure As A Service (IAAS) layer. This framework supplies cloud services such as those proposed in Slim [5] and Claudia [11]. These frameworks take into account the configuration and infrastructure establishment on demand through the process of service deployment.

However, none of the existing works presents a practical model to reconfigure the cloud applications at run-time by using a modeling formalism, a graph of dependencies and the use of intelligent agents.

III. Proposed Contribution

In this section, we present our proposed contribution implemented by a multi-agent architecture.

A. Motivation

In CC, we encounter two major problems: computing and storage, and what interests us most is storage. In this case, we have the memory allocation and the devices status (free or busy). In this paper, two aspects will be dealt with consequences that are storage and memory performance factor where the goal of our contribution is to minimize the power consumption and the computing time. For storage, there are many works addressing these three methods: Deduplication, Compression (dealing with files) and Snapshot (treating devices while ensuring safety).

According to the work of Meyer and al. [22], the deduplication method is used to remove duplicated files. In this case, this method provides a gain of space of, e.g., X% and if we combine it with the compression method that is used to compress the files after deduplicating them, then it will guarantee a Y% gain. To deal with the problem of memory capacity, we will use the method of reconfiguration by proposing the use of a dependency graph to show the relationships between objects or components in VMs, with a weight of all dependencies (arcs) that predict the starting or not of these components and ultimately ensure the order of scheduling of these components or objects with topological sort. In this case, we must be able to propose a formal solution that ensures that the order to stop and start the components/objects or VMs must be coherent. We have to construct a graph of dependencies between components. This graph G = (V, E) is oriented where the vertices (V) are the components and arcs (E) are pairs of components (C_i, C_j). The starting, stopping, or removing of a component C_j should depend on the component C_i.

To construct the sequence diagram, we proceed to the topological sort of the dependency graph. The order of nodes indicates the coherent order of stopping or starting components or objects. The topological sort imposes Depth First Search (DFS) of the dependency graph. Then, we propose the use of a weighted graph G = (V, E, c) where c is the cost function defined by: $c : E \Longrightarrow \{0, 1\}$, where for each arc (C_i, C_j) we associate 1 the stopping of C_j requires stopping C_i and 0 otherwise. For each arc of the dependency graph, we add an information that specifies if the shutdown of destination component of this arc imposes or not the shutdown of the source component. In this case, when a component needs to be stopped, stopping the component that precedes will no longer be required, which allows a performance gain in memory. We take an example of n VMs composed of n components as shown in Fig. 1. Then, we apply the graph of dependencies,

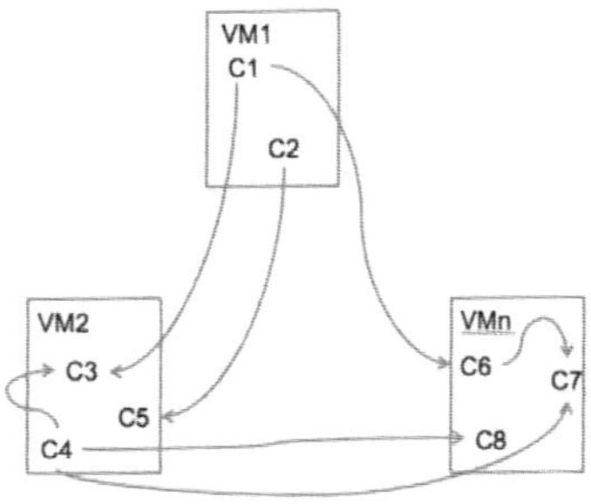

Figure 1. Example of components running in many VMs.

presented in Fig. 2. After that, we apply the second method of the topological sort as shown in Fig. 3.

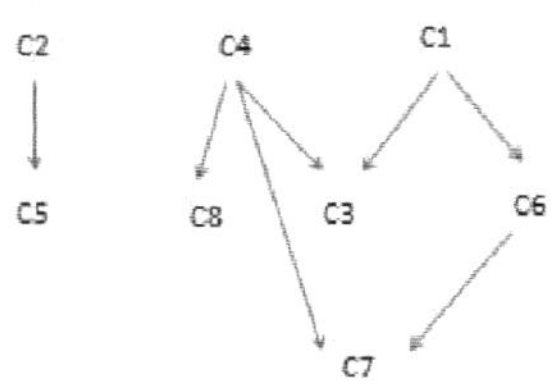

Figure 2. The graph of dependencies.

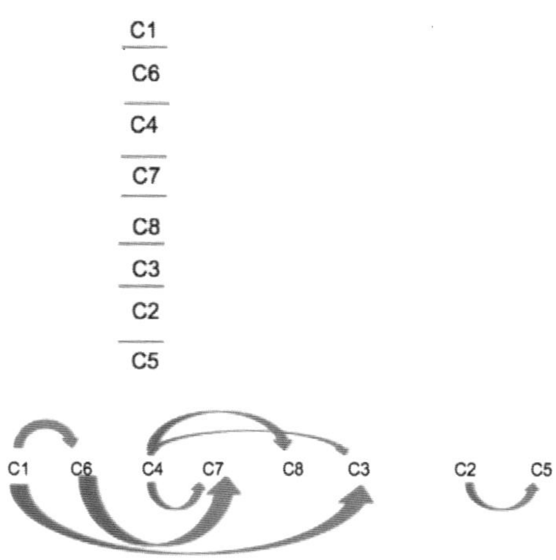

Figure 3. The topological sort.

B. Multi-Agent Architecture

To handle all possible types of reconfigurations, predictable or unpredictable, we propose an approach based on an intelligent agent-based architecture for real-time reconfiguration of CC and IoT applications. Our architecture is based on a hardware part composed of objects/components, a software part composed of VMs and the third part is cloud services including IAAS, Platform As A Service (PAAS) and Software As A Service (SAAS). We define five agents managing reconfiguration scenarios, as follows:

1) Hypervisor Agent (AH) in charge of creating VMs and controlling the cloud manager agent,
2) Cloud Manager Agent (ACM) in charge of the reconfiguration process and monitoring the status of deployed VMs, by controlling and assuring the interactions between the rest of the agents (the decisive agent, the evaluation agent and the executive agent),
3) EValuation Agent (AEV) which subsequently sends the request of reconfiguration operation to the executive agent and indicates success or failure against the following performance criteria: minimized energy criterion, maintenance and storage.
4) Decisive Agent (AD) according to the result of AEV, the AD decides to reconfigure again or not.
5) EXecutive Agent(AEX) runs components or operations in each VM and controls the relationships between them.

The proposed architecture of CC based on intelligent agents is shown in Fig. 4. Our architecture of IoT based on CC can be

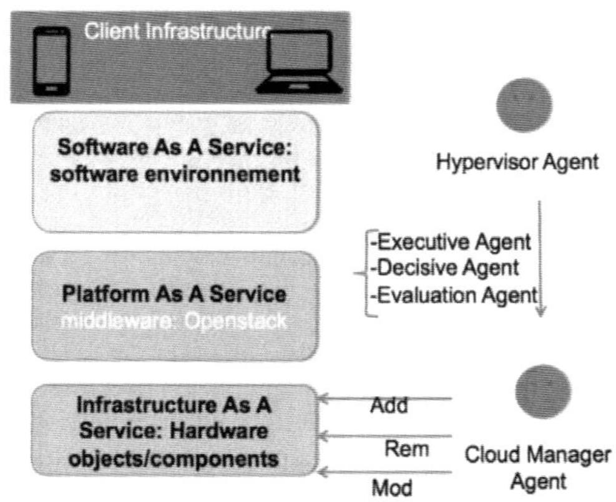

Figure 4. Architecture of cloud computing based on intelligent agent.

illustrated as shown in Fig. 5, where we take a smart hospital as a use case.

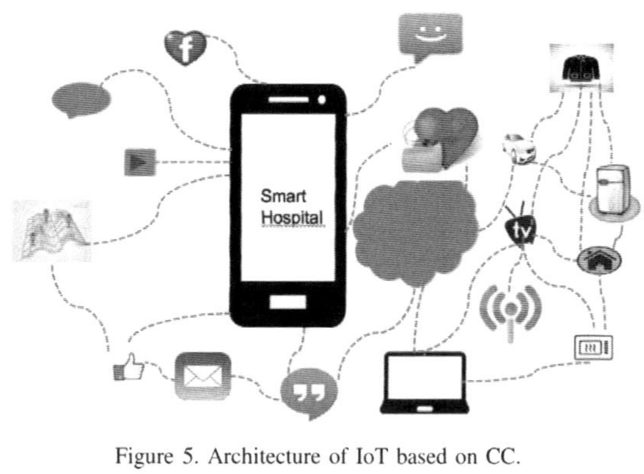

Figure 5. Architecture of IoT based on CC.

C. Formalization

We describe four dimensions of reconfigurations at run-time: reconfiguration of VMs, reconfiguration of objects or components, reconfiguration of relations (bindings) and reconfiguration of environment. Also, we consider the following reconfiguration operations: instantiation or destruction of VMs, addition or removal of a component to/from an existing VM, and addition or removal of liaisons. Now, let **Sys** be a distributed reconfigurable system composed of n VMs noted VM_n, where each VM is composed of m objects/components denoted C_m. We denote **NbCp_i** the number of components in each VM. Let A_{rs} be the agents to handle heterogeneous reconfiguration scenarios with **rs = [H,EX,EV,D,CM]** (rs: reconfiguration scenario). Let **E** be a finite set of states of each VM as follows: Active, Inactive or Suspended where **E = [A, I, S]**. Let **R** be the different reconfiguration operations: Addition, Removal, or Modification, where **R = [Add, Rem, Mod]**. Given the following matrix of size (n, 5) which defines scenarios that can be applied simultaneously by the different agents where each line corresponds to a reconfiguration scenario and the columns correspond to the VM_i, E, R, A_{rs}, and $NbCp\_i$ as described in Table I: We denote in the following

TABLE I. ARCHITECTURE DESCRIPTION

VM_i	E	R	A_{rs}	NbCp_i
VM_1	I	Mod/Add	A_{ex}	10
VM_2	A	Mod	A_{ev}	2
..	..	..	..	..

by: (i) $Instan^{AH}_{VM_n}$: a reconfiguration scenario applied by AH, (ii) $Reconf^{ACM}_{VM_n}$: a reconfiguration scenario applied by ACM, (iii) $Reconf^{AEX}_{VM_n}$: a reconfiguration scenario applied by AEX, (iv) $Reconf^{AEV}_{VM_n}$: a reconfiguration scenario applied by AEV, (v) $Reconf^{AD}_{VM_n}$: a reconfiguration scenario applied by AD.

Let Reconf be: $Reconf^{A_{rs},Cond}_{VM_i,C_j}$: a reconfiguration scenario applied by agents under two conditions: the finite state E and the different reconfiguration operations R, where i = [1, n] and j = [1, m]. A priority level must be defined between the different agents given as follows: (i) A_H: its priority is 1; (ii) A_{CM}: its priority is 2; (iii) A_{EV}: its priority is 3; (iv) A_D: its priority is 4; (v) A_{EX}: its priority is 5; We also define INT a set of interactions, where we distinguish two phases shown in Fig. 6: (i) Trigger phase: an agent which decides what direct interaction to launch and with which agent to interact, (ii) Interaction resolution phase: when an interaction is instantiated, to collectively choose an action from those proposed by the interaction, this action will be called the result of the interaction and its implementation will change the state of the overall system. For this reason, we must also define a transition function **Tr** between different VMs and that we characterize as follow:

If Sending **Then** Tr(VM_n, VM_{n-1}) = 1
Else Tr(VM_n, VM_{n-1}) = 0. An example is following:
1st step: $Instan^{AH}_{VM_i}$
2nd step: AEX may apply the following reconfiguration scenario :
$Reconf^{AEX,Cond}_{VM_i,C_j}$ where **Cond = [A, Rem]**, A corresponds to the state machine (Active) and **Rem** is the removal reconfiguration operation on the corresponding VM_i of the component C_j. We have to associate the following interactions between the different agents involved in the reconfiguration operation as follows:
$Int_{AEV \to AD}$. $Int_{AD \to AEX}$ if Tr(VM_i, VM_{i-1}) = 1.
3rd step: C_i = 0 (component is stopped) *Case 1:* $Reconf^{AEX,RemRi}_{VM_i,C_j}$: is a reconfiguration scenario of links where Rem_{R_i}: is the removal of links R_i. *Case 2:* $Reconf^{AEX,RemCj}_{VM_i,C_j}$, where Rem_{C_j} is the removal of the component C_j.
4th Step: C_j = 1 (component is active) *Case 1* : $Reconf^{AEX,cond}_{VM_i,C_j}$, where Cond = [A, Add]. *Case 2* : $Reconf^{AEX,AddR'i}_{VM_i,C_j}$.

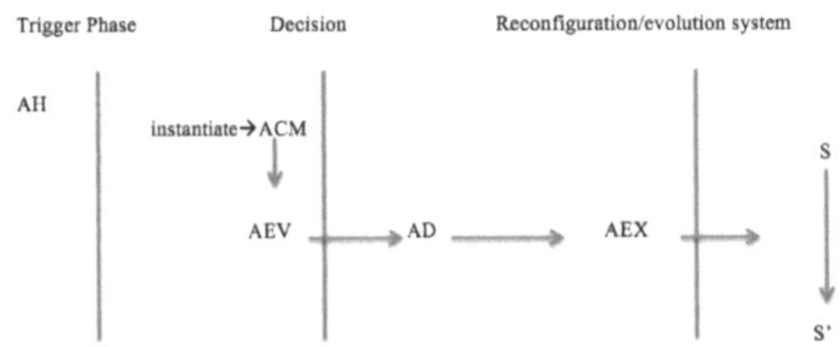

Figure 6. Interaction between agents.

```
Data:
Result:
begin
    date = 0; stack.init(); foreach x ∈ S do
        c[x] = WHITE;
        p[x] = NULL;
    foreach x ∈ S do
        if c[x] = WHITE then
            DFS(x);
```

Figure 7. Topological sort algorithm.

D. Implementation

In this section, based on the proposed work [25], we implement the DFS algorithm which models our protocol described by the topological sort present in Fig. 7. The strategy of the DFS is to search in depth in the graph whenever possible. The path of a graph ends when all nodes have been visited. DFS will process the vertices first deep and then wide. After processing a vertex it recursively processes all of its descendants. The complexity of this algorithm shown in Fig. 8 is: T(n) = O(n + m), where n is the number of vertices (components) and m is the number of edges (liaisons between components).

IV. CASE STUDY

In this section, we present an evaluation of our proposed contribution by a case study in the healthcare filed.

A. Presentation

Healthcare is an example where IoT technologies are used to accelerate and coordinate management of medical

```
Data: x : a node
Result:
begin
    c[x] = GREY;
    date = date + 1;
    d[x] = date;
    foreach y ∈ a[x] do
        if c[y] = WHITE then
            p[y] = x;
            DFS(y)
    c[x] = BLACK;
    date = date + 1;
    stack.push(x);
    f[x] = date;
```

Figure 8. DFS algorithm.

information and patient care. Our use case is composed of:
(i) Different services (cardiology, pediatric, etc.).
(ii) For each service, there are different applications. Some examples include the pacemaker which is in charge of the measurement and regulation of the patients heart beats, an electronic bracelet to track Alzheimers patients, etc.

Our proposed architecture of this use case is a private cloud where we modeled every service by a VM and each application is modeled by objects/components, as shown in Fig. 9. Each object (e.g. electronic bracelet) has an agent that controls the application composed of various agents to be distributed. These agents interact with asynchronous messages to exchange necessary information for starting/stopping the component. Each application has two FIFO buffers, one for incoming messages and one for outgoing messages. These applications interact together in a point to point mode (no broadcast or multi-way communication). Based on the case study discussed above, a simulation and a performance evaluation will be presented later.

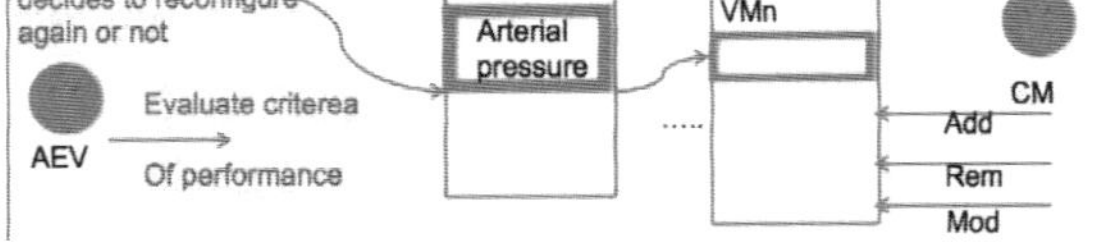

Figure 9. Architecture of smart hospital (Private Cloud).

We present a reconfiguration scenario shown in Fig. 10 and illustrated by the following steps:
(i) **1st step**: AH instantiates all VMs and controls the ACM.
(ii) **2nd step**: AEV failures on the balance of storage performance, as a consequence, AD demands to the AEX to reconfigure again. Then, AEX adds the required liaisons between the VMs.
(iii) **3rd step**: AEX removes the component C_j. (1) *Case 1:* AEX sends messages to VM2 for the removal of R_i. (2) *Case 2:* AEX sends messages to VM1 for the removal of R_1. (3) *Case 3:* AEX stops the execution of component C_1 and removes R_1. (4) *Case 4:* AEX stops the execution of component C_2 and removes R_2. (5) *Case 5:* AEX stops the execution of component C_j.
(iv) **4th step**: (1) *Case 1:* AEX adds a new C'_j. (2) *Case 2:* AEX executes the component C'_j. (3) *Case 3:* AEX adds a new relation R'_2. (4) *Case 4:* AEX executes the component C_2. (5) *Case 5:* AEX adds a new liaison R'_1. (6) *Case 6:* AEX executes the component C_1.

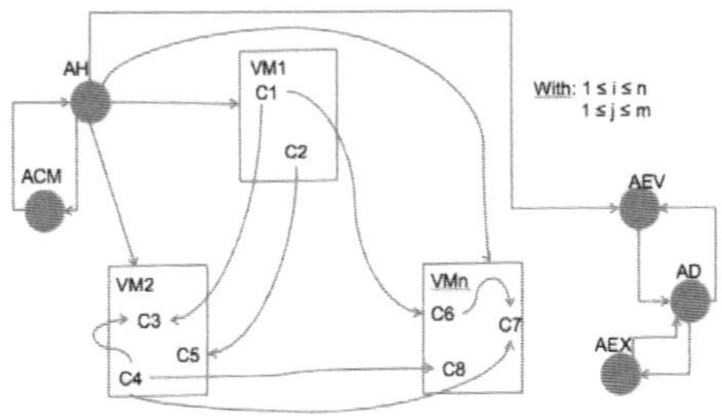

Figure 10. A reconfiguration scenario.

B. Application

In this section, we discuss the performance of our original proposed approach by simulation tests and we discuss its efficiency and effectiveness. We assume an environment of cluster with 27 heterogeneous physical machines (PMs) where three VMs are hosted. This environment includes 9 LENOVO hosts with AMD Athlon(tm) 64 X2 3600+ 1.9GHz, 9 DELL hosts with Intel(R) Core(TM)2 Duo 2.83GHz and 9 DELL machines with Intel(R) Core(TM)2 Duo 2.33GHz. We are varying our test parameters from 50 to 300 components and applying the test for each value and every result is the average of 20 trials of the experiment. This paper just discusses computing time and power consumption for each online reconfiguration scenario. Note that how to choose the most suitable values for each experimentation test is beyond the scope of this paper. Each type of the three VMs is simulated where each type of applications deployed in is referred to TPC-W benchmark [23].

C. Evaluation of Performance

In this section, we evaluate the efficiency and effectiveness of our online reconfiguration of IoT and CC applications approach. In Fig. 11, we show our proposed approach takes less computing time than the computing time required in [26]. Also, if we consider the A_{rs} parameter as a modification operation and the other three parameters (E, R and $NbCp\_i$) are assigned to fixed values, the computing time of our proposed approach is almost linearly increasing with the increase of interactions, which confirms that our approach has high scalability. Also, our online reconfiguration conserves the power consumption by up to 20% compared to the related approach of Tang et al. [27], as shown in Fig. 12.

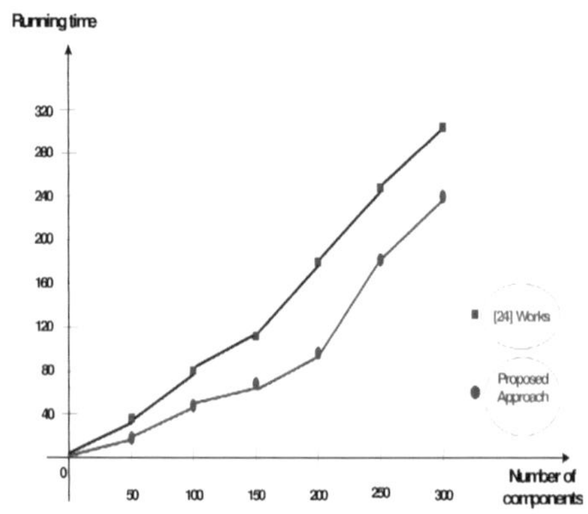

Figure 11. Running time evolution.

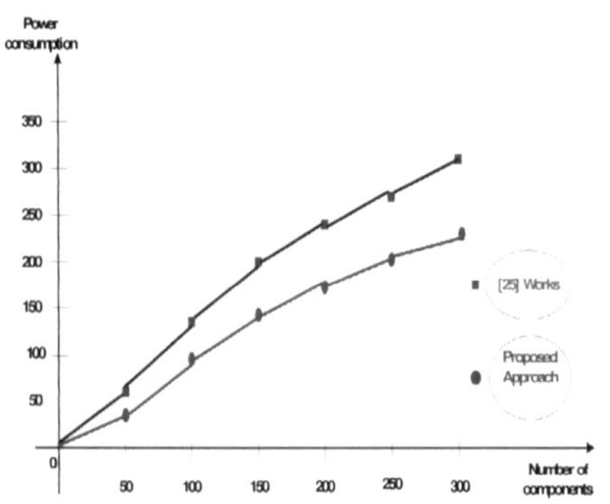

Figure 12. Power consumption evolution.

V. Conclusion and Future Work

This paper dealt with the performance criteria based on computing time and power consumption. We proposed an intelligent agent-based real-time reconfiguration able to manage applications in cloud and modeling formalism with algorithm to optimize these criteria. Our work assumes different applications deployed on VMs dependent on each other which is valid in reality and especially for current applications hosted in CC data centers and IoT applications. In our future work, we will continue our research taking into account real-time constraints that will occur in the capture of data from the sensors, storage capacity and security performance.

References

[1] N. Khanghahi and R. Ravanmehr, "Cloud Computing Performance Evaluation: Issues and Challenges". IJCCSA, vol.3, no.5, pp. 29-41, 2013.

[2] B. de Bruini and L. Floridi, "The Ethics of Cloud Computing". Sci. Eng. Ethics, pp. 1-19, 2016.

[3] I. Malhotra and J. Bakal, "A Survey and Comparative Study of Data Deduplication Techniques". IEEE Inter. Conf. on Pervasive Computing (ICPC), pp. 1-5, 2015.

[4] Y. Kim, A. Gupta, B. Urgaonkar, P. Berman, and A. Sivasubramaniam, "Hybridstore: A Cost-Efficient, High-Performance Storage System Combining SSDs and HDDs". in IEEE 19th Inter. Symp. on MASCOTS'11, pp. 227-236, Singapore, 2011.

[5] Z. Li, A. Mukker, and E. Zadok, "On the Importance of Evaluating Storage Systems Costs". 6th USENIX Workshop on HotStorage'14, pp. 6-6, Philadelphia, 2014.

[6] Y. Li and D.D.E. Long, "Which Storage Device is the Greenest? Modeling the Energy Cost of I/O Workloads". IEEE 22nd Inter. Symp. on MASCOTS'14, pp. 100-105, Paris, 2014.

[7] N. Aguirre and T. Maibaum, "A Logical Basis for the Specification of Reconfigurable Component-Based Systems". In Proc. of FASE03, vol. 2621 of LNCS, pp. 37-51. Springer, 2003.

[8] A. Ketfi and N. Belkhatir, "A Metamodel-Based Approach for the Dynamic Reconfiguration of Component-Based Software". In Proc. of ICSR04, vol. 3107 of LNCS, pp. 264-273. Springer, 2004.

[9] T. Bures, P. Hnetynka, and F. Plasil, "SOFA 2.0: Balancing Advanced Features in a Hierarchical Component Model". In Proc. of SERA06, pp. 40-48. IEEE Comp. Society, 2006.

[10] J. Magee and J. Kramer, "Dynamic Structure in Software Architectures". In Proc. of the 4th ACM SIGSOFT Symp. on Found. of Soft Eng. SIGSOFT96, pp. 3-14, 1996.

[11] J. Magee, J. Kramer, and D. Giannakopoulou, "Behaviour Analysis of Software Architectures". In Proc. of WICSA199, vol. 12 of IFIP Conf. Proc., pp. 35-49, 1999.

[12] R. Allen, R. Douence, and D. Garlan, "Specifying and Analyzing Dynamic Software Architectures". In Proc. of FASE98, vol. 1382 of LNCS, pp. 21-37. Springer, 1998.

[13] G. Salaun, X. Etchevers, N. De Palma, F. Boyer, and T. Coupaye, "Verification of a Self-configuration Protocol for Distributed Applications in the Cloud". In SAC12 Proceedings of the 27th Annual ACM Symp. on App. Comp., pp. 1278-1283, ACM Press, 2012.

[14] F. Boyer, O. Gruber, and G. Salaun, "Specifying and Verifying the Synergy Reconfiguration Protocol with LOTOS NT and CADP". In Proc. of FM11, vol. 6664 of LNCS, pp. 103-117, Springer, 2011.

[15] L. Srivastava, "The Internet of Things-Back to the Future", 2012, URL: http://www.youtube.com/watch?V=CJdNq.7uSdd.Mandfeature=related, [accessed 01-08-2016].

[16] "Green Goose", 2012, URL: http://www.greengoose.com, [accessed 04-08-2016].

[17] F. Boyer, O. Gruber, and D. Pous, "Robust Reconfigurations of Component Assemblies". In Proc. of ICSE13, pp. 13-22, IEEE/ACM, 2013.

[18] J. Kirschnick, J.M. Alcaraz-Calero, L. Wilcock, and N. Edwards, "Towards an Architecture for the Automated Provisioning of Cloud Services". In Proc. of ICSE13, pp. 13-22. IEEE Commun. Mag. 48, 124-131, 2010.

[19] L.R. Merino et al., "From Infrastructure Delivery to Service Management in Clouds". Future Generation Comput. Syst. 26, pp. 1226-1240, 2010.

[20] F. Duran and G. Salaun, "Robust Reconfiguration of Cloud Applications". The 17th Inter. ACM Sigsoft Symposium on CBSE'14, pp. 179-184, France 2014.

[21] P.P. Kumar, A.R. Reddy, and A. Rupa, "Snapshot Based Virtualization Mechanism for Cloud Computing". IJCSI, vol. 9, Issue 5, pp. 226-231, 2012.

[22] D.T. Meyer and W.J. Bolosky, "A Study of Practical Deduplication". ACM Trans. on Storage, vol. 7, no 4, Article 14, pp. 14:1-14:20, 2012.

[23] D.A. Menasc, "TPC-W: A Benchmark for E-commerce". IEEE Internet Computing, vol. 6, no 3: pp. 83-87, 2002.

[24] S.R. Kodituwakku and U.S. Amarasinghe, "Comparison of Lossless Data Compression Algorithms for Text Data". Indian Journal of Computer Science and Engineering, vol. 1, no 4, pp. 416-425, 2014.

[25] "Depth-First Search (DFS)", 2002, URL: http://www.cs.toronto.edu/~heap/270F02/node36.html [accessed: 06-08-2016].

[26] D. Kusic, J.O. Kephart, J.E. Hanson, N. Kandasamy, and G. Jiang, "Power and Performance Management of Virtualized Computing Environments via Lookahead Control". Journal of Cluster Computing, vol. 12, no 1: pp. 1-15, 2009.

[27] C. Tang, M. Steinder, M. Spreitzer, and G. Pacifici, "A Scalable Application Placement Controller for Enterprise Data Centers". In Proc. of the 16th WWW'07, pp. 331-340, NY USA 2007.

Role of Mobile OS and LBS Platform in Design of e-Tourism Smart Services

Ekaterina Balandina[1], Sergey Balandin[2,3], Yevgeni Koucheryavy[1], Mark Zaslavskiy[2,3]
[1] Tampere University of Technology, [2] ITMO University, [3] FRUCT Ltd
Tampere, Finland; Saint-Petersburg, Russia; Helsinki, Finland
e-mail: Ekaterina.Dashkova@student.tut.fi; yk@cs.tut.fi; Sergey.Balandin@fruct.org; Mark.Zaslavskiy@fruct.org

Abstract – **The paper discusses opportunities and challenges in development of the current ecosystem of digital services. Special attention is paid to analysis of the role of Location Based Services (LBS) platforms for service ecosystems in the Internet of Things (IoT) era. We study architectures of LBS-enabled smart systems and analyze factors that could enable faster adoption of new service paradigms by the industry. The paper discusses potential roles of the IoT infrastructure for addressing this problem. One of the supporting questions is the role of mobile operational systems in development of a future ecosystem of the services, which we study by reviewing two approaches implemented in two open source mobile operational systems: Sailfish OS and Tizen OS. One of the starting observations was that the "cold start" problem is one of the top factors that block services from successful development. The problem refers to the case when a new service lacks relevant content. We propose to address this problem by providing developers with a toolkit for accessing relevant content available in various open databases. Development of a method for efficient data importing from open databases and content management is one of the practical results of this study. We implemented the proposed method as an extension to the open source LBS platform Geo2Tag. Now, it is available for free use and illustrates really good performance. Results of our study were tested on the most typical use cases of services for tourists and hospitality industry. The practical results of projects are available for use by business and helped us formulate priorities for further research.**

Keywords: LBS; Internet of Things; Geo2Tag; Sailfish OS; import of open data.

I. INTRODUCTION

Nowadays, the service market is in the middle of a major transformation towards smart and proactive services. This transformation is supported by higher availability of powerful mobile devices with broadband network access, large memory and significant processing power, which allow to store and efficiently process large volume of data. Moreover, the development of the Internet of Things (IoT) ecosystem enables modern services to collect most relevant local content and manage the environment around the user. But, despite the fact that the opportunity is there, in practice, we still see only a few examples of services that take this opportunity to practice. So, let us analyze potential reasons for the slow adoption of new technologies and present our solutions that are targeted to improve the situation.

The absolute majority of available services are based on the interaction of a user with mobile devices. The user does not only consume deliverables, but is actively involved in content creating, knowledge management and decision making. However, we evaluate that this approach has reached its limits due to the explosive growth of volume and complexity of data. The services shall autonomously and efficiently search, filter and process the data and so become more intelligent and proactive.

Therefore, the motivation for this study is to take part in the definition of design for the new generation of mobile services ecosystem [1], which, in particular, fulfils the following criteria:

- provides innovative pro-active smart services that improve quality of life, are highly personalized, taking over the most difficult and boring work from the user, helping to save natural resources and wherever possible allow to use prophylaxis instead of curing a damage created by a problem;
- is stable, efficient and scalable to enable broad deployment of Internet of Things paradigm that will connect by two orders of magnitude more devices than the number of humans on the planet.

The development of such ecosystem for smart services demands to find solutions for the following two domains:

- mobile operational system (OS) that is functionally rich, flexible and efficient to provide required low-level support for the smart services;
- availability of a tool to define the accurate context of the user and collect the corresponding contextual information.

In complex ecosystems, such as smart spaces, mobile devices are considered primary as a tool for accessing services [2]. However, development of the smart services ecosystem demands more active role of mobile devices, i.e., they shall become center of the personal smart space and the personal management hub for the surrounding IoT devices [3]. Consequently the mobile devices shall become more powerful and the mobile OS be more efficient, functional-reach and flexible to provide the required support. In the next section of this paper we provide the corresponding analysis and comparison of the available mobile OS ecosystems.

Also, in the last years, we have seen that the role of location-aware services is increasing and the corresponding ecosystem is growing fast and developing in all aspects. Most of mass-market mobile devices have embedded technologies for detecting location. This creates a huge opportunity to develop services and solutions that associate virtual tags to the real physical objects and processing most relevant content based on the geographical context. This domain is called Location Based Services (LBS) and it very natural approach for development of smart services of next generation, which can be used for various use cases, e.g., for the cultural heritage management systems [1][4].

The third section of the paper discusses the potential role of LBS platform for development of smart services. As a result of IoT ecosystem development, we expect significant rise of the demand for LBS support, as IoT solutions need to monitor the geographical position of the things in time and attach them with a set of relevant attributes. This is exactly what LBS platforms provide from the box. For this study we particularly discuss how the LBS platform can address the "cold-start" problem. It is well known problem for newly launched services that do not have critical mass of relevant content. Lack of relevant content makes services less attractive for the users and often lead to the complete fail of a project.

For this study, we took as an example the IoT-enabled open source LBS platform Geo2Tag [5]. The platform already provides most of required service primitives, so importing function could be delivered with reasonable efforts. The additional advantage of the platform is that it provides efficient toolkit for development of services based on the Smart Spaces principles.

As a source of content, we are offering the universal importer from largest databases of open data. Open data is fast growing model of content delivery, where content is generated by volunteers and in projects funded by government and public funding, which makes the generated content available for free use. Already now thus model is strong competitor to the classical schemes of paid access to the content and it is expected that its role will increase in the future [6]. So the third section provides general presentation of our solution and discusses benefits that it delivers to the services. The fourth section presents implementation of the corresponding solution and discusses its performance characteristics. The key findings and results of our study are summarized in the conclusion section, followed by acknowledgments and list of references.

II. Role of Mobile OS

The root of this study is based on observation that the mobile device shall not be any longer seen as a pure service consumption point. Nowadays, personal mobile devices are powerful enough to take role of a manager of IoT environment around the user. Smart spaces technology provides the best infrastructure for it [7]. However, for deployment of personal smart space its core part - Semantic Information Broker (SIB) shall be installed on the mobile device. Such architecture does not contradict to the smart spaces reference model [2], but so far this case has not been studied. The main reason is that previously mobile devices were not powerful enough and most mobile OS could not provide required low-level support and flexibility. Nowadays, technically smartphones are powerful enough, but the main question whether mobile OS could efficiently use the device hardware and provide all basic functional required for proper operation of smart spaces SIB.

We started this part of study by making review of the leading mobile OS. Analysis of iOS and Windows ecosystems discovered that both are not suitable, as do not provide the required access to the low-level interfaces, the provide privacy tools are insufficient and the overall performance is not insufficient. The first results for Android OS were much more promising. One can find a number of publications on using Android devices for smart spaces applications [8]. Moreover, our initial tests show that it is possible to make SIB working on Android devices. However, Android sets to many restrictions on use of the low-level functions. Consequently due to inefficient use of resources we end-up with situation that smartphone cannot provide sufficient processing power for proper management of the personalized smart spaces by SIB even on most powerful Android phones. Moreover, Android architecture is not good for implementation of the proper privacy solution. As a result Android OS was excluded from further consideration.

But, further study of this topic discovered that, nowadays, there are two open source mobile OS that could fulfill our requirements. The first candidate is Tizen OS that is the best of available mobile OS adopted for use in resource restricted devices and IoT environment. For the last two years, Tizen OS is clearly positioned to take the dominant role as operational system for Internet of Things [9]. Nowadays, one can find a lot of IoT devices on Tizen and the system ensures seamless device-to-device connectivity and address needs of the whole Internet of Things environment. Tizen OS is target to remove border between the personal mobile device and surrounding IoT devices, as all devices operate under the same OS and mobile device can be seen just as one of IoT devices. Such flat peer-to-peer architecture is very scalable and well fits to the general IoT scenarios. However, it is not optimal for deployment of smart spaces that are done on principles of client-server architecture. As a consequence Tizen smartphones are not so much optimized for heavy computations and the privacy model does not directly match to the smart spaces needs. Moreover, nowadays there are not many Tizen-enabled smartphones and none of them is powerful enough to run SIB of the personal smart space. So as a conclusion we admit that Tizen OS is very promising mobile OS with great potential for our needs, but at the moment it is not suitable and there are no Tizen smartphones that can be used even for prototyping purposes. We are going to keep eye on further development of Tizen OS ecosystem, but had to drop it for the purpose of this study.

Sailfish OS is the optimized development of principles defined in MeeGo OS [10]. Sailfish OS is focusing on smartphone as a primary type of target device. Nowadays, Sailfish OS is the most efficient and fast mobile OS where the additional key priorities are privacy and usability. The system is based on Linux kernel and provides most of required basic primitives for accessing low-level functional and interfaces. Smartphone under Sailfish OS can provide efficient hosting for SIB and at the same time perform role of a hub when accessing to the various IoT services. The open architecture allows developing and integrating the missing primitives to the system core. These are exactly the features we are looked from a mobile OS. Nowadays, there is more than half a dozen of high-end smartphones on Sailfish OS. So it was possible to find required device for our study.

As a result, we confirmed that modern mobile OS can enable the new organization of smart spaces, where the core of the smart space is hosted by the mobile device. Also, we can conclude that, currently, Sailfish OS provides the best ecosystem for building personalized M3-enabled smart spaces. Within scope of the study, we defined all basic elements of the smart spaces that dynamic personalize the virtual and physical environment based on users' preferences. Based on results of this study, our next step will be to implement a fully functional IoT management architecture in personal smart space developed on top of the open source Smart-M3 platform [11].

III. Role of Location-based Context Information

The recent progress in volumes of available data storages and speed and availability of telecommunication technologies enable development of the new generation of services. Potentially this service in any place at any time can access any piece of knowledge created by the humankind. But, the volume of knowledge is so huge that it would flood any service. There are multiple technologies to address this need, starting from efficient data search algorithms to advanced methods of data mining and big data management. However, by applying even the best methods to the full set of data we end up in unacceptable delays and low relevancy of the results. The only way to significantly help this situation is by applying efficient filtering of the content. Context is the most natural filtering. Generally we took definition of the context as any information that can be used to characterize the situation of an entity, where an entity is a person, place, or object that is considered relevant to the interaction between a user and an application, including the user and application themselves [12]. For this study we focus on a subset of the context information that can be derived based on the geographical location of an entity. As it was shown by the previous studies, in majority of practical use cases the location-based context gives the most relevant filtering of the content [13]. Moreover, according to the analytical forecast in the next 3 years the demand for LBS-context driven solutions among developers will increase by at least 22% [14].

As an illustration of the role of the location-based context in smart services, we decided to address well-known problems, typical for current services. We target to propose a solution for the lack-of-content (also known as "cold-start") problem of new services. To make the story clearer for understanding and results more creditable, we illustrate the demand for such solution, the proposed idea and our implementation, on an example of services for the tourists and hospitality industry.

The recent reviews of tourist expectations done by tourist offices and agencies, as well as general analytic reports for the hospitality industry discovering clear trend that modern tourist is willing to see advanced e-tourism ecosystem that would enable personalization of service with minimal cost overhead. For example, one can easily see success of the simple trip planning web sites, which created a new market of online travel sales, with volume only in the USA of over $150B/year [15]. Generally there are many services for tourists and hospitality industry. But, basic services are not sufficient anymore. Tourists demand smart pro-active services for planning trips, onsite supporting, managing memories and sharing experience after the trip.

At the same time, there is demand from developers to reduce the complexity and the amount of resources required for development and maintenance of such services. For example, because of the development complexity, most services are missing on-site support and are isolated from each other. In this study, we target to come up with the toolkit for efficient development of such services. As a result, the development cycle shall be shortened and on-site support of the tourists and data exchange between the services provided from the box will take place. In the following, we start summarizing the main identified problems for this domain:

1) "cold start" as most services cannot collect the critical mass of relevant content;
2) update delays, which might results in significant decrease of relevance of the content and sometimes be even misleading;
3) user's content and settings cannot easily be shared between the apps;
4) development of smart services related to very high implementation and maintenance complexity.

Due to the above listed problems current e-Tourism ecosystem is highly fragmented and slow in adoption ideas of advanced smart services. As a solution we propose to use LBS platform that provides common ground for tourist services and services of the hospitality industry.

Most of available LBS platforms have high entrance threshold for developers, i.e., license fee, high complexity of development or both. This stops developers from broad adoption of LBS-enabled architecture in the services. Also most of available LBS platforms are lacking efficient mechanisms for keeping data up-to-date and only a few LBS platform are IoT-enabled, which is strict requirement for the future-proved services.

Based on earlier performed analysis of various LBS ecosystems [16], we selected Geo2Tag LBS Platform [5]. Nowadays, Geo2Tag is the most popular open source LBS platform in the world [17]. Geo2Tag is recommended by IEEE Internet of Things technical community for prototyping IoT solutions in City tagging scenarios [18]. Moreover, Geo2Tag is available for deployment in clouds, can be provided as PaaS, or configured on standalone server or even on the network of regular PCs. This provides developers and users with widest possible choice of architectures and development approaches for their solutions.

A number of services and applications are implemented on top of Geo2Tag, including a few cultural heritage systems and tourist services, e.g., Open Karelia network [19] and New Moscow cultural heritage system [20]. What is important is that these solutions are not just stand alone museum systems, but a service overlay on top of LBS platform. Such design is very scalable and provides complete infrastructure for the development of LBS services for networks of regional museums. So far, a number of regional museum networks and wide variety of supporting services were created on top of Geo2Tag cultural overlay. A few local SME and independent developers use the system and are able to exchange relevant content between the services and share functional primitives published in community-developed open source libraries.

Content is the key asset for all tourist services and its availability has core meaning for the popularity of a service. Building critical mass of content for new services is currently a complex task that requires a lot of time and resources. At the same time there is a lot of open data on culture and history (as well as in many other application domains). In this study we target to make content of open databases available for services in LBS platforms.

The goal of this project is to provide developers with the enhanced set of tools for importing cultural heritage information to the Geo2Tag database. We developed an efficient content importing tool that was tested with popular European open databases and Wikipedia. Further details of the developed toolkit are discussed in the next section.

We are going to continue this work by expanding the list of supported open databases. Finally, we target to provide import access to major open data on cultural heritage [21][22][23], plus add support of data import from Europeana and make in-depth analysis of additional sources of relevant content. Moreover, to help with content management we are going to provide developers with special Geo2Tag modules (agents) for automatic search and filling of the missing fields (with unspecified/null content). Plus, we target to release a special content kick-off admin tool to help create an initial set of content for a service based on most relevant open data, and these new results will be included to our next publication.

IV. Implementation of the Proposed Extensions

Implementation of the open data importer for Geo2Tag is done based on definition of import API on top of user's plug-in subsystem available in the platform. The interface includes module that defines general import algorithm, library of abstract classes for all steps of import process and the set of REST-interfaces for controlling and managing the import procedure. Implementation of the import procedure has total length of 1113 lines of code and is available for free download as open source extension included to the default main package of the Geo2Tag platform [5]. The algorithm developed in the import API use the following source data:

- Channel ID (the named set of data);
- Link to the original set of open data;
- Name of the Geo2Tag service - destination of the imported data.

The import algorithm implements the following four steps:

1. Downloading data. This step contains all actions required for establishing connection, authorization and downloading data from an open data database.
2. Fragmentation of the downloaded open data set to the level of individual elements. At this step the algorithm performs de-serialization of the initial set of data.
3. One by one translates each individual element from the set of open data to Geo2Tag compatible format. At this step, the algorithm extracts geo-location and time-stamps attributes from the original open data element and saves them to the newly created geo-tag element in Geo2Tag database. In addition, content of the new geo-tag is associated with metadata on current import session, i.e., link to the original data set and the time-stamp of the import procedure.
4. Saves created set of geo-tags in the Geo2Tag database available for direct access by the service.

The set of abstract classes of the import API contains logic of each step of the import algorithm plus templates for implementation of REST-interfaces for controlling import procedure. Further details on the design of this part of the algorithm are discussed by Zaslavskiy and Mouromtsev [24].

The proposed method includes procedure for geo-context layout of the open data. Implementation of this procedure shall be supported by the set of corresponding basic primitives and tools provided by Geo2Tag platform. Moreover, due to specifics of organization of open data the location information could be stored in various formats, starting from geo-coordinates and up to street address or even textual description of a place. This creates the new challenge of building universal solution for extracting geographical coordinates for the street address (this is relatively easy as the corresponding libs are available) and the text description. To address this demand (which could be also useful as independent service for some application) we have developed special Geo2Tag plug-in, that solving the problem of direct geo-coding. This plug-in extends functional of Geo2Tag platform by the following two REST-interfaces:

- /instance/plugin/geocoding/service/<string:serviceName>/job – creates task on packet geo-coding of data for the specified service channel serviceName;
- /instance/plugin/geocoding/service/<string:serviceName>/job/<string:jobId> - provides control of the created task.

As an example of the real use case created on top of the developed API we developed a plug-in to import data from the Open Karelia public museum overlay to make it available for use by any services in Geo2Tag. This source of open data has been selected for the first pilot as its objects contain information about the location in the form of geographical coordinates and time presented in an interval-based format of dates with "B.C." trigger. This let us to confirm that the developed algorithm works and could successfully process complex data structures of the open data defined in formats that are unfriendly for machine processing.

The next step was to confirm that the proposed method is efficient enough to be executed even on the mobile devices, i.e., so that this import procedure could be directly used by smart services on smartphones. We tested implementation of the method on the low-performance home PC with the following formal characteristics:

- Dual-core CPU processor @ 2.10GHz – this corresponds to the top clock frequency for smartphones;
- RAM: 3Gb – this volume was selected as it is maximum volume of RAM on modern smartphones.

We choose to use this PC instead of direct testing on the smartphone as it helped us to save time on implementation of the test environment plus let us use most well known and verified monitoring tools. And the PC parameters were selected in a way to formally match to the top smartphones on the market. But, as we know smartphones are able to more efficiently use memory and processing power, so the obtained results could be safely referred as a "bottom" performance estimate for modern smartphones.

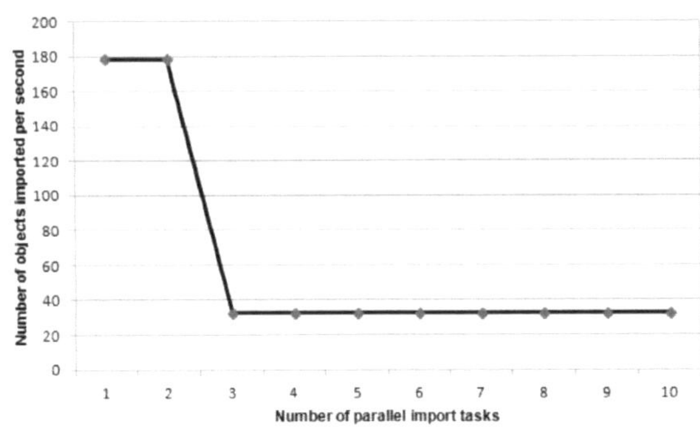

Figure 1. Dependency of the number of imported objects per second on the number of parallel import tasks.

The first set of performance tests is measuring performance of the import plug-in when serving a number of parallel import tasks. This test case simulated situation when a few services have to perform parallel importing of the content from open data databases.

In fact, the most typical scenarios for smartphones is that there is one or two parallel tasks that might need to simultaneously import content. But, we decided to makes the corresponding simulations for up to 10 parallel import tasks. The result dependency of the number of imported objects per second on the number of parallel import tasks is presented in Fig. 1. The algorithm shows really good performance of approximately 180 imported objects per second for the cases of one and two parallel tasks. When the number of parallel tasks exceeds the number processor cores we see step degradation of performance, which is direct result of multi-flow scheduling that has to be used in such cases. But, good news is that all modern smartphones are multi-core so we can expect similar level of per task performance, but for a larger number of parallel tasks, which is very important as with development of smart proactive services we can expect to see up to 10 parallel tasks on importing additional content to support efficient decision making.

The next analyzed key indicator was the time expectancy for the complete import procedure. The corresponding experimental results are shown in Fig. 2, where one can see the dependency of the maximum, minimum and average import time on the number of parallel tasks.

The results presented in Fig. 2 show that despite the restriction of the maximum number of concurrent executed threads and the Global Interpreter Lock (GIL) technology in Python [25], the average import time is growing slowly.

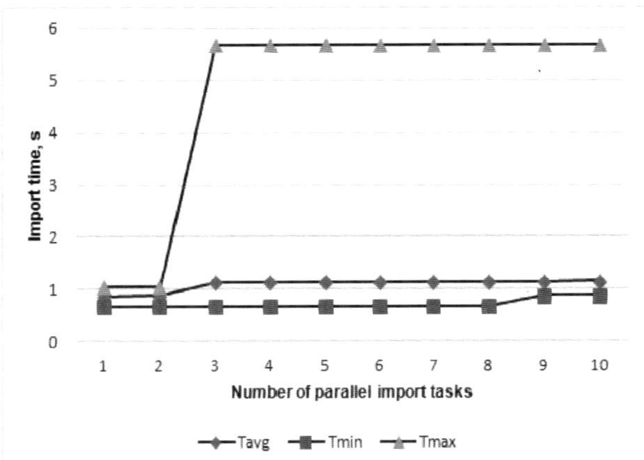

Figure 2. Dependency of the maximum, minimum and average import time on the number of parallel tasks.

When the number of parallel tasks exceeds the number of processor cores we observe sharp step increase for the maximum time of import. As discussed above, it is caused by the fact that in this experiment we used only built-in mechanism for managing connections to the web server Apache and the GIL and have not apply advanced scheduling tools. This leads to inefficient performance when one core has to process multiple tasks. At the same time one can notice that after this step change the value of maximum import time remained virtually unchanged with the growth of the number of parallel import tasks. This can be explained by the operation of the MongoDb cache [26].

Based on the received good performance levels and stable results without strict dependency on the number of parallel tasks, we can conclude that the proposed import method can be used for on-fly support of multiple smart services when executed directly on a smartphone with Geo2Tag support. As a result the developed solution can significantly simplify and speeds-up development and testing of services and enable "hot start" of new services. The proposed import extension has been committed to the open source LBS platform Geo2Tag and currently it is included to the default installation set of the platform.

V. Conclusion and Future Work

This paper proposes a new reference architecture for personal smart spaces, where the center of smart space is hosted by the smartphone. This idea is not new, but such architecture could not be implemented in the past. The main reasons were lack of efficient mobile platform to host SIB and infrastructure for efficient management of context data based on geographical location of the user. Within the scope of this study, we developed all basic elements to enable dynamic personalization of the virtual and physical environment based on the preferences of the user. As a result, we can conclude that this study gives a valuable scientific contribution to the development of architectures for various use cases of smart services in the Internet of Things environment. There is still the unsolved problem of collaborative personalization as the environment has to adapt itself to multiple users. The size of gravity field of each personal smart space shall be dynamically defined at any moment in time. This is an important topic for study that we are planning to address in the future.

Another direct conclusion of this study is that, currently, Sailfish OS provides the best ecosystem for implementing personalized M3-enabled smart spaces. Based on analysis and received practical results, our next step will be to implement a fully functional IoT management architecture in personal smart space deployed on top of the Smart-M3 platform.

Another aspect that we are going to address in the follow up study is the development of business model that takes into account interests of smartphone and IoT-devices producers. Our preliminary analysis shows that the discussed technical architecture provides a very reasonable solution, as it does not demand reallocation of business niches. In this case, one can see the personal smart spaces architecture on Sailfish OS as the business peacemaker for mobile device producers and manufactures of IoT devices. But, in-depth study of these issues is required and we also target to develop a solid proposal on the monetization scheme for personal smart spaces services. Moreover, we would like to come up with an analysis of possible roadmaps that combine smartphones and IoT ecosystems into a solid personalized service provision infrastructure that will surround users 24/7.

Finally, the paper makes an important step forward in the development of the LBS-ecosystem by offering an universal solution for importing most relevant content using open data databases and defining relevance based on geo-context. As a result, this helps to address the "cold start" problems as well as a few other problems highly relevant for the service developers. The developed content importing algorithm was implemented on the Geo2Tag LBS platform. The performance tests show that the proposed import method can be used for on-fly support of multiple smart services, when executed directly on a smartphone. Our import extension has been committed to Geo2Tag and currently it is included to the default installation set of the platform. A task for further study is to analyze the dependency of import tasks performance characteristics on the number of parallel tasks when executed on Sailfish OS operated multi-core mobile device.

ACKNOWLEDGMENT

Authors of ITMO University are thankful for the financial support provided by Government of Russian Federation, Grant 074-U01. Ekaterina Balandina is grateful for support provided by the Graduate School DELTA via Tampere University of Technology. The authors thank Geo2Tag community for great work on development and maintenance of the open source LBS platform Geo2Tag.

REFERENCES

[1] K. Kulakov, O. Petrina, D. Korzun, and A. Varfolomeyev, "Towards an Understanding of Smart Service: The Case Study for Cultural Heritage e-Tourism", in Proc. of the 18th FRUCT & ISPIT Conference, 18-22 April 2016, Saint-Petersburg, Russia. IEEE, pp. 145-152. 2016.

[2] S. Balandin and H. Waris, "Key properties in the development of smart spaces," in Proc. 5th Int'l Conf. Universal Access in Human-Computer Interaction (UAHCI '09). Part II: Intelligent and Ubiquitous Interaction Environments, LNCS 5615, C. Stephanidis, Ed. Springer-Verlag, pp. 3–12. 2009.

[3] G. Kortuem, F. Kawsar, V. Sundramoorthy, and D. Fitton, "Smart objects as building blocks for the Internet of Things," IEEE Internet Computing, vol. 14, no. 1, pp. 44–51, Jan. 2010.

[4] E. Balandina, S. Balandin, Y. Koucheryavy, and D. Mouromtsev, "Innovative e-Tourism Services on top of Geo2Tag LBS Platform", the 11th International Conference on Signal Image Technology & Internet Systems (SITIS 2015), Bangkok, Thailand. pp. 752-759. 2015.

[5] "Web portal of Geo2Tag developers community", FRUCT Ltd, URI: www.geo2tag.org. retrieved: August, 2016.

[6] "Market value Open Data to reach 286 billion by 2020", European data portal, URI: http://www.consultancy.uk/news/3019/market-value-open-data-to-reach-286-billion-by-2020, 9 December 2015. retrieved: August, 2016.

[7] D. Korzun, S. Balandin, and A. Gurtov, "Deployment of Smart Spaces in Internet of Things: Overview of the design challenges", in Proc. of the 13th Conf. Next Generation Wired/Wireless Networking and 6th Conf. on Internet of Things and Smart Spaces (NEW2AN/ruSMART 2013), LNCS 8121, Springer. pp. 48–59. Aug. 2013.

[8] N. Lebedev, I. Timofeev, and I. Zavialova, "Design and Implementation of the First Aid Assistance Service Based on Smart-M3 Platform", in Proc. of the 18th FRUCT & ISPIT Conference (FRUCT18), IEEE, pp. 174-180. Apr. 2016.

[9] C. Weinschenk, "Tizen: We Can Be the OS of the IoT", ITBusinessEdge. URI: http://www.itbusinessedge.com/blogs/data-and-telecom/tizen-we-can-be-the-os-of-the-iot.html. Jun 2014. retrieved: August, 2016.

[10] D. Luis, "Sailfish OS discovers its MeeGo roots on the Nokia N9", phoneArena.com, URI: http://www.phonearena.com/news/Sailfish-OS-discovers-its-MeeGo-roots-on-the-Nokia-N9_id50240. 11 December 2013. retrieved: August, 2016.

[11] D. Korzun, A. Kashevnik, S. Balandin, and A. Smirnov, "The Smart-M3 platform: Experience of smart space application development for Internet of Things", in Proc. of the 15th Conf. Next Generation Wired/Wireless Networking and 8th Conf. on Internet of Things and Smart Spaces (NEW2AN/ruSMART 2015). LNCS 9247. Springer. pp. 56–67. Aug. 2015.

[12] A. K. Dey, "Understanding and using context," Personal and ubiquitous computing, Vol. 5, No. 1, pp. 4–7, 2001.

[13] I. Paramonov, A. Vasilyev, and E. Mamedov, "A conceptual framework for development of context-aware location-based services on smart-M3 platform," in Proc. of 17th conference of Open Innovations Association FRUCT. IEEE, pp. 142-150. Apr 2015.

[14] J. Ellacott, "Global LBS Platform Market 2015-2019 - Increased Demand for Location-based Services", BusinessWire. URI: http://www.businesswire.com/news/home/20150716005694/en/Increased-Demand-Location-Based-Services-Improve-Global-LBS, 16 July 2015. retrieved: August, 2016.

[15] M.C. Rodriguez-Sanchez, J. Martinez-Romo, S. Borromeo, and J.A. Hernandez-Tamames, "GAT: Platform for automatic context-aware mobile services for m-tourism", Expert Systems with Applications, Vol. 40, pp. 4154–4163. 2013.

[16] E. Balandina, S. Balandin, Y. Koucheryavy, and D. Mouromtsev, "IoT Use Cases in Healthcare and Tourism", in Proc. of the 17th IEEE Conference on Business Informatics (CBI 2015), Lisbon, Portugal. pp. 37-44. 2015.

[17] "Open Source LBS Platforms", MetricsKey rating, URI: http://metricskey.com/open/open-source-location-based-services/, retrieved: August, 2016. & and "LBS Platform" keyword search, Google, URI: https://www.google.fi/search?q=LBS+Platform. retrieved: August, 2016.

[18] "Recommended LBS platforms for prototyping IoT solutions in City tagging scenarios", the reference is in the bottom of the first page of PDF, IEEE Internet of Things, URI: http://iot.ieee.org/iot-scenarios.html?prp=6. retrieved: August, 2016.

[19] "Open Karelia cross-border museum network", Hypertext ENPI CBC project, URI: www.openkarelia.org. retrieved: August, 2016.

[20] "New Moscow cultural heritage system", Mosart, URI: http://www.novmosdata.ru/. retrieved: August, 2016.

[21] Set of Open Culture Data in Netherlands databases, URI: http://www.opencultuurdata.nl/datasets. retrieved: August, 2016.

[22] Database of open data in Italy, URI: http://www.iccd.beniculturali.it. retrieved: August, 2016.

[23] Set of Open Culture Data in Russia databases, URI: http://mkrf.ru/opendata/. retrieved: August, 2016.

[24] M. Zaslavskiy and D. Mouromtsev, "Implementation of the new REST API for open source LBS-platform Geo2Tag", in Proc of Artificial Intelligence and Natural Language and Information Extraction, Social Media and Web Search FRUCT Conference (AINL-ISMW FRUCT), IEEE. pp. 125-130. Nov. 2015.

[25] D. Beazley, "Understanding the python GIL", PyCON Python Conference. Atlanta, Georgia. 2010.

[26] K. Banker, "MongoDB in action", Manning Publications Co, 2011.

An Experimental Study of Personalized Mobile Assistance Service in Healthcare Emergency Situations

Alexander Borodin*, Nikolay Lebedev*, Andrew Vasilyev*†, Yulia Zavyalova*, Dmitry Korzun*
* Petrozavodsk State University (PetrSU), Petrozavodsk, Russia
† P.G. Demidov Yaroslavl State University (YarSU), Yaroslavl, Russia
Email: aborod@cs.petrsu.ru, lebedev@cs.petrsu.ru, andrey.vasilyev@fruct.org, yzavyalo@cs.petrsu.ru, dkorzun@cs.karelia.ru

Abstract—**Chronic diseases currently account for most deaths in the world. Despite the fact that these illnesses are generally incurable, they are often preventable and manageable, and concomitant risks are reducible. In particular, acute out-of-hospital complications of the chronic conditions can pose a threat to health and life. Nevertheless, in the case of early detection and timely treatment the remote patient has a good chance to survive. The success of the early management and resuscitation is directly related to the arrival time of the emergency medical services. In our approach, a mobile health (m-Health) service is introduced to healthcare. The service supports involvement of trained volunteers to first aid and resuscitation, dispatching them depending on the proximity to the patient, and provide a guidance. Our design concept of this service is heavily relies upon the smart spaces paradigm, namely, the personalized assistance in medical emergencies is delivered to mobile participants operated in networked environment as a result of knowledge reasoning over the shared information. In this paper, we study the architecture and key features of the service and its smart m-Health space. We experimentally evaluate the Smart-M3 based implementation to analyze the feasibility and applicability of such mobile information services for the case of medical emergencies.**

Keywords–healthcare; medical emergency; m-Health; personalized assistance service; smart spaces; Internet of Things; Smart-M3; performance evaluation

I. Introduction

Over the last few decades, mortality of chronic diseases has decidedly risen and now they are the leading cause of death and disability worldwide, surpassing the infectious and acute ilnesses [1][2]. Almost half of the total chronic disease deaths are attributable to cardiovascular diseases (CVD), which is umbrella term for all diseases related to heart and circulation, including, but not limited to, coronary heart disease, heart failure, stroke and atrial fibrillation [3].

Due to the long-term and, mostly, outpatient treatment, complications of these diseases can be developed between visits to the doctor and resulted in acute worsening of chronic conditions. According to statistics, most heart disease deaths occur suddenly outside the hospital [4]. Most sudden deaths from CVDs are caused by a heart attack or acute myocardial infarction (AMI) with the survival rate 60–70% [5], and out-of-hospital cariac arrest (OHCA) with the survival rate 7–11% [6][7].

It is proven that the survival from OHCA is utterly time-sensitive and in case of immediate treatment the chance of survival is roughly 67% [8]. However, it rapidly decreases and after 12 minutes the patient dies almost inevitably [8]. Due to the hospital locations, traffic conditions and lack of free ambulance staff, the ambulance response time may vary over a wide range. Moreover, for better survival rate the so-called "chain of survival", namely, a particular sequence of actions should be carried out. Among the links of this chain, the cardiopulmonary resuscitation (CPR) should be fulfilled, and being provided by bystanders, it extremely increases the survival chances [9][10].

Decreasing the emergency response time can be based on an integrated approach to healthcare. The approach aims at achieving the following properties.

1) Remote tracking out-of-hospital CVD events and outpatient care by means of continuous monitoring of the vital signs with personal wearable sensors and reliable identification of health state worsening.
2) Involving the bystanders and trained volunteers to the process of early management in healthcare emergency situations.
3) Supervising patients and caregivers with recommendations provided by personal digital assistants—information services—running on mobile devices.

The above properties characterize the growing class of mobile health (m-Health) systems, where the classic style of patient's health monitoring by visiting a hospital is substituted with more effective and intelligent solutions [11]. They are essentially enabled by the progress in technologies of the Internet of Things (IoT) and smart spaces. An mHealth system is responsible to support and provision of healthcare services using mobile communication devices, such as mobile phones and tablet computers. Mobile devices are primarily responsible for collecting medical data, delivery of healthcare information to participants, real-time monitoring of patient vital signs, and direct provision of care (via mobile telemedicine).

In addition to the patient mobility requirement, mHealth services are essentially data-driven. They should produce "smart assistance" decisions on the basis of individual health data and a context information gathered from a variety of sources [12][13]. In this paper, we study the problem of reducing IT set-up costs and improve the quality of such mHealth services. Specifically, our approach is directed to the minimization of risk of CVD complications due to improvement of prevention, early diagnostics, forecasting of development of the disease. The service implementation is based on Smart-M3 platform [14]. The platform provides a promising open source solution for smart spaces based systems in IoT environments [15][16].

We consider a smart spaces based system for assistance in healthcare emergency situations. The use cases and system design were proposed in our previous work [13][17][18]. The focus of this paper is on experimental study of the architecture, the key features of the service and the created smart m-Health space for the patient. We experimentally evaluate our Smart-M3 based implementation to analyze the feasibility and applicability of the approach to mHealth development in the particular healthcare case of emergency assistance.

The rest of the paper is organized as follows. Section II introduces enabler solutions that are used in the service development. Section III describes our pilot implementation of the mHealth assistance service for emergency situations. Section IV provides the key results of the experimental evaluation. Finally, Section V concludes the study.

II. Enabler Solutions and Related Work

Let us consider solutions from IoT and smart spaces that enable development of the considered class of mHealth services. Most of the discussed solutions have been elaborated in our previous work.

The possibility to provide mobile healthcare service, outside of hospital, is a clear result of the emerging IoT technology, including the use of wireless sensors and personal mobile devices. As a reference health parameter the service can use the electrocardiogram (ECG) recordings obtained from personal cardiomonitor. An example mobile application of this health parameter monitoring is CardiaCare [19]. The application runs on a smartphone communicating with a heart activity monitor used by the patient. This variant of assistant service with heart rhythm analysis is pure local: arrhythmias detection for the heart function is performed directly on the smartphone.

The data heterogeneity problem for personal and body-area medical and well-being devices is discussed in [20][21]. One solution [20] is the enterprise service that guarantees interoperability and integration. For this purpose the intermediate semantic middleware is provided. Our solution [21] involves the architecture of the background service running on the smartphone. The architecture supports mashup health parameters gathered from a variety wirelessly connected sensors. Furthermore, a relational data model is proposed in [22], which is agnostic to the stored health parameters and supports introducing new vital signs with no need to redesign the backend database schema.

In [23], mobile and web applications are proposed to improve the efficiency of emergency services. Current location of the patient and his/her name and age are sent to the emergency command center for the purpose of better dispatching of emergency units. A particular design and its implementation are described in [14][24], where the service acts as a digital assistant aimed to dispatch closely located volunteers to the patients in healthcare emergency situations.

A smart spaces based platform is introduced by Vergary et al. [25]. The platform aims at the information interoperability between existing smart spaces based solutions in healthcare. The concept is illustrated with a simple demo application for the Smart-M3 platform. In particular, they focused on solutions to ensure an autonomous life to patients who would normally be placed in hospital. These solutions are based on ambient intelligence techniques and try to adapt the technology to peoples needs by building on three basic concepts: ubiquitous computing, ubiquitous communication, and intelligent user interfaces.

Reference scenarios for constructing emergency and other mHealth services are considered in [13][17][18]. The construction is essentially based on the mechanisms of semantic information sharing in smart spaces. The role of service intelligence and semantic relation of all available information when constructing assistance mHealth services is discussed in [11]. When a lot of data appears, then, knowledge reasoning over these data collections becomes inevitable part of the service. Based on deduced knowledge, recommendations to assist a patient can be constructed. A special form is prediction, which is important for early detection of patient state changes.

III. Personalized Mobile Assistance Service in Healthcare Emergency Situations

The analyzed mHealth service aims at providing personalized information assistance in healthcare emergency situations. The assistance is in the form of recommendations, both to the patient and involved medical professionals. According to the smart spaces approach proposed by Korzun et al. [13], the system is deployed at a set of networked devices, including, but not limited to, standalone or cloud-based server equipment, desktops, laptops and personal mobile devices, such as smartphones and tablets. The multi-agent Smart-M3-based architecture is shown in Fig. 1.

The basic software unit is an agent acting as a Knowledge Processor (KP). Such KPs run on the digital devices as a part of the application or background service. The KPs interact with users, sensor equipment, external information sources and other KPs. The data, gathered and processed by one KP, can be shared with other KPs by means of so-called Semantic Information Broker (SIB). SIB provides the functionality of ontology-driven common storage for the information shared by KPs and presented in machine-readable form of RDF-triples, the Resource Description Framework. Also, it support-sSPARQL queries for accessing the RDF-data.

As a result of this cooperative information sharing, a semantic network is formed in the smart space. The network integrates various heterogeneous data sources and their consumers.

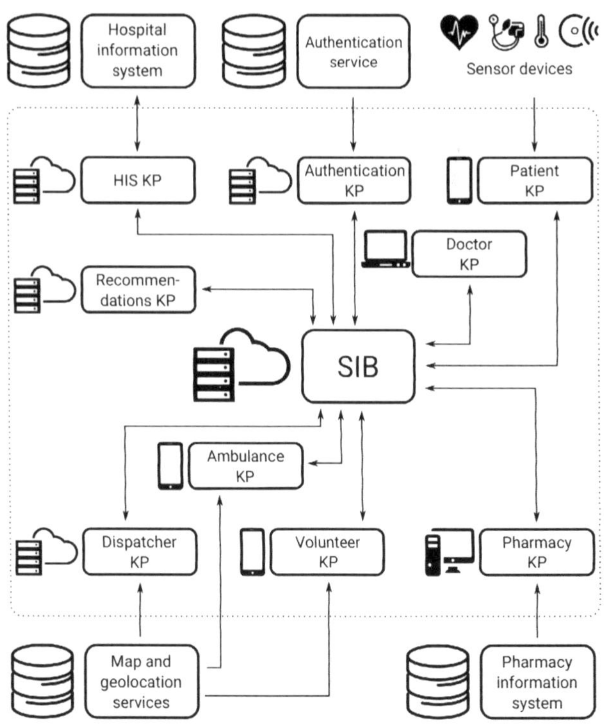

Figure 1. Multi-agent system architecture for personalized information assistance in healthcare emergency situations

In addition, this semantic information sharing provides high scalability in the condition of current trends in development of IoT technologies and the explosive growth of the market of m-Health equipment and applications.

The patient is equipped with a set of personal sensor devices that are able to continuously register the vital signs and send the recordings wirelessly to the personal mobile device. The mobile device has positioning capabilities, therefore, the location of the patient is also known. Besides, the health state is regularly assessed based on the questionnaire-based survey. The digital recordings of health parameters and the survey data are preprocessed on the local hardware and risk factors are identified. The Patient KP operates as a part of the mobile application, collects and shares the location and the risk factors in the smart space. The patient is also able to use the "panic button" to send an emergency alarm. The purpose is to address to the doctor timely and obtain further guidelines (e.g., call the ambulance or to take medications independently). Along with the alarm, the patient is able to send the complaints, selecting them from the predefined list, if in consciousness. The patient receives the machine-generated guidelines from the Recommentations KP.

The health data, provided by the patient is linked with the information from patient's electronic health record (EHR) elicited from the hospital information system (HIS) and published to the SIB by the HIS KP and is available to the physician via Doctor KP.

Alarms, locations and concomitant health data are available to EMS and, in certain limits, to volunteers. Bystanders, able to provide a first aid are guided by first aid assistant. Trained volunteers, able to assess the heaviness of the health state and provide resuscitation procedures, are informed on the important peculiarity of the patient, e.g., individual contraindications. Volunteer KPs also publish the locations to the SIB, as a result, volunteers receive alarms based on their proximity to the patient expressed in time to arrive the patient, elicited from the external map service. Both location of the patient, and locations of the appointed volunteers are accessible by ambulance squad through the Ambulance KP.

So far, the mobile applications for patients, volunteers, ambulances and physicians have been developed along with the authentication and dispatcher services. Current version of HIS KP interacts with the HIS mockup due to the lack of API of available HISes. For the same reason, the development of the Pharmacy KP is postponed. Scenarios of personal recommendations for the hypertension management and decreasing the risk of complications in hypertensive patients are currently discussing with the cardiologists from the Institute of Medicine of Petrozavodsk State University, preliminary discussion can be found in [26].

IV. Experimental Study

A. Experiment Setup

The experiments with the implemented pilot mHealth service services in medical emergencies aim to analyze the applicability of smart spaces based approach to mHealth service implementation, as it was described in Section III.

Since the personal mobile device (e.g., smartphone) of a patient is continuously used for collecting and preprocessing of the vital signs from a number of health sensors, a problem of fast battery drain can arise due to the computational load. During our experiments electrocardiogram recordings were being continuously and wirelessly obtained from the portable ECG monitor to the smartphone. These recordings were being preprocessed to extract the R-R intervals for the purposes of further HRV analysis. Calculated HRV-metrics were then publishing to the SIB.

For the extraction of R peaks from the ECG recording, the one-pass algorithm based on the Teager energy operator developed in our previous work was used [27]. The performance of the algorithm was evaluated on the well-known MIT-BIH Arrhythmia Database containing 48 half-hour annotated two-channel ambulatory ECG recordings freely available online. According to the tests, the average sensitivity on these recordings is 98.94 ($\min = 92.03$) and the average positive precision is 99.47 ($\min = 97.13$). These results are comparable to the well-known algorithms of R peaks extraction.

In the tests, we have used the wearable 1-lead ECG recorder with Bluetooth LE connectivity. The discharge rate of the smartphone battery was being measured during the tests using standard tools provided by Android OS. There were 10 four-hour tests with lengths of R-R intervals extracting alternated with 10 four-hour tests with no preprocessing. Before the tests were started, the negligible difference in the battery discharge rate had been forecasted due to the features of used R peak detection algorithm.

The information shared by KPs is presented in the SIB in the form of RDF triples. Real world entities may need hundreds of triples to be represented in the semantic and machine-processible form. Therefore, the problem of evaluation of SIB performance regarding domain-specific information entities. In the proposed service, semantic descriptions of the questionnaires for the regular health state audit and alarm accompanying complaints, are those complex information structures. In the second experiment, the questions of the health state questionnaire were publishing to the SIB and then they were consumed by other KP. The time of readiness of the questionnaire to other KPs and the time of extracting the questionnare-related triples from the SIB were being measured in each test. The tests differed in the number of requested questions.

Since the purpose of these tests is to evaluate the performance of the SIB, they were fulfilled in artificial conditions, namely, the influence of the network load has been eliminated, the KP and the SIB were run on the same desktop computer. For the experiments 10 tests were constructed with 10, 20 and up to 100 questions. There were 100 runs for each questionnaire. Before the tests were started, we had predicted SIB to be able to deal with the semantic description of the questionnaire of any reasonable size.

Participants of the smart space operate in distributed networked environment and gain an access to the external services, and so, the third experiment is devoted to the evaluation of the functionality of remote access to the EHR that is stored in an external HIS. The EHR consists of the set of documents and for the purposes of reasoning a subset of these documents may be published to the SIB. During the tests, measurements of arterial blood pressure (ABP) were extracted from the HIS mockup and published to the SIB. For the purposes of the further data processing, patients were divided into the several groups depending on the number of ABP measurements in their EHRs, as it is shown in Fig. 2. The query processing time for all measurements of one patient was evaluated against the number of simultaneous queries for each group of the patients.

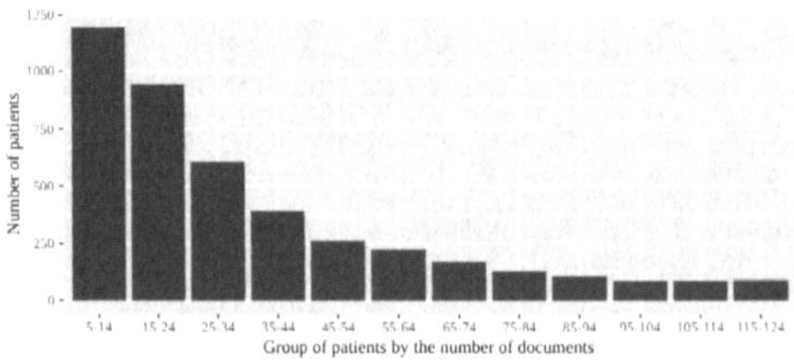

Figure 2. A histogram of the number of documents in patient accounts

The main service scenario is to appoint the volunteers to the emergency patients depending on locations in order to reduce the response time. Therefore, the process of volunteer dispatching was profoundly studied. In this experiment, the randomly distributed to the fictional map volunteers were being appointed to the patients. The patients were simulated with different rates of alarm arrivals. The waiting times of patients in the queue were being measured in each test. The tests differed in the number of available volunteers.

B. Functional Testing

The results of the battery discharge rate evaluation experiment are summarized in Table I. We observe the difference within the small bounds. It leads to conclusion that the ECG preprocessing on the smartphone has no significant affect on the battery drain. Therefore, the computational resources of the smartphone can be used in smart services for sensor data processing taking into account battery usage.

The box plot for the experiment with the questionnaire publication is shown in Fig. 3. It shows a linear dependence between the publication/consumption time and the number of questions. The box plot demonstrates low variation in samples that can be explained by the absence of the influence of outside fluctuation sources such as network load.

Since the semantic representation of the questionnaire was constructed of up to 500 RDF triples, the overall time needed to publish the questionnaire to the SIB was quite inappropriate and amounted about 10 seconds for the 50 questions. Nevertheless, operations of publishing and reading of the questionnaires are quite rare and are carried out only when the questionnaire is modified, the semantic representation can be used in smart healthcare service for medical emergencies. It should be noted that the experiments were be carrying out with CuteSIB 0.2.0 [28] that has limitations in SPARQL support and the triples were publishing and consuming with a set of queries that could affect the performance.

The HIS KP was under study in the third experiment. Results of the query processing time evaluations are displayed on the box plots, as it is shown in Fig. 4. The linear dependence between query processing and the number of simultaneous queries was estimated. At the same time, 10 simultaneous

TABLE I. BATTERY DISCHARGE RATE EVALUATION

Test run	Battery discharge, %
1	9
2	10
3	10
4	8
5	9
6	11
7	9
8	10
9	9
10	9

(a) Battery discharge with R peaks detection

Test run	Battery discharge, %
1	9
2	11
3	10
4	9
5	9
6	10
7	9
8	10
9	10
10	9

(b) Battery discharge with no ECG preprocessing

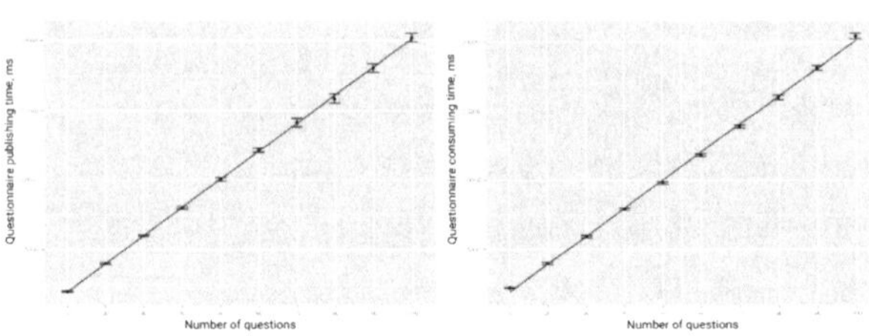

(a) Plot of the publishing time against the questionnaire size

(b) Plot of the consuming time against the questionnaire size

Figure 3. mHealth smart space: SIB performance evaluation

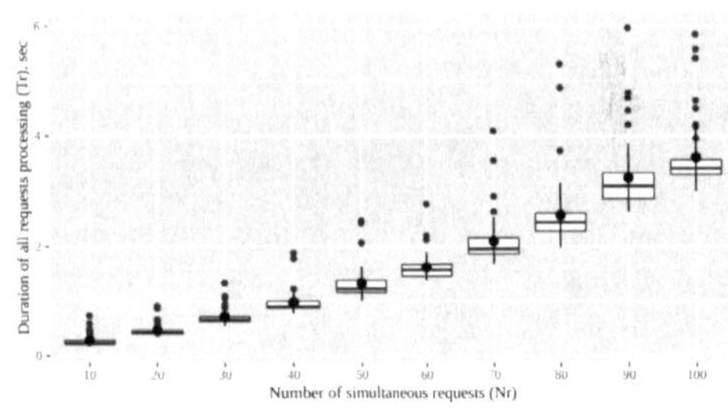

(a) Patients with 5–14 documents

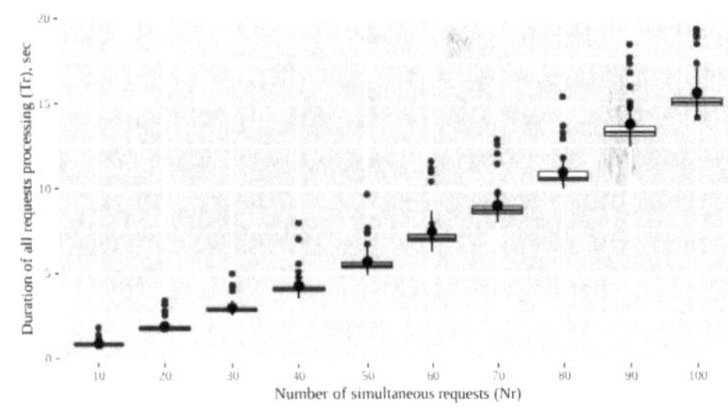

(b) Patients with 45–54 documents

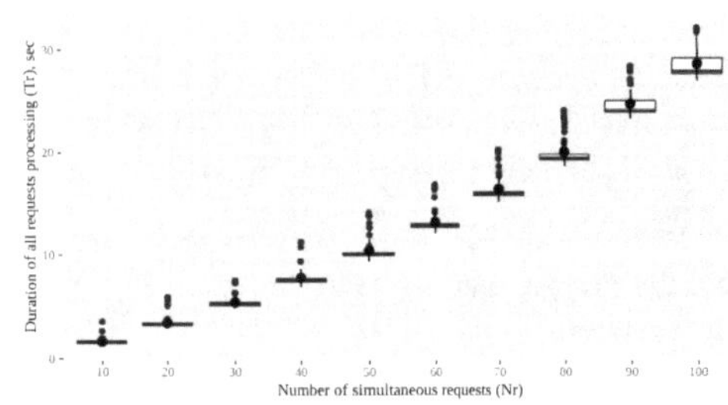

(c) Patients with 85–94 documents

Figure 4. Performance of query processing in dependence on the number of simultaneous queries for several groups of patients requests result in readiness of the documents within the bounds of one second. It allows to conclude that developed HIS KP can be used in the assistance in medical emergency.

In the experiment with the dispatching volunteers to the patients, the exponential dependence between alarm waiting times before the volunteer is chosen versus the number of patients was estimated. At the same time, according to the statistics, Petrozavodsk EMS receive a call every 5–15 minutes on average. At this rate of alarm arrival, the dispatcher allows to appoint the volunteers to the patients in a few seconds, and thus, is quite fast to be used in reference scenario.

Hereinabove, the results of four experiments are presented and briefly discussed. In the example of emergency assistance service, we showed that such a mHealth service can be constructed using smart spaces and, in particular, based on the Smart-M3 platform.

C. Emergency Response Time

The proposed system is aimed to the increasing of the efficiency of the first aid providing due to the mobilization of the trained volunteers. The volunteers that are located nearby to the scene of an accident receive an alarm along with the details and have the chance to arrive in a timely manner, and, in turn, to promote the increasing the survival rate in life-threatening conditions. Therefore, one of the goals of the experimental study is the evaluation of decreasing of emergency response times when using of the proposed system.

Simulation analysis was chosen as the method for assessing the merits of the approach. The process of receiving alarms and dispatching them to the volunteers was considered on the example of one of the urban residential districts of Petrozavodsk with the population of at least 50 thousand.

Since departure points of the emergency vehicles are known, the assessment of the emergency response time without the support of the volunteers can be obtained from the external map services taking into account the traffic conditions. We obtained the assessment of the arrival time of emergency vehicle to the scene in 9–17 minutes depending on the location of the patient on condition of lack of transport traffic jams. We have found out that this assessment is in accord with the statistics of the local Ministry of Healthcare claiming that the average response time in Petrozavodsk is approximately 14 minutes.

We had predicted the significant decreasing of the response times before simulations runs were started, as it is shown in Fig. 5. Using the map services we also obtained the assessments of the arrival times for all pairs of addresses of the selected residential district.

The simulation model is based on the assumptions that the patients and volunteers are distributed along the district according to the residential density and all the volunteers are available for alarm dispatching. In each series of simulation runs 20, 30, and so on, up to 100 volunteers were distributed over all the district map. During the simulation it is revealed that on condition of presence of the trained local volunteers the emergency response time decreases to 3–9 minutes depending on the density of volunteers.

V. CONCLUSION

This paper presented the experimental evaluation of personalized mobile assistance service healthcare emergency situations. For the service development, we reviewed the mHealth use cases, IoT-enabled solutions, and information-drive multi-agent system models. The evaluated implementation is Smart-M3 based pilot that aims at demonstrating the feasibility and applicability of the smart spaces approach to mHealth service development for deploying in emerging IoT environments. The presented experiment results indicate the possibility for creating a personalzied mHealth smart space around its mobile patients. We confirmed that the efficiency of the Smart-M3 platform is enough to implement and deploy such services even in complicated settings of IoT environments.

For the analysis of advantages of the approach, the developed personalized mobile assistance service is planned to be approved among the patients of Petrozavodsk Hospital of Emergency Care.

ACKNOWLEDGMENT

This research is financially supported by the Ministry of Education and Science of the Russian Federation: project # 14.574.21.0060 (RFMEFI57414X0060) of Federal Target Program "Research and development on priority directions of scientific-technological complex of Russia for 2014–2020"

REFERENCES

[1] Centers for Disease Control and Prevention, "Chronic disease overview," Feb. 2016. [Online]. Available: http://www.cdc.gov/chronicdisease/overview/index.htm [retrieved: Aug. 2016]

[2] World Health Organization, "Preventing chronic diseases: a vital investment: WHO global report," 2005. [Online]. Available: http://www.who.int/chp/chronic_disease_report/full_report.pdf [retrieved: Aug. 2016]

[3] R. Busse, M. Bluemel, D. Sheller-Kreinsen, and A. Zentner, "Tackling chronic disease in europe," 2010. [Online]. Available: http://www.euro.who.int/__data/assets/pdf_file/0008/96632/E93736.pdf [retrieved: Aug. 2016]

[4] J. P. Ornato and M. A. Peberdy, "Cardiopulmonary resuscitation," 2005.

[5] K. Smolina, F. L. Wright, M. Rayner, and M. J. Goldacre, "Determinants of the decline in mortality from acute myocardial infarction in england between 2002 and 2010: linked national database study," BMJ, vol. 344, 2012. [Online]. Available: http://www.bmj.com/content/344/bmj.d8059 [retrieved: Aug. 2016]

[6] D. Mozaffarian et al., "Executive summary: Heart disease and stroke statistics–2015 update a report from the american heart association," Circulation, pp. 434–441, Jan. 2015. [Online]. Available: http://circ.ahajournals.org/content/circulationaha/131/4/434.full.pdf [retrieved: Aug. 2016]

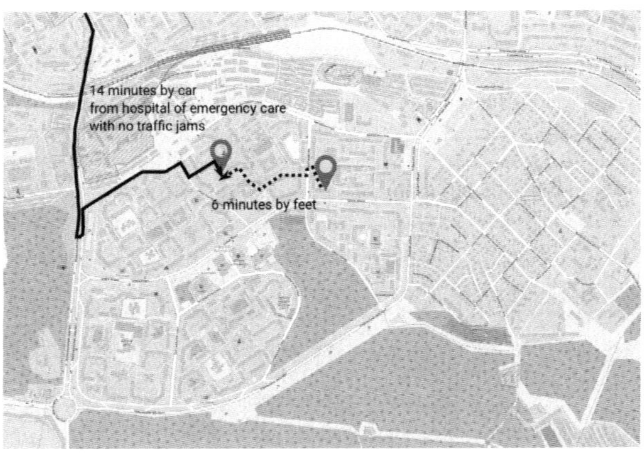

Figure 5. A district map: alarm and volunteer locations and response time assessments

[7] European Society of Cardiology, "Out-of-hospital cardiac arrest survival just 7 percent," 2013. [Online]. Available: https://www.sciencedaily.com/releases/2013/09/130901154147.htm [retrieved: Aug. 2016]

[8] B. Sund, "Effect of response times on survival from out-of-hospital cardiac arrest: using geographic information systems," Department of Economics, Karlstad University, Karlstad University Working Papers in Economics 4, May 2012. [Online]. Available: http://www.diva-portal.org/smash/get/diva2:372865/FULLTEXT01.pdf [retrieved: Aug. 2016]

[9] R. O. Cummins, J. P. Ornato, W. H. Thies, and P. E. Pepe, "Improving survival from sudden cardiac arrest: the "chain of survival" concept. a statement for health professionals from the advanced cardiac life support subcommittee and the emergency cardiac care committee, american heart association." Circulation, vol. 83, no. 5, pp. 1832–1847, 1991. [Online]. Available: http://circ.ahajournals.org/content/83/5/1832 [retrieved: Aug. 2016]

[10] L. W. Boyce et al., "High survival rate of 43% in out-of-hospital cardiac arrest patients in an optimised chain of survival," Netherlands Heart Journal, vol. 23, no. 1, pp. 20–25, 2015. [Online]. Available: http://dx.doi.org/10.1007/s12471-014-0617-x [retrieved: Aug. 2016]

[11] D. Korzun, A. Borodin, I. Paramonov, A. Vasiliev, and S. Balandin, "Smart spaces enabled mobile healthcare services in internet of things environments," International Journal of Embedded and Real-Time Communication Systems (IJERTCS), vol. 6, no. 1, pp. 1–27, 2015.

[12] H. Demirkan, "A smart healthcare systems framework," IT Professional, vol. 15, no. 5, pp. 38–45, Sep. 2013. [Online]. Available: http://dx.doi.org/10.1109/MITP.2013.35 [retrieved: Aug. 2016]

[13] D. Korzun, A. Borodin, I. Timofeev, I. Paramonov, and S. Balandin, "Digital assistance services for emergency situations in personalized mobile healthcare: Smart space based approach," in Proc. 2015 Int'l Conf. on Biomedical Engineering and Computational Technologies (SIBIRCON/SibMedInfo). IEEE, pp. 62–67, Oct. 2015.

[14] N. Lebedev, I. Timofeev, and I. Zavialova, "Design and implementation of the first aid assistance service based on smart-m3 platform," in Proc. 18th Conf. Open Innovations Framework Program FRUCT. ITMO University, pp. 174–180, Apr. 2016.

[15] J. Honkola, H. Laine, R. Brown, and O. Tyrkkö, "Smart-M3 information sharing platform," in Proc. IEEE Symp. Computers and Communications (ISCC'10). IEEE Computer Society, pp. 1041–1046, Jun. 2010.

[16] D. Korzun, A. Kashevnik, S. Balandin, and A. Smirnov, "The Smart-M3 platform: Experience of smart space application development for Internet of Things," in Internet of Things, Smart Spaces, and Next Generation Networks and Systems. Proc. 15th Int'l Conf. Next Generation Wired/Wireless Networking and 8th Conf. on Internet of Things and Smart Spaces (NEW2AN/ruSMART 2015), LNCS 9247, S. Balandin, S. Andreev, and Y. Koucheryavy, Eds. Springer, pp. 56–67, Aug. 2015.

[17] E. Balandina, S. Balandin, Y. Koucheryavy, and D. Mouromtsev, "IoT use cases in healthcare and tourism," in Proc. IEEE 17th Conf. on Business Informatics (CBI), vol. 2, pp. 37–44, Jul. 2015.

[18] I. Paramonov, A. Vasilyev, and I. Timofeev, "Communication between emergency medical system equipped with panic buttons and hospital information systems: Use case and interfaces," in Proc. the AINL-ISMW FRUCT 2015. ITMO Univeristy, pp. 36–43, Nov. 2015.

[19] A. Borodin, A. Pogorelov, and Y. Zavyalova, "The Cross-platform Application for Arrhythmia Detection," in Proc. 12th Conf. of Open Innovations Association FRUCT and Seminar on e-Tourism, S. Balandin and A. Ovchinnikov, Eds. SUAI, pp. 26–30, Nov. 2012.

[20] P. Castillejo, J.-F. Martnez, L. Lpez, and G. Rubio, "An internet of things approach for managing smart services provided by wearable devices," International Journal of Distributed Sensor Networks, vol. 2013, p. 9, 2013.

[21] A. Borodin, Y. Zavyalova, A. Zaharov, and I. Yamushev, "Architectural approach to the multisource health monitoring application design," in Proc. 17th Conf. of Open Innovations Association FRUCT. ITMO Univeristy, pp. 36–43, Apr. 2015.

[22] A. Borodin and Y. Zavyalova, "On an EAV based approach to designing of medical data model for mobile healthcare service," in Proc. 9th Int'l Conf. on Mobile Ubiquitous Computing, Systems, Services and Technologies (UBICOMM 2015). IARIA XPS Press, pp. 20–23, Jul. 2015.

[23] J. B. de Guzman, R. C. C. de Guzman, and E. R. G. Ado, "Mobile emergency response application using geolocation for command centers," International Journal of Computer and Communication Engineering, vol. 3, no. 4, pp. 235–238, Jul. 2014.

[24] I. Zavialova, N. Lebedev, and A. Borodin, "First aid assistance service," in Proc. 18th Conf. Open Innovations Framework Program FRUCT. ITMO Univeristy, pp. 638–638, Apr. 2016.

[25] F. Vergari et al., "An integrated framework to achieve interoperability in person-centric health management," International Journal of Telemedicine and Applications, vol. 2011, pp. 5:1–5:10, Jan. 2011.

[26] E. Andreeva, A. Borodin, and T. Kuznetsova, "Mobile system for the management of hypertension in remote patients and evaluation of the risk markers for hypertension-related complications," in Proc. 18th Conf. Open Innovations Framework Program FRUCT. ITMO Univeristy, pp. 419–420, Apr. 2016.

[27] A. Borodin and A. Rudenya, "A study of teager-kaiser energy operator pertinence for r peak detection in ecg recordings," in Proc. AINL-ISMW FRUCT, S. Balandin, T. Tyutina, and U. Trifonova, Eds. ITMO University, pp. 144–146, Nov. 2015.

[28] D. G. Korzun, I. V. Galov, and A. A. Lomov, "CuteSIB: a functional platform that provides a cross domain search extent for triple based informationy," https://sourceforge.net/projects/smart-m3/, 2009–2016, [retrieved: Aug. 2016].

Personalizing the Internet of Things Using Mobile Information Services

Dmitry G. Korzun
Department of Computer Science
Petrozavodsk State University
Petrozavodsk, Russia
e-mail: dkorzun@cs.karelia.ru

Sergey I. Balandin
ITMO National Research University
St. Petersburg, Russia
FRUCT Oy
Helsinki, Finland
e-mail: sergey.balandin@fruct.org

Abstract—**A smart space enables semantics-oriented information sharing in a networked computing environment, including the case of mobile settings. In this paper, we consider the emerging case of Internet of Things (IoT) environments. We introduce our study on personalization of such environments using mobile information services within a smart space. Such advanced services are defined now as "smart" or "intelligent". Their construction and delivery are provided by participants themselves, following the concepts of multiagent systems, peer-to-peer networks, and autonomic computing. This study identifies the key properties of a smart space to serve its mobile users and to provide them with all needed information assistance.**

Keywords–Smart Spaces; Internet of Things; Information Services; Personalization; Mobile OS.

I. INTRODUCTION

We consider the emerging case of Internet of Things (IoT) environments [1]. An IoT environment is associated with a physical spatial-restricted place equipped with and consisting of a variety of devices personal mobile devices, multimodal systems, etc.). In addition to local networking, the environment has access to the global Internet with its diversity of services and resources. Evolving from the world of embedded electronic devices, an IoT environment includes many mobile participants, each acts as an autonomous decision-making entity: a smart object in the IoT terms [2] or agent in the multiagent system terms [3]. In these IoT settings, the role of personalized mobile information services becomes growing.

Smart spaces form a programming paradigm for creating a wide class of ubiquitous computing environments [4]–[8]. Nowadays, smart spaces become more and more closely integrated with IoT. More precisely, a smart space enables information sharing in a given IoT environment, supporting construction of advanced information services by the participants themselves. Such services are often referred as "smart", emphasizing the new level of service recognition (detection of user needs), construction (automated preprocessing of large data amounts) perception (derived information provision to the user for decision-making). In this paper, we study personalization of IoT environments using mobile information services constructed within smart spaces.

Our study essentially exploits the known opportunities of M3 architecture [1], [9], [10], which represents a particular approach to creation of smart spaces [11]–[13]. Participants are software agents that act as Knowledge Processors (KPs) over the information of the entire given IoT environment. The central component is a Semantic Information Broker (SIB). It maintains a knowledge corpus cooperatively collected and produced by the KPs themselves, following the concept of Peer-to-Peer (P2P) networking and implementing an information hub of the environment. We characterize mobile information services by their ability (i) to find a proper information fragment (e.g., a situation-aware recommendation) in the knowledge corpus over the information available in the whole IoT environment and (ii) to deliver the result to the mobile end-user with effectively perceived visual representation on the personal mobile device (e.g., a widget on smartphone).

The M3-based approach achieves semantic interoperability even in the challenging IoT settings when the large number of mobile participants are involved as well as a lot of surrounding devices and remote Internet services are used in computations. Service construction can be personalized for a mobile user based on recognition and own interpretation of the collected information by the KPs resided on the user's personal mobile device. Service delivery and consumption by a mobile user essentially depends on processing and visualization methods supported on the user's personal mobile device and its mobile Operating System (OS).

The rest of the paper is organized as follows. Section II introduces mobile information services constructed within smart spaces. Section III discusses the properties of service construction and delivery in the case of IoT environments. Section IV studies the role and opportunities of mobile operating systems to form our approach to service-oriented personalization of IoT environments. Section V motivates the value offering of personal smart spaces that virtually accompany the users providing them advanced mobile information services. Finally, Section VI concludes the presented study.

II. MOBILE INFORMATION SERVICES

The amount of information is growing in the Internet such that users cannot efficiently manage the existing multitude of resources. The observable lack of mechanisms for information exchange between Internet services results in high fragmentation, i.e., information collected in one service is rarely accessible in another. In this section, we consider the M3-based approach to mobile information services constructed within smart spaces. Such services are called "smart" aiming at intelligent use of all available information in various situations that the mobile user can get [5], [6], [8].

The first property is an information service, i.e., the service provides the information fragment appropriate to the user in the current environment. The user—not the service—applies this fragment for situational decision-making. Consequently, such services provides a kind of informational and analytical support. The intellectual role of human is not replaced but auxiliary assistance is performed, similarly as it has happened in automated and autonomic computing [14]. The key challenge is information search, construction of the appropriate information fragment, and its visualization to the user.

The second property is a mobile service. The mobility essentially increases the number of situations which the users can get in. Consequently, such services are acting as a mobile assistant that accompanies the user. The latter follows the style "make everything from my personal mobile device", and the user may have no idea which other devices (surrounding or remote) are involved into the service construction and delivery. The key challenge is making the participation easy and transparent, as well as the service delivery becomes essentially aware of the visualization capabilities of the user's device.

Smart spaces support provision of advanced information services [12]. A smart space is created in a given computing environment, which is typically localized by being associated with a physical spatial-restricted place (office, room, home, city square, etc.). The environment is equipped with a variety of devices, including the essential share of mobile ones. Smart spaces aim at supporting cooperation of all devices in the environment in order to provide its users with convenience, safety, and comfort. The underlying computing environment is enhanced to handle the growth of the number of mobile devices and the amount of multi-source information to be processed.

The required cooperation of devices is supported by establishing a shared view of resources in the environment. Every device can join and leave the space dynamically. Software part of a smart environment includes two sides:

1) Agents to make autonomous information processing,
2) An information hub to provide a shared view on all available information.

Participation of a device is determined by its software agent running on the device. The users participate using their personal mobile devices as primary means to consume services. Each agent produces its share of information and makes it available to others via the hub. Similarly, the agent consumes information of its own interest from the hub. That is, a hub is a server that realizes a shared information space (i.e., an associative memory for agents) for the required cooperation.

The M3 architecture provides a particular approach for creating smart spaces [1], [9]. Rather than promoting the compatibility within one specific service-level solution in terms of protocols or software stacks, the M3 architecture addresses information-level compatibility and the collaboration between different producers and consumers of information on more abstract level [5], [8]. Agents interact on a semantic level, utilizing (potentially different) existing underlying services.

Smart-M3 platform [13], [15] is open source middleware for implementing smart spaces that follow the M3 architecture and take the mobile settings into account; see Fig. 1. The key architectural component is SIB that implements an information hub for agents of a given environment. Agents act as KPs running on devices of the environment. Some of them act on behalf of external data sources, resources, and services. Network communication between a KP and its SIB uses Smart Space Access Protocol (SSAP) or other M3-aware protocols [16] for information access and exchange.

Each KP communicates with a SIB using the blackboard interaction model [17]. This SIB maintains semantic information of the environment and its applications. The information

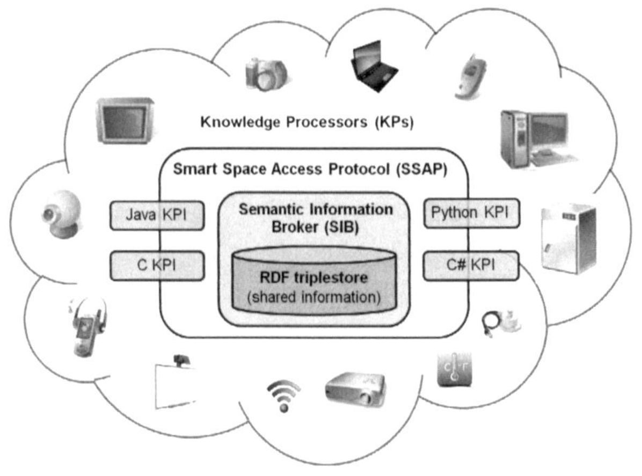

Figure 1. Smart-M3 concept model of a smart space.

is represented in accordance with the Resource Description Framework (RDF); see [18]. The basic data unit is a triple. A set of such RDF triples is considered as a graph, allowing representing semantics as relations. As a result, a shared knowledge corpus is formed in an RDF triplestore.

Communication between KPs is indirect, it occurs through the insertion and removal of triples into or from the SIB. This blackboard model is complemented by the Pub/Sub model [7], [17], which allows KPs to subscribe to specific triples. A subscribe operation creates a persistent query that is stored in the SIB and is re-evaluated automatically after each change to the shared content. Every subscribed KP is notified when the specified triples are added, removed, or updated.

The content representation in the form of RDF graph makes the ability to reason existing knowledge and infer new knowledge by means of ontologies. The Web Ontology Language (OWL) from the Semantic Web is used for creating ontologies [18]. Following [19], let us formally define a smart space as (I, O), where I is factual data (smart space content) and ontology O provides their logical representation structure. Ontology provides a tool to make use of the shared data and their semantics. Thus, the KPs can focus on the semantics of processed information.

In the multi-agent case, the notion of common ontology for the entire smart space becomes more or less virtual. Explicit maintenance of a space-wide large ontology O is impractical. Each KP may use own ontology o, though partially agreed with others. The partial ontology o describes the structure of content accessible by this KP (or a group of KPs). This property leaves freedom for a mobile KP to make own interpretation of the shared knowledge corpus, e.g., depending on the local user's context observed on the personal mobile device.

Operations on shared content I are essentially based on semantic search: any operation with an information fragment i first requires finding i in I. Table I shows basic smart space access primitives. SIB supports search queries using SPARQL query language. The result of the query is a list of all triples that match the query. In fact, it makes any SIB a SPARQL endpoint [18]. If the ontology-oriented type of interaction is used then the smart space access primitives are enriched with ontology, e.g., for $q = q(o)$ the search query becomes subject to the given logical structure of factual data in I.

TABLE I. SMART SPACE ACCESS PRIMITIVES.

Primitive	Notation	Description	Search factor
join, leave	—	KP initiates a session establishing a network connection to SIB. KP may use own ontology o for structural representation of exchanged information between KP and SIB.	Scope determination: part of I that the given KP may access.
insert	$I := I + x$	Insertion of new facts. A set of triples x is added to I on the assumption that no triple of x already exists in I.	Existence check: I does not contain x.
remove	$I := I - x$	Remove existing facts. A set of triples x is deleted from I on the assumption that x already exists in I.	Existence check: I contains x.
update	$I := \langle I + x \rangle$	Update of existing facts. A set of triples x is updated in I (non-interrupted remove and insert) on the assumption that the triples already exist in I.	Search: triples x to update.
query	$x := [q \to I]$	Instant content retrieval. The query returns all existing in I triples x specified by q.	Search: triples x matching to the specification q.
subscribe, unsubscribe	Await $x := [q \to I]$	Persistent content retrieval. Whenever the specified by q content in I is changed the query returns the affected triples x	Search: appearance of triples x matching to the specification q.

In summary, construction of an information service requires iterative search-and-process manipulations of several KPs on the shared content. Eventually, a needed information fragment becomes derivable by a KP on the user side.

III. SERVICES IN INTERNET OF THINGS ENVIRONMENTS

An IoT environment is a computing environment associated with a physical spatial-restricted place. The surrounding "things" are Internet-enabled devices that can perform computations. In addition to local networking, the environment has access to the global Internet with its diversity of services and resources. In this section, we formalize construction and delivery of mobile information services in smart spaces deployed in a given IoT environments.

Although the term IoT was initially proposed to refer to uniquely identifiable interoperable connected objects with Radio-Frequency IDentification (RFID) technology, now the most common view of IoT refers to a dynamic global network infrastructure for the ubiquitous connection of numerous physical objects (e.g., everyday things equipped with RFIDs, various sensors and actuators, embedded and mobile electronic devices, low capacity and powerful computers) that rely on advanced wireless communication and information processing technologies. Furthermore, IoT aims at fusion of real (physical) and virtual (information) worlds. As a result, IoT is evolving to service-oriented information interconnection and convergence on the global level [2], [20], [21].

Involvement of many surrounding devices of the IoT environment is one of the essential properties that the smart spaces approach has to take into account in service development. Even low-capacity devices act in service construction on the equal basic with more powerful computers. As a result, it opens the services for data coming from the physical world (embedded and other IoT devices) and from such an overlapped area of the physical and information worlds as human-related and social activity [22] (smartphones and other personal mobile computers, various carried and wearable devices). Many edge IoT devices become responsible for a significant part of system computations, in accordance to the vision of smart objects in IoT [2], [23] and of human-centered information systems in edge-centric computing [24].

The interoperability becomes one of the key issues. For a smart space deployed in an IoT environment, the interoperability is defined as the ability for software agents (written in different programming languages, running on different devices with different operating systems) to communicate and interact with one another (over different networks). In the previous

Require: Ontology o to access information content I of the smart space. The set U of available UI devices.
1: Await $[q_{\text{act}}(o) \to I] = \text{true}$ {event-based activation}
2: Query $x := [q_{\text{info}}(o) \to I]$ {information selection}
3: Select $d \in U$ {target UI devices}
4: Visualization $v_d := v_d + x$ {service delivery to end-user}

Figure 2. Information service construction for the end-user.

Require: Ontology o to access smart space information content I. The set U of available UI devices.
1: Await $[q_{\text{act}}(o) \to I] = \text{true}$ {event-based activation}
2: Query $x := [q_{\text{info}}(o) \to I]$ {information selection}
3: Decide $y := f(x, o)$ {formulation of processing action}
4: Update $I := I + y$ {new shared information}

Figure 3. Content search & processing in the smart space.

section, we showed that having a shared view on available resources an information service can be considered as information search and knowledge reasoning over the content I with subsequent delivery of the result to the end-users. Let us formalize conceptual steps of the service construction.

The algorithm in Fig. 2 defines construction of an information service for the end-user. Step 1 detects when the service is needed based on the current situation in the smart space. Step 2 makes selection of knowledge x to deliver to the user. Step 3 decides which UI elements are target devices for the service delivery. Step 4 updates recent visualization v_d to include x on device d.

The algorithm in Fig. 3 defines construction of an information service responsible for eventual production of appropriate information fragments in the smart space. Step 1 analyzes the space content to detect when a processing action is needed. Steps 2 and 3 are reasoning in context of the current situation, and the service decides what updates (possibly without human intervention) are needed in the recent system state. The updates become available to the participants.

Therefore, KPs of the smart space apply available knowledge in constructing and delivering the services, without necessarily identification who finds and provides the knowledge. Algorithms 2 and 3 of generic services assume that some part of available knowledge is shared in the smart space and the other part is kept locally by KPs themselves (i.e., non-shared). To make a further step in the service design we need to clarify the structure of I. In the extreme case, all data a service needs are accessed via its smart space, which provides search query interfaces to reason knowledge over I and its instant structure.

Based on the ontological modeling approach, one can consider I consisting of various information objects and semantic relations among them [1], [11], [25]. Its basic structure is defined by problem domain and activity ontologies (OWL classes, relations, restrictions). Factual objects in I are represented as instances (OWL individuals) of ontology classes and their object properties represent semantic relations between objects.

For modeling IoT objects (their resources and processing activity), P2P methods can be applied for representing the inferred knowledge [19]. Any object $i \in I$ is treated as a peer. Each i keeps some data (values of data properties) and has links to some other objects j (object properties). Therefore, a P2P network G_I is formed on top of I. Contributions to the smart space (insert, update, remove) change the network of objects, similarly as it happens in P2P due to peers churn and neighbors selection. This P2P model extends the notion of ontology graph (interrelated classes and instances of them) kept implicitly in I and in ontologies o at the KPs to a dynamic self-organized system. That is, content I is considered as interacting objects, which are active entities (make actions) on one hand and are subject to information changes (actions consequence) on the other hand.

Consequently, service construction can be formulated in terms of flows of information changes. Given a starting object $s \in I$ and its initial change. Let $D(s)$ be a graph routable from s in G_I. Construction of a service corresponds to a routing path $s \to^* d$. Injection of the change starts the service (like a P2P node starting a lookup query). The sequence of changes flows in G_I. Note that parallel paths are possible. Any point when an agent reads an object can be considered a final step of the service construction since the agent consumes an outcome.

In summary, the service construction in an IoT environment needs virtualization of all related processes and resources. In addition to the straightforward virtualization, the semantics are shared to describe relations observed by involved participants in ongoing processes and available resources. The shared content is a knowledge corpus represented as a semantic network (represented objects and their relations). It becomes a dynamic evolving system with properties similar to P2P networks. A service construction process is reflected in the smart space as routes in the semantic network.

IV. Personalization Approach

The users are more and more interested in context-aware, situational, and personalized services. In this section, we study the opportunities of mobile devices and mobile operating systems in the proposed service-oriented personalization of IoT environments On one hand, the personalization approach is based on the smart space properties, which we described in the previous sections. On the other hand, the role of mobile operating systems is crucial for customizing a service to the user's needs in the current situation.

Nowadays, the personal mobile devices are seen as the primary tool for accessing services in the smart space [13]. Moreover, in the near future personal handheld devices could become not just an interface to the mobile and Internet services, but the master devices for personalized management of IoT environment, and play in the world of devices the same role as browsers play in the world of Internet services. In fact a modern smartphone is the closest and very powerful device that can manage surrounding IoT environment, so creating a personal smart space around the user. The personal mobile device shall not be anymore seen as a pure service consumption point. In fact it is the best source of situational and other personal information that can be used in delivery or even personalized construction of various services.

Our work on smart spaces-based development has already indicated the distinctive role of smartphones and tablets for such emerging IoT application domains as collaborative work systems [26], e-Tourism recommendation services [27], and mobile healthcare assistance [28]. Many studied use cases of the smart spaces based applications for IoT consider smartphone as a device for handling processing of the most personal data, which is done by the corresponding KPs that are executed on the device [29].

Consider the personal smart spaces created by placing the smartphone in the center to take role of the SIB host. This architectural change enables a number of benefits for the end-users, which we discuss in the next section. At the same time the use case is quite demanding for the smartphone. Let us study whether the new architecture can be supported by the available smartphone ecosystems. Even the quick analysis of the iOS and Windows ecosystems illustrated that they are not properly suitable, as it is not possible to get required access to the low-level interfaces and functions.

The next considered candidate is the Android ecosystem. One can find a number of studies that use KPs on Android devices in M3-enabled smart spaces, e.g., see [30], [31]. Moreover, it is possible to make SIB working on Android devices. Unfortunately, Android sets too many restrictions on the use of low-level functions. Due to these restrictions the implementation of a personal smart space cannot be done efficiently. The Android ecosystem provides insufficient processing power for proper management of a smart space by SIB installed even on the most powerful Android smartphones.

Another candidate is Tizen OS ecosystem [32]. Since the last two years it has become one of the leaders OS for IoT devices, which is important advantage for programming smart spaces. Moreover, Tizen is an open source platform that enables efficient implementation of SIB. The only strong disadvantage of the current Tizen OS ecosystem is that it is too much focused on compatibility with resource-restricted devices and they pay less attention to OS optimization for the high-end smartphone devices. As a result, although Tizen OS is a very promising candidate, it is impossible to find powerful enough high-end smartphone on Tizen OS.

Finally, Sailfish OS [33] is yet another ecosystem for personal mobile devices in IoT. This OS can be seen as a close "relative" of Tizen OS, as the root of both systems is in MeeGo OS. Nevertheless, Sailfish OS focuses on smartphones as a primary target device with setting the key goal in optimization of the system performance. As a result, Sailfish OS provides currently the most efficient and fast mobile OS ecosystem. The system is based on Linux kernel and includes most of required basic primitives for accessing low-level functions and interfaces. The open architecture enables us to develop and integrate the missing primitives to the system core. Moreover, other key priorities of Sailfish OS are privacy and usability. These are exactly the "bonus" features that this mobile OS we are expected to provide to the smart spaces. Nowadays, the

Sailfish OS ecosystem is supported by half a dozen of high-end smartphones. Although these smartphones are not well-known among regular users so far, one can get Sailfish OS devices and even have a few options.

In summary, this preliminary study of mobile operating systems indicates that potentially the Sailfish OS provides the best-suited candidate for implementing personalized M3-enabled smart spaces.

V. VALUE OFFERING BY PERSONAL SMART SPACES

The personal smart spaces aim at automatic dynamic personalization of the whole virtual and physical environment around the user. The personalization is done based on the individual preferences as well as on physical location and other relevant context information available for the smart space. The idea is that the smart space makes continuously monitoring of all services and devices that are available for the user at any moment of time and automatically forms environment management requests to maximize comfort and safety of the user. In particular, the personal smart space provides a middleware to help the user to most efficiently interact with the surround IoT environment.

Consider an example of user interaction with physical environment. When the user enters to the shopping mall the personal smart space can check what large interaction screens are available. As a result, when the user is passed by, she/he can take control over the available screens as a temporarily interface for more comfortable interaction with services provided by the shopping mall.

The example can be continued for the user interaction with the virtual environment. While the user interacts with the shopping mall services, the personal smart space makes monitoring what is searched by the user, request for personal discounts from the shops of interest, and build the optimal path for visiting places of interest.

The mixed user interactions with virtual and physical environment are also possible. When the user is done with search the personal smart space activates navigation services on the smartphone plus available visualization. Other appropriate tools can also be activated, e.g., to highlight the path in the shop or to call elevators.

By the above illustrative example we describe our idea of the new type of value offering delivered by the personal smart spaces. Everyone can imagine a number of other use cases for various application domains. Importantly that such use case scenarios fully fit to the basic reference model of smart spaces [4], [5], with assumption that SIB could be fully operational on the personal mobile device.

The definition of personal smart spaces creates a new problem of collaborative personalization, as multiple users will interact with IoT environments in public places. The environment has to adopt itself to the multiple users at the same time. As a result, we come with definition of a new key parameter—the size of the gravity field of the personal smart spaces. In other words, the individual gravity field shows the influence level of the user to the collaborative decision making and control in the IoT environment.

An interesting case study for collaborative personalization is the microphone service of SmartRoom system [26], [30]. Each user can use her/his smartphone as a microphone collaboratively working in multimedia equipped room during a conference session, work group meeting, or seminar. The audio system in the room is a shared resource with mutual exclusion. User access to this resource is subject to personalization, which, in turn, depends on the situational role and interests of the user.

In summary, defining the optimal size for each individual gravity field is an open research topic for our further work, which we are planning to accomplish within the scope of studying collaborative use of the personal smart spaces.

VI. CONCLUSION AND FUTURE WORK

This paper elaborated the fundamental concept of mobile information services that are constructed and delivered within smart spaces. We introduced the theoretical properties of such services that enable personalization of the IoT environment. The properties are essentially based on semantic-driven multi-agent iterative search-and-process manipulations on the shared knowledge corpus with virtualization of IoT environment processes and resources. The important direction of our further theoretical research is new data mining and knowledge reasoning methods for effective service personalization in the large-scale IoT settings. Such methods need to be implemented as cooperative activity of many KPs with knowledge sharing support from SIB. In particular, it needs extending the function of SIB, which is recently limited with information access and exchange mediation.

From the applied research and development point of view, a promising option for applications is personal smart spaces when the user's smartphone is placed in the center. We considered the main available mobile OS ecosystems and concluded that most of them cannot provide the required support for the personalized smart spaces. Nevertheless, the Sailfish OS seems a suitable ecosystem for creating personal smart spaces with the M3 architecture. This option provides the most straightforward solution to enable personalization of IoT environments based on the user's preferences. At the same time, we are faced with a new research problem of collaborative personalization when the IoT environment adapts itself to multiple users. Its solutions need extending the SIB with the gravity field support for the personal smart spaces. In particular, definition of an optimal size for each individual gravity field is an important research topic of our future work.

As the next development step we are planning to implement a full version of Smart-M3 SIB for Sailfish OS. Then, a set of reference use cases will be created and experimentally evaluated on top of the personalized smart spaces.

ACKNOWLEDGMENT

The reported concept elaboration study was funded by Russian Fund for Basic Research (RFBR) according to research project # 14-07-00252. The work of D. Korzun on the presented applied solutions was financially supported by the Ministry of Education and Science of the Russian Federation within project # 2.2336.2014/K from the project part of state research assignment.

REFERENCES

[1] D. Korzun, S. Balandin, and A. Gurtov, "Deployment of Smart Spaces in Internet of Things: Overview of the design challenges," in Proc. 13th Int'l Conf. Next Generation Wired/Wireless Networking and 6th Conf. on Internet of Things and Smart Spaces (NEW2AN/ruSMART 2013), LNCS 8121, Springer, pp. 48–59, Aug. 2013.

[2] G. Kortuem, F. Kawsar, V. Sundramoorthy, and D. Fitton, "Smart objects as building blocks for the Internet of Things," IEEE Internet Computing, vol. 14, no. 1, pp. 44–51, Jan. 2010.

[3] V. Gorodetsky, "Agents and distributed data mining in smart space: Challenges and perspectives," in Agents and Data Mining Interaction (ADMI 2012), LNAI 7607, Springer-Verlag, pp. 153–165, Jun. 2013.

[4] A. Smirnov *et al.*, "Context-aware smartspace: Reference model," in Proc. 2009 Int'l Conf. Advanced Information Networking and Applications Workshops (WAINA'09). IEEE Computer Society, pp. 261–265, May 2009.

[5] S. Balandin and H. Waris, "Key properties in the development of smart spaces," in Proc. 5th Int'l Conf. Universal Access in Human-Computer Interaction (UAHCI '09). Part II: Intelligent and Ubiquitous Interaction Environments, LNCS 5615, C. Stephanidis, Ed. Springer-Verlag, pp. 3–12, Jul. 2009.

[6] J. Augusto, V. Callaghan, D. Cook, A. Kameas, and I. Satoh, "Intelligent environments: a manifesto," Human-centric Computing and Information Sciences, vol. 3, no. 1, pp. 1–18, 2013.

[7] L. Roffia *et al.*, "A semantic publish-subscribe architecture for the Internet of Things," IEEE Internet of Things Journal, vol. PP, no. 99, pp. 1–23, 2016.

[8] D. Korzun, "On the smart spaces approach to semantic-driven design of service-oriented information systems," in Proc. 12th Int'l Baltic Conf. on Databases and Information Systems (DB&IS 2016), G. A. et al., Ed. Springer International Publishing, pp. 181–195, Jul. 2016.

[9] I. Oliver and J. Honkola, "Personal semantic web through a space based computing environment," Computing Research Repository (CoRR), vol. abs/0808.1455, pp. 1–14, Aug. 2008.

[10] J. Kiljander, A. Ylisaukko-oja, J. Takalo-Mattila, M. Eteläperä, and J.-P. Soininen, "Enabling semantic technology empowered smart spaces," Journal of Computer Networks and Communications, vol. 2012, pp. 1–14, 2012.

[11] E. Ovaska, T. S. Cinotti, and A. Toninelli, "The design principles and practices of interoperable smart spaces," in Advanced Design Approaches to Emerging Software Systems: Principles, Methodology and Tools. IGI Global, pp. 18–47, 2012.

[12] D. Korzun, "Service formalism and architectural abstractions for smart space applications," in Proc. 10th Central & Eastern European Software Engineering Conference in Russia (CEE-SECR 2014). ACM, pp. 19:1–19:7, Oct. 2014.

[13] D. Korzun, A. Kashevnik, S. Balandin, and A. Smirnov, "The Smart-M3 platform: Experience of smart space application development for Internet of Things," in Internet of Things, Smart Spaces, and Next Generation Networks and Systems. Proc. 15th Int'l Conf. Next Generation Wired/Wireless Networking and 8th Conf. on Internet of Things and Smart Spaces (NEW2AN/ruSMART 2015), LNCS 9247, Springer, pp. 56–67, Aug. 2015.

[14] J. Bicevskis *et al.*, "A practitioner's approach to achieve autonomic computing goals," Baltic Journal of Modern Computing, vol. 3, no. 4, pp. 273–293, 2015.

[15] J. Honkola, H. Laine, R. Brown, and O. Tyrkkö, "Smart-M3 information sharing platform," in Proc. IEEE Symp. Computers and Communications (ISCC'10). IEEE Computer Society, pp. 1041–1046, Jun. 2010.

[16] J. Kiljander, F. Morandi, and J.-P. Soininen, "Knowledge sharing protocol for smart spaces," International Journal of Advanced Computer Science and Applications (IJACSA), vol. 3, pp. 100–110, 2012.

[17] A. Smirnov *et al.*, "Anonymous agent coordination in smart spaces: State-of-the-art," in Smart Spaces and Next Generation Wired/Wireless Networking. Proc. 9th Int'l Conf. NEW2AN'09 and 2nd Conf. on Smart Spaces ruSMART 2009. LNCS 5764. Berlin, Heidelberg: Springer-Verlag, pp. 42–51, Sep. 2009.

[18] C. Gutierrez, C. A. Hurtado, A. O. Mendelzon, and J. Pérez, "Foundations of semantic web databases," J. Comput. Syst. Sci., vol. 77, no. 3, pp. 520–541, May 2011.

[19] D. Korzun and S. Balandin, "A peer-to-peer model for virtualization and knowledge sharing in smart spaces," in Proc. 8th Int'l Conf. on Mobile Ubiquitous Computing, Systems, Services and Technologies (UBICOMM 2014). IARIA XPS Press, pp. 87–92, Aug. 2014.

[20] L. Atzori, A. Iera, and G. Morabito, "The Internet of Things: A survey," Computer Networks, vol. 54, no. 15, pp. 2787–2805, Oct. 2010.

[21] C. Perera, A. Zaslavsky, P. Christen, and D. Georgakopoulos, "Context aware computing for the Internet of Things: A survey," IEEE Communications Surveys Tutorials, vol. 16, no. 1, pp. 414–454, Feb. 2014.

[22] C. Evers, R. Kniewel, K. Geihs, and L. Schmidt, "The user in the loop: Enabling user participation for self-adaptive applications," Future Generation Computer Systems, vol. 34, pp. 110–123, 2014.

[23] J. Tervonen, K. Mikhaylov, S. Pieska, J. Jamsa, and M. Heikkila, "Cognitive Internet-of-Things solutions enabled by wireless sensor and actuator networks," in 5th IEEE Conference on Cognitive Infocommunications (CogInfoCom). IEEE, pp. 97–102, Nov. 2014.

[24] P. Garcia Lopez *et al.*, "Edge-centric computing: Vision and challenges," SIGCOMM Comput. Commun. Rev., vol. 45, no. 5, pp. 37–42, Sep. 2015.

[25] M. Palviainen and A. Katasonov, "Model and ontology-based development of smart space applications," Pervasive Computing and Communications Design and Deployment: Technologies, Trends, and Applications, pp. 126–148, May 2011.

[26] D. Korzun, I. Galov, A. Kashevnik, and S. Balandin, "Virtual shared workspace for smart spaces and M3-based case study," in Proc. 15th Conf. of Open Innovations Association FRUCT. ITMO University, pp. 60–68, Apr. 2014.

[27] A. G. Varfolomeyev, A. Ivanovs, D. G. Korzun, and O. B. Petrina, "Smart spaces approach to development of recommendation services for historical e-tourism," in Proc. 9th Int'l Conf. on Mobile Ubiquitous Computing, Systems, Services and Technologies (UBICOMM). IARIA XPS Press, pp. 56–61, Jul. 2015.

[28] D. Korzun, A. Borodin, I. Paramonov, A. Vasiliev, and S. Balandin, "Smart spaces enabled mobile healthcare services in internet of things environments," International Journal of Embedded and Real-Time Communication Systems (IJERTCS), vol. 6, no. 1, pp. 1–27, 2015.

[29] E. Balandina, S. Balandin, Y. Koucheryavy, and D. Mouromtsev, "IoT use cases in healthcare and tourism," in Proc. IEEE 17th Conf. on Business Informatics (CBI 2015), vol. 2, pp. 37–44, Jul. 2015.

[30] P. Kovyrshin and D. Korzun, "Android smartphone as a microphone in SmartRoom system," in Proc. 15th Conf. Open Innovations Framework Program FRUCT. ITMO University, pp. 198–199, Apr. 2014.

[31] P. Bellavista, V. Conti, C. Giannelli, and J. Honkola, "The Smart-M3 semantic information broker (SIB) plug-in extension: Implementation and evaluation experiences," in Proc. IEEE Int'l Conf. on Green Computing and Communications (GreenCom). IEEE, pp. 704–711, Nov. 2012.

[32] C. Weinschenk, "Tizen: We can be the OS of the IoT," Jun. 2014, URL: http://www.itbusinessedge.com/blogs/data-and-telecom/tizen-we-can-be-the-os-of-the-iot.html [accessed: 2016-08-30].

[33] D. Luis, "Sailfish OS discovers its MeeGo roots on the Nokia N9," Dec. 2013, URL: http://www.phonearena.com/news/Sailfish-OS-discovers-its-MeeGo-roots-on-the-Nokia-N9_id50240 [accessed: 2016-08-30].

Performance Evaluation Suite for Semantic Publish-Subscribe Message-oriented Middlewares

Fabio Viola*, Alfredo D'Elia*, Luca Roffia† and Tullio Salmon Cinotti*†
*ARCES - University of Bologna, Bologna, Italy - 40125
†DISI - University of Bologna, Bologna, Italy - 40126
Email: {fabio.viola2, alfredo.delia4, luca.roffia, tullio.salmoncinotti}@unibo.it

***Abstract*—The emerging Internet of Things paradigm is driving the industry and the research towards Information and Communication Technologies (ICT) scenarios supporting high heterogeneity and interoperability. We claim that software architectures based on Semantic Publish-Subscribe Message-Oriented Middlewares (SPS-MoMs) are a powerful approach to address the requirements of such scenarios. While benchmarks and frameworks are available to evaluate the performance of MoMs, Semantic Web tools (i.e., SPARQL endpoints and RDF stores) and publish-subscribe systems, there are still no de-facto standards for the evaluation of SPS-MoMs, due to the novelty of this approach. In this paper, we propose Performance Evaluation Suite (PES), a benchmarking framework aimed at retrieving relevant performance indicators about a generic SPS-MoM. The feasibility of the proposed approach is proved by using PES to compare different implementations of a Semantic Information Broker (SIB), the core component of a SPS-MoM named Smart-M3.**

***Keywords*—Message-oriented middleware; benchmark; performance evaluation; semantics; IoT.**

I. INTRODUCTION

In the last decade, the Information and Communication Technologies (ICT) world has seen the birth of a new paradigm known as Internet of Things (IoT) [1]. Researchers from different areas have been involved in studying and strengthening the vision behind IoT. This new paradigm revolutionized the way the Internet worked up to ten years ago: laptops, PCs, tablets and smart phones are surrounded by (and need to communicate with) heterogeneous smart objects (i.e., things) spread in the physical environment. Smart objects continuously produce (i.e., sensors) and consume (i.e., actuators) data in order to provide services in different application domains (Asin and Gascon listed more than 50 application domains [2]) ranging from transportation [3][4] to logistics [5], from healthcare [6][7] to entertainment [8], from agriculture [9][10] to smart buildings [11][12], just to name a few.

Dealing with such heterogeneity in terms of application domains (e.g., different requirements), networks and protocols (e.g., DASH7 [13], 6LoWPAN [14], MQTT [15], COAP [16], XMPP [17], AMQP [18]) and device capabilities (e.g., power consumption [19]) ask for new interoperable and scalable solutions. We claim that the level of interoperability, dynamicity, flexibility, expressivity and extendibility required in IoT could be provided by a Message-Oriented Middleware (MoM) [20], more specifically a Semantic Publish-Subscribe MOM (SPS-MoM). On one hand, the MOM interaction paradigm allows to cope with events generated by IoT devices and the publish-subscribe mechanism provides an asynchronous and highly scalable many-to-many communication model, granting decoupling in terms of space, time and synchronization. On the other hand, the use of Semantic Web [21] technologies (i.e., Resource Description Framework (RDF) [22], Web Ontology Language (OWL) ontologies [23] and SPARQL 1.1 language [24]) is functional to achieve interoperability at information level. In fact, OWL ontologies allow the representation rich and complex knowledge about application domains in the form of RDF graphs that can be queried and updated using the SPARQL 1.1 language.

The main drawback of Semantic Web technologies concerns the low level of performance that makes it difficult to achieve responsiveness and scalability required in many IoT applications. The main reason for the poor performance is that Semantic Web technologies have been designed to process data sets consisting of big amounts of RDF triples that evolve constantly but at a much slower rate compared to the rate of elementary events occurring in the physical environment. Frameworks, benchmarks and methods for performance evaluation of Semantic Web systems, in general, and Semantic Publish-Subscribe systems, in particular, have been proposed in the literature. Unfortunately, these methods are not suitable for analyzing the performance of a Semantic Publish-Subscribe MOM. In fact, the former (e.g., [25][26][27][28]) are mainly designed to evaluate the performance of a SPARQL endpoint on answering a predefined set of queries with reference to several data sets and they do not include any SPARQL Update. The latter are instead focused on analyzing the performance of specific publish-subscribe systems (e.g., [29][30]).

In this paper we present, a suite dedicated to the evaluation of the performance of Semantic Publish-Subscribe MOMs. The implementation of this general suite was then specialized, without loss of generality, on the Smart-M3 platform [31], where publish and subscribe primitives are both expressed using SPARQL 1.1 (i.e., respectively as SPARQL Update and SPARQL Query) or through a RDF triple pattern serialization formalisn named RDF-M3. The main contribution of our work consists in a set of tools and methods to evaluate all the relevant performance metrics by executing existing benchmarks or creating user defined ones, specific to the target application domain. A benchmark definition includes the definition of the updates and queries (e.g., SPARQL) along with the definition of the RDF data set (e.g., OWL, N3). Tools are used to populate the knowledge base and to run the benchmarks. The evaluation outcome is in the form of graphical representations of the main results (i.e., SVG or PNG files) and includes the statistical analysis on the measured timing components (e.g., mean, variance, maximum and minimum values included in a CSV file). Finally, an example of the evaluation of two Smart-M3 SIBs (i.e., OSGi SIB [32], RedSIB [33]) is presented.

The article is organized as follows: after a review of the related work, an overview of the reference platform is reported in Section III. Then, a detailed description of the evaluation suite software architecture is presented in Section IV. The subsequent section reports on the evaluation of existing SIBs. We conclude in section VI.

II. RELATED WORK

As stated by Guo et al. in [34], benchmarking a Semantic Web system is a challenging task. The main research questions concern the benchmark definition and the design of a suite able to run the same benchmark on different systems. The answers to these two questions become also more difficult moving from Semantic Web systems to Semantic Publish-Subscribe Message-Oriented Middlewares (SPS-MoMs). In fact, in a Semantic Web system, the aim is in general evaluating the performance of the query mechanism implemented by the underpinning SPARQL endpoint, while in a SPS-MoM the focus is more on the subscription mechanism. The latter assume that the benchmark defines not just the set of queries (i.e., that can be used as set of subscriptions), but also the set of updates and how these two sets interact (i.e., which updates trigger which subscriptions). Concerning the benchmark definition, Guo et al. proposed the Leigh University Benchmark (LUBM) [35] aimed at benchmarking Semantic Web knowledge base systems in large OWL applications. LUBM provides a knowledge base (whose ontology is called *univ-bench*) and a set of 14 queries designed to validate the knowledge base management system and its query engine. The starting knowledge is provided by the Univ-Bench Artificial Data generator (UBA), a tool generating a complete data set regarding the University domain. The correctness, response time and completeness (evaluated on explicit statements or implicit knowledge available through reasoning) are taken in consideration to provide the performance profile for the knowledge base. Considering SPS-MoMs, this benchmark allows to evaluate the time response of SPARQL queries, but it is not suitable to evaluate the subscription mechanism (i.e., it does not specify any SPARQL update).

The University of Freiburg proposed a Benchmark for SPARQL endpoints called SP^2B [36]. This benchmark is based on the DBLP dataset containing open bibliographic information on major computer science journals and proceedings [37]. SP^2B is provided with a data generator that produces an N3 file [38] containing n triples (where $n \in \{10k, 50k, 250k, 1M, 5M, 25M\}$). The query set is made up of 17 SPARQL queries (14 SELECT, 3 ASK) for which is known the exact number of results, depending on the dimension of the knowledge base. This benchmark is designed to assess the performance of the SPARQL query engine (functionality and processing speed). Another relevant benchmark for the SPARQL language is [39] but the research objective originating the benchmark definition was not to evaluate or compare SPS-MOMs, but to choose between a native Semantic architecture or one obtained through a SPARQL to SQL rewriter.

Concerning the design of a benchmarking suite for semantic publish-subscribe systems, to the best of our knowledge, [40] is the most representative work. Despite the approach being quite similar to the one here presented, some differences can be clearly appreciated. First, the update sequence is supposed to be generated pseudo-randomly, while we specify the update profile as an input. Having a predefined update set allows to better control the experiment. Second, there is not a clear distinction between the software modules and this can limit the extensibility and flexibility of the solution. Third, it is not possible to configure complex sequences of operations in order to make the performance analysis deeper. Instead our Performance Evaluation Suite (PES) is specifically designed to be modular. The user is able to configure the experiments and to obtain charts and detailed log files including important statistics such as the variance of the elapsed time, the minimum, maximum and mean value. Since the performance in SPS-MoMs are often affected by the content and size of the knowledge base, PES also allows to repeat every experiment on different data sets.

III. THE REFERENCE PLATFORM

The Performance Evaluation Suite has been designed with a general approach and the first target platform chosen has been Smart-M3 [31]. Smart-M3 is an interoperability platform developed since 2008. This platform has been adopted in several past and ongoing research projects, like Internet of Energy [41], Arrowhead [42] and CHIRON [43] just to name a few. The development of Smart-M3 is currently carried on by several European universities and the proposed solution has been applied in different application domains like e-health, smart energy systems [44] and tourism [45][46].

The central component of the Smart-M3 platform is the Semantic Information Broker (SIB) that is aimed at storing the shared knowledge base in the form of an RDF graph. Several implementations of the SIB exist: 1) RedSIB [47] is a C general-purpose implementation, fast and nowadays very diffused; 2) the OSGi SIB [32] is a more recent work oriented at IoT gateways; 3) pySIB [48] is a lightweight Python implementation developed for low-powered computing nodes as, for example, System on Chips (SoCs) devices; 4) CuteSIB [49] is another recent implementation born as a fork of the old RedSIB.

Knowledge Processors (KPs) represent the client side of each application: they share data through the SIB and interoperate thanks to proper messages encoded with the Smart Space Access Protocol (SSAP). KPs can be developed exploiting one of the many existing APIs (currently available for Java, Python, C, C#, Ruby, Javascript, PHP).

The architecture of the Smart-M3 platform is summarized in Fig. 1.

The Smart-M3 interoperability platform allows to update and retrieve data using primitives based on SPARQL or on a formalism known in the Smart-M3 literature as RDF-M3, based on the concept of triple patterns. A triple pattern traces the model of an RDF triple, but allows the use of wild cards for the subject, the predicate and the object. If B, U and L are respectively the sets of the possible BNodes, URIs and Literals, a triple is defined as: $t = (s, p, o)$ where $s \in B \cup U$, $p \in U$, and $o \in U \cup B \cup L$. Introducing the wild card "Any" or "*" (that corresponds to a specific URI and matches every term) a triple pattern can be defined as: $t = (s, p, o)$ where $s \in B \cup U \cup \{*\}$, $p \in U \cup \{*\}$, and $o \in U \cup B \cup L \cup \{*\}$. In example a pattern

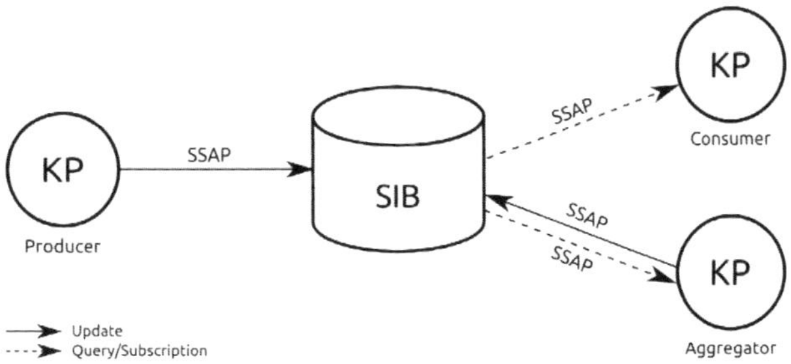

Fig. 1. The architecture of the Smart-M3 interoperability platform

based query $(*, rdf : type \in U, ns : Person \in U)$ retrieves every triple where the predicate is the URI rdf:type and the object is the URI ns:Person allowing to build a list of all the persons stored in the SIB. The SIB can be queried using a list of triple patterns: the result is made up by all the triples matching at least one of the provided triple patterns. In some cases pattern based interaction is more intuitive and simple for developers, however for inserting or retrieving complex graphs the SPARQL language [24] is always the best choice.

In Section V, the proposed PES is used to benchmark the performance of the RDF-M3 query and update mechanism of two SIBs. The results of these benchmarks are then compared with similar tests performed against the SPARQL query and update engines of the same SIBs. The results demonstrates how in some cases RDF-M3 outperforms SPARQL.

IV. Software Architecture

The PES is a free set of software modules released under the GNU General Public License 3.0. The entire suite is developed with the Python programming language and it is based on the C implementation of the Python interpreter, often referred to as CPython. PES is multiplatform, so it supports all the major operating systems. The PES software architecture is shown in Fig. 2 and described in the following subsections.

A. The Configuration Manager

The PES behavior depends on the directives specified in its configuration files (compliant with the specifications contained in [50]) and from the command line. The principal parameters specified from the command-line or through the global configuration file are the list of the SIBs to be tested (composed by IP address and port and by the required interaction protocol, e.g., SSAP [31] or JSSAP [48]) and the type of test to be performed (e.g., a query test).

Other configuration files are test-specific and are used to configure the desired benchmark. A benchmark is defined by proper configuration files. Each of these configuration files allows to specify the initial knowledge base, the number of iterations to perform, the desired output format for the chart (i.e., SVG or PNG) and if the CSV output file should be produced or not. Depending on the type of test to be performed, the configuration file may include different sections.

B. The KB Loader

The Knowledge Base Loader (KB Loader) is used to load the triples that initially constitute the knowledge base when a performance test is started. This component currently supports the N3 and the OWL KB serialization formats. The first allows to be compatible with the SP^{2}B benchmark [36], since its data generator produces an N3 file. The KB Loader sends n triples at a time to the SIB, where n is a parameter whose value depends on the trade off between KB size, number of operations to load it and efficiency of the target SIB to process large input files.

C. The PES Core

The core of PES is composed of the test modules. This extensible set of modules is currently composed of an Update Test, a Query Test and a Subscription Test.

1) Update Test: allows to measure the performance of an update request with either SPARQL or RDF-M3. For all the SIBs to be tested, the module performs a series of insertions of n triples where n ranges from n_{MIN} to n_{MAX} with step s. Each of these parameters is configured exploiting the Configuration Manager described in Subsection IV-A. Every test is repeated I times, here I is the number of iterations requested to obtain sufficient statistical samples. The mean value, the minimum and maximum and the variance are then calculated.

The time elapsed to perform the update operation is measured at the client side, so it can be considered as the sum of different components:

$$\begin{aligned} t_{update} = & t_{kp\_req} + t_{net\_req} + \\ & t_{sib\_req} + t_{sib\_elab} + t_{sib\_rep} + \\ & t_{net\_rep} + t_{kp\_rep} \end{aligned} \quad (1)$$

where t_{kp_req} and t_{kp_rep} respectively represent the time needed by the Knowledge Processor to encode the request and parse the reply, t_{net_req} and t_{net_rep} are the number of milliseconds used to transfer the packets over the network and t_{sib_req}, t_{sib_elab} and t_{sib_rep} represent the time used by the context broker to parse the received request, elaborate the request and produce a reply. The current implementation of the PES only measures t_{update}.

Measuring the time elapsed to perform an update allows to assess whether or not the SIB is able to timely store and share the information sent by the KP. The module can be configured to run with active subscriptions to evaluate their impact on the platform.

2) Query Test: The Query Test module measures the performance of the SPARQL engine (whether the requested query is a SPARQL one) or of the underlying RDF store (in case the requested query formalism is RDF-M3). For each formalism, two kinds of tests can be performed:

- *Simple test*: the knowledge base is loaded, then the query is performed;
- *Complex test*: the knowledge base is loaded in several steps and at the end of each step the specified query is performed.

The module can be configured, as in the previous case, exploiting the Configuration Manager described in Subsection

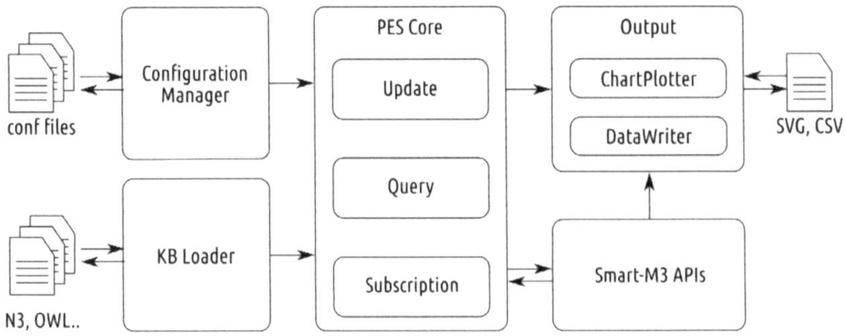

Fig. 2. The Software Architecture of the Performance Evaluation Suite

IV-A. The parameters used to set the behavior of the module are:

- The type of query test to perform (i.e., *simple* or *complex*);
- The files containing the knowledge base to load together with their format (i.e., N3 or OWL) and the desired step;
- The query to perform together with its type (i.e., SPARQL or RDF-M3);
- The number of iterations to perform.

The measured time t_{query} can be considered as the sum of different components, the same highlighted for the Update Test. For each test the minimum, the maximum and mean values of the time elapsed are returned, together with the variance. A CSV file gathers all the information deriving from the execution of a test and, if desired, an SVG chart is plotted according to the settings in the test configuration file.

3) Subscription Test: represents our most significant contribution since, to the best of our knowledge, none of the existing benchmarks allows to properly characterize the performance of a semantic publish-subscribe platform.

This test allows to subscribe to a given triple pattern using RDF-M3 or to a subgraph using the SPARQL QUERY language, then to perform updates of the knowledge base and measure the time in milliseconds required by the KP to receive the expected notification. The Subscription Test can also be used to instantiate a variable number n of KPs, each one with the same subscription, in order to calculate a notification loss ratio or to perform stress tests.

The Subscription Test can be configured with a dedicated configuration file that states the initial knowledge base (a list of n3 or OWL files to load), the subscriptions and the updates to perform and the desired number of iterations.

D. The Ouptut module

The Output module reports the results of the tests performed by plotting the related charts and writing all the measured values on a CSV file. The module relies on the pygal library that allows to render the charts on SVG or PNG files.

In Section V, it is possible to observe the charts rendered by this module, while in the following listing it is reported an example of a CSV file produced during the execution of a subscription test. The first field is the name of the SIB tested and from the second field a list of the collected notification times. The row is concluded by the mean value, minimum and the maximum values and the variance. All the values here reported are expressed in ms.

```
S0,2.819,...,2.986,1.792,3.948,0.281
S1,3.789,...,2.538,1.381,3.789,0.57
S2,1.054,...,2.392,1.003,3.51,0.673
```

E. The Smart-M3 APIs

Knowledge Processors are developed through proper APIs that make possible the interaction with the SIB. The APIs are not developed ad-hoc for the purpose of this project, but are external modules included into the PES. Since PES is developed in Python, the APIs adopted by the suite are the Python Smart-M3 APIs (including the one providing support for the JSSAP introduced by pySIB [48]).

The update mechanisms, the query functionalities and the subscription engine represents the targets of the tests modules forming the PES Core. The PES is not constrained to the Smart-M3 platform, but replacing this module with the proper APIs (and replacing the function calls to such APIs) can be used to evaluate the performance of other Semantic Publish-Subscribe MOMs.

V. EVALUATION

The configuration adopted for these benchmarks is composed of a server called `mml` and a host called `desmodue` connected in a Local Area Network at 1GBps. The former, `mml`, is a server provided with 12 core Intel Xeon CPU E5-2430 v2 at 2.50 GHz, 15.360 Kb cache and 32 GB RAM and 280 GB hard disk. The latter, `desmodue`, is a laptop PC with a CPU Intel Core(TM) i5-2520 at 2.50 GHz with 3.072 KB of cache for every core. This host is provided with 4 GB RAM and 160 GB hard disk. `desmodue` runs Linux Mint 17 Qiana, while `mml` Ubuntu Server 16.04.

PES runs on the host named `desmodue`, while the SIBs to be tested runs on `mml`. In this demonstrative tests we decided to take into account the C implementation of the SIB named RedSIB [47] and the Java one, called the OSGi SIB [32], both supporting the standard SSAP protocol and both executed without a persistent storage.

A. Update Test

A demonstration of the Update Test is shown in Fig. 3. The test perfomed on the two above-mentioned SIBs consists in measuring the time elapsed to insert a block composed by n triples with an RDF-M3 update; n varies from 250 to 2500 with a step of 250. No subscriptions were active during the test. Three iterations of the test have been performed. The RDF-M3 update builds the triples exploiting information coming from the configuration file that contains the desired namespace (i.e., `ns` bound to `http://ns#`) the template for subject, predicate and object (i.e., `ns:SubN`, `ns:PredN` and `ObjN`) and their type (i.e., URI, URI and Literal).

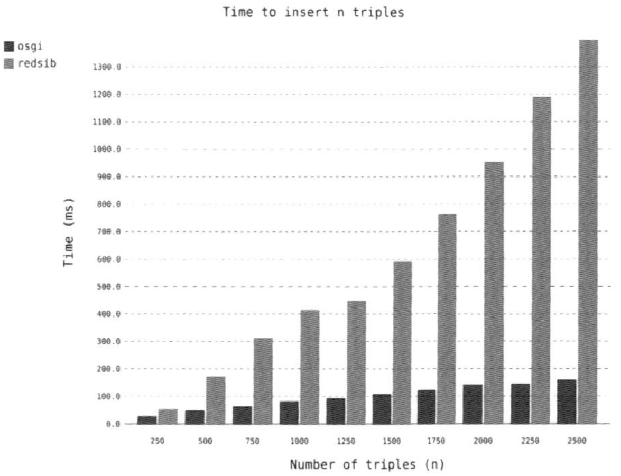

Fig. 3. The Update test performed on RedSIB and OSGi SIB

An example of the textual output represented by the related CSV file is shown below. The first field identifies the SIB, the second the number of triples. After the list of the collected values, the mean value, the minimum and maximum values and the variance are reported.

```
osgi,250,28.14,..,28.38,28.14,28.82,0.09
osgi,500,53.28,..,56.29,56.10,59.00,4.09
osgi,750,66.93,..,65.77,62.72,67.67,4.74
osgi,1000,78.53,..,77.30,76.37,78.53,0.82
osgi,1250,88.98,..,87.56,85.95,88.98,1.55
...
```

Fig. 4 shows the results of repeating the update test with only 1000 triples to insert on both the SIBs. The different kind of graph is the result of a different configuration set up by the user in the configuration manager.

B. Query Test

Two further tests have been performed on the OSGi SIB and on RedSIB, both consisting in retrieving the entire content of the knowledge base with RDF-M3 (Fig. 5) and with SPARQL (Fig. 6). With RDF-M3 the triple pattern is ($\star$, $\star$, $\star$), while the SPARQL query is:

```
SELECT ?s ?p ?o
WHERE {
    ?s ?p ?o
}
```

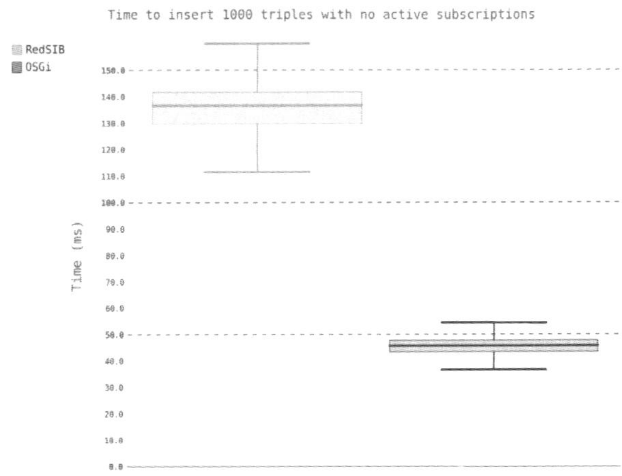

Fig. 4. The Update test performed on RedSIB and OSGi SIB with box chart output

The two charts allow to identify a better behavior of the RDF-M3 queries with respect to the given use case and, in general, a higher timeliness of the OSGi SIB.

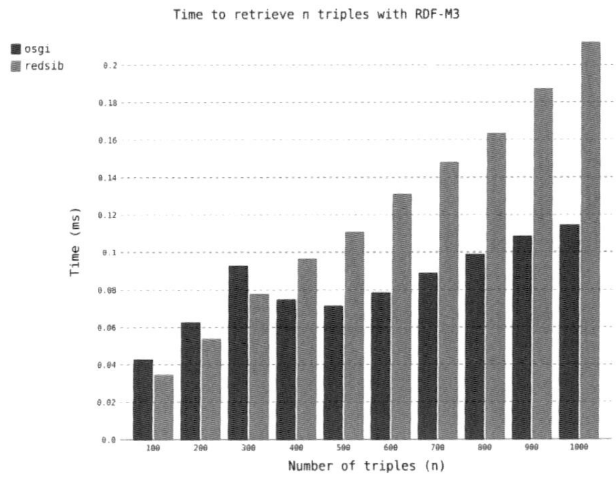

Fig. 5. The Query test performed on RedSIB and OSGi SIB to retrieve the entire RDF store content using the RDF-M3 query formalism

C. Subscription Test

The most relevant contribution of the PES, as mentioned in the introduction, is the ability to measure the time needed to receive a notification about an update of the RDF store. An example of the Subscription Test is shown in Fig. 7. In this example, a reference scenario of electric mobility was used and the time required to receive a notification about the registration of a new user was measured. In the chart is possible to observe the minimum notification time (in milliseconds), the maximum one and the mean value.

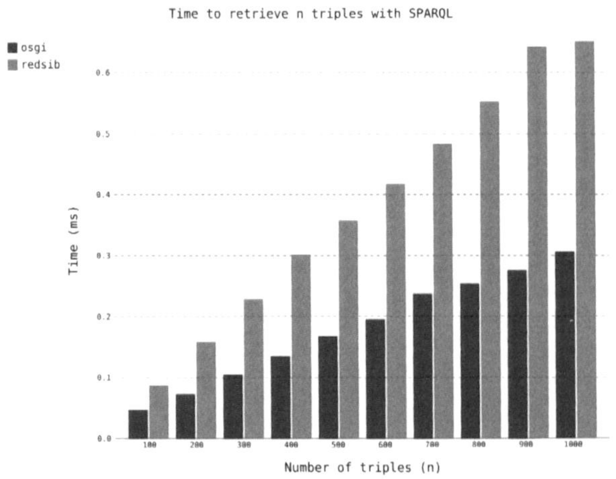

Fig. 6. The Query test performed on RedSIB and OSGi SIB to retrieve the entire RDF store content using the SPARQL query formalism

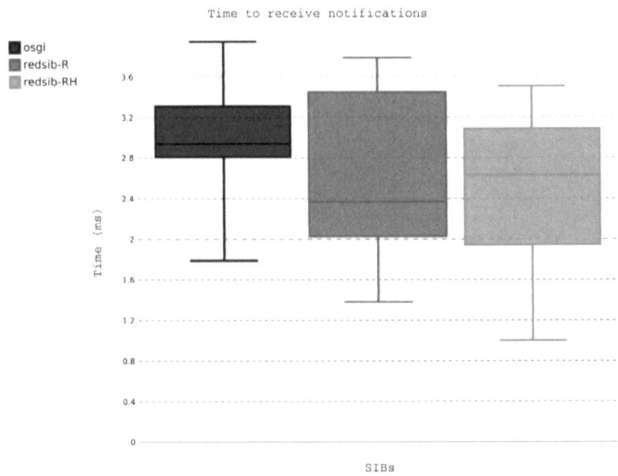

Fig. 7. The Subscription Test performed on RedSIB (with options `--ram` and `--ram-hash`) and OSGi SIB

It is possible to observe the presence in the box chart of two different boxes for RedSIB: the one labeled with `redsib-R` is related to the volatile storage without support for hash tables, while `redsib-RH` allows to test RedSIB with a volatile storage exploiting these data structures. The results show a little performance improvement in subscription management if the hash tables are used.
The SPARQL update is:

```
PREFIX ns: <http://.../ioe-ontology.owl#>
PREFIX rdf: <http://.../22-rdf-syntax-ns#>
INSERT DATA {
ns:User1_URI rdf:type ns:Person .
    ns:User1_URI ns:hasName "User Name" .
    ns:User1_URI ns:hasPasswd "UserPasswd"
}
```

while SPARQL subscription is:

```
PREFIX ns: <http://.../ioe-ontology.owl#>
PREFIX rdf: <http://.../22-rdf-syntax-ns#>
SELECT ?s
WHERE {
    ?s rdf:type ns:Person
}
```

VI. Conclusion and Future Work

A suite of software modules, named Performance Evaluation Suite (PES), aiming at evaluating the performance of Semantic Publish-Subscribe Message-Oriented Middlewares (SPS-MoMs) has been presented. A first implementation of the PES has been used to evaluate and compare the performance of two instances of the Smart-M3 Semantic Information Broker (SIB). The proposed platform allows to run existing benchmarks (e.g., SP^2B or LUBM) and to extend these benchmarks to evaluate the subscription mechanism provided by the broker. Future works include the definition of a set of benchmarks specific for IoT scenarios that can be used to perform an extensive performance analysis of available SPS-MoMs, including the several SIB implementations. The PES will be extended to provide a set of Key Performance Indicators (e.g., the average number of updates, or queries or subscriptions processed per unit time) that, along with current statistical analysis of the timing components, will allow to identify bottlenecks and limits of current SPS-MoMs driving the research towards an efficient and effective IoT solution.

References

[1] R. Minerva, A. Biru, and D. Rotondi, "Towards a definition of the internet of things (iot)," May 2015. [Online]. Available: http://iot.ieee.org/definition.html, [retrieved: April 2016]

[2] A. Asin and D. Gascon, "50 sensor applications for a smarter world," *Libelium Comunicaciones Distribuidas, Tech. Rep*, 2012.

[3] X.-Y. Liu and M.-Y. Wu, "Vehicular cps: an application of iot in vehicular networks," *Jisuanji Yingyong/ Journal of Computer Applications*, vol. 32, no. 4, pp. 900–904, 2012.

[4] W. He, G. Yan, and L. Da Xu, "Developing vehicular data cloud services in the iot environment," *Industrial Informatics, IEEE Transactions on*, vol. 10, no. 2, pp. 1587–1595, 2014.

[5] P. Ferreira, R. Martinho, and D. Domingos, "Iot-aware business processes for logistics: limitations of current approaches," in *Inforum*, vol. 3, 2010, pp. 612–613.

[6] S. Amendola, R. Lodato, S. Manzari, C. Occhiuzzi, and G. Marrocco, "Rfid technology for iot-based personal healthcare in smart spaces," *IEEE Internet of Things Journal*, vol. 1, no. 2, pp. 144–152, April 2014.

[7] C. Doukas and I. Maglogiannis, "Bringing iot and cloud computing towards pervasive healthcare," in *Innovative Mobile and Internet Services in Ubiquitous Computing (IMIS), 2012 Sixth International Conference on*, July 2012, pp. 922–926.

[8] C. L. Hu, H. T. Huang, C. L. Lin, N. H. M. Anh, Y. Y. Su, and P. C. Liu, "Design and implementation of media content sharing services in home-based iot networks," in *Parallel and Distributed Systems (ICPADS), 2013 International Conference on*, Dec 2013, pp. 605–610.

[9] J. Burrell, T. Brooke, and R. Beckwith, "Vineyard computing: Sensor networks in agricultural production," *Pervasive Computing, IEEE*, vol. 3, no. 1, pp. 38–45, 2004.

[10] Z. Liqiang, Y. Shouyi, L. Leibo, Z. Zhen, and W. Shaojun, "A crop monitoring system based on wireless sensor network," *Procedia Environmental Sciences*, vol. 11, pp. 558–565, 2011.

[11] G. T. Costanzo, G. Zhu, M. F. Anjos, and G. Savard, "A system architecture for autonomous demand side load management in smart buildings," *IEEE Transactions on Smart Grid*, vol. 3, no. 4, pp. 2157–2165, Dec 2012.

[12] L. Schor, P. Sommer, and R. Wattenhofer, "Towards a zero-configuration wireless sensor network architecture for smart buildings," in *Proceedings of the First ACM Workshop on Embedded Sensing Systems for Energy-Efficiency in Buildings*, ser. BuildSys '09. New York, NY, USA: ACM, 2009, pp. 31–36. [Online]. Available: http://doi.acm.org/10.1145/1810279.1810287

[13] M. Weyn, G. Ergeerts, L. Wante, C. Vercauteren, and P. Hellinckx, "Survey of the dash7 alliance protocol for 433mhz wireless sensor communication," *International Journal of Distributed Sensor Networks*, 2013.

[14] E. Kim, D. Kaspar, D. Gomez, and C. Bormann, "Problem statement and requirements for ipv6 over low-power wireless personal area network (6lowpan) routing," RFC 6606, October 2015. [Online]. Available: https://rfc-editor.org/rfc/rfc6606.txt

[15] A. Banks and R. Gupta, "Mqtt version 3.1.1," October 2014, [retrieved: April 2016]. [Online]. Available: http://docs.oasis-open.org/mqtt/mqtt/v3.1.1/os/mqtt-v3.1.1-os.html. Latest version: http://docs.oasis-open.org/mqtt/mqtt/v3.1.1/mqtt-v3.1.1.html.

[16] Z. Shelby, K. Hartke, and C. Bormann, "The constrained application protocol (coap)," RFC 7252, June 2014. [Online]. Available: https://tools.ietf.org/html/rfc7252

[17] P. Saint-Andre, "Extensible Messaging and Presence Protocol (XMPP): Core," RFC 6120, October 2015. [Online]. Available: https://rfc-editor.org/rfc/rfc6120.txt

[18] "Advanced message queuing protocol (amqp) version 1.0. 29," October 2012, [retrieved: April 2016]. [Online]. Available: http://docs.oasis-open.org/amqp/core/v1.0/os/amqp-core-complete-v1.0-os.pdf

[19] A. D'Elia, L. Perilli, F. Viola, L. Roffia, F. Antoniazzi, R. Canegallo, and T. S. Cinotti, "A self-powered wsan for energy efficient heat distribution," in *2016 IEEE Sensors Applications Symposium (SAS)*, April 2016, pp. 1–6.

[20] M. Albano, L. L. Ferreira, L. M. Pinho, and A. R. Alkhawaja, "Message-oriented middleware for smart grids," *Computer Standards & Interfaces*, vol. 38, pp. 133–143, 2015. [Online]. Available: http://www.sciencedirect.com/science/article/pii/S0920548914000804

[21] T. Berners-Lee, J. Hendler, and O. Lassila, "The Semantic Web," pp. 34–43, 2001.

[22] "Rdf 1.1 concepts and abstract syntax," February 2014, [retrieved: April 2016]. [Online]. Available: https://www.w3.org/TR/2014/REC-rdf11-concepts-20140225/

[23] "Owl 2 web ontology language primer (second edition)," December 2012, [retrieved: April 2016]. [Online]. Available: https://www.w3.org/TR/2012/REC-owl2-primer-20121211/

[24] "Sparql 1.1 overview," March 2013, [retrieved: April 2016]. [Online]. Available: https://www.w3.org/TR/sparql11-overview/

[25] Y. Guo, Z. Pan, and J. Heflin, "LUBM: A benchmark for OWL knowledge base systems," *Web Semantics*, vol. 3, no. 2-3, pp. 158–182, 2005.

[26] Y. Guo, A. Qasem, Z. Pan, and J. Heflin, "A requirements driven framework for benchmarking Semantic Web knowledge base systems," *IEEE Transactions on Knowledge and Data Engineering*, vol. 19, no. 2, pp. 297–309, 2007.

[27] R. Garcìa-Castro and E. al., *Web Semantics: Science, Services and Agents on the World Wide Web, Special Issue on Evaluation of Semantic Technologies*. Elsevier, 2013, vol. 21.

[28] C. Bizer and A. Schultz, "The Berlin SPARQL Benchmark," *International Journal on Semantic Web & Information Systems*, vol. 5, no. 2, pp. 1–24, 2009.

[29] M. Murth, D. Winkler, S. Biffl, E. Kühn, and T. Moser, "Performance Testing of Semantic Publish / Subscribe Systems," *Journal Of Web Semantics*, pp. 45–46, 2010.

[30] M. Murth, "K{ü}hn, e.: A Semantic Event Notification Service for Knowledge-Driven Coordination," in *Proc. of 1st Int'l. workshop on emergent semantics and cooperation in open systems (ESTEEM), co-operation with the 2nd Int'l. Conf. on Distributed Event-Based Systems (DEBS 2008), Rome, Italy*, 2008.

[31] J. Honkola, H. Laine, R. Brown, and O. Tyrkko, "Smart-M3 information sharing platform," in *The IEEE symposium on Computers and Communications*. IEEE, 2010, pp. 1041–1046.

[32] D. Manzaroli, L. Roffia, T. S. Cinotti, E. Ovaska, P. Azzoni, V. Nannini, and S. Mattarozzi, "Smart-m3 and osgi: The interoperability platform," in *Computers and Communications (ISCC), 2010 IEEE Symposium on*. IEEE, 2010, pp. 1053–1058.

[33] "Redsib," [retrieved: April 2016]. [Online]. Available: https://sourceforge.net/projects/smart-m3/files/Smart-M3-RedSIB_0.9.2/

[34] Y. Guo, A. Qasem, Z. Pan, and J. Heflin, "A requirements driven framework for benchmarking semantic web knowledge base systems," *IEEE Transactions on Knowledge and Data Engineering*, vol. 19, no. 2, pp. 297–309, 2007.

[35] Y. Guo, Z. Pan, and J. Heflin, "Lubm: A benchmark for owl knowledge base systems," *Web Semantics: Science, Services and Agents on the World Wide Web*, vol. 3, no. 2, pp. 158–182, 2005.

[36] M. Schmidt, T. Hornung, G. Lausen, and C. Pinkel, "Sp2bench: A sparql performance benchmark," in *2009 IEEE 25th International Conference on Data Engineering*, March 2009, pp. 222–233.

[37] M. Ley, "The dblp computer science bibliography: Evolution, research issues, perspectives," in *String Processing and Information Retrieval*. Springer, 2002, pp. 1–10.

[38] T. Berners-Lee and D. Connolly, "Notation3 (n3): A readable rdf syntax," *W3C Team Submission: http://www. w3. org/TeamSubmission*, no. 3, 1998.

[39] C. Bizer and A. Schultz, "The berlin sparql benchmark," 2009.

[40] M. Murth, D. Winkler, S. Biffl, E. Kühn, and T. Moser, "Performance testing of semantic publish/subscribe systems," in *OTM Confederated International Conferences" On the Move to Meaningful Internet Systems"*. Springer, 2010, pp. 45–46.

[41] "Ioe." [Online]. Available: http://www.artemis-ioe.eu/ [retrieved: April 2016]

[42] "Arrowhead ahead of the future," http://www.arrowhead.eu/ [retrieved: April 2016].

[43] "Chiron." [Online]. Available: http://www.unibo.it/en/research/projects-and-initiatives/unibo-projects-under-7th-framework-programme/cooperation-1/information-and-communication-technology-ict-1/chiron [retrieved: April 2016]

[44] A. D'Elia, F. Viola, F. Montori, M. Di Felice, L. Bedogni, L. Bononi, A. Borghetti, P. Azzoni, P. Bellavista, D. Tarchi *et al.*, "Impact of interdisciplinary research on planning, running, and managing electromobility as a smart grid extension," *Access, IEEE*, vol. 3, pp. 2281–2305, 2015.

[45] A. Varfolomeyev, D. Korzun, A. Ivanovs, and O. Petrina, "Smart personal assistant for historical tourism," in *RECENT ADVANCES in ENVIRONMENTAL SCIENCES and FINANCIAL DEVELOPMENT. 9-15 Nov, 2014*, 2014, p. 9.

[46] A. Smirnov, A. Kashevnik, S. I. Balandin, and S. Laizane, "Intelligent mobile tourist guide," in *Internet of Things, Smart Spaces, and Next Generation Networking*. Springer Berlin Heidelberg, 2013, pp. 94–106.

[47] F. Morandi, L. Roffia, A. DElia, F. Vergari, and T. S. Cinotti, "Redsib: a smart-m3 semantic information broker implementation," in *Proc. 12th Conf. of Open Innovations Association FRUCT and Seminar on e-Tourism*. SUAI, 2012, pp. 86–98.

[48] F. Viola, A. D'Elia, L. Roffia, and T. Salmon Cinotti, "A modular lightweight implementation of the smart-m3 semantic information broker," in *18th FRUCT*, 2016, pp. 370–377.

[49] I. V. Galov, A. A. Lomov, and D. G. Korzun, "Design of semantic information broker for localized computing environments in the internet of things," in *Open Innovations Association (FRUCT), 2015 17TH Conference of*. IEEE, 2015, pp. 36–43.

[50] D. Crocker, "Standard for the format of ARPA Internet text messages," Internet Requests for Comments, RFC Editor, RFC 822, August 1982. [Online]. Available: https://tools.ietf.org/html/rfc822

Supporting Environmental Analysis and Requalification of Taranto Sea: an Integrated ICT Platform

Floriano Scioscia, Agnese Pinto, Filippo Gramegna,
Giovanna Capurso, Danilo De Filippis, Raffaello Perez de Vera, Eugenio Di Sciascio

DEI - Politecnico di Bari
via E. Orabona 4, I-70125, Bari, Italy
Email: floriano.scioscia@poliba.it, agnese.pinto@poliba.it, filippo.gramegna@poliba.it,
giovanna.capurso@gmail.com, danilo.defilippis@poliba.it, raffaello.perez@hotmail.it, eugenio.disciascio@poliba.it

Abstract—**Pollution in Taranto Sea must be monitored constantly to detect potential issues to public health, marine biology and economic activities in the basin. A recent environmental analysis and intervention initiative is performing a systematic and multidisciplinary research on the area. This paper describes the support software platform, which is being devised for the project. It is based on the crowdsourcing paradigm and on open source software and open data formats. The platform collects heterogeneous data from different research units and presents them as multiple georeferenced and timestamped information layers, which can be combined for advanced analysis. The overall architecture, developed tools and prospected integration of Radio Frequency Identification (RFID) technologies for survey sample tracking are discussed in detail.**

Keywords - ***Environmental monitoring; OpenSeaMap; Crowdsourcing; Geographic Information System.***

I. INTRODUCTION

Human settlements and activities have an impact on the coastal and marine environment. Marine litter and industrial waste impair the sea ecosystem and economic activities based on it. The Taranto Sea is one of the most critical situations in Italy and an internationally relevant case study [1], due to the Taranto basin having low water circulation [2]. Pollution can affect the health of the local population, as well as the wildlife and the traditionally relevant seafood breeding activity in the area. Authorities have set up a program [3] for the requalification of Taranto Sea. In order to accurately plan the best and safest intervention strategies, systematic analysis of seawater and seabed is needed with an interdisciplinary approach, including geological, geotechnical, physical, chemical and biological investigations. Borehole sampling of the seafloor is one of the most important and sensitive activities: stocking samples and moving them to the various analysis laboratories requires accurate and timely tracking. Furthermore, collected data need to be stored systematically and shared among the different research units in order to allow the discovery of relevant patterns and correlations providing the needed insight to operate effectively and efficiently.

This paper presents an integrated Information and Communication Technology (ICT) platform supporting the ongoing environmental analysis and intervention activities in Taranto Sea. The proposal is based on the principle of information *crowdsourcing*. In the last years, this paradigm has established itself thanks to the ICT progress increasing large-scale information sharing possibilities. Experience with crowdsourcing has shown that a large, loosely coupled and heterogeneous community of users is able to produce and maintain a data or knowledge base, which is superior in size and quality w.r.t. a narrow team of dedicated professionals. The key for crowdsourcing success lies in three factors: (i) a motivated community, which globally possesses the required skills; (ii) an ICT support platform; (iii) a decentralized organization model respecting individual autonomy but promoting shared policies and mechanisms to maintain high quality of information as size grows. This work proposes an integrated ICT support platform based on open source software and open data formats. The core of the platform consists of tools and technologies derived from *OpenSeaMap*, a worldwide collaborative project for marine cartography creation. It allows to collect heterogeneous data about points of the Taranto Sea basin into a unified, general data model, where results from the different investigations appear as multiple layers of information, wildwhich are individually georeferenced and timestamped, in order to support space-oriented, time-oriented and attribute-oriented queries. A further capability is to allow cross-checking data from different domains in order to perform interdisciplinary analysis and find hidden correlations. The whole platform is accessible through a uniform and user-friendly interface.

Functional requirements of large-scale research projects go beyond those of typical cartographers or Geographic Information System (GIS) users. First of all, security was of paramount importance, therefore a Virtual Private Network (VPN) link protects all communications from/to the server hosting the proposed platform. Access is granted only to the staff of involved research units. Furthermore, the need to work on massive data required specialized tools for (i) automating repetitive entry and import operations, and (ii) performing advanced search and data mining. Finally, integrating sample tracking management with the platform was studied through the use of Radio Frequency IDentification (RFID) technologies. The developed and proposed solutions constitute an integrated ICT platform to support the whole workflow of environmental analysis and monitoring, from field to laboratory. The platform is under use in the Taranto Sea marine environment requalification initiative, but it provides a general solution which can be exported to a number of analogous scenarios with minimal or no modification.

The rest of the paper is as follows: the next section discusses related work. Section III describes the core components of the integrated crowdsourcing platform, while Section IV provides details on data management tools. RFID-based traceability solutions are outlined in Section V, then conclusion is in Section VI.

II. Related work

GIS systems allow georeferencing data, performing various kinds of analysis and producing chart-based reports. GIS technology is constantly improving and its adoption has been rising for several years. They have been used successfully in a wide range of scenarios, from urban planning [4] and transportation [5] to epidemiology [6] and environmental monitoring [7]. Nevertheless, available solutions are usually based on closed software, which is expensive to purchase and even more to customize to the peculiar needs of a particular project. Even though open standards exist for georeferenced data, not all tools support them, so requiring format conversions with the risk of losing valuable information.

Crowdsourcing approaches and platforms propose a radically different approach, based on the contribution of large numbers of –often volunteer– participants to solve a complex problem or collect large bodies of information [8]. Since the concept is quite recent, defining characteristics of the crowdsourcing paradigm is still openly debated [9]. Anyway, the need to facilitate global-scale collaboration directs crowdsourcing ICT platforms toward open data formats and often open source software. This creates opportunities for customizations and extensions in order to satisfy specific requirements.

Environmental collaborative monitoring networks were proposed in [10], combining traditional environmental monitoring with the principles of crowdsourcing. They were based on three key elements: (i) motivated citizens, (ii) sensing devices and (iii) a back-end information infrastructure. Although that work is more limited in scope w.r.t. the one proposed here, it shares the same basic perspective.

Among map-based crowdsourcing projects, *OpenSeaMap* [11] and OpenStreetMap [12] (OSM henceforth) are likely the largest and most successful. They are worldwide collaborative initiatives for shared creation of cartographic corpuses, respectively dedicated to sea and land mapping. They are based on World Wide Web technologies and follow *open data* license models, granting anyone the right to use, expand and modify the data. The core software components were originally designed and developed for OpenStreetMap since 2004 and then adopted –with some adjustments– by OpenSeaMap in 2009. They are freely available through open source software licenses.

The complete OpenSeaMap solution comprises several components, including:

- PostgreSQL [13], an efficient and scalable database management system with support for georeferenced data;
- Overpass [14], a geospatial query engine with a very flexible language and Application Programming Interface (API);
- a Web-based interface, mainly for information visualization and exploration;
- various editors for classical computers and mobile devices to modify and add cartography data.

Among the editors, the Java OpenStreetMap editor (JOSM) [15] is particularly relevant: it was developed in Java technology, making it compatible with Windows, Mac OS, Linux and other UNIX-like operating systems. It has a user-friendly interface, depicted in Fig. 1. Finally, it adopts a modular extensible architecture: *plug-ins* add new functionality without altering the whole software tool.

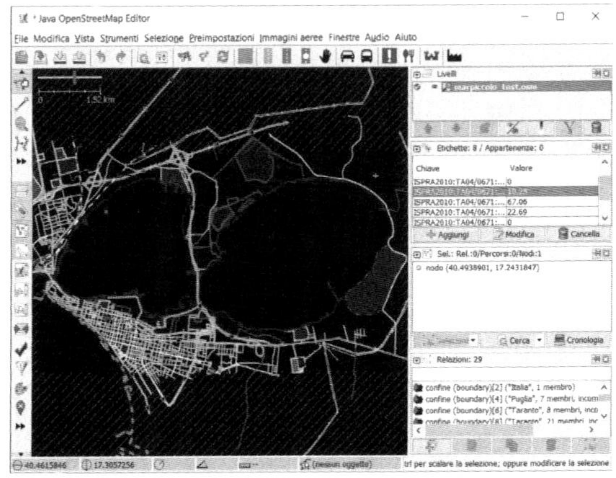

Figure 1. JOSM cartography editor

An important evolution of software platforms for environmental data management is the integration with automated information gathering devices and infrastructures. Wireless sensor networks [16], Internet of Things technologies [17] and robotics [18] have been adopted for this purpose in various projects, exploiting their respective peculiarities. RFID can be similarly integrated and is the most suitable technology whenever there is the need to track physical objects such as collected samples.

III. Requirements, strategy, architecture

Supporting the characterization of Taranto Sea for monitoring and requalification requires the development of a distributed information system capable of storing and retrieving gathered data efficiently. All the relevant information for the different research units should be stored along with geospatial and temporal references for each point as a stack of superimposed informative layers, in order to ensure full data traceability.

The support platform should also facilitate the systematic upload of information. This functional requirement posed the first significant challenge for the project, due to the sheer size and heterogeneity of the raw data at stake. Information characterizing the probed seabed points actually pertains to several disciplines, including geotechnics, hydraulics, hydrogeology, hydrology, chemistry, marine biology and biodiversity. Data must be properly stored, through an annotation process capable of making their nature and information content as explicit as possible. A second challenge involves querying the information system for systematic and interdisciplinary investigation. Complex environmental analysis needs searching techniques able to discover correlations and links between different attributes, acquired by separate teams with diverse tools and in variable time spans. The information system must allow users to express complex queries in order to retrieve the point(s) matching more closely a specific set of characteristics within the area of interest. This requires data mining capabilities and cross-checking all information produced in the investigations carried out by the various research units.

A preliminary analysis of necessities and desiderata of the marine environmental monitoring tasks has elicited further important non-functional requirements:

- security and privacy of data and communications between users and the system, allowing to share information only among teams involved in the project;
- support for open and interoperable data formats, due to the diversity of tools and platforms to be used;
- general and flexible data storage models and schemes, to support heterogeneous sources and allow integrated analysis;
- high performance scalability;
- easily usable and accessible interface, as the main users of the platform will be scientists but not necessarily trained in computer science.

The above constraints have led to consider *crowdsourcing* as the most appropriate information sharing model. Global distributed collaborative projects have already shown it to be scalable, reliable and effective. After an extensive survey of the state of the art, the overall proposal was based on the OpenSeaMap, with appropriate custom extensions to meet the specific requirements of the project. A careful audit has shown OSM technologies and tools fully meet the identified requirements of generality, openness, reliability, scalability, usability and security.

The OSM data model adheres to a simple and extensible Extensible Markup Language (XML) Schema, comprising three basic element types: (i) *nodes*, *i.e.*, single geospatial points; (ii) *ways*, representing ordered sequences of nodes; (iii) *relations*, grouping logically multiple nodes and/or ways. Each element includes latitude and longitude coordinates, a unique identity code and versioning fields. The basic model can be extended through optional informative *tags*, *i.e.*, key-value pairs of Unicode strings of up to 255 characters. The OSM community has defined a large number of tags to describe a wide range of entities and attributes, but new ones can be introduced freely to meet new and unforeseen use cases. The base model was therefore extended exploiting tags to create a general-purpose schema for environmental data and their geographical and temporal metadata. It is structured as follows:

- **Key:** unique prefix currently unused in OSM (according to the community-managed Wiki [19]), concatenated with a timestamp of the data entry.
- **Value:** concatenation of sub-fields, each with the same key-value structure, including:
  - `sur`: survey identifier (ID);
  - `sid`: sample ID;
  - `sts`: survey extraction time;
  - `dmi`: minimum depth;
  - `dma`: maximum depth;
  - `a`: attribute name;
  - `v`: attribute value.

Including a timestamp in the key makes each data insertion unique, so creating a traceable record of all editing operations. Furthermore, as data concern samples extracted at different values of marine or seabed depth, a depth range attribute was added in order to evolve the basic two-dimensional coordinate system of OSM into a three-dimensional one. Finally, general-purpose attributes obtained through laboratory analysis are stored individually for each point on the map and each depth range, in every survey campaign (both historical and ongoing ones). The above data model allows spatial, temporal and attribute-oriented queries to support a wide range of use cases.

In order to further optimize the analysis of data from different sources distributed at large scale, ongoing developments are assessing the possibility of using artificial intelligence techniques. The adoption of automated techniques to extract high-level knowledge from raw georeferenced data through mining algorithms allows building knowledge-based tools for environmental monitoring, decision support and control. A promising direction is grounded on the combination of machine learning and knowledge representation techniques [20], exploiting non-standard inference services for the analysis of information streams [21].

IV. Data Editing Tools

JOSM was selected as the main data editing tool in the proposed integrated platform. Two extensions to the basic editor developed for the project are discussed in this section. They are devoted to massive data import and advanced search, respectively.

A. Survey data importer

Population of the proposed environmental information system involves high volumes of data. Therefore it is necessary to provide tools to automate the process of information migration and integration from existing sources. In order to facilitate data entry, the proposed platform includes a JOSM plug-in allowing users to import georeferenced data from common formats, such as Comma Separated Values (CSV) and Microsoft Excel. This enables importing in the proposed system not only data gathered in past surveys, but also the output of analysis processes currently used by the involved research units. Such an approach removes time-consuming and error-prone computerized data entry procedures, and enhances automation in laboratory workflows.

After opening a data source file, the tool lets the user choose the set of records to import and select the fields of interest, through an assisted procedure, after which loading is performed automatically in batch mode. The main steps are as follows:

1) determination of fields and records to be imported from the data source, as shown in Fig. 2;
2) selection of coordinates and reference system, which are mandatory features, as depicted in Fig. 3,;
3) selection of further optional features, concerning the survey the imported records refer to (see Fig. 4).

At the end of the assisted procedure, individual nodes are imported. When import is complete, nodes can be viewed directly on the map as shown in Fig. 5. When a point is selected on the map, its records are shown in the boxes on the right hand side of the user interface.

Initially loading procedures will involve historical data, collected by surveys carried out on Taranto Sea sites in the past. Subsequently, in the same way new data will be uploaded progressively during the environmental observation period.

B. Advanced query interface

A second JOSM plug-in was developed to support retrieval and analysis in the environmental data management platform.

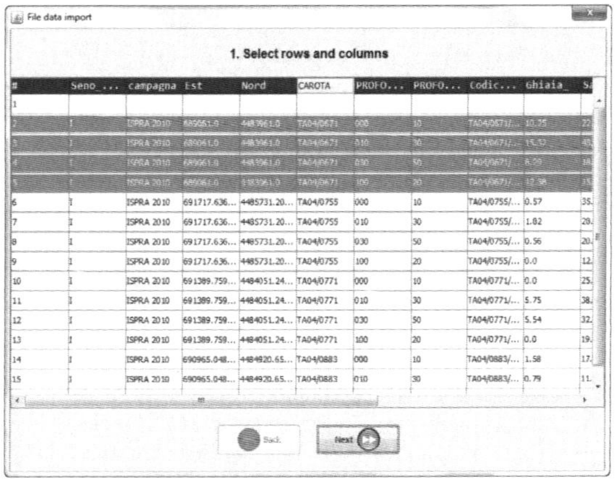

Figure 2. Import plug-in: record selection

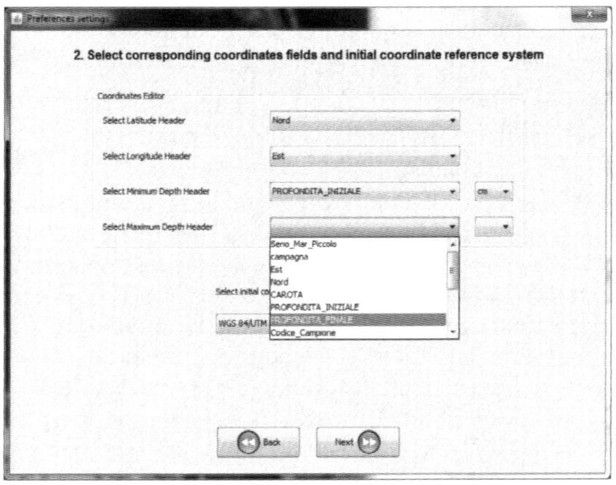

Figure 3. Import plug-in: geographical attributes selection

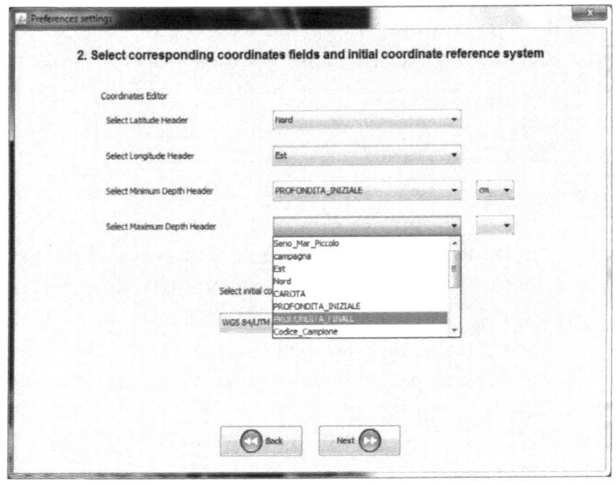

Figure 4. Import plug-in: optional attributes selection

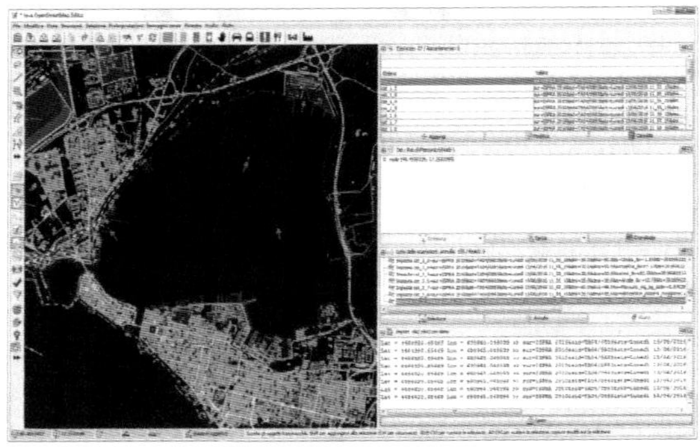

Figure 5. Import plug-in: result panel

It was designed to enable the advanced search of points of interest through the combination of multiple criteria. The built-in search functionality in JOSM provides a very basic interface, accepting just a query string as input. This poses a high usability barrier, since the user is required to have a working knowledge of the OSM data model, regular expressions and logical operators. This cannot be taken for granted for typical users, even for scientists and engineers working on environmental data. Furthermore, the limited syntax does not allow several kinds of complex queries. A different kind of search interface is needed, to enhance both user-friendliness and query flexibility.

As depicted in Fig. 6, the devised tool allows to express complex queries with:

- a filter on depth range;
- a filter on survey metadata, particularly useful for historical analysis;
- user-specified filters on any attribute stored in the system, both for number and string types.

Individual filters can be joined through logical connectors in a simplified, fully visual fashion. The tool hides the complexity of query composition behind a straightforward user interface. Users are not required to master the Overpass language in order to be able to compose articulated queries. After confirmation, search starts. The tool displays in red on the map the points of interest matching the query criteria.

V. ENVIRONMENTAL SAMPLE TRACKING VIA RFID

As tracking of seabed samples is a challenging logistic task, the proposed ICT platform is open to the integration of RFID technologies. RFID allows the identification and tracking of

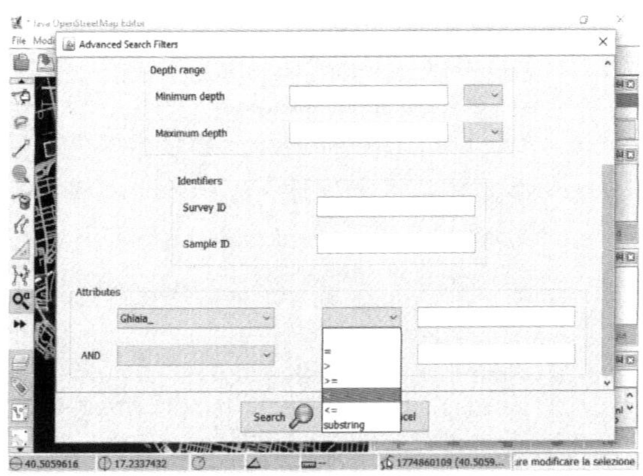

Figure 6. Advanced query user interface

objects equipped with transponders (*tags*), by means of fixed or mobile interrogators (*readers*) able to read and write data. Each tag stores a unique code which identifies the object throughout its life cycle. Compared to traditional technologies such as bar codes, RFID has a fundamental advantages, because reading occurs at a distance, with a range depending on the device technical specifications, and it does not require the optical alignment of the reader with the tag. Each RFID tag can be equipped with an enclosure capable of tolerating the operating environment conditions, making this technology suitable for processes with risk of exposure to liquids or acids and saline vapors, wide temperature changes, mechanical vibrations and shocks.

The RFID products market is very large and diversified: specialized offerings exist for a wide range of industrial sectors. A complete RFID solution typically includes: (i) a set of tags suitable for the objects to identify and the environment in which they will be used; (ii) a set of fixed readers to be placed appropriately, to detect objects crossing passages or presence in confined environments such as trucks or shelves; (iii) a set of portable readers, for operators in the field who have to read and write tags; (iv) a back-end software receiving real-time alerts of reading events from connected readers. A typical reading event consists of at least three elements: the identification code read from the tag (which uniquely identifies an object); a reader identification code (used to determine the location of the reading); a timestamp. In this way, the back-end software is able to build and manage a history of all handling operations on objects equipped with RFID tags. On this data, rules and queries of varying complexity can be specified to meet business needs. Furthermore, semantic annotations could be written into RFIDs attached to objects so that a meaningful articulated description accompanies the item the tag adheres to [22]. In such semantic-enhanced contexts, tagged objects act as actual resources, revealing –in addition to their identification code– a semantic annotation to nearby RFID readers; this allows them to describe themselves on the fly even when a central support infrastructure is not available. Semantic-based sensory data dissemination and query processing technologies could enable advanced solutions for environmental monitoring.

For marine environment analysis, RFID tags must be applicable to the containers of samples extracted from the seabed. The writing of the identification code will be performed on the pontoon hosting the extraction tools, as soon as a sample is placed in its container equipped with an initially empty RFID tag. From then on, each sample will be identifiable and traceable along the following planned steps:

- from the extraction workers to the logistics supervisor, on the pontoon;
- from the supervisor to a staff member of an analysis laboratory which takes charge of the samples directly on the pontoon;
- from the logistics supervisor on the pontoon to the warehouse;
- from the warehouse to analysis laboratories, where staff takes charge of the samples in their premises, and back again to the warehouse;
- from a laboratory to another laboratory directly, with possible partitioning of a sample into smaller ones (which have to be tracked individually thereafter).

In detail, a process analysis step revealed the following requirements for the proposed RFID solution:

- a set of tags attached to the body and the cap of each container. The container and cap identification codes will be strongly correlated to allow verifying the simultaneous presence of both elements. Tags must be resistant to sea water also in the presence of any pollutants;
- portable readers for writing tags on the pontoon;
- fixed readers on each warehouse gates as well as on shelves, to monitor the arrival and the departure of samples and to check how many samples are currently present;
- fixed readers at the gates of each laboratory to monitor sample movements;
- fixed or portable readers for writing operations, dedicated to laboratories which must be able to divide a sample into smaller ones, each with its own container.

Among the different available RFID tag families, the EPCglobal Generation II Ultra High Frequency (Gen2 UHF) standard from GS1 Consortium [23] emerges as the most advisable, since it guarantees secure read/write operations and the compatibility with the majority of readers and software tools. Examples of different types of tags available on the market are reported in Table I. They are all enclosed in a waterproof plastic material resistant to dust and water immersion, and equipped with user memory for the storage of additional data beyond the Electronic Product Code (EPC) identification code.

TABLE I. RFID TAG EXAMPLES (PRODUCT NAMES OMITTED)

Storage	Packaging	Reading range	Operating temperature	Cost
EPC 128 bit, 512 bit of user memory	Plastic (IP 68 certification)	up to 9 meters	From -40 to 80 °C	€450 for 100 tags
EPC 96 bit, 512 bit of user memory	Thermoplastic (IP 68 certification)	up to 6 meters	From -40 to 85 °C	€60 for 10 tags
EPC 96 bit, 512 bit of user memory	Polypropylene (IP 68 certification)	up to 7 meters	From -40 to 85 °C	€32 for 10 tags

Back-end software solutions are currently divided in two main categories: full packages to be installed and run on one's own computing infrastructure; Platform-as-a-Service (PaaS) cloud offerings, with elastic computing resources and pay-as-you-go fees. Anyway, the general architecture of RFID software compliant with GS1 standards is shown in Fig. 7. The main elements are:

- Low-Level Reader Protocol (LLRP), ensuring compatibility with interrogator hardware from multiple manufacturers;
- Application Level Events (ALE) compliant middleware to catch and manage RFID reading events; it embeds a rule engine for declarative specification of customized business rules;
- Electronic Product Code Information Services (EPCIS) for describing, gathering and sharing data associated with tracked objects, also across computer networks.

As back-end software tools support custom extensions, real-time RFID event tracking can be integrated with the OSM-based software solution described in Section III, in order

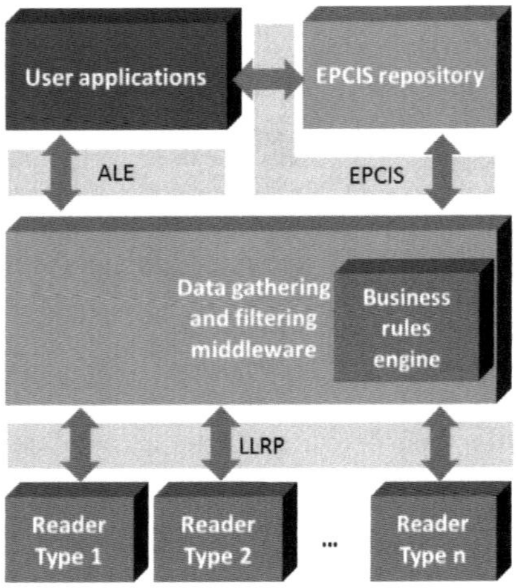

Figure 7. RFID management software architecture

to provide a unified platform for the whole environmental analysis workflow, from field to laboratory.

VI. CONCLUSION

The paper presented an integrated ICT platform supporting analysis of the marine environment in Taranto Sea, Italy. The proposal is based on principles of crowdsourcing and comprises an information system –based on OpenSeaMap– for managing georeferenced and timestamped data, as well as specialized tools –as plug-ins for the JOSM editor– for massive data import and advanced queries. Furthermore, the feasibility of integrating RFID technologies to track survey samples in all steps of their life cycle was evaluated.

Future work includes a full validation of the proposed platform in all activities of the environmental analysis and requalification program. As the devised platform provides a general solution for many analogous scenarios of environmental monitoring and decision support, it is possible to export it to other contexts beyond the Taranto Sea, with minimal effort.

ACKNOWLEDGMENT

Authors acknowledge the project "Accordo con il Commissario Straordinario per gli interventi urgenti di bonifica, ambientalizzazione e riqualificazione della città di Taranto".

REFERENCES

[1] G. Alabiso, M. Giacomini, M. Milillo, and P. Ricci, "The taranto sea system: 8 years of chemical–physical measurements," *Biol. mar. medit*, vol. 12, no. 1, pp. 369–373, 2005.

[2] N. Cardellicchio, S. Covelli, and T. Cibic, "Integrated environmental characterization of the contaminated marine coastal area of taranto, ionian sea (southern italy)," *Environmental Science and Pollution Research*, pp. 1–4, 2016.

[3] Commissario Straordinario per la bonifica, ambientalizzazione e riqualificazione di Taranto. (last access: 2016-09-20). [Online]. Available: http://www.commissariobonificataranto.it

[4] I.-A. Yeo, S.-H. Yoon, and J.-J. Yee, "Development of an environment and energy geographical information system (e-gis) construction model to support environmentally friendly urban planning," *Applied Energy*, vol. 104, pp. 723–739, 2013.

[5] S. Erdogan, I. Yilmaz, T. Baybura, and M. Gullu, "Geographical information systems aided traffic accident analysis system case study: city of afyonkarahisar," *Accident Analysis & Prevention*, vol. 40, no. 1, pp. 174–181, 2008.

[6] H. M. Khormi and L. Kumar, "Assessing the risk for dengue fever based on socioeconomic and environmental variables in a geographical information system environment," *Geospatial health*, vol. 6, no. 2, pp. 171–176, 2012.

[7] E. Chuvieco, I. Aguado, M. Yebra, H. Nieto, J. Salas, M. P. Martín, L. Vilar, J. Martínez, S. Martín, P. Ibarra *et al.*, "Development of a framework for fire risk assessment using remote sensing and geographic information system technologies," *Ecological Modelling*, vol. 221, no. 1, pp. 46–58, 2010.

[8] D. C. Brabham, "Crowdsourcing as a model for problem solving an introduction and cases," *Convergence: the international journal of research into new media technologies*, vol. 14, no. 1, pp. 75–90, 2008.

[9] E. Estellés-Arolas and F. González-Ladrón-De-Guevara, "Towards an integrated crowdsourcing definition," *Journal of Information science*, vol. 38, no. 2, pp. 189–200, 2012.

[10] C. Gouveia and A. Fonseca, "New approaches to environmental monitoring: the use of ict to explore volunteered geographic information," *GeoJournal*, vol. 72, no. 3-4, pp. 185–197, 2008.

[11] OpenSeaMap. (last access: 2016-09-20). [Online]. Available: http://www.openseamap.org/

[12] M. Haklay and P. Weber, "Openstreetmap: User-generated street maps," *IEEE Pervasive Computing*, vol. 7, no. 4, pp. 12–18, 2008.

[13] PostreSQL. (last access: 2016-09-20). [Online]. Available: https://www.postgresql.org/

[14] Overpass API. (last access: 2016-09-20). [Online]. Available: http://wiki.openstreetmap.org/wiki/Overpass_API

[15] JOSM. (last access: 2016-09-20). [Online]. Available: https://josm.openstreetmap.de/

[16] G. Xu, W. Shen, and X. Wang, "Applications of wireless sensor networks in marine environment monitoring: A survey," *Sensors*, vol. 14, no. 9, pp. 16 932–16 954, 2014.

[17] S. Fang, L. Da Xu, Y. Zhu, J. Ahati, H. Pei, J. Yan, and Z. Liu, "An integrated system for regional environmental monitoring and management based on internet of things," *IEEE Transactions on Industrial Informatics*, vol. 10, no. 2, pp. 1596–1605, 2014.

[18] M. Dunbabin and L. Marques, "Robots for environmental monitoring: Significant advancements and applications," *IEEE Robotics & Automation Magazine*, vol. 19, no. 1, pp. 24–39, 2012.

[19] OpenStreetMap Wiki - OpenSeaMap. (last access: 2016-09-20). [Online]. Available: http://wiki.openstreetmap.org/wiki/OpenSeaMap

[20] A. Pinto, F. Scioscia, G. Loseto, M. Ruta, E. Bove, and E. Di Sciascio, "A semantic-based approach for machine learning data analysis," *Semantic Computing (ICSC), 2015 IEEE International Conference on*, pp. 324–327, 2015.

[21] M. Ruta, S. Colucci, F. Scioscia, E. Di Sciascio, and F. Donini, "Finding commonalities in rfid semantic streams," *Procedia Computer Science*, vol. 5, pp. 857–864, 2011.

[22] R. De Virgilio, E. Di Sciascio, M. Ruta, F. Scioscia, and R. Torlone, "Semantic-based RFID Data Management," *Unique Radio Innovation for the 21st Century: Building Scalable and Global RFID Networks*, pp. 111–141, 2011.

[23] GS1. (last access: 2016-09-20). [Online]. Available: http://www.gs1.org

An Ontology-Based Affective Computing Approach for Passenger Safety Engagement on Cruise Ships

Annarita Cinquepalmi

DEI - Politecnico di Bari
Via E. Orabona 4
Bari, Italy I-70125
Email: annarita.cinquepalmi@poliba.it

Umberto Straccia

Istituto di Scienza e Tecnologie dell'Informazione
Consiglio Nazionale delle Ricerche
ISTI-CNR, Pisa, Italy
Email: straccia@isti.cnr.it

Abstract—**The safety of cruise passengers is a key element for a cruise company. Among various aspects, the ability to interpret and recognize cruisers' emotions, so that he/she feel safe, plays a central role in human communication. Affective computing addresses the computational processing of emotions. Current automatic emotion recognizers basically use automated classification tools to label emotions without capturing relations between biosignals and observations measured by the various sensors. This work proposes instead an Ontology Web Language (OWL) ontology-based emotion recognition framework by (i) monitoring human body vital signals through wearable, non-invasive sensors; and then the (ii) emotion detection is based on a ontology-based matchmaking process via non-standard automated reasoning services. A key factor is the use of so-called vague/fuzzy concepts, which are intrinsic in the realm of emotions and their dynamic evolution. To this end, we exploit Fuzzy Description Logics (Fuzzy DLs), which are the logical foundation of fuzzy OWL ontologies, i.e., OWL ontologies extended with vague/fuzzy concepts. An early prototype has been implemented w.r.t. a reference dataset and a preliminary experiment has being carried out with the aim to monitor the emotions experienced by cruise passengers while viewing safety video instructions.**

Keywords - Affective Computing; Semantic Matchmaking; Fuzzy OWL 2.

I. Introduction

The number of people taking cruises across the world has increased year-on-year. The Cruise Lines International Association [1] estimates that 24 million passengers are expected to cruise this year. Despite statistics, passengers opinion about cruise ship safety changed since Costa Concordia accident in January 2012 off the coast of Italy (32 people died). Among others, passenger safety training is crucial for cruise company. To this end, it appears to be useful to monitor and capture passengers emotions, when viewing safety video instructions, to improve the emotional condition or prevent harmful health states of the passengers. According to [2], *Affective Computing* (AC) aims to create computational systems, which are *Emotionally Intelligent* (EmI), *i.e.*, capable to recognize, understand and express emotions in order to improve users' well-being. EmI systems may establish empathy with the user, *e.g.*, through an interactive automated agent, *i.e.*, affective avatar designed to perceive user emotional experiences when engaged in specific activities.

Physiological signals have been used increasingly in AC thanks to technological improvements in low-cost miniaturized unobtrusive wearable biosensors for continuous monitoring. Recently, manufacturers have being developing increasingly robust and cost-effective biosensors for fast and sensitive analysis of human body vital signals. Over the last decade, EmI systems have gained momentum for a wide number of applications in several important companies, *e.g.*, NeuroFocus [3] utilized electroencephalography (EEG), eye tracking, and biometrics to capture the non-conscious aspects, emotions, and preferences of consumer decision-making; and EmSense [4] developed the proprietary unobtrusive EmBand^{TM}hardware for measuring positive/negative emotional response and cognitive engagement to advertising.

Emotion-aware systems identify specific outcomes from biosensors and respond by triggering appropriate actions within a given context. Additional examples include: (i) monitoring the elderly to recognize signs of health issues [5], such as sadness bouts as a symptom in depressed patients, and alerting healthcare providers; (ii) increasing safety of drivers by observing their emotions [6] and, suggesting a relaxation technique if a state of anger or frustration is detected (*biofeedback*); and (iii) improving user satisfaction in smart home environments [7], by controlling domotic devices to favor comfort and resting.

Nevertheless, most existing approaches are still quite intrusive. Furthermore, studies are tipically carried out in controlled laboratory conditions, hardly transferable to real scenarios. Basically, they rely on conventional computing architectures running procedures for signal processing and features extraction, which have high computational costs, affecting the performance in real time applications.

This paper proposes a quasi-real-time computing framework, which only leverages off-the-shelf technology for biosignal monitoring and analysis, attempting to go beyond current simple emotion classification by exploiting fuzzy OWL Ontologies [8][9]. Biosignals and features are described through semantic annotations based on a reference ontology. In particular, fuzzy OWL enables the description and manipulation of vague concepts, such as emotions. Semantic-based processing of raw sensor data makes them machine-understandable and allows ontology-based knowledge to be processed efficiently, even in mobile and pervasive contexts with severe resource limitations in memory, storage and energy consumption. For this purpose, the optimized Mini-ME embedded reasoning engine [10] is adopted.

Our framework works in three fundamental stages: (i) detect most relevant biosignals features; (ii) build an annotated description of the emotional dimensional model in terms of *valence* (V) and *arousal* (A) [11] via the FuzzyDL-Learner [12][13][14][15]; and (iii) use matchmaking to recognize the emotion from its dimensional features. Non-standard inference services [16] are exploited to compare annotations of the valence/arousal (VA) space, discovering the most emotion(s) experienced by the user.

The ultimate goal of the framework is to provide helpful and timely user feedback and/or provide customized services. The free public DECAF data set [17] was used for the initial implementation and experimentation of the proposed framework, in order to build a Fuzzy OWL ontology of emotions correlated with biosignals and the continuous VA model. Experiments on the proposed framework are still ongoing; this paper provides a proof of concept on the feasibility of our approach.

The remainder of the paper is organized as follows. In Section II, a literature analysis is given, Section III describes the framework in detail, while a representative case study for passenger safety engagement on cruise ships is described in Section IV. The conducted experiment is illustrated in Section V. The paper closes with concluding remarks and future perspectives.

II. Related Work

Biosignals are multichannel time-varying recordings of parameters of the central and/or the autonomic nervous system. They are known to convey information that can be used for emotion assessment [18]. Using biosignals has some advantages over other methods: (i) they are relatively robust to voluntary control and manipulation, because they are governed by the human autonomous nervous system; (ii) using wireless wearable sensors they can be collected anytime and anywhere without active user input; (iii) they can be easily correlated with external channels like facial expression.

The literature about emotion recognition through biosensors shows a standardized procedure to build EmI systems, summarized in the four following stages: (i) signal acquisition; (ii) preprocessing (iii) feature extraction; and (iv) machine learning based classification [2][19]. They exploit conventional fixed computer architectures, thus preventing many realistic application scenarios.

Recent developements in Body Area Network (BAN) allow data gathered from wearable sensors routed through multi-hop wireless links toward a portable computing device (*e.g.*, a smartphone) [20]. In mobile real-time emotion detection systems, performance of the processing pipeline is critical in terms of both computational efficiency and classification accuracy. Furthermore, classification yields trivial labels, without a formally structured description about the characteristics of the elicited user emotion.

The Semantic Web initiative generated standard logic-based languages for the representation of ontologies to enable machine-understandable characterization of knowledge domains. Emotion recognition approaches exploiting Semantic Web technologies exist in literature, although they are a minority. Zhang *et al.* [21] proposed a system based on reasoning rules applying a Decision Tree, but mining was exploited only to map data to a single class. Furthermore, a rule-based system is useful only if there is an exact match between rules and the data: this is quite rare in complex domains like emotion characterization.

The complexity of emotions, the non-linearity of biosignals, the impossibility to find a single model to represent emotions can be faced by adopting fuzzy systems [22]. They are generally robust and have the ability to process inaccurate and vague data.

Let us recap that, although a large amount of work has been carried out about fuzzy logic-based machine learning [23], fuzzy ontology-based machine learning techniques have been scarcely investigated in general [8] and not at all in the context of EmI. Together with the adoption of non-standard inference services, supporting approximate matches, this appears to be an interesting ingredient to improve EmI system performance in terms of fine-graned emotion categorization, flexible classification and logic-based explanation of the outcomes.

III. Emotionally Intelligent System: Framework and Approach

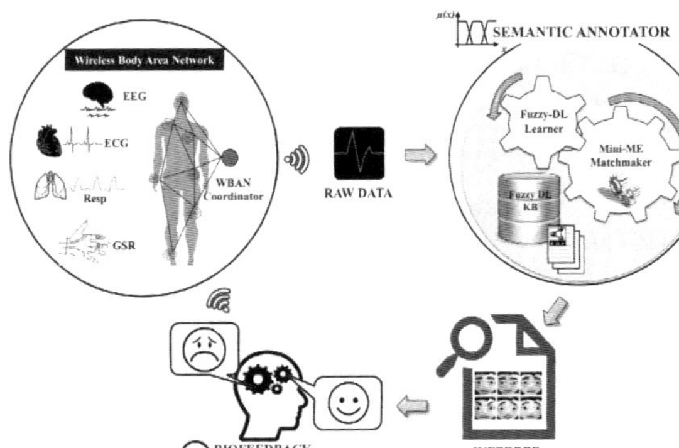

Figure 1. Proposed Framework.

Our framework extends the standard emotion recognition works discussed in Section II. Workflow steps are basically the same, but semantic-based enhancements change the way each step is performed. The main peculiarities of the proposed approach are: (i) a real-time emotional patterns detection based on *Fuzzy DLs* [8]. Fuzzy DLs are the logical foundation of fuzzy OWL ontologies, i.e., OWL ontologies extended with vague/fuzzy concepts [9][24]; (ii) a semantic-based matchmaking process to recognize the most likely emotion, and (iii) a feedback action to improve the user's emotional state.

The overall architecture is depicted in Fig. 1. Autonomous and unobtrusive sensor nodes can form a body area network or body sensor network (BSN) [25]. Gathered physiological parameters are routed through multiple wireless links in the BAN to a portable device (*e.g.*, a smartphone) with constrained computational resources for real-time DAQ (Data Acquisition). Physiological signals in response to stimuli are collected and used as the EmI system input. Before these data streams are fed into the computational model, feature extraction techniques are exploited.

The first efforts toward affect recognition have focused on finding the link between users emotional state and its corresponding physiological state, translating low-level data captured by sensing devices to high-level abstractions expressed by a semantic annotation. The goal of the *semantic annotator* component is to build a semantic annotation combining physiological features and bidimensional emotion parameters: *valence* or *evaluation* and *arousal* or *activation*. Valence represents how positive or negative (*i.e.*, pleasant or unpleasant) an emotion is, while arousal represents a passive/active scale, ranging from calm to excited. The key idea in the above model is to represent emotions with just a coordinate system conveying basic attributes. As a consequence, any emotion could be represented as a point in this space [11]. Thus, each emotional state can be defined as a combination of these dimensions, *e.g.*, anger can be characterized by high arousal and negative valence, happiness by low arousal and positive valence, and sadness by low arousal and negative valence. If the emotion is completely neutral it should be assigned to the center point of the space.

Exploiting the FuzzyDL-Learner [13][14][15], concept emotion descriptions are automatically learned from biosignal features compiled into an OWL 2 [26] ontology. Through non-standard inference services [16], the semantic annotation is compared with emotion descriptions contained in the ontology, created in a training step from a reference biosignal dataset. Non-standard inference services for semantic matchmaking, implemented in the Mini-ME reasoner [10], produce the most appropriate elicited user emotion(s). The system captures the best action to enhance user's affective states, giving a user feedback.

A prototypical fuzzy ontology modeling the domain of interest has been defined, using fuzzy OWL [9]. The logical foundation of fuzzy OWL are Fuzzy DLs, an extension to classical DLs with the aim of dealing with *fuzzy/vague/imprecise information* (for more details see [8][24]). Roughly, in Fuzzy DLs, there are *fuzzy concepts* (representing classes of objects), *fuzzy roles* (a.k.a. *properties*, joining pairs of objects), *individuals* (specific named objects) and *fuzzy datatypes* (or fuzzy concrete domains defined over an interval of the rational numbers). The important aspect to know is that, unlike usually, objects may be an instance of a fuzzy concept to some degree in $[0, 1]$, while in the non-fuzzy case an object is either instance or not an instance of a concept. *Axioms* are statements which represent is-a relations between concepts. The logical statement has a *degree of truth* allowing to define new fuzzy concepts from other ones during the learning process. It is beyond the scope of this work to illustrate the details of Fuzzy DLs. We refer the reader to [8].

The FuzzyDL-Learner system is used to learn automatically to identify relationship between human affective states and bidimensional emotional characteristics. The main feature of the FuzzyDL-Learner system is that it allows to learn graded fuzzy OWL 2 descriptions of a selected target class in terms of specific inclusion axioms expressed in OWL $\mathcal{EL}$ [27], in which, fuzzy concepts may occur to improve both the accuracy of the description, as well as their readability. The learner uses the pFOIL-DL learning algorithm [15] to automatically induce fuzzy concepts descriptions. pFOIL-DL is inspired on FOIL [28], a popular Inductive Logic Programming algorithm for learning sets of rules. The three main differences from FOIL are: (i) pFOIL-DL uses a probabilistic measure to score concept expressions, (ii) it does not remove positive examples covered from the training set, but leaves it unchanged after each learned rule and (iii) it evaluates the goodness of an induced rule not independently of previously learned rules, but considering the whole set of learnt expressions. Additionally, FuzzyDL-Learner automatically fuzzifies the range of the real-valued bidimensional emotion parameters and finds relationship between emotions and the VA space. Furthermore, it may provide an automatic natural language translation of the learned classification emotion rules. The conjunction of the dimensional value intervals associated to each emotion – as determined by the training set– becomes the annotation for that emotion. In this way, each emotion can be described as the conjunction of qualitative features, valence and arousal. For instance, the following is a learned description for the emotion $Fear$

$$\begin{aligned} &\exists hasArousal.Arousal\_low \sqcap \\ &\exists hasValence.Valence\_high \quad \sqsubseteq \quad Fear \end{aligned}$$

dictating that $Fear$ is identified by low arousal values and high valence values, where low arousal (resp. high valence) are automatically determined as illustrated in Fig. 2. The output constitutes the *annotated dataset* and is the factual knowledge in the reference fuzzy Ontology.

The subsequent classification task exploits a semantic-based matchmaking process computing non-standard inferences, implemented in the Mini-ME embedded reasoning engine [10]. In a generic setting, given a request *R* and a set of resources *S* expressed w.r.t. a reference ontology, semantic matchmaking allows to find and rank the best matching resources through non-standard inference procedures called *Concept Contraction* and *Concept Abduction* [16]. If *R* and *S* have conflicting characteristics, Concept Contraction determines new concepts *G* (*Give up*) and *K* (*Keep*); *G* is the explanation about what in *R* is incompatible with *S*, while *K* represents the compatible part. In addition, a penalty value is computed, which is the semantic distance of the description w.r.t. the request. Otherwise, if there is compatibility between *R* and *S* but *R* does not match *S* fully, *Concept Abduction* extracts the concept expression *H* (*Hypothesis*), expressing what should be hypothesized in *S* in order to completely satisfy *R*. A related penalty value of a service A w.r.t. a request B is computed as:

$$d(A, B) = 100(1 - \frac{penalty_{(c)} + penalty_{(a)}}{max\ penalty_{(a)}}) \qquad (1)$$

where $penalty_{(c)}$ and $penalty_{(a)}$ are the penalty induced by Concept Contraction and Concept Abduction between

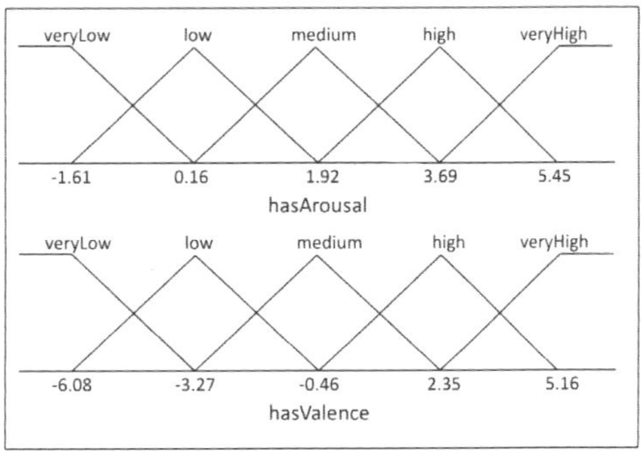

Figure 2. Fuzzy concepts obtained from the datatype properties *hasArousal* and *hasValence*.

each service/resource annotation and the request. Penalty is normalized w.r.t. the maximum possible semantic distance from the request A, *i.e.*, the one of the most generic DL concept (denoted $\top$); this distance depends only on the reference ontology. Finally, semantic affinity is expressed by a percentage of scores and the service with highest rank is selected by the requester.

We have adapted the semantic matchmaking problem to the discovery of user emotions in the following way. The request is defined by a semantic description expressed as the logical conjunction of information about emotional bidimensional features extracted from unlabeled user input. Resources are the semantic descriptions populating the previously annotated dataset. The annotated dataset and fuzzy concepts descriptions are fed to the matchmaking reasoner, and ranked penalty values associated with a logic-based explanation are obtained from the semantic matchmaking process. The emotion with the lowest penalty is identified as the best matching emotion from the current user's biosignals.

IV. Case study: Emotions in Viewing Safety Video Instructions

The proposal explores how emotions affect consumer decision making in *Emotional or Experiental Marketing* [29]. In contrast to traditional marketing, emotional marketers focus to understand what influences consumer decision-making and stimulates their sense and minds. Consumer experience is not often caused by rational choice: typically, emotional responses drive human opinion and experience. The selected reference scenario and case study aims to capture passengers cruise emotions when viewing safety video instructions immediately after sailing. The video provides clear instructions and explains in detail the actions each person on board should follow in the event of an emergency. Passengers convey the emotion elicited, after viewing, in terms of valence and arousal. The subsequent FuzzyDL-Learner in conjunction with semantic-based matchmaking make a detailed analysis of emotions and behaviors fully transparent to the user. The feedback is to suggest what parts of the safety video should be changed and in what way in order to favor cruiser engagement and serenity, so that he/she feel safe to travel with a cruise company and will enjoy their stay.

TABLE I. pFoil LEARNED CONCEPT DESCRIPTIONS.

Target Class	Induced Axiom
Fear	$\exists hasArousal.Arousal\_low \sqcap \exists hasValence.Valence\_high$
	$\exists hasArousal.Arousal\_medium \sqcap \exists hasValence.Valence\_veryHigh$
	$\exists hasArousal.Arousal\_low \sqcap \exists hasValence.Valence\_veryHigh$
Amusement	$\exists hasArousal.Arousal\_low \sqcap \exists hasValence.Valence\_medium$
	$\exists hasArousal.Arousal\_low \sqcap \exists hasValence.Valence\_veryLow$
	$\exists hasArousal.Arousal\_low$
Shock	$\exists hasArousal.Arousal\_low \sqcap \exists hasValence.Valence\_high$
	$\exists hasArousal.Arousal\_veryLow \sqcap \exists hasValence.Valence\_high$
Disgust	$\exists hasArousal.Arousal\_low \sqcap \exists hasValence.Valence\_high$
	$\exists hasArousal.Arousal\_veryLow \sqcap \exists hasValence.Valence\_high$
	$\exists hasArousal.Arousal\_high \sqcap \exists hasValence.Valence\_veryHigh$
Fun	$\exists hasArousal.Arousal\_low$
	$\exists hasArousal.Arousal\_medium \sqcap \exists hasValence.Valence\_veryLow$
Anger	$\exists hasArousal.Arousal\_high$
	$\exists hasArousal.Arousal\_medium \sqcap \exists hasValence.Valence\_high$
	$\exists hasArousal.Arousal\_veryHigh$
	$\exists hasArousal.Arousal\_high \sqcap \exists hasValence.Valence\_veryHigh$
Excitement	$\exists hasArousal.Arousal\_high$
	$\exists hasArousal.Arousal\_medium \sqcap \exists hasValence.Valence\_low$
	$\exists hasArousal.Arousal\_veryLow \sqcap \exists hasValence.Valence\_high$

The freely accessible DECAF [17] database for affect recognition and tagging was used to assess the feasibility of our approach. It is a multimodal dataset for decoding user physiological responses to multimedia content: it consists of a collection of peripheral physiological signals and multi-modal recordings, taken from 30 healthy subjects. The records incorporate magnetoencephalogram, horizontal electrooculogram, electrocardiogram, trapezius electromyogram, and near infrared facial video signals. The participants watched 36 emotional videos and gave feedback in terms of valence and arousal. Arousal expresses the intensity of the emotional feeling built up when a subject watched a safety video, ranging on a discrete scale of 0 (very calm) to 4 (very aroused), valence refers to how was the feeling after watching a clip on a scale of -2 (unpleasant) to 2 (very pleasant). The chosen video clips are also associated with emotional tags.

Our prototypal system exploits the Fuzzy-DL Learner and the Mini-ME matchmaker for emotion detection. The workflow starts with valence, arousal participants' self-assessment ratings information. To make sense of the data, z-score normalization rescaling is required. For each video normalized arousal and valence scores are calculated by taking the mean and standard deviation of arousal and valence ratings listed in [17], considered as ground truth. In order to enable a fully automated emotion annotation and matchmaking process, the above meaningful emotional features are translated to an OWL ontology. A two-step modeling was devised to tie VA parameters to emotions. The former exploits bidimensional features as input to the FuzzyDL-Learner in order to fuzzify valence and arousal and to create a fuzzy OWL ontology by identifying axioms that express each emotional label. The latter maps the DECAF dataset to an *annotated dataset* to transform raw data into higher level knowledge according to previous fuzzified arousal/valence space.

Seven emotional classes were considered to induce concept descriptions: *Amusement, Anger, Disgust, Excitement, Fear, Fun and Shock*. The discretization method adopted by pFOIL-DL partitioned valence and arousal numeric datatypes into 5 fuzzy sets (*veryLow, low, medium, high, veryHigh*) with associated membership functions, as depicted in Figure 2. The learned expressions are reported in Table I. These axioms form our fuzzy OWL ontology. As a matter of example, *e.g.*, *anger* has been characterized by high arousal and negative valence while *amusement* by low arousal and positive valence.

The goal of the second step is to build the *annotated dataset*, connoting each valence, arousal value according to the fuzzy interval obtained in the previous phase. For example, assume subject with ID 9, after viewing a video, may reports *V=0* and *A=2*. Then, self-assessment valence/arousal ratings provided by participants are processed as follows:

1) Valence/arousal ratings are z-score normalized considering ground truth mean and standard deviation in the training set. The chosen video clip has μ_A=1.20, σ_A=0.96, μ_V=1.56 and σ_V=0.50. The normalized ratings are, thus, $\overline{A}$=*0.83* and $\overline{V}$=*-3.12*.
2) The semantic description of the subject, according to the reference ontology, is composed. According to fuzzy concepts obtained previously, normalized ratings are both in the *low* range, so a semantic description is expressed as:
   SubjectId_9: $\forall hasArousal.low \sqcap \exists hasArousal \sqcap \forall hasValence.low \sqcap \exists hasValence$
3) Annotated dataset and concept descriptions learned by FuzzyDL-Learner are then fed to the matchmaker in order to detect the subject's emotion(s). In the case under examination, ranked penalty obtained from the semantic matchmaking process are: *Amusement:16.18, Fun:27.27, Excitement:36.36, Disgust:42.86, Fear:45.45, Shock:57.18, Anger:60.53*. Amusement has the lowest semantic distance and therefore the best matching emotion.
4) Finally, based on the elicited emotion, the most suitable feedback could be applied in order to improve the emotional condition or prevent harmful health states of the passengers.

V. EXPERIMENTS

The experimental setup used to test the accuracy of our implementation consisted of a smaller sample number than DECAF [17]. 30 subjects were involved in the experiment watching 20 emotional videos, making a total of 600 individual records. The chosen video clips were shown in random order eliciting 7 emotions, namely amusement, anger, disgust, excitement, fear, fun ad shock.

TABLE II. CONFUSION MATRIX. a)AMUSEMENT b)ANGER c)DISGUST d)EXCITEMENT e)FEAR f)FUN g)SHOCK

Real/Predict	a	b	c	d	e	f	g
a	102	6	3	4	3	0	2
b	5	111	0	1	3	0	0
c	19	7	21	5	4	4	0
d	4	15	3	36	1	0	1
e	1	11	2	5	40	0	1
f	41	21	4	5	1	46	2
g	11	12	2	5	8	5	17

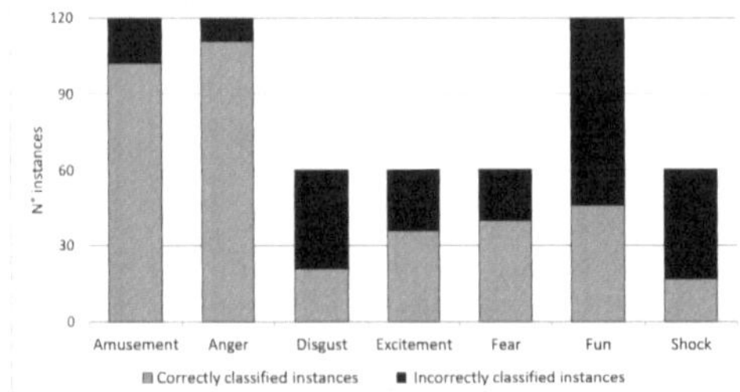

Figure 3. Classification result.

Table II shows thee confusion matrix of emotions classification. On a total of 600 instances, 373 were correctly classified with an accuracy of 62.17%. A graphical representation of the results is shown in Fig. 3. The overall weighted classification precision, recall and F-Measure are 0.735, 0.660 and 0.695 respectively.

A relevant issue is the user subjectivity associated with emotional perception: values assigned to a given impression may be subjective. For instance, *Fun* emotion has been mistakenly classified as *Amusement* because both are pleasant and not aroused emotions. For this reason, tolerance is a crucial factor to be considered. In summary, our preliminary results reveal that the semantic-based approach in conjunction with fuzzy ontology-based approach seems to be a promising route towards improving standard machine learning based emotion classification techniques.

VI. CONCLUSION AND FUTURE WORK

The paper presented early work on a novel framework for emotion recognition from biosignals via semantic annotation and matchmaking in conjunction with a fuzzy ontology-based approach. Raw sensor data, without any descriptive metadata, have limited use as they are hard to discover, integrate or interpret. One challenge is to develop and test a framework for expressing and classifying complex patterns from biosignals, allowing emotion recognition through emotional model. To this end, FuzzyDL-Learner extracts fuzzy emotional concepts creating a fuzzy OWL ontology. Then, by exploiting a matchmaker, the semantic descriptions of the test sample are compared with annotations contained in the fuzzy ontology. The matchmaker returns then the most similar emotion as output.

The proposed approach is currently under prototypical implementation. Experimental evaluation on proper testbeds is ongoing and will allow to assess effectiveness w.r.t. the state of the art in AC. A further endeavor is validating the reference dataset quality and improving the accuracy of the proposed framework.

REFERENCES

[1] Cruise Lines International Association. [Online]. Available: http://www.Cruising.org 2016.09.28

[2] R. W. Picard, E. Vyzas, and J. Healey, "Toward machine emotional intelligence: Analysis of affective physiological state," *IEEE Transactions on Pattern Analysis and Machine Intelligence*, vol. 23, no. 10, pp. 1175–1191, 2001.

[3] Consumer Neuroscience. [Online]. Available: http://www.neurofocus.com 2016.09.28

[4] EmSense Corporation. [Online]. Available: http://www.emsense.com 2016.08.05

[5] V. Stanford, "Biosignals offer potential for direct interfaces and health monitoring," *Pervasive Computing, IEEE*, vol. 3, no. 1, pp. 99–103, 2004.

[6] J. A. Healey and R. W. Picard, "Detecting stress during real-world driving tasks using physiological sensors," *IEEE Transactions on Intelligent Transportation Systems*, vol. 6, no. 2, pp. 156–166, 2005.

[7] D. J. Cook *et al.*, "Assessing the quality of activities in a smart environment," *Methods Inf Med*, vol. 48, no. 5, pp. 480–485, 2009.

[8] U. Straccia, *Foundations of Fuzzy Logic and Semantic Web Languages*. CRC Press, 2013.

[9] F. Bobillo and U. Straccia, "Fuzzy ontology representation using OWL 2," *International Journal of Approximate Reasoning*, vol. 52, pp. 1073–1094, 2011.

[10] F. Scioscia *et al.*, "A mobile matchmaker for the Ubiquitous Semantic Web," *International Journal on Semantic Web and Information Systems (IJSWIS)*, vol. 10, no. 4, pp. 77–100, 2014.

[11] J. A. Russell, "A circumplex model of affect," *Journal of personality and social psychology*, vol. 39, no. 6, pp. 1161–1178, 1980.

[12] The FuzzyDL-Learner System. [Online]. Available: http://www.umbertostraccia.it/cs/software/FuzzyDL-Learner/index.html 2016.09.28

[13] F. A. Lisi and U. Straccia, "A FOIL-Like Method for Learning under Incompleteness and Vagueness," *23rd International Conference on Inductive Logic Programming*, vol. 8812, pp. 123–139, 2014, revised Selected Papers.

[14] F. A. Lisi and U. Straccia, "Learning in description logics with fuzzy concrete domains," *Fundamenta Informaticae*, vol. 140, no. 3-4, pp. 373–391, 2015.

[15] U. Straccia and M. Mucci, "pFOIL-DL: Learning (Fuzzy) $\mathcal{EL}$ Concept Descriptions from Crisp OWL Data Using a Probabilistic Ensemble Estimation," *Proceedings of the 30th Annual ACM Symposium on Applied Computing (SAC-15)*, pp. 345–352, 2015.

[16] M. Ruta, E. Di Sciascio, and F. Scioscia, "Concept abduction and contraction in semantic-based P2P environments," *Web Intelligence and Agent Systems*, vol. 9, no. 3, pp. 179–207, 2011.

[17] M. K. Abadi *et al.*, "DECAF: MEG-based multimodal database for decoding affective physiological responses," *IEEE Transactions on Affective Computing*, vol. 6, no. 3, pp. 209–222, 2015.

[18] J. Healey, "Physiological sensing of emotion," *The Oxford handbook of affective computing*, pp. 204–216, 2014.

[19] F. Nasoz, K. Alvarez, C. L. Lisetti, and N. Finkelstein, "Emotion recognition from physiological signals using wireless sensors for presence technologies," *Cognition, Technology & Work*, vol. 6, no. 1, pp. 4–14, 2004.

[20] M. Chen, S. Gonzalez, A. Vasilakos, H. Cao, and V. C. Leung, "Body area networks: A survey," *Mobile networks and applications*, vol. 16, no. 2, pp. 171–193, 2011.

[21] X. Zhang, B. Hu, P. Moore, J. Chen, and L. Zhou, "Emotiono: an ontology with rule-based reasoning for emotion recognition," *Neural Information Processing*, pp. 89–98, 2011.

[22] R. L. Mandryk and M. S. Atkins, "A fuzzy physiological approach for continuously modeling emotion during interaction with play technologies," *International Journal of Human-Computer Studies*, vol. 65, no. 4, pp. 329–347, 2007.

[23] M. E. Cintra, M. C. Monard, and H. A. Camargo, "On rule learning methods: a comparative analysis of classic and fuzzy approaches," *Soft Computing: State of the Art Theory and Novel Applications*, pp. 89–104, 2013.

[24] F. Bobillo and U. Straccia, "The Fuzzy Ontology Reasoner *fuzzyDL*," *Knowledge-Based Systems*, vol. 95, pp. 12–34, 2016.

[25] B. Latré, B. Braem, I. Moerman, C. Blondia, and P. Demeester, "A survey on wireless body area networks," *Wireless Networks*, vol. 17, no. 1, pp. 1–18, 2011.

[26] W3C OWL Working Group. OWL 2 Web Ontology Language Document Overview (Second Edition). W3C Recommendation 11 December 2012. [Online]. Available: http://www.w3.org/TR/owl2-overview/

[27] OWL 2 Web Ontology Language Profiles, *http://www.w3.org/TR/2009/REC-owl2-profiles-20091027/*, W3C, 2009 (accessed Semptember 27, 2016).

[28] J. R. Quinlan, "Learning logical definitions from relations," *Machine Learning*, vol. 5, pp. 239–266, 1990.

[29] B. H. Schmitt, *Experiential marketing: How to get customers to sense, feel, think, act, relate*. Simon and Schuster, 2000.

From the Physical Web to the Physical Semantic Web: knowledge discovery in the Internet of Things

Michele Ruta, Saverio Ieva, Giuseppe Loseto, Eugenio Di Sciascio
Politecnico di Bari
via E. Orabona 4, Bari (I-70125), Italy
email:{michele.ruta,saverio.ieva,giuseppe.loseto,eugenio.disciascio}@poliba.it

Abstract—**The *Physical Semantic Web* is proposed as a paradigm enhancing the Google Physical Web approach for the Internet of Things. It allows semantic annotations to be associated to beacons instead of trivial identifiers, in order to enable more powerful expressiveness in human-things and things-things interactions. This paper presents a general framework for the Physical Semantic Web, based on machine-understandable annotations of physical resources and novel logic-guided resource discovery capabilities. Possible application scenarios are outlined to highlight the benefits of induced enhancements and the effectiveness of theoretical solutions.**

Keywords–Physical Web; Knowledge Representation; Ubiquitous computing

I. INTRODUCTION AND MOTIVATION

The Physical Web is a paradigm in the Internet of Things framework devised by Google Inc. to enhance the interaction capabilities with real-world objects. A discovery service, running on a mobile device, retrieves Uniform Resource Locators (URLs) of nearby things through the *Eddystone* Bluetooth beacon protocol [1]. This requires neither centralized archives nor special-purpose applications. Finding URLs via Wi-Fi using mDNS (multicast DNS) and uPnP (Universal Plug and Play) is also supported. The Google Physical Web approach tends to preserve legacy applications: it empowers the human-thing interaction when native software is unfeasible or even impractical to be used: every smart object owns a web address, and this makes possible a simple and direct interaction bypassing dedicated apps and on-line backends. Although such an approach induces not negligible enhancements in the object networks manageability, several issues restrain a powerful adoption in even more complex Internet of Things (IoT) scenarios. Particularly, things-things interaction is not enabled yet and discovery mechanisms are too simplistic with respect to what needed in really autonomic IoT scenarios. Basically, interoperability problems have to be taken into account when coping with contexts evolving and modifying continuously.

This paper proposes to extend the Physical Web project exploiting the Semantic Web approach and theory, so enabling advanced resource advertisement and discovery features. Knowledge Representation (KR) promotes interoperability, being a possible means to overcome internal peculiarities of interacting entities. As of now, more and more studies indicate this could be also exploited in the Internet of Things. The so-called *Semantic Web of Things* (SWoT) [2] refers to scenarios where intelligence is embedded in the environment by deploying in the field a plethora of heterogeneous micro-devices, each acting as dynamic knowledge micro-repository.

In the proposed approach semantic annotations are encapsulated in beacons, to enhance representation capabilities of objects in the Physical Web. This adds the possibility of more complex interactions: things become resources exposing knowledge characterizing themselves without depending on any centralized actor and/or infrastructure. In addition, user agents running on mobile personal devices are able to dynamically discover the best available objects according to user's profile and preferences; not simply resources in the surroundings, but the ones better supporting users tasks and needs. The proposed approach still maintains the reference URL-based mechanism detecting all Eddystone-URL beacons in a given environment. Legacy applications are preserved, any off-the-shelf beacon and mobile device supporting the base Eddystone protocol can be adopted. Hence, each URL could target: (i) a basic web page where users access the document via browser; (ii) an annotated web page, where users may view the page and/or exploit features allowed by metadata semantics; (iii) a semantic annotation to be used by agents. Retrieved annotations are exploited in a semantic-based matchmaking [3] setting to compare a request (*e.g.*, user profile) with multiple beacon annotations (*i.e.*, object descriptions). Proper compression techniques are adopted to cope with verbosity of annotations and minimize data transfers. Any resource domain (shopping, transportation, gaming, points of interest, work, and so on) can be explored by simply selecting the conceptualization (*i.e.*, ontology) annotations are grounded on. For each <user profile, resource> pair, a score is the outcome of matchmaking: it assesses the affinity of the beacon with user preferences. Concept Abduction [4] non-standard inference provides also a full explanation about the score, evidencing compatible and missing features. Analogously, in case of incompatibility between preferences and beacon, the Concept Contraction inference [4] detects properties of the beacons causing the mismatch.

The remainder of the paper is organized as follows. The next section frames the background of the proposal, while the following Section III presents the envisioned Physical Semantic Web protocol and framework. Then Section IV introduces reference application scenarios to corroborate the comprehension of what proposed before Section V which closes the paper sketching future work.

II. RELATED WORK

In latest years, interesting approaches were developed to integrate knowledge-based frameworks in Wireless Sensor Networks and the Internet of Things. Resulting architectures largely vary in scope, but usually aim to: (i) exploit ontologies –*e.g.*, [5]– to annotate data, devices and services; (ii) share sensor data along the Linked Open Data (LOD) [6] guidelines by means of RESTful [7] or OGC's Sensor Web Enablement (SWE) [8] web service interfaces. *Sense2Web* [9] is a LOD-based platform to publish sensor data and link them to existing resources on the Semantic Web. Different ontologies were used to describe physical resources, query data and relations to deduce implicit knowledge and integrate sensor information coming from various sources. Likewise, the *Linked Stream Middleware* (LSM) platform [10] fuses data produced by sensors with other LOD sources, by enriching both sensor sources and data streams with semantic annotations. A processing engine is used to perform queries across both dataset types, mashup the data and compute results. Finally, [11] describes an application of knowledge representation to automatically create sensor compositions: user goals, functional and non-functional properties of sensors are described w.r.t. an OWL (Web Ontology Language) ontology so that the envisioned orchestration system is able to combine sensors and processes to satisfy a user request. In [12] ontology-based sensor descriptions allow the users to express requests in terms of device characteristics. Quantitative querying and semantic-based reasoning techniques are combined to improve the resource discovery and select appropriate sensors through exploratory search.

From a communication standpoint, the present paper is based on Bluetooth Low Energy (BLE) and Eddystone. Valid and supported alternatives include 6LoWPAN [13] at the network level and CoAP [14] at the application one. 6LoWPAN enables IPv6 packets to be carried on top of low-power wireless networks, while CoAP is an HTTP-like protocol for interconnected objects, designed for machine-to-machine interoperation of resource-constrained nodes. It follows the REST (REpresentational State Transfer) paradigm for making resources accessible, exploiting a binary data representation and a subset of HTTP methods. Each resource is a server-controlled abstraction, unambiguously identified by a URI (Uniform Resource Identifier). 6LoWPAN can be interfaced to IPv6 and CoAP/UDP to HTTP/TCP, so that sensor data can be accessed also from the classic Web. As an example, the *SPITFIRE* project [15] combines Semantic Web and networking technologies to build a service infrastructure aiming to develop advanced applications exploiting Internet-connected sensors and lightweight protocols, as CoAP. In that framework, sensors are described as RDF triples and service discovery is based on metadata (referred for example to device features or location).

A major issue of most proposals is the requirement for a stable Internet connection and/or a support infrastructure to enable discovery features. This makes them unsuitable connectionless scenarios and to mobile ad-hoc networks of resource-constrained objects. As an example, the work in [16] proposes "IoT gateways" to expose resources between CoAP and HTTP nodes; peer-to-peer (P2P) overlay network techniques are used to enable large-scale discovery among different networks. A key issue is that the approach is based only on a resource name resolution scheme, not allowing the use of articulate resource features for discovery, selection and ranking. Actually, all the above solutions except [12] only allow elementary queries on annotations, and then only basic discovery is possible.

Flags (3 Bytes)			Service UUIDs (4 Bytes)				Service Data (4 Bytes)			
Len	Type	Flags	Len	Type	Eddystone UUID		Len	Type	Eddystone UUID	
0x02	0x01	0x06	0x03	0x03	0xAA	0xFE	0x??	0x16	0xAA	0xFE
Eddystone Frame (up to 20 Bytes)										

Figure 1: Eddystone Beacon message format

Ontology-based *complex event processing* [17] and *semantic matchmaking* [4] could be used to improve knowledge and object discovery in mobile and pervasive contexts. The latter exploits logic-based reasoning to support approximated matches, resource ranking and explanation of outcomes.

III. The Physical Semantic Web: proposed approach

This section recalls the original Physical Web and outlines the proposed Physical Semantic Web evolution as a comprehensive framework for knowledge management in agent-based IoT environments.

A. Protocol

The Physical Web (PW) is an open approach, initially proposed and implemented by Google, aiming to enable on-demand interaction among objects and user devices. Every PW object should be able to expose information to surrounding devices, which can process it without requiring any specific application. The current PW is grounded on two basic elements: a wirelessly broadcast resource identifier (typically a URL) and a mobile device agent able to discover and show collected nearby URLs to the user. *Bluetooth Low Energy* (BLE)[1] beacons supporting the open *Eddystone* [1] application-level protocol are used to expose generic URLs. BLE was introduced in 2010 within the Bluetooth 4.0 Core Specification for Internet of Things scenarios. It uses the same 2.4 GHz Bluetooth radio with a simpler modulation scheme (strongly reducing power usage), ensuring multi-vendor interoperability and a long life-cycle for low-cost devices with standard coin-cell batteries. Over BLE, Eddystone protocol specification defines different formats for proximity beacon messages. All messages share a common PDU (Protocol Data Unit) format, reported in Figure 1. It is composed by: (i) 3 bytes for flags as defined in [18, Part A]; (ii) 4 bytes for service Universally Unique IDentifier (UUID) advertisement, containing the Eddystone Service UUID `0xFEAA`; (iii) resource data, comprising 4 bytes for data advertisement (also in this case the Eddystone Service UUID is included) and up to 20 bytes for the data message payload.

The protocol defines the following Eddystone message types, identified by means of the four most significant bits of the first octet in the data message.

- *Eddystone-UID* (`0x00`): broadcasts a unique 16-byte beacon ID as shown in Figure 2a. Namespace ID can be used to group a set of beacons, while the instance ID identifies individual devices in the group.

[1] https://www.bluetooth.com/what-is-bluetooth-technology/bluetooth-technology-basics/low-energy

This partition is useful to improve discovery and filter beacons according to one or more namespaces.

- *Eddystone-URL* (`0x10`): exposes an encoded schema prefix and a compressed and encoded URL (up to 17 bytes), fitting the message format reported in Figure 2b. The URL can be decoded and used by clients to manage the related resource (typically, open a Web page).
- *Eddystone-TLM* (`0x20`): transmits telemetry data useful for monitoring the health and operation of the beacon: battery voltage, device temperature and count of broadcast packets. TLM messages can be either *unencrypted* (version field `0x00`) or *encrypted* (`0x01`), following the format shown in Figure 2c and Figure 2d respectively. In the latter case, beacons must have been previously configured as Eddystone-EID and an identity key should be set during the configuration step.
- *Eddystone-EID* (`0x30`): includes an encrypted ephemeral identifier refreshing periodically during the beacon life-cycle (Figure 2e). This message type is used for security issues (*e.g.*, with encrypted TLM) and privacy-enhanced devices.

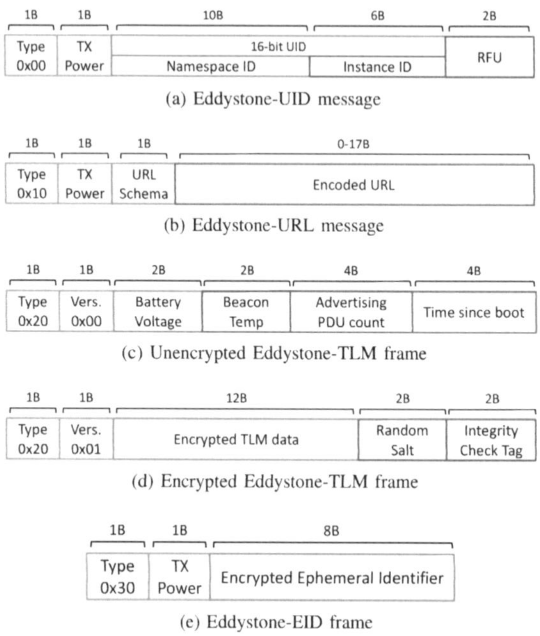

(a) Eddystone-UID message

(b) Eddystone-URL message

(c) Unencrypted Eddystone-TLM frame

(d) Encrypted Eddystone-TLM frame

(e) Eddystone-EID frame

Figure 2: Format of Eddystone messages

In the current Physical Web proposal, any client supporting BLE can scan the surrounding environment and discover resources (exposed through Eddystone-URL messages) without requiring a directory service or dedicated apps, which are deemed impractical for simple interactions. Google provided reference client implementations for iOS, Android and Node.js. Eventually, scanners should be implemented as background services in operating systems, so as to require no software installation by users. Beacons broadcast URLs pointing to Web pages for informative purposes or to Web apps using advanced technologies to offer interactive user experiences, *e.g.*, push notifications, direct connection and remote control of smart devices via *Web Bluetooth* [19] specification, which enables Web pages to access Bluetooth 4 devices using the *Generic ATTribute (GATT)* Profile to read and/or write attribute values. When multiple beacons are detected in the same area, ranking is based on beacon proximity. Eddystone allows estimating distance by comparing the RSSI (Received Signal Strength Indicator) with the nominal transmitted power recorded in beacon messages (see Figure 2a and 2b). Previous user actions can be also taken into account by implementing the following optional features: (i) *history*, a cache of recently visited URLs; (ii) *favorites*, a list of bookmarked URLs; (iii) *spam*, a list of URLs marked as undesired.

Despite the benefits of a general-purpose and technologically open approach, the Physical Web has several limits: (i) explicit interaction with the user is always required; (ii) beacons can only broadcast a simple URL, not rich resource descriptions; (iii) beacon ranking is based on simplistic distance criteria, without considering common and/or conflicting characteristics of the advertised resources w.r.t. a discoverer's profile or request. This paper proposes an extension of the PW vision, the *Physical Semantic Web* (PSW), exploiting Semantic Web technologies to enable advanced resource discovery. Particularly, in the approach presented here, along with classic and standard web pages each Eddystone beacon could also target annotated web pages or logic-based resource annotations. Both could be used to perform a semantic-based matchmaking [4], which exploits standard and non-standard inferences to give a logic-based ranking of nearby resources w.r.t. a request based on the meaning of their descriptions.

From a communication standpoint, the usage of Eddystone-URL beacons presumes an Internet connection will be available to retrieve resources pointed by broadcast URLs. In several real-world scenarios MANETs (Mobile Ad-hoc NETworks) and point-to-point infrastructure-less connections provide a more flexible and effective solution for wireless low-power networking. They can be particularly useful in ubiquitous scenarios, where mobile objects must provide quick decision support and/or on-the-fly organization in such intrinsically unpredictable environments. As shown in Figure 3, the PSW exploits Eddystone-UID beacon messages to transmit: MAC address of the device exposing the resource; instance ID, adopted to identify a specific local resource provided by the object; the protocol to be used to retrieve the resource annotation (*e.g.*, Bluetooth, Wi-Fi Direct). Such an approach considerably increases the flexibility and autonomicity of the basic PW for what concerns resource management, dissemination and discovery.

B. Framework

The proposed framework enhancing the standard PW solution is based on four elements.

A. **Machine-understandable standard language** to express information with rich and unambiguous semantics. The devised PW extension supports both human-to-machine and machine-to-machine interactions. This grants flexibility for accommodating a wider range of scenarios, including agent-based systems with implicit interaction patterns or with no

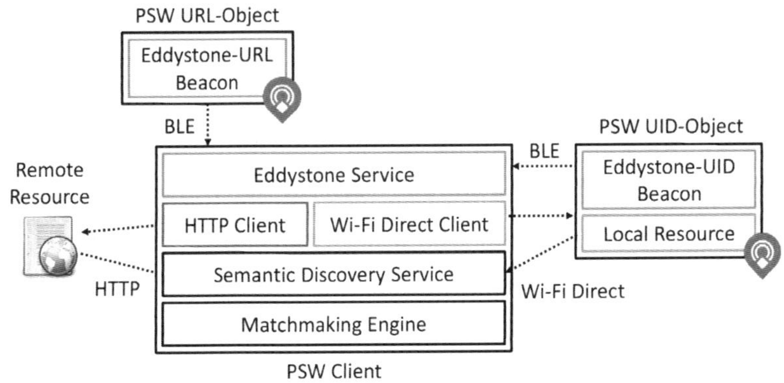

Figure 3: Physical Semantic Web architecture

user involvement at all. The proposal relies on Semantic Web languages, and particularly on Resource Description Framework (RDF) [20] and Web Ontology Language (OWL) [21]. RDF defines a general knowledge assertion model for characterizing and linking resources through statements structured as *subject-predicate-object* triples. OWL allows defining *ontologies* on top of RDF, *i.e.*, expressive vocabularies for modeling structured knowledge about particular domains. The semantics of OWL is formally grounded on the Description Logics (DLs) family of logical languages. An ontology and a set of individuals build the *Knowledge Base* (KB) used for automated *reasoning* supporting discovery in the reference domain.

B. Objects exposing semantic annotations. From now on, the term object will not refer to the RDF-specific meaning, but will denote material things equipped with storage, processing and communication facilities. Ontologies are assumed as stable background knowledge, available either through direct wireless exchange between smart objects or through the Web. Every object exposes a semantic annotation describing its state, capabilities and/or factual knowledge collected from the context it is dipped in. Each annotation corresponds to a KB individual, expressed w.r.t. a particular domain ontology. Objects materialize structured information with rigorous semantics and make it discoverable to nearby devices through BLE via Eddystone-UID frames, as explained in Section III-A. In this way, knowledge exchange can occur through point-to-point connectivity, even without Internet connection. Whenever Internet access is available, they also publish the same knowledge fragments on the Web and advertise them via Eddystone-URL frames, in order to make them retrievable through the standard PW mechanism. No customized application-level protocols are needed to mediate interactions and knowledge sharing: starting from a logical core information grounded on a reference ontology, an object is able to update and enrich its annotation during its lifecycle, in order to reflect evolution in its perceptions, goals and functionalities.

C. Knowledge discovery and sharing. When an object exposes a semantic-based annotated information, agents running on nearby devices and objects can discover it via PSW, as outlined in Section III. The PSW push policy allows agents to be notified of nearby annotation instances. Nevertheless, discovery is driven by application requirements, expressed as a semantic-based request in a matchmaking problem. The discoverer agent collects UIDs and URLs from neighboring devices and preselects only the ones corresponding to semantic annotations having the same reference ontology as the request. This preliminary filter sets the general knowledge domain for the current discovery session and excludes irrelevant knowledge fragments, so reducing the communication and computational load of the subsequent matchmaking step. The matchmaking outcome is a list of annotations ranked by semantic similarity w.r.t. the request. In classical PW scenarios, the user is in control of the discovery process: she selects one of the returned results pointing to a Web page with human-readable information and possible actions. In more advanced scenarios, the discovery process is performed autonomously by an agent device, equipped with knowledge representation tools to select the best result(s) and guide automatic interactions between objects.

D. Semantic matchmaking. Knowledge discovery is supported by a rigorous semantic matchmaking framework to rank a set of *resources* according to relevance with respect to a *request*, where the resources and the request must be satisfiable concept expressions with respect to a common ontology. Standard reasoning services for matchmaking include *Subsumption* and *Satisfiability*. Given a request R and a resource S, Subsumption verifies whether all features in R are included in S: its outcome is either *full match* or not. Satisfiability checks whether any constraint in R contradicts some specification in S, hence it divides resources in *compatible* (a.k.a. *potential matches*) and *incompatible* (a.k.a. *partial matches*) w.r.t. the request. This approach is inadequate for fully autonomic scenarios, because full matches seldom occur and incompatibility is frequent when dealing with complex expressions from independent heterogeneous sources. One would like to determine *what* constraints caused incompatibility or missed full match. In order to produce a finer resource ranking and a logic-based explanation of outcomes, the framework exploits *Concept Abduction* and *Concept Contraction* non-standard inference services [4]. Given a request R incompatible with an available resource S, Contraction detects what part G (for *Give up*) of R is conflicting with S. If one retracts G from R, K (for *Keep*) is obtained, which represents a contracted version of the original request, such that it is compatible with S. On the other hand, if R and S are compatible but S does not match R completely, Abduction identifies what additional feature set H (for *Hypothesis*) should be assumed in S in order to reach a full match. *Penalty functions* are associated to Abduction and Contraction, in order to compute a semantic distance metric for ranking a set of resources w.r.t. a given request. The overall matchmaking process is summarized in Figure 4. Efficient implementations of the above inferences exist for mobile and embedded computing architectures on moderately expressive DLs [3]. The final ranking score integrates semantic distance with context-aware data-oriented attributes:

$$f(R,S) = 100[1 - \frac{penalty(R,S)}{penalty(R,\top)}(1 + dist(R,S))]$$

where $penalty(R,S)$ is the penalty induced by Abduction and Contraction from request R and resource S; this value is normalized dividing by the penalty between R and the universal concept (a.k.a. *Top* or *Thing*), which depends exclusively on axioms in the reference ontology. The $dist(R,S)$ term is the physical distance between the discoverer agent and the discovered resource's owner. Nearer resources are usually preferred, because (i) knowledge locality is often important in pervasive applications and (ii) shorter hops in wireless communications are more reliable and less energy-consuming. The formula for f translates the semantic distance measure into a *relevance* 0-100% ascending scale.

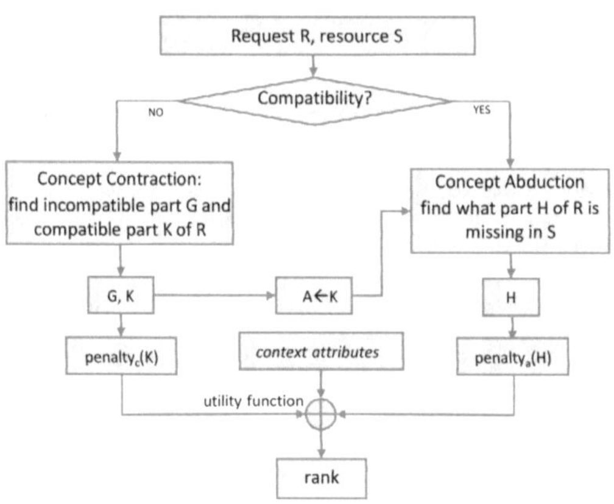

Figure 4: Semantic context-aware matchmaking

The above elements implement a *ubiquitous Knowledge Base* (u-KB) model [2] where the classical components of a KB (ontologies and individuals) are attached to ubiquitous smart objects and no centralized storage or processing infrastructure is required. At the *field layer*, mobile hosts extract information from the environment through embedded sensing and identification technologies. At the *discovery layer*, hosts communicate by exposing and searching knowledge fragments through the Physical Semantic Web. Since objects can expose multiple resources referring to different ontologies, several u-KBs can co-exist in the same physical space: the PSW protocol allows to materialize a proper subset of the u-KB of interest when needed for reasoning.

IV. Application Scenarios

Several reference scenarios are now outlined to exemplify practical applications of the Physical Semantic Web approach. Basically, proposed scenarios exploit two different architectures:

- Internet-based scenarios: a wireless Internet connection is available on the user's mobile device (*e.g.*, via 3G, LTE, Wi-Fi communication). Moreover, the user installed the PSW mobile app to discover and interact with nearby beacons;
- Connection-less scenarios: an Internet connection is not available and PSW objects can communicate via peer-to-peer connections in infrastructure-less networks.

It is important to notice that basic PW framework only considers Internet-based scenarios whereas PSW also enables to exploit BLE beacons in many real-world IoT environments.

1. Distributed Sea Surveillance. Monitoring large marine areas is essential to prevent environmental emergencies and rescue victims of nautical disasters. Innovative surveillance strategies leverage multimodal sensor platforms mounted on water drones or on buoys placed in strategic locations. In such scenarios, Internet connectivity is generally unavailable: *nomadic networks* are a more effective paradigm to minimize data transfers. This can save both bandwidth and power of stationary nodes (*e.g.*, buoys), which must run unattended for long time spans. Each sensor node must be able to perform a mining and summarization process on the potentially large streams of raw data, in order to extract only interesting events and patterns. Such summaries can be expressed with short, high-level formal annotations in Semantic Web languages. Exploiting the PSW proposal, the mobile nodes of the nomadic network (*e.g.*, drones) patrolling an area can discover and collect annotations of relevant events and conditions from stationary nodes. If intervention is required, mobile nodes can provide immediate assistance for minor issues or alert the command center in case of more complex operations.

2. Precision Agriculture. Let us consider a simple case study where an agricultural land is divided into several fields, farmed with different type of products each characterized by a set of features (*e.g.*, age, growth stage). Each field is managed autonomously by a team of robots (sensors and actuators), acting as smart objects and able to process data to produce shareable useful knowledge. *Monitor* robots collect data in the field, create a local semantic-based annotation and expose an *Eddystone-UID* beacons indicating how to retrieve the description. In particular the beacon message contains the MAC address of a Bluetooth device (not necessarily the same BLE device exposing the beacon) and the ID of the file to be retrieved by means of the Bluetooth File Transfer profile. These descriptions are discovered, downloaded through a P2P connection and then processed by *actuators*, equipped with a mobile matchmaker, to identify the most suitable areas where perform required actions (*e.g.*, irrigation, fertilization).

3. Self-driving vehicles. An application of the Physical Semantic Web will be proposed to support long-term performance evaluation tests of vehicles. Currently this kind of tests deals with several issues, as continuous long-term road test sessions are a very intensive physical and mental task for human drivers often spanning several weeks. Self-driving vehicles can overcome these limitations, also extending the maximum duration of tests. However novel challenges must be taken in consideration. Autonomous driving requires many complex interactions with the surrounding environment. The vehicle has to check its status, understand the external context and decide how to respond to the detected conditions. By embedding BLE beacons in the road surface, self-driving cars can be not only guided to remain on track, but also informed about context conditions in an articulated way. Some test centers, like *Porsche Nardò Technical Center* (http://www.porscheengineering.com/nardo/), are already starting investigations in this direction. Further developments could be then applied to real-world self-driving scenarios. By embedding a BLE beacon in a car, the vehicle becomes a *moving beacon* able to annotate and share both context and vehicles properties in order to dynamically adapt its driving style in presence of modifications of the test environment (*e.g.*, change of weather conditions and wear of vehicle components).

V. Conclusion and Future Work

The paper proposed a theoretical framework enabling the Physical Semantic Web, a novel paradigm enhancing the Physical Web program by Google. It basically applies the Semantic Web of Things vision to the real world. Models for knowledge sharing and discovery have been extended to fully autonomic environments populated by smart objects. Application scenarios have been also presented to make evident benefits the approach could drive to reach. Future work will be oriented to: (i) validate the approach through an extensive experimentation (supported by Google Inc.) with native Physical Web devices; (ii) align the early Physical Semantic Web proposal to the latest PW features (*e.g.*, *FatBeacon* specification); (iii) further investigate objects interaction schemes in order to enable more effective data management; (iv) extend the current PW Android client (http://github.com/google/physical-web/tree/master/android) integrating the proposed semantic-based discovery of BLE beacons; (v) implement and test the multi-robot scenario, described in IV, exploiting both simulation software and off-the-shelf robots. Robot Operating System (ROR) will be used as reference platform.

More information about the Physical Semantic Web project can be found on the reference web page (http://sisinflab.poliba.it/swottools/physicalweb) whereas all software updates will be uploaded on the GitHub repository (http://github.com/sisinflab-swot/physical-semantic-web), created as a fork of the official Physical Web project.

Acknowledgment

The authors acknowledge partial support of Google Inc. for valuable endorsements within the frame of IoT Research Award.

References

[1] "Eddystone protocol specification," http://github.com/google/eddystone, [Online; accessed 20-Sep-2016].

[2] M. Ruta, F. Scioscia, and E. Di Sciascio, "Enabling the Semantic Web of Things: framework and architecture," in 2012 IEEE Sixth International Conference on Semantic Computing. IEEE, 2012, pp. 345–347.

[3] F. Scioscia, M. Ruta, G. Loseto, F. Gramegna, S. Ieva, A. Pinto, and E. Di Sciascio, "A mobile matchmaker for the Ubiquitous Semantic Web," International Journal on Semantic Web and Information Systems, vol. 10, no. 4, dec 2014, pp. 77–100.

[4] M. Ruta, E. Di Sciascio, and F. Scioscia, "Concept abduction and contraction in semantic-based P2P environments," Web Intelligence and Agent Systems, vol. 9, no. 3, 2011, pp. 179–207.

[5] M. Compton, P. Barnaghi, L. Bermudez, R. Garcia-Castro, O. Corcho, S. Cox, J. Graybeal, M. Hauswirth, C. Henson, A. Herzog et al., "The SSN Ontology of the W3C Semantic Sensor Network Incubator Group," Web Semantics: Science, Services and Agents on the World Wide Web, vol. 17, 2012.

[6] T. Heath and C. Bizer, "Linked data: Evolving the web into a global data space," Synthesis lectures on the semantic web: theory and technology, vol. 1, no. 1, 2011, pp. 1–136.

[7] K. Janowicz, A. Bröring, C. Stasch, S. Schade, T. Everding, and A. Llaves, "A restful proxy and data model for linked sensor data," International Journal of Digital Earth, vol. 6, no. 3, 2013, pp. 233–254.

[8] A. Bröring, P. Maué, K. Janowicz, D. Nüst, and C. Malewski, "Semantically-enabled sensor plug & play for the sensor web," Sensors, vol. 11, no. 8, 2011, pp. 7568–7605.

[9] P. Barnaghi, M. Presser, and K. Moessner, "Publishing linked sensor data," in CEUR Workshop Proceedings: Proceedings of the 3rd International Workshop on Semantic Sensor Networks (SSN), Organised in conjunction with the International Semantic Web Conference, vol. 668, 2010.

[10] D. Le-Phuoc, H. Q. Nguyen-Mau, J. X. Parreira, and M. Hauswirth, "A middleware framework for scalable management of linked streams," Web Semantics: Science, Services and Agents on the World Wide Web, vol. 16, Nov. 2012, pp. 42–51.

[11] K.-N. Tran, M. Compton, and R. G. Jemma Wu, "Semantic Sensor Composition," in 3rd International Workshop on Semantic Sensor Networks. Proceedings of the 9th International Semantic Web Conference (ISWC 2010), ser. CEUR Workshop Proceedings, D. R. D. Taylor K., Ayyagari A., Ed., vol. 668. CEUR-WS, nov 2010, pp. 33–48.

[12] C. Perera, A. Zaslavsky, C. Liu, M. Compton, P. Christen, and D. Georgakopoulos, "Sensor Search Techniques for Sensing as a Service Architecture for the Internet of Things," Sensors Journal, IEEE, vol. 14, no. 2, 2014, pp. 406–420.

[13] N. Kushalnagar, G. Montenegro, and C. P. Schumacher, "IPv6 over Low-Power Wireless Personal Area Networks (6LoWPANs): Overview, Assumptions, Problem Statement, and Goals," Internet proposed standard RFC, vol. 4919, August 2007.

[14] C. Bormann, A. Castellani, and Z. Shelby, "CoAP: An Application Protocol for Billions of Tiny Internet Nodes," IEEE Internet Computing, vol. 16, no. 2, 2012, pp. 62–67.

[15] D. Pfisterer, K. Romer, D. Bimschas, O. Kleine, R. Mietz, C. Truong, H. Hasemann, A. Kroller, M. Pagel, M. Hauswirth et al., "SPITFIRE: Toward a Semantic Web of Things," Communications Magazine, IEEE, vol. 49, no. 11, 2011, pp. 40–48.

[16] S. Cirani, L. Davoli, G. Ferrari, R. Léone, P. Medagliani, M. Picone, and L. Veltri, "A scalable and self-configuring architecture for service discovery in the internet of things," Internet of Things Journal, IEEE, vol. 1, no. 5, 2014, pp. 508–521.

[17] K. Taylor and L. Leidinger, "Ontology-driven complex event processing in heterogeneous sensor networks," The Semanic Web: Research and Applications, 2011, pp. 285–299.

[18] Bluetooth SIG, "Supplement to the Bluetooth Core Specification, Version 5," 2014. [Online]. Available: https://www.bluetooth.org/DocMan/handlers/DownloadDoc.ashx?doc_id=291904

[19] W3C Draft Community Group, "Web Bluetooth," https://webbluetoothcg.github.io/web-bluetooth/, Tech. Rep., Sep. 2016.

[20] G. Schreiber and Y. Raimond, "RDF 1.1 Primer," W3C, W3C Note, Jun. 2014, http://www.w3.org/TR/rdf11-primer.

[21] B. Parsia, S. Rudolph, M. Krötzsch, P. Patel-Schneider, and P. Hitzler, "OWL 2 Web Ontology Language Primer (Second Edition)," W3C Recommendation, Dec. 2012, http://www.w3.org/TR/owl2-primer.

AUTHOR INDEX

International Academy, Research, and Industry Association (IARIA)
412 Derby Way
Wilmington, DE 19810

CURRAN ASSOCIATES INC.
proceedings.com

ISBN 978-1-5108-3085-1
9 781510 830851

Third International Conference on Advances in Signal, Image and Video Processing (SIGNAL 2018)

Held at InfoSys 2018

Nice, France
20 - 24 May 2018

IARIA